American
Conservative Thought
in the Twentieth Century

THE AMERICAN HERITAGE SERIES

THE

American Heritage

Series

UNDER THE GENERAL EDITORSHIP OF
Leonard W. Levy & Alfred Young

Did You Ever See a Dream Walking?

American
Conservative Thought
in the Twentieth Century

edited by

William F. Buckley, Jr.

Bobbs-Merrill Educational Publishing

Indianapolis

First Edition
Fifth Printing—1978

Library of Congress Catalog Card Number 76-99163
ISBN 0-672-51327-7
Designed by Starr Atkinson

To Christopher Taylor Buckley

Cujus ingenium, si amore non
fallor, magnum quiddam
pollicetur

◎ *Acknowledgments*

The introduction contains parts of an essay I published in *The Jeweler's Eye* (New York: G. P. Putnam's Sons, 1968), and a few passages from an address published in *Actions Speak Louder* (New Rochelle, N.Y.: Arlington House, 1968).

I wish to record my special gratitude to Professor Jeffrey Hart and Miss Agatha Schmidt for, respectively, his invaluable counsel and her ingenious help with the research, and of course my thanks to Professor Leonard W. Levy for his patience and for the excellence of his advice, which, if he had given any more of it, this would have been a book about twenty-first-century American thought.

✒ Foreword

America celebrates itself as a nation of the liberal tradition, yet that tradition has, in fact, a strong conservative base. One of the most revealing American traits is moving forward while facing backward—a conservative posture. For example, new rights that should exist are established on the fictitious pretence that they can be traced to the Magna Carta. Historical roots, preferably the imprimatur of Thomas Jefferson, are sought to justify innovative policies. We rely on the future to redeem the promises of the past. We revere the memory of our rebels but only if they are long dead. America is one of the youngest of the major powers yet has the oldest written Constitution, the oldest democracy, the oldest republic, the oldest party system, and the oldest federal system. And every generation thrusts forward its liberal prophets of doom and gloom who claim that rigor mortis is setting in. If America has, as is commonly supposed, been an uncongenial environment for conservatism, conservatism has, nevertheless, demonstrated an extraordinary tenacity in politics, literature, law, religion, economics, and social thought.

Liberalism, however, confidently believing that it rides the waves of the future, has regarded conservatism with an amused if sometimes embittered tolerance. The armory of liberal clichés is rich in quips and ripostes that put conservatism down. To the perennial conservative charge that liberalism is creeping social-ism in disguise, the liberal reply is that conservatism is the por-tent of galloping reaction. When the conservative thanks God that the Constitution still stands, the liberal query is whether the Constitution can stand still. When the conservative charges liberalism with having one foot firmly planted in the clouds, the retort is that conservatism is the art of keeping up with yes-terday. History, says the liberal, repeats itself first as tragedy, second as farce, and finally as conservatism. The debate persists generation after generation, its malicious humor enlivening its antagonisms and seriousness.

The American Heritage Series has thus far kept its thumb on the liberal side of the scales. As editors we have opened our pages to the voices of Abolitionism, libertarian theory, agrarian revolt, literary radicalism, the New Left, Black nationalism, Negro protest thought, the tradition of nonviolent civil disobedience, and other forms of dissent. Conservatism, ironically a form of dissent within the liberal tradition, also deserves a hearing from any serious student of American history. We believe that every age needs men who redeem their time by living with a vision of things that were as well as things that ought to be. We believe, too, that wisdom derives from a variety of sources, even from those who see little good in the world, think that almost everything is going to the dogs, and believe that most people are rascals. Belatedly we add to the American Heritage Series a volume that provides a new perspective by offering the best of American conservative thought in the twentieth century, under the editorship of William F. Buckley, Jr. The result will force many readers to defend cherished first principles against incisive attack.

Mr. Buckley is the foremost expositor of rational, humanistic conservative thought in America today. He is a man for all conservative seasons: author, politician, TV star, popular lecturer, and editor-in-chief of the nation's leading journal of conservative opinion, *National Review*. In every capacity he is an outstanding educator, though not an academician. Famed as a tough-minded adversary, an entertaining and brilliant conversationalist, and a scintillating stylist, he is also an enormously learned man and a serious thinker. His introduction to this book is written with his characteristic charm, wit, ego, trenchancy, and, of course, strong bias.

His subject is a slippery one, being almost indefinable, as is the case with liberalism or almost any other "ism." Even to its practitioners and philosophers, conservatism comes in as many varieties as Heinz foods. Mr. Buckley is eclectic, but clearly within bounds. He flatly rejects the intolerant and rigid dogmatism of Ayn Rand, the extreme and unrealistic anti-statism of conservatives who verge on anarchism, and the apoplectic and reckless reactionarism of the John Birchers with their conspiracy theories. Mr. Buckley's conservatism shares nothing in common with the conservatism of Big Business or of the self-appointed super-patriots, bigots, and xenophobes. As his introduction, section prefaces, and documentary selections make clear, his conservatism is sophisticated and complex, although not always consistent. At times he appears to be defending a status quo or, at least, those highly selected aspects of it, in terms of values and institutions, that meet his approval; at other times he seems to be defending a status quo ante—values and institutions of the past that have been subordinated, even lost, by modern developments. He variously describes conservatism as a position, an attitude, and an ideology. Whether he is defending fixed positions or fixed principles, or both, Mr. Buckley's conservatism is vigorously individualistic, in favor of ordered liberty, hostile to promiscuous equalitarianism, and pronouncedly tolerant. While theistic in character, it welcomes non-believers. Though tradition-oriented and partial to continuity rather than experiment, it has a deep streak of romantic utopianism. Mr. Buckley believes that conservative thought is addressed to shaping a visionary or paradigmatic society; he finds the twentieth century to be a hideously science-centered age with a passion for equality that subverts the ideal society.

A pluralist should welcome Mr. Buckley's pluralistic approach to conservatism. Any thoughtful reader should find in the authors whom he has selected considerable intellectual force, conviction, and even beauty. To ignore, to be unmoved, or to be unprovoked by Mr. Buckley and his fellow conservatives within these covers is to risk the charge of being dead to ideas or, what is equally damning, so prejudiced that nothing can move or remove encrusted, ritualistic beliefs of whatever hue.

This book is one of a series of which the aim is to provide the essential primary sources of the American experience, especially of American thought. The series, when completed, will constitute a documentary library of American history, filling a need

long felt among scholars, students, libraries, and general readers
for authoritative collections of original materials. Some volumes
will illuminate the thought of significant individuals, such as
James Madison or Louis Brandeis; some will deal with movements, such as those of the Antifederalists or the Populists; others will be organized around special themes, such as Puritan political thought, or American Catholic thought on social questions. Many volumes will take up the large number of subjects
traditionally studied in American history for which, surprisingly, there are no documentary anthologies; others will pioneer
in introducing new subjects of increasing importance to scholars
and to the contemporary world. The series aspires to maintain
the high standards demanded of contemporary editing, providing authentic texts, intelligently and unobtrusively edited. It
will also have the distinction of presenting pieces of substantial
length that give the full character and flavor of the original.
The series will be the most comprehensive and authoritative
of its kind.

Leonard W. Levy
Alfred Young

✍ Contents

Introduction ✍ Did You Ever See a Dream Walking?

The idea of this book is obvious enough. Notwithstanding efforts, some of them greatly ingenious, either to make American "conservatism" go away or to deprive it of substantial meaning, it is still very much with us. Sometimes it seems as if half the academic and journalistic communities were engaged in demonstrating that the term "conservative" is meaningless while the other half engages in attempting to define its meaning. Neither camp has succeeded. Nor will this book succeed in so forbidding a venture in taxonomy as to fix forever the meaning of an elusive and glamorous term. This doesn't mean that the idea ("conservatism") is empty of structural content, merely that people disagree about what the content is. And there is, of course, no final authority on the matter qualified to act as arbiter; nor should there be. The purpose of this volume is not therefore to assert that content apodictically. Merely to say: here is a single student's understanding of what is the flesh and blood of conservatism in America, and here are a few essays by contemporaries of whom only one or two (Oakeshott and Meyer) understand themselves as engaged in the very act of distilling the essence of conservatism. The others are merely saying what they want to say, and it is the exclusive responsibility of the editor to have corralled them into a single volume that attempts to describe the conservative position: its attitudes, its tones, its— to use a word I loathe but which we are no longer permitted to live without except in self-conscious essays concerning its objectionability—its "ideology."

There are several points to be made here, briefly. One is that reasonable and well-informed men differ in their understanding not merely of what conservatism is, but of what are its provenances, political, historical, and philosophical. Another is that, notwithstanding such disagreements, the term is practically useful; that is to say, the term does communicate sufficiently to keep it in use, which would not be the case if it were regularly used to mean contradictory things. Another is that every student of conservatism charged with putting together a book containing quintessential samplings of conservative thought would come up with different and differing selections, though not, I think, with totally dissonant selections. Whereas it is predictably the case that the conservative who reads this book will wish that Mr. Jones had been left out and Mr. Smith included, he is not, in my judgment, likely to think of Mr. Jones's presence here as heretical. Not, at least, the conservative whose views are generally accepted as "conservative" on the American scene. Confusion tends to arise less on account of disagreements about this emphasis or that than from categorical objections by anti-conservative militants who either insist (a) on illegitimizing the entire enterprise (on the grounds of its intellectual inexactitude), or (b) on identifying contemporary American conservatism with altogether eccentric political modalities (a dissociation from which is a ritual form of self-elevation, particularly in the academy).

This volume is an honest effort to transcribe one American conservative's understanding of some of the recent sources of the illumination he lives by. The discipline of the book (as set down by the master editor of the series) is both constricting and reasonable. We are concerned with *American* conservative thought—not, say, English or European conservative thought (and there *are* differences). The contributors should (it was stipulated) be more or less contemporary Americans, although exceptions have been permitted—but only where sticking by the rule would have required ethnocentric bitterendedness (how can you Buy American when making the case against rationalism in politics, when over there, within easy reach, is

Oakeshott?). The authors (the rules continue) must have written in the twentieth century (exit Burke, and Adams, and Burckhardt, just for instance). On the other hand, I ruled (and got away with it) that an individual who figured seminally in the formation of twentieth-century conservative attitudes was not necessarily to be preferred, notwithstanding his traceable personal-intellectual influence, over one of his disciples who speaks to us more idiomatically. This liberty I have taken licentiously. Not merely because I know better the works of the very contemporary conservatives, some of them younger than myself, but because I am attracted to their way of saying things in preference to that of some of our venerable elders (I can't, for instance, read Santayana, even though I know he is beautiful); a personal preference I certainly should not undertake to defend by the use of purely conservative arguments.

One's own experience is of course relevant in such a selection as I have here attempted. Unlike most of the editors of the other volumes in the series, my experience has been not in the academic world but in the more agitated outside, as editor of a conservative journal of opinion, *National Review*. I think it prudent under the circumstances to highlight some of my own experiences as an editor, insofar as they shed light on the definition of contemporary conservatism.

I am asked most frequently by members of the lecture audience, "What is conservatism?" Sometimes the questioner, guarding against the windy evasiveness one comes to expect from lecturers, will add, "preferably in one sentence." On which occasions I have replied, "I could not give you a definition of Christianity in one sentence, but that does not mean that Christianity is undefinable." Usually that disposes of the hopes of those who wish a neatly packaged definition of conservatism which they can stow away. Those who are obstinate I punish by giving, with a straight face, Professor Richard Weaver's definition of conservatism as "the paradigm of essences towards which the phenomenology of the world is in continuing approximation"—as noble and ingenious an effort as any I have ever

read. The point is, of course, that we are at the stage danger-
ously close to mere verbal gambiting. I have never failed, I am
saying, to dissatisfy an audience that asks the meaning of conservatism.

Yet I feel I know, if not what conservatism is, at least who a
conservative is. I confess that I know who is a conservative less
surely than I know who is a liberal. Blindfold me, spin me about
like a top, and I will walk up to the single liberal in the room
without zig or zag and find him even if he is hiding behind the
flower pot. I am tempted to try to develop an equally sure nose
for the conservative, but I am deterred by the knowledge that
conservatives, under the stress of our times, have had to invite
all kinds of people into their ranks to help with the job at hand,
and the natural courtesy of the conservative causes him to treat
such people not as janissaries, but as equals; and so, empirically,
it becomes difficult to see behind the khaki, to know surely
whether that is a conservative over there doing what needs to
be done, or a radical, or merely a noisemaker, or pyrotechnician,
since our ragtag army sometimes moves together in surprising
uniformity, and there are exhilarating moments when everyone's eye is Right. (Thus we hear Professor Daniel Patrick Moynihan calling on liberals and conservatives to unite behind a
"politics of stability.") I have, after all, sometimes wondered
whether I am myself a true conservative. I feel that I qualify
spiritually and philosophically; but temperamentally I am not of
the breed, and so I need to ask myself, among so many other
things, how much it matters what one is temperamentally. There
are other confusions.

Whittaker Chambers, for instance, distinguished sharply between a conservative and a "man of the Right." "You," he wrote
me on resigning as an editor of *National Review*, "are a conservative, and I know no one with better title to the word. But I
am not one, never was. I call myself, on those occasions when I
cannot avoid answering the question, a man of the Right." I
reflected on that letter, needless to say, as would you if you were
the editor of a journal from which Whittaker Chambers had
just withdrawn, and remarked an interesting thing: In the five-
year history of the journal, Chambers was the only man to resign

from its senior board of editors explicitly because he felt he could no longer move within its ideological compass; and yet he never wrote a piece for us (or in the last dozen years of his life, that I know of, for anyone else) that was out of harmony with the thrust of *National Review*'s position.

Oh yes, people withdraw, and write and denounce you, and swear that green grass will never grow over your grave on account of this or that offensive article or editorial or book review; but these losses are merely a part of the human attrition of outspoken journalism. They prove nothing, in our case, that has anything to do with ideological fecklessness. What I am saying is that, notwithstanding the difficulty in formulating the conservative position and the high degree of skepticism from our critics before *National Review* was launched, *National Review*'s position was, I believe, instantly intelligible from the very first issue. *He would probably say that anyway* (the skeptic will charge), *it being in his and the journal's interest to say so*. But I make that statement on empirical grounds, as I propose to make others in this introduction on the meaning of conservatism which will reason *a posteriori* from the facts to the theory—and which will be based exclusively on my own experiences as editor of *National Review*. Since I shall not allude to it again, let me say so now unambiguously: This part of this essay is about the experiences of *National Review* and their bearing, by the processes of exclusion, on a workable definition of contemporary conservatism. I do not by any means suggest that *National Review* is the only functioning alembic of modern conservatism, merely that it is the only one whose experiences I can relate with any authority, and that its experiences may be interesting enough to be worth telling.

Roughly the same group of men, representing the same vested interests in certain ideas and attitudes, continue to be the major participants in *National Review*. The magazine found instantly and expanded an audience which seemed intuitively to grant and to understand the happy eclecticism of the magazine's guiding ideas; whereas the critics, whose delighted line at the beginning was one or another variant on the theme, "This country needs a conservative magazine and, having read *National Re-*

view, we *still* say what this country needs is a conservative magazine," finally, except for the bitterenders, gave up and began to refer to *National Review* as, plain and simple, a "conservative journal." Others who, as I say, refuse to give up, will continue to refer to it only after a ritualistic pejorative: "the McCarthyite *National Review*," "the ultrarightist *National Review*," and so on. But it being so that in language the governing law is usage, it is by now predictable that those who feel that Peter Viereck or Clinton Rossiter or Walter Lippmann is the true architect of American conservatism are bound to enter the ranks of eccentricity, like the rightwing gentlemen who, because they continue to insist on referring to themselves as "liberals," have difficulty communicating with the rest of the world, which for two generations now has understood liberalism to mean something else, beginning, roughly, from the time Santayana observed that the only thing the modern liberal is concerned to liberate is man from his marriage contract.

Since this is an empirical probe, based on my own experience as editor of *National Review,* I shall speak about people and ideas with which *National Review* has had trouble making common cause. In 1957, Whittaker Chambers reviewed *Atlas Shrugged,* the novel by Miss Ayn Rand wherein she explicates the philosophy of "Objectivism," which is what she has chosen to call her creed. Man of the Right, or conservative, or whatever you wish to call him, Chambers did in fact read Miss Rand right out of the conservative movement. He did so by pointing out that her philosophy is in fact another kind of materialism—not the dialectical materialism of Marx, but the materialism of technocracy, of the relentless self-server who lives for himself and for absolutely no one else, whose concern for others is explainable merely as an intellectualized recognition of the relationship between helping others and helping oneself. Religion is the first enemy of the Objectivist and, after religion, the state—respectively, "the mysticism of the mind" and "the mysticism of the muscle." "Randian Man," wrote Chambers, "like Marxian Man, is made the center of a godless world."

Her exclusion from the conservative community was, I am

sure, in part the result of her desiccated philosophy's conclusive incompatibility with the conservative's emphasis on transcendence, intellectual and moral; but also there is the incongruity of tone, that hard, schematic, implacable, unyielding dogmatism that is in itself intrinsically objectionable, whether it comes from the mouth of Ehrenburg, or Savonarola, or Ayn Rand. Chambers knew that specific ideologies come and go but that rhetorical totalism is always in the air, searching for the ideologue-on-the-make; and so he said things about Miss Rand's tone of voice which, I would hazard the guess, if they were true of anyone else's voice, would tend to make it *eo ipso* unacceptable for the conservative. ". . . The book's [*Atlas Shrugged*] dictatorial tone . . . ," Chambers wrote,

> is its most striking feature. Out of a lifetime of reading, I can recall no other book in which a tone of overriding arrogance was so implacably sustained. Its shrillness is without reprieve. Its dogmatism is without appeal . . . resistance to the Message cannot be tolerated because disagreement can never be merely honest, prudent, or just humanly fallible. Dissent from revelation so final can only be willfully wicked. There are ways of dealing with such wickedness, and, in fact, right reason itself enjoins them. From almost any page of *Atlas Shrugged*, a voice can be heard, from painful necessity, commanding: "To a gas chamber—go!" The same inflexibly self-righteous stance results, too, in odd extravagances of inflection and gesture. . . . At first we try to tell ourselves that these are just lapses, that this mind has, somehow, mislaid the discriminating knack that most of us pray will warn us in time of the difference between what is effective and firm, and what is wildly grotesque and excessive. Soon we suspect something worse. We suspect that this mind finds, precisely in extravagance, some exalting merit; feels a surging release of power and passion precisely in smashing up the house.[1]

As if according to a script, Miss Rand's followers jumped *National Review* and Chambers in language that crossed the *i*'s and dotted the *t*'s of Mr. Chambers's point. (It is not fair to hold

[1]Several years later, a graduate student in philosophy, a disciple of Hayek, von Mises, and Friedman, analyzed the thought and rhetoric of Miss Rand and came to similar conclusions. Miss Rand, he wrote, is "hate blinded," "suffocating in her invective" (Bruce Goldberg, "Ayn Rand's 'For the New Intellectual,' " *New Individualist Review*, I, No. 3 [1961], 17–24).

the leader responsible for the excesses of the disciples, but this reaction from Miss Rand's followers, never repudiated by Miss Rand, suggested that her own intolerance is easily communicable to other Objectivists.) One correspondent, denouncing him, referred to "Mr. Chambers's 'break' with Communism"; a lady confessed that on reading his review she thought she had "mistakenly picked up the *Daily Worker*"; another accused him of "lies, smears, and cowardly misrepresentations"; still another saw in him the "mind-blanking, life-hating, unreasoning, less-than-human being which Miss Rand proves undeniably is the cause of the tragic situation the world now faces. . ."; and summing up, one Objectivist wrote that "Chambers the Christian communist is far more dangerous than Chambers the Russian spy."

What the experience proved, it seems to me, beyond the unacceptability of Miss Rand's ideas and rhetoric, is that no conservative cosmology whose every star and planet is given in a master book of coordinates is very likely to sweep American conservatives off their feet. They are enough conservative and anti-ideological to resist totally closed systems, those systems that do not provide for deep and continuing mysteries. They may be pro-ideology and unconservative enough to resist such asseverations as that conservatism is merely "an attitude of mind," as one contributor to this volume once upon a time asserted. But I predict, on the basis of a long association with American conservatives, that there isn't anybody around scribbling into his sacred book a series of all-fulfilling formulae which will serve the conservatives as an Apostles' Creed. Miss Rand tried it, and *because* she tried it, she compounded the failure of her ideas. She will have to go down as an Objectivist; my guess is she will go down as a novelist or, possibly, just plain go down, period.

The conservative's distrust of the state, so richly earned by it and so energetically motivated in this volume, raises inevitably the question, How far can one go? This side, the answer is, of anarchism—that should be obvious enough. But one man's anarchism is another man's statism. *National Review* will never define to everyone's satisfaction what are the tolerable limits of the state's activity; and we never expected to do so. We got into the problem, as so often is the case, not by going forward to meet it, but by backing up against it.

There exists a small breed of men whose passionate distrust of the state has developed into a theology of sorts, or at least into a demonology, to which they adhere as devotedly as any religious fanatic ever attempted to adhere to the will of the Lord. I do not feel contempt for the endeavor of either type. It is intellectually stimulating to discuss alternatives to municipalized streets, even as it is to speculate on whether God's wishes would better be served if we ordered fried or scrambled eggs for breakfast on this particular morning. Yet conservatives must concern themselves not only with ideals, but with matters of public policy, and I mean by that something more than the commonplace that one must maneuver within the limits of conceivable action. We can read and take pleasure in the recluse's tortured deliberations on what will benefit his soul. Bernanos's *Diary of a Country Priest* was not only a masterpiece; it was also a bestseller. And we can read with more than mere amusement Dr. Murray Rothbard's suggestion that lighthouses be sold to private tenants who will then chase down the light beam in speed boats and collect a dollar from the storm-tossed ship whose path it illuminates. Chesterton reminds us that many dogmas are liberating because the damage they do when abused cannot compare with the damage that might have been done had whole peoples not felt their inhibiting influence. If our society seriously wondered whether to denationalize the lighthouses, it would not wonder at all whether to nationalize the medical profession.

But Dr. Rothbard and his merry anarchists wish to *live* their fanatical antistatism, and the result is a collision between the basic policies they urge and those urged by conservatives who recognize that the state sometimes is the necessary instrument of our proximate deliverance. The defensive strategic war in which we have been engaged over a number of years on myriad fronts cannot be prosecuted by voluntary associations of soldiers and scientists and diplomats and strategists, and when this obtrusive fact enters into the reckonings of our state-haters, the majority, sighing, yield to reality, whereas the small minority, obsessed by their antagonism to the state, refuse to give it even the powers necessary to safeguard the community. Dr. Rothbard and a few others have spoken harshly of *National Review*'s complacency before the twentieth-century state in all matters that have to do with anticommunism, reading their litanies about the necessity for refusing at any cost to countenance the growth of the state. Thus, for instance, Mr. Ronald Hamowy of the University of Chicago complained about *National Review* in 1961: ". . . The Conservative movement has been straying far under *National Review* guidance . . . leading true believers in freedom and individual liberty down a disastrous path . . . and in so doing they are causing the Right increasingly to betray its own traditions and principles."[2]

And Mr. Henry Hazlitt, reviewing enthusiastically Dr. Rothbard's magnum opus, *Man, Economy, and State* for *National Review* in 1962 paused to comment, sadly, on the author's "extreme apriorism," citing, for instance, Dr. Rothbard's opinion that libel and slander ought not to be illegalized, and that even blackmail,

> "would not be illegal in the free society. For blackmail is the receipt of money in exchange for the service of not publicizing certain information about the other person. No violence or threat of violence to person or property is involved." . . . When Rothbard [Mr. Hazlitt comments] wanders out of the strictly economic realm, in which his scholarship is so rich and his reasoning so rigorous, he is misled by his epistemological doctrine of "extreme apriorism" into trying to substitute his own instant jurisprudence for the common law principles built up through generations of human experience.

"Extreme apriorism"—a generic bull's-eye. If *National Review*'s experience is central to the growth of contemporary con-

    [2]Ronald Hamowy, "National Review: Criticism and Reply," *New Individualist Review*, I, No. 3 [1961].

servatism, extreme apriorists will find it difficult to work with conservatives except as occasional volunteers helping to storm specific objectives. They will not be a part of the standing army, rejecting as they do the burden of reality in the name of a virginal antistatism. I repeat, I do not deplore their influence intellectually; and tactically, I worry not at all. The succubi of world communism are quite active enough to compel the attention of all but the most confirmed solipsists. The virgins have wriggled themselves outside the mainstream of American conservatism. Mr. Hamowy, offering himself up grandly as a symbol of the undefiled conservative, has joined the Committee for a Sane Nuclear Policy.

We ran into the John Birch Society—or, more precisely, into Mr. Robert Welch. Mr. Welch's position is very well known. Scrubbed down, it is that one may reliably infer subjective motivation from objective result; e.g., if the West loses as much ground as demonstrably it has lost during the past twenty years to the enemy, it can only be because those who made policy for the West were the enemy's agents. The *ultima ratio* of this position was the public disclosure—any 300-page document sent to hundreds of people can only be called an act of public disclosure —that Dwight Eisenhower was a communist (to which the most perfect retort—was it Russell Kirk's?—was not so much analytical as artistic: "Eisenhower isn't a communist—he is a golfer").

In criticizing Mr. Welch, we did not move into a hard philosophical front, as for instance we did in our criticisms of Miss Rand or of the neo-anarchists. Rather, we moved into an organizational axiom, the conservative equivalent of the leftists' *pas d'ennemi à gauche*. The position has not, however, been rigorously explicated or applied. Mr. Welch makes his own exclusions; for instance, Gerald L. K. Smith, who, although it is a fact that he favors a number of reforms in domestic and foreign policy which coincide with those favored by Mr. Welch (and by *National Review*), is dismissed as a man with an *idée fixe,* namely, the role of Perfidious Jew in modern society. Many rightwingers (and many liberals, and all communists) believe in a *deus ex machina*. Only introduce the single tax and our problems will wither away, say the followers of Henry George. . . . Only expose the Jew and the international conspiracy will be broken, say others. . . . Only abolish the income tax and all will be well. . . . Forget everything else, but restore the gold standard. . . . Abolish compulsory taxation and we shall all be free. . . . They are called nostrum peddlers by some; certainly they are obsessed. Because whatever virtue there is in what they call for—and some of their proposals strike me as highly desirable, others as mischievous—no one of them (or dozen of them) can begin to do the whole job. Many such persons, because inadequate emphasis is given to their pandemic insight, the linchpin of social reconstruction, are dissatisfied with *National Review*. Others react more vehemently; our failure to highlight *their* solution has the effect of distracting from its unique relevance and so works positively against the day when the great illumination will show us the only road forward. Accordingly, *National Review* is, in their eyes, worse than merely useless.

The defenders of Mr. Welch who are also severe critics of *National Review* are not by any means all of them addicts of the conspiracy school. They do belong, however inconsistently, to the school that says that we must all work together—as a general proposition, sound advice. Lenin distinguished between the sin of "sectarianism," from which suffer all those who refuse to cooperate with anyone who does not share their entire position right down to the dependent clauses, and the sin of "opportunism," the weakness of those who are completely indiscriminate about their political associates.

The majority of those who broke with *National Review* as the result of our criticisms of Mr. Welch believe themselves to have done so in protest against *National Review*'s sectarianism. In fact, I believe their resentment was primarily personal. They were distressed by an attack on a man who had ingratiated himself with them and toward whom their loyalty hardened in proportion as he was attacked. So their bitterness ran over, and now it is widely whispered that *National Review* has been "infiltrated."

The questions we faced at *National Review* were two. The first, to which the answer was always plainly no, was whether Mr. Welch's views on public affairs were sound. The editors knew from experience that they were not. Enough of us had recently been to college, or were in continuing touch with academic circles, to know that the approaches to the internal security and to foreign relations that have been practiced by successive administrations after the Second World War were endorsed by the overwhelming majority of the intellectuals in this country. Therefore, any assumption that only a communist (or a fool, as Mr. Welch allowed) could oppose the House Committee on Un-American Activities or favor aid to Poland and Yugoslavia must deductively mean that the nation's academies are staffed, primarily, by communists (or fools). It is not merely common sense that rejects this assumption, but a familiarity with the intricate argumentation of almost the entire intellectual class (who, of course, are not fools, at least not in the sense in which Mr. Welch uses the word).

The second question then arose—whether it was necessary explicitly to reject Mr. Welch's position as an unrealistic mode of thought. And that had to be answered by asking whether at the margin it contributed to the enlightenment of rightwing thought. The answer was not as obvious as one might suppose. Ironically, the assumptions that reason will prevail and that logic and truth are self-evident—the constituent assumptions of those who believe that that syllogism is correct which says, "(A) We were all-powerful after World War II; (B) Russia is now as powerful as we are; therefore, (C) We willed the enemy's ascendancy" (the essence of Mr. Welch's methodology)—argued in favor of leaving Mr. Welch alone. Thus might one reason if one believed that the truth will triumph: If Mr. Welch merely succeeds in drawing people's attention, which otherwise would not be drawn, to public events, if he scourges them to read about and think about public affairs—then those same people, though introduced to public concern by Mr. Welch, will by the power of reason reject, upon examination, Mr. Welch's specific counsels and graduate as informed members of the anticommunist community.

But reason is *not* king (and many of those who have shrunk from Mr. Welch have done so less because on reflection they repudiate his analysis than because public scandal of a kind has in fact attached to discipleship in a movement dominated by a man with a very special set of views that reality rejects). And so it seemed necessary to say what one hoped would be obvious: that the Welch view is wrong, that it is wrong irrespective of the many personal virtues of Mr. Welch, and wrong irrespective of how many people who were otherwise politically lethargic are now, thanks to Mr. Welch, politically animated.

In consequence, *National Review* was widely criticized for "throwing mud" at Mr. Welch (a curious way to refer to the act of throwing at Mr. Welch his own statements), and some battle lines (and some necks) were broken. Whom did we actually alienate? A body of people? A body of thought? I tend to think not, for the reasons I have suggested. If we alienated those who genuinely believe in *pas d'ennemi à droite,* why do these same people (a) applaud Mr. Welch's exclusion of Gerald L. K. Smith, and (b) proceed to exclude us? It is no answer to the latter inconsistency that the penalty of turning against someone on your side excuses the turning away against the offender; and Mr. Welch, although failing to be consistent on point (a) above, *was* consistent in respect of (b). Aside from a few aggrieved references to *National Review*'s naïveté and to the communists' need of conservative frontmen to implement the smear of the John Birch Society, he has not, as yet, anyway, excluded us from the anticommunist community.

For this reason I tend to put down our encounter with Mr. Welch as having no philosophical significance in an empirical probe of the contemporary locus of American conservatism— except to the extent it can be said that *National Review* rejects as out of this world what goes by the name of the conspiracy view of history. Most of the followers of Mr. Welch who broke with *National Review* on account of our criticisms of him showed themselves, by the inconsistency of their own position, to have acted primarily out of personal pique—to which, of course, they are entitled. But perhaps this brief analysis is relevant, if only because it explains why *National Review's* noisiest collision did not serve any great purpose in the construction of an empirical definition of conservatism.

A few years ago, Mr. Max Eastman, the author and poet, wrote sadly[3] that he must withdraw from the masthead of *National Review:*

> There are too many things in the magazine—and they go too deep—that directly attack or casually side-swipe my most earnest passions and convictions. It was an error in the first place to think that, because of political agreements, I could collaborate formally with a publication whose basic view of life and the universe I regard as primitive and superstitious. That cosmic, or chasmic, difference between us has always troubled me, as I've told you, but lately its political implications have been drawn in ways that I can't be tolerant of. Your own statement in the issue of October 11 [1958] that Father Halton labored "for the recognition of God's right to His place in Heaven" invited me into a world where neither my mind nor my imagination could find rest. That much I could take, although with a shudder, but when you added that "the struggle for the world is a struggle, essentially, by those who mean to unseat Him," you voiced a political opinion that I think is totally and dangerously wrong. . . .

Can you be a conservative and believe in God? Obviously. Can you be a conservative and not believe in God? This is an empirical essay, and so the answer is, as obviously, yes. Can you be a conservative and despise God and feel contempt for those who believe in Him? I would say no. True, Max Eastman is the only man who has left the masthead of *National Review* in protest against its pro-religious sympathies, but it does not follow that this deed was eccentric; he, after all, was probably the only man on *National Review* with that old-time hostility to religion associated with evangelical atheism—with, e.g., the

[3] A letter to the editor.

names of Theodore Dreiser, Upton Sinclair, Henry Mencken, and Clarence Darrow, old friends of Eastman. If one dismisses religion as intellectually contemptible, it becomes difficult to identify oneself wholly with a movement in which religion plays a vital role; and so the moment came when Max Eastman felt he had to go, even while finding it difficult to answer the concluding observation I made to him: "I continue to feel that you would be at a total loss as to what to criticize in the society the editors of *National Review* would, had they the influence, establish in America."

Mr. Eastman's resignation brought up an interesting point, to which I also addressed myself in my reply to my old friend:

> You require that I take your letter seriously, and having done so I must reproach myself rather than you. For if it is true that you cannot collaborate formally with me, then it must be true that I ought not to have collaborated formally with you; for I should hate for you to think that the distance between atheism and Christianity is any greater than the distance between Christianity and atheism. And so if you are correct, that our coadjutorship was incongruous, I as editor of *National Review* should have been the first to spot it and to act on it. All the more because my faith imposes upon me more rigorous standards of association than yours does.

I know now, several years after this exchange of letters, that my point here, that the reciprocal of the proposition that a God-hater cannot associate fully with a Christian, is not in fact true —for reasons that are not easy to set down without running the risk of spiritual or philosophical condescension. But the risk must be taken, and I choose the Christian rather than the secular formulation because, although the latter can very handily be made,[4] it remains debatable in a way that the Christian formulation does not. The reason why Christian conservatives can associate with atheists is because we hold that, above all, faith is a gift and that, therefore, there is no accounting for the bad fortune that has beset those who do not believe or the good

---

[4]See, e.g., Eric Voegelin's "On Readiness to Rational Discussion," *Freedom and Serfdom: An Anthology of Western Thought*, ed. Albert Hunold (Dordrecht, Holland: D. Reidel, 1961), pp. 269–284.

fortune that has befallen those who do. The pro-religious conservative can therefore welcome the atheist as a full-fledged member of the conservative community even while feeling that at the very bottom the roots do not interlace, so that the sustenance that gives a special bloom to Christian conservatism fails to reach the purely secularist conservatism. Voegelin will argue on purely intellectual grounds, taking as his lesson the Socratic proposition that virtue can be taught, but only if virtue is defined as knowledge. Socrates defined knowledge, Voegelin reminds us, as transcendental cognition, as, in fact, requiring the ability to see far enough into the nature of things to recognize transcendence, a view he elaborated in *Protagoras*.

The God-hater, as distinguished from the agnostic (who says merely that he doesn't know) or simply the habitual atheist (who knows there is no God, but doesn't much care about those who disagree), regards those who believe in or tolerate religion as afflicted with short-circuited vision. Their faith is the result of a combination of intellectual defectiveness and psychological immaturity, leading to the use of such analysis and rhetoric as Max Eastman "can't be tolerant of."

The agnostic can shrug his shoulders about the whole thing, caring not whether, in his time, the conflict between the pro-religious and anti-religious elements within conservatism will be resolved. There are so many other things to do than think about God. "Are you anything?" a lady flightily addressed at her dinner table a scholarly gentleman and firebrand conservative who has always managed to nudge aside questions or deflect conversational trends that seemed to be moving into hard confrontations involving religion. He smiled. "Well, I guess I'm not *nothing*," and the conversation went on pleasantly. Max Eastman *was* nothing; and he could no more resist the opportunity to incant his nonbelief than the holy priest can resist the opportunity to proselyte; and so the tension.

Mr. Eastman, like many other programmatic conservatives, based his defense of freedom primarily on pragmatic grounds. Mr. Erik von Kuehnelt-Leddihn once remarked that Friedrich Hayek's *Constitution of Liberty* seemed to be saying that, if freedom were not pragmatically productive, there would be no *reason* for freedom. It appears to be the consensus of religious-minded conservatives that ordered freedom is desirable quite apart from its demonstrable usefulness as the basis for economic and political association. The research of the past fifteen years on Edmund Burke appears to have liberated him from the social pragmatists by whom he had been co-opted. Not to stray too far from the rules of this discussion, I cite a poll a few years ago which showed that the great majority of the readers of *National Review* think of themselves formally as religious people, suggesting that conservatism, of the kind I write about, is planted in a religious view of man.

Though as I say only a single resignation has been addressed to *National Review* in protest against the magazine's friendliness to religion, there is much latent discord, particularly in the academic world, centering on the question not so much of whether God exists or doesn't (only a few continue to explore the question consciously, let alone conscientiously, and most of the latter are thought of as *infra dig*), but on the extent to which it is proper to show toward religion the intellectual disdain the God-haters believe it deserves. Russell Kirk was not allowed inside the faculty of a major university in which, *mirabile dictu,* conservatives (specifically: libertarians) had control of the social science department—because of his "religiosity."

Although I say the antagonism is here and there seen to be hardening, I have grounds for optimism based not merely on *National Review's* own amiable experiences with all but the most dedicated atheists, but on the conviction that the hideousness of a science-centered age has resulted in a stimulation of religious scholarship and of all of those other impulses, intellectual and spiritual, by which man is constantly confounding the most recent wave of neoterics who insist that man is merely a pandemoniac conjunction of ethereal gases. The atheists have not got around to answering Huxley's self-critical confession that neither he nor his followers had succeeded in showing how you can deduce Hamlet from the molecular structure of a mutton chop.

I repeat what is obvious: These are merely notes, though not, I hope, altogether desultory, suggesting where are some of the confines of contemporary conservatism, the walls it runs up against and bounces away from. The freeway remains large, large enough to accommodate very different players with highly different prejudices and techniques. The differences are now tonal, now substantive, but they do not appear to be choking each other off. The symbiosis may yet be a general consensus on the proper balance between freedom, order, and tradition of the kind Mr. Frank Meyer talks about in his contribution to this volume.

To the student who may at this point be saying that he now has some idea of what conservatism is not but very little idea of what it is, I say: be patient. Not only because at this point there are so many unread pages in this volume, each one of which, I am confident, he will find suggestive of something that conservatism is. But patient even after finishing this book: patient especially throughout the course of his academic experience because there he will find that the general assumption is that conservatism is the habit of mind of the heavy people who make up the bourgeois order and the intellectual plaything of here and there a dilettante writer or poet whose idea of chic is sort of perverted.

I think of one student who graduated recently from Exeter, which is one of our finest preparatory schools, and matriculated at a venerable Ivy League college where, after two months, he approached the local conservative professor—most colleges tolerate one (1)—and told him that forsooth he was the first intelligent conservative he had ever met. Now of course by "intelligent" one must understand that the boy meant somebody who could do his academic arpeggios; said boy, almost surely, would have said the same thing even if he had grown up next door to Henry Ford the Elder. America is teeming with highly intelligent conservatives who, however, aren't thought of as "intelligent" because all *they* do is build bridges, develop cyclotrons, understand the national budget, argue before the Supreme Court, or fathom the will of God. Because they are, in general terms, well integrated into a part of the national culture.

Now I take it that one of the reasons why academicians tend to be liberals is that many of those who choose to take up scholarship are also rejecting alternative professions, the professions which are tied in to the existing culture. That is to say, they are influenced in part by the desire to learn and to teach, and in part by the desire to dissociate from their culture and, up until now, the politics of dissociation have been liberal, even as teaching has been the vocational form of dissent.

What then does the student do face to face with the minds he will encounter in this volume? Obviously he will not agree with all of them (they do not agree among themselves). But he will not doubt that most of them speak with considerable intellectual force; will not doubt that all of them speak competently, that some of them express themselves brilliantly, some with great beauty. That will come as something of a surprise to many readers, and the more they are surprised, the more they need to acquaint themselves with some of the literature, the existence and the scope of which is suggested by these essays.

To conservatives, I would say that this volume at least suggests that the struggle availeth, having said which I hasten to add that the struggle is also permanent. Surely Mr. Weaver's intricate definition of conservatism seems to suggest the twin conservative concerns for advance and prudence. A conservative is properly concerned simultaneously with two things, the first being the shape of the visionary or paradigmatic society toward which we should labor; the second, the speed with which it is thinkable to advance toward that ideal society with the foreknowledge that any advance upon it is necessarily asymptotic; that is, we cannot hope for ideological home runs and definitive victories. What American conservatives have achieved is not only the dismay of local radicals but of European intellectuals, who find the rise of conservative thought in America utterly baffling.

To be sure, it is quite widely believed in Europe that the principal contribution America can make to Western thought is not to think at all. I grant the generality that the world would probably be better off, not worse, if a lot of people who are currently hard at work thinking, should desist from doing so, and spend their time, instead, cultivating the elevated thought of others. I remember an occasion not long ago when an editor of *National Review* remarked, on hearing the news that $600,000 had been allocated to bring together in seclusion for one year a dozen top American philosophers at Santa Barbara just to think about thinking, that the expenditure of $60,000-odd per year apiece toward the withdrawal of the average modern philosopher from public life was a price America could ill afford not to pay.

It is quite widely thought in Europe that America, in the modern era, has taken the place of Rome in the ancient era; that it is we who have successfully organized the resources of nature, in order to guard the peace, and who have produced the greatest share of the world's material goods, in order that others might indicate how best they might be enjoyed in usufruct. But unlike Ancient Rome it is said sadly—truthfully—America has not acquired the mien, let alone the habit, of great power. We have not even acquired *gravitas.* Nor has America shown a proper veneration for the values of the Old World, to compare, for instance, with the Romans' humility before the civilization of Greece. America, it is generally agreed, can contribute to Western thought only the physical shelter under which Westerners can continue their dialogues; to that extent, it is believed, America can be useful. But even then—hark the dissent—the danger lies that in an excess of zeal, out of a fatuous idealism which distinguishes our exuberant moralism, it is altogether possible—altogether likely in the opinion of some—altogether predictable, if we are to listen to such as Bertrand Russell—that we will end up triggering a conclusive holocaust, which would forever interrupt that purposeful intercourse between the blither spirits of the West, the continuing hope of an upward-mobile mankind, the dialogue between C. P. Snow and Yevtushenko.

The existence of much conservative scholarship, and of the conservative movement in America, is a phenomenon concerning which European intellectuals—most particularly I would

charge the English, since it is their ignorance I am most educated in—are in a state of innocence so total that one might be
tempted in earthier circumstances to regard it as vulgar, which,
under the present circumstances, we had better merely call distracting. They do not know that there is growing in America a
spirit of resistance to the twentieth century, and it is just possible
that that development will prove the most significant of our
time.

I grant that I am involved in an uneasy figure of speech. It is
hardly possible to "resist" the twentieth century, as the term is
commonly used, any more than it is possible to "resist" gravity
or death. But the figure is useless only insofar as it invokes a
mechanistic view of history, which presupposes that it is the inescapable destiny of the twentieth century to codify certain
trends, social and philosophical, economic and organizational,
trends that are irresistible even as the passage of time is irresistible: trends which issue out of the very genes of history.

It is a common epithet to say of a man whose views are
deemed out of fashion that he "resists the twentieth century."
There are any number of lively polemical variations on the
theme. Senator Goldwater, it has tirelessly been said, entered
the twentieth century kicking and screaming. Russell Kirk, it
has been said one thousand times, though to be sure mostly by
those who are unfamiliar with the Middle Ages, "has a brilliant
fourteenth-century mind." And so on.

The friction arises, of course, when two essentially different
attitudes toward history are rubbed together. We of the Right
do not doubt that history is in fact tendentious, that the vectors
of social thought and action nowadays point to monolithic government and the atomization of norms. And it is certainly true
that most of the intellectuals in America appear to be disposed
to submit to the apparent imperatives of the twentieth century.
Apocalypse is in the air; and the cost of hitchhiking along with
the century, in Europe, in Asia, in America, is tacitly acknowledged to be the surrender of one's potty old self (the New
Left, to its credit, gags). The older intellectuals in America
grew into a world that seemed to be headed inescapably toward

social self-destruction; and then, when the Bomb came, toward physical self-destruction. Ten years ago Whittaker Chambers drew my attention to a note in the *Journal of the Goncourt Brothers,* one of whom had been taken that day by Madame Curie to see radium in the laboratory in which she had discovered it and had intuited where it would all leave us: "I thought I heard the voice of God, ringing out as clearly as the doorkeeper's at the Louvre at five o'clock every weekday afternoon, and uttering the same solemn words, 'Closing time, gentlemen!' "

Indeed no one of those who would resist the twentieth century would be so foolish as to say that it is the ideal arena in which to make the struggle. "If you wish to lead a quiet life," Trotsky said to a contemporary, "you picked the wrong century to be born in." "And indeed," Chambers commented, "the point was finally proved when a pickaxe mauled the brain of the man who framed those words."

So it is not an escapist's ignorance of the distinctive darkness of this century's shadows that makes possible the traces of whiggish optimism which are here and there discernible in this book. The spirit of defiance doesn't issue from a romantic American ignorance of the gloomy composure of the times we live in: but it does, I think, issue from distinctively American patterns of thought, from the essence of the American spirit. In America it is quite true that a substantial number of people are dragging their feet, resisting, kicking, complaining, hugging on to our ancient moorings. Consider:

(1) It is essentially the modernist view that only the state can negotiate the shoals that lie ahead of twentieth-century man. We are accordingly urged to believe in the state as the primary agent of individual concerns, a belief that is embedded in the analysis and rhetoric of socialism. Yet we are resisting, in America, the beatification of the state, most particularly in the past few years, when American conservatives have been joined by prominent liberals in expressing skepticism for the capacities of the state. Even though the statists did lull the general public into accepting the state as a genial servant, the state was never truly integrated as a member of the American household. The

native distrust the majority of Americans hold for the genus state has not, I am suggesting, completely dissipated. We are still reluctant to accept the state as a sacramental agent for transubstantiating private interest into public good.

Consider the course of postwar American history:

—The call for the nationalization of basic industries, so insistent in the immediate postwar years, is still, utterly stilled, droning away only in the fever swamps of the dogmatic Left.

—With all its power, the ideological Establishment has failed in its efforts to ease over to the federal government the primary responsibility for education, or health, or even housing.

Through inertia we might indeed end up, as de Tocqueville predicted we would, as minions of an omnipotent government; but it may yet be that American resistance by the minority is nowadays more remarkable than American acquiescence by the majority. At any typical gathering of Americans there are members in the audience who know prescriptively what you are talking about when you warn of the danger in relying on the state. Something, somehow, kept us from accepting the state, as the trend of the twentieth century seemed to dictate that we should do, as the sanctifying force in political affairs.

(2) Probably no country in the history of the world was ever so devoutly secularist as our own in its practical affairs; and yet the spiritual side of life, which the twentieth century is here to anachronize, is an unshakable part of us. The worst failure in America is the man who aspires to true cynicism. Let the lushest bloom of the twentieth century stand before a typical nonacademic American audience and declare his fidelity to materialism, and the audience will divide between those in whom he has aroused pity and those in whom he has aroused contempt. It is as fashionable in America as in Europe to declare that truth is not knowable, that the freedom of inquiry is the nearest we can hope to come to the truth. And yet, although the American people tolerate and even support universities dedicated in effect to the proposition that no truth is knowable, still, the majority of the universities' supporters and alumni organize their lives with reference to certitudes, certitudes which for reasons some-

times of humility, sometimes of laziness, sometimes of awe, they decline to identify. But that these certitudes are there, underlying human experience, they do not seem to doubt; and that—the faith of our fathers, it is sometimes called—gives the cast to our—to be sure equivocal—foreign policy: relieves us of tortured doubts over the question whether we had rather be dead than red, or red than dead. The utter failure of the collaborators in our midst to engage the public in a trauma of self-doubt over the issue of Red or Dead finally suggests that adamant resistance of the American people to submission to the twentieth century.

And finally, (3). There is what this book is about. There is an American renaissance of thought, a grinding of wheels, an on-going commotion. What is coming is the intellectualization of the spirit I speak of. Modern formulations are necessary even in defense of very ancient truths. Not because of any alleged anachronisms in the old ideas—the Beatitudes remain, surely, the essential statement of the Western code—but because the idiom of life is always changing, and we need to say things in such a way as to get inside the vibrations of modern life.

For years Americans seemed woefully incapable of speaking for themselves. The great apostles of the twentieth century are not American. With perhaps the exceptions of Oliver Wendell Holmes and John Dewey, no matter how hard they practise in the American idiom, our own intellectuals for the most part speak a derivative speech; speak in European accents. Adlai Stevenson was for reasons perfectly clear to me a greater hero in England than in America. So is John Kenneth Galbraith and David Riesman. So—dare I say it?—was Franklin Delano Roosevelt, notwithstanding the genius with which he seemed to be fashioning indigenous American ideals, though all the time he used an alien clay. In the past fifteen years in America a literature has emerged which taken together challenges root and branch the presumptions of the twentieth century. The intuitive wisdom of the founders of the American republic and of the European giants from whom they learned the art of statecraft is being rediscovered. The shallowness of the nineteenth-century social abstractionists has been penetrated, and their followers are thrown on the defensive. The meaning of the spirit of the West is being exhumed; impulses that never ceased to beat in the American heart are being revitalized.

Will we all be saved then? "Whom knows," as Leo Durocher once thoughtfully put it. I hope so, caring as I do that we shall be saved from this dreadful century, whose name stands for universal ignominy in the name of equality; and, in the name of freedom, a drab servitude to anonymous institutional idealisms. I hope and pray that, as time goes by, the twentieth century will shed the odium that clings to its name, that it may crystallize as the century in which the individual overtook technology —the century in which all the mechanical ingenuity of man, even when fired by man's basest political lusts, proved insufficient to sunder man's essential reliance on his Maker, the century in which we learned finally (no, not finally; we never learn finally), or at least for a period, how useless it is, how dangerous it is, to strut about ideologizing the world when we need to know that it was born intractable and will die intractable.

W.F.B.

✒ Selected Bibliography

The Contributors

I list here the published books of the authors whose works appear in this volume when these books touch, directly or indirectly, on the theme of conservatism.

L. BRENT BOZELL

With William F. Buckley, Jr., *McCarthy and His Enemies* (Chicago: Henry Regnery, 1954); *The Warren Revolution* (New Rochelle, N. Y.: Arlington House, 1966).

JAMES BURNHAM

The Managerial Revolution (New York: John Day, 1941); *The Machiavellians* (New York: John Day, 1943); *The Struggle for the World* (New York: John Day, 1947); *The Coming Defeat of Communism* (New York: John Day, 1950); *Containment or Liberation?* (New York: John Day, 1953); *The Web of Subversion* (New York: John Day, 1954); *Congress and the American Tradition* (Chicago: Henry Regnery, 1959); *Suicide of the West* (New York: John Day, 1964); *The War We Are In* (New Rochelle, N. Y.: Arlington House, 1967).

WHITTAKER CHAMBERS

Witness (New York: Random House, 1952); *Cold Friday* (New York: Random House, 1964); *Odyssey of a Friend,* edited by William F. Buckley, Jr. (New York: G. P. Putnam's Sons, 1970).

CHRISTOPHER DAWSON

The Age of the Gods (Boston: Houghton, Mifflin, 1928); *Progress and Religion* (London: Sheed & Ward, 1929); *The Making of Europe* (London: Sheed & Ward, 1932); *The Modern Dilemma* (London: Sheed & Ward, 1933); *The Spirit of the Oxford Movement* (New York: Sheed & Ward, 1933); *Enquiries into Religion and Culture* (New York: Sheed & Ward, 1933);

Mediaeval Religion (London: Sheed & Ward, 1934); *Religion and the Modern State* (London: Sheed & Ward, 1935); *Beyond Politics* (New York: Sheed & Ward, 1939); *Religion and Culture* (New York: Sheed & Ward, 1948); *Education and the Crisis of Christian Culture* (Chicago: Henry Regnery, 1949); *Religion and the Rise of Western Culture* (New York: Sheed & Ward, 1950); *Understanding Europe* (New York: Sheed & Ward, 1952); *The Dynamics of World History* (New York: Sheed & Ward, 1957, c1956); *The Crisis of Western Education* (New York: Sheed & Ward, 1961); *The Dividing of Christendom* (New York: Sheed & Ward, 1965); *The Historic Reality of Christian Culture* (New York: Harper and Row, 1965); *The Formation of Christendom* (New York: Sheed & Ward, 1967).

MAX EASTMAN
Since Lenin Died (New York: Boni and Liveright, 1925); *Leon Trotsky* (New York: Greenberg, 1925); *Marx, Lenin and the Science of Revolution* (London: Allen and Unwin, 1926); *The End of Socialism in Russia* (Boston: Little, Brown, 1937); *Marxism, Is It Science?* (New York: Norton, 1940); *Stalin's Russia and the Crisis in Socialism* (New York: Norton, 1940); *Reflections on the Failure of Socialism* (New York: Devin-Adair, 1955); *Love and Revolution* (New York: Random House, 1964).

MILTON FRIEDMAN
Essays in Positive Economics (Chicago: University of Chicago Press, 1953); *A Theory of the Consumption Function* (Princeton, N. J.: Princeton University Press, 1957); *A Program for Monetary Stability* (New York: Fordham University Press, 1959); *Price Theory* (Chicago: Aldine Publishing Company, 1962; rev. ed., 1968); *Capitalism and Freedom* (Chicago: University of Chicago Press, 1962); *Inflation: Causes and Consequences* (Bombay, N. Y.: Asia Publishing House, 1963); *Post War Trends in Monetary Theory and Policy* (Athens: Center for Economic Research, 1963); *Dollars and Deficits* (Englewood Cliffs, N. J.: Prentice-Hall, 1968); *The Optimum Quantity of Money* (Chicago: Aldine Publishing Company, 1969); with Walter W. Heller, *Monetary vs. Fiscal Policy* (New York: Norton, 1969).

JEFFREY HART

Political Writers of Eighteenth-Century England (New York: Alfred A. Knopf, 1964); *Viscount Bolingbroke: Tory Humanist* (Toronto: University of Toronto Press, 1965); *The American Dissent* (Garden City, N. Y.: Doubleday, 1966).

HENRY HAZLITT

Editor, *A Practical Program for America* (New York: Harcourt, Brace, 1932); *Will Dollars Save the World?* (New York: D. Appleton-Century Co., 1947); *The Great Idea* (New York: Appleton-Century-Crofts, 1951); *The Failure of the New Economics* (Princeton, N. J.: Van Nostrand, 1959); *What You Should Know About Inflation* (rev. ed.; Princeton, N. J.: Van Nostrand, 1960); *Economics in One Lesson* (rev. ed.; New York: Macfadden Books, 1962); *The Foundations of Morality* (Princeton, N. J.: Van Nostrand, 1964); *Time Will Run Back* (New Rochelle, N. Y.: Arlington House, 1966); *Man Vs. the Welfare State* (New Rochelle, N. Y.: Arlington House, 1970).

JANE JACOBS

The Death and Life of Great American Cities (New York: Random House, 1961); *The Economy of Cities* (New York: Random House, 1969).

HARRY V. JAFFA

Thomism and Aristotelianism (Chicago: University of Chicago Press, 1952); editor, with Robert W. Johannsen, *In the Name of the People* (Columbus: Ohio State University Press, 1959); *Crisis of the House Divided* (Garden City, N. Y.: Doubleday, 1959); with Allan Bloom, *Shakespeare's Politics* (New York: Basic Books, 1964).

WILLMOORE KENDALL

With Austin Ranney, *Democracy and the American Party System* (New York: Harcourt, Brace and World, 1956); *John Locke and the Doctrine of Majority Rule* (Urbana: University of Illinois Press, 1959); *War and the Use of Force* (Denver: Swallow Press, 1959); *The Conservative Affirmation* (Chicago: Henry Regnery, 1963); editor, with George W. Carey, *Liberalism Versus Conservatism* (Princeton, N. J.: Van Nostrand, 1966); with George W. Carey, *Basic Symbols of the American Political*

Tradition (Baton Rouge: Louisiana State University Press, 1970).

HUGH KENNER

Paradox in Chesterton (New York: Sheed & Ward, 1947); *The Poetry of Ezra Pound* (Norfolk, Conn.: New Directions, 1951); *Wyndham Lewis* (Norfolk, Conn.: New Directions, 1954); *Dublin's Joyce* (Bloomington: Indiana University Press, 1956); editor, *The Art of Poetry* (New York: Rinehart, 1959); *The Invisible Poet: T. S. Eliot* (New York: McDowell, Obolensky, 1959); *Samuel Beckett* (New York: Grove Press, 1962, c1961); editor, *Seventeenth-Century Poetry* (New York: Holt, Rinehart and Winston, 1964); *Flaubert, Joyce and Beckett: The Stoic Comedians* (London: Witt, Allen, 1964); editor, *Studies in Change* (Englewood Cliffs, N. J.: Prentice-Hall, 1965); *The Counterfeiters* (Bloomington: Indiana University Press, 1968).

RUSSELL KIRK

Randolph of Roanoke (Chicago: University of Chicago Press, 1951); *The Conservative Mind* (Chicago: Henry Regnery, 1953); *A Program for Conservatives* (Chicago: Henry Regnery, 1954); *Academic Freedom* (Chicago: Henry Regnery, 1955); *Beyond the Dreams of Avarice* (Chicago: Henry Regnery, 1956); *The Intelligent Woman's Guide to Conservatism* (New York: Devin-Adair, 1957); *The American Cause* (Chicago: Henry Regnery, 1957); *Confessions of a Bohemian Tory* (New York: Fleet Publishing Corp., 1963); *Edmund Burke: A Genius Reconsidered* (New Rochelle, N. Y.: Arlington House, 1967); with James McClellan, *The Political Principles of Robert A. Taft* (New York: Fleet Press, 1967); *Enemies of the Permanent Things* (New Rochelle, N. Y.: Arlington House, 1969).

FRANK S. MEYER

The Moulding of Communists (New York: Harcourt, Brace and World, 1961); *In Defense of Freedom* (Chicago: Henry Regnery, 1962); editor, *What Is Conservatism?* (New York: Holt, Rinehart and Winston, 1964); editor, *The African Nettle* (New

York: John Day, 1965); *The Conservative Mainstream* (New Rochelle, N. Y.: Arlington House, 1969).

JOHN COURTNEY MURRAY, S. J.
Morality and Modern War (New York: The Church Peace Union, 1959); *We Hold These Truths* (New York: Sheed & Ward, 1960); *The Problem of God: Yesterday and Today* (New Haven: Yale University Press, 1964); *The Problem of Religious Freedom* (Westminster, Md.: Newman Press, 1965); editor, *Freedom and Man* (New York: P. J. Kenedy, 1965).

ALBERT JAY NOCK
The Myth of a Guilty Nation (New York: Huebach, 1922); *Jefferson* (New York: Harcourt, Brace, 1926); *On Doing the Right Thing* (New York: Harper, 1928); with C. R. Wilson, *Francis Rabelais, the Man and His Work* (New York: Harper, 1929); *A Journey into Rabelais' France* (New York: Morrow and Company, 1934); *A Journal of These Days, June 1932-December 1933* (New York: Morrow and Company, 1934); *Our Enemy, The State* (New York: Morrow and Company, 1935; reprinted 1959); *Free Speech and Plain Language* (New York: Morrow and Company, 1937); *Henry George* (New York: Morrow and Company, 1939); *Journal of Forgotten Days, May 1934-October 1935* (Chicago: Henry Regnery, 1948); *Snoring as a Fine Art, and Twelve Other Essays* (Rindge, N. J.: R. R. Smith, 1958); *Selected Letters,* edited by Francis J. Nock (Caldwell, Idaho: Caxton Printers, 1962); *Memoirs of a Superfluous Man* (Chicago: Henry Regnery, 1964).

MICHAEL OAKESHOTT
Experience and Its Modes (Cambridge: The University Press, 1933); *The Social and Political Doctrines of Contemporary Europe* (New York: Macmillan, 1942); editor, *Hobbes's Leviathan* (New York: Macmillan, 1947); *Political Education* (Cambridge: Bowes and Bowes, 1951); *The Voice of Poetry in the Conversation of Mankind* (London: Bowes and Bowes, 1959); *Rationalism in Politics* (New York: Basic Books, 1962).

MORTIMER SMITH

And Madly Teach (Chicago: Henry Regnery, 1949); *William Jay Gaynor, Mayor of New York* (Chicago: Henry Regnery, 1951); *The Diminished Mind* (Chicago: Henry Regnery, 1954); *The Public Schools in Crisis* (Chicago: Henry Regnery, 1956).

LEO STRAUSS

On Tyranny (New York: Political Science Classics, 1948); *Natural Right and History* (Chicago: University of Chicago Press, 1950); *The Political Philosophy of Hobbes* (Chicago: University of Chicago Press, 1952); *What Is Political Philosophy?* (Glencoe, Ill.: The Free Press, 1959); editor, with Joseph Cropsey, *History of Political Philosophy* (Chicago: Rand McNally, 1963); *The City and the Man* (Chicago: Rand McNally, 1964); *Spinoza's Critique of Religion* (New York: Schocken Books, 1965); *Socrates and Aristophanes* (New York: Basic Books, 1966); *Thoughts on Machiavelli* (2nd ed.; Seattle: University of Washington Press, 1969).

ERNEST VAN DEN HAAG

Education as an Industry (New York: A. M. Kelley, 1956); with Ralph Ross, *The Fabric of Society* (New York: Harcourt, Brace and World, 1957); *Passion and Social Constraint* (New York: Stein and Day, 1963).

ERIC VOEGELIN

The Nature of the American Spirit (*Ueber die Form des Amerikanischen Geistes* [Tubingen: Mohr, 1928]); *The New Science of Politics* (Chicago: University of Chicago Press, 1952); *Order and History* (4 vols.; Baton Rouge: Louisiana State University Press, 1956–71); *Science, Politics, and Gnosticism* (Chicago: Henry Regnery, 1968).

FREDERICK D. WILHELMSEN

Hilaire Belloc: No Alienated Man (New York: Sheed & Ward, 1953); *Man's Knowledge of Reality* (Englewood Cliffs, N. J.: Prentice-Hall, 1956); *The Metaphysics of Love* (New York: Sheed & Ward, 1962); *Seeds of Anarchy* (Dallas: Argus Press, 1969).

GARRY WILLS

Chesterton, Man and Mask (New York: Sheed & Ward, 1961); *Solomon the Wise* (Garden City, N. Y.: Doubleday, 1961); *Politics and Catholic Freedom* (Chicago: Henry Regnery, 1964); *Roman Culture* (New York: Braziller, 1966); with Ovid Demaris, *Jack Ruby* (New York: New American Library, 1967); *The Second Civil War: Arming for Armageddon* (New York: New American Library, 1968.)

Further Reading

American conservatism is distinctive, conditioned of course by the special features of American history. But it is also continuous with the orthodox moral and political traditions of Western civilization, and serious students should therefore know something of that tradition. As a prolegomenon to readings in more recent conservative thought, one should read some Plato, particularly, the *Republic*, and the Socratic dialogues—*Euthyphro, Apology, Crito*—Aristotle's *Ethics*, St. Augustine's *Confessions*, Virgil's *Aeneid*, and the New Testament. Highly recommended seminal interpretations are Werner Jaeger's *Paideia* (3 vols.; New York: Oxford University Press, 1939–1945), and Eric Voegelin's *Order and History* (4 vols.; Baton Rouge: Louisiana State University Press, 1956–1971).

Reading in post-Renaissance political theory is indispensable if only to gain command over some of the terms of the modern controversy. Include Hobbes' *Leviathan*, Locke's *Essay Concerning Civil Government*, Burke's *Reflections*, Mill's *On Liberty*, Nietzsche's *Will to Power*, Rousseau's *Confessions*, Newman's *Apologia Pro Vita Sua*.

A number of narrative histories are helpful, e.g., Macaulay's and Churchill's. A revolution in the understanding of history was brought about in our time largely by Herbert Butterfield's *The Whig Interpretation of History* (New York: Charles Scribner's Sons, 1951). The older Whig history depicted "progressive" heroes (Luther, Drake, Woodrow Wilson) in combat with conservative villains (The Council of Trent, the Spanish Armada,

xlviii   Selected Bibliography

Philip II). Butterfield argues for a profounder view of the concrete historical realities. Butterfield's book has resulted in a
more accurate view of the behavior of real men under actual
historical conditions, and helped to liberate us from Whig historical melodrama.

Turning to America, a close acquaintance, please, with the
Declaration of Independence, the Federalist Papers, and the
Constitution. (They are readily available in many editions.)
Max Farrand's *The Framing of the Constitution* (New Haven:
Yale University Press, 1913; rev. ed., 1962) is the standard
source for the necessary information about the Philadelphia
Convention, but it should be supplemented by the major forth-
coming study of constitutional tradition and the tensions within
it by Willmoore Kendall, *Basic Symbols of the American Politi-
cal Tradition*, with George W. Carey (Baton Rouge: Louisiana
State University Press, 1970), and by Harry Jaffa's *Crisis of the
House Divided* (Garden City, N. Y.: Doubleday, 1959), a
masterful analysis of the crucial issues at stake in the Lincoln-
Douglas debates.

The student desiring to survey the general area of conservative thought since the Second World War is handicapped by
the fact that most comprehensive attempts to deal with the subject have been polemical. Clinton Rossiter's *Conservatism in
America* (New York: Alfred A. Knopf, 1955; rev. ed., 1962) is
mildly sympathetic, but a little evasive. Industrious attempts
have been made to discredit conservatives by linking them with
the extremist fringes—present in any broad political movement.
The specimen of this approach is *Danger on the Right* (New
York: Random House, 1964) by Arnold Forster and Benjamin
Epstein. At a more sophisticated level, *The New American
Right* (New York: Criterion Books, 1955; revised and updated
as *The Radical Right* [Garden City, N. Y.: Doubleday, 1963]),
edited by Daniel Bell, seeks to discredit the entire American
Right through a process of sociologization: the Right is "losing
status" and is therefore angry, etc., etc.

Morton M. Auerbach's *The Conservative Illusion* (New York:
Columbia University Press, 1959) is a polemical work against

the ideas of Burke as these influence modern conservatism, but it is not very firm in its scholarly or analytical grasp.

Jeffrey Hart's *The American Dissent* (Garden City, N. Y.: Doubleday, 1966) is a good critical survey of contemporary American conservatism, especially as that has been articulated by the various contributors to *National Review*. M. Stanton Evans addresses himself to the American political scene in *The Future of Conservatism* (New York: Holt, Rinehart and Winston, 1968) and shows that the constantly reported death of American conservatism is, to say the least, an exaggeration. Allen Guttmann in *The Conservative Tradition in America* (New York: Oxford University Press, 1967) tries to show that while it is thought that there was an important conservative tradition, in fact that tradition is nevertheless entirely liberal; but his view of the American political tradition is drawn entirely from liberal sources, *QED*.

It frequently is said that modern conservatism was born as a response to the French Revolution and its doctrines. Those doctrines constituted—and still do—a powerful challenge to the orthodox Western tradition. The student should therefore acquaint himself with the French Revolution and some of the analytical and controversial writing surrounding it. The very abundance of histories of the Revolution may constitute an impediment to knowledge, that abundance plus the ferocious controversial nature of many of them. For a single responsible and readable history of the Revolution I would suggest M. J. Sydenham's *The French Revolution* (New York: G. P. Putnam's Sons, 1965), or *Paris in the Terror* by Stanley Loomis (Philadelphia: Lippincott, 1964). Burke's *Reflections* and Joseph de Maistre's *Works*, edited by Jack Lively (New York: Macmillan, 1965), should be read as important contemporary responses to the Revolution.

Crane Brinton's *The Anatomy of Revolution* (rev. ed.; Englewood Cliffs, N. J.: Prentice-Hall, 1952) is a historical analysis of the structure of revolution. Brinton deals in detail with the French Revolution but shows how the pattern revealed there, and the evolution from reform through the use of force to the use of terror, is exhibited by other revolutions as well. *The Socio-logical Tradition* by Robert A. Nisbet (New York: Basic Books, 1967), is an important study of such nineteenth-century sociologists as Durkheim, Weber, and de Tocqueville, and has as its central theme the fact that these seminal writers were part of a conservative reaction to the events and doctrines of the French Revolution. In *The Origins of Totalitarian Democracy* (New York: Praeger, 1960), J. L. Talmon demonstrates that modern totalitarianism has its roots in doctrines central to the French Revolution. *The Brave New World of the Enlightenment* (Ann Arbor: University of Michigan Press, 1961) by Louis I. Bredvold shows the intellectual pedigree in seventeenth- and eighteenth-century radical doctrine of some characteristic modern radical illusions, and *The Relevance of Edmund Burke*, edited by Peter Stanlis (New York: P. J. Kenedy, 1964), shows the continuing viability of Burke's moral and political insights.

A powerful current of thought on the Left has endeavored to depict the United States as the contemporary analogue of the *Ancien Régime,* and it is worth getting acquainted with the best works of this vein. Martin Oppenheimer's *The Urban Guerrilla* (Chicago: Quadrangle Books, 1969) has two principal aspects: a most able sociological analysis of the various kinds of contemporary revolutionary movements, and also recommendations to contemporary American revolutionists on how to go about destroying America. In *Empire and Revolution* (New York: Random House, 1969), David Horowitz argues along largely traditional Marxist lines that capitalism is necessarily expansionist, to the destruction of underdeveloped countries and their culture, and therefore must be destroyed.

Modern conservatism exhibits two main aspects, which are really responses to two challenges. One aspect, sometimes called the traditionalist, arises out of the struggle to preserve traditional Western moral and social values against the disintegrative assault of liberal doctrine and the disintegrative effect of certain modern social conditions. Both British and American writings have figured prominently here. I would recommend G. K. Chesterton's *Orthodoxy* (Garden City, N. Y.: Doubleday, 1959), and

C. S. Lewis's *The Abolition of Man* (New York: Macmillan, 1947) and *The Case for Christianity* (New York: Macmillan, 1943) as profound works in defense of orthodox Christianity. From Christopher Dawson's voluminous writings I would single out *The Crisis of Western Education* (New York: Sheed & Ward, 1961) and *Enquiries Into Religion and Culture* (New York: Sheed & Ward, 1933). Like T. S. Eliot's *Notes Toward the Definition of Culture* (New York: Harcourt, Brace and World, 1949), these explore the profound relationship that exists between Christianity and the historic values of Western civilization.

Not surprisingly, poets have exhibited a special awareness of the roots of meaning in our civilization, and some of them have been particularly effective in raising them into conscious awareness. T. S. Eliot's essays are generally to be recommended, especially his "Tradition and the Individual Talent" (*The Sacred Wood* [New York: Alfred A. Knopf, 1930]), and the essays on humanism in *Selected Essays* (rev. ed.; New York: Harcourt, Brace and World, 1950). Other important poets have written out of analogous traditionalist impulses, for instance, Allen Tate's *Essays of Four Decades* (Chicago: Swallow Press, 1969) and John Crowe Ransom's *The World's Body* (Baton Rouge: Louisiana State University Press, 1968).

In *We Hold These Truths* (New York: Sheed & Ward, 1960), John Courtney Murray investigates the importance of the tradition of natural law in the history of American culture and politics (see Essay 2) and concludes that a revival of this tradition is essential. In *The Problem of God: Yesterday and Today* (New Haven: Yale University Press, 1964), Father Murray addresses himself effectively and analytically to the historical and cultural sources of modern disbelief, showing that the pervasive atheistic and agnostic assumptions of much of contemporary society are culturally and historically conditioned.

Russell Kirk's *The Conservative Mind* (Chicago: Henry Regnery, 1953) is a study of English and American conservative thought from Burke to Santayana, and a successful attempt to define a conservative intellectual tradition.

The revival of serious interest in political theory in American academic and intellectual circles is largely due to the teaching and writing of Leo Strauss, whose characteristic approach is a close and critical reading of the original text. His *Natural Right and History* (Chicago: University of Chicago Press, 1950), is a profound study of the evolution of the tradition of the natural law, of the great tensions within the classic tradition of Western political thought, and his collection of essays, *What Is Political Philosophy?* (Glencoe, Ill.: The Free Press, 1959), continues his investigation of that classic tradition. In an entirely different vein, but just as seriously concerned with political theory, is *The New Science of Politics* (Chicago: University of Chicago Press, 1952), in which Eric Voegelin traces the revolutionary and utopian impulses within Western history to the ancient heresy of gnosticism.

A mention is in order on the unique presence of George Santayana, a writer and thinker not easy to situate, yet profoundly civilized and civilizing. I recommend his autobiographical *Persons and Places* (3 vols.; New York: Charles Scribner's Sons, 1944) as an introduction to this deeply traditional sensibility.

The above writers have been concerned mainly with the recovery and/or preservation of our central moral, religious, and cultural values. Others have been primarily concerned to resist the encroachments of the leviathan state on the freedoms of the individual. Much of this resistance has come from the work of economists. Mr. Hazlitt (Essay 7, pp. 144–189) gives a complete bibliography for those who want to pursue this tradition. Frank Meyer has written profoundly on the requirements and problems of freedom and modern conditions. See especially his *In Defense of Freedom* (Chicago: Henry Regnery, 1962).

Within American conservatism, Willmoore Kendall set himself the task of defining in a precise and systematic way the distinctive features of American conservatism. The essays collected in his *The Conservative Affirmation* (Chicago: Henry Regnery, 1963) make original contributions to our understanding of the American political and constitutional traditions, and these essays are a valuable introduction to his thought. The tensions

Kendall defines within our constitutional tradition are those that are formed political controversies at this time. In *Congress and the American Tradition* (Chicago: Henry Regnery, 1959), James Burnham discusses the gradual preemption of legislative sovereignty within the American historical situation. In *Suicide of the West* (New York: John Day, 1964), he examines deeply the conflict between Western civilization and Communist doctrine backed by Russian power, and he probes the crisis in Western morale which has caused the West, rather than the Communist world, to emerge as the principal victim of that antagonism. No understanding of modern conservatism is possible without an appreciation of the profundity of the issues involved in this conflict.

For deeply moving and illuminating expressions of the individual experience of Communism I would recommend: *The Case of Comrade Tulayev* by Victor Serge (Garden City, N. Y.: Doubleday, 1950); *I Speak for the Silent* by Vladimir B. Tchernavin (Boston: Hale, Cushman & Flint, Inc., 1935); *Speak Memory: An Autobiography Revisited* by Vladimir Nabokov (New York: G. P. Putnam's Sons, 1966); *The Captive Mind* by Czeslaw Milosz (New York: Alfred A. Knopf, 1953); *Doctor Zhivago* by Boris Pasternak (New York: Pantheon Books, 1958); *Assignment in Utopia* by Eugene Lyons (rev. ed.; New York: Twin Circle Publishing, 1967); *One Day in the Life of Ivan Denisovich* by Alexander Solzhenitsyn (New York: Praeger, 1963); *The Burned Bramble* by Manès Sperber (Garden City, N. Y.: Doubleday, 1951); *Homage to Catalonia* by George Orwell (New York: Harcourt, Brace and World, 1952); *The Cypresses Believe in God* by José Maria Gironella (New York: Alfred A. Knopf, 1955); *Bread and Wine* by Ignazio Silone (rev. ed.; New York: Atheneum, 1962); *Witness* by Whittaker Chambers (New York: Random House, 1952); *I Chose Freedom* by Victor Kravchenko (New York: Charles Scribner's Sons, 1946); *Darkness at Noon* by Arthur Koestler (New York: Macmillan, 1941); *The Journals of André Gide* (New York: Alfred A. Knopf, 1956); *Ward 7* by Valeriy Tarsis (New York: E. P. Dutton, 1965); *On Socialist Realism* by Abram Tertz (Andrei Sinyavsky)

(New York: Random House, 1960); *The Penkovskiy Papers* by Oleg Penkovskiy (Garden City, N. Y.: Doubleday, 1965); *Moscow Summer* by Mihajlo Mihajlov (New York: Farrar, Straus & Giroux, 1965); *Conversations with Stalin* by Milovan Djilas (New York: Harcourt, Brace and World, 1962).

For a strategic understanding of the problem, see also James Burnham's *The Struggle for the World* (New York: John Day, 1947), Henry Kissinger's *The Necessity for Choice* (New York: Harper & Row, 1961), Robert Strausz-Hupé's *Protracted Conflict* (New York: Harper & Row, 1959), Gerhart Niemeyer's *An Inquiry into Soviet Mentality* (New York: Praeger, 1956). For a sample of the psychological impulses behind much of the heterodox revolutionary enterprises in the so-called Third World, see Franz Fanon's *The Wretched of the Earth* (New York: Grove Press, 1965), which is both representative and valuable.

Conservative insight into social reality is frequently confirmed by the best work in the social sciences though this work is often produced by authors who think of themselves as liberals. In *Beyond the Melting Pot* (Cambridge, Mass.: The MIT Press, 1963), Nathan Glazer and Daniel P. Moynihan study the ethnic structure of New York City and show convincingly that the "melting pot"—i.e., integrationist theory of American society—does not reflect the social reality. Professor Will Herberg writes with enormous insight in *Protestant, Catholic, Jew* (rev. ed.; Garden City, N. Y.: Doubleday Anchor, 1960) to the same effect, and to others equally illuminating. Martin Anderson in his influential *The Federal Bulldozer* (Cambridge, Mass.: The MIT Press, 1964) devastatingly confirms the thesis of Jane Jacobs already suggested in the text. In *Lament for a Generation* (New York: Farrar, Straus & Giroux, 1960), Ralph de Toledano brilliantly illuminates the philosophical and cultural evolution of a conservative. In *The Conflict of Generations* (New York: Basic Books, 1969), Lewis Feuer has light to shed on contemporary youthful turbulence which he places in both a psychological and historical perspective. See also *Seeds of Anarchy* by F. D. Wilhelmsen (Dallas: Argus Press, 1969).

American
Conservative Thought
in the Twentieth Century

Part One

The Historical and Intellectual Background

Garry Wills's breathtaking essay, "The Convenient State," marshals arguments against assigning to the state responsibilities it is metaphysically incapable of exercising—unless the state were to achieve such relations with the people as the people and their right-minded political philosophers (their friends) have eloquently warned against throughout deliberated time. *"For the Christian,"* Wills notes after surveying classical and early Christian thought (Wills's Ph.D. degree, taken at Yale, was in the classics), *"the state can no longer fill up man's failings or aim at self-sufficiency and ideal justice. The earthly order must be identified as temporal, an area of trial and transition."*

"When ideal justice is set before the community as its political end," he concludes, *"the only efficient path towards that ever receding goal is the marshaling of force in the state."* Under the circumstances, *". . . the end of the state* [should be] *. . . the orderly advancement and discipline of society as the necessary ground of human activity. . . .* [The] *system of checks is worked out by each community,"* Wills concludes, *"but it is based on the general truth that the state's role is to enforce equity and order, rather than justice and charity."*

3

Thus—precisely—the "convenient" state—the state with which Michael Oakeshott is comfortable (see below, p. 103). Mr. Wills's essay was originally published as a part of a symposium edited by Frank S. Meyer entitled *What Is Conservatism?* Mr. Wills has written several books on disparate subjects (*Roman Culture, Jack Ruby*), teaches at Johns Hopkins University, and writes for *Esquire* magazine, *National Review*, and the scholarly journals.

John Courtney Murray was an aristocratic New Yorker who though a Jesuit priest is widely acknowledged as the principal apostle of the separation of church and state within a New World Catholic context. His special relevance here is as a noble advocate of the crucial role of society, which sets him up in opposition to the obdurate individualism of such as Albert Jay Nock and William Graham Sumner. Father Murray's best-known essays were collected and published in 1960 in the volume *We Hold These Truths*. In making the case for "social freedom" and for the idea of the consensus, he reminds us that the earliest Americans rejected by anticipation the nineteenth-century notion of the "outlaw conscience" ("*conscientia exlex,* the conscience that knows no law higher than its own subjective imperatives"). "*Part of the inner architecture of the American ideal of freedom has been,*" Father Murray points out, "*the profound conviction that only a virtuous people can be free. It is not an American belief,*" he reminds Wilsonian liberals sharply, "*that free government is inevitable, only that it is possible, and that its possibility can be realized only when the people as a whole are inwardly governed by the recognized imperatives of the universal moral law.*" That is a conservative *aperçu*, plain and simple; and although it is ungentlemanly to argue against the co-optors who have so deeply desired to have Father Murray as one of their own for reasons (a) admirable (they liked and admired him for his emphasis on secular pluralism, which they took to signify a tacit acquiescence in philosophical relativism binding at all levels in civil society) and, (b) less than admirable (Whee! A Catholic priest who speaks like us!).

Although others (notably F. A. Hayek) have done it more meticulously, Father Murray's eloquent repudiation of the French revolutionary tradition is quite good enough, flatly rejecting it as, if you can bear it, un-American: *"In considerable part,"* he writes of the Declaration of the Rights of Man, *"the letter was a parchment-child of the Enlightenment, a top-of-the-brain concoction of a set of men who did not understand that a political community, like man himself, has roots in history and in nature. They believed that a state could be simply a work of art, a sort of absolute beginning, an artifact of which abstract human reason could be the sole artisan. Moreover, their exaggerated individualism had shut them off from a view of the organic nature of the human community; their social atomism would permit no institutions or associations intermediate between the individual and the state."* It has been said at greater length, but not, since Burke (see Hart below, p. 461), better.

L. Brent Bozell was driven to inquire into the origins of judicial review by what he deemed the excesses of the Supreme Court under the leadership of Earl Warren. He produced a little-noticed book, *The Warren Revolution*, excerpts from the first chapter of which are here reproduced. It is the finest recent statement I have seen on the idea of federalism, incorporating the traditional arguments against abstractionist government, and showing how the framers consciously understood themselves to be engaged in devising mechanisms that would mesh together, geared less to abstractionist paradigms than to real situations. The chapter is cut off at the point where Mr. Bozell asks rhetorically, *"Where as a practical matter do we go from here?"*—the reason being that his answer is, essentially— nowhere. Mr. Bozell's interest subsequently turned to essentially religious matters; indeed he now feels that his own book is irrelevant on the grounds that it does not ask what he deems to be the deeper question, namely, how does a society set out consciously to guide itself by the precepts of the natural law?[1] He appears to have approached theocracy, but en route he de-

[1]See *Triumph,* III, No. 2 (February 1968), pp. 10–14.

vised a majestic statement of the altogether conservative disposition of the framers to launch a republic of separated powers,
and Mr. Bozell was certainly not alone in the conviction that the
Warren Court ushered in what might be called a new age in
American politics; that, by the aggrandizement of its own role,
it caused organic dislocations, and that it is not yet known what
will be their consequences.

Mr. Frank Meyer's essay, "What Is Conservatism?", is his own
contribution to a symposium organized a few years ago under
the title *Left, Right and Center.* He gives his own answer to the
question he posed, tracing the contemporary efforts to fuse
once more the objective moral order (the kind of thing Father
Murray stresses) and the liberalism of the nineteenth century
(which flowed into contemporary conservatism via such as
William Graham Sumner and Albert Jay Nock): to reunite what
the nineteenth century sundered. Mr. Meyer goes so far as to
reproduce the credo of a contemporary political society (the
American Conservative Union), which he deems a thoroughly
satisfactory statement of the principles of American conservatism. Mr. Meyer came to conservatism through the agony of
communism (he is the author of the memorable, *The Moulding
of Communists*). He is thought by some to have emerged over-
touched by ideological rigidity. In fact, close students of his
journalism (he writes regularly for *National Review,* of which
he is a senior editor), have remarked the diligence with which
he pursues the fusionists' dream of a conservatism that is both
assertive in its commitment to individual freedom and yet
aware of the mitigating roles of tradition and culture.

1 The Convenient State

Garry Wills

The liberal and the conservative who would sort out their differences, for some constructive purpose, encounter from the outset an unusual problem: the very things that seem to unite them are a cause of confusion and deeper cleavage. Even when we of the West fall out, we select our weapons from the same armory; and, as (in the stock jibe) the same medieval God heard the prayers of opposed armies, so Plato and Aristotle seem to hover over the ranks of every possible faction in the civilization they helped to create. Even when men undermine our citadel, they do it with our engines; and, in greatest part, unconsciously. This brings the bitterness of fratricide into the dispute over our inheritance. The conservative claims guardianship over the storehouse of Western wisdom. The liberal contends that the genius of the West lies in its capacity for innovation, in a daring reliance on reason and a resiliency toward change.

Because these two forces share a vocabulary and, to some extent, a vision, the discovery that they are saying different things in the same words leads, on either side, to suspicion of betrayal; and the variations in meaning that the common vocabulary suffers seem to open an unbridgeable chasm. In no case is this so clear as in the allegiance of both sides to the principles of freedom and order; for neither party denies the necessity of some polarity and balance between the two. The liberal is traditionally considered the spokesman of freedom, the conservative of

From *What Is Conservatism?*, edited by Frank S. Meyer (New York: Holt, Rinehart and Winston, 1964), Chapter 9, pp. 152–177. Copyright © 1964 by the Intercollegiate Society of Individualists. Reprinted by permission of Holt, Rinehart and Winston, Inc.

order. But, even aside from the shifting maneuvers these terms have lately performed, no one ever claimed that such a simplistic division was absolute. The most partisan liberal cannot, if he claims to speak responsibly, deny that conservatives are concerned with guaranteeing freedom. And the archest reactionary this side of insanity cannot claim that the liberal is not trying to construct a social order. In fact, as time wears on, the stress on principles ancillary to their professed ones makes liberals and conservatives seem to change places, so that liberals now champion a strong central government, and conservatives speak for economic and political individualism. Is the difference between these two, then, merely accidental at any moment because it is, in the long run, only a matter of degree, the conservative laying heavy emphasis on the prescriptive, the liberal on the spontaneous, elements in political life? Given the same set of ingredients, do the cooks simply vary their recipes? No; the shared language disguises, and so perpetuates, fundamental differences.

Freedom and order, justice and settled interests, progress and tradition . . . the words are used of different things in the different camps; and when these concepts cluster to form more complex groupings of ideas—republic, democracy, self-determination, aristocracy—the differences undergo a staggering multiplication. It is true that freedom and order will be correlates in any of the systems advanced. But this, again, impedes communication, since the varieties of meaning in the one word will exact an answering variation in the other. It is useless, therefore, to debate whether the emphasis should be on freedom or order, or to adjudicate between major political systems by discussing the *degree* of freedom desired, or the *extent* of order, as if these were constant substances varying only in quantity. The question should be *what kind* of order, *what kind* of freedom, is at issue. Our history is littered with defeated varieties of each virtue. To take an obvious case, there is the theocratic definition of freedom and order—principles which become, under this rubric, Virtue and Providence. In such a scheme, freedom is freedom to be virtuous, and order is the right to exact virtue from man as his proper attribute. At another extreme of our experience is anarchism, which (read the paradox how you will) is a system for avoiding system. It, too, has a principle of order—the removal and continued negation of political coercion—corresponding to its untrammeled freedom.

These systems are both unworkable, since virtue that is enforced is not virtue, and anarchy that is guaranteed against control is to that extent controlled. But their *ignis fatuus* has drawn men down tragic paths, and they will continue to beckon. The important thing is to see that there is no use distinguishing such schemes by *degree,* as having a different internal disposition of freedom and order. The anarchist does not err in exalting freedom over order, but in exalting the wrong kind of freedom and the wrong kind of order. It is his whole philosophical framework that is incorrectly established. He is right about the machinery of these correlates; he is only wrong about the world. To put it another way, the relation of freedom to order is a dynamic one that can manifest itself in any number of consistent programs; and a political system is therefore to be judged by its substance, not by its dynamics.

Thus Mill cripples his discourse from the start when he calls the treatise on liberty an attempt to adjudicate the ancient "struggle between Liberty and Authority,"—as if these were two things of perduring and permanent meaning, but with shifting relations, toward each other, of supremacy or subjection. The real difference, for instance, between the historically normative polities of ancient Greece and the "barbarians" was not simply one of liberty as opposed to tyranny. The ancient empires had a mystical sanction. Their art and customs show no awareness of the individualism that emerged in Hellas' statues of man. Liberty, in such a society, has another meaning than it was to take on in the debates of the Hellenes. And in the primitive societies so thoroughly scrutinized by modern anthropologists, the instruments for educating and preserving the individual, under severe disadvantages, are the very disciplines for initiation into the political order on which all life depends. In such a world, the relation of freedom to order continues to exist, but as a drastically reduced version of the religious maxim, *cui servire regnare*. A similar paradox is worked out in the Marxist dialectic, and summarized, satirically, in Orwell's "Freedom is slavery." Far from being a game of the mind, this slogan expresses the only possible approach to freedom in the Marxist world; the Communist paradox has the same consistency as the Christian language used to describe a freedom heightened to indefectible obedience in the beatific vision. The only error is trying to acclimatize heaven to the intemperate regions of practical politics. Again, men are right about the relation of freedom to order, and only wrong about the world.

Since freedom and order are correlates, an absolutism at one pole leads to an absolutism at the other. The Marxist starts from order and asserts that "freedom is slavery." The absolutists of individualism start at the other pole but end in the same contradiction. Even the most extreme libertarian must justify his position by an appeal to order. Mill, for instance, advocates a free market of ideas as the most infallible guide to certitude— enough-talk automatically producing truth, triumphant over all pretenders and "self-evident." Thus freedom becomes authority and arms itself with all the instruments the liberal state has taken to itself in order to advance man's "self-evident" rights.

But if freedom always implies order in any consistent system, why has Western civilization made freedom a separate aim and motto, so that the boast of Greece was to have invented freedom, and a war of national liberation like America's could float the banner "liberty or death"? The reason is that the Western tradition—as opposed to all others, even the most sophisticated Oriental disciplines—has exalted the individual person. This civilization, centered in the primacy of the private soul, brought a whole new ordering of society into human history. The difference is immediately apparent when Greek thought and art enter the world. Impersonal pattern, hieratic system, absorption in the eternity of the Ideal give way to the naked splendor and particularity of man; even the gods assumed those anthropomorphic forms still vital in Western imaginations. The Greek "idea" was first detached and delineated in the cult statues given various gods' names, but in reality sharing one title: Man. No longer did man achieve his manhood by religio-political initiation into secrets of order. The individual reason became the test of reality with the Greeks, and this reason asserted itself by defying the order of magic and mystery. The state religion was secularized; it sloughed off its feral elements, boasting of this liberation under the symbol of battle with centaurs and other half-human powers. The individual reason, thus exalted, ventured on the distinctive Western achievements—systematic logic and science, a philosophy freed of superstition.

The discovery of the individual's unique resources, the testing of the world against the private reason, forced the state into a new role. Formerly, man's hard-won achievements had been stored up in the authority of the community, kept under sacred leadership and symbols. But the Greek mind freed itself from this total dependence on tradition, and man's sights were set on the uncharted areas where no collective approach to mystery could lead him. The state took on a humbler function, keeping order among the individuals whose free quest gave late Greek cities their divided, spontaneous, almost anarchic individuality.

Thus freedom became an assertion of the individual's right to pursue his own vision; and liberty became a prior demand for all human speculation or education. This demand did not lessen as the Hellenic world spread and was transmuted by Christianity. In fact, the Christian emphasis on the individual soul's worth, and its other-worldly goal, deepened the cleavage between man and the religious state. The Christian recognizes a divided loyalty, giving to Caesar what is Caesar's, but to God the inestimably vaster reaches of the soul that belong to God.

But if the state's order is no longer, in the Greek world, coextensive with man's attempt to order his private world, what role is government to play? Where does the supremacy of the private person find its frontier, or verge on other claims? How do the sacred areas of each man's individuality meet and adjust to each other? It is this question that has put the problem of freedom at the center of Western political dispute. And, in a kind of slovenly philosophical shorthand, this problem has been cast as a search for the *amount* of freedom man is to enjoy. But the problem is that the Greek world introduced an entirely new conception of human life, one still novel today; a conception that runs into contradiction if pushed by a ruthless logic. The autonomy of the individual, the fight against tradition, seem to make government at worst a causeless evil, at best a necessary evil. But experience has taught that a "freedom" which travels down the road of anarchy is never seen again. Thus the problem of the Western world has been to find a new kind of order to act as foundation for its fugitive new kind of freedom. Many attempts at the solution of this problem have been short-lived, because they did not come to grips with the particular kind of freedom—with its almost impossible demands—that the West has chosen to pursue. The attempts which remain in the central line of Western experiment cluster into two main groups. These continuing schools of thought, or lines of approach, correspond in some degree with the popular division of political thinkers into liberal and conservative. In some degree, but not exactly; and the popular terms are no longer precise. It will be better, then, to give unequivocal if unfamiliar names to the two, calling them the Order of Justice and the Order of Convenience.

I. The Order of Justice

If the state is not meant to initiate man into his place in the world, what is its function? The earliest and most arresting answer is Plato's: the end of the state is justice. The liberated intellect of man discerns, behind all disciplines of mystery, an order whose sole force is its claim upon the reason. This is the order of each thing's due, of justice as an Idea. But some intellects are not capable of grasping this ideal form; and so it is the task of human society to find and put in office the intellects fitted for communion with the Idea of justice. The rest of men will have to take what these rulers dispense, as they mediate the light of justice to men bewildered by shadows.

Plato wrote when the Greek adventure into individuality seemed to be reaching a suicidal point of fission. He wrote to meet the practical demand for order, and to forestall the resurge of sheer mystery—in this case, the mystery of force—as a claim on man's obedience. He makes the claims of the state meet the challenge of reason; but the Platonic state answers this challenge so successfully that it again becomes the entire area of man's endeavor. The state brings justice into the flux of history. Theocracy has returned, and absolutism; but reason is the new deity and absolute. The assertion of the individual intellect leads to an equal assertion of the state's power as the seat of truth. Men throw off mystery, only to be ruled by Idea.

Aristotle, though he introduced empirical elements of observation and psychological realism into political theory, nonetheless based the state on metaphysical principles as two-edged as Plato's. The Greeks had advanced the boast of the individual's self-sufficiency against the hieratic absolutism of less rational civilizations. Aristotle considered reason's own claim to autonomy with rigor and found that man, isolated, cannot meet the test of self-sufficiency, or *autarkeia*, either economically or psychologically. The smallest unit that can make a pretense at *autarkeia* is the state that is armed against foreign aggression and able to supply internal economic needs. Then, translating human dependence into logical dependence, Aristotle argues: "By the very order of things, the state is prior in right to the family, and to each of us singly, since the whole is of necessity prior to the part" (1253a19–20). Man, without the *polis* to complete him, is not even a man: perhaps an animal, perhaps a god (1253a29). Like "an isolated piece at draughts," such a man has no function aside from the action of the total set of markers. The entire business of being man, which is to be just (1253a16–18), is only fulfilled in the state, the guardian of justice: "The virtue of justice has, as its sphere, the *polis*. For the virtue of justice *(dikaiosunē)* establishes what is just *(to dikaion)*, and this order of justice *(dikē)* gives men's relations their political pattern *(politikēs koinōnias taxis)*" (1253a37–39). Therefore the state alone is equipped to achieve the highest good (1252a4–6).

In his own way, Aristotle repeats the Platonic recoil of a complete individuality into a new state absolutism. Both systems tried to achieve freedom of the will through the free exercise of reason. But the reason is not free. It is an instrument for reaching an outside and objective reality, which is single under single aspects. Man can refuse to think, or think confusedly; but once the evidences of reality are received within the intellect, it is not free to think anything it pleases. Thus any attempt to base political freedom on the claims of man's intellect makes the state the center of truth—in Plato, truth as moral enlightenment; in Aristotle, truth as a set of logical imperatives—and nothing is more absolute than the claim of truth upon man.

The empirical observations of Aristotle gave rise to a certain political realism, but the authoritarian principle hidden in his definition of the state still haunts us. The Christian Aristotelian could no longer take *autarkeia* as the test of man's achievement. For the Christian, man's nobility comes from the fact that he is out of place in the world, meant for another City, with a higher and lasting citizenship. There is a further problem. Aristotle wrote that the state is prior to man "by nature," or in the order of things. The Christian doctrines of Creation, the Fall, and Heaven give a range of meanings to the word "nature" that Aristotle could never have imagined. In the new scheme, "nature" can mean the proper ordination of things as intended in the pristine state of man. Or nature is *fallen* nature—the human condition weighted by tendencies toward sin; the rest of creation scarred, and subject to catastrophe, as a result of man's rebellion. Or nature can mean the evidences of original order still asserting themselves in, and adapting themselves to, the present state of man. Nature can mean the good product of God's hand or the twisted remains of man's work. It can be contrasted with "unnatural" acts, as the model of ordination; or it can be contrasted with grace, as the frustrated thing unable to rise to its goal without redemption from a supernatural source.

For the Christian, the state can no longer fill up man's failings or aim at self-sufficiency and ideal justice. The earthly order must be identified as temporal, an area of trial and transition. As Augustine posed the problem, citizens of the two eternal Cities, the heavenly and the diabolic, must live together and mix in earthly polities, the wheat and chaff growing together before the final sifting. The earthly political community must concentrate on a limited agreement to ensure tranquillity, a state of truce in which citizens of both eternal Cities work out the mystery of their salvation or damnation.

But Aquinas, after putting Aristotle's politics in a context which transmutes it entirely, an existential context of theological drama, let the Aristotelian terms and transitions stand as a model analysis in the order of intellect. To be useful as a practical science, this analysis must be applied, in concrete instances and by the use of prudence, to a real world radically altered in the light of revelation. The trouble is that the followers of Aquinas could not or would not follow the alterations that must be made when an Aristotelian politics is put in the existential framework of Christian theology. By the same process that dehydrated the entire Thomist metaphysics, the logical terms of Aristotle were once more applied to reality without the mediation of metaphysical realism and the moral act of prudence. *Autarkeia* clashed too obviously with the Christian mentality; but "the common good" took over the content of that key term, as an ideal order perfecting the "individual good." And justice is treated as the aim of the state, almost as simply as in Aristotle's time, by many modern Thomists.[1]

As the Thomist politics was denatured, "natural law" became the sanction of "divine right" theories of government. Here, the Christian religion replaced reason in the Hellenic scheme, making the ruler the source of justice for other men.[2] Then the "laws

[1] An example of this simplistic reading of Scholastic theory is Robert M. Hutchins' *Saint Thomas and the World State,* Aquinas Lecture (Milwaukee, Wis.: Marquette University Press, 1949). Hutchins argues that the principle of *autarkeia* makes the entire world—now so interdependent and threatened with mutual annihilation—the smallest possible unit for a just political constitution. "Saint Thomas" is pictured as demanding this, though there is, in the lecture, no recognition of the limits put on the principle of *autarkeia* by revelation or philosophical realism.

[2] This doctrine of divine legitimacy was diluted, in certain forms of eighteenth- and nineteenth-century "conservatism," to the view that Providence invariably manifests itself in the history of states, sanctioning established power. Whatever is, is good; the *status quo* is sacred. Burke, and even Tocqueville, tread on or near this dangerous ground whenever they in-

of nature" were totally emptied of realistic content to become the ideal "Nature" of the eighteenth century. The rebellion against a monarch's "natural" legitimacy turned political union into a free contract, arising from the insufficiencies of the "natural" condition. But Rousseau treads the same perilous circle that Plato first traced—out from the state as mystery and back to supreme political authority in the form of reason.. In the eighteenth-century myth of a "state of nature," reason, in a vacuum, constructs a "case" for government, draws up a contract, insists on its terms as if they were points in logic, then consents to this invention of the mind.

Those things which have been criticized as inconsistencies in Rousseau—his union of extreme individualism with collective tyranny—are actually the result of his penetrating logic. He saw that Locke's doctrine (of natural rights surrendered by agreement) leads to a state that is either absolutely just, or—when the state fails in some particular, and tries to prevent dissolution of the agreement by force—absolutely unjust. Society and the state are coextensive terms. Prior to the social contract, each man is a world apart; and the absolute autonomy of this condition can only be surrendered to a custodian who discerns and demands absolute right. That is why the eighteenth-century reformers had to believe that Nature's intent was clear, everywhere "self-evident," in order to embark on their experiments. It is fascinating to watch this antinomy at work, individualism reaching an extreme where it is automatically transmuted into governmental absolutism:

> No more perfect union is possible, and no associate has any subsequent demand to make. For if the individual retained any rights whatever, this is what would happen: there being no common superior able to say the last word on any issue between him and the public, he would be his own judge on this or that point, and so would try before long to be his own judge on all points. . . .

---

voke Providence; and Professor Russell Kirk, in his *The Conservative Mind*, seems to say that one denies the existence of a divine Providence by maintaining that its workings are mysterious, not readily traced in the achievement of political power.

Each gives himself to everybody so that he gives himself to nobody.[3]

Because man's reason is not of itself free, the state based on "pure reason" only recognizes the freedom to be right; the state must, in Rousseau's famous phrase, "force men to be free":

> In and of itself, a people always wills, but does not always see, what is good; while the general will is always well-intentioned, the judgment that directs it is not always an instructed judgment. It must be brought to see things as they are. It must be brought, sometimes, to see things as they ought to appear. It must be shown the right road, which it is seeking.[4]

Since, in the purely rational world of Socrates and Rousseau, men only do wrong through some mistake in judgment or information, putting them on the right way is not forcing the will but "freeing the mind of error." Once again, the fallacy of extreme individualism, or simple democracy—society's attempt to make its circumference, or whole area, its own center—results in a reverse reading of the riddle: the center, source of truth, becomes the circumference enclosing all human activities in a rigid rule.

The enduring attractiveness of the Order of Justice arises from its total reliance on reason. Rationalism flatters the individual; it is particularly seductive in the Western tradition, where the unfettered reason has accomplished so much; and it always produced spokesmen of the highest logical dexterity. Men of this school can invoke the great political theoreticians—Plato, Aristotle, Rousseau—though they find little support in the great political institutions of the past, in the achievements of the real order, usually wrought by slow accumulation of constitutional safeguards, or by a system of compromise and enlightened expedience.

Perhaps an even deeper source of inspiration for this view of the state is the fact that it taps moral, religious, and humanitarian enthusiasms. When a man argues that the state should

[3]J. J. Rousseau, *Social Contract,* trans. Willmoore Kendall (Chicago, 1954), I, 6.
[4]*Ibid.,* II, 6; cf. II, 3.

not be an oracle of justice, a teacher of morals, or a dispenser of human comfort, the defenders of the Order of Justice frequently represent such a man's stand as an attack on justice itself, or a lack of moral principle, or an insensitivity to the demands of the human heart. Of course, it is precisely the state's usurpation of a religious and moral role that leads to its betrayal of freedom. Proponents of such a state always demand a hard orthodoxy of its subjects. Plato makes a grasp of ideal justice the qualification for political office. The "divine right" theories of government rest on a common profession of faith. The Enlightenment theories are based on the certitude that the "laws of Nature" are easily discernible and universally recognized. The beginnings of a Paine-Jefferson orthodoxy in America, based on these "self-evident" laws, were aborted by the religious fundamentalism of Americans and the system of compromise that effected the federalist union.[5] But modern liberals have reintroduced an orthodoxy of self-evident rights by their credal insistence on the universal validity and viability of certain concepts, like "democracy," "equality," and "self-determination."

It will be seen that the Order of Justice I have described corresponds, accidental usages aside, to what is generally termed the liberal strand in Western political discourse.[6] The title arises from the initial stress, in all these systems, on reason and the free individual. But the turning of a rationalist freedom into a tyranny of intellect is not, as has so often been supposed, a mere

[5] It is necessary to distinguish between the *consensus* which must exist to give union to a polity, and the *orthodoxy* exacted by rationalist systems. A consensus, as the word's form indicates, is a meeting of several views on common ground; an orthodoxy is the reduction of all views to a single view. Consensus implies compromise, establishing a minimal ground of agreement on which to base political organization. Orthodoxy goes to the roots of metaphysical and religious awareness and demands a "right view" on these things, not merely a *modus vivendi*. (The contemporary word for this is "ideology," according to the fine anger and bad etymology of John Adams, "the science of idiocy.")

[6] The "conservative" belief in a manifest (as opposed to mysterious) Providence is not normally classed with the ideal systems of the liberals, but it should be. The theological naïveté of such "conservatism" makes the real world ideal, so that "the King's Justice" *is* justice.

accident or relapse of human weakness under the demands of a great ideal. The seeds of tyranny were in the ideal from the beginning. Robespierre and the Terror are the logical consequence of Rousseau and the Social Contract. When men realize this, they will cease wondering at the "inconsistencies" in Plato's or Rousseau's authoritarian state, or at the conversion of "divine right" into sheer might under a simplistic reading of the natural law. The Order of Justice is like the statue of Justice; its attributes are a blindfold, and the sword.

II. *The Order of Convenience*

The title I have given this second form of order will strike some as frivolous; and "convenience" is, I admit, susceptible to misunderstanding. But other words that suggest themselves are even more misleading—rule by the expedient or the opportune (which now connote a lack of moral probity), government by concurrence (which gets mixed up, now, with dogmas of democratic procedure, though I would use the word in Calhoun's sense), or the principle of community (a word now desiccated by abstract definitions of the "common good"). So there is nothing for it but to choose a comparatively neutral word, at first glance trivial, and give it a specific function for this discussion.[7]

The problem of finding a single word is not accidental, not a quibble over method. The lack of an accepted term indicates a chronic failure in political discourse, the chasm between theory and practice; for the order I am considering is not nameless because unimportant, or absent from our history. In fact, each highest form of political community succeeded because this order informed and stiffened it invisibly. The Greek democracy was not doctrinaire. There is no theorist of Athenian democracy, no proponent of a doctrine. All the major political theorists of Hellas formed their ideal systems as alternatives to the real order, admittedly fallible, that was stimulating their investiga-

[7]Hooker and Cardinal Newman use the term for their concept of government, but not with sufficient regularity to make it the leading characterization of their descriptions.

tions. Thucydides, Plato, Aristotle—"oligarchs" all. It is true that there are some democratic speeches put in the mouths of Herodotean and Euripidean characters. But the speculative recommendations of democracy are very few; perhaps the most famous is the speech Thucydides invented for Pericles, a boast ironically voiced under the shadow of defeat. The Roman Empire actually professed a spurious theory, maintaining the façade of a republic. Medieval theory tried to redeem feudal and merchant practice but acted merely as a component force working for balance.[8] England is notoriously the producer and product of a kind of unconscious constitution. And America, after the *furor ideologicus* had passed that lifted the colonies on wings of war, based its Constitution on an unashamed profession of compromise. The political ideal of *The Federalist* elevates compromise to a principle of harmony. It is one of the major attempts to articulate an Order of Convenience.

Do these preliminary remarks mean that politics must simply be opposed to theory; in the foolish modern word, "anti-intellectual"?[9] No. But the Order of Convenience must be built on a basic truth that is even more scandalous to modern ears: the particular aim of the state is not to achieve justice, and certainly not to dispense it. In the words of Newman, "satisfaction, peace, liberty, conservative interests [are] the supreme end of the law, not mere raw justice as such."[10] This, of course, does not mean that the state is to be unjust, or free of the imperatives of the moral law. The state, like the family, like the corporation, like

[8]In romantic idealizations of medieval society, for instance, it is largely forgotten that the Scholastic theologians were virtually unanimous in condemning the guilds as centers of monopoly power. See the important collection of texts in Raymond de Roover's "The Concept of the Just Price: Theory and Economic Policy," *Journal of Economic History*, XVIII (1958).

[9]Conservatives are generally distrustful of speculatists' rules for the practical science of politics; as artists are skeptical about the "rules" of academic aestheticians. In both cases, the distrust has been amply justified. In politics, conservatives often find their allies are religious thinkers, artists, and orators rather than the philosophers.

[10]"Who's To Blame?" *Discussions and Arguments* (London: Longmans, 1907), p. 351. The state is to seek "such a justice . . . as may not be inconsistent with the interests of a large conservatism" (p. 350).

the labor union, is bound by the laws of morality that are incumbent on all human endeavor, corporate as well as individual. In carrying out its function, the state must act with justice. But its specific aim is not to enforce justice as such. The family, too, must observe right order—the child obeying, the parent avoiding undue laxity or severity; husband and wife helping each other, yet observing measure in their demands upon each other. This due measure, this order of right, is achieved by the observance of justice; yet the formal aim of the family is not sheer justice as such. Its aim is to give birth and education to new members of our race, to recruit partners in the human adventure. Only when this purpose is clearly understood can the order of claims and the areas of just activity be discerned in the life of the family.

In the same way, the state must observe justice in its activities; but its aim is more limited, more concretely specified. And unless that aim is made clear, there is no way of knowing what justice is for the state; politics becomes an instrument for seeking every kind of good thing, for bringing ideal justice itself down to earth. We have seen the theocratic consequences of such an undertaking. These consequences make the rule of what Newman called "raw justice" the source of every tyranny that is not sheer outlawry, and the permanent temptation of every state. The nineteenth-century liberals found something evil in power itself, as if tyranny customarily advanced by some brutal and naked appeal of its own nature. But every truly powerful system of oppression was shaped by an ideal that can recruit talent, can use other energies than the thirst of a few for the acme of human rule. When ideal justice is set before the community as its political end, the only efficient path toward that ever-receding goal is the marshaling of force in the state. All tyrannies give legitimacy to oppression by making it a transitional period through which men must pass on their way to Utopia, a kind of induced labor that is to bring forth the new order. So it was with the despots who had to "establish divine right," so with the Terror, so with the Utilitarian acceptance of the "growing pains" of industrialism, so with the dictatorship of the proletariat.

I do not mean to minimize, no conservative can, the effects of original sin in the life of society; but the most heartbreaking, and politically far-reaching, of these effects is not the drive of sheer evil, but the misguided and desperate grasping after good —the enthusiasms, heresies, crusades that can mobilize human generosity. The optimistic liberal does not recognize that society is ultimately hurt less by individuals who catch at instant advantage than by the messiahs who undertake great missions with long-range planning, ingenuity, patient endurance, and conviction of ultimate triumph. We are witnessing the scale of this menace in the fiery spread and intensity of the Communist vision.[11]

The talk of "power" as a constant factor everywhere to be minimized is as self-defeating as the quantitative approach to freedom (as something everywhere to be increased). The two views are, in fact, reverse sides of a single coin. Power arms itself for the long pull, invades the mind, and gives structure to human effort, not when it is a spasm leading to dissolution, but when it is summoned up by a false god, with rights over the whole man and all men. Nero is personally more despicable, but politically less destructive, than Robespierre or Lenin.[12]

But if the state is not to be founded on an ideal order of justice, what is its basis? Obviously, the real order—the order of man's needs. The individual only finds his natural fulfillment in society. As Aristotle pointed out, even language is a convention, a "coming together." Language is itself society. And all man's other achievements involve a similar social opportunity for the individual's self-expression. But if there is a society, there must

[11]The liberal often speaks of replacing selfishness with principle as the final solution to human problems—not seeing that principle, codes and creeds, moral fervor and fanaticism can be devouring flames. Cf. Ronald Knox's *Enthusiasm*.

[12]The modern liberal lost the fear of power as he came to exercise it; but the "individualist" branch of American conservatism retains it, along with Acton's unfortunate dictum. (What "absolute power" and "absolute corruption" are supposed to mean in the mouth of an historian, no one can say.)

be a state. As a necessary physical regimen keeps the individual alive, so there must be a regime, an order, a discipline in society. That regime is the state.

The fallacy of the rationalists is that they begin the construction of their political models with the isolated reason of the individual. They make the pure autonomy of the individual clash and, finally, merge with the autonomy of a just order. But man does not start with a formed and pure freedom. Man "free" of society is man free of air; free, that is, to suffocate. The rationalist pits the individual against an abstract order of justice in the state, instead of tracing the spontaneous growth and grouping of social forms that give the individual a field for expression and activity. The state appears, apocalyptically, in such theories, bringing justice "new-born" into prior chaos. But in the real order, the state arises from a hierarchy of social organizations, of groups formed to fill particular needs. The state stabilizes this spontaneous social expression. It answers a natural demand for unity. It cannot initiate such unity, or carve countries out of the map by legislative fiat.

Although it is a commonplace that man is a "social animal," the rationalist theories contradict this commonplace. For if the state arises out of man's social instinct, then the state destroys its own roots when it denies free scope to the other forms of social life. The state, when it is made the source of justice, must be equally and instantly available to all citizens; and, in achieving this, in sweeping away the confusion of claims raised by families, economic orders, educational conventions, codes of conduct, natural gradations of privilege, the liberal leaves society atomized, each man isolated, with all the weight of political power coming unintercepted upon him.[13] The higher forms of organization do not grow out of and strengthen the lower, but counter and erase them. This is what has happened under the Order of Justice from the time when Plato pitted the state

[13]Rousseau, *op. cit.*, II, 12: "Each citizen should be completely independent vis-à-vis each of the others, and as dependent as can be vis-à-vis the city."

against the family to the modern breakdown of divided jurisdiction in the centralized state. As usual, Rousseau follows the logic of this position to its fated end:

> Where, however, blocs are formed, lesser associations at the expense of the broader one, the will of each of these associations comes to be general with respect to its members and particular with respect to the state. . . . If, then, we are to have a clear declaration of the general will, we must see to it that there are no partial societies within the state, so that each citizen forms his own opinions.[14]

By this route, the liberal state arrives, everywhere, at contradiction: though the state is instituted to assure the development of personality, societies that embrace the rationalist ideal are marked by a cult of impersonality. Plato attempted to erase the distinction between the sexes. The French and Russian revolutions came up with titles meant to attack titles: "Citizen" in one case, "Comrade" in the other. Since political justice conditions all of a man's life in such societies, men rejoice in the reduction of persons to a minimal legal status and equality. In such communities, loyalty to the state is expressed as duty toward abstract justice, not as patriotism.

For the realist, on the other hand, the state, by disciplining a particular society, expresses the character of that society, protects its spontaneity and symbolic self-confrontation at all levels of life, draws on the society's specific resources, and commands a loyalty that is personalized as patriotism. How does the state accomplish this? How complement the multiple, spontaneous, or consanguineous forms of social coherence? As all things complement: by supplying what is lacking. Other social groups than the political have a positive bond of mutual affection or defined and positive interest. This is their strength, but it circumscribes their

[14]*Ibid.*, II, 3. Rousseau applies, in the modern world and in a totalistic way, the historically conditioned techniques for replacing clan law that are analyzed by Aristotle in the *Politics:* democracy was advanced in Hellas, we are told, when men saw that "private cults should be reduced to a minimum or transformed into public ones, and every device is to be explored for throwing everyone together with everyone as much as possible, for shattering other, older loyalties" (*Pol.* 1319b24–27).

appeal. Only those qualify to take part who share the interests of a family or a class, of a school of thought or a creed. But conflicts of interest arise in the common area of life in which these activities take place. The task of adjudicating these conflicts by a shared code, and of including all the strata of society in a single frame of minimal order, must be entrusted to an agent of order with force at its disposal. This agency circumscribes a larger community than the partial groupings; it is not voluntary from moment to moment; it can enforce its judgments in the name of the very social forces that become obstreperous. The state is necessary because the other, overlapping social forms extend across a field of human activity that no one of them can circumscribe. Thus the end of the state is the orderly advancement and discipline of society as the necessary ground of human activity. And the necessary, basic condition for the formation of a state is a shared good that must be protected if all social and individual effort is to thrive. That is why Newman calls a common possession the basis of the state.[15]

The state, as extending throughout all other levels of social solidarity, must have a certain neutrality toward them all, and as the order-enforcing agent, it must take upon itself a certain negative, punitive function. This neutral and negative aspect of the state will be perverted, and become a positive push—as life-giving, rather than life-preserving—if the other forms of spontaneous activity wither; or if the state officials try to use their power to call up a positive vision of their own; or if poli-

---

[15]*Historical Sketches*, I, p. 161: "A society is a collection of individuals made one by their participation in some common possession." The common possession may be race, religion, language, or shared historical experience, as well as possession of a naturally defined area of the earth. Newman's definition should be compared to Augustine's realistic way of defining the state (*City of God*, XIX, 24): "A political community is a gathering of rational creatures united by the things for which they have a shared love." Acton, in one of his file-card aphorisms, remarked that "Liberty is the creation of property, not religion." This is true only if Newman's and Augustine's wide concept of property—as some good thing shared, commanding a fixed loyalty from the community at large—be accepted; and only if a religion refusing to give to Caesar what is God's can be considered, at the political level, such a "property."

tics is considered the all-inclusive area of man's achievement of excellence. To continue the comparison of individual regimen to social regime, such a society is like the health crank, who expends all his energy on the achievement of an ideal physical equilibrium, not using the body's forces for the essentially human tasks.

To prevent this usurpation on the part of the state, every society that is long-lived or successful finds ways of limiting the action of political force. The disciplinary agent of society is itself disciplined by society; the rulers are ruled. This system of checks is worked out by each community, but it is based on the general truth that the state's role is to enforce equity and order, rather than ideal justice. The free agencies of society must preserve their function by circumscribing the state's role in the totality of social activity. This fact has been instinctively recognized by all those theorists who, after talking about ideal forms of government, recommend a mixture of forms, striking a balance between all possible ruling forces in the state. This roundabout descent from the ideal to the real is clumsy. The true form of society is not to be found in a mixture of pure components, but in the particular aim and energy of each real community.

Each society must form a unique *constitution,* an "agreed station" of components, growing out of the resources it can command. The ideal state—of a justice or a freedom defined outside any particular human context—is as meaningless as some uniform ideal of individual fulfillment. Is monarchy, aristocracy, or democracy the best form of government? Such a question simply breeds further questions: Best for what society? And what kind of monarchy, or democracy? These questions are as hopeless as similar ones would be in the case of an ideal life for individuals. Is it better that man be an artist or philosopher, monk or martyr, doctor or teacher, worker or statesman? And if he is a doctor, should he engage in research, psychology, or compassionate work among the poor? If an artist, should he write or paint in an austere or demonstrative style? To attempt an abstract answer to these questions is to deny the mystery of individuality, the secret springs of motive, that make up the human fact of freedom. As ever, rationalism leads to sterile paradox, to an ideal freedom that is a denial of freedom. Calhoun rightly says:

> The great and broad distinction between governments is,—not that of the one, the few, or the many,—but of the constitutional and the absolute.[16]

And what is meant by a constitutional government? According to Calhoun, it is that government in which all the free forms and forces of society—or as many as possible—retain their life and "concur" in a political area of peaceful co-operation and compromise. According to Newman, it is that society in which the character of those "concurring" is best allowed for and given scope for development:

> As individuals have characters of their own, so do races. . . . Moreover, growing out of these varieties or idiosyncrasies, and corresponding to them, will be found in these several races, and proper to each, a certain assemblage of beliefs, convictions, rules, usages, traditions, proverbs, and principles . . . tending to some definite form of government. . . . It is something more than law; it is the embodiment of special ideas, ideas perhaps which have been held by a race for ages, which are of immemorial usage, which have fixed themselves in its innermost heart, which are in its eyes sacred. . . . They are the creative and conservative influences of Society; they erect nations into States, and invest States with Constitutions.[17]

Absolutism, or despotism, is a sheer thrust of force across the grain of these free and preservative influences, a defiance of the spontaneous life that checks government even as it impels it forward. A constitutional regime gives both *life* and *limit* to government; it maintains a system that rules even society's rulers. The force exercised by despots may be, and often is, the assertion of an ideal, but of an ideal unrooted, unembodied in the flesh and substance of society. It is, literally, a ghostly thing seeking to haunt or possess the body politic by unnatural forces. For this reason, the answer to Lincoln's question must be that

[16] *A Disquisition of Government* (New York: Appleton, 1853), p. 37.
[17] "Who's To Blame?" pp. 315–16.

no nation *can* long endure if it is only "dedicated to a proposition." It must be dedicated to a people, to its particular human possibilities, since

> that must be pronounced no State, but a mere fortuitous collection of individuals, which has no unity stronger than despotism, or deeper than law.[18]

One cannot simply ask whether a thing is just (as abolition of slavery is just, whether in fifth-century Athens, first-century Rome, or nineteenth-century Richmond); whether it is desirable (as better education of the young is desirable); whether it is moral (as sexual continence is moral). In politics one must ask at the same time, always, whether it is constitutional. Should the state act, and if so to what extent, with what precautions, and following what precedents; in conjunction with what tempering and expanding activity on the part of spontaneous organizations? If these questions are not asked, if the state enters the private area of morals, then censorship and orthodoxy give the political guardian a divine character. There is no limitation of the state but by the single test of constitutionality.

The constitution is not always, and is never merely, a written document.[19] It is the "shared situation" of society, that continuous arrangement whereby men preserve their common stake in a political regime. It is composed of all the influences that make a state continue to express the character of its people; that recruit and give room for the development of talent; that develop the resources of personality through society. Newman even wrote that "bribery" (*i.e.*, the buying of titles and offices), after it had

[18]*Ibid.*, pp. 351–52.

[19]American society offers a special situation, since it brought a high degree of political wisdom into a new and unsettled area. To make up for the lack of checks and balances of native growth, the American Constitution aimed more specifically at an internal balancing of governmental activities than was necessary in communities of more gradual growth. This gives to the written Constitution of America a force and focal position that would not normally belong to a state's explicit political charter. The American Constitution *is* the American tradition, reaching back to Europe and articulated through an extraordinary act of conscious statesmanship; and departure from it is the more dangerous because the country has little other tradition to give it form.

been systematized as a recognized and efficient part of the British government's balanced operation, was part of the English constitution; and therefore to be used as a tool of the community, provided no specific act of immorality is committed, like the breaking of an oath.[20] In the same way, a society that is basically tribal in organization must have a state that is based on the tribes. Otherwise, the society has no way of meshing with its political order, of making its character felt, of maintaining identity while it grows toward a different mode of articulating itself, politically. Such a society proves the

> inexpediency of suffering the tradition of Law to flow separate from that of popular feeling . . . there ought to be a continual influx of the national mind into the judicial conscience; and, unless there was this careful adjustment between law and politics, the standards of right and wrong set up at Westminster would diverge from those received by the community at large, and the Nation might some day find itself condemned and baffled by its own supreme oracle. . . .[21]

As an instance, the "democratic" regimes being established in Africa, over inchoate areas arbitrarily defined as nations, perfectly exemplify Calhoun's maxim that the only realistic division of governments is into constitutional and absolute. These "democracies," imported from a Hellenic-Christian tradition of many centuries' growth, and imposed on stray parts of the tribal labyrinth of Africa, are not based on any real consensus. So-called popular support and "nationalism" do not express the genius of Africa itself, of any real nation. The native groups who "express their will" so simply with the marking of a ballot have merely expressed a hope that Western material comforts will magically be made theirs by this method. The result is an absolutism—an enlightened one, it may be claimed, but surely an absolutism. The term "democracy" means little or nothing in such a context; whereas other forms of government, today condemned out of hand as "dictatorships," may have a very effective constitutional system.

Does this mean that society must settle, always, for what it

[20]"Who's To Blame?" pp. 351–52.
[21]*Ibid.*, p. 349.

has, never push out toward higher achievement; must it forswear leadership in order to avoid loss of "constitution," treat all hope of better things as a temptation to visionary absolutism?

On the contrary, a constitution fosters not only liberty but leadership. In an integral community, the leaders really lead; they are followed. There is no chasm between the masses and the intelligentsia. One of the principal ironies of modern democracy is that egalitarian doctrine has driven a greater wedge between thinkers and the populace than most systems of privilege ever did, so that it seems almost necessary that "clerks" be traitors. The interplay of various groups within accepted tradition makes talent serve the community, not seek a false elevation by institutionalizing rebellion. When a nation has no tradition to appeal to but a "tradition of revolution," it has confessed bankruptcy; it can no longer marshal the potentials of the populace to serve the common stake, the constitution. When artists and philosophers and churchmen cannot find a meaningful area of mutual enrichment, then politicians must supply the social cohesion *ex nihilo,* and enforce it by militant centralization of power. In this situation, the boasts of broad franchise or democratic ritual do not give substance to man's liberty. For liberty is not the product of mechanical instruments like the electoral process.[22]

In modern democratic myth, man's freedom is given him entire at birth, a thing solid and circular in its perfection, but shattered and dispersed as time goes on. To prevent the final dissolution of all freedom, men form polities by chipping off a piece of liberty and surrendering it to the state, which is thus constructed out of the surrendered quantities of individual rights. The art of constructing a just state consists in finding how

[22]John Courtney Murray, S. J., *We Hold These Truths* (New York: Sheed and Ward, 1960), p. 208: "The totalitarianizing tendency is inherent in the contemporary idolatry of the democratic process. . . . What is urged is a monism, not so much of the political order itself, as of a political technique. The proposition is that all the issues of human life—intellectual, religious, and moral issues as well as formally political issues—are to be regarded as, or resolved into, political issues and are to be settled by the single omnicompetent political technique of majority vote."

to sacrifice the thinnest possible slices of individual "sovereignty," and the most uniform, so that all these contribute to the central storehouse of national sovereignty. But man's freedom is not whole nor homogeneous. It is as complex as man himself, since it makes him man.

First, there is the basic freedom which consists in possession of a will. This will can never be taken away, or tampered with at its source. It can be killed, but only by killing the man, or reducing him to a subhuman level. Even in prison, the will is free so long as it exists.

Second, there is the last fulfillment of liberty, the state of continual choice that uses and never abuses freedom. This, according to Christian teaching, is the freedom of man at rest in his eternal reward. But according to authoritarian state systems, it is also a political ideal. All such systems imply, or, if pushed to logic, assert that man's freedom is freedom to do good. As Rousseau put it, the state forces man to be free.

In a third sense, freedom means the condition that encourages and allows for the active exercise of the will. This condition is achieved by education, by surroundings that stimulate and nurture free choice, by social discipline that gives man a peaceful area of movement. This is the freedom to which political discipline makes essential contributions. It is the freedom of a nation; not given by the state, but protected by it. Those who isolate a particular "political freedom" from the rest of man's self-extension into social institutions are usually reduced to the worship of various absolutes—the franchise, a widespread press, a public education—without regard to the genius of the groups and individuals finding common ground and seeking expression in the particular society. These absolutes can be as imprisoning as the authoritarian systems.[23] Plato says that freedom for "lead men" consists in obedience to the "gold men," the modern liberal

[23]One of Acton's numberless file cards, studied by Herbert Butterfield, contains the statement that the real conflict acted out in the course of the French Revolution was "the great struggle between liberty and democracy"—not between monarchy and democracy, tradition and liberty, but between man's desire to be free and the doctrinaire channels into which this thrust was guided and expended.

insists that freedom for the Congolese consists in an electoral and parliamentary system not geared to mesh with regional, tribal, emotional and intellectual differences or difficulties. The result in both cases is a union of chaos and compulsion, both impinging on the real exercise of freedom.

There is a fourth definition of freedom—this one spurious—as a mere lack of outside compulsion. But freedom is a spontaneity toward several alternatives, a principle of action. To define it as a lack is absurd. This leads to the ideal of the "open society," in which definite intellectual and cultural molds are avoided or broken, throwing the individual back on his own resources and responsibility at each step of his life. The ideal society, it is suggested, would be a kind of Great Books Club in which each person chooses his favorite historical and intellectual milieu, or browses among them all with an ultimate choice in mind. Such a society is impossible. There would be no agreed language, no common terms for contracts, no shared understanding of the way to get work done, no possibility of educational discipline. That is, there would be no society.[24] *Identity* would disappear, first in the society, then in the individual.

Freedom is not a mere lack; it is an urge to extend one's self by the exercise of choice, and unless there is a defined and delim-

---

[24]Even Ernst Cassirer, in arguing for the moral unity of Rousseau's work, admits contradiction on the "literal" level in Rousseau's concept of an open society as the milieu for education: "From the very outset, the work stands outside the conditions of human society. It releases the pupil from every kind of relationship to human society; it places him, as it were, in a vacuum. The walls of this prison close in on him ever more confiningly . . . to lead him back to the simplicity and plainness of nature. But is it not the height of unnaturalness thus to hide the existing order of things from the child? And furthermore, is this attempt not doomed to failure from the outset? . . . At decisive turning points of spiritual and ethical development, such external aid is required and employed—we may recall, for example, the conversation between Emile and the gardener, which is designed to convey and to make comprehensible to Emile the first idea of property. Thus the fanatical love of truth, which was to guide this system of education, ends up by degenerating into a curiously complicated system of deceptions of carefully calculated pedagogical tricks" (*The Question of Jean-Jacques Rousseau*, trans. Peter Gay, New York: Columbia, 1954).

ited self, no extension is possible. There is no range of choice or reach of possibilities unless man operates from an established base of some sort. Unless a society can retain and enrich its identity, it does not admit the possibility of human fulfillment within its continuity, or even the luxury of revolt. All rebels would hate a genuinely open society; there would be nothing to rebel against. Tradition, what Burke calls "prejudice," is necessary to give freedom range in the real order, just as an individual, with all his limitations, is the necessary vehicle for the free will itself. And so, by another route, we find that freedom and order are correlates; and that rationally limited freedom is the partner of a humanly limited order, the limits being set by man's effort to achieve a fully human life under each society's historical conditions. The attempts at an absolute freedom recoil, logically and in experience, toward a political absolutism. Freedom must be concrete because man is; freedom is man.

Only the Order of Convenience, of enlightened expedience, of prejudice mobilized toward improvement, can give the practical art of politics a combination of flexibility and stability. The Order of Convenience can take the findings of the great political theorists and use them, without incurring the results of mistaken metaphysics. It can learn from Plato the importance, to society, of education and morality, without making the state a New Jerusalem of the intellect. It can take from Aristotle a realistic grasp of social psychology, of the uses of property, of moderation in reform, without making the state prior in right to the individual. It can learn from Rousseau the need for constant adjustment of political forms to the structure of society, without basing all forms on an explicit and rational "contract." Perhaps most significant of all, this kind of politics can return to the real genius of natural-law theory. It will recognize the laws of nature, not as dictates for an ideal life, but as the structure of reality calling, at each moment, for a real response, individual and social. It will seek "the common good," not as some ideal scheme of order, or quantitative accumulation of individual goods, but as the real life of the "commonalty," of community in all its mutually enriching forms. This true politics of the natural law is, as a modern exponent of that obscured system reminds us, rooted in a metaphysics vastly different from the eighteenth-century definition of Nature. Taking the American Republic as a concrete example, John Courtney Murray writes:

> Its basis was not the philosophic rationalism that called itself Enlightenment, but only a political pragmatism more enlightened than the Enlightenment ever was, because it looked to the light of experience to illuminate the prudential norms necessary to guide it in handling a concrete social reality that is vastly complicated.[25]

The political realist also preserves the virtue of justice, by assigning it its true place in the life of the state. This justice is primarily a matter of equity and procedure, of the fair enforcement of the constitution. This is not a role as inspiring or ambitious as justice plays in the states aiming at an ideal order. It is primarily a matter of fair rules for the free development of a society's particular impulses, the virtues of an umpire or a policeman; and, under threat of foreign aggression, the virtues of a watchdog. In fact, the disappointment of idealists, when faced with this system, is violent. Even Lord Acton, the moralist of liberty, considered Newman's politics "immoral"; and Augustine's attack on the *just* state of Plato has largely been ignored, or dismissed as a "deplorable lapse" in an otherwise great thinker.[26] But this recognition of the state's limited function is the means for freeing man in his extra-political and supra-political roles.

The Greeks sundered man from the hieratic order of politics, secularizing the state by an exercise of reason. But the order of reason, in the final theorists of Hellas, became as strict a political regimen as the religious state had been. Christianity completed

---

[25] Murray, *op. cit.,* p. 164.

[26]Cf. *Letters of Lord Acton to Mary Gladstone* (London: Macmillan, 1905) for Acton's "deep aversion" (p. 243) to the "sophist, the manipulator, not the servant, of truth" (p. 70). A. J. Carlyle called Augustine's denial of the concept that the state's characteristic attribute is justice "a deplorable error for a great Christian teacher" (*Social and Political Ideas of Some Great Mediaeval Thinkers,* ed. F. J. C. Hearnshaw, London, 1923, p. 51).

the secularization of the state by placing man's goal on the other side of time, distinguishing, finally, the things of God from the things of Caesar. This duality, approached variously under the understandings and misunderstandings of the Two Cities or the Two Swords, led Christian wisdom to define and defy political absolutism. "Two there are," wrote Gelasius I to Anastasius I, "by which this world is ruled on title of sovereign right" —the area of priestly ministration, that is, of the individual soul and its divine freedom; and the order of kingly authority, that is, of temporal peace, establishing the condition in which men can discern and exercise their ultimate freedom.[27]

The effects of this new, and final, secularization were farther-reaching than the establishment of religious freedom. Once the state lost its primacy as an interpreter of the eternal order, it lost the claim by which it cowed all intermediate societies—the family, the free organizations of groups in which man seeks the answer to his own mysteries. As John Courtney Murray says, in a chapter called "Are There Two Or One?", "this comprehensive right [of the Church] asserted within the political community requires as its complement that all the intrapolitical sacredness (*res sacra in temporalibus*) be assured of their proper immunity from politicization."[28]

Although the medieval limitation on the state arose out of the state's recognition of the Church's mission, the Christian ordina-

[27]Murray, *op. cit.*, p. 209: "Christianity has always regarded the state as a limited order of action for limited purposes, to be chosen and pursued under the direction and correction of the organized moral conscience of society, whose judgments are formed and mobilized by the Church, an independent and autonomous community, qualified to be the interpreter of man's nature and destiny." Cf. Acton, *The History of Freedom and Other Essays* (London: Macmillan, 1907), p. 205: "In the Jewish as in the Gentile world, political and theological obligations were made to coincide; in both, therefore,—in the theocracy of the Jews as in the *politeia* of the Greeks,—the State was absolute. Now it is the great object of the Church, by keeping the two spheres permanently distinct,—by rendering to Caesar the things that are Caesar's, and to God the things that are God's—to make all absolutism, of whatever kind, impossible."
[28]Murray, *op. cit.*, p. 203. For a psychological presentation of the fact that liberty arises from creatively divided loyalties, *cf.* T. S. Eliot's discussion of religion in *Notes Towards a Definition of Culture.*

tion of man has left a sacredness about the individual soul that has survived the breakup of a single center for Christendom. The modern state, in its best manifestations (like the American Constitution), retains the secularization paradoxically created by Christianity's otherworldliness. The state must be agnostic, if nothing else, about the possibilities and final goal of the individual; and allow the human adventure to proceed, not preempting the place of that unknown City that may be calling man. Thus the apparently mincing ideal of the state that shocks liberals is the charter of freedom for the spirit of man. By foregoing the inspirational political theories, man taps other and more enduring sources of inspiration. Such are the virtues of convenience. For "convenience," in its older English usage, meant consonance, especially the correspondence of things with thought. The convenient state has constant reference to man, and is adjusted to his real endeavors. It is the meeting of political institutions with the mystery and activity of man, a standing-together (constitution) of political discipline and the individual discipline of exercised freedom.

It would be useless to claim that the term "conservative" always means, or should mean, the advocacy of such a convenient state. As we have seen, the "divine right" and providential branch of conservatism belongs rather with the proponents of an Order of Justice. But I think it is true that the really great conservatives were not believers in the sacredness of the *status quo*. What distinguishes them—look at Augustine and Johnson, Burckhardt and Ruskin, Randolph and Calhoun, Adams and Newman—is a pungent sense of reality, of man's real needs and achievements. The great conservatives were not powerful, with personal stock in the *status quo*; they were, almost all of them, the foes of current fads, of enthusiasms that commanded the power centers of their day as liberalism has swept the world in our time. The caricature of the conservative as a mere lover of his own person and privilege will not stand. If you want to find the jealous embrace of attained power, go to the liberal ideologue, who must have total power in order to achieve his total reform, his rapid creation of Utopia. Go to Pericles, to Caesar, to Robespierre, to Bonaparte; to Lenin, or Mao Tse-Tung, or

Castro; go, for that matter, to Wilson and Franklin Roosevelt. The conservative is typically moderate, skeptical, critical. He forms a permanent opposition to that permanent new theory or new regime that promises escape from the hard human realities.

To say that the enduringly important conservatives of the past were believers in a politics of convenience is to imply that the conservatism offering most to the future will be of this same kind; and I think the implication is a sound one.

2   E Pluribus Unum: The American Consensus

John Courtney Murray, S. J.

As it arose in America, the problem of pluralism was unique in the modern world, chiefly because pluralism was the native condition of American society. It was not, as in Europe and in England, the result of a disruption or decay of a previously existent religious unity. This fact created the possibility of a new solution; indeed, it created a demand for a new solution. The possibility was exploited and the demand was met by the American Constitution. . . .

The Nation Under God

The first truth to which the American Proposition makes appeal is stated in that landmark of Western political theory, the

From John Courtney Murray, S. J., *We Hold These Truths: Catholic Reflections on the American Proposition* (New York: Sheed & Ward, 1960), Chapter 1, pp. 27–43. Copyright © 1960 by Sheed & Ward, Inc. Reprinted by permission of Sheed & Ward, Inc.

Declaration of Independence. It is a truth that lies beyond politics; it imparts to politics a fundamental human meaning. I mean the sovereignty of God over nations as well as over individual men. This is the principle that radically distinguishes the conservative Christian tradition of America from the Jacobin laicist tradition of Continental Europe. The Jacobin tradition proclaimed the autonomous reason of man to be the first and the sole principle of political organization. In contrast, the first article of the American political faith is that the political community, as a form of free and ordered human life, looks to the sovereignty of God as to the first principle of its organization. In the Jacobin tradition religion is at best a purely private concern, a matter of personal devotion, quite irrelevant to public affairs. Society as such, and the state which gives it legal form, and the government which is its organ of action are by definition agnostic or atheist. The statesman as such cannot be a believer, and his actions as a statesman are immune from any imperative or judgment higher than the will of the people, in whom resides ultimate and total sovereignty (one must remember that in the Jacobin tradition "the people" means "the party"). This whole manner of thought is altogether alien to the authentic American tradition.

From the point of view of the problem of pluralism this radical distinction between the American and the Jacobin traditions is of cardinal importance. The United States has had, and still has, its share of agnostics and unbelievers. But it has never known organized militant atheism on the Jacobin, doctrinaire Socialist, or Communist model; it has rejected parties and theories which erect atheism into a political principle. In 1799, the year of the Napoleonic *coup d'état* which overthrew the Directory and established a dictatorship in France, President John Adams stated the first of all American first principles in his remarkable proclamation of March 6:

> . . . it is also most reasonable in itself that men who are capable of social arts and relations, who owe their improvements to the social state, and who derive their enjoyments from it, should, as a society, make acknowledgements of dependence and obligation to Him

who hath endowed them with these capacities and elevated them in the scale of existence by these distinctions. . . .

President Lincoln on May 30, 1863, echoed the tradition in another proclamation:

> Whereas the Senate of the United States, devoutly recognizing the supreme authority and just government of Almighty God in all the affairs of men and nations, has by a resolution requested the President to designate and set apart a day for national prayer and humiliation; And whereas it is the duty of nations as well as of men to own their dependence upon the overruling power of God, to confess their sins and trespasses in humble sorrow, yet with the assured hope that genuine repentance will lead to mercy and pardon. . . .

The authentic voice of America speaks in these words. And it is a testimony to the enduring vitality of this first principle—the sovereignty of God over society as well as over individual men— that President Eisenhower in June, 1952, quoted these words of Lincoln in a proclamation of similar intent. There is, of course, dissent from this principle, uttered by American secularism (which, at that, is a force far different in content and purpose from Continental laicism). But the secularist dissent is clearly a dissent; it illustrates the existence of the American affirmation. And it is continually challenged. For instance, as late as 1952 an opinion of the United States Supreme Court challenged it by asserting: "We are a religious people whose institutions presuppose a Supreme Being." Three times before in its history— in 1815, 1892, and 1931—the Court had formally espoused this same principle.

The Tradition of Natural Law

The affirmation in Lincoln's famous phrase, "this nation under God," sets the American proposition in fundamental continuity with the central political tradition of the West. But this continuity is more broadly and importantly visible in another, and related, respect. In 1884 the Third Plenary Council of Baltimore made this statement: "We consider the establishment of our country's independence, the shaping of its liberties and laws, as a work of special Providence, its framers 'building better than they knew,' the Almighty's hand guiding them." The providential aspect of the matter, and the reason for the better building can be found in the fact that the American political community was organized in an era when the tradition of natural law and natural rights was still vigorous. Claiming no sanction other than its appeal to free minds, it still commanded universal acceptance. And it furnished the basic materials for the American consensus.

The evidence for this fact has been convincingly presented by Clinton Rossiter in his book, *Seedtime of the Republic,** a scholarly account of the "noble aggregate of 'self-evident truths' that vindicated the campaign of resistance (1765–1775), the resolution for independence (1776), and the establishment of the new state governments (1776–1780)." These truths, he adds, "had been no less self-evident to the preachers, merchants, planters, and lawyers who were the mind of colonial America." It might be further added that these truths firmly presided over the great time of study, discussion, and decision which produced the Federal Constitution. "The great political philosophy of the Western world," Rossiter says, "enjoyed one of its proudest seasons in this time of resistance and revolution." By reason of this fact the American Revolution, quite unlike its French counterpart, was less a revolution than a conservation. It conserved, by giving newly vital form to, the liberal tradition of politics, whose ruin in Continental Europe was about to be consummated by the first great modern essay in totalitarianism.

The force for unity inherent in this tradition was of decisive importance in what concerns the problem of pluralism. Because it was conceived in the tradition of natural law the American Republic was rescued from the fate, still not overcome, that fell upon the European nations in which Continental Liberalism, a deformation of the liberal tradition, lodged itself, not least by the aid of the Lodges. There have never been "two Americas,"

---

*New York: Harcourt, Brace and Co., 1953.

in the sense in which there have been, and still are, "two Frances," "two Italys," "two Spains." Politically speaking, America has always been one. The reason is that a consensus was once established, and it still substantially endures, even in the quarters where its origins have been forgotten.

Formally and in the first instance this consensus was political, that is, it embraced a whole constellation of principles bearing upon the origin and nature of society, the function of the state as the legal order of society, and the scope and limitations of government. "Free government"—perhaps this typically American shorthand phrase sums up the consensus. "A free people under a limited government" puts the matter more exactly. It is a phrase that would have satisfied the first Whig, St. Thomas Aquinas.

To the early Americans government was not a phenomenon of force, as the later legal positivists would have it. Nor was it a "historical category," as Marx and his followers were to assert. Government did not mean simply the power to coerce, though this power was taken as integral to government. Government, properly speaking, was the right to command. It was authority. And its authority derived from law. By the same token its authority was limited by law. In his own way Tom Paine put the matter when he said, "In America Law is the King." But the matter had been better put by Henry of Bracton (d. 1268) when he said, "The king ought not to be under a man, but under God and under the law, because the law makes the king." This was the message of Magna Charta; this became the first structural rib of American constitutionalism.

Constitutionalism, the rule of law, the notion of sovereignty as purely political and therefore limited by law, the concept of government as an empire of laws and not of men—these were ancient ideas, deeply implanted in the British tradition at its origin in medieval times. The major American contribution to the tradition—a contribution that imposed itself on all subsequent political history in the Western world—was the written constitution. However, the American document was not the *constitution octroyée* of the nineteenth-century Restorations—

a constitution graciously granted by the King or Prince-President. Through the American techniques of the constitutional convention and of popular ratification, the American Constitution is explicitly the act of the people. It embodies their consensus as to the purposes of government, its structure, the extent of its powers and the limitations on them, etc. By the Constitution the people define the areas where authority is legitimate and the areas where liberty is lawful. The Constitution is therefore at once a charter of freedom and a plan for political order.

The Principle of Consent

Here is the second aspect of the continuity between the American consensus and the ancient liberal tradition; I mean the affirmation of the principle of the consent of the governed. Sir John Fortescue (d. 1476), Chief Justice of the Court of King's Bench under Henry VI, had thus stated the tradition, in distinguishing between the absolute and the constitutional monarch: "The secounde king [the constitutional monarch] may not rule his people by other laws than such as thai assenten to. And therefore he may set uppon thaim non imposicions without their consent." The principle of consent was inherent in the medieval idea of kingship; the king was bound to seek the consent of his people to his legislation. The American consensus reaffirmed this principle, at the same time that it carried the principle to newly logical lengths. Americans agreed that they would consent to none other than their own legislation, as framed by their representatives, who would be responsible to them. In other words, the principle of consent was wed to the equally ancient principle of popular participation in rule. But, since this latter principle was given an amplitude of meaning never before known in history, the result was a new synthesis, whose formula is the phrase of Lincoln, "government by the people."

Americans agreed to make government constitutional and therefore limited in a new sense, because it is representative, republican, responsible government. It is limited not only by law but by the will of the people it represents. Not only do the people adopt the Constitution; through the techniques of representation, free elections, and frequent rotation of administrations they also have a share in the enactment of all subsequent statutory legislation. The people are really governed; American political theorists did not pursue the Rousseauist will-o'-the-wisp: how shall the individual in society come to obey only himself? Nevertheless, the people are governed because they consent to be governed; and they consent to be governed because in a true sense they govern themselves.

The American consensus therefore includes a great act of faith in the capacity of the people to govern themselves. The faith was not unrealistic. It was not supposed that everybody could master the technical aspects of government, even in a day when these aspects were far less complex than they now are. The supposition was that the people could understand the general objectives of governmental policy, the broad issues put to the decision of government, especially as these issues raised moral problems. The American consensus accepted the premise of medieval society, that there is a sense of justice inherent in the people, in virtue of which they are empowered, as the medieval phrase had it, to "judge, direct, and correct" the processes of government.

It was this political faith that compelled early American agreement to the institutions of a free speech and a free press. In the American concept of them, these institutions do not rest on the thin theory proper to eighteenth-century individualistic rationalism, that a man has a right to say what he thinks merely because he thinks it. The American agreement was to reject political censorship of opinion as unrightful, because unwise, imprudent, not to say impossible. However, the proper premise of these freedoms lay in the fact that they were social necessities. "Colonial thinking about each of these rights had a strong social rather than individualistic bias," Rossiter says. They were regarded as conditions essential to the conduct of free, representative, and responsible government. People who are called upon to obey have the right first to be heard. People who are to bear burdens and make sacrifices have the right first to pronounce on the purposes which their sacrifices serve. People who are summoned to contribute to the common good have the right first to pass their own judgment on the question, whether the good proposed be truly a good, the people's good, the common good. Through the technique of majority opinion this popular judgment becomes binding on government.

A second principle underlay these free institutions—the principle that the state is distinct from society and limited in its offices toward society. This principle too was inherent in the Great Tradition. Before it was cancelled out by the rise of the modern omnicompetent society-state, it had found expression in the distinction between the order of politics and the order of culture, or, in the language of the time, the distinction between *studium* and *imperium.* The whole order of ideas in general was autonomous in the face of government; it was immune from political discipline, which could only fall upon actions, not ideas. Even the medieval Inquisition respected this distinction of orders; it never recognized a crime of opinion, *crimen opinionis;* its competence extended only to the repression of organized conspiracy against public order and the common good. It was, if you will, a Committee on un-Christian Activities; it regarded activities, not ideas, as justiciable.

The American Proposition, in reviving the distinction between society and state, which had perished under the advance of absolutism, likewise renewed the principle of the incompetence of government in the field of opinion. Government submits itself to judgment by the truth of society; it is not itself a judge of the truth in society. Freedom of the means of communication whereby ideas are circulated and criticized, and the freedom of the academy (understanding by the term the range of institutions organized for the pursuit of truth and the perpetuation of the intellectual heritage of society) are immune from legal inhibition or government control. This immunity is a civil right of the first order, essential to the American concept of a free people under a limited government.

A Virtuous People

"A free people": this term too has a special sense in the American Proposition. America has passionately pursued the ideal of freedom, expressed in a whole system of political and civil rights, to new lengths; but it has not pursued this ideal so madly as to rush over the edge of the abyss, into sheer libertarianism, into the chaos created by the nineteenth-century theory of the "outlaw conscience," *conscientia exlex,* the conscience that knows no law higher than its own subjective imperatives. Part of the inner architecture of the American ideal of freedom has been the profound conviction that only a virtuous people can be free. It is not an American belief that free government is inevitable, only that it is possible, and that its possibility can be realized only when the people as a whole are inwardly governed by the recognized imperatives of the universal moral law.

The American experiment reposes on Acton's postulate, that freedom is the highest phase of civil society. But it also reposes on Acton's further postulate, that the elevation of a people to this highest phase of social life supposes, as its condition, that they understand the ethical nature of political freedom. They must understand, in Acton's phrase, that freedom is "not the power of doing what we like, but the right of being able to do what we ought." The people claim this right, in all its articulated forms, in the face of government; in the name of this right, multiple limitations are put upon the power of government. But the claim can be made with the full resonance of moral authority only to the extent that it issues from an inner sense of responsibility to a higher law. In any phase civil society demands order. In its highest phase of freedom it demands that order should not be imposed from the top down, as it were, but should spontaneously flower outward from the free obedience to the restraints and imperatives that stem from inwardly possessed moral principle. In this sense democracy is more than a political experiment; it is a spiritual and moral enterprise.

And its success depends upon the virtue of the people who undertake it. Men who would be politically free must discipline themselves. Likewise institutions which would pretend to be free with a human freedom must in their workings be governed from within and made to serve the ends of virtue. Political freedom is endangered in its foundations as soon as the universal moral values, upon whose shared possession the self-discipline of a free society depends, are no longer vigorous enough to restrain the passions and shatter the selfish inertia of men. The American ideal of freedom as ordered freedom, and therefore an ethical ideal, has traditionally reckoned with these truths, these truisms.

Human and Historical Rights

This brings us to the threshold of religion, and therefore to the other aspect of the problem of pluralism, the plurality of religions in America. However, before crossing this threshold one more characteristic of the American Proposition, as implying a consensus, needs mention, namely, the Bill of Rights. The philosophy of the Bill of Rights was also tributary to the tradition of natural law, to the idea that man has certain original responsibilities precisely as man, antecedent to his status as citizen. These responsibilities are creative of rights which inhere in man antecedent to any act of government; therefore they are not granted by government and they cannot be surrendered to government. They are as inalienable as they are inherent. Their proximate source is in nature, and in history insofar as history bears witness to the nature of man; their ultimate source, as the Declaration of Independence states, is in God, the Creator of nature and the Master of history. The power of this doctrine, as it inspired both the Revolution and the form of the Republic, lay in the fact that it drew an effective line of demarcation around the exercise of political or social authority. When government ventures over this line, it collides with the duty and right of resistance. Its authority becomes arbitrary and therefore nil; its act incurs the ultimate anathema, "unconstitutional."

One characteristic of the American Bill of Rights is important for the subject here, namely, the differences that separate it from the Declaration of the Rights of Man in the France of '89. In considerable part the latter was a parchment-child of the Enlightenment, a top-of-the-brain concoction of a set of men who did not understand that a political community, like man himself, has roots in history and in nature. They believed that a state could be simply a work of art, a sort of absolute beginning, an artifact of which abstract human reason could be the sole artisan. Moreover, their exaggerated individualism had shut them off from a view of the organic nature of the human community; their social atomism would permit no institutions or associations intermediate between the individual and the state.

In contrast, the men who framed the American Bill of Rights understood history and tradition, and they understood nature in the light of both. They too were individualists, but not to the point of ignoring the social nature of man. They did their thinking within the tradition of freedom that was their heritage from England. Its roots were not in the top of anyone's brain but in history. Importantly, its roots were in the medieval notion of the *homo liber et legalis*, the man whose freedom rests on law, whose law was the age-old custom in which the nature of man expressed itself, and whose lawful freedoms were possessed in association with his fellows. The rights for which the colonists contended against the English Crown were basically the rights of Englishmen. And these were substantially the rights written into the Bill of Rights.

. . . Freedom of speech, assembly, association, and petition for the redress of grievances, security of person, home, and property—these were great historical as well as civil and natural rights. So too was the right to trial by jury, and all the procedural rights implied in the Fifth- and later in the Fourteenth-Amendment provision for "due process of law." The guarantee of these and other rights was new in that it was written, in that it envisioned these rights with an amplitude, and gave them a priority, that had not been known before in history. But the Bill of Rights was an effective instrument for the delimitation of government authority and social power, not because it was written on paper in 1789 or 1791, but because the rights it proclaims had already been engraved by history on the conscience of a people. The American Bill of Rights is not a piece of eighteenth-century rationalist theory; it is far more the product of Christian history. Behind it one can see, not the philosophy of the Enlightenment but the older philosophy that had been the matrix of the common law. The "man" whose rights are guaranteed in the face of law and government is, whether he knows it or not, the Christian man, who had learned to know his own personal dignity in the school of Christian faith.

The American Consensus Today

Americans have been traditionally proud of the earlier phases of their history—colonial and Revolutionary, constitutional and Federalist. This pride persists today. The question is, whether the American consensus still endures—the consensus whose essential contents have been sketched in the foregoing. A twofold answer may be given. The first answer is given by Professor Rossiter:

"Perhaps Americans could achieve a larger measure of liberty and prosperity and build a more successful government if they were to abandon the language and assumptions of men who lived almost two centuries ago. Yet the feeling cannot be downed that rude rejection of the past, rather than levelheaded respect for it, would be the huge mistake. Americans may eventually take the advice of their advanced philosophers and adopt a political theory that pays more attention to groups, classes, public opinion, power-élites, positive law, public administration, and other realities of twentieth-century America. Yet it seems safe to predict that the people, who occasionally prove themselves wiser than their philosophers, will go on thinking about the political community in terms of unalienable rights, popular sovereignty, consent, constitutionalism, separation of powers, morality, and limited government. The political theory of the American Revolution—a theory of ethical, ordered liberty —remains the political tradition of the American people."

This is a cheerful answer. I am not at all sure that it is correct, if it be taken to imply that the tradition of natural law, as the foundation of law and politics, has the same hold upon the mind of America today that it had upon the "preachers, merchants, planters, and lawyers who were the mind of colonial America." There is indeed talk today about a certain revival of this great tradition, notably among more thoughtful men in the legal profession. But the talk itself is significant. One would not talk of reviving the tradition, if it were in fact vigorously alive. Perhaps the American people have not taken the advice of their advanced philosophers. Perhaps they are wiser than their philosophers. Perhaps they still refuse to think of politics and law as their philosophers think—in purely positivist and pragmatist terms. The fact remains that this is the way the philosophers think. Not that they have made a "rude rejection of the past." They are never rude. And they can hardly be said to have rejected what they never knew or understood, because it was never taught to them and they never learned it. The tradition of natural law is not taught or learned in the American university. It has not been rejected, much less refuted. We do not refute our adversaries, said Santayana; we quietly bid them goodbye. I think . . . that the American university long since bade a quiet goodbye to the whole notion of an American consensus, as implying that there are truths that we hold in common, and a natural law that makes known to all of us the structure of the moral universe in such wise that all of us are bound by it in a common obedience.

There is, however, a second answer to the question, whether the original American consensus still endures. It is certainly valid of a not inconsiderable portion of the American people, the Catholic community. The men of learning in it acknowledge certain real contributions made by positive sociological analysis of the political community. But both they and their less learned fellows still adhere, with all the conviction of intelligence, to the tradition of natural law as the basis of free and ordered political life. Historically, this tradition has found, and still finds, its intellectual home within the Catholic Church. It is indeed one of the ironies of history that the tradition should have so largely languished in the so-called Catholic nations of Europe at the same time that its enduring vigor was launching a new Republic across the broad ocean. There is also some paradox in the fact that a nation which has (rightly or wrongly) thought of its own genius in Protestant terms should have owed its origins and the stability of its political structure to a tradition whose genius is alien to current intellectualized versions of the Protestant religion, and even to certain individualistic exigencies of Protestant religiosity. These are special questions, not to be pursued here. The point here is that Catholic participation in the American consensus has been full and free, unreserved and unembarrassed, because the contents of this consensus—the ethical and political principles drawn from the tradition of natural law—approve themselves to the Catholic intelligence and conscience. Where this kind of language is talked, the Catholic joins the conversation with complete ease. It is his language. The ideas expressed are native to his own universe of discourse. Even the accent, being American, suits his tongue.

Another idiom now prevails. The possibility was inherent from the beginning. To the early American theorists and politicians the tradition of natural law was an inheritance. This was its strength; this was at the same time its weakness, especially since a subtle alteration of the tradition had already commenced. For a variety of reasons the intellectualist idea of law as reason had begun to cede to the voluntarist idea of law as will. One can note the change in Blackstone, for instance, even though he still stood within the tradition, and indeed drew whole generations of early American lawyers into it with him. (Part of American folklore is Sandburg's portrait of Abraham Lincoln, sitting barefoot on his woodpile, reading Blackstone.) Protestant Christianity, especially in its left wing (and its left wing has always been dominant in America), inevitably evolved away from the old English and American tradition. Grotius and the philosophers of the Enlightenment had cast up their secularized versions of the tradition. Their disciples were to better their instruction, as the impact of the methods of empirical science made itself felt even in those areas of human thought in which knowledge is noncumulative and to that extent recalcitrant to the methods of science. Seeds of dissolution were already present in the ancient heritage as it reached the shores of America.

Perhaps the dissolution, long since begun, may one day be consummated. Perhaps one day the noble many-storeyed mansion of democracy will be dismantled, levelled to the dimensions of a flat majoritarianism, which is no mansion but a barn, perhaps even a tool shed in which the weapons of tyranny may be forged. Perhaps there will one day be wide dissent even from the political principles which emerge from natural law, as well as dissent from the constellation of ideas that have historically undergirded these principles—the idea that government has a moral basis; that the universal moral law is the foundation of society; that the legal order of society—that is, the state—is subject to judgment by a law that is not statistical but inherent in the nature of man; that the eternal reason of God is the ultimate origin of all law; that this nation in all its aspects—as a society, a state, an ordered and free relationship between governors and governed—is under God. . . .

3   The Unwritten Constitution

L. Brent Bozell

. . . Our intention is to speak of method, to inquire whether the responsibility for diagnosis and cure, in the public sphere, has been entrusted to the people and to the institutions—the "machinery," to summon the contemporary figure—that are likely to do the best job.

. . . The method of public policy-making in the United States has undergone a fundamental change in the past decade without the change having been widely commented on, or, by most of us, even noticed. True, the change is not apparent at the stages of policy-making we ordinarily think of as decisive. "We the people" still elect or indirectly appoint our public officials as we have done in the past. Our officials, in turn, enact and administer the laws much as they always have—allowing, of course, for the continuing expansion of the bureaucracy's role, and for the increasing influence of non-governmental "opinion molders." In the total business of governing a society, however, these dimensions are not nearly so important as they must seem to those who move in them. We may recall the famous husband who, challenged to disprove the sociologists' thesis that the woman rules the modern American family, replied that in *his* family *he* made the decisions on the major issues—e.g., whether the U.S. should continue to belong to the United Nations, and what should be done about right-to-work. But the sociologists' concern, as we know, was not so much to distinguish between "major" and "minor" decisions as to demonstrate that most day-

From L. Brent Bozell, *The Warren Revolution* (New Rochelle, N.Y.: Arlington House, 1966), Introduction, pp. 15–37. Copyright © 1966 by L. Brent Bozell. Reprinted by permission of Arlington House, Publishers.

to-day decisions are *derivative,* that they are made in the context of and are therefore largely determined by the family's peculiar character, or ethos—its ethical substructure—which, according to the thesis, is largely established and defined by the woman.

In dealing with political societies, we properly speak of the society's ethical substructure as its "constitution." It is in the matter of *constitution-making* that the fundamental change in American public life has recently occurred.

Before indicating the nature of the change, let us be as clear as we can about what a "constitution," in the generic sense in which we are using the term, is. And perhaps the best way of getting at that is to state what a constitution does, or may do.

In part, it is a scheme under which public authority in a society is divided up: it sets forth who, in the conduct of public business, shall have power to do what to whom.

Second, it may establish, or attempt to establish, the boundary lines of the public business, beyond which no public authority is expected to venture; that is, it may reserve certain areas of private freedom.

Third, it may grant certain privileges of a public nature— what we are accustomed to call "civil rights."

And fourth—a function that both underlies the first three and also extends far beyond them—a constitution embodies an understanding among the society's members about the *kind* of society it is. What are the society's purposes? Or does it have any purpose beyond merely surviving? What does it "believe in"? Or does it consider itself to be "open" and thus, as a society, to believe in nothing? Does it relate, or seek to relate, its individual members as "equals"? Or according to various "structures" that have been established by its organic processes? Is the society expected to serve the interests of its members, or are the members expected to serve the society's interest? And so on.

Now regardless of which of these roles it performs—whether it dispenses authority, or reserves freedom, or grants rights, or reflects a consensus about the society's underlying character— a constitutional provision is superior to ordinary acts of government in this respect: it is a *standard* to which the ordinary governmental act is expected to conform—conformity being the condition on which the society's members have agreed to be governed at all. A constitution, then, is a society's internal treaty of peace. If the peace terms are honored, the society may look forward to tranquility, order, obedience: the expressions of peace. If they are breached, the society may anticipate, according to the gravity of the matter, discord, violence, rebellion: the expressions of war.

Let us probe a little further. Everyone knows that constitutions may be written, as in the United States, or unwritten, as in Great Britain. What is less often noticed is that a society that has a written constitution also has an unwritten one: in a society like ours, that is to say, only *part* of the Constitution is written down. In the United States, moreover, this is true with respect to each of the four constitutional functions we have mentioned.

The division and granting of power, to take the first, is largely taken care of in our written Constitution; but the authority of Cabinet members and of the various bureaucracies is not specified there—and is not less secure, or "constitutional," for the fact it is not specified. Nor, to anticipate our thesis a little, does the written Constitution say anything about our society's *supreme* authority—the one that is meant to construe its *Constitution*. As we shall see, this is a matter that has always been the exclusive concern of our unwritten constitution.

As for reserving freedom, our Bill of Rights does indeed purport to safeguard certain areas, at least against federal intrusion; but there are other private freedoms of constitutional status— the right to marry whom one chooses and the right to move freely about the country are two of them—to which neither the Bill of Rights nor the Constitution proper makes allusion.*

Regarding public privileges, the right to a jury trial is con-

*We do not suggest that these freedoms are absolute under the unwritten constitution, but that it is largely the unwritten constitution, rather than the reservation clauses (the Ninth and Tenth Amendments) of the written one, that determines where the lines are drawn. This may be appreciated by a moment's reflection on how our society handled Mormon polygamy on the one hand, and the supposed danger of sabotage by Japanese-Americans during World War II, on the other.

ferred by the written Constitution, as is the right not to be excluded from the franchise because of race or sex; but the right
to vote itself, or, to cite an even more recent entry, the right to
a free formal education, are assured, if at all, only by our unwritten constitution.*

Finally, the matters that fall under the heading of a society's
character or credo are largely the concern, in the United States
anyway, of our unwritten constitution. For example, as significant a characteristic of our society as that it is "religious," i.e.,
that the generality of its members acknowledge God, certainly
can not be discovered in the written Constitution proper—nor,
for that matter, in the First Amendment which treats the subject
in a back-handed fashion, which is to say in language clearly
more appropriate for protecting a minority than for affirming
the belief of a majority. The written Constitution, however, is
not altogether silent on such matters. The "obligation of contracts" clause, for instance, says a lot about what we now call the
Protestant ethic, and has played no small role in causing its observance in American public life. Still other matters of this kind
are merely hinted at, as the provision limiting the importation
of slaves hinted that our society was already developing doubts,
although somewhat diffidently, about slavery, and as the equal
protection clause later hinted that our beliefs were moving in
the direction, not merely of freedom (for that is another matter),
but of equality.

But saying this much takes us to a consideration that is even
less frequently noticed, with the result that an important element of our political machinery is generally misunderstood.
What must be said now is that *some matters—and they are
momentous matters—appear to be dealt with, and settled, by
our written Constitution, but in point of fact are not settled by
it.* Perhaps the best example is the matter of free speech. We
have been taught to believe that the constitutional status of
freedom of speech in the United States is set forth in the First

---

*Of course such rights may be expressly conferred by written state
constitutions or laws; but this fact does not detract from their status as
elements of an unwritten *national* consensus.

Amendment. That this is not and could not be true is apparent from the language of the Amendment, which is recognizably unserviceable as a working constitutional directive. To be sure, there is a school of thought that contends the words "Congress shall make *no* law abridging the freedom of speech" were intended by the framers to be taken literally. But sober students have a different understanding of the matter: they know, a priori, that no responsible group of law givers would deprive their society of the means to protect itself against speech that endangered its survival; and they know, a posteriori, that this particular group of law givers did not think of themselves to be doing so, as witness that the Congress that wrote the First Amendment also wrote, a scant five years later, the Alien and Sedition Acts. But if the framers' formulation was not meant to be taken literally, then it was merely metaphorical—an indication that the society for which the framers spoke thought highly of free speech. But if only metaphorical, it is, we repeat—and has proved to be—quite useless as a constitutional standard. Actually, our constitutional rule about freedom of speech, to the extent it has proved capable of being written down at all, is embodied in the "clear and present danger" doctrine which was first put into words by a Supreme Court justice in the twentieth century. Justice Holmes did not, however, invent the rule. He found it, as we still find it today, in a consensus that has been hammered out over the years by legislatures, Presidents, courts; the rule was to be found, in a word, in our *un*written constitution.

The free speech matter is, as we say, merely illustrative. That much the same point must be made about the reach of the commerce clause, the balance of the First Amendment, and parts of the Fifth and the Fourteenth Amendments—to mention a few of our written Constitution's more important provisions—does not require elaboration. It follows that to try to distinguish between our "written" and "unwritten" constitutions—since a provision may appear formally in one, but actually be in the other—is not particularly helpful, and may be misleading. We are better advised to draw the line, for distinctions indeed must be made, between what we shall henceforth call our *fixed* constitution and our *fluid* constitution, it being understood that while all "fixed" provisions are written, not all written provisions are fixed. So let us turn to the differences, which are fundamental, between our fixed and fluid constitutions.

The principal differences arise out of the method by which the two types of constitution are *made,* and thus the method by which they may be *unmade,* or changed. A fixed constitutional provision, under our system, is made by *formal* procedures which have been designed a) to define the proposed provision unambiguously; b) to subject it to open, deliberative debate by the appointed constitution-makers; c) to dispose of the proposal definitively by public tabulation of the constitution-makers' votes. A fluid provision, on the other hand, is made by *informal* procedures which are calculated, precisely, to *avoid* exact definition, deliberative debate, and public vote-taking.

We may spell this out a little. In the case of a fixed provision, our society has in effect convened itself in extraordinary session —either in special constitutional convention or by summoning Congress and the state legislatures to act in that capacity—to consider issuing a binding policy directive to its various public authorities. The task of the session is to determine whether there exists, at this time and place, a sufficiently broad consensus about the desirability of a given policy to warrant placing that policy beyond the reach of the society's ordinary political processes. And the test of sufficiency will be whether a clear statement of the policy, after its meaning and implications have been fully explored and weighed in open debate, can command the support of a "constitutional majority" of the society, as measured by the formal constitution-making machinery set forth in Articles V and VII of the written Constitution. Moreover, and most important of all, the society has made a prior *"moral"* commitment that should the required majority affirm the statement, the decision will thenceforth be binding, not only on its individual members, but on every public authority—*until such time as a contrary-minded constitutional majority has been mobilized and has recorded a new consensus through the same arduous, exacting procedures.* Thus, on July 12, 1909, two-thirds of the Congress proposed an amendment to the Constitution that would permit the levying of a federal tax on incomes; by February 25, 1913, three-quarters of the state legislatures had ratified the proposal, thereby incorporating it into the fixed constitution as the Sixteenth Amendment. And thus it has been understood ever since, no less by the enemies of the federal income tax than by its friends, that the power conferred by the Sixteenth Amendment cannot be withdrawn, or modified, except in compliance with the Amendment procedures stipulated in Article V.

It is quite otherwise with the fluid constitution. Here we are dealing with "provisions" such as our constitutional rule about freedom of speech, that are fashioned gradually, subtly, often imperceptibly, by the society's organic process. There is no moment—no "time and place"—at which the provision may be said to have been framed and adopted; rather it has *developed,* the product of the society's inner dynamics of experience, growth and change. It may have had, at its point of departure, a "principle" set forth in the written Constitution, such as "freedom of speech," "due process of law," "equal protection of the law"; but except as the framers made clear their expectations as to how the principle was to be applied, the provision will not become *effective,* until the rivalries, the interplay, the give and take among the society's diverse forces and factions, have hammered out a working consensus about the concrete particulars of application.

Nor is it likely, either in the process of its adoption or thereafter, that a fluid provision will, or can, be reduced to a neat formulation that establishes, with equal clarity for everybody, its exact dimensions and implications. *For the distinctive characteristic of a fluid provision is precisely that it carries shadings of meaning, provisos, exceptions, qualifications—a hundred nuances that will permit different interpretations by different people in different situations, and without which general acceptance could not be expected.* Any attempt to spell out the nuances would probably prevent a constitutional consensus from taking shape, and so destroy the possibility of giving *the principle* in question effective constitutional status.

This is why a fluid provision cannot prudently be "put to a vote," why no one seeks to measure the consensus by a mathematica' formula. Adoption is accomplished, rather, by an *accumulation* of actions taken over a period of years by various public authorities, as well as by private citizens and groups— actions that may often be in sharp conflict with each other, but which may eventually produce a broad synthesis. Congress and the state legislatures—for example—may indicate a preference for one course of action; the courts may resist, or perhaps try to go the other way; the President may join one side or the other, or possibly bring his weight to bear on behalf of compromise; community practice, meanwhile, is recording its own judgment. And as each participant in the process absorbs the impact of the others' behavior, sufficient veerings and withdrawals may occur to produce a common course along which the society as a whole can be seen to be traveling. Once this has happened one of our constitution's fluid provisions has come into being.

But mark well two aspects of the process that bear heavily on today's problems. The first is that the establishment of this kind of constitutional consensus does not preclude divergences from the fluid provision's principal thrust; rather, as we have noted, the consensus may depend precisely on the recognition and toleration of disparities, of meanderings from the main stream. It is in the very nature of a fluid provision, since it springs from the organic pressures of a diversified society, that it contemplates some front-runners, some laggards, even some die-hards who try still to move in the opposite direction. The American colonies, toward the end of the seventeenth century, were moving toward a general rule of religious toleration, and the emergence of the rule was no less apparent for the fact that Massachusetts, unlike the more enlightened colonies further south, was still hanging witches. The second thing to remember is that the substance and direction of the flow are established, not by the action of one force, but by the *interaction* of many. Thus while the fluid constitution is subject to constant change, the change is always a community undertaking. A fluid constitutional provision is unmade, or revised, in the same fashion it was made—by a shift in the consensus, brought about and registered by the society's organic processes.

The gradual emergence of our national government as a "welfare state" illustrates the making of a fluid provision. Our fixed constitution simply does not deal with the subject of federal welfarism. To be sure, certain passages of the written document—the Preamble, the taxing power, the commerce clause, the due process clause, and the Tenth Amendment—can be and have been read, in net impact, as authorizing welfare measures; but they also can be and have been read as forbidding such measures. Careful commentators on both sides, moreover, have always acknowledged the inconclusiveness of the evidence. Therefore, the existence and scope of the national government's power in this area have necessarily been the product of an *informal* constitutional consensus.

And note that while that consensus, historically, has changed very little from year to year, it has undergone a substantial change over the course of many years. At the turn of the century the notion that Congress is constitutionally competent to "wage war on poverty" would have been laughed out of court. Today it is probably correct to say that our society recognizes a congressional *power* to undertake any welfare measure that can be accomplished by the appropriation and allocation of public funds. The sharpest shift in the consensus occurred, of course, in the nineteen-thirties, and was reflected in a dramatic struggle between the President and Congress on the one hand, and the Supreme Court on the other, with the state governments (though their interests were as deeply involved as any) meekly watching the contest from the sidelines. The mechanics of that shift—for instance as it affected the field of agriculture—are worth remembering. Congress and the President attempted to aid the agricultural community by the imposition of certain production controls, said to be justified under the taxing power. The Supreme Court denied the taxing power was that extensive, and so declared the first AAA unconstitutional. Congress then retaliated with the second AAA—this time, however, advancing its plan under the cover of the commerce clause. The Court retreated, clearly not because it believed Congress now to be on superior constitutional ground, but because community sentiment, as reflected in part by President Roosevelt's "court-packing" threat, had rallied to the support of New Deal legislation. The Court's capitulation thus *ratified* a revision of the fluid constitutional consensus. This pattern of settlement, moreover, seems sure to be followed in the future: whether the trend towards increased welfarism is sustained or reversed, the American people will continue to make constitutional decisions on such matters through the informal, organic processes of the fluid constitution, rather than by formal, rigid declarations of policy set forth in the fixed constitution.

At this point a general observation may be in order about how constitutions ought to be made. It would appear that certain kinds of problems are more appropriately and successfully handled by the informal procedures of a fluid constitutional provision, while certain other kinds of problems lend themselves more readily to the rigid affirmations of a fixed constitution. There are some matters, that is to say, in which continuing growth and change, and not always in the same direction, or with the same impact on all parts of our society, can be expected. In these matters the *flexibility* of the fluid constitution allows our various governmental structures to absorb and reflect the diverse shifts in community consensus that are going on down below, and may thus be an indispensable condition of stability and order, as well as of maximum freedom. For this reason, such bottom-level and fundamentally ethical decisions as those that determine the kind of economic system the society will sustain, the type of social order it will observe, how it will handle the problem of political orthodoxy and dissent, its approach to religion, the code of personal morality it will sanction—such matters are usually better left to adjudication in the fluid constitution. The fixed constitution, on the other hand, is usually the more appropriate place for allocating the public authority to various branches and levels of government; for providing means of preserving the allocation—e.g., our system of "checks and balances"; for prescribing the conditions of conferring authority —e.g., the qualifications of public officials and the mode of selecting them (which would include the problem of the franchise); for describing certain details of government organization —minutiae such as the date Congress is to convene; and finally for asserting those strictly juridical or "courtroom" rights that are designed to assure individuals, irrespective of changing historical currents, an even-handed administration of justice. To be sure, such matters can become intertwined with bottom-level questions: an allocation of power—of the taxing power, for instance—may affect a society's basic economic structure; the franchise may affect its social structure; a guarantee of juridical rights may affect the underlying balance between orthodoxy and dissent; and so on; and when such complications occur a society will understandably be at sixes and sevens in deciding whether to deal with the problem in its fixed or in its fluid constitution. But on the whole the type of question just mentioned, unlike the bottom-level questions, can be succinctly posed and resolved by a "hard," relatively permanent constitutional consensus; for that reason, the interests of stability, order and maximum freedom are normally better served by a fixed provision.

There is a corollary to all of this. A *mixing* of constitutional categories—a failure to deal with a given matter by the type of provision suited to it—may lead to unhappy consequences.*
On the one hand, failure to formalize a hard constitutional con-

---

*We speak here only of the United States; quite different generalizations might apply to other societies. For example, a more religiously homogenous society, like Spain, might find the State's relations with a given religion a proper subject for its fixed constitution. And on the other hand, the political systems of the Continent have never been particularly successful in giving fixed constitutional status to allocations of authority and limitations on the State's power generally. When formal constitution-making came into vogue in Europe in the early part of the nineteenth century, Prince Metternich persuasively argued that only the Anglo-Saxon peoples had sufficient self-restraint to maintain a meaningful distinction between the "state" and "society," and thus to observe fixed constitutional limitations on the State's power.

sensus by recording it in a fixed provision may permit a simple, transitory majority temporarily to defy the consensus for want of enforcement machinery. Prior to 1940 the President's tenure was limited to two terms by what most Americans thought to be a very hard "consensus." But since the consensus had been sanctioned by tradition only, the two-term rule was, in effect, a fluid constitutional provision. Consequently, Franklin Roosevelt was able to side-step the rule on the approval of a simple majority. A decade later the framers of the Twenty-second Amendment sought to repair the oversight by placing the question of Presidential tenure where a constitutional majority has now formally decided it belongs—in our fixed constitution. On the other hand, attempts to give fixed constitutional status to policies that do not lend themselves to that treatment will be at best futile, and at worst productive of great mischief. The attempt to define a constitutional rule about freedom of speech in the First Amendment settled nothing. The attempt to deal with the country's drinking problem by constitutional fiat in the Eighteenth Amendment led to a breakdown of the public order and was in due course withdrawn by the Twenty-first Amendment.

[My thesis, then,] . . . is a) that until a dozen years ago the constitution-makers of the United States by and large observed the distinction between the type of provision that is suited to the country's fixed constitution and the type that is suited to its fluid constitution, with the result that the country for the better part of this 165-year period enjoyed internal peace. The notable exceptions are the Civil War and, less calamitously, the Prohibition Era, when the distinction broke down. And it is b) that during the past . . . years the Supreme Court, with the encouragement of the country's intellectual establishment, has instituted a *third* kind of constitution-making, which is revolutionary both in its method and in its consequences. This new kind of constitution-making, to state the phenomenon broadly, *has sought to transfer the solution of some of the most momentous problems of contemporary public policy from the fluid constitution to the fixed constitution—by judicial decree.* The result is that the internal peace of the country has been gravely disturbed, and the country's potential for peaceful growth in the future seriously jeopardized. This is not the place to document the thesis in detail, but it will be helpful to indicate here some of its configurations.

One of the more remarkable aspects of the American political system is how little our fixed constitution has been altered since the first ten amendments were added on November 3, 1791, and thus how much of the country's growth and development and accommodation to changing times has been accomplished through the organic processes of our fluid constitution. In over a century and a half, the American Constitution has been amended by formal procedures only fourteen times—a record that becomes even more remarkable when we consider the kind of amendments those fourteen were.

One of them, the Twelfth Amendment, merely corrected an oversight in the original document regarding the method of electing the President, and thus made no substantive change in the system.

Another, the Twentieth, was a decision of administrative convenience, bringing Congress' annual meeting date into line with the date of the President's inauguration; it, too, reflected no substantive change in the country's political system.

A third, the Twenty-second, may be said to have affected the Constitution's original allocation of authority by potentially limiting the power of an individual President; but the two-term rule, as we have just remarked, did not so much change the system as recognize that the better way to guard an ancient consensus about how the system should operate was to remove the rule from the fluid into the fixed constitution.

Three other amendments dealt, in their principal effect, with the distribution of power between the national and state governments. The earliest, the Eleventh, reflected a decentralization tendency. The States, as sovereign entities, were not to be subject to suit in the national courts. Two later amendments, the Sixteenth and Seventeenth, reflected the centralization tendencies of the present century. The Sixteenth permitted Congress to levy an income tax without regard to the former rule that direct taxes be assessed in proportion to each State's population. The Seventeenth made senators popular representatives rather than representatives, in effect, of the state governments.

Another group of four, the Fifteenth, the Nineteenth, the Twenty-third and the Twenty-fourth, dealt with the franchise. Note, however, that the first of these four had origins of a very different character from the latter three, with the result that until recently it enjoyed a very different status in our constitutional system. The Fifteenth Amendment was conceived and promoted as an instrument of the Northern radicals' Reconstruction program; it was one of the conditions of peace laid down by the victors in the Civil War. While the Fifteenth's proponents formally observed the prescribed amendment procedures, they did not really command the support of a hard constitutional consensus. The country as a whole in 1870 was little more prepared to welcome Negroes to the franchise than the deep South was in 1960. As a result, the Fifteenth Amendment's status in the fixed constitution was extremely shaky until the present decade. It was honored as much in the breach as in the observance precisely because it lacked the sanction of a bona fide consensus. To be sure, recognition of Negro voting rights steadily increased over the years, but this development proceeded apace with changing social attitudes and economic conditions in various parts of the country—which means that the problem, in reality, was being adjudicated over a period of ninety years by our fluid constitution. Today, at last, a hard constitutional consensus about Negro voting has come into being, an event that was memorialized in 1964 by the adoption of the Twenty-fourth—the anti-poll tax—Amendment.

Now the Twenty-fourth is similar in this respect to the Nineteenth and the Twenty-third which, respectively, forbade the exclusion of women from the franchise, and gave the vote in Presidential elections to residents of the District of Columbia: all three merely formalized a consensus that had already been brought into being by the operation of the society's organic processes. It is not to disparage the suffragette movement or the agitations of disenfranchised Washingtonians, to recognize that their successes had been assured by a prior evolution of attitudes and practices in the country's economic and social structures. The franchise amendments, in a word, show that meaningful provisions of the written Constitution must have the support of a broadly-based consensus—that while the written Constitution can record, it cannot peaceably *produce* a change in the society's underlying ethical substructure.

The Thirteenth and Fourteenth Amendments were also conditions of peace imposed by the winning side in the Civil War. But each of them has peculiar aspects of which we should take careful account. The Thirteenth, unlike the Fifteenth, appears to have had the support of an authentic constitutional consensus at the time it was adopted. To be sure, a hard national consensus concerning the status of slavery had not emerged before the War, and the unwillingness of intransigents on both sides to allow the problem to be "worked out" through the organic processes precipitated the war. But the verdict of the war produced a consensus that Negroes should be free, which was no less authentic for the fact it was hammered out by force of arms. The problem of Negro slavery was thus adjudicated by our fixed constitution—notwithstanding the modern thesis that if wiser heads had prevailed the same result would have been achieved less painfully through the organic processes. Much the same may be said about one aspect of the Fourteenth on which we shall be commenting at some length below; suffice to note here that the Fourteenth's framers viewed certain elemental juridical rights as necessary concomitants of Negro emancipation, and these rights, like the Thirteenth itself, enjoyed fixed constitutional status from the beginning. However, the Amendment's broader implications, as suggested by the due process and equal protection clauses, were left for future implementation to the organic processes of the fluid constitution.

There are, finally, the Eighteenth Amendment which is the *reductio ad absurdum* example of the kind of problem that should never be thrust into the rigid prescriptions of a fixed constitution, and the Twenty-first which recognized and corrected the error.

For the rest, American constitution-making, up until 1954, proceeded in "fluid" channels. Our fixed constitution survived more or less intact, according to the framers' original plan and apparent expectations. It served us well, not only as a guarantor of stability and peace, but as a firmly grounded launching pad for innovation and relevant response to changing situations and changing times. This is not to say the framers would have felt altogether at home in our mid-twentieth-century American society: a century and a half had brought about profound changes in our insights and our outlooks, in our social, economic, and political organization, even in the substantive values we embraced. But it is to say that the framers, with remarkable shrewdness, seem to have anticipated the areas in which the changes might take place, and to have left those areas open—"flexible"—and unguarded by prescriptive dogma. It is also to say that the framers' successors had by and large recognized the wisdom of keeping things that way. The elastic clauses of the written Constitution remained flexible instruments of government. Our major policy decisions continued to be the product of an interaction—a series of organic tensions—between the wills of all branches of government. Our governors, whether in courts, legislatures or executive mansions, showed a remarkable reluctance to obstruct the flow of the fluid constitution by trying to give fixed constitutional status to policies around which an authentic consensus had not yet formed.

The Supreme Court's new method of constitution-making has exposed the country to a quite different experience during the past . . . years.

We have seen certain matters, of which the race problem is the one that comes most readily to mind, that were in the process of adjudication by the country's varied and intricate organic mechanisms, suddenly subjected to the rigid imperatives of a judge-defined "supreme law."

We have seen matters, like the relationship between church and state, that in the American experience have always defied simplistic, doctrinaire solutions, suddenly chained to abstract formulas that may be familiar to the rhetoric but are altogether alien to the customs and underlying attitudes of the people.

We have seen matters, like the apportionment of legislative representatives, that have traditionally been handled according to local needs and desires and thus disparately, suddenly laced into a single theory of politics that must be uniformly enforced alike in situations where the theory is helpful according to the community's lights and in those where it is not.

We have seen matters, like our national policy toward political dissidence, that have always been a function of competing concerns—in this case usually a compromise between each man's concern for personal freedom and the society's concern for consensus and self-preservation—suddenly treated as though only one concern were involved—in this case the First Amendment's paradigmatic statement about freedom.

Above all, in every such case, we have seen matters about which a hard constitutional consensus does *not* exist treated as though such a consensus *did* exist: we have been summoned to accord merely *judge*-endorsed policies the same dignity we accord policies that have passed the muster of the Constitution's formal amendment procedures.

This momentous innovation has been accomplished through the quietest of revolutions. The Warren Court, with the approval of much of the country's intellectual leadership, has simply expanded an old judicial function into a new one. From the earliest days of the Republic, the Supreme Court was a major participant in the making of our fluid constitution. Principally through the power of *judicial review*, the Court helped discover and develop working consensuses in areas not covered by the fixed constitution. Its decisions, strictly speaking, adjudicated nothing more than the rights of the litigants in the case at hand: nonetheless they were understood to be affirming a "judicial policy" that would govern similar cases in the future. And since that policy carried the sanction of the Court's considerable prestige as a putatively disinterested party, it is understandable that other policy-makers—Congress, the President, the States—were reluctant to repudiate judicial policy by ignoring or resisting the Court's rulings. The Court's views, to be sure, did not always prevail. But they were always an important factor in determining how the country should be run in those areas governed by the organic processes of the fluid constitution. Today, however, the Court claims not just a participant's role in the making of the fluid constitution, but the *umpire's* role. From its old job of being *an* expounder of the constitution, it has become *the* expounder. Its judgments are not simply a *factor,* along with the judgments of other public authorities, in the making of the fluid constitution; the Court now insists that its judgments are final and binding, not only on the litigants in the case at hand, but on all public authorities. The only recourse for those who disagree with the Court, under the new understanding, is to the formal amendment procedures of the written Constitution. *Thus, a Supreme Court decision has become equivalent to a provision of the fixed Constitution.*

In all respects, that is, save one. Like a fixed provision, it is binding on all public authorities. Like a fixed provision, it can be changed only by invoking the arduous amendment machinery of Article V. *The one respect in which a Court decision differs from other provisions of the fixed constitution is that it has acquired that status, not by securing the endorsement of a hard national consensus, but by securing the certification of a nine-man tribunal.*

The race problem is an instructive instance of how this new method of constitution-making has affected our society's traditional way of doing business. Prior to the Civil War there were only two fixed constitutional provisions affecting the relationship between the white and Negro races. One dealt with the importation of slaves, forbidding Congress to ban the slave trade prior to 1808, and permitting (but not requiring) it to do so thereafter.* The other provided that slaves were to be counted

---

*This has been our only experience with an "executory" constitutional provision. The consensus of 1787 asserted, in effect, that the country had made up its mind to place the slave trade under the control of the national

as three-fifths of a white person for the purposes of apportioning representatives and levying direct taxes. For the rest, the original framers in effect decided that the problem should be dealt with by the machinery of what we are calling the fluid constitution: while later generations might adopt a fixed constitutional provision to govern this or that aspect of the problem, this would require the emergence of a hard constitutional consensus that was not present in 1787. Regarding the fundamental issues of whether slavery should be extended, and whether there should be slavery at all, no such consensus ever took shape through the organic processes; and as we have noted the Civil War occurred because neither side was prepared to wait for the consensus machinery to work out a solution. This judgment is not entirely hindsight. At the moment of crisis, in his first Inaugural Address, Mr. Lincoln made a last plea for submission to the true constitutional morality. The Union had thus far survived, Lincoln thought, because the country had refrained from forcing explosive issues to premature conclusions. It had not resolved its great disputes by submitting them to some final arbiter—whether to a popular majority as reflected by Congress, or to the individual States asserting their sovereign prerogatives, or to the Supreme Court that had recently handed down the Dred Scott decision—but by entrusting them to the consensus machinery that could speak and act for the whole. Lincoln's counsel, however, fell on deaf ears: the country was impatient with the consensus machinery, and the country fought.

The Civil War itself, as we have seen, produced two additions to the fixed constitution: Negroes were to be free—the Thir-

---

government, but that this decision was to take effect at a fixed future date. Note that this does not mean the framers anticipated the emergence of a *new* constitutional consensus in 1808, but rather that the forces favoring national control were already of consensus proportions in 1787, and that the achievement of their goals was merely postponed as part of the ratification strategy. The curious codicil to Article V, forbidding alteration of the importation provision even by constitutional amendment, is inexplicable except as an acknowledgment that the forces favoring national control would probably have the votes to write a fixed provision from the first moment the Constitution went into operation.

teenth Amendment; and they were to have the elemental juridical rights enjoyed by white persons—the Fourteenth. But until the adoption of the Twenty-fourth Amendment in 1964, which confirmed the inclusion of Negro voting rights in the fixed constitution, it was impossible to mobilize a hard constitutional consensus around any further rule for governing race relations. This does not mean, of course, that relations between the Negro and white races during these years remained frozen where the Civil War amendments left them; it simply means that all further developments took place under the aegis of the fluid constitution. It does not mean, to take a concrete example, that the implications of the equal protection clause were restricted to the narrow aims of the Fourteenth Amendment's framers. It does mean, however, that the expansion of the concept of equal protection occurred through evolution, through our society's organic processes.

It is worth noting why this evolutionary process, although it moved slowly by the standards of modern civil rights enthusiasts, succeeded both in generating progress and in keeping the peace. The changes that were brought about between the Civil War and 1954 were the end product of many forces, acting through many agents, operating by different methods, often moving in different directions. These changes never eliminated "racial tensions"; on the contrary, it was precisely the organic dynamics of the tension between political, social, economic and moral forces that produced and shaped the changes. Congresses, Presidents, courts, state governments, schools, churches, trade unions, private philanthropies, crusaders, agitators—all made their separate contributions; combined, they produced a relationship between the races that proved to be, in the jargon of today, "viable." They produced solutions that were far from perfect—that differed from place to place and from situation to situation—but solutions that the country, at any given moment, could live with. The reason, at bottom, why the country could live with imperfect solutions was that they were open to further change *as the country's attitudes and practices changed:* the organic processes had produced a *living* law; they had produced

rules for governing the relations of the races that closely reflected, and promised to continue to reflect, the going beliefs,
practices, capacities, and desires of the people. And so the
country, instead of fragmenting from the tensions, paradoxically found successive formulas for unity and peace and future
progress, through preservation of the tensions.

Then came *Brown v. Board of Education.* In May, 1954, the
country was very far from having made up its mind on the
question of segregated schools. It was divided in its practices in
this matter because it was still profoundly divided in its beliefs.
No hard constitutional consensus had been reached, or was
likely to be reached in the foreseeable future. Therefore neither
side, neither the "integrationists" nor the "segregationists," insofar as they were then identified as distinct groups, could realis-
tically hope for the adoption of a constitutional amendment—
a provision, that is, of the fixed constitution—that would embody its views and make them thenceforth the supreme and
uniform law of the land. In this situation, the Supreme Court,
visibly moved by the ideology of equality, took matters into its
own hands and sought to impose upon the country a uniform
solution to the problem of mixing the races in the public schools.
The Court not only decided that the Negro plaintiffs in the
Brown case were entitled to admission to white schools. It also,
the following year, ordered a staged desegregation of public
schools throughout the land, an order the judicial system itself
proceeded to administer. And that was not all: although the
claim had been implicit in the logic of the *Brown* opinion, the
Warren Court, in 1958, formally proclaimed that its own views
about segregated schools—or on any other subject for that
matter—were binding on other public authorities in the country's political system. In the Little Rock school case of *Cooper v.
Aaron,* the Supreme Court, for the first time, entered its own
explicit claim to judicial supremacy:

> [*Marbury v. Madison*] declared the basic principle that the fed-
> eral judiciary is supreme in the exposition of the law of the
> Constitution, and that principle has ever since been respected by
> this Court and the Country as a permanent and indispensable

feature of our constitutional system. It follows that the interpretation of the Fourteenth Amendment, enunciated by this Court in
the *Brown* case is the supreme law of the land, and Article VI of
the Constitution makes it of binding effect on the States any
Thing in the Constitution or Laws of any State to the Contrary
notwithstanding.

Thus, as Professor Charles Hyneman has written, "the judges
regarded their statement as to what the Constitution means to
be identical with the words of the Constitution itself in capacity
to impose obligation upon the rest of the nation." Thus the
Court abandoned the organic processes of the fluid constitution
with respect to this aspect of the race problem, and would do
so later on with respect to others. Thus these explosive issues
were transferred to the fixed constitution—by judicial fiat. And
the country's most learned commentators counseled obedience
to the fiat. They asserted there was no alternative to obeying
except to amend the Constitution.

With what practical consequences? Our experience with race
conflict during the past decade speaks for itself. Before the
desegregation decisions withdrew the problem from the organic
processes, the country's practices by and large had kept abreast
of the country's attitudes; the progress that had been made
toward improving race relations was thus progress in depth,
progress bound to endure because it was rooted in the consent
and behavior of those directly concerned. After the decisions,
the possibilities of consensual adjustment and accommodation
were greatly diminished because of the wide gap between what
was commanded and what was desired; and that gap inevitably
became filled with hostility. Before the desegregation decisions,
our society could respond relevantly to the concrete challenges
that changing times produced: it could develop a living law on
the race issue because the law, by definition, was attuned to the
lives of the people. After the decisions, the people, Negroes and
whites alike, were required to conform their lives to the prescriptions of ideology. Before the desegregation decisions, different sections of the country could deal with the race problem
according to the capacities of their own districts which had

been destined by history and geography to be disparate. After the decisions, dissimilars were treated as similars, diversity was expunged in favor of a superficial uniformity. Before the desegregation decisions, the country had approached the race issue as part of a multi-dimensional problem: there was not only the matter of giving the Negro his due, but also the matters of preserving the integrity of community life, of maintaining the country's federal political structure, of improving the country's schools, of maintaining the public order, of keeping the country's economic system flourishing, and so on. After the decisions, the issue became single-dimensional: all related problems became subordinate to the goal of satisfying the Negroes' claims.

Nor is this all. Consider the central commitment of American political thought, the idea that just government requires the consent of the governed. What the granting of fixed constitutional status to the Supreme Court's desegregation decisions has done to the concept of consensual government can best be appreciated by recalling the obstacles to *withdrawing* that status. The great anomaly in the Court's new method of constitution-making is that while nine judges can draw up a fixed constitutional provision, *without* the authority of a hard constitutional consensus, their decision cannot be reversed *except* on the authority of a hard constitutional consensus. Remember that before the *Brown* case, neither the proponents of the mandatory integration of public schools, nor its opponents, could muster sufficient popular support to overcome the obstacles of Article V and incorporate their point of view in the fixed constitution. But thanks to the proponents' success in enlisting the aid of the Supreme Court in the role of "final arbiter," the opponents must now corral a hard constitutional majority, as reflected by Article V's formal amendment procedures, in order to restore the *status quo ante*. They must either do that, or persuade the Court to change its mind. That is why we may speak today of Judicial Supremacy.

The ultimate concern of these pages is with the *wisdom* of the Supreme Court's new method of constitution-making. . . .

Do we wish to make it a permanent feature of our political system? (And let us not suppose, on the strength of what has been said so far, that an answer on the merits must all that surely be, No. Some of our most eminent thinkers have recently advanced powerful arguments in defense of the Court's new role, and we shall want to weigh those arguments carefully.) Or, is it the wiser course to restore consensus rule to the United States? If so, we shall need to acquire a better understanding of the consensus society than most contemporary commentary betrays. We shall also need to know what concrete demands Restoration will make upon us: Where, as a practical matter, do we go from here?

4   The Recrudescent American Conservatism

Frank S. Meyer

To discuss conservatism in America today is to plunge at once into a tangle of semantic confusion. There have been over the past few years so many efforts, often contradictory, by scholars and journalists to extract its essence and define its limits that it is with some diffidence I begin with a rather broad and general description of it.

What Is Conservatism?

This essay is concerned with conservatism as a political, social, and intellectual movement—not as a cast of mind or a tempera-

From *Left, Right and Center,* edited by Robert Goldwin (Chicago, Ill.: Rand McNally, 1965), Chapter 1, pp. 1–17. Reprinted by permission of Rand McNally & Company.

mental inclination. Such a movement arises historically when the unity and balance of a civilization are riven by revolutionary transformations of previously accepted norms of polity, society, and thought. Conservatism comes into being at such times as a movement of consciousness and action directed to recovering the tradition of the civilization. This is the essence of conservatism in all the forms it has assumed in different civilizations and under differing circumstances. Sometimes such movements are successful, as was the return to the basic Egyptian tradition after Akhnaton's revolutionary changes. Sometimes they succeed for a time and modulate the later and further development of the revolutionary impulse, as did the Stuart restoration after the English Revolution or the European consolidation after the French Revolution and the reign of Napoleon. Sometimes they have little effect on contemporary events but make a tremendous impress on the consciousness of the future, as did the Platonic reaction to the destruction of the balance of civilization brought about by the overweening power drive of the Athenian *demos* and the arrogance of Sophistical thought. Sometimes they fail utterly and are lost to history.

In any era the problem of conservatism is to find the way to restore the tradition of the civilization and apply it in a new situation. But this means that conservatism is by its nature two-sided. It must at one and the same time be reactionary and presentist. It cannot content itself with appealing to the past. The very circumstances that call conscious conservatism into being create an irrevocable break with the past. The many complex aspects of the past had been held together in tension by the unity of the civilization, but that particular tension, that particular suspension in unity, can never be recreated after a revolutionary break. To attempt to recreate it would be pure unthinking reaction (what Toynbee calls "archaism") and would be bound to fail; nor could reaction truly restore the civilizational tradition to the recovery of which it was putatively directed. But while conservatism is not and cannot be naked reaction, neither can its concern with contemporary circumstances lead it, if it is to be true to itself, to be content with the status quo, with serving as a "moderating wing" within the existing situation. For that situation is the result of a revolutionary break with the tradition of the civilization, and to "conserve" it is to accept the radical break with tradition that conservatism exists to overcome.

Conservatism is neither reactionary yearning for an irremediably lost past, nor is it trimming acquiescence in the consolidation of revolution, just so long as the revolution does not go too fast. It is a vindication and renewal of the civilizational tradition as the fundament upon which reason must build to solve the problems of the present.

It is absurd, therefore, because one conservative voice in one period showed an underlying hostility to reason, to maintain, as is today so often done, that Edmund Burke's attitude to reason is an essential element of any definition of conservatism. True, no conservatism can accept utopian reliance upon the limited reason of one generation (or one school of thought within that generation), which ignores the tradition and builds upon arrogant confidence in its own experience and its own ratiocination. But conservatism is not antirational. It demands only that reason operate upon the foundation of the tradition of civilization, that is, upon the basis of the accumulated reason, experience, and wisdom of past generations.

From the point of view of contemporary "liberalism," it may indeed seem that any respect for tradition is *ipso facto* a repudiation of reason. This, together with the fact that Burke was to a rather strong degree critical of the claims of reason and that nineteenth-century conservatism often tended in this direction, may explain, although it does not excuse, the insistence of author after author in late years (most recently, Morton Auerbach in *The Conservative Illusion*) that no movement has a right to the name of conservatism if it does not fit the mould of an exaggerated representation of Burke's views on reason. Thus, the contemporary American conservative movement has consistently been denied its right to its self-chosen name by critics who refuse to think deeply and seriously about the phenomenon of conservatism, preferring instead facilely to derive their criteria from ephemeral characteristics of the conservatism of a single historical period.

It is easy to show that contemporary American conservatism is not a replica of nineteenth-century European conservatism; while it resembles it in some ways, it also resembles nineteenth-century European liberalism in its commitment to individual liberty and its corollary commitment to an economic system free of state control. But to show that, is to prove nothing of substance. The claim of the contemporary American conservative movement to the title conservative does not have to be based upon a surface resemblance to the conservative movement of another period. It is based upon its commitment to the recovery of a tradition, the tradition of Western civilization and the American republic which has been subjected to a revolutionary attack in the years since 1932.

The Contemporary American Conservative Movement

The crystallization in the past dozen years or so of an American conservative movement is a delayed reaction to the revolutionary transformation of America that began with the election of Franklin Roosevelt in 1932. That revolution itself has been a gentler, more humane, bloodless expression in the United States of the revolutionary wave that has swept the globe in the twentieth century. Its grimmest, most total manifestations have been the phenomena of Communism and Nazism. In rather peculiar forms in late years it has expressed itself in the so-called nationalism typified by Nasser, Nkrumah, and Sukarno; in Western Europe it has taken the forms of the socialism of England or that of Scandinavia. Everywhere, however open or masked, it represents an aggrandizement of the power of the state over the lives of individual persons. Always that aggrandizement is cloaked in a rhetoric and a program putatively directed to and putatively concerned for "the masses."

The American form of that revolution differs little in its essentials from Western European democratic socialism. But, by an ironic twist of history, it has become known as "liberalism." (So far is it removed from the classical liberalism of the nineteenth century, with its overriding concern for individual liberty and the limitation of the state, that clear discourse requires some mode of differentiation; and I shall for that reason, through the rest of this essay, refer to this twentieth-century American development as Liberalism, with a capital L, reserving the lower case for classical liberalism.) Ushered in by the election of 1932, so thorough was the victory of Liberalism that for many years afterwards it met with no concerted resistance, in either the intellectual or political spheres. True, islands of resistance remained—in the Congress, in the academy among some economists and humanists, in the business community, in the endemic mass anti-Communist movement among some strata of the population. These were rearguard actions; by and large, Liberalism dominated the scene, took over the academy and the organs of mass communication, controlled the Democratic party, and slowly penetrated the Republican party. Only in recent years has there emerged a consistent, cohesive conservative movement, based upon a broad consensus of principle, challenging Liberal assumptions and Liberal power all along the line.

In its origins intellectual, centered among a group of writers gathered around the old *Freeman, National Review,* and *Modern Age,* it early attracted a following and guided a movement in the universities, and gradually focused and channelized the energies of disparate tendencies opposed to Liberalism through all levels of society. During the past half dozen years its attitude began to be reflected among a group of young Congressmen, and it fully emerged on the national political arena with the nomination of Barry Goldwater at the Republican convention of 1964.

There are many strands in this movement, many trends in its thought. In particular there exists within it a continuing tension between an emphasis on tradition and virtue, on the one hand, and an emphasis on reason and freedom, on the other. I will return to this problem a little farther on; here I want only to say that these differences are but differences of emphasis, creating tensions within a common consensus, not sharply opposed points of view.

That common consensus of the contemporary American conservative movement is reflected, with different degrees of understanding and depth, at every level of the conservative movement. It underlies the principled positions of the consciously intellectual as it does the empirical positions and the instinctive attitudes of the political activists and the broad constituency of that movement. The clearest way, I think, to summarize this consensus is to contrast it with the beliefs and attitudes of the Liberal world outlook, which sets the prevailing tone of contemporary American society. I do not assert that every conservative accepts every one of the articles of belief I am positing or that every Liberal accepts each of the contrasted articles. But I would maintain that the attitudes adumbrated do reflect the over-all opposition between the conservative and Liberal consensuses in America today.

A. Conservatism assumes the existence of an objective moral order based upon ontological foundations. Whether or not individual conservatives hold theistic views—and a large majority of them do—this outlook is derived from a theistic tradition. The essential point, however, is that the conservative looks at political and social questions with the assumption that there are objective standards for human conduct and criteria for the judgment of theories and institutions, which it is the duty of human beings to understand as thoroughly as they are able and to which it is their duty to approximate their actions.

The Liberal position, in contrast, is essentially operational and instrumental. As the conservative's world is, in Richard Weaver's phrase, a world of essences to be approximated, the Liberal's world is a world of problems to be solved. Hence, the conservative's concern with such questions of essence as individual liberty and civilizational tradition. Hence, the Liberal's concern with modes and operations, such as democracy (a mode or means of government which implies that what is morally right is what fifty per cent plus one think is right), or progress (a concept that derives norms from the operation of historical events, establishing as the good the direction in which events have been moving and seem presently to be moving).

B. Within the limits of an objective moral order, the primary reference of conservative political and social thought and action is to the individual person. There may be among some conservatives a greater emphasis upon freedom and rights, as among others a greater emphasis upon duties and responsibilities; but whichever the emphasis, conservative thought is shot through and through with concern for the person. It is deeply suspicious of theories and policies based upon the collectivities that are the political reference points of Liberalism—"minorities," "labor," "the people." There may be tension between those conservatives who stress individual freedom and those who stress community as a fabric of individual rights and responsibilities, but both reject the ideological hypostasization of associations of human beings into entities and the collectivist politics based upon it.

C. The cast of American conservative thought is profoundly antiutopian. While it recognizes the continuing historical certainty of change and the necessity of basic principle being expressed under different circumstances in different ways, and while it strives always for the improvement of human institutions and the human condition, it rejects absolutely the idea that society or men generally are perfectible. In particular, it is perennially suspicious of the utopian approach that attempts to *design* society and the lives of human beings, whether in the light of abstract rationalist ideas or operational engineering concepts. It therefore rejects the entire Liberal *mystique* of "planning," which, no matter how humanitarian the motives of the planners, perforce treats human beings as faceless units to be arranged and disposed according to a design conceived by the planner. Rather, the conservative puts his confidence in the free functioning of the energies of free persons, individually and in voluntary cooperation.

D. It is on the basis of these last two points—concern for the individual person and rejection of utopian design—that the contemporary American conservative attitude to the state arises. For the state, which has the ultimate power of enforcement of its dictates, is the necessary implement for successful Liberal planning and for effective control of the lives of individual human beings. Conservatives may vary on the degree to which the power of the state should be limited, but they are agreed upon the principle of limitation and upon the firmest opposition to the Liberal concept of the state as the engine for the fixing of ideological blueprints upon the citizenry. There is much difference among them on the manner and mode in which the state should be limited, but in opposition to the prevailing Liberal tendency to call upon it to act in every area of human life, from automation to social relations, they are firmly united upon the principle of limitation.

E. Similarly, American conservatives are opposed to state control of the economy, in all its Liberal manifestations, whether direct or indirect. They stand for a free economic system, for two reasons. In the first place, they believe that the modern state is politically so strong, even without controls over the economy, that it concentrates power to a degree that is incompatible with the freedom of its citizens. When to that power is added control over the economy, such massive power is created that the last defenses against the state becoming a monstrous Leviathan begin to crack. Second—though this is subsidiary in the conservative outlook to the danger to freedom—conservatives in general believe, on the basis of classical and neoclassical economic theory, that a free economy is much more productive of material wealth than an economy controlled directly or indirectly by the state.

F. American conservatism derives from these positions its firm support of the Constitution of the United States as originally conceived—to achieve the protection of individual liberty in an ordered society by limiting the power of government. Recognizing the many different partial outlooks that went into its inception, adoption, and execution, the conservative holds that the result was a constitutional structure concerned simultaneously with limiting the power of the individual states and of the federal government, and of the tripartite elements in both—through the careful construction of a tension of separate powers, in which ultimate sovereignty rested in no single part, but in the tension itself. Conservatives believe that this conception was the closest that human beings have come to establishing a polity which gives the possibility of maintaining at one and the same time individual liberty, underlying norms of law, and necessary public order. Against the Liberal endeavor to establish sovereignty, nominally in the democratic majority, actually in the executive branch of a national government, they strive to re-establish a federal system of strictly divided powers, so far as government itself is concerned, and to repulse the encroachment of government, federal or state, over the economy and the individual lives of citizens.

G. In their devotion to Western civilization and their unashamed and unself-conscious American patriotism, conservatives see Communism as an armed and messianic threat to the very existence of Western civilization and the United States. They believe that our entire foreign and military policy must be based upon recognition of this reality. As opposed to the vague internationalism and the wishful thinking about Communist "mellowing" or the value of the United Nations that characterize Liberal thought and action, they see the defense of the West and the United States as the overriding imperative of public policy.

It is difficult to summarize in a short space the consensus of a variegated and living movement, especially when it is by its very nature opposed to ideology. I have attempted, however, to give here the best description of the contemporary American conservative movement that I have been able to derive from observation and experience. In confirmation of my summary, I would present from the actual political life of the conservative movement a statement which I think bears me out. It is the Statement of Principles of the American Conservative Union, founded in December, 1964, with the aim of coordinating and guiding American conservatism. I believe it states in brief compass the position I have been endeavoring to analyze, and as a practical political document shows the essential congruity of conservative thought with that analysis.

The American Conservative Union holds firm the truth that all men are endowed by their Creator with unalienable rights. To a world floundering in philosophical anarchy, we therefore commend a transcendent moral order against which all human institutions in every commonwealth, may confidently be judged.

We believe that government is meant to serve men: by securing their rights under a rule of law that dispenses justice equally to all; and in times of danger by marshalling the might of the commonwealth against its enemies.

We remark the inherent tendency of government to tyranny. The prudent commonwealth will therefore labor tirelessly, by means agreeable to its peculiar genius and traditions, to limit and disperse the power of government. No task should be confided to a higher authority that can be performed at a subsidiary level; and whatever the people can do for themselves should not be confided to government at all.

We believe that the Constitution of the United States is the ideal charter for governing the American commonwealth. The checks and balances that distribute the power of our national authority, and the principle of federalism that reserves to the states or to the people all power not confided to the national authority, are the cornerstones of every freedom enjoyed in this commonwealth. To their integrity we pledge a jealous defense.

We have learned that man's liberty, no less than his material interests, is promoted by an economic system based on private property and directed by a free, competitive market. Such a system not only enlarges the scope of individual choice but by dispersing economic decisions provides a further bulwark against the concentration of political power. And no other system can assure comparable living standards and growth. As against the encroachments of the welfare state, we propose a state of welfare achieved by free, collaborative endeavor.

Today the American commonwealth, as well as the civilization that illuminated it, are mortally threatened by the global Communist revolution. We hold that permanent co-existence with Communism is neither honorable nor desirable nor possible. Communism would enslave the world by any means expedient to that end. We deem no sacrifice too great to avoid that fate. We would parry the enemy's thrusts—but more: by maintaining American military superiority and exerting relentless pressure against the Communist empire, we would advance the frontiers of freedom.

Traditionalist and Libertarian Emphases Within the Conservative Movement

There is, then, a consensus that gives the contemporary American conservative movement unity. As I argued at the beginning of this essay, it is a consensus that reflects a legitimate conservative outlook, in the sense that conservatism properly considered is not confined to the limited doctrines of the conservatism of any given historical period, but represents the effort to refresh and renew the tradition of a civilization and a nation in response to a radical challenge to that tradition. Nevertheless, although there is a conservative consensus today, there are stresses and strains within it, reflecting the differing emphases partially derived from variant strands of the tradition. Most of these stresses and strains within the conservative movement center around one fundamental clash of emphasis, that between what can be called the "traditionalist" and the "libertarian" elements within it.

The specifically American form of the Western tradition, which is the source and inspiration of contemporary American conservatism, is the consensus established by the Founding Fathers and incorporated in the constitutional settlement. While it is true that something of the tension between the traditionalist and libertarian emphases exists throughout the Western tradition and therefore exists within that consensual settlement, it had always been and remained at the time of the establishment of the Republic precisely that—a tension *within* a basic civilizational consensus. It is from that integrated foundation that the over-all consensus of the American conservatism of today is built. To some degree therefore the traditionalist-libertarian opposition within it is directly derived from its source. But many of the characteristics of that opposition, characteristics often threatening the maintenance of consensus, are derived from a very different source, from the naturalization in the United States, during this century and the last part of the nineteenth century, of the nineteenth-century conflict between European conservatism and European liberalism. This is historically ironic because that European conflict was the aftermath of the French Revolution, and neither that revolution nor the system which it overthrew had relevance for the American situation. By the same token, the positions of European liberalism and European conservatism of the nineteenth century are also irrelevant here.

The philosophical position upon which the American constitutional settlement was based had already brought into a common synthesis concepts which were placed in radical opposition by the European conservative-liberal struggle: a respect for the tradition together with a respect for reason, the acceptance of the authority of an organic moral order together with a fierce concern for the freedom of the individual person. That synthesis is neither liberal nor conservative in the nineteenth-century sense. Efforts of writers like Louis Hartz to maintain that it is essentially "liberal" either in the nineteenth-century European sense or the twentieth-century American sense are based on a misunderstanding of the Constitutional consensus— as well as being historically anachronistic; and this is also true of those who would equate that consensus with the point of view of nineteenth-century European conservatism.

Nineteenth-century conservatism defended values based upon a fundamental moral order and the authority of tradition, standing firmly against the corrosive attack of utilitarianism, positivism, and scientism. But it did not recognize as a truth corollary to its defense of moral values that acceptance by individual persons of the moral authority of objective standards of the good must be voluntary; when it is a mere surface acceptance imposed by external power, it is without meaning or content. Nineteenth-century conservatism was all too willing to substitute for the authority of the good the authoritarianism of human rulers, and to support an authoritarian political and social structure.

Nineteenth-century liberalism, on the other hand, stood firmly for the freedom of the individual person and, in defense of that freedom, developed the doctrine and practice of limited state power and the free economy. But as it did so, it corroded by its utilitarianism belief in an objective moral order as the foundation of respect for the value and integrity of the individual person and therefore the only firm foundation of individual freedom.

The traditionalist and the libertarian within the contemporary American conservative movement are not heirs of European conservatism and European liberalism because they draw from a common source in the American constitutional consensus. Their common effort to achieve a philosophical clarification of the consensus that underlies their actual empirical participation in the single movement is, however, impeded by the importation of the nineteenth-century European categories. As I have written elsewhere:

> The misunderstandings between libertarian and traditionalist are to a considerable degree the result of a failure to understand the differing levels on which classical liberal doctrines are valid and invalid. Although the classical liberal forgot—and the contemporary libertarian conservative sometimes tends to forget—that in the *moral* realm freedom is only a means whereby men can pursue their proper end, which is virtue, he did understand that in the *political* realm freedom is the primary end. If, with Acton, we 'take the establishment of liberty for the realization of moral duties to be the end of civil society,' the traditionalist conservative of today, living in an age when liberty is the last thought of our political mentors, has little cause to reject the contributions to the understanding of liberty of the classical liberals, however corrupted their understanding of the ends of liberty. Their error lay largely in the confusion of the temporal with the transcendent. They could not distinguish between the *authoritarianism* with which men and institutions suppress the freedom of men, and the *authority* of God and truth.[1]

The divergent emphases of traditionalist and libertarian are, however, gradually being resolved in the life of the American

[1]"Freedom, Tradition, Conservatism," in *What Is Conservatism?*, ed. Frank S. Meyer (New York: Holt, Rinehart and Winston, Inc., 1964), pp. 15–16.

conservative movement. Several factors contribute to this resolution: common action in the political struggle against Liberalism; a conscious return to a study of the founding tradition of
the Republic; and a deepening of contemporary conservative
thought itself.

Problems of the American Conservative Movement

The deepening of conservative thought, however, is only at its
beginnings. This is understandable, because in the dozen years
or so that this conscious conservative movement has been in
existence, its first intellectual task has been to fight for recognition as a legitimate position in an intellectual climate of conformity to Liberal norms. A movement striving to gather its
forces in a hostile environment will quite naturally tend in the
first instance to concentrate upon the simple statement and
restatement of its basic principles, and upon elaborating those
principles only insofar as it is necessary to sustain a critique of
the principles and practices against which the movement is
arrayed. When, following such a primary period of constitution,
the intellectual sector of such a movement finds itself rather
suddenly and somewhat unexpectedly involved in a serious
political development like the Goldwater surge of 1960 to 1964,
there arises an overwhelming temptation to turn aside from
further development of fundamental thought and occupy itself
with practical political questions of skills and techniques. It is
true that the skills and techniques of political organization are
essential to the success of a political movement, and that conservatives have only recently begun to cultivate them; but they
are only auxiliaries for a movement which, by its nature, stands
for nothing less than a radical transformation of the consciousness of an age.

This is what the contemporary American conservative movement exists to do. It has no other excuse for being. Concentration on method, without greater emphasis on transforming
consciousness, could lead only to practical political rivalry with

Liberalism on its own grounds. Such a development of conservatism would end by making it a right-wing of the Liberal consensus, not a challenge to its essence. The conservative movement in coming into being has set itself a greater and much more difficult task: to appeal to the civilizational instincts and beliefs that it feels survive half-smothered in the American people. But this cannot be done except upon the basis of a broad and profound development of the conservative world view.

That task is complex. Although, simply stated, the world view of conservatism is the world view of Western civilization, conservatism in a revolutionary age cannot be content with pious repetition of a series of received opinions. Too much has been shattered for it to be possible ever merely to return to the forms and modes of the past. Conservatism needs to be more than preservative; its function is to restore, and to do so by creating new forms and modes to express, in contemporary circumstances, the essential content of Western civilization. To do this it cannot confine itself to a broad attack upon established Liberalism. It has to meet the pretensions of Liberalism area by area and point by point at the level that *conservative* pretensions to be the heirs of Western civilization demand. This requires nothing less than a critical appraisal of the corpus of the intellectual activity of the twentieth century, with the aim of applying ageless principles to it and thereby deepening those principles.

This is a task of which conservative scholars are becoming more and more aware. Nor would I want to give the impression that a good deal of work in this direction has not already been done. I emphasize the task, however, because upon a serious endeavor to fulfill it depends the growth to maturity of the American conservative movement.

Another problem corollary to this one, or more accurately derivative from it, confronts conservatism on a more immediate practical level. What I am referring to is the translation of conservative principles into specific alternatives to the accepted Liberal public policies. The weakness here is one of execution, a weakness which could be characteristic of any young and fresh movement and is not generically a conservative weakness. There is, however, a difficulty in overcoming it that derives from the underlying political stance of conservatism as compared with the stance of Liberalism, and from the tone of approach to social and political problems that prevails today because of the influence of Liberalism. Liberalism finds in every social situation problems to be collectively solved by planned action, usually action involving the use of the power of government. Conservatism considers some of these situations natural manifestations of the human spirit and not "problems" to be solved at all; others it recognizes as situations that can be improved, but only by time and the working of free human energies individually or in voluntary association; above all, it considers the greatest social and political problem the increasing provenance and power of the state and therefore considers a further increase of that provenance and power a greater evil than the specific evils against which the state is called into action.

Since regnant Liberalism creates an atmosphere in which positive solutions to every conceivable problem are demanded, to be "negative" is the greatest of sins. But if conservatism is to be true to its vision, a large portion of its program will be negative insofar as proposing governmental action to remedy social situations is concerned. It will propose the limitation of government in order to free the energies of citizens to go about remedying these situations in their several ways as they see best. In the Liberal atmosphere this can easily be made to sound callous, hard-hearted, uncaring. But to maintain that hardships, deprivations, social imbalances are not properly or effectively solved by state action is not to deny their existence. Rather it is to call upon the imaginative exercise of voluntary altruistic effort to restore a widespread sense of responsibility for social well-being and to guard against the moral degradation of citizens as direct clients of the state or as indirect petitioners for community largesse.

Some examples of what can be done may be seen in the recent work of the Foundation for Voluntary Welfare, headed by Richard C. Cornuelle. It has already brought to completion one project and begun another, each of which is directed to the remedy of social situations through voluntary effort. The United Student Aid Fund has already been established through the agency of the Foundation for Voluntary Welfare, with the assistance of bankers, businessmen, and administrators, to preempt a large part of the field of loans to students, which would otherwise have become an additional activity of expanding government. Mr. Cornuelle's next project is to take Marion County, Indiana, as a pilot community and there to enlist all available private resources in an all-out attempt to eliminate hard-core unemployment in that county.

This is conservative action of a kind which cannot be incorporated in a neat "positive program" for the political arena (similarly, the enormous constructive thrust of private industry, which we have come to take for granted, does not lend itself to neat political packaging). But such action could and would be multiplied a thousandfold if a conservatively directed citizenry ceased to look to government and if the corollary shrinkage of government left in the hands of the citizens resources now taxed from them to support government programs.

But even when the charge of callousness to human distress is countered, the charge of negativity still remains. The only answer conservatives can make to this charge, unless they wish to descend to unprincipled demagogy, is to show that a positive program for the preservation of freedom and the expansion of human energies requires a series of negative programs directed towards the dismantling of smothering governmental activities. Such a program can be effectively presented only if it analyzes compellingly and specifically the actuality of government activities area by area; otherwise, no matter how generally correct the criticism, it gives the impression of being merely destructive criticism. It is here that the conservative movement still lacks fully adequate programmatic development. It needs studies, such as those of Martin Anderson on urban renewal, of Arnold W. Green on governmental programs for the young, the old, for recreation, for automation, or of Roger A. Freeman on federal aid to education, in every field where Liberalism invokes state action. And further, it needs to develop means of effectively transmitting the conclusions of such studies to the electorate. Only in a few areas, such as national defense or the handling of crime, where government is the natural organ for positive action, can conservative programs be intrinsically "positive." Here, too, a great deal more development of general conservative positions is needed.

Such specification of a conservative program, negative or positive, is as necessary as the deepening and enriching of conservative thought on a higher level, which I discussed earlier. Until it is done, the statement of sharp conservative principle, which obviously demands deep-going change in the existing situation, can sound like irresponsible radicalism. If it is not backed up by a sober, specific, and conservatively restrained program of gradually phased transformation, the considered conservative position on limited government and resistance to Communism is in danger of being translated into such nightmares as the immediate cutting off of every Social Security check or the instigation of nuclear war against the Soviet Union.

Both in fundamental thought and in practical programmatics, the present need of the American conservative movement is to intensify its development. Its essential principles are clear; they constitute a doctrine that is truly conservative in that it is directed towards the recovery of the civilizational tradition. Its future depends upon its ability to deepen its understanding of those principles and achieve full maturity.

Part Two The
Limitations
of the State

The second part of this book explores the "limitations of the state," the state being, for contemporary liberal activists, the chosen instrument of action. In the opening chapter Garry Wills warns against attempts by the state to make justice. Professor Michael Oakeshott is renowned for going further: he doubts the competence of the state to ordain any strategic policies at all, that is to say, to devise them pursuant to an act of will. This is rationalism in politics, and Mr. Oakeshott takes rationalism in politics to mean, really, ideology in politics. In this curious conclusion Oakeshott, the organic conservative, and Milton Friedman, the rigorous individualist, reach congruent conclusions. Mr. Friedman delights in pointing out that almost inevitably when the federal government sets out to help, the intended beneficiary emerges as the victim: when the government sets out to increase the wages of poor people through minimum wage laws, it ends up causing unemployment, i.e., in fact diminishing the wages of the poorest elements rather than increasing them.

Mr. Oakeshott, as I say, goes further—by denying that there

is any available historical experience which suggests that the state in fact can make politics "rationally," i.e., ideologically; his challenging aphorism being that rationalism in politics is making politics as the crow flies. His most celebrated essay is called just that, "Rationalism in Politics"; although I found the most trenchant (and exhilarating) contraction of his larger statements on the role of the conservative in his essay "On Being Conservative" (*Rationalism in Politics,* pp. 191–194). I reproduce, impatiently, three paragraphs here and now, together with the sublime analytical climax. They are the finest distillate I know of traditional conservatism.

"*To some people,*" Oakeshott observes, "'*government*' *appears as a vast reservoir of power which inspires them to dream of what use might be made of it. They have favorite projects, of various dimensions, which they sincerely believe are for the benefit of mankind, and to capture this source of power, if necessary to increase it, and to use it for imposing their favorite projects upon their fellows is what they understand as the adventure of governing men. They are, thus, disposed to recognize government as an instrument of passion; the art of politics is to inflame and direct desire.*"

The wisdom—already—in these three sentences, is at least for this conservative overpowering; so much falls into place. But he is not nearly done:

"*Now* [Oakeshott continues], *the disposition to be conservative in respect of politics reflects a quite different view of the activity of governing. The man of this disposition understands it to be the business of a government not to inflame passion and give it new objects to feed upon; but to inject into the activities of already too passionate men an ingredient of moderation; to restrain, to deflate, to pacify, and to reconcile; not to stoke the fires of desire, but to damp them down. And all this, not because passion is vice and moderation virtue, but because moderation is indispensable if passionate men are to escape being locked in an encounter of mutual frustration.*" Why mutual frustration? Because rationalist politics beckons one way and leads another; does so necessarily, in the view of conservatives, because leading a people indisposed from Point A to Point B is an impossible undertaking for a government, considering the fractiousness of The People, some of whom desire different destinations, or if not that, different velocities in approaching their chosen destinations. "*Where activity is bent upon enterprise,*" Oakeshott concludes, "*the indispensable counterpart is another order of activity, bent upon restraint, which is unavoidably corrupted (indeed, altogether abrogated) when the power assigned to it is used for advancing favorite projects. An 'umpire' who at the same time is one of the players is no umpire; 'rules' about which we are not disposed to be conservative are not rules but incitements to disorder; the conjunction of dreaming and ruling generates tyranny.*" It has never been better stated.

It nevertheless seemed sensible to include in this collection not the essay "On Being Conservative" or the classic "Rationalism in Politics," but Mr. Oakeshott's provocative "The Masses in Representative Democracy." Here Oakeshott takes us through his historical hypothesis, namely, that the discovery of the individual was the pre-eminent fact of modern European history. But that that discovery also had the effect of leaving us with the "individual manqué"—indisposed to endure the pains of independence. When the individuals manqués discovered that they were a majority—that they were in fact mass man—they started to take over. "*For, although the 'mass man' is specified by his disposition,*" Mr. Oakeshott explains, "*—a disposition to allow in others only a replica of himself, to impose upon all a uniformity of belief and conduct that leaves no room for either the pains or the pleasures of choice—and not by his numbers, he is confirmed in this disposition by the support of others of his kind. He can have no friends (because friendship is a relation between individuals), but he has comrades. The 'masses' as they appear in modern European history are not composed of individuals; they are composed of 'anti-individuals' united in a revulsion from individuality.*"

Conservatism—bear in mind the thread of the argument—is, by Oakeshott's reckoning (and mine), the politics of the individual. But "*'anti-individuality,' long before the 19th century,*" *had established itself as one of the major dispositions of the modern European moral character."* Oakeshott is introducing the concept of individual power in the pre-free market sense into which the individual was primarily situated by the nineteenth-century liberals and such of their successors, quoted here, as Hazlitt and Friedman and Eastman. Ever since the anti-individualists took over, the role of government has changed. It began to assume, as Oakeshott sees it, *"the role of architect and custodian, not of 'public order' in an 'association' of individuals pursuing their own activities, but of 'the public good' of a 'community.' The ruler was recognized to be, not the referee of the collisions of individuals, but the moral leader and managing director of 'the community.' . . . And if we call the manner of government that has been generated by the aspirations of individuality 'parliamentary government,' we may call the modification of it under the impact of the 'mass man,' 'popular government.' But it is important to understand that these are two wholly different manners of government."*

Mr. Oakeshott's point is of obvious importance to the conservatism that disdains "popular government" when it essays the subsumption of the individual in the name of the collectivity. Mr. Oakeshott goes on to discuss the forms of popular democracy and the "ventriloquism" which is the device by which leaders nowadays lead: *"Moreover it is known in advance what offer will collect the most votes: the character of the 'mass man' is such that he will be moved only by the offer of release from the burden of making choices for himself, the offer of 'salvation.' And anyone who makes this offer may confidently demand unlimited power: it will be given him."*

Oakeshott then goes on with a definition of mass man which it is useful to compare with Ortega's. *"The 'mass man,' as I understand him,"* says Oakeshott, *"is specified by his character, not by his numbers. He is distinguished by so exiguous an individuality that when it meets a powerful experience of individuality it revolts into 'anti-individuality.' He has generated for himself an appropriate morality, an appropriate understanding of the office of government, and appropriate modifications of* '*parliamentary government.*' *He is not necessarily 'poor,' nor is he envious only of 'riches'; he is not necessarily 'ignorant,' often he is a member of the so-called* intelligentsia; *he belongs to a class which corresponds exactly with no other class. He is specified primarily by a moral, not an intellectual, inadequacy. He wants 'salvation'; and in the end will be satisfied only with release from the burden of having to make choices for himself. He is dangerous, not on account of his opinions or desires, for he has none: but on account of his submissiveness. His disposition is to endow government with power and authority such as it has never before enjoyed: he is utterly unable to distinguish a 'ruler' from a 'leader.' In short, the disposition to be an 'anti-individual' is one to which every European man has* [read: most American men have] *a propensity; the 'mass man' is merely one in whom this propensity is dominant.*"

Ortega and Oakeshott: the phenomena they are looking at are distinct even though there is some overlapping. There is a misleading similarity in terminology which suggests that they are closer than in fact they are. Oakeshott's target is ideology, which he thinks of as a shortcut kind of knowledge, or pseudo-knowledge; Ortega's target is the democratization of authority, entailing an erosion of standards in culture, politics, and morals; as he puts it, "*the characteristic of the hour is that the commonplace mind, knowing itself to be commonplace, has the assurance* (denuedo) *to proclaim the rights of the commonplace, and to impose them wherever it will.*"[1]

Elsewhere he says. "*The ordinary man, hitherto guided by others, has resolved to govern the world himself.*"[2] The "*psychological structure of this new type of mass-man*" he gives as: "*1) an inborn, root-impression that life is easy, plentiful, without any grave limitations; consequently, each average man finds within himself a sensation of power and triumph which, 2) invites him to stand up for himself as he is, to look upon his moral and intellectual endowment as excellent, complete. This con-*

[1]José Ortega y Gasset, *The Revolt of the Masses* (New York: W. W. Norton, 1932), p. 18.
[2]*Ibid.,* p. 97.

tentment with himself leads him to shut himself off from any external court of appeal; not to listen, not to submit his opinions to judgment; not to consider others' existence. His intimate feeling of power urges him always to exercise predominance. He will act then as if he and his like were the only beings existing in the world; and, consequently, 3) will intervene in all matters, imposing his own vulgar views without respect or regard for others, without limit or reserve, that is to say, in accordance with a system of 'direct action.'"[3]

Writing in 1930, Ortega sees both Bolshevism and fascism as a part of this development. Both put mass-man mediocrities in power instead of the traditional elite. Oakeshott's argument is different, however harmonious. He takes as his starting point the break-up of the medieval community. The effect was to form two kinds of persons—the man who welcomed his freedom and the man who experienced freedom as pain. Oakeshott's masses are composed of the latter. They turn to ideology, which gives them an illusory sense of security and certainty and excuses them from facing the complexities of actual existence. For Oakeshott, genuine knowledge as contrasted with the nescience of ideology is not "transportable"—it is acquired in the course of performing some activity.

Where is the overlapping? Both observed the emergence of a different kind of modern man. For Oakeshott, the danger is that this new man will be driven, through ignorance, inexperience, and a desire for certainty, to simplistic ideology; for Ortega, this new man is incapable of maintaining the structure of value. He is self-indulgent, undisciplined, sure of himself even though a mediocrity. Oakeshott sees the danger of mass fanaticism; Ortega, of widespread vulgarization and of ethical breakdown.

Albert Jay Nock is at this point introduced on account of the arrant lengths to which he takes his opposition to the state and because the lengths to which he takes his position achieve an in-

[3]*Ibid.*

tellectual clarity in antistatism that is also valuable sentimentally. He is little known nowadays; in fact he was never widely known, although he is one of those few who are survived by a cult. There is indeed a Nockian Society, whose members pass along to each other the parerga of the master. Some of those who admire him do so exclusively on account of his prose style, which was one of the best ever, though there are those who think of it as rather too lacy; and who decry his Americanizations as self-conscious, something like the Duke of Windsor saying ain't. But it is a striking style, and I love it.

Mr. Nock was the editor of the original *Freeman* magazine, which is not easily situated in the spectrum of American politics as currently drawn. It lasted four years, from 1920 to 1924, and made a singular impression on the literary set. Mr. Nock affected to take no interest in the political direction of the *Freeman*, pledging himself only to publish what was good, never mind the point of view of the writer. Throughout his life, he recalled in his intellectual autobiography, *Memoirs of Superfluous Man*, he was a poor judge of character—"*A person might be a survivor of the saints or he might be the devil's rag-baby, for all I should know. . . . [But] if a captain of industry made me his personnel-manager he would find me worth a ducal salary.*" The talent was however not enough to keep the journal afloat, and Mr. Nock walked away from the *Freeman* toward a position of elitist individualism. He cherished the memory of Henry George the single-taxer, whom he considered the most original social thinker of modern times. He maintained that if ten thousand critically situated people in America would only read the *Social Statics* of Herbert Spencer, the world would forever after be relieved of the blight of statism. He wrote a strangely unknown tract called *Our Enemy, the State,* of which the essay here published is an autobiographically adapted précis. His literary passions were always pre-eminent, and to the scholarly community Mr. Nock is known as the translator and exegete of Rabelais, as well as the author of *A Journey into Rabelais' France,* a charming, brilliant little volume in the tradition, assuming there were such a tradition, of Henry Adams's *Mont-St.-Michel and Chartres.*

In his essay on the "Anarchist's Progress," Nock uses the idiom of the total individualist, well known in the conservative American tradition, who rejects almost completely the claims of the state. For the sake of intellectual clarity, it is sometimes valuable to extend an argument to its extreme. Nock is all-American in the use of the tall tale. "*His general sense of political duty*"— he is referring to the town drunkard of a youthful experience, whom he contrasts with the public official—"*I must say, still seems to me as intelligent and as competent as that of any man I have met in the many, many years that have gone by since then, and his mode of expressing it still seems about as effective as any I could suggest.*" On he goes into dogmatical antistatism, carried so far as to conclude that what's wrong even with the church and the family is "*mostly due to the historical connection of these two institutions with the State.*" He makes the provocative point that crime is the monopoly of the state. He undertakes to explain the institution of the state as a device by which money is taken from one set of pockets in order to put into another set of pockets (he was a lifelong friend of Charles Beard).

But then, concerning political action, even for the sainted sake of anarchy, he was indisputably conservative. Among the final essays in this book is another by Nock which is striking in its beauty and in its programmatic resignation. It is adumbrated in this essay. Far from hoisting the black banner of the anarchist and sounding the tocsin of revolt, he passes action by: "*I was never much for evangelization; I am not sure enough that my opinions are right, and even if they were, a second-hand opinion is a poor possession.*" He makes, in effect, a conservative's concession to the existing order. He would not tear down that order even if he had the power to do so, he says, because it is, after all, the product of the American mind. And off he goes, into the mists of privacy, from which, one supposes—one hopes—he will someday be rescued, if not because of what he has to say about the state, although that is indisputably illuminating, then because of his wit and style and the quiet, authoritative scholarship that conferred such unobtrusive distinction on all of his writings.[4]

Henry Hazlitt has written probably the all-time best seller in the field, the primer, *Economics in One Lesson*. What is more, it is not only popular, it is highly regarded, for instance, by Milton Friedman, notwithstanding its ideological implacability (Hazlitt and Friedman, for example, disagree on the uses of Keynes, the former dismissing him altogether as a nefarious confuser, the latter crediting him with genuinely useful insights and a liberating technical vocabulary). Hazlitt's is the definitive modern short-form presentation of the classical arguments for classical economics, and no matter how abstruse economics can become, the *basic* points are, by the standard of any conservative—basic: basic to the maximization of individual leverage on economic arrangements.

Although his book is a popular classic, Mr. Hazlitt's arguments are by no means unpolished. Indeed such exacting scholars as Ludwig von Mises have remarked Hazlitt's total domination of his subject. The point to remember is that flawless though it is, *Economics in One Lesson* suffers from the inadequacies of a single lesson in anything. I have selected a few excerpts from Hazlitt's famous work and, in addition, reprint Hazlitt's recommended library for those who desire to pursue the study of classical economics.

Max Eastman's many careers have included radical journalism, in which he engaged with zest as a young man, as editor of *The Masses*. His interests were not only ideological but literary and philosophical, and in the course of a very long career he published dozens of books on almost as many themes, including a book of poetry. He saw at firsthand, while he was in Russia in the twenties, the disintegration of the socialists' dream. For a

[4]Robert Crunden has written a book, *The Mind and Art of Albert Jay Nock* (Chicago: Henry Regnery, 1964), which may trigger a revival of interest in Nock.

few years he put down the totalitarianization of Russia to the evil character of the man unfortunately cast as the revolution's protagonist, Joseph Stalin. But one day in the thirties he woke to find himself not merely anti-Stalinist, but also antisocialist. And it is from a little book, *Reflections on the Failure of Socialism* published in 1955, that I draw a few excerpts touching on the insight that economic and political freedoms are inseparable.

The conviction of Max Eastman that political freedom is not feasible without economic freedom is shared by Professor Milton Friedman of the University of Chicago—at this point, excepting only Paul Samuelson, perhaps the best known living American economist. The excerpt here is harmonious with Oakeshott's antirationalism. Friedman contends that centralist policies tend to achieve effects different from those planned. Friedman's insistence on the point, deriving as it sometimes seems to do from the religion of antistatism, acquires an off-putting aprioristic flavor. *"Resistance,"* Oakeshott has observed, *"has now itself been converted into an ideology. This is, perhaps, the main significance of Hayek's* Road To Serfdom—*not the cogency of his doctrine, but the fact that it is a doctrine. A plan to resist all planning may be better than its opposite but it belongs to the same style of politics."* Still, somewhere between the absolutism of Nock and Friedman and Oakeshott's abhorrence of political doctrine (an abhorrence which is itself an inchoate doctrine) there is the conservatives' *presumption* against state activity; and the reasons for cherishing that presumption are lucidly expounded by all the contributors to this section—by Michael Oakeshott, Albert Jay Nock, Henry Hazlitt, Max Eastman, and Milton Friedman.

5 The Masses in Representative Democracy

Michael Oakeshott

I

The course of modern European history has thrown up a character whom we are accustomed to call the "mass man." His appearance is spoken of as the most significant and far-reaching of all the revolutions of modern times. He is credited with having transformed our way of living, our standards of conduct and our manners of political activity. He is, sometimes regretfully, acknowledged to have become the arbiter of taste, the dictator of policy, the uncrowned king of the modern world. He excites fear in some, admiration in others, wonder in all. His numbers have made him a giant; he proliferates everywhere; he is recognized either as a locust who is making a desert of what was once a fertile garden, or as the bearer of a new and more glorious civilization.

All this I believe to be a gross exaggeration. And I think we should recognize what our true situation is in this respect, what precisely we owe to this character, and the extent of his impact, if we understood more clearly who this "mass man" is and where he has come from. And with a view to answering these questions, I propose to engage in a piece of historical description.

It is a long story, which has too often been made unintelligible

From *Freedom and Serfdom: An Anthology of Western Thought,* edited by Albert Hunold (Dordrecht, Holland: D. Reidel, 1961), pp. 151–170. Reprinted by permission of D. Reidel Publishing Company.

by being abridged. It does not begin (as some would have us understand) with the French Revolution or with the industrial changes of the late eighteenth century; it begins in those perplexing centuries which, because of their illegibility, no historian can decide whether they should properly be regarded as a conclusion or a preface, namely the fourteenth and fifteenth centuries. And it begins, not with the emergence of the "mass man," but with an emergence of a very different kind, namely, that of the human individual in his modern idiom. You must bear with me while I set the scene for the entry of the character we are to study, because we shall mistake him unless we prepare ourselves for his appearance.

II

There have been occasions, some of them in the distant past, when, usually as a consequence of the collapse of a closely integrated manner of living, human individuality has emerged and has been enjoyed for a time. An emergence of this sort is always of supreme importance; it is the modification not only of all current activities, but also of all human relationships from those of husband, wife and children to those of ruler and subject. The fourteenth and fifteenth centuries in Western Europe were an occasion of this kind. What began to emerge, then, were conditions so pre-eminently favourable to a very high degree of human individuality, and human beings enjoying (to such a degree and in such numbers) the experience of "self-determination" in conduct and belief, that it overshadows all earlier occasions of the sort. Nowhere else has the emergence of individuals (that is, persons accustomed to making choices for themselves) either modified human relationships so profoundly, or proved so durable an experience, or provoked so strong a reaction, or explained itself so elaborately in the idiom of philosophical theory.

Like everything else in modern Europe, achievement in respect of human individuality was a modification of medieval conditions of life or thought. It was not generated in claims and assertions on behalf of individuality, but in sporadic divergencies from a condition of human circumstance in which the opportunity for choice was narrowly circumscribed. To know oneself as the member of a family, a group, a corporation, a church, a village community, as the suitor at a court or as the occupier of a tenancy, had been, for the vast majority, the circumstantially possible sum of self-knowledge. Not only were ordinary activities, those concerned with getting a living, communal in character, but so also were decisions, rights and responsibilities. Relationships and allegiances normally sprang from status and rarely extricated themselves from the analogy of kinship. For the most part anonymity prevailed; individual human character was rarely observed because it was not there to be observed. What differentiated one man from another was insignificant when compared with what was enjoyed in common as members of a group of some sort.

This situation reached something of a climax in the twelfth century. It was modified slowly, sporadically and intermittently over a period of about seven centuries, from the thirteenth to the twentieth century. The change began earlier and went more rapidly in some parts of Europe than in others; it penetrated some activities more readily and more profoundly than others; it affected men before it touched women; and during these seven centuries there have been many local climaxes and corresponding recessions. But the enjoyment of the new opportunities of escape from communal ties gradually generated a new idiom of human character.

It emerged first in Italy: Italy was the first home of the modern individual who sprang from the break-up of medieval communal life. "At the close of the thirteenth century," writes Burckhardt, "Italy began to swarm with individuality; the ban laid upon human personality was dissolved; a thousand figures meet us, each in his own special shape and dress." The *uomo singolare,* whose conduct was marked by a high degree of self-determination and a large number of whose activities expressed personal preferences, gradually detached himself from his fellows. And together with him appeared, not only the *libertine* and the *dilettante,* but also the *uomo unico,* the man who, in the mastery of his circumstances, stood alone and was a law to himself. Men examined themselves and were not dismayed by their own want of perfection. This was the character which Petrarch dramatized for his generation with unmatched skill and unrivalled energy. A new image of human nature appeared —not Adam, not Prometheus, but Proteus—a character distinguished from all others on account of his multiplicity and of his endless power of self-transformation.

North of the Alps, events took a similar course, though they moved more slowly and had to contend with larger hindrances. In England, in France, in the Netherlands, in Spain, in Switzerland, in Poland, Hungary and Bohemia, and particularly in all centres of municipal life, conditions favourable to individuality, and individuals to exploit them, appeared. There were few fields of activity untouched. By the middle of the sixteenth century they had been so firmly established that they were beyond the range of mere suppression: not all the severity of the Calvinist *régime* in Geneva was sufficient to quell the impulse to think and behave as an independent individual. The disposition to regard a high degree of individuality in conduct and in belief as the condition proper to mankind and as the main ingredient of human "happiness," had become one of the significant dispositions of modern European character. What Petrarch did for one century, Montaigne did for another.

The story of the vicissitudes of this disposition during the last four centuries is exceedingly complex. It is a story, not of steady growth, but of climaxes and anti-climaxes, of diffusion to parts of Europe at first relatively ignorant of it, of extension to activities from which it was at first excluded, of attack and defence, of confidence and of apprehension. But, if we cannot pursue it in all its detail, we may at least observe how profoundly this disposition imposed itself upon European conduct and belief. In the course of a few hundred years, it was magnified into an ethical and even into a metaphysical theory, it gathered to itself an appropriate understanding of the office of government, it modified political manners and institutions, it settled itself upon art, upon religion, upon industry and trade and upon every kind of human relationship.

In the field of intellectual speculation the clearest reflection of this profound experience of individuality is to be seen in ethical theory. Almost all modern writing about moral conduct begins with the hypothesis of an individual human being choosing and pursuing his own directions of activity. What appeared to require explanation was not the existence of such individuals, but how they could come to have duties to others of their kind and what was the nature of those duties; just as the existence of other minds became a problem to those who understood knowledge as the residue of sense experience. This is unmistakable in Hobbes, the first moralist of the modern world to take candid account of the current experience of individuality. He understood a man as an organism governed by an impulse to avoid destruction and to maintain itself in its own characteristic and chosen pursuits. Each individual has a natural right to independent existence: the only problem is how he is to pursue his own chosen course with the greatest measure of success, the problem of his relation to "others" of his kind. And a similar view of things appeared, of course, in the writings of Spinoza. But even where an individualistic conclusion was rejected, this autonomous individual remained as the starting point of ethical reflection. Every moralist in the seventeenth and eighteenth centuries is concerned with the psychological structure of this assumed "individual": the relation of "self" and "others" is the common form of all moral theory of the time. And nowhere is this seen more clearly to be the case than in the writings of Kant. Every human being, in virtue of not being subject to natural necessity, is recognized by Kant to be a Person, an end in himself, absolute and autonomous. To seek his own happiness is the natural pursuit of such a person; self-love is the motive of the choices which compose his conduct. But as a rational human being he will recognize in his conduct the universal conditions of autonomous personality; and the chief of these conditions is to use humanity, as well in himself as in others, as an end and never as a means. Morality consists in the recognition of individual personality whenever it appears. Moreover, personality is so far sacrosanct that no man has either a right or a duty to promote the moral perfection of another: we may promote the "happiness" of others, but we cannot promote their "good" without destroying their "freedom" which is the condition of moral goodness.

In short, whatever we may think of the moral theories of modern Europe, they provide the clearest evidence of the overwhelming impact of this experience of individuality.

But this pursuit of individuality, and of the conditions most favourable to its enjoyment, was reflected also in an understanding of the proper office of government and in appropriate manners of governing and being governed, both modifications of an inheritance from the Middle Ages. We have time only to notice them in their most unqualified appearance, namely, in what we have come to call "modern representative democracy." This manner of governing and being governed appeared first in England, in the Netherlands and in Switzerland, and was later (in various idioms) extended to other parts of Western Europe and the United States of America. It is not to be understood either as an approximation to some ideal manner of government, or as a modification of a manner of government (with which it has no connection whatever) current for a short while in certain parts of the ancient world. It is simply what emerged in Western Europe where the impact of the aspirations of individuality upon medieval institutions of government was greatest.

The first demand of those intent upon exploring the intimations of individuality was for an instrument of government capable of transforming the interests of individuality into rights and duties. To perform this task government required three attributes. First, it must be single and supreme; only by a concentration of all authority at one centre could the emergent individual escape from the communal pressures of family and guild, of church and local community, which hindered his enjoyment of his own character. Secondly, it must be an instrument of government not bound by prescription and therefore with authority to abolish old rights and create new: it must be a "sovereign" government. And this, according to current ideas, meant a government in which all who enjoyed rights were partners, a government in which the "estates" of the realm were direct or indirect participants. Thirdly, it must be powerful—able to preserve the order without which the aspirations of individuality could not be realized; but not so powerful as itself to constitute a new threat to individuality. In an earlier time, the recognized methods of transforming interests into rights had been judicial; the "parliaments" and "councils" of the Middle Ages had been pre-eminently judicial bodies. But from these "courts of law" emerged an instrument with more emphatic authority to recognize new interests by converting them into new rights and duties; there emerged legislative bodies. Thus, a ruler, and a parliament representative of his subjects, came to share the business of "making" law. And the law they made was favourable to the interests of individuality: it provided the detail of what became a well-understood condition of human circumstance, commonly denoted by the word "freedom." In this condition every subject was secured of the right to pursue his chosen directions of activity as little hindered as might be by his fellows or by the exactions of government itself, and as little distracted by communal pressures. Freedom of movement, of initiative, of speech, of belief and religious observance, of association and disassociation, of bequest and inheritance; security of person and property; the right to choose one's own occupation and dispose of one's labour and goods; and over all the "rule of law": the right to be ruled by a known law, applicable to all subjects alike. And these rights, appropriate to individuality, were not the privileges of a single class; they were the property of every subject alike. Each signified the abrogation of some feudal privilege.

This manner of governing, which reached its climax in the "parliamentary" government which emerged in England and elsewhere in the late eighteenth and early nineteenth centuries, was concurrently theorized in an understanding of the proper office of government. What had been a "community" came to be recognized as an "association" of individuals: this was the counterpart in political philosophy of the individualism that had established itself in ethical theory. And the office of government was understood to be the maintenance of arrangements favourable to the interests of individuality, arrangements (that is) which emancipated the subject from the "chains" (as Rousseau put it) of communal allegiances, and constituted a condition of human circumstance in which the intimations of individuality might be explored and the experience of individuality enjoyed.

Briefly, then, my picture is as follows. Human individuality is an historical emergence, as "artificial" and as "natural" as the landscape. In modern Europe this emergence was gradual, and the specific character of the individual who emerged was determined by the manner of his generation. He became unmistakable when the habit appeared of engaging in activities identified as "private"; indeed, the appearance of "privacy" in human conduct is the obverse of the desuetude of the communal arrangements from which modern individuality sprang. This experience of individuality provoked a disposition to explore its own intimations, to place the highest value upon it, and to seek security in its enjoyment. To enjoy it came to be recognized as the main ingredient of "happiness." The experience was magnified into an ethical theory; it was reflected in manners of governing and being governed, in newly acquired rights and duties and in a whole pattern of living. The emergence of this disposition to be an individual is the pre-eminent event in modern European history.

III

There were many modest manners in which this disposition to be an individual might express itself. Every practical enterprise and every intellectual pursuit revealed itself as an assemblage of opportunities for making choices: art, literature, philosophy, commerce, industry and politics each came to partake of this character. Nevertheless, in a world being transformed by the aspirations and activities of those who were excited by these opportunities, there were some people, by circumstance or by temperament, less ready than others to respond to this invitation; and for many the invitation to make choices came before the ability to make them and was consequently recognized as a burden. The old certainties of belief, of occupation and of status were being dissolved, not only for those who had confidence in their own power to make a new place for themselves in an association of individuals, but also for those who had no such confidence. The counterpart of the agricultural and industrial *entrepreneur* of the sixteenth century was the displaced labourer; the counterpart of the *libertine* was the dispossessed believer. The familiar warmth of communal pressures was dissipated for all alike—an emancipation which excited some, depressed others. The familiar anonymity of communal life was replaced by a personal identity which was burdensome to those who could not transform it into an individuality. What some recognized as happiness, appeared to others as discomfort. The same condition of human circumstance was identified as progress and as decay. In short, the circumstances of modern Europe, even as early as the sixteenth century, bred, not a single character, but two obliquely opposed characters: not only that of the individual, but also that of the "individual *manqué*." And this "individual *manqué*" was not a relic of a past age; he was a "modern" character, the product of the same dissolution of communal ties as had generated the modern European individual.

We need not speculate upon what combination of debility, ignorance, timidity, poverty or mischance operated in particular cases to provoke this character; it is enough to observe his appearance and his efforts to accommodate himself to his hostile environment. He sought a protector who would recognize his predicament, and he found what he sought, in some measure, in "the government." From as early as the sixteenth century the governments of Europe were being modified, not only in response to the demands of individuality, but in response also to the needs of the "individual *manqué*." The "godly prince" of the Reformation and his lineal descendant, the "enlightened despot" of the eighteenth century, were political inventions for making choices for those indisposed to make choices for themselves; the Elizabethan Statute of Labourers was designed to take care of those who were left behind in the race.

The aspirations of individuality had imposed themselves upon conduct and belief and upon the constitutions and activities of governments, in the first place, as demands emanating from a powerful and confident disposition. There was little attempt to moralize these demands, which in the sixteenth century were clearly in conflict with current moral sentiment, still fixed in its loyalty to the morality of communal ties. Nevertheless, from the experience of individuality there sprang, in the course of time, a morality appropriate to it—a disposition not only to explore individuality but to approve of the pursuit of individuality. This constituted a considerable moral revolution; but such was its force and vigour that it not only swept aside the relics of the morality appropriate to the defunct communal order, but left little room for any alternative *to itself.* And the weight of this moral victory bore heavily upon the "individual *manqué.*" Already outmanoeuvred in the field (in conduct), he now suffered a defeat at home, in his own character. What had been no more than a doubt about his ability to hold his own in a struggle for existence, became a radical self-distrust; what had been merely a hostile prospect, disclosed itself as an abyss; what had been the discomfort of ill-success was turned into the misery of guilt.

In some, no doubt, this situation provoked resignation; but in others it bred envy, jealousy and resentment. And in these emotions a new disposition was generated: the impulse to escape from the predicament by imposing it upon all mankind. From the frustrated "individual *manqué*" there sprang the militant "anti-individual," disposed to assimilate the world to his own character by deposing the individual and destroying his moral prestige. No promise, or even offer, of self-advancement could tempt this "anti-individual"; he knew his individuality was too poorly furnished to be explored or exploited with any satisfaction whatever. He was moved solely by the opportunity of complete escape from the anxiety of not being an individual, the opportunity of removing from the world all that convicted him of his own inadequacy. His situation provoked him to seek release in separatist communities, insulated from the moral pressure of individuality. But the opportunity he sought appeared fully when he recognized that, so far from being alone, he belonged to the most numerous class in modern European society, the class of those who had no choices of their own to make. Thus, in the recognition of his numerical superiority the "anti-individual" at once recognized himself as the "mass man" and discovered the way of escape from his predicament. For, although the "mass man" is specified by his disposition—a disposition to allow in others only a replica of himself, to impose upon all a uniformity of belief and conduct that leaves no room for either the pains or the pleasures of choice—and not by his numbers, he is confirmed in this disposition by the support of others of his kind. He can have no friends (because friendship is a relation between individuals), but he has comrades. The "masses" as they appear in modern European history are not composed of individuals; they are composed of "anti-individuals" united in a revulsion from individuality. Consequently, although the remarkable growth of population in Western Europe during the last four hundred years is a condition of the success with which this character has imposed itself, it is not a condition of the character itself.

Nevertheless, the "anti-individual" had feelings rather than thoughts, impulses rather than opinions, inabilities rather than passions, and was only dimly aware of his power. Consequently, he required "leaders": indeed, the modern concept of "leadership" is a concomitant of the "anti-individual," and without him it would be unintelligible. An association of individuals requires a ruler, but it has no place for a "leader." The "anti-individual" needed to be told what to think; his impulses had to be transformed into desires, and these desires into projects; he had to be made aware of his power; and these were the tasks of his leaders. Indeed, from one point of view, "the masses" must be regarded as the invention of their leaders.

The natural submissiveness of the "mass man" may itself be

supposed to have been capable of prompting the appearance of appropriate leaders. He was unmistakably an instrument to be played upon, and no doubt the instrument provoked the *virtuoso*. But there was, in fact, a character ready to occupy this office. What was required was a man who could at once appear as the image and the master of his followers; a man who could more easily make choices for others than for himself; a man disposed to mind other people's business because he lacked the skill to find satisfaction in minding his own. And these, precisely, were the attributes of the "individual *manqué*," whose achievements and whose failures in respect of individuality exactly fitted him for this task of leadership. He was enough of an individual to seek a personal satisfaction in the exercise of individuality, but too little to seek it anywhere but in commanding others. He loved himself too little to be anything but an egoist; and what his followers took to be a genuine concern for their salvation was in fact nothing more than the vanity of the almost selfless. No doubt the "masses" in modern Europe have had other leaders than this cunning frustrate who has led always by flattery and whose only concern is the exercise of power; but they have had none more appropriate—for he only has never prompted them to be critical of their impulses. Indeed, the "anti-individual" and his leader were the counterparts of a single moral situation; they relieved one another's frustrations and supplied one another's wants. Nevertheless it was an uneasy partnership: moved by impulses rather than by desires, the "mass man" has been submissive but not loyal to his leaders: even the exiguous individuality of the leader has easily aroused his suspicion. And the leader's greed for power has disposed him to raise hopes in his followers which he has never been able to satisfy.

Of all the manners in which the "anti-individual" has imposed himself upon Western Europe two have been pre-eminent. He has generated a morality designed to displace the current morality of individuality; and he has evoked an understanding of the proper office of government and manners of governing appropriate to his character.

The emergence of the morality of the "anti-individual," a morality, namely, not of "liberty" and "self-determination," but of "equality" and "solidarity" is, of course, difficult to discern; but it is already clearly visible in the seventeenth century. The obscurity of its beginnings is due in part to the fact that its vocabulary was at first that of the morality of the defunct communal order; and there can be little doubt that it derived strength and plausibility from its deceptive affinity to that morality. But it was, in fact, a new morality, generated in opposition to the hegemony of individuality and calling for the establishment of a new condition of human circumstance reflecting the aspirations of the "anti-individual."

The nucleus of this morality was the concept of a substantive condition of human circumstance represented as the "common" or "public" good, which was understood, not to be composed of the various goods that might be sought by individuals on their own account, but to be an independent entity. "Self-love," which was recognized in the morality of individuality as a legitimate spring of human activity, the morality of the "anti-individual" pronounced to be evil. But it was to be replaced, not by the love of "others," or by "charity" or by "benevolence" (which would have entailed a relapse into the vocabulary of individuality), but by the love of "the community."

Round this nucleus revolved a constellation of appropriate subordinate beliefs. From the beginning, the designers of this morality identified private property with individuality, and consequently connected its abolition with the condition of human circumstance appropriate to the "mass man." And further, it was appropriate that the morality of the "anti-individual" should be radically equalitarian: how should the "mass man," whose sole distinction was his resemblance to his fellows and whose salvation lay in the recognition of others as merely replicas of himself, approve of any divergence from an exact uniformity? All must be equal and anonymous units in a "community." And, in the generation of this morality, the character of this "unit" was tirelessly explored. He was understood as a "man" *per se,* as a "comrade," as a "citizen." But the most acute diagnosis, that of

Proudhon, recognized him as a "debtor"; for in this notion what was asserted was not only the absence of distinction between the units who composed the "community" (all are alike "debtors"), but also a debt owed, not to "others" but to the "community" itself: at birth he enters into an inheritance which he had played no part in accumulating, and whatever the magnitude of his subsequent contribution, it never equals what he has enjoyed: he dies necessarily insolvent.

This morality of the "anti-individual," the morality of a *solidarité commune*, began to be constructed in the sixteenth century. Its designers were mostly visionaries, dimly aware of their purposes, and lacking a large audience. But a momentous change occurred when the "anti-individual" recognized himself as the "mass man," and perceived the power that his numerical superiority gave him. The recognition that the morality of the "anti-individual" was, in the first place, the morality not of a sect of aspirants, but of a large ready-made class in society (the class, not of the "poor," but of those who by circumstance or by occupation had been denied the experience of individuality), and that in the interests of this class it must be imposed upon all mankind, appears unmistakably, first in the writings of Marx and Engels.

Before the end of the nineteenth century, then, a morality of "anti-individualism" had been generated in response to the aspirations of the "mass man." It was, in many respects, a rickety construction: it never achieved a design comparable to that which Hobbes or Kant or Hegel gave the morality of individuality; and it has never been able to resist relapse into the inappropriate concepts of individuality. Nevertheless it throws back a tolerably clear reflection of the "mass man," who by this means became more thoroughly acquainted with himself. But we are not concerned with its merits or defects, we are concerned only to notice it as evidence of the power with which the "mass man" has imposed himself on modern Europe over a period of about four centuries. "Anti-individuality," long before the nineteenth century, had established itself as one of the major dispositions of the modern European moral character. And this disposition was evident enough for it to be recognized unequivocally by Sorel, and to be identified by writers such as Nietzsche, Kierkegaard and Burckhardt as the image of a new barbarism.

From the beginning (in the sixteenth century) those who exerted themselves on behalf of the "anti-individual" perceived that his counterpart, a "community" reflecting his aspirations, entailed a "government" active in a certain manner. To govern was understood to be the exercise of power in order to impose and maintain the substantive condition of human circumstance identified as "the public good"; to be governed was, for the "anti-individual," to have made for him the choices he was unable to make for himself. Thus, "government" was cast for the rôle of architect and custodian, not of "public order" in an "association" of individuals pursuing their own activities, but of "the public good" of a "community." The ruler was recognized to be, not the referee of the collisions of individuals, but the moral leader and managing director of "the community." And this understanding of government has been tirelessly explored over a period of four and a half centuries, from Thomas More's *Utopia* to the Fabian Society, from Campanella to Lenin. But the leaders who served the "mass man" were not merely theorists concerned to make his character intelligible in a moral doctrine and in an understanding of the office of government; they were also practical men who revealed to him his power and the manner in which the institutions of modern democratic government might be appropriated to his aspirations. And if we call the manner of government that had been generated by the aspirations of individuality "parliamentary government," we may call the modification of it under the impact of the "mass man," "popular government." But it is important to understand that these are two wholly different manners of government.

The emergent individual in the sixteenth century had sought new rights, and by the beginning of the nineteenth century the rights appropriate to his character had, in England and elsewhere, been largely established. The "anti-individual" observed these rights, and he was persuaded that his circumstances (chiefly his poverty) had hitherto prevented him from sharing them. Hence the new rights called for on his behalf were, in the first place, understood as the means by which he might come to participate in the rights won and enjoyed by those he thought of as his better placed fellows. But this was a great illusion; first, because in fact he had these rights, and secondly because he had no use for them. For the disposition of the "mass man" was not to become an individual, and the enterprise of his leaders was not to urge him in this direction. And what, in fact, prevented him enjoying the rights of individuality (which were as available to him as to anyone else) was not his "circumstances" but his character—his "anti-individuality." The rights of individuality were necessarily such that the "mass man" could have no use for them. And so, in the end, it turned out: what he came to demand were rights of an entirely different *kind,* and of a kind which entailed the abolition of the rights appropriate to individuality. He required the right to enjoy a substantive condition of human circumstance in which he would not be asked to make choices for himself. He had no use for the right to "pursue happiness"—that could only be a burden to him: he needed the right to "enjoy happiness." And looking into his own character he identified this with Security—but again, not security against arbitrary interference in the exercise of his preferences, but Security against having to make choices for himself and against having to meet the vicissitudes of life from his own resources. In short, the right he claimed, the right appropriate to his character, was the right to live in a social protectorate which relieved him from the burden of "self-determination."

But this condition of human circumstances was seen to be impossible unless it were imposed upon all alike. So long as "others" were permitted to make choices for themselves, not only would his anxiety at not being able to do so himself remain to convict him of his inadequacy and threaten his emotional security, but also the social protectorate which he recognized as his counterpart would itself be disrupted. The Security he needed entailed a genuine equality of circumstances imposed upon all. The condition he sought was one in which he would meet in others only a replica of himself: what he was, everybody must become.

He claimed this condition as a "right," and consequently he sought a government disposed to give it to him and one endowed with the power necessary to impose upon all activities the substantive pattern of activity called "the public good." "Popular government" is, precisely, a modification of "parliamentary government" designed to accomplish this purpose. And if this reading is correct, "popular government" is no more intimated in "parliamentary government" than the rights appropriate to the "anti-individual" are intimated in the rights appropriate to individuality: they are not complementary but directly opposed to one another. Nevertheless, what I have called "popular government" is not a concrete manner of government established and practised; it is a disposition to impose certain modifications upon "parliamentary government" in order to convert it into a manner of government appropriate to the aspirations of the "mass man."

This disposition has displayed itself in specific enterprises, and in less specific habits and manners in respect of government. The first great enterprise was the establishment of universal adult suffrage. The power of the "mass man" lay in his numbers, and this power could be brought to bear upon government by means of "the vote." Secondly, a change in the character of the parliamentary representative was called for: he must be not an individual, but a *mandataire* charged with the task of imposing the substantive condition of human circumstances required by the "mass man." "Parliament" must become a "work-shop," not a debating assembly. Neither of these changes was intimated in "parliamentary government"; both, in so far as they have been achieved, have entailed an assembly of a new character. Their immediate effect has been twofold: first, to confirm the authority of mere numbers (an authority alien to the practice of "parliamentary government"); and secondly, to give governments immensely increased power.

But the institutions of "parliamentary government" proved to have only a limited eligibility for conversion into institutions appropriate to serve the aspirations of the "mass man." And an assembly of instructed delegates was seen to be vulnerable to a much more appropriate contrivance—the *plébiscite*. Just as it lay in the character of the "mass man" to see everyman as a "public official," an agent of "the public good," and to see his representatives not as individuals but instructed delegates, so he saw every voter as the direct participant in the activity of governing: and the means of this was the *plébiscite*. An assembly elected on a universal adult suffrage, composed of instructed delegates and flanked by the device of the *plébiscite* was, then, the counterpart of the "mass man." They gave him exactly what he wanted: the illusion without the reality of choice; choice without the burden of having to choose. For, with universal suffrage have appeared the massive political parties of the modern world, composed not of individuals but of "anti-individuals." And both the instructed delegate and the *plébiscite* are devices for avoiding the necessity for making choices. The "mandate" from the beginning was an illusion. The "mass man," as we have seen, is a creature of impulses, not desires; he is utterly unable to draw up instructions for his representative to follow. What in fact has happened, whenever the disposition of "popular government" has imposed itself, is that the prospective representative has drawn up his own mandate and then, by a familiar trick of ventriloquism, has put it into the mouth of his electors: as an instructed delegate he is not an individual, and as a "leader" he relieves his followers of the need to make choices for themselves. And similarly, the *plébiscite* is not a method by which the "mass man" imposes his choices upon his rulers; it is a method of generating a government with unlimited authority to make choices on his behalf. In the *plébiscite* the "mass man" achieved final release from the burden of individuality: he was told emphatically what to choose.

Thus, in these and other constitutional devices, and in less formal habits of political conduct, was generated a new art of politics: the art, not of "ruling" (that is, of seeking the most practicable adjustments for the collisions of "individuals"), nor even of maintaining the support of a majority of individuals in a "parliamentary" assembly, but of knowing what offer will collect most votes and making it in such a manner that it appears to come from "the people"; the art, in short, of "leading" in the modern idiom. Moreover, it is known in advance what offer will collect the most votes: the character of the "mass man" is such that he will be moved only by the offer of release from the burden of making choices for himself, the offer of "salvation." And anyone who makes this offer may confidently demand unlimited power: it will be given him.

The "mass man," as I understand him, then, is specified by his character, not by his numbers. He is distinguished by so exiguous an individuality that when it meets a powerful experience of individuality it revolts into "anti-individuality." He has generated for himself an appropriate morality, an appropriate understanding of the office of government, and appropriate modifications of "parliamentary government." He is not necessarily "poor," nor is he envious only of "riches"; he is not necessarily "ignorant," often he is a member of the so-called *intelligentsia;* he belongs to a class which corresponds exactly with no other class. He is specified primarily by a moral, not an intellectual, inadequacy. He wants "salvation"; and in the end will be satisfied only with release from the burden of having to make choices for himself. He is dangerous, not on account of his opinions or desires, for he has none: but on account of his submissiveness. His disposition is to endow government with power and authority such as it has never before enjoyed: he is utterly unable to distinguish a "ruler" from a "leader." In short, the disposition to be an "anti-individual" is one to which every European man has a propensity; the "mass man" is merely one in whom this propensity is dominant.

IV

Of the many conclusions which follow from this reading of the situation the most important is to dispose of the most insidious of our current political delusions. It has been said, and it is commonly believed, that the event of supreme importance in modern European history is "the accession of the masses to complete social power." But that no such event has taken place is evident when we consider what it would entail. If it is true (as I have contended) that modern Europe enjoys two opposed moralities (that of individuality and that of the "anti-individual"), that it enjoys two opposed understandings of the office of government, and two corresponding interpretations of the current institutions of government, then, for the "mass man" to have won for himself a position of undisputed sovereignty would entail the complete suppression of what, in any reading, must be considered the strongest of our moral and political dispositions and the survival of the weakest. A world in which the "mass man" exercised "complete social power" would be a world in which the activity of governing was understood *solely* as the imposition of a single substantive condition of human circumstance, a world in which "popular government" had altogether displaced "parliamentary government," a world in which the "civil" rights of individuality had been abrogated by the "social" rights of anti-individuality—and there is no evidence that we live in such a world. Certainly the "mass man" has emerged and has signified his emergence in an appropriate morality and an appropriate understanding of the office of government. He has sought to transform the world into a replica of himself, and he has not been entirely unsuccessful. He has sought to enjoy what he could not create for himself, and nothing he has appropriated remains unchanged. Nevertheless, he remains an unmistakably derivative character, an emanation of the pursuit of individuality, helpless, parasitic and able to survive only in opposition to individuality. Only in the most favourable circumstances, and then only by segregating him from all alien influences, have his leaders been able to suppress in him an unquenched propensity to desert at the call of individuality. He has imposed himself emphatically only where the relics of a morality of communal ties survived to make plausible his moral and political impulses. Elsewhere, the modifications he has provoked in political manners and moral beliefs have been extensive, but the notion that they have effaced the morality of individuality and "parliamentary government" is without foundation. He loves himself too little to be able to dispose effectively of the only power he has, namely, his numerical superiority. He lacks passion rather than reason. He has had a past in which he was taught to admire himself and his antipathies; he has a present in which he is often the object of the ill-concealed contempt of his "leaders"; but the heroic future forecast him is discrepant with his own character. He is no hero.

On the other hand, if we judge the world as we find it (which includes, of course, the emergence of the "mass man") the event of supreme and seminal importance in modern European history remains the emergence of the human individual in his modern idiom. The pursuit of individuality has evoked a moral disposition, an understanding of the office of government and manners of governing, a multiplicity of activity and opinion and a notion of "happiness," which have impressed themselves indelibly upon European civilization. The onslaught of the "mass man" has shaken but not destroyed the moral prestige of individuality; even the "anti-individual," whose salvation lies in escape, has not been able to escape it. The desire of "the masses" to enjoy the products of individuality has modified their destructive urge. And the antipathy of the "mass man" to the "happiness" of "self-determination" easily dissolves into self-pity. At all important points the individual still appears as the substance and the "anti-individual" only as the shadow.

6 Anarchist's Progress

Albert Jay Nock

I

When I was seven years old, playing in front of our house on
the outskirts of Brooklyn one morning, a policeman stopped and
chatted with me for a few moments. He was a kindly man, of a
Scandinavian blonde type with pleasant blue eyes, and I took
to him at once. He sealed our acquaintance permanently by telling me a story that I thought was immensely funny; I laughed
over it at intervals all day. I do not remember what it was, but
it had to do with the antics of a drove of geese in our neighbourhood. He impressed me as the most entertaining and delightful
person that I had seen in a long time, and I spoke of him to my
parents with great pride.

At this time I did not know what policemen were. No doubt I
had seen them, but not to notice them. Now, naturally, after
meeting this highly prepossessing specimen, I wished to find
out all I could about them, so I took the matter up with our old
colored cook. I learned from her that my fine new friend represented something that was called the law; that the law was very
good and great, and that everyone should obey and respect it.
This was reasonable; if it were so, then my admirable friend just
fitted his place, and was even more highly to be thought of, if
possible. I asked where the law came from, and it was explained
to me that men all over the country got together on what was

From Albert Jay Nock, *On Doing the Right Thing and Other Essays* (New
York: Harper & Brothers, 1928), pp. 123–160. Copyright © 1928 by
Harper & Brothers; renewed 1956 by Samuel A. Nock and Francis J. Nock.
Reprinted by permission of Harper & Row, Publishers, Incorporated.

called election day, and chose certain persons to make the law
and others to see that it was carried out; and that the sum-total of
all this mechanism was called our government. This again was
as it should be; the men I knew, such as my father, my uncle
George, and Messrs. So-and-so among the neighbours (running
them over rapidly in my mind), could do this sort of thing handsomely, and there was probably a good deal in the idea. But
what was it all for? Why did we have law and government, anyway? Then I learned that there were persons called criminals;
some of them stole, some hurt or killed people or set fire to
houses; and it was the duty of men like my friend the policeman
to protect us from them. If he saw any he would catch them and
lock them up, and they would be punished according to the law.

A year or so later we moved to another house in the same
neighbourhood, only a short distance away. On the corner of
the block—rather a long block—behind our house stood a large
one-story wooden building, very dirty and shabby, called the
Wigwam. While getting the lie of my new surroundings, I considered this structure and remarked with disfavour the kind of
people who seemed to be making themselves at home there.
Some one told me it was a "political headquarters," but I did
not know what that meant, and therefore did not connect it with
my recent researches into law and government. I had little curiosity about the Wigwam. My parents never forbade my going
there, but my mother once casually told me that it was a pretty
good place to keep away from, and I agreed with her.

Two months later I heard some one say that election day
was shortly coming on, and I sparked up at once; this, then, was
the day when the lawmakers were to be chosen. There had
been great doings at the Wigwam lately; in the evenings, too, I
had seen noisy processions of drunken loafers passing our house,
carrying transparencies, and tin torches that sent up clouds of
kerosene-smoke. When I had asked what these meant, I was
answered in one word, "politics," uttered in a disparaging tone,
but this signified nothing to me. The fact is that my attention
had been attracted by a steam-calliope that went along with one
of the first of these processions, and I took it to mean that

there was a circus going on; and when I found that there was no circus, I was disappointed and did not care what else might be taking place.

On hearing of election day, however, the light broke in on me. I was really witnessing the august performances that I had heard of from our cook. All these processions of yelling hoodlums who sweat and stank in the parboiling humidity of the Indian-summer evenings—all the squalid goings-on in the Wigwam—all these, it seemed, were part and parcel of an election. I noticed that the men whom I knew in the neighbourhood were not prominent in this election; my uncle George voted, I remember, and when he dropped in at our house that evening, I overheard him say that going to the polls was a filthy business. I could not make it out. Nothing could be clearer than that the leading spirits in the whole affair were most dreadful swine; and I wondered by what kind of magic they could bring forth anything so majestic, good and venerable as the law. But I kept my questionings to myself for some reason, though, as a rule, I was quite a hand for pestering older people about matters that seemed anomalous. Finally, I gave it up as hopeless, and thought no more about the subject for three years.

An incident of that election night, however, stuck in my memory. Some devoted brother, very far gone in whisky, fell by the wayside in a vacant lot just back of our house, on his way to the Wigwam to await the returns. He lay there all night, mostly in a comatose state. At intervals of something like half an hour he roused himself up in the darkness, apparently aware that he was not doing his duty by the occasion, and tried to sing the chorus of "Marching Through Georgia," but he could never get quite through three measures of the first bar before relapsing into somnolence. It was very funny; he always began so bravely and earnestly, and always petered out so lamentably. I often think of him. His general sense of political duty, I must say, still seems to me as intelligent and as competent as that of any man I have met in the many, many years that have gone by since then, and his mode of expressing it still seems about as effective as any I could suggest.

II

When I was just past my tenth birthday we left Brooklyn and went to live in a pleasant town of ten thousand population. An orphaned cousin made her home with us, a pretty girl who soon began to cut a fair swath among the young men of the town. One of these was an extraordinary person, difficult to describe. My father, a great tease, at once detected his resemblance to a chimpanzee, and bored my cousin abominably by always speaking of him as Chim. The young man was not a popular idol by any means, yet no one thought badly of him. He was accepted everywhere as a source of legitimate diversion, and in the graduated, popular scale of local speech was invariably designated as a fool—a born fool, for which there was no help. When I heard he was a lawyer, I was so astonished that I actually went into the chicken-court one day to hear him plead some trifling case, out of sheer curiosity to see him in action; and I must say I got my money's worth. Presently the word went around that he was going to run for Congress, and stood a good chance of being elected; and what amazed me above all was that no one seemed to see anything out of the way about it.

My tottering faith in law and government got a hard jolt from this. Here was a man, a very good fellow indeed—he had nothing in common with the crew who herded around the Wigwam —who was regarded by the unanimous judgment of the community, without doubt, peradventure, or exception, as having barely sense enough to come in when it rained; and this was the man whom his party was sending to Washington as contentedly as if he were some Draco or Solon. At this point my sense of humour forged to the front and took permanent charge of the situation, which was fortunate for me, since otherwise my education would have been aborted, and I would perhaps, like so many who have missed this great blessing, have gone in with the reformers and uplifters; and such a close shave as this, in the words of Rabelais, is a terrible thing to think upon. How many reformers there have been in my day; how nobly and absurdly busy they were, and how dismally unhumorous! I can dimly remember Pingree and Altgeld in the Middle West, and Godkin, Strong, and Seth Low in New York. During the 'nineties, the goodly fellowship of the prophets buzzed about the whole country like flies around a tar-barrel—and, Lord! where be they now?

III

It will easily be seen, I think, that the only unusual thing about all this was that my mind was perfectly unprepossessed and blank throughout. My experiences were surely not uncommon, and my reasonings and inferences were no more than any child, who was more than half-witted, could have made without trouble. But my mind had never been perverted or sophisticated; it was left to itself. I never went to school, so I was never indoctrinated with pseudo-patriotic fustian of any kind, and the plain, natural truth of such matters as I have been describing, therefore, found its way to my mind without encountering any artificial obstacle.

This freedom continued, happily, until my mind had matured and toughened. When I went to college I had the great good luck to hit on probably the only one in the country (there certainly is none now) where all such subjects were so remote and unconsidered that one would not know they existed. I had Greek, Latin, and mathematics, and nothing else, but I had these until the cows came home; then I had them all over again (or so it seemed) to make sure nothing was left out; then I was given a bachelor's degree in the liberal arts, and turned adrift. The idea was that if one wished to go in for some special branch of learning, one should do it afterward, on the foundation laid at college. The college's business was to lay the foundation, and the authorities saw to it that we were kept plentifully busy with the job. Therefore, all such subjects as political history, political science, and political economy were closed to me throughout my youth and early manhood; and when the time came that I wished to look into them, I did it on my own, without the interference of instructors, as any person who has gone through a course of training similar to mine at college is quite competent to do.

That time, however, came much later, and meanwhile I thought little about law and government, as I had other fish to fry; I was living more or less out of the world, occupied with literary studies. Occasionally some incident happened that set my mind perhaps a little farther along in the old sequences, but not often. Once, I remember, I ran across the case of a boy who had been sentenced to prison, a poor, scared little brat, who had intended something no worse than mischief, and it turned out to be a crime. The judge said he disliked to sentence the lad; it seemed the wrong thing to do; but the law left him no option. I was struck by this. The judge, then, was doing something as an official that he would not dream of doing as a man; and he could do it without any sense of responsibility, or discomfort, simply because he was acting as an official and not as a man. On this principle of action, it seemed to me that one could commit almost any kind of crime without getting into trouble with one's conscience. Clearly, a great crime had been committed against this boy; yet nobody who had had a hand in it—the judge, the jury, the prosecutor, the complaining witness, the policemen and jailers—felt any responsibility about it, because they were not acting as men, but as officials. Clearly, too, the public did not regard them as criminals, but rather as upright and conscientious men.

The idea came to me then, vaguely but unmistakably, that if the primary intention of government was not to abolish crime but merely to monopolize crime, no better device could be found for doing it than the inculcation of precisely this frame of mind in the officials and in the public; for the effect of this was to exempt both from any allegiance to those sanctions of humanity or decency which anyone of either class, acting as an individual, would have felt himself bound to respect—nay, would have wished to respect. This idea was vague at the moment, as I say, and I did not work it out for some years, but I think I never quite lost track of it from that time.

Presently I got acquainted in a casual way with some officeholders, becoming quite friendly with one in particular, who held a high elective office. One day he happened to ask me how I would reply to a letter that bothered him; it was a query about the fitness of a certain man for an appointive job. His recommendation would have weight; he liked the man, and really wanted to recommend him—moreover, he was under great political pressure to recommend him—but he did not think the man was qualified. Well, then, I suggested offhand, why not put it just that way?—it seemed all fair and straightforward. "Ah yes," he said, "but if I wrote such a letter as that, you see, I wouldn't be reëlected." This took me aback a bit, and I demurred somewhat. "That's all very well," he kept insisting, "but I wouldn't be reëlected." Thinking to give the discussion a semi-humorous turn, I told him that the public, after all, had rights in the matter; he was their hired servant, and if he were not reëlected it would mean merely that the public did not want him to work for them any more, which was quite within their competence. Moreover, if they threw him out on any such issue as this, he ought to take it as a compliment; indeed, if he were reëlected, would it not tend to show in some measure that he and the people did not fully understand each other? He did not like my tone of levity, and dismissed the subject with the remark that I knew nothing of practical politics, which was no doubt true.

IV

Perhaps a year after this I had my first view of a legislative body in action. I visited the capital of a certain country, and listened attentively to the legislative proceedings. What I wished to observe, first of all, was the kind of business that was mostly under discussion; and next, I wished to get as good a general idea as I could of the kind of men who were entrusted with this business. I had a friend on the spot, formerly a newspaper reporter who had been in the press gallery for years; he guided me over the government buildings, taking me everywhere and showing me everything I asked to see.

As we walked through some corridors in the basement of the Capitol, I remarked the resonance of the stonework. "Yes," he said thoughtfully, "these walls, in their time, have echoed to the uncertain footsteps of many a drunken statesman." His words were made good in a few moments when we heard a spirited commotion ahead, which we found to proceed from a good-sized room, perhaps a committee room, opening off the corridor. The door being open, we stopped, and looked in on a strange sight.

In the centre of the room, a florid, square-built, portly man was dancing an extraordinary kind of break-down, or *kazák* dance. He leaped straight up to an incredible height, spun around like a teetotum, stamped his feet, then suddenly squatted and hopped through several measures in a squatting position, his hands on his knees, and then leaped up in the air and spun around again. He blew like a turkey-cock, and occasionally uttered hoarse cries; his protruding and fiery eyes were suffused with blood, and the veins stood out on his neck and forehead like the strings of a bass-viol. He was drunk.

About a dozen others, also very drunk, stood around him in crouching postures, some clapping their hands and some slapping their knees, keeping time to the dance. One of them caught sight of us in the doorway, came up, and began to talk to me in a maundering fashion about his constituents. He was a loathsome human being; I have seldom seen one so repulsive. I could make nothing of what he said; he was almost inarticulate; and in pronouncing certain syllables he would slaver and spit, so that I was more occupied with keeping out of his range than with listening to him. He kept trying to buttonhole me, and I kept moving backward; he had backed me thirty feet down the corridor when my friend came along and disengaged me; and as we resumed our way, my friend observed for my consolation that "you pretty well need a mackintosh when X talks to you, even when he is sober."

This man, I learned, was interested in the looting of certain valuable public lands; nobody had heard of his ever being interested in any other legislative measures. The florid man who was dancing was interested in nothing but a high tariff on certain manufactures; he shortly became a Cabinet officer. Throughout my stay I was struck by seeing how much of the real business of legislation was in this category—how much, that is, had to do with putting unearned money in the pockets of beneficiaries—and what fitful and perfunctory attention the legislators gave to any other kind of business. I was even more impressed by the prevalent air of cynicism; by the frankness with which everyone seemed to acquiesce in the view of Voltaire, that government is merely a device for taking money out of one person's pocket and putting it into another's.

V

These experiences, commonplace as they were, prepared me to pause over and question certain sayings of famous men, when subsequently I ran across them, which otherwise I would perhaps have passed by without thinking about them. When I came upon the saying of Lincoln, that the way of the politician is "a long step removed from common honesty," it set a problem for me. I wondered just why this should be generally true, if it were true. When I read the remark of Mr. Jefferson, that "whenever a man has cast a longing eye on office, a rottenness begins in his conduct," I remembered the judge who had sentenced the boy, and my officeholding acquaintance who was so worried about reëlection. I tried to reëxamine their position, as far as possible putting myself in their place, and made a great effort to understand it favorably. My first view of a parliamentary body came back to me vividly when I read the despondent observation of John Bright, that he had sometimes known the British Parliament to do a good thing, but never just because it was a good thing. In the meantime I had observed many legislatures, and their principal occupations and preoccupations seemed to me precisely like those of the first one I ever saw; and while their personnel was not by any means composed throughout of noisy and disgusting scoundrels (neither, I hasten to say, was the first one), it was so unimaginably inept that it would really have to be seen to be believed. I cannot think of a more powerful stimulus to one's intellectual curiosity, for instance, than to sit in the galleries of the last Congress, contemplate its general run of membership, and then recall these sayings of Lincoln, Mr. Jefferson, and John Bright.[1]

It struck me as strange that these phenomena seemed never to stir any intellectual curiosity in anybody. As far as I know, there is no record of its ever having occurred to Lincoln that the fact he had remarked was striking enough to need accounting for; nor yet to Mr. Jefferson, whose intellectual curiosity was almost boundless; nor yet to John Bright. As for the people around me, their attitudes seemed strangest of all. They all disparaged politics. Their common saying, "Oh, that's politics," always pointed to something that in any other sphere of action they would call shabby and disreputable. But they never asked themselves why it was that in this one sphere of action alone they took shabby and disreputable conduct as a matter of course. It was all the more strange because these same people still somehow assumed that politics existed for the promotion of the highest social purposes. They assumed that the State's primary purpose was to promote through appropriate institutions the general welfare of its members. This assumption, whatever it amounted to, furnished the rationale of their patriotism, and they held to it with a tenacity that on slight provocation became vindictive and fanatical. Yet all of them were aware, and if pressed, could not help acknowledging, that more than 90 per cent of the State's energy was employed directly against the general welfare. Thus one might say that they seemed to have one set of credenda for week-days and another for Sun-

[1]As indicating the impression made on a more sophisticated mind, I may mention an amusing incident that happened to me in London two years ago. Having an engagement with a member of the House of Commons, I filled out a card and gave it to an attendant. By mistake I had written my name where the member's should be, and his where mine should be. The attendant handed the card back, saying, "I'm afraid this will 'ardly do, sir. I see you've been making yourself a member. It doesn't go quite as easy as that, sir—though from some of what you see around 'ere, I wouldn't say as 'ow you mightn't think so."

days, and never to ask themselves what actual reasons they had for holding either.

I did not know how to take this, nor do I now. Let me draw a rough parallel. Suppose vast numbers of people to be contemplating a machine that they had been told was a plough, and very valuable—indeed, that they could not get on without it— some even saying that its design came down in some way from on high. They have great feelings of pride and jealousy about this machine, and will give up their lives for it if they are told it is in danger. Yet they all see that it will not plough well, no matter what hands are put to manage it, and in fact does hardly any ploughing at all; sometimes only, with enormous difficulty and continual tinkering and adjustment can it be got to scratch a sort of furrow, very poor and short, hardly practicable, and ludicrously disproportionate to the cost and pains of cutting it. On the other hand, the machine harrows perfectly, almost automatically. It looks like a harrow, has the history of a harrow, and even when the most enlightened effort is expended on it to make it act like a plough, it persists, except for an occasional six or eight per cent of efficiency, in acting like a harrow.

Surely such a spectacle would make an intelligent being raise some enquiry about the nature and original intention of that machine. Was it really a plough? Was it ever meant to plough with? Was it not designed and constructed for harrowing? Yet none of the anomalies that I had been observing ever raised any enquiry about the nature and original intention of the State. They were merely acquiesced in. At most, they were put down feebly to the imperfections of human nature which render mismanagement and perversion of every good institution to some extent inevitable; and this is absurd, for these anomalies do not appear in the conduct of any other human institution. It is no matter of opinion, but of open and notorious fact, that they do not. There are anomalies in the church and in the family that are significantly analogous; they will bear investigation, and are getting it; but the analogies are by no means complete, and are mostly due to the historical connection of these two institutions with the State.

Everyone knows that the State claims and exercises the monopoly of crime that I spoke of a moment ago, and that it makes this monopoly as strict as it can. It forbids private murder, but itself organizes murder on a colossal scale. It punishes private theft, but itself lays unscrupulous hands on anything it wants, whether the property of citizen or of alien. There is, for example, no human right, natural or Constitutional, that we have not seen nullified by the United States Government. Of all the crimes that are committed for gain or revenge, there is not one that we have not seen it commit—murder, mayhem, arson, robbery, fraud, criminal collusion and connivance. On the other hand, we have all remarked the enormous relative difficulty of getting the State to effect any measure for the general welfare. Compare the difficulty of securing conviction in cases of notorious malfeasance, and in cases of petty private crime. Compare the smooth and easy going of the Teapot Dome transactions with the obstructionist behaviour of the State toward a national child-labour law. Suppose one should try to get the State to put the same safeguards (no stronger) around service-income that with no pressure at all it puts around capital-income: what chance would one have? It must not be understood that I bring these matters forward to complain of them. I am not concerned with complaints or reforms, but only with the exhibition of anomalies that seem to me to need accounting for.

VI

In the course of some desultory reading I noticed that the historian Parkman, at the outset of his volume on the conspiracy of Pontiac, dwells with some puzzlement, apparently, upon the fact that the Indians had not formed a State. Mr. Jefferson, also, who knew the Indians well, remarked the same fact—that they lived in a rather highly organized society, but had never formed a State. Bicknell, the historian of Rhode Island, has some interesting passages that bear upon the same point, hinting that the collisions between the Indians and the whites may have been largely due to a misunderstanding about the nature of land-tenure; that the Indians, knowing nothing of the British system of land-tenure, understood their land-sales and land-grants as merely an admission of the whites to the same communal use of land that they themselves enjoyed. I noticed, too, that Marx devotes a good deal of space in *Das Kapital* to proving that economic exploitation cannot take place in any society until the exploited class has been expropriated from the land. These observations attracted my attention as possibly throwing a strong side light upon the nature of the State and the primary purpose of government, and I made note of them accordingly.

At this time I was a good deal in Europe. I was in England and Germany during the Tangier incident, studying the circumstances and conditions that led up to the late war. My facilities for this were exceptional, and I used them diligently. Here I saw the State behaving just as I had seen it behave at home. Moreover, remembering the political theories of the eighteenth century, and the expectations put upon them, I was struck with the fact that the republican, constitutional-monarchical and autocratic States behaved exactly alike. This has never been sufficiently remarked. There was no practical distinction to be drawn among England, France, Germany, and Russia; in all these countries the State acted with unvarying consistency and unfailing regularity against the interests of the immense, the overwhelming majority of its people. So flagrant and flagitious, indeed, was the action of the State in all these countries, that its administrative officials, especially its diplomats, would immediately, in any other sphere of action, be put down as a professional-criminal class; just as would the corresponding officials in my own country, as I had already remarked. It is a noteworthy fact, indeed, concerning all that has happened since then, that if in any given circumstances one went on the assumption that they were a professional-criminal class, one could predict with accuracy what they would do and what would happen; while on any other assumption one could predict almost nothing. The accuracy of my own predictions during the war and throughout the Peace Conference was due to nothing but their being based on this assumption.

The Liberal party was in power in England in 1911, and my attention became attracted to its tenets. I had already seen something of Liberalism in America as a kind of glorified mugwumpery. The Cleveland Administration had long before proved what everybody already knew, that there was no essential difference between the Republican and Democratic parties; an election meant merely that one was in office and wished to stay in, and the other was out and wished to get in. I saw precisely the same relation prevailing between the two major parties in England, and I was to see later the same relation sustained by the Labour Administration of Mr. Ramsay MacDonald. All these political permutations resulted only in what John Adams admirably called "a change of impostors." But I was chiefly interested in the basic theory of Liberalism. This seemed to be that the State is no worse than a degenerate or perverted institution, beneficent in its original intention, and susceptible of restoration by the simple expedient of "putting good men in office."

I had already seen this experiment tried on several scales of magnitude, and observed that it came to nothing commensurate with the expectations put upon it or the enormous difficulty of arranging it. Later I was to see it tried on an unprecedented scale, for almost all the Governments engaged in the war were Liberal, notably the English and our own. Its disastrous results in the case of the Wilson Administration are too well known to need comment; though I do not wish to escape the responsibility of saying that of all forms of political impostorship, Liberalism always seemed to me the most vicious, because the most pretentious and specious. The general upshot of my observations, however, was to show me that whether in the hands of Liberal or Conservative, Republican or Democrat, and whether under nominal constitutionalism, republicanism or autocracy, the mechanism of the State would work freely and naturally in but one direction, namely: against the general welfare of the people.

VII

So I set about finding out what I could about the origin of the State, to see whether its mechanism was ever really meant to work in any other direction; and here I came upon a very odd fact. All the current popular assumptions about the origin of the State rest upon sheer guesswork; none of them upon actual investigation. The treatises and textbooks that came into my hands were also based, finally, upon guesswork. Some authorities guessed that the State was originally formed by this-or-that mode of social agreement; others, by a kind of muddling empiricism; others, by the will of God; and so on. Apparently none of these, however, had taken the plain course of going back upon the record as far as possible to ascertain how it actually had been formed, and for what purpose. It seemed that enough information must be available; the formation of the State in America, for example, was a matter of relatively recent history, and one must be able to find out a great deal about it. Consequently I began to look around to see whether anyone had ever anywhere made any such investigation, and if so, what it amounted to.

I then discovered that the matter had, indeed, been investigated by scientific methods, and that all the scholars of the Continent knew about it, not as something new and startling, but as a sheer commonplace. The State did not originate in any form of social agreement, or with any disinterested view of promoting order and justice. Far otherwise. The State originated in conquest and confiscation, as a device for maintaining the stratification of society permanently into two classes—an owning and exploiting class, relatively small, and a propertyless dependent class. Such measures of order and justice as it established were incidental and ancillary to this purpose; it was not interested in any that did not serve this purpose; and it resisted the establishment of any that were contrary to it. No State known to history originated in any other manner, or for any other purpose than to enable the continuous economic exploitation of one class by another.[2]

[2]There is a considerable literature on this subject, largely untranslated. As a beginning, the reader may be conveniently referred to Mr. Charles A. Beard's *Rise of American Civilization* and his work on the Constitution of the United States. After these he should study closely—for it is hard reading—a small volume called *The State* by Professor Franz Oppenheimer, of the University of Frankfort. It has been well translated and is easily available.

This at once cleared up all the anomalies which I had found so troublesome. One could see immediately, for instance, why the hunting tribes and primitive peasants never formed a State. Primitive peasants never made enough of an economic accumulation to be worth stealing; they lived from hand to mouth. The hunting tribes of North America never formed a State, because the hunter was not exploitable. There was no way to make another man hunt for you; he would go off in the woods and forget to come back; and if he were expropriated from certain hunting-grounds, he would merely move on beyond them, the territory being so large and the population so sparse. Similarly, since the State's own primary intention was essentially criminal, one could see why it cares only to monopolize crime, and not to suppress it; this explained the anomalous behaviour of officials, and showed why it is that in their public capacity, whatever their private character, they appear necessarily as a professional-criminal class; and it further accounted for the fact that the State never moves disinterestedly for the general welfare, except grudgingly and under great pressure.

Again, one could perceive at once the basic misapprehension which forever nullifies the labors of Liberalism and Reform. It was once quite seriously suggested to me by some neighbours that I should go to Congress. I asked them why they wished me to do that, and they replied with some complimentary phrases about the satisfaction of having someone of a somewhat different type "amongst those damned rascals down there." "Yes, but," I said, "don't you see that it would be only a matter of a month or so—a very short time, anyway—before I should be a damned rascal, too?" No, they did not see this; they were rather taken aback; would I explain? "Suppose," I said, "that you put in a Sunday-school superintendent or a Y.M.C.A. secretary to run an assignation-house on Broadway. He might trim off some of the coarser fringes of the job, such as the badger game and the panel game, and put things in what Mayor Gaynor used to call a state of 'outward order and decency,' but he *must* run an assignation-house, or he would promptly hear from the owners." This was a new view to them, and they went away thoughtful.

Finally, one could perceive the reason for the matter that most puzzled me when I first observed a legislature in action, namely, the almost exclusive concern of legislative bodies with such measures as tend to take money out of one set of pockets and put it into another—the preoccupation with converting labour-made property into law-made property, and redistributing its ownership. The moment one becomes aware that just this, over and above a purely legal distribution of the ownership of natural resources, is what the State came into being for, and what it yet exists for, one immediately sees that the legislative bodies are acting altogether in character, and otherwise one cannot possibly give oneself an intelligent account of their behaviour.[3]

Speaking for a moment in the technical terms of economics, there are two general means whereby human beings can satisfy their needs and desires. One is by work—*i.e.*, by applying labour and capital to natural resources for the production of wealth, or to facilitating the exchange of labour-products. This is called the economic means. The other is by robbery—*i.e.*, the appropriation of the labour-products of others without compensation. This is called the political means. The State, considered functionally, may be described as *the organization of the political means,* enabling a comparatively small class of beneficiaries to satisfy their needs and desires through various delegations of the taxing power, which have no vestige of support in natural right, such as private land-ownership, tariffs, franchises, and the like.

It is a primary instinct of human nature to satisfy one's needs and desires with the least possible exertion; everyone tends by

[3]When the Republican convention which nominated Mr. Harding was almost over, one of the party leaders met a man who was managing a kind of dark-horse, or one-horse, candidate, and said to him, "You can pack up that candidate of yours, and take him home now. I can't tell you who the next President will be; it will be one of three men, and I don't just yet know which. But I can tell you who the next Secretary of the Interior will be, and that is the important question, because there are still a few little things lying around loose that the boys want." I had this from a United States Senator, a Republican, who told it to me merely as a good story.

instinctive preference to use the political means rather than the economic means, if he can do so. The great desideratum in a tariff, for instance, is its license to rob the domestic consumer of the difference between the price of an article in a competitive and a non-competitive market. Every manufacturer would like this privilege of robbery if he could get it, and he takes steps to get it if he can, thus illustrating the powerful instinctive tendency to climb out of the exploited class, which lives by the economic means (exploited, because the cost of this privilege must finally come out of production, there being nowhere else for it to come from), and into the class which lives, wholly or partially, by the political means.

This instinct—and this alone—is what gives the State its almost impregnable strength. The moment one discerns this, one understands the almost universal disposition to glorify and magnify the State, and to insist upon the pretence that it is something which it is not—something, in fact, the direct opposite of what it is. One understands the complacent acceptance of one set of standards for the State's conduct, and another for private organizations; of one set for officials, and another for private persons. One understands at once the attitude of the press, the Church and educational institutions, their careful inculcations of a specious patriotism, their nervous and vindictive proscriptions of opinion, doubt or even of question. One sees why purely fictitious theories of the State and its activities are strongly, often fiercely and violently, insisted on; why the simple fundamentals of the very simple science of economics are shirked or veiled; and why, finally, those who really know what kind of thing they are promulgating, are loth to say so.

VIII

The outbreak of the war in 1914 found me entertaining the convictions that I have here outlined. In the succeeding decade nothing has taken place to attenuate them, but quite the con-

trary. Having set out only to tell the story of how I came by
them, and not to expound them or indulge in any polemic
for them, I may now bring this narrative to an end, with a word
about their practical outcome.

It has sometimes been remarked as strange that I never
joined in any agitation, or took the part of a propagandist for
any movement against the State, especially at a time when I
had an unexampled opportunity to do so. To do anything of
the sort successfully, one must have more faith in such processes
than I have, and one must also have a certain dogmatic turn of
temperament, which I do not possess. To be quite candid, I
was never much for evangelization; I am not sure enough that
my opinions are right, and even if they were, a second-hand
opinion is a poor possession. Reason and experience, I repeat,
are all that determine our true beliefs. So I never greatly cared
that people should think my way, or tried much to get them to
do so. I should be glad if they *thought*—if their general turn,
that is, were a little more for disinterested thinking, and a little
less for impetuous action motivated by mere unconsidered pre-
possession; and what little I could ever do to promote disinterested thinking has, I believe, been done.

According to my observations (for which I claim nothing but
that they are all I have to go by) inaction is better than wrong
action or premature right action, and effective right action
can only follow right thinking. "If a great change is to take
place," said Edmund Burke, in his last words on the French
Revolution, "the minds of men *will be fitted to it.*" Otherwise
the thing does not turn out well; and the processes by which
men's minds are fitted seem to me untraceable and imponder-
able, the only certainty about them being that the share of
any one person, or any one movement, in determining them is
extremely small. Various social superstitions, such as magic, the
divine right of kings, the Calvinist teleology, and so on, have
stood out against many a vigorous frontal attack, and thrived on
it; and when they finally disappeared, it was not under attack.
People simply stopped thinking in those terms; no one knew

just when or why, and no one even was much aware that they had stopped. So I think it very possible that while we are saying, "Lo, here!" and "Lo, there!" with our eye on this or that revolution, usurpation, seizure of power, or what not, the superstitions that surround the State are quietly disappearing in the same way.

My opinion of my own government and those who administer it can probably be inferred from what I have written. Mr. Jefferson said that if a centralization of power were ever effected at Washington, the United States would have the most corrupt government on earth. Comparisons are difficult, but I believe it has one that is thoroughly corrupt, flagitious, tyrannical, oppressive. Yet if it were in my power to pull down its whole structure overnight and set up another of my own devising— to abolish the State out of hand, and replace it by an organization of the economic means—I would not do it, for the minds of Americans are far from fitted to any such great change as this, and the effect would be only to lay open the way for the worse enormities of usurpation—possibly, who knows? with myself as the usurper! After the French Revolution, Napoleon!

Great and salutary social transformations, such as in the end do not cost more than they come to, are not effected by political shifts, by movements, by programs and platforms, least of all by violent revolutions, but by sound and disinterested thinking. The believers in action are numerous, their gospel is widely preached, they have many followers. Perhaps among those who will see what I have here written, there are two or three who will agree with me that the believers in action do not need us— indeed, that if we joined them, we should be rather a dead weight for them to carry. We need not deny that their work is educative, or pinch pennies when we count up its cost in the inevitable reactions against it. We need only remark that our place and function in it are not apparent, and then proceed on our own way, first with the more obscure and extremely difficult work of clearing and illuminating our own minds, and second, with what occasional help we may offer to others whose faith, like our own, is set more on the regenerative power of thought than on the uncertain achievements of premature action.

7   Economics in One Lesson

Henry Hazlitt

THE LESSON

Economics is haunted by more fallacies than any other study known to man. This is no accident. The inherent difficulties of the subject would be great enough in any case, but they are multiplied a thousandfold by a factor that is insignificant in, say, physics, mathematics or medicine—the special pleading of selfish interests. While every group has certain economic interests identical with those of all groups, every group has also, as we shall see, interests antagonistic to those of all other groups. While certain public policies would in the long run benefit everybody, other policies would benefit one group only at the expense of all other groups. The group that would benefit by such policies, having such a direct interest in them, will argue for them plausibly and persistently. It will hire the best buyable minds to devote their whole time to presenting its case. And it will finally either convince the general public that its case is sound, or so befuddle it that clear thinking on the subject becomes next to impossible.

In addition to these endless pleadings of self-interest, there is a second main factor that spawns new economic fallacies every day. This is the persistent tendency of men to see only the immediate effects of a given policy, or its effects only on a special group, and to neglect to inquire what the long-run effects of that policy will be not only on that special group but on all groups. It is the fallacy of overlooking secondary consequences.

In this lies almost the whole difference between good economics and bad. The bad economist sees only what immediately strikes the eye; the good economist also looks beyond. The bad economist sees only the direct consequences of a proposed course; the good economist looks also at the longer and indirect consequences. The bad economist sees only what the effect of a given policy has been or will be on one particular group; the good economist inquires also what the effect of the policy will be on all groups.

The distinction may seem obvious. The precaution of looking for all the consequences of a given policy to everyone may seem elementary. Doesn't everybody know, in his personal life, that there are all sorts of indulgences delightful at the moment but disastrous in the end? Doesn't every little boy know that if he eats enough candy he will get sick? Doesn't the fellow who gets drunk know that he will wake up next morning with a ghastly stomach and a horrible head? Doesn't the dipsomaniac know that he is ruining his liver and shortening his life? Doesn't the Don Juan know that he is letting himself in for every sort of risk, from blackmail to disease? Finally, to bring it to the economic though still personal realm, do not the idler and the spendthrift know, even in the midst of their glorious fling, that they are heading for a future of debt and poverty?

Yet when we enter the field of public economics, these elementary truths are ignored. There are men regarded today as brilliant economists, who deprecate saving and recommend squandering on a national scale as the way of economic salvation; and when anyone points to what the consequences of these policies will be in the long run, they reply flippantly, as might the prodigal son of a warning father: "In the long run we are all dead." And such shallow wisecracks pass as devastating epigrams and the ripest wisdom.

But the tragedy is that, on the contrary, we are already suffering the long-run consequences of the policies of the remote or recent past. Today is already the tomorrow which the bad economist yesterday urged us to ignore. The long-run consequences of some economic policies may become evident in a few months. Others may not become evident for several years. Still others may not become evident for decades. But in every case those long-run consequences are contained in the policy as surely as the hen was in the egg, the flower in the seed.

From this aspect, therefore, the whole of economics can be reduced to a single lesson, and that lesson can be reduced to a single sentence. *The art of economics consists in looking not merely at the immediate but at the longer effects of any act or policy; it consists in tracing the consequences of that policy not merely for one group but for all groups.*

2

Nine-tenths of the economic fallacies that are working such dreadful harm in the world today are the result of ignoring this lesson. Those fallacies all stem from one of two central fallacies, or both: that of looking only at the immediate consequences of an act or proposal, and that of looking at the consequences only for a particular group to the neglect of other groups.

It is true, of course, that the opposite error is possible. In considering a policy we ought not to concentrate *only* on its long-run results to the community as a whole. This is the error often made by the classical economists. It resulted in a certain callousness toward the fate of groups that were immediately hurt by policies or developments which proved to be beneficial on net balance and in the long run.

But comparatively few people today make this error; and those few consist mainly of professional economists. The most frequent fallacy by far today, the fallacy that emerges again and again in nearly every conversation that touches on economic affairs, the error of a thousand political speeches, the central sophism of the "new" economics, is to concentrate on the short-run effects of policies on special groups and to ignore or belittle the long-run effects on the community as a whole. The "new" economists flatter themselves that this is a great, almost a revolutionary advance over the methods of the "classical" or "orthodox" economists, because the former take into consideration short-run effects which the latter often ignored. But in themselves ignoring or slighting the long-run effects, they are making the far more serious error. They overlook the woods in their precise and minute examination of particular trees. Their methods and conclusions are often profoundly reactionary. They are sometimes surprised to find themselves in accord with seventeenth-century mercantilism. They fall, in fact, into all the ancient errors (or would, if they were not so inconsistent) that the classical economists, we had hoped, had once for all got rid of.

3

It is often sadly remarked that the bad economists present their errors to the public better than the good economists present their truths. It is often complained that demagogues can be more plausible in putting forward economic nonsense from the platform than the honest men who try to show what is wrong with it. But the basic reason for this ought not to be mysterious. The reason is that the demagogues and bad economists are presenting half-truths. They are speaking only of the immediate effect of a proposed policy or its effect upon a single group. As far as they go they may often be right. In these cases the answer consists in showing that the proposed policy would also have longer and less desirable effects, or that it could benefit one group only at the expense of all other groups. The answer consists in supplementing and correcting the half-truth with the other half. But to consider all the chief effects of a proposed course on everybody often requires a long, complicated, and dull chain of reasoning. Most of the audience finds this chain of reasoning difficult to follow and soon becomes bored and inattentive. The bad economists rationalize this intellectual debility and laziness by assuring the audience that it need not even attempt to follow the reasoning or judge it on its merits because it is only "classicism" or "laissez faire" or "capitalist apologetics" or whatever other term of abuse may happen to strike them as effective.

We have stated the nature of the lesson, and of the fallacies that stand in its way, in abstract terms. But the lesson will not be driven home, and the fallacies will continue to go unrecognized, unless both are illustrated by examples. Through these examples we can move from the most elementary problems in economics to the most complex and difficult. Through them we can learn to detect and avoid first the crudest and most palpable fallacies and finally some of the most sophisticated and elusive. To that task we shall now proceed.

THE LESSON APPLIED

The Broken Window

Let us begin with the simplest illustration possible: let us, emulating Bastiat, choose a broken pane of glass.

A young hoodlum, say, heaves a brick through the window of a baker's shop. The shopkeeper runs out furious, but the boy is gone. A crowd gathers, and begins to stare with quiet satisfaction at the gaping hole in the window and the shattered glass over the bread and pies. After a while the crowd feels the need for philosophic reflection. And several of its members are almost certain to remind each other or the baker that, after all, the misfortune has its bright side. It will make business for some glazier. As they begin to think of this they elaborate upon it. How much does a new plate glass window cost? A hundred dollars? That will be quite a sum. After all, if windows were never broken, what would happen to the glass business? Then, of course, the thing is endless. The glazier will have $100 more to spend with other merchants, and these in turn will have $100 more to spend with still other merchants, and so ad infinitum. The smashed window will go on providing money and employment in ever-widening circles. The logical conclusion from all this would be, if the crowd drew it, that the little hoodlum who threw the brick, far from being a public menace, was a public benefactor.

Now let us take another look. The crowd is at least right in its first conclusion. This little act of vandalism will in the first instance mean more business for some glazier. The glazier will be no more unhappy to learn of the incident than an undertaker to learn of a death. But the shopkeeper will be out $100 that he was planning to spend for a new suit. Because he has had to replace a window, he will have to go without the suit (or some equivalent need or luxury). Instead of having a window and $100 he now has merely a window. Or, as he was planning to buy the suit that very afternoon, instead of having both a window and a suit he must be content with the window and no suit. If we think of him as a part of the community, the community has lost a new suit that might otherwise have come into being, and is just that much poorer.

The glazier's gain of business, in short, is merely the tailor's loss of business. No new "employment" has been added. The people in the crowd were thinking only of two parties to the transaction, the baker and the glazier. They had forgotten the potential third party involved, the tailor. They forgot him precisely because he will not now enter the scene. They will see the new window in the next day or two. They will never see the extra suit, precisely because it will never be made. They see only what is immediately visible to the eye. . . .

Who's "Protected" by Tariffs?

A mere recital of the economic policies of governments all over the world is calculated to cause any serious student of economics to throw up his hands in despair. What possible point can there be, he is likely to ask, in discussing refinements and advances in economic theory, when popular thought and the actual policies of governments, certainly in everything connected with international relations, have not yet caught up with Adam Smith? For present-day tariff and trade policies are not only as bad as those in the seventeenth and eighteenth centuries, but incomparably worse. The real reasons for those tariffs and other trade barriers are the same, and the pretended reasons are also the same.

Since *The Wealth of Nations* appeared nearly two centuries ago, the case for free trade has been stated thousands of times, but perhaps never with more direct simplicity and force than it was stated in that volume. In general Smith rested his case on one fundamental proposition: "In every country it always is and must be the interest of the great body of the people to buy whatever they want of those who sell it cheapest." "The proposition is so very manifest," Smith continued, "that it seems ridiculous to take any pains to prove it; nor could it ever have been called in question, had not the interested sophistry of merchants and manufacturers confounded the common-sense of mankind."

From another point of view, free trade was considered as one aspect of the specialization of labor:

> It is the maxim of every prudent master of a family, never to attempt to make at home what it will cost him more to make than to buy. The tailor does not attempt to make his own shoes, but buys them of the shoemaker. The shoemaker does not attempt to make his own clothes, but employs a tailor. The farmer attempts

to make neither the one nor the other, but employs those different artificers. All of them find it for their interest to employ their whole industry in a way in which they have some advantage over their neighbors, and to purchase with a part of its produce, or what is the same thing, with the price of a part of it, whatever else they have occasion for. What is prudence in the conduct of every private family can scarce be folly in that of a great kingdom.

But whatever led people to suppose that what was prudence in the conduct of every private family *could* be folly in that of a great kingdom? It was a whole network of fallacies, out of which mankind has still been unable to cut its way. And the chief of them was the central fallacy with which this book is concerned. It was that of considering merely the immediate effects of a tariff on special groups, and neglecting to consider its long-run effects on the whole community.

2

An American manufacturer of woolen sweaters goes to Congress or to the State Department and tells the committee or officials concerned that it would be a national disaster for them to remove or reduce the tariff on British sweaters. He now sells his sweaters for $20 each, but English manufacturers could sell here sweaters of the same quality for $15. A duty of $5, therefore, is needed to keep him in business. He is not thinking of himself, of course, but of the thousand men and women he employs, and of the people to whom their spending in turn gives employment. Throw them out of work, and you create unemployment and a fall in purchasing power, which would spread in ever-widening circles. And if he can prove that he really would be forced out of business if the tariff were removed or reduced, his argument against that action is regarded by Congress as conclusive.

But the fallacy comes from looking merely at this manufacturer and his employes, or merely at the American sweater industry. It comes from noticing only the results that are immediately seen, and neglecting the results that are not seen because they are prevented from coming into existence.

The lobbyists for tariff protection are continually putting forward arguments that are not factually correct. But let us assume that the facts in this case are precisely as the sweater manufacturer has stated them. Let us assume that a tariff of $5 a sweater is necessary for him to stay in business and provide employment at sweater-making for his workers.

We have deliberately chosen the most unfavorable example of any for the removal of a tariff. We have not taken an argument for the imposition of a new tariff in order to bring a new industry into existence, but an argument for the retention of a tariff *that has already brought an industry into existence,* and cannot be repealed without hurting somebody.

The tariff is repealed; the manufacturer goes out of business; a thousand workers are laid off; the particular tradesmen whom they patronized are hurt. This is the immediate result that is seen. But there are also results which, while much more difficult to trace, are no less immediate and no less real. For now sweaters that formerly cost $20 apiece can be bought for $15. Consumers can now buy the same quality of sweater for less money, or a much better one for the same money. If they buy the same quality of sweater, they not only get the sweater, but they have $5 left over, which they would not have had under the previous conditions, to buy something else. With the $15 that they pay for the imported sweater they help employment—as the American manufacturer no doubt predicted—in the sweater industry in England. With the $5 left over they help employment in any number of industries in the United States.

But the results do not end there. By buying English sweaters they furnish the English with dollars to buy American goods here. This, in fact (if I may here disregard such complications as multilateral exchange, loans, credits, gold movements, etc. which do not alter the end result) is the only way in which the British can eventually make use of these dollars. Because we have permitted the British to sell more to us, they are now able to buy more from us. They are, in fact, eventually *forced* to buy more from us if their dollar balances are not to remain perpetually unused. So, as a result of letting in more British goods, we must export more American goods. And though fewer people are now employed in the American sweater industry, more people are employed—and much more efficiently employed— in, say, the American automobile or washing-machine business. American employment on net balance has not gone down, but American and British production on net balance has gone up. Labor in each country is more fully employed in doing just those things that it does best, instead of being forced to do things that it does inefficiently or badly. Consumers in both countries are better off. They are able to buy what they want where they can get it cheapest. American consumers are better provided with sweaters, and, British consumers are better provided with motor cars and washing machines.

3

Now let us look at the matter the other way round, and see the effect of imposing a tariff in the first place. Suppose that there had been no tariff on foreign knit goods, that Americans were accustomed to buying foreign sweaters without duty, and that the argument were then put forward that we could *bring a sweater industry into existence* by imposing a duty of $5 on sweaters.

There would be nothing logically wrong with this argument so far as it went. The cost of British sweaters to the American consumer might thereby be forced so high that American man- ufacturers would find it profitable to enter the sweater business. But American consumers would be forced to subsidize this in- dustry. On every American sweater they bought they would be forced in effect to pay a tax of $5 which would be collected from them in a higher price by the new sweater industry.

Americans would be employed in a sweater industry who had not previously been employed in a sweater industry. That much is true. But there would be no net addition to the country's in- dustry or the country's employment. Because the American con- sumer had to pay $5 more for the same quality of sweater he would have just that much less left over to buy anything else. He would have to reduce his expenditures by $5 somewhere else. In order that one industry might grow or come into existence, a hundred other industries would have to shrink. In order that 20,000 persons might be employed in a sweater industry, 20,000 fewer persons would be employed elsewhere.

But the new industry would be *visible*. The number of its employes, the capital invested in it, the market value of its product in terms of dollars, could be easily counted. The neighbors could see the sweater workers going to and from the factory every day. The results would be palpable and direct. But the shrinkage of a hundred other industries, the loss of 20,000 other jobs somewhere else, would not be so easily noticed. It would be impossible for even the cleverest statistician to know precisely what the incidence of the loss of other jobs had been —precisely how many men and women had been laid off from each particular industry, precisely how much business each particular industry had lost—because consumers had to pay more for their sweaters. For a loss spread among all the other productive activities of the country would be comparatively minute for each. It would be impossible for anyone to know precisely how each consumer *would* have spent his extra $5 if he had been allowed to retain it. The overwhelming majority of the people, therefore, would probably suffer from the optical illusion that the new industry had cost us nothing.

4

It is important to notice that the new tariff on sweaters would not raise American wages. To be sure, it would enable Americans to work *in the sweater industry* at approximately the average level of American wages (for workers of their skill), instead of having to compete in that industry at the British level of wages. But there would be no increase of American wages *in general* as a result of the duty; for, as we have seen, there would be no net increase in the number of jobs provided, no net increase in the demand for goods, and no increase in labor productivity. Labor productivity would, in fact, be *reduced* as a result of the tariff.

And this brings us to the real effect of a tariff wall. It is not merely that all its visible gains are offset by less obvious but no less real losses. It results, in fact, in a net loss to the country. For contrary to centuries of interested propaganda and disinterested confusion, the tariff *reduces* the American level of wages.

Let us observe more clearly how it does this. We have seen that the added amount which consumers pay for a tariff-protected article leaves them just that much less with which to buy all other articles. There is here no net gain to industry as a whole. But as a result of the artificial barrier erected against foreign goods, American labor, capital, and land are deflected from what they can do more efficiently. Therefore, as a result of the tariff wall, the average productivity of American labor and capital is reduced.

If we look at it now from the consumer's point of view, we find that he can buy less with his money. Because he has to pay more for sweaters and other protected goods, he can buy less of everything else. The general purchasing power of his income has therefore been reduced. Whether the net effect of the tariff is to lower money wages or to raise money prices will depend upon the monetary policies that are followed. But what is clear is that the tariff—though it may increase wages above what they would have been in *the protected industries*—must on net balance, when *all* occupations are considered, *reduce real wages*.

Only minds corrupted by generations of misleading propaganda can regard this conclusion as paradoxical. What other result could we expect from a policy of deliberately using our resources of capital and manpower in less efficient ways than we know how to use them? What other result could we expect from deliberately erecting artificial obstacles to trade and transportation?

For the erection of tariff walls has the same effect as the erection of real walls. It is significant that the protectionists habitually use the language of warfare. They talk of "repelling an invasion" of foreign products. And the means they suggest in the fiscal field are like those of the battlefield. The tariff barriers that are put up to repeal this invasion are like the tank traps, trenches and barbed-wire entanglements created to repel or slow down attempted invasion by a foreign army.

And just as the foreign army is compelled to employ more expensive means to surmount those obstacles—bigger tanks, mine detectors, engineer corps to cut wires, ford streams and build bridges—so more expensive and efficient transportation means must be developed to surmount tariff obstacles. On the one hand, we try to reduce the cost of transportation between England and America, or Canada and the United States, by developing faster and more efficient planes and ships, better roads and bridges, better locomotives and motor trucks. On the other hand, we offset this investment in efficient transportation by a tariff that makes it commercially even more difficult to transport goods than it was before. We make it a dollar cheaper to ship the sweaters, and then increase the tariff by two dollars to prevent the sweaters from being shipped. By reducing the freight that can be profitably carried, we reduce the value of the investment in transport efficiency.

5

The tariff has been described as a means of benefiting the producer at the expense of the consumer. In a sense this is correct. Those who favor it think only of the interests of the producers immediately benefited by the particular duties involved. They forget the interests of the consumers who are immediately injured by being forced to pay these duties. But it is wrong to think of the tariff issue as if it represented a conflict between the interests of producers as a unit against those of consumers as a unit. It is true that the tariff hurts all consumers as such. It is not true that it benefits all producers as such. On the contrary, as we have just seen, it helps the protected producers at the expense of all other American producers, *and particularly of those who have a comparatively large potential export market.*

We can perhaps make this last point clearer by an exaggerated example. Suppose we make our tariff wall so high that it becomes absolutely prohibitive, and no imports come in from the outside world at all. Suppose, as a result of this, that the price of sweaters in America goes up only $5. Then American consumers, because they have to pay $5 more for a sweater, will spend on the average five cents less in each of a hundred other American industries. (The figures are chosen merely to illustrate a principle: there will, of course, be no such symmetrical distribution of the loss; moreover, the sweater industry itself will doubtless be hurt because of protection of still *other* industries. But these complications may be put aside for the moment.)

Now because foreign industries will find their market in America *totally* cut off, they will get no dollar exchange, and therefore they will be *unable to buy any American goods at all.* As a result of this, American industries will suffer in direct proportion to the percentage of their sales previously made abroad. Those that will be most injured, in the first instance, will be such industries as raw cotton producers, copper producers, makers of sewing machines, agricultural machinery, typewriters, commercial airplanes, and so on.

A higher tariff wall, which, however, is not prohibitive, will produce the same kind of results as this, but merely to a smaller degree.

The effect of a tariff, therefore, is to change the *structure* of American production. It changes the number of occupations, the kind of occupations, and the relative size of one industry as compared with another. It makes the industries in which we are comparatively inefficient larger, and the industries in which we are comparatively efficient smaller. Its net effect, therefore, is to reduce American efficiency, as well as to reduce efficiency in the countries with which we would otherwise have traded more largely.

In the long run, notwithstanding the mountains of argument pro and con, a tariff is irrelevant to the question of employment. (True, sudden *changes* in the tariff, either upward or downward, can create temporary unemployment, as they force corresponding changes in the structure of production. Such sudden changes can even cause a depression.) But a tariff is not irrelevant to the question of wages. In the long run it always reduces real wages, because it reduces efficiency, production and wealth.

Thus all the chief tariff fallacies stem from the central fallacy with which this book is concerned. They are the result of looking only at the immediate effects of a single tariff rate on one group of producers, and forgetting the long-run effects both on consumers as a whole and on all other producers.

(I hear some reader asking: "Why not solve this by giving tariff protection to *all* producers?" But the fallacy here is that this cannot help producers uniformly, and cannot help at all domestic producers who already "outsell" foreign producers: these efficient producers must necessarily suffer from the diversion of purchasing power brought about by the tariff.)

6

On the subject of the tariff we must keep in mind one final precaution. It is the same precaution that we found necessary in examining the effects of machinery. It is useless to deny that a tariff does benefit—or at least *can* benefit—*special interests.* True, it benefits them *at the expense of everyone else.* But it does benefit them. If one industry alone could get protection, while its owners and workers enjoyed the benefits of free trade in everything else they bought, that industry would benefit, even on net balance. As an attempt is made to *extend* the tariff blessings, however, even people in the protected industries, both as producers and consumers, begin to suffer from other people's protection, and may finally be worse off even on net balance than if neither they nor anybody else had protection.

But we should not deny, as enthusiastic free traders have so often done, the possibility of these tariff benefits to special groups. We should not pretend, for example, that a reduction of the tariff would help everybody and hurt nobody. It is true that its reduction would help the country on net balance. But *somebody* would be hurt. Groups previously enjoying high protection would be hurt. That in fact is one reason why it is not good to bring such protected interests into existence in the first place. But clarity and candor of thinking compel us to see and acknowledge that some industries are right when they say that a removal of the tariff on their product would throw them out of business and throw their workers (at least temporarily) out of jobs. And if their workers have developed specialized skills, they may even suffer permanently, or until they have at long last learnt equal skills. In tracing the effects of tariffs, as in tracing the effects of machinery, we should endeavor to see *all* the chief effects, in both the short run and the long run, on *all* groups.

As a postscript to this chapter I should add that its argument is not directed against *all* tariffs, including duties collected mainly for revenue, or to keep alive industries needed for war; nor is it directed against all arguments for tariffs. It is merely directed against the fallacy that a tariff on net balance "provides employment," "raises wages," or "protects the American standard of living." It does none of these things; and so far as wages and the standard of living are concerned, it does the precise opposite. But an examination of duties imposed for other purposes would carry us beyond our present subject.

Nor need we here examine the effect of import quotas, exchange controls, bilateralism and other devices in reducing, diverting or preventing international trade. Such devices have, in general, the same effects as high or prohibitive tariffs, and often worse effects. They present more complicated issues, but their net results can be traced through the same kind of reasoning that we have just applied to tariff barriers. . . .

"Enough to Buy Back the Product"

Amateur writers on economics are always asking for "just" prices and "just" wages. These nebulous conceptions of economic justice come down to us from medieval times. The classical economists worked out instead, a different concept—

the concept of *functional* prices and *functional* wages. Functional prices are those that encourage the largest volume of production and the largest volume of sales. Functional wages are those that tend to bring about the highest volume of employment and the largest payrolls.

The concept of functional wages has been taken over, in a perverted form, by the Marxists and their unconscious disciples, the purchasing-power school. Both of these groups leave to cruder minds the question whether existing wages are "fair." The real question, they insist, is whether or not they will *work*. And the only wages that will work, they tell us, the only wages that will prevent an imminent economic crash, are wages that will enable labor "to buy back the product it creates." The Marxist and purchasing-power schools attribute every depression of the past to a preceding failure to pay such wages. And at no matter what moment they speak, they are sure that wages are still not high enough to buy back the product.

The doctrine has proved particularly effective in the hands of union leaders. Despairing of their ability to arouse the altruistic interest of the public or to persuade employers (wicked by definition) ever to be "fair," they have seized upon an argument calculated to appeal to the public's selfish motives, and frighten it into forcing employers to grant their demands.

How are we to know, however, precisely when labor does have "enough to buy back the product"? Or when it has more than enough? How are we to determine just what the right sum is? As the champions of the doctrine do not seem to have made any real effort to answer such questions, we are obliged to try to find the answers for ourselves.

Some sponsors of the theory seem to imply that the workers in each industry should receive enough to buy back the particular product they make. But they surely cannot mean that the makers of cheap dresses should have enough to buy back cheap dresses and the makers of mink coats enough to buy back mink coats; or that the men in the Ford plant should receive enough to buy Fords and the men in the Cadillac plant enough to buy Cadillacs.

It is instructive to recall, however, that the unions in the automobile industry, at a time when most of their members were already in the upper third of the country's income receivers, and when their weekly wage, according to government figures, was already 20 per cent higher than the average wage paid in factories and nearly twice as great as the average paid in retail trade, were demanding a 30 per cent increase so that they might, according to one of their spokesmen, "bolster our fast-shrinking ability to absorb the goods which we have the capacity to produce."

What, then, of the average factory worker and the average retail worker? If, under such circumstances, the automobile workers needed a 30 per cent increase to keep the economy from collapsing, would a mere 30 per cent have been enough for the others? Or would they have required increases of 55 to 160 per cent to give them as much per capita purchasing power as the automobile workers?

(We may be sure, if the history of wage bargaining even *within individual unions* is any guide, that the automobile workers, if this last proposal had been made, would have insisted on the maintenance of their existing differentials; for the passion for economic equality, among union members as among the rest of us, is, with the exception of a few rare philanthropists and saints, a passion for getting as much as those above us in the economic scale already get rather than a passion for giving those below us as much as we ourselves already get. But it is with the logic and soundness of a particular economic theory, rather than with these distressing weaknesses of human nature, that we are at present concerned.)

2

The argument that labor should receive enough to buy back the product is merely a special form of the general "purchasing power" argument. The workers' wages, it is correctly enough contended, are the workers' purchasing power. But it is just as true that everyone's income—the grocer's, the landlord's, the employer's—is his purchasing power for buying what others have to sell. And one of the most important things for which others have to find purchasers is their labor services.

All this, moreover, has its reverse side. *In an exchange economy everybody's money income is somebody else's cost.* Every increase in hourly wages, unless or until compensated by an equal increase in hourly productivity, is an increase in costs of production. An increase in costs of production, where the government controls prices and forbids any price increase, takes the profit from marginal producers, forces them out of business, means a shrinkage in production and a growth in unemployment. Even where a price increase is possible, the higher price discourages buyers, shrinks the market, and also leads to unemployment. If a 30 per cent increase in hourly wages all around the circle forces a 30 per cent increase in prices, labor can buy no more of the product than it could at the beginning; and the merry-go-round must start all over again.

No doubt many will be inclined to dispute the contention that a 30 per cent increase in wages can force as great a percentage increase in prices. It is true that this result can follow only in the long run and only if monetary and credit policy permit it. If money and credit are so inelastic that they do not increase when wages are forced up (and if we assume that the higher wages are not justified by existing labor productivity in dollar terms), then the chief effect of forcing up wage rates will be to force unemployment.

And it is probable, in that case, that total payrolls, both in dollar amount and in real purchasing power, will be lower than before. For a drop in employment (brought about by union policy and not as a transitional result of technological advance) necessarily means that fewer goods are being produced for everyone. And it is unlikely that labor will compensate for the absolute drop in production by getting a larger relative share of the production that is left. For Paul H. Douglas in America and A. C. Pigou in England, the first from analyzing a great mass of statistics, the second by almost purely deductive methods, arrived independently at the conclusion that the elasticity of the demand for labor is somewhere between —3 and —4. This means, in less technical language, that "a 1 per cent reduction in the real rate of wage is likely to expand the aggregate demand for labor by not less than 3 per cent."[1] Or, to put the matter the other way, "If wages are pushed up above the point of marginal productivity, the decrease in employment would normally be from three to four times as great as the increase in hourly rates"[2] so that the total incomes of the workers would be reduced correspondingly.

Even if these figures are taken to represent only the elasticity of the demand for labor revealed in a given period of the past, and not necessarily to forecast that of the future, they deserve the most serious consideration.

3

But now let us suppose that the increase in wage rates is accompanied or followed by a sufficient increase in money and credit to allow it to take place without creating serious unemployment. If we assume that the previous relationship between wages and prices was itself a "normal" long-run relationship, then it is altogether probable that a forced increase of, say, 30 per cent in wage rates will ultimately lead to an increase in prices of approximately the same percentage.

The belief that the price increase would be substantially less than that rests on two main fallacies. The first is that of looking only at the direct labor costs of a particular firm or industry and assuming these to represent all the labor costs involved. But this is the elementary error of mistaking a part for the whole. Each "industry" represents not only just one section of the productive process considered "horizontally," but just *one* section of that process considered "vertically." Thus the *direct* labor cost of making automobiles in the automobile factories themselves may

[1]A. C. Pigou, *The Theory of Unemployment* (1933), p. 96.
[2]Paul H. Douglas, *The Theory of Wages* (1934), p. 501.

be less than a third, say, of the total costs; and this may lead the incautious to conclude that a 30 per cent increase in wages would lead to only a 10 per cent increase, or less, in automobile prices. But this would be to overlook the indirect wage costs in the raw materials and purchased parts, in transportation charges, in new factories or new machine tools or in the dealers' mark-up.

Government estimates show that in the fifteen-year period from 1929 to 1943, inclusive, wages and salaries in the United States averaged 69 per cent of the national income. In the five-year period 1956–1960 they also averaged 69 per cent of the national income! These wages and salaries, of course, had to be paid out of the national product. While there would have to be both deductions from this figure and additions to it to provide a fair estimate of "labor's" income, we can assume on this basis that labor costs cannot be less than about two-thirds of total production costs and may run above three-quarters (depending upon our definition of "labor"). If we take the lower of these two estimates, and assume also that dollar profit margins would be unchanged, it is clear that an increase of 30 per cent in wage costs all around the circle would mean an increase of nearly 20 per cent in prices.

But such a change would mean that the dollar profit margin, representing the income of investors, managers and the self-employed, would then have, say, only 84 per cent as much purchasing power as it had before. The long-run effect of this would be to cause a diminution of investment and new enterprise compared with what it would otherwise have been, and consequent transfers of men from the lower ranks of the self-employed to the higher ranks of wage-earners, until the previous relationships had been approximately restored. But this is only another way of saying that a 30 per cent increase in wages under the conditions assumed would eventually mean also a 30 per cent increase in prices.

It does not necessarily follow that wage-earners would make no relative gains. They would make a relative gain, and other elements in the population would suffer a relative loss, *during the period of transition.* But it is improbable that this relative gain would mean an absolute gain. For the kind of change in the relationship of costs to prices contemplated here could hardly take place without bringing about unemployment and unbalanced, interrupted or reduced production. So that while labor might get a broader slice of a smaller pie, during this period of transition and adjustment to a new equilibrium, it may be doubted whether this would be greater in absolute size (and it might easily be less) than the previous narrower slice of a larger pie.

4

This brings us to the general meaning and effect of economic *equilibrium.* Equilibrium wages and prices are the wages and prices that equalize supply and demand. If, either through government or private coercion, an attempt is made to lift prices above their equilibrium level, demand is reduced and therefore production is reduced. If an attempt is made to push prices below their equilibrium level, the consequent reduction or wiping out of profits will mean a falling off of supply or new production. Therefore, an attempt to force prices either above or below their equilibrium levels (which are the levels toward which a free market constantly tends to bring them) will act to reduce the volume of employment and production below what it would otherwise have been.

To return, then, to the doctrine that labor must get "enough to buy back the product." The national product, it should be obvious, is neither created nor bought by manufacturing labor alone. It is bought by everyone—by white collar workers, professional men, farmers, employers, big and little, by investors, grocers, butchers, owners of small drug stores and gasoline stations—by everybody, in short, who contributes toward making the product.

As to the prices, wages and profits that should determine the distribution of that product, the best prices are not the highest prices, but the prices that encourage the largest volume of production and the largest volume of sales. The best wage rates for labor are not the highest wage rates, but the wage rates that permit full production, full employment and the largest sustained payrolls. The best profits, from the standpoint not only of industry but of labor, are not the lowest profits, but the profits that encourage most people to become employers or to provide more employment than before.

If we try to run the economy for the benefit of a single group or class, we shall injure or destroy all groups, including the members of the very class for whose benefit we have been trying to run it. We must run the economy for everybody. . . .

The Assault on Saving

From time immemorial proverbial wisdom has taught the virtues of saving, and warned against the consequences of prodigality and waste. This proverbial wisdom has reflected the common ethical as well as the merely prudential judgments of mankind. But there have always been squanderers, and there have apparently always been theorists to rationalize their squandering.

The classical economists, refuting the fallacies of their own day, showed that the saving policy that was in the best interests of the individual was also in the best interests of the nation. They showed that the rational saver, in making provision for his own future, was not hurting, but helping, the whole community. But today the ancient virtue of thrift, as well as its defense by the classical economists, is once more under attack, for allegedly new reasons, while the opposite doctrine of spending is in fashion.

In order to make the fundamental issue as clear as possible, we cannot do better, I think, than to start with the classic example used by Bastiat. Let us imagine two brothers, then, one a spendthrift and the other a prudent man, each of whom has inherited a sum to yield him an income of $50,000 a year. We shall disregard the income tax, and the question whether both brothers really ought to work for a living or give most of their income to charity, because such questions are irrelevant to our present purpose.

Alvin, then, the first brother, is a lavish spender. He spends not only by temperament, but on principle. He is a disciple (to go no further back) of Rodbertus, who declared in the middle of the nineteenth century that capitalists "must expend their income to the last penny in comforts and luxuries," for if they "determine to save . . . goods accumulate, and part of the workmen will have no work."[3] Alvin is always seen at the night clubs; he tips handsomely; he maintains a pretentious establishment, with plenty of servants; he has a couple of chauffeurs, and doesn't stint himself in the number of cars he owns; he keeps a racing stable; he runs a yacht; he travels; he loads his wife down with diamond bracelets and fur coats; he gives expensive and useless presents to his friends.

To do all this he has to dig into his capital. But what of it? If saving is a sin, dissaving must be a virtue; and in any case he is simply making up for the harm being done by the saving of his pinchpenny brother Benjamin.

It need hardly be said that Alvin is a great favorite with the hat check girls, the waiters, the restaurateurs, the furriers, the jewelers, the luxury establishments of all kinds. They regard him as a public benefactor. Certainly it is obvious to everyone that he is giving employment and spreading his money around.

Compared with him brother Benjamin is much less popular. He is seldom seen at the jewelers, the furriers or the night clubs, and he does not call the head waiters by their first names. Whereas Alvin spends not only the full $50,000 income each year but is digging into capital besides, Benjamin lives much more modestly and spends only about $25,000. Obviously, think the people who see only what hits them in the eye, he is providing less than half as much employment as Alvin, and the other $25,000 is as useless as if it did not exist.

But let us see what Benjamin actually does with this other

[3]Karl Rodbertus, *Overproduction and Crises* (1850), p. 51.

$25,000. He does not let it pile up in his pocketbook, his bureau drawers, or in his safe. He either deposits it in a bank or he invests it. If he puts it either into a commercial or a savings bank, the bank either lends it to going businesses on short term for working capital, or uses it to buy securities. In other words, Benjamin invests his money either directly or indirectly. But when money is invested it is used to buy or build capital goods —houses or office buildings or factories or ships or motor trucks or machines. Any one of these projects puts as much money into circulation and gives as much employment as the same amount of money spent directly on consumption.

"Saving," in short, in the modern world, is only another form of spending. The usual difference is that the money is turned over to someone else to spend on means to increase production. So far as giving employment is concerned, Benjamin's "saving" and spending combined give as much as Alvin's spending alone, and put as much money in circulation. The chief difference is that the employment provided for Alvin's spending can be seen by anyone with one eye; but it is necessary to look a little more carefully, and to think a moment, to recognize that every dollar of Benjamin's saving gives as much employment as every dollar that Alvin throws around.

A dozen years roll by. Alvin is broke. He is no longer seen in the night clubs and at the fashionable shops; and those whom he formerly patronized, when they speak of him, refer to him as something of a fool. He writes begging letters to Benjamin. And Benjamin, who continues about the same ratio of spending to saving, not only provides more jobs than ever, because his income, through investment, has grown, but through his investment he has helped to provide better-paying and more productive jobs. His capital wealth is greater also. Because of his investments, the national wealth and income are greater. He has, in brief, added to the nation's productive capacity; Alvin has not.

So many fallacies have grown up about saving in recent years that they cannot all be answered by our example of the two brothers. It is necessary to devote some further space to them. Many stem from confusions so elementary as to seem incredible, particularly when found in economic writers of wide repute. The word "saving," for example, is used sometimes to mean mere *hoarding* of money, and sometimes to mean *investment*, with no clear distinction, consistently maintained, between the two uses.

Mere hoarding of hand-to-hand money, if it takes place irrationally, causelessly, and on a large scale, is in most economic situations harmful. But this sort of hoarding is extremely rare. Something that looks like this, but should be carefully distinguished from it, often occurs *after* a down-turn in business has got under way. Consumptive spending and investment are then *both* contracted. Consumers reduce their buying. They do this partly, indeed, because they fear they may lose their jobs, and they wish to conserve their resources: they have contracted their buying not because they wish to consume less but because they wish to make sure that their power to consume will be extended over a longer period if they do lose their jobs.

But consumers reduce their buying for another reason. Prices of goods have probably fallen, and they fear a further fall. If they defer spending, they believe they will get more for their money. They do not wish to have their resources in goods that are falling in value, but in money which they expect (relatively) to rise in value.

The same expectation prevents them from investing. They have lost their confidence in the profitability of business; or at least they believe that if they wait a few months they can buy stocks or bonds cheaper. We may think of them either as refusing to hold goods that may fall in value on their hands, or as holding money itself for a rise.

It is a misnomer to call this temporary refusal to buy "saving." It does not spring from the same motives as normal saving. And it is a still more serious error to say that this sort of "saving" is the *cause* of depressions. It is, on the contrary, the *consequence* of depressions.

It is true that this refusal to buy may intensify and prolong a depression once begun. But it does not itself originate the

°depression. At times when there is capricious government intervention in business, and when business does not know what the government is going to do next, uncertainty is created. Profits are not reinvested. Firms and individuals allow cash balances to accumulate in their banks. They keep larger reserves against contingencies. This hoarding of cash may seem like the cause of a subsequent slowdown in business activity. The real cause, however, is the uncertainty brought about by the government policies. The larger cash balances of firms and individuals are merely one link in the chain of consequences from that uncertainty. To blame "excessive saving" for the business decline would be like blaming a fall in the price of apples not on a bumper crop but on the people who refuse to pay more for apples.

But when once people have decided to deride a practice or an institution, any argument against it, no matter how illogical, is considered good enough. It is said that the various consumers' goods industries are built on the expectation of a certain demand, and that if people take to saving they will disappoint this expectation and start a depression. This assertion rests primarily on the error we have already examined—that of forgetting that what is saved on consumers' goods is spent on capital goods, and that "saving" does not necessarily mean even a dollar's contraction in *total* spending. The only element of truth in the contention is that *any* change that is *sudden* may be unsettling. It would be just as unsettling if consumers suddenly switched their demand from one consumers' good to another. It would be even more unsettling if former savers suddenly switched their demand from capital goods to consumers' goods.

Still another objection is made against saving. It is said to be just downright silly. The Nineteenth Century is derided for its supposed inculcation of the doctrine that mankind through saving should go on making itself a larger and larger cake without ever eating the cake. This picture of the process is itself naive and childish. It can best be disposed of, perhaps, by putting before ourselves a somewhat more realistic picture of what actually takes place.

Let us picture to ourselves, then, a nation that collectively saves every year about 20 per cent of all it produces in that year. This figure greatly overstates the amount of net saving that has occurred historically in the United States,[4] but it is a round figure that is easily handled, and it gives the benefit of every doubt to those who believe that we have been "oversaving."

Now as a result of this annual saving and investment, the total annual production of the country will increase each year. (To isolate the problem we are ignoring for the moment booms, slumps, or other fluctuations.) Let us say that this annual increase in production is 2½ percentage points. (Percentage points are taken instead of a compounded percentage merely to simplify the arithmetic.) The picture that we get for an eleven-year period, say, would then run something like this in terms of index numbers:

Year	Total Production	Consumers' Goods Produced	Capital Goods Produced
First	100	80	20[*]
Second	102.5	82	20.5
Third	105	84	21
Fourth	107.5	86	21.5
Fifth	110	88	22
Sixth	112.5	90	22.5
Seventh	115	92	23
Eighth	117.5	94	23.5
Ninth	120	96	24
Tenth	122.5	98	24.5
Eleventh	125	100	25

[*]This of course assumes the process of saving and investment to have been already under way at the same rate.

[4]Historically 20 per cent would represent approximately the *gross* amount of the gross national product devoted each year to capital formation (excluding consumers' equipment). When allowance is made for capital consumption, however, *net* annual savings have been closer to 12 per cent. Cf. George Terborgh, *The Bogey of Economic Maturity* (1945). For 1960 gross savings (or gross investment) was officially estimated at 18 per cent of the national income.

The first thing to be noticed about this table is that total production increases each year *because of the saving,* and would not have increased without it. (It is possible no doubt to imagine that improvements and new inventions merely in *replaced* machinery and other capital goods of a value no greater than the old would increase the national productivity; but this increase would amount to very little and the argument in any case assumes enough *prior* investment to have made the existing machinery possible.) The saving has been used year after year to increase the quantity or improve the quality of existing machinery, and so to increase the nation's output of goods. There is, it is true (if that for some strange reason is considered an objection), a larger and larger "cake" each year. Each year, it is true, not *all* of the currently produced "cake" is consumed. But there is no irrational or cumulative consumer restraint. For each year a larger and larger cake is in fact consumed; until, at the end of eleven years (in our illustration), the annual consumer's cake alone is equal to the combined consumers' and producers' cakes of the first year. Moreover, the capital equipment, the ability to produce goods, is itself 25 per cent greater than in the first year.

Let us observe a few other points. The fact that 20 per cent of the national income goes each year for saving does not upset the consumers' goods industries in the least. If they sold only the 80 units they produced in the first year (and there were no rise in prices caused by unsatisfied demand) they would certainly not be foolish enough to build their production plans on the assumption that they were going to sell 100 units in the second year. The consumers' goods industries, in other words, are *already geared* to the assumption that the past situation in regard to the rate of savings will continue. Only an unexpected *sudden and substantial increase* in savings would unsettle them and leave them with unsold goods.

But the same unsettlement, as we have already observed, would be caused in the *capital* goods industries by a sudden and substantial *decrease* in savings. If money that would previously have been used for savings were thrown into the purchase of consumers' goods, it would not increase employment but merely lead to an increase in the price of consumption goods and to a decrease in the price of capital goods. Its first effect on net balance would be to force shifts in employment and temporarily to *decrease* employment by its effect on the capital goods industries. And its long-run effect would be to reduce production below the level that would otherwise have been achieved.

3

The enemies of saving are not through. They begin by drawing a distinction, which is proper enough, between "savings" and "investment." But then they start to talk as if the two were independent variables and as if it were merely an accident that they should ever equal each other. These writers paint a portentous picture. On the one side are savers automatically, pointlessly, stupidly continuing to save; on the other side are limited "investment opportunities" that cannot absorb this saving. The result, alas, is stagnation. The only solution, they declare, is for the government to expropriate these stupid and harmful savings and to invent its own projects, even if these are only useless ditches or pyramids, to use up the money and provide employment.

There is so much that is false in this picture and "solution" that we can here point only to some of the main fallacies. "Savings" can exceed "investment" only by the amounts that are actually *hoarded in cash.*[5] Few people nowadays, in a modern industrial community like the United States, hoard coins and bills in stockings or under mattresses. To the small extent that this may occur, it has already been reflected in the production plans of business and in the price level. It is not ordinarily

[5]Many of the differences between economists in the diverse views now expressed on this subject are merely the result of differences in definition. "Savings" and "investment" may be so defined as to be identical, and therefore necessarily equal. Here I am choosing to define "savings" in terms of money and "investment" in terms of goods. This corresponds roughly with the common use of the words, which is, however, not consistent.

even cumulative: dishoarding, as eccentric recluses die and their hoards are discovered and dissipated, probably offsets new hoarding. In fact, the whole amount involved is probably insignificant in its effect on business activity.

If money is kept either in savings banks or commercial banks, as we have already seen, the banks are eager to lend and invest it. They cannot afford to have idle funds. The only thing that will cause people generally to try to increase their holdings of cash, or that will cause banks to hold funds idle and lose the interest on them, is, as we have seen, either fear that prices of goods are going to fall or the fear of banks that they will be taking too great a risk with their principal. But this means that signs of a depression have already appeared, and have caused the hoarding, rather than that the hoarding has started the depression.

Apart from this negligible hoarding of cash, then (and even this exception might be thought of as a direct "investment" in money itself) "savings" and "investment" are brought into equilibrium with each other in the same way that the supply of and demand for any commodity are brought into equilibrium. For we may define "savings" and "investment" as constituting respectively the supply of and demand for new capital. And just as the supply of and demand for any other commodity are equalized by price, so the supply of and demand for capital are equalized by interest rates. The interest rate is merely the special name for the price of loaned capital. It is a price like any other.

This whole subject has been so appallingly confused in recent years by complicated sophistries and disastrous governmental policies based upon them that one almost despairs of getting back to common sense and sanity about it. There is a psychopathic fear of "excessive" interest rates. It is argued that if interest rates are too high it will not be profitable for industry to borrow and invest in new plants and machines. This argument has been so effective that governments everywhere in recent decades have pursued artificial "cheap money" policies. But the argument, in its concern with increasing the demand for capital, overlooks the effect of these policies on the supply of capital. It is one more example of the fallacy of looking at the effects of a policy only on one group and forgetting the effects on another.

If interest rates are artificially kept too low in relation to risks, there will be a reduction in both saving and lending. The cheap-money proponents believe that saving goes on automatically, regardless of the interest rate, because the sated rich have nothing else that they can do with their money. They do not stop to tell us at precisely what personal income level a man saves a fixed minimum amount regardless of the rate of interest or the risk at which he can lend it.

The fact is that, though the volume of saving of the very rich is doubtless affected much less proportionately than that of the moderately well-off by changes in the interest rate, practically everyone's saving is affected in some degree. To argue, on the basis of an extreme example, that the volume of real savings would not be reduced by a substantial reduction in the interest rate, is like arguing that the total production of sugar would not be reduced by a substantial fall of its price because the efficient, low-cost producers would still raise as much as before. The argument overlooks the marginal saver, and even, indeed, the great majority of savers.

The effect of keeping interest rates artificially low, in fact, is eventually the same as that of keeping any other price below the natural market. It increases demand and reduces supply. It increases the demand for capital and reduces the supply of real capital. It creates economic distortions. It is true, no doubt, that an artificial reduction in the interest rate encourages increased borrowing. It tends, in fact, to encourage highly speculative ventures that cannot continue except under the artificial conditions that gave them birth. On the supply side, the artificial reduction of interest rates discourages normal thrift, saving, and investment. It reduces the accumulation of capital. It slows down that increase in productivity, that "economic growth," that "progressives" profess to be so eager to promote.

The money rate can, indeed, be kept artificially low only

by continuous new injections of currency or bank credit in place of real savings. This can create the illusion of more capital just as the addition of water can create the illusion of more milk. But it is a policy of continuous inflation. It is obviously a process involving cumulative danger. The money rate will rise and a crisis will develop if the inflation is reversed, or merely brought to a halt, or even continued at a diminished rate. Cheap money policies, in short, eventually bring about far more violent oscillations in business than those they are designed to remedy or prevent.

If no effort is made to tamper with money rates through inflationary governmental policies, increased savings create their own demand by lowering interest rates in a natural manner. The greater supply of savings seeking investment forces savers to accept lower rates. But lower rates also mean that more enterprises can afford to borrow because their prospective profit on the new machines or plants they buy with the proceeds seems likely to exceed what they have to pay for the borrowed funds.

4

We come now to the last fallacy about saving with which I intend to deal. This is the frequent assumption that there is fixed limit to the amount of new capital that can be absorbed, or even that the limit of capital expansion has already been reached. It is incredible that such a view could prevail even among the ignorant, let alone that it could be held by any trained economist. Almost the whole wealth of the modern world, nearly everything that distinguishes it from the pre-industrial world of the seventeenth century, consists of its accumulated capital.

This capital is made up in part of many things that might better be called consumers' durable goods—automobiles, refrigerators, furniture, schools, colleges, churches, libraries, hospitals and above all private homes. Never in the history of the world has there been enough of these. Even if there were enough homes from a purely numerical point of view, *quali-*

tative improvements are possible and desirable without definite limit in all but the very best houses.

The second part of capital is what we may call capital proper. It consists of the tools of production, including everything from the crudest axe, knife or plow to the finest machine tool, the greatest electric generator or cyclotron, or the most wonderfully equipped factory. Here, too, quantitatively and especially qualitatively, there is no limit to the expansion that is possible and desirable. There will not be a "surplus" of capital until the most backward country is as well equipped technologically as the most advanced, until the most inefficient factory in America is brought abreast of the factory with the latest and finest equipment, and until the most modern tools of production have reached a point where human ingenuity is at a dead end, and can improve them no further. As long as any of these conditions remain unfulfilled, there will be indefinite room for more capital.

But how can the additional capital be "absorbed"? How can it be "paid for"? If it is set aside and saved, it will absorb itself and pay for itself. For producers invest in new capital goods—that is, they buy new and better and more ingenious tools—because these tools *reduce costs of production*. They either bring into existence goods that completely unaided hand labor could not bring into existence at all (and this now includes most of the goods around us—books, typewriters, automobiles, locomotives, suspension bridges); or they increase enormously the quantities in which these can be produced; or (and this is merely saying these things in a different way) they reduce *unit* costs of production. And as there is no assignable limit to the extent to which unit costs of production can be reduced—until everything can be produced at no cost at all—there is no assignable limit to the amount of new capital that can be absorbed.

The steady reduction of unit costs of production by the addition of new capital does either one of two things, or both. It reduces the costs of goods to consumers, and it increases the wages of the labor that uses the new equipment because it increases the productive power of that labor. Thus a new machine benefits both the people who work on it directly and the great body of consumers. In the case of consumers we may say either that it supplies them with more and better goods for the same money, or, what is the same thing, that it increases their real incomes. In the case of the workers who use the new machines it increases their real wages in a double way by increasing their money wages as well. A typical illustration is the automobile business. The American automobile industry pays the highest wages in the world, and among the very highest even in America. Yet (until recently) American motor car makers could undersell the rest of the world, because their unit cost was lower. And the secret was that the capital used in making American automobiles was greater per worker and per car than anywhere else in the world.

And yet there are people who think we have reached the end of this process,[6] and still others who think that even if we haven't, the world is foolish to go on saving and adding to its stock of capital.

It should not be difficult to decide, after our analysis, with whom the real folly lies.

THE LESSON RESTATED

Economics, as we have now seen again and again, is a science of recognizing *secondary* consequences. It is also a science of seeing *general* consequences. It is the science of tracing the effects of some proposed or existing policy not only on some *special* interest *in the short run,* but on the *general* interest *in the long run.*

This is the lesson that has been the special concern of this book. We stated it first in skeleton form, and then put flesh and skin on it through more than a score of practical applications.

But in the course of specific illustration we have found hints

[6]For a statistical refutation of this fallacy consult George Terborgh, *The Bogey of Economic Maturity* (1945). The "stagnationists" whom Dr. Terborgh was refuting have been succeeded by the Galbraithians with a similar doctrine.

of other general lessons; and we should do well to state these lessons to ourselves more clearly.

In seeing that economics is a science of tracing consequences, we must have become aware that, like logic and mathematics, it is a science of recognizing inevitable *implications*.

We may illustrate this by an elementary equation in algebra. Suppose we say that if $x = 5$ then $x + y = 12$. The "solution" to this equation is that y equals 7; but this is so precisely because the equation *tells* us in effect that y equals 7. It does not make that assertion directly, but it inevitably implies it.

What is true of this elementary equation is true of the most complicated and abstruse equations encountered in mathematics. *The answer already lies in the statement of the problem.* It must, it is true, be "worked out." The result, it is true, may sometimes come to the man who works out the equation as a stunning surprise. He may even have a sense of discovering something entirely new—a thrill like that of "some watcher of the skies, when a new planet swims into his ken." His sense of discovery may be justified by the theoretical or practical consequences of his answer. Yet the answer was already contained in the formulation of the problem. It was merely not recognized at once. For mathematics reminds us that inevitable implications are not necessarily obvious implications.

All this is equally true of economics. In this respect economics might be compared also to engineering. When an engineer has a problem, he must first determine all the facts bearing on that problem. If he designs a bridge to span two points, he must first know the exact distance between those two points, their precise topographical nature, the maximum load his bridge will be designed to carry, the tensile and compressive strength of the steel or other material of which the bridge is to be built, and the stresses and strains to which it may be subjected. Much of this factual research has already been done for him by others. His predecessors, also, have already evolved elaborate mathematical equations by which, knowing the strength of his materials and the stresses to which they will be subjected, he can determine the necessary diameter, shape, number and structure of his towers, cables and girders.

In the same way the economist, assigned a practical problem, must know both the essential facts of that problem and the valid deductions to be drawn from those facts. The deductive side of economics is no less important than the factual. One can say of it what Santayana says of logic (and what could be equally well said of mathematics), that it "traces the radiation of truth," so that "when one term of a logical system is known to describe a fact, the whole system attaching to that term becomes, as it were, incandescent."[7]

Now few people recognize the necessary implications of the economic statements they are constantly making. When they say that the way to economic salvation is to increase "credit," it is just as if they said that the way to economic salvation is to increase debt: these are different names for the same thing seen from opposite sides. When they say that the way to prosperity is to increase farm prices, it is like saying that the way to prosperity is to make food dearer for the city worker. When they say that the way to national wealth is to pay out governmental subsidies, they are in effect saying that the way to national wealth is to increase taxes. When they make it a main objective to increase exports, most of them do not realize that they necessarily make it a main objective ultimately to increase imports. When they say, under nearly all conditions, that the way to recovery is to increase wage rates, they have found only another way of saying that the way to recovery is to increase costs of production.

It does not necessarily follow, because each of these propositions, like a coin, has its reverse side, or because the equivalent proposition, or the other name for the remedy, sounds much less attractive, that the original proposal is under all conditions unsound. There may be times when an increase in debt is a minor consideration as against the gains achieved with the

[7]George Santayana, *The Realm of Truth* (1938), p. 16.

borrowed funds; when a government subsidy is unavoidable to achieve a certain military purpose; when a given industry can afford an increase in production costs, and so on. But we ought to make sure in each case that both sides of the coin have been considered, that all the implications of a proposal have been studied. And this is seldom done.

2

The analysis of our illustrations has taught us another incidental lesson. This is that, when we study the effects of various proposals, not merely on special groups in the short run, but on all groups in the long run, the conclusions we arrive at usually correspond with those of unsophisticated common sense. It would not occur to anyone unacquainted with the prevailing economic half-literacy that it is good to have windows broken and cities destroyed; that it is anything but waste to create needless public projects; that it is dangerous to let idle hordes of men return to work; that machines which increase the production of wealth and economize human effort are to be dreaded; that obstructions to free production and free consumption increase wealth; that a nation grows richer by forcing other nations to take its goods for less than they cost to produce; that saving is stupid or wicked and that squandering brings prosperity.

"What is prudence in the conduct of every private family," said Adam Smith's strong common sense in reply to the sophists of his time, "can scarce be folly in that of a great kingdom." But lesser men get lost in complications. They do not re-examine their reasoning even when they emerge with conclusions that are palpably absurd. The reader, depending upon his own beliefs, may or may not accept the aphorism of Bacon that "A little philosophy inclineth man's mind to atheism, but depth in philosophy bringeth men's minds about to religion." It is certainly true, however, that a little economics can easily lead to the paradoxical and preposterous conclusions we have just rehearsed, but that depth in economics brings men back to common sense. For depth in economics consists in looking for all the consequences of a policy instead of merely resting one's gaze on those immediately visible.

3

In the course of our study, also, we have rediscovered an old friend. He is the Forgotten Man of William Graham Sumner. The reader will remember that in Sumner's essay, which appeared in 1883:

> As soon as A observes something which seems to him to be wrong, from which X is suffering. A talks it over with B, and A and B then propose to get a law passed to remedy the evil and help X. Their law always proposes to determine what C shall do for X or, in the better case, what A, B and C shall do for X. . . . What I want to do is to look up C. . . . I call him the Forgotten Man. . . . He is the man who never is thought of. He is the victim of the reformer, social speculator and philanthropist, and I hope to show you before I get through that he deserves your notice both for his character and for the many burdens which are laid upon him.

It is an historic irony that when this phrase, the Forgotten Man, was revived in the nineteen thirties, it was applied, not to C, but to X; and C, who was then being asked to support still more X's, was more completely forgotten than ever. It is C, the Forgotten Man, who is always called upon to stanch the politician's bleeding heart by paying for his vicarious generosity.

4

Our study of our lesson would not be complete if, before we took leave of it, we neglected to observe that the fundamental fallacy with which we have been concerned arises not accidentally but systematically. It is an almost inevitable result, in fact, of the division of labor.

In a primitive community, or among pioneers, before the division of labor has arisen, a man works solely for himself or his immediate family. What he consumes is identical with what he produces. There is always a direct and immediate connection between his output and his satisfactions.

But when an elaborate and minute division of labor has set in, this direct and immediate connection ceases to exist. I do not make all the things I consume but, perhaps, only one of them. With the income I derive from making this one commodity, or rendering this one service, I buy all the rest. I wish the price of everything I buy to be low, but it is in my interest for the price of the commodity or services that I have to sell to be high. Therefore, though I wish to see abundance in everything else, it is in my interest for scarcity to exist in the very thing that it is my business to supply. The greater the scarcity, compared to everything else, in this one thing that I supply, the higher will be the reward that I can get for my efforts.

This does not necessarily mean that I will restrict my own efforts or my own output. In fact, if I am only one of a substantial number of people supplying that commodity or service, and if free competition exists in my line, this individual restriction will not pay me. On the contrary, if I am a grower of wheat, say, I want my particular crop to be as large as possible. But if I am concerned only with my own material welfare, and have no humanitarian scruples, I want the output of all *other* wheat growers to be as *low* as possible; for I want scarcity in wheat (and in any foodstuff that can be substituted for it) so that my particular crop may command the highest possible price.

Ordinarily these selfish feelings would have no effect on the total production of wheat. Wherever competition exists, in fact, each producer is compelled to put forth his utmost efforts to raise the highest possible crop on his own land. In this way the forces of self-interest (which, for good or evil, are more persistently powerful than those of altruism) are harnessed to maximum output.

But if it is possible for wheat growers or any other group of producers to combine to eliminate competition, and if the government permits or encourages such a course, the situation changes. The wheat growers may be able to persuade the national government—or, better, a world organization—to force all of them to reduce pro rata the acreage planted to wheat. In this way they will bring about a shortage and raise the price of wheat; and if the rise in the price per bushel is proportionately greater, as it well may be, than the reduction in output, then the wheat growers as a whole will be better off. They will get more money; they will be able to buy more of everything else. Everybody else, it is true, will be worse off; because, other things equal, everyone else will have to give more of what he produces to get less of what the wheat grower produces. So the nation as a whole will be just that much poorer. It will be poorer by the amount of wheat that has not been grown. But those who look only at the wheat farmers will see a gain, and miss the more than offsetting loss.

And this applies in every other line. If because of unusual weather conditions there is a sudden increase in the crop of oranges, all the consumers will benefit. The world will be richer by that many more oranges. Oranges will be cheaper. But that very fact may make the orange growers as a group poorer than before, unless the greater supply of oranges compensates or more than compensates for the lower price. Certainly if under such conditions my particular crop of oranges is no larger than usual, then I am certain to lose by the lower price brought about by general plenty.

And what applies to changes in supply applies to changes in demand, whether brought about by new inventions and discoveries or by changes in taste. A new cotton-picking machine, though it may reduce the cost of cotton underwear and shirts to everyone, and increase the general wealth, will mean the employment of fewer cotton pickers. A new textile machine, weaving a better cloth at a faster rate, will make thousands of old machines obsolete, and wipe out part of the capital value invested in them, so making poorer the owners of those machines. The development of nuclear power, though it could confer unimaginable blessings on mankind, is something that is dreaded by the owners of coal mines and oil wells.

Just as there is no technical improvement that would not hurt someone, so there is no change in public taste or morals, even for the better, that would not hurt someone. An increase in sobriety would put thousands of bartenders out of business. A decline in gambling would force croupiers and racing touts to seek more productive occupations. A growth of male chastity would ruin the oldest profession in the world.

But it is not merely those who deliberately pander to men's vices who would be hurt by a sudden improvement in public morals. Among those who would be hurt most are precisely those whose business it is to improve those morals. Preachers would have less to complain about; reformers would lose their causes: the demand for their services and contributions for their support would decline. If there were no criminals we should need fewer lawyers, judges and firemen, and no jailers, no locksmiths, and (except for such services as untangling traffic snarls) even no policemen.

Under a system of division of labor, in short, it is difficult to think of a greater fulfillment of any human need which would not, at least temporarily, hurt some of the people who have made investments or painfully acquired skill to meet that precise need. If progress were completely even all around the circle, this antagonism between the interests of the whole community and of the specialized group would not, if it were noticed at all, present any serious problem. If in the same year as the world wheat crop increased, my own crop increased in the same proportion; if the crop of oranges and all other agricultural products increased correspondingly, and if the output of all industrial goods also rose and their unit cost of production fell to correspond, then I as a wheat grower would not suffer because the output of wheat had increased. The price that I got for a bushel of wheat might decline. The total sum that I realized from my larger output might decline. But if I could also because of increased supplies buy the output of everyone else cheaper, then I should have no real cause to complain. If the price of everything else dropped in exactly the same ratio as the decline in the price of my wheat, I should be better off, in fact, exactly in proportion to my increased total crop; and everyone else, likewise, would benefit proportionately from the increased supplies of all goods and services.

But economic progress never has taken place and probably never will take place in this completely uniform way. Advance occurs now in this branch of production and now in that. And if there is a sudden increase in the supply of the thing I help to produce, or if a new invention or discovery makes what I produce no longer necessary, then the gain to the world is a tragedy to me and to the productive group to which I belong.

Now it is often not the diffused gain of the increased supply or new discovery that most forcibly strikes even the disinterested observer, but the concentrated loss. The fact that there is more and cheaper coffee for everyone is lost sight of; what is seen is merely that some coffee growers cannot make a living at the lower price. The increased output of shoes at lower cost by the new machine is forgotten; what is seen is a group of men and women thrown out of work. It is altogether proper—it is, in fact, essential to a full understanding of the problem—that the plight of these groups be recognized, that they be dealt with sympathetically, and that we try to see whether some of the gains from this specialized progress cannot be used to help the victims find a productive role elsewhere.

But the solution is never to reduce supplies arbitrarily, to prevent further inventions or discoveries, or to support people for continuing to perform a service that has lost its value. Yet this is what the world has repeatedly sought to do by protective tariffs, by the destruction of machinery, by the burning of coffee, by a thousand restriction schemes. This is the insane doctrine of wealth through scarcity.

It is a doctrine that may always be privately true, unfortunately, for any particular group of producers considered in isolation—if they can make scarce the one thing they have to sell while keeping abundant all the things they have to buy. But it is a doctrine that is always publicly false. It can never be applied all around the circle. For its application would mean economic suicide.

And this is our lesson in its most generalized form. For many things that seem to be true when we concentrate on a single economic group are seen to be illusions when the interests of everyone, as consumer no less than as producer, are considered.

To see the problem as a whole, and not in fragments: that is the goal of economic science.

A NOTE ON BOOKS

Those who desire to read further in economics should turn next to some work of intermediate length. A good work of this class, which was designed as an introductory college-economic textbook, is *An Introduction to Economics* by John V. Van Sickle and Benjamin Rogge (746 pages). An even simpler book, written as a text for high school students, but an ideal elementary introduction to the subject, is *Understanding Our Free Economy*, by F. R. Fairchild and T. J. Shelly (589 pages).

After reading one of these volumes the student who aims at thoroughness will go on to some advanced work. *Human Action*, by Ludwig von Mises (889 pages), extends the logical unity and precision of economics beyond any other work. Not to be missed is Philip Wicksteed's *The Common Sense of Political Economy* (two volumes, 871 pages), as remarkable for the ease and lucidity of its style as for the penetration and power of its reasoning. Still a third volume in this distinguished class is Frank H. Knight's *Risk, Uncertainty and Profit* (381 pages).

Short books which discuss special economic subjects in a simple way are *Planning for Freedom*, by Ludwig von Mises, *The Theory of Collective Bargaining*, by W. H. Hutt, and *Why Wages Rise*, by F. A. Harper. For those who wish a simple explanation of inflation the present author has written *What You Should Know About Inflation*. There is an excellent little book on the same subject by Melchior Palyi, *A Primer on Inflation*.

Among recent works which discuss current ideologies and developments from a point of view similar to that of the present volume are the present author's *The Failure of the "New Economics": An Analysis of the Keynesian Fallacies;* F. A. Hayek,

The Road to Serfdom, and the same author's monumental *Constitution of Liberty;* Lionel Robbins, *Economic Planning and International Order;* Wilhelm Röpke, *A Humane Economy;* and Ludwig von Mises, *Planned Chaos.* Mises' *Socialism* is the most thorough and devastating critique of collectivist doctrines ever written.

The reader should not overlook, finally, Frédéric Bastiat's classic *Economic Sophisms,* and particularly his essay on *What Is Seen and What Is Not Seen.* Under the title *The Free Man's Library,* the present author has compiled a descriptive and critical bibliography of 550 outstanding books on the philosophy of individualism, free trade, free enterprise, free markets, and individual liberty.

Those who are interested in working through the economic classics might find it most profitable to do this in the reverse of their historical order. Presented in this order, the chief works to be consulted, with the dates of their first editions, are: John Bates Clark, *The Distribution of Wealth,* 1899; Alfred Marshall, *Principles of Economics,* 1890; Eugen von Böhm-Bawerk, *The Positive Theory of Capital,* 1888; Karl Menger, *Principles of Economics,* 1871; W. Stanley Jevons, *The Theory of Political Economy,* 1871; John Stuart Mill, *Principles of Political Economy,* 1848; David Ricardo, *Principles of Political Economy and Taxation,* 1817; and Adam Smith, *The Wealth of Nations,* 1776.

Economics broadens out in a hundred directions. Whole libraries have been written on specialized fields alone, such as money and banking, foreign trade and foreign exchange, taxation and public finance, government control, capitalism and socialism, wages and labor relations, interest and capital, agricultural economics, rent, prices, profits, markets, competition and monopoly, value and utility, statistics, business cycles, wealth and poverty, social insurance, housing, public utilities, mathematical economics, studies of special industries and of economic history. But no one will ever properly understand any of these specialized fields unless he has first of all acquired a firm grasp of basic economic principles and the complex interrelationship of all economic factors and forces. When he has done this by his reading in general economics, he can be trusted to find the right books in his special field of interest.

8 Freedom and the Planned Economy

Max Eastman

It is the bureaucratic socializers—if I may devise that label for the champions of a lawyer-manager-politician-intellectual revolution—who constitute a real and subtle threat to America's democracy. It is their dream that is moving into focus as that of Lenin grows dim.

The assumption common to these two dreams is that society can be made more free and equal, and incidentally more orderly and prosperous, by a state apparatus which takes charge of the economy, and runs it according to a plan. And this assumption, though alluringly plausible, does not happen to be true. A state apparatus which plans and runs the business of a country must have the authority of a business executive. And that is the authority to tell all those active in the business where to go and what to do, and if they are insubordinate put them out. It must be an authoritarian state apparatus. It may not want to be, but the economy will go haywire if it is not.

From Max Eastman, *Reflections on the Failure of Socialism* (New York: Devin-Adair, 1955), Chapter 1, pp. 23–28; Chapter 2, pp. 29–35; Chapter 5, pp. 57–67. Copyright © 1955 by Max Eastman. Reprinted by permission of the Devin-Adair Co.

That much was foreseen by many cool-headed wise men during the hundred-odd years since the idea of a "socialized" economy was broached. But the world was young, and the young can not be told—they have to learn by experience. (I was among the least willing to be told.) However, the actual experience of state-run economies, popping up one after another in the last thirty-five years, should be enough, it seems to me, to bring home this simple fact to the most exuberant. It is a fact which you can hardly fail to realize if you watch the operation of any big factory, or bank, or department store, or any place of business where a large number of people are at work. There has to be a boss, and his authority within the business has to be recognized, and when not recognized, enforced.

Moreover, if the business is vast and complex, his authority has to be continuous. You cannot lift him out of his chair every little while, tear up his plans, and stick in somebody else with a different idea of what should be done or how it should be done. The very concept of a plan implies continuity of control. Thus the idea that a periodic election of the boss and managing personnel is consistent with a planned national economy is lacking both in logic and imagination—you need only define the word "plan," or present a plan to your mind's eye. The thing is conceivable perhaps in a small enterprise, but where would you be if the nation's entire wealth production and distribution were a single business? Even supposing elections could be genuine when those in office controlled all the jobs in the country. Suppose they were genuine—you might as well explode a bomb under the economy as hold an election.

The phony elections in totalitarian countries, the ballots with only one party and one list of candidates, are not the mere tricks of a cynical dictator—they are intrinsic to a state-planned economy. Either phony elections or no elections at all—that is what thoroughgoing socialism will mean, no matter who brings it in— hard-headed Bolsheviks, soft-headed Social Democrats, or genteel liberals. . . . How could you unseat an administration with every enterprise and every wage and salary in the country in its direct control? Not only private self-interest would prevent it, and that would be a force like gravitation, but public prudence also—patriotism! "Don't change horses in midstream," we say. But we'd be in midstream all the time with the entire livelihood of the nation dependent upon an unfulfilled plan in the hands of those in office. "Don't rock the boat" would be the eternal slogan, the gist of political morals. That these morals would have to be enforced by the criminal law is as certain as that mankind is man. . . .

A false and undeliberated conception of what man is lies at the bottom, I think, of the whole bubble-castle of socialist theory. Although few seem to realize it, Marxism rests on the romantic notion of Rousseau that nature endows men with the qualities necessary to a free, equal, fraternal, family-like living together, and our sole problem is to fix up the external conditions. All Marx did about this with his dialectic philosophy was to change the tenses in the romance: Nature *will* endow men with these qualities *as soon as* the conditions are fixed up. Because of his stress upon economic conditions, Marx is commonly credited with the cynical opinion that economic self-interest is dominant in human nature. Marx was far from a cynic about human nature. He believed that human nature is a function of the economic conditions, completely variable and capable of operating, once these conditions are "ripe," on the divinely rational and benign principle: "From each according to his abilities, to each according to his needs." It was to protect this optimistic dogma about human nature that the Stalin government felt obliged to stamp out the true science of genetics. According to that science, traits acquired during the lifetime of an organism are not appreciably transmitted in heredity. Only by selective breeding, whether artificial or natural, can profound changes be made in the nature of any species. While men's acquired characters may, and undoubtedly do, change with changing economic (and other) conditions, the underlying traits of human nature remain the same. There is little doubt that the Marxian bigots in the Kremlin were moved by this consideration in liquidating the world-famous geneticist, Avilov, and supporting the charlatan, Lysenko, in popularizing a belief in the wholesale heredity of acquired characteristics. Without such belief, the whole Marxian myth that economic evolution will bring us to the millennium falls to the ground.*

Once we have abandoned this myth, we can give heed to the real contribution of Karl Marx: his sense of the great part played by economic relations in determining political and cultural ways of life. His own sagacity will conduct us, then, to a genuinely scientific study of the economic foundations of political freedom. This study has been made by various economists of the "neo-liberal" school—Wilhelm Roepke, F. A. Hayek, Ludwig von Mises and others. Taking human nature as it functions in average life, they have shown that the competitive market and the price system are the basis of whatever real political freedom exists, or can be imagined to exist, where there is an elaborate division of labor.

I am not an economist, but I have watched with some care the destinies of these men's earnest writings. There has been no answer, and I don't see how there can be an answer, to their assertion that mankind is confronted with a choice between two and only two business systems—a choice which involves the fate of democratic civilization. We can choose a system in which the amount and kind of goods produced is determined by the *impersonal* mechanism of the market, issuing its decrees in the form of fluctuating prices. Or we can choose a system in which this is determined by commands issuing from a *personal* authority backed by armed force. You cannot dodge this issue by talking about a "mixed economy." The economy is inevitably mixed; nobody in his right mind proposes a total abandonment of government enterprise. You can not dodge it by insisting the state must *regulate* the market or *intervene* in its operations. If carefully defined, that statement is obvious. The question is whether the economy is mixed to the point of destroying the es-

---

*I pointed out this vital conflict between Marxism and modern science in my early book *Marx and Lenin, the Science of Revolution* in 1925, anticipating by twenty years—although far indeed from expecting—the physical liquidation of the scientists. The passage will be found unchanged in *Marxism Is It Science* (pp. 267–269).

The question of Marxism and the present conception of man is more fully discussed in my last chapter: "Socialism and Human Nature."

sential directing function of the market, whether the regulations are a substitute for the market or a framework within which it shall operate, whether intervention is compatible or incompatible with the general control of the economy by the whole people as consumers of goods. That is the difference between collectivism and the market economy. That is the alternative with which mankind is confronted. You can not dodge it, or pray it away, or hide it from yourself with smokescreens of ideas. It is a fact, not an idea. We have to choose. And the choice is between freedom and tyranny.

There is no conflict between freedom so conditioned and a humane regard on the part of the state for people who fail utterly in the competitive struggle. No one need starve, no one need be destitute, in order to preserve the sovereignty of the market. The principle of collective responsibility for those actually in want can be maintained without violating the principle of competition. But we need no longer deceive ourselves that liberty in a human world is compatible with economic equality. Liberty means absence of external restraint. To democrats, it meant absence of arbitrary governmental restraint, and was to a degree synonymous with equality before the law. But to the Socialists it meant absence of all governmental restraint, and also of those more subtle restraints imposed by a minority who own the land and the wealth-producing machinery. Who, in the absence of these restraints, is going to impose equality? What is to bring it about that men, once granted leave to behave as they please, will behave as though the whole human race were a loving family? We have to make up our minds, if we are going to defend this free world against an oncreeping totalitarian state control, whether, in fact, our primary interest is in freedom from state control, or in an attempt at economic equality enforced by a controlling state. We have to accept such inequalities as are presumed by, and result from, economic competition.

Equality apart, however, there is something vitally democratic, as well as impersonal, in the control exercised by the market. When a man buys something on a free market, he is casting his vote as a citizen of the national economy. He is making a choice which, by influencing prices, will enter into the decision as to how, and toward what ends, the economy shall be conducted. His choice may be outweighed by others who buy more; that is inevitably true. But in placing the major economic decisions in the hands of the whole people as consumers, recording these decisions automatically through the mechanism of price, the market makes freedom possible in a complex industrial society. It is the only thing that makes it possible.

Strangely enough Marx himself as a historian was the first to perceive this. Looking backward, he observed that all our freedoms had evolved together with, and in dependence upon, private capitalism with its free competitive market. Had he been a man of science instead of a mystic believer in the inevitability of a millennium, he might have guessed at what is so clearly obvious now: that this dependence of other freedoms upon the free market extends into the future also. It is a brief step indeed from Marxism—once the Hegelian wishful thinking is weeded out of it—to such a passage as this from Wilhelm Roepke:

> It is hardly forgivable naiveté to believe that a state can be all-powerful in the economic sphere without also being autocratic in the political and intellectual domain and vice versa. . . . It therefore makes no sense to reject collectivism politically, if one does not at the same time propose a decidedly non-socialist solution of the problems of economic and social reform. If we are not in earnest with this relentless logic, we have vainly gone through a unique and costly historical object-lesson.

The failure of the Social Democrats, and still more in America of the "left" liberals, to learn this lesson is now a major threat to freedom in the western world.* I am not sure it is always a

---

*Sadly enough, the Social Democrats, though trained in "economic interpretation," are least of all able to learn this lesson. Even those emerging from their imprisonment in Marxian dogma take the wrong road. They reject what was sagacious and scientific about the master, his insistence on the importance of economic relations, and cling to his wishful dream, contradicted by all we now know about economics, of freedom under the planning state. Instead of going forward from their pseudo-scientific socialism to an expert, modern attempt to create a better society, they shrink back, clinging to a word and an emotion, into an attitude hardly distinguishable from that of the utopian socialists whom Marx superseded.

failure to learn. I think a good number of these Fabians and crypto-socialists—a new breed to which political expediency under the New Deal gave rise—have a suspicion that freedom will go down the drain. Travers Clement, one of the old-timers, has explicitly proposed hauling down the watchwords: "Liberty, Equality, Fraternity," and running up: "Cradle-to-grave Security. Full Employment and Sixty Million Jobs."* It was no accident of old age that both Sidney and Beatrice Webb and their brilliant colleague and co-evangelist in Fabian socialism, Bernard Shaw, ended their careers as loyal defenders of the most complete and ruthless tyranny mankind has known.

However, our American creepers toward socialism are most of them less bold and forthright than that. Often they don't even know where they are creeping. They see with the tail of an eye that political liberty is incompatible with economic subjection, but they refuse to look straight in the face of this fact. They refuse to learn the lesson that the history of these last thirty years has been spread out on the table, it almost seems, to teach them. They remain indecisive, equivocal—lured by the idea of security, orderly production, and universal welfare under a planning state, yet not quite ready to renounce in behalf of it those rights and liberties of the individual which stand or fall with the free market economy.

An ironical truth is that these socializers will not achieve security, orderly production, or the prosperity that makes universal welfare possible, by sacrificing freedom. They will be duped and defeated on all fronts. For me that also is proven by the history of the last three decades. But that is not the theme of this chapter.

Its theme is that our progress in democracy is endangered by democratic enthusiasts who imagine that they can preserve freedom politically while hacking away at its economic foundations. More even than the fellow travelers with their vicarious flair for violent revolution, or the Communists with their courageous belief in it, these piously aspiring reformers are undermining our

*In the *New Leader* for August 4, 1945, answering my argument that democratic socialism is impossible.

hopes. Yearning to do good and obsessed by the power of the state to do it, relieved by this power of their age-old feeling of futility, they are destroying in the name of social welfare the foundations of freedom.

Arthur Koestler warned us some years ago against the "men of good will with strong frustrations and feeble brains, the wishful thinkers and idealistic moral cowards, the fellow-travelers of the death train." We have accepted his warning. At least we have learned the meaning of the word fellow traveler, and are no longer falling in droves for these unlovely accomplices of the tyrant. We must arm our minds now against the less obvious, the more strong and plausible and patriotic enemies of freedom, the advocates of a state-planned economy. They are not on the train and have no thought of getting on, but they are laying the tracks along which another death train will travel. . . .

There occurred no change in my feeling on this subject when I abandoned the idea of proletarian revolution. I still think the worst enemy of human hope is not brute facts, but men of brains who will not face them. For that reason I had no high expectations of the liberal intelligentsia when it came to acknowledging that the "revolution of our times," as so far conceived and conducted, is, has been, and will be, a failure. I never dreamed, however, that they could sink to the depths of maudlin self-deception and perfectly abject treason to truth, freedom, justice, and mercy that many of them have reached in regard to the Russian debacle. That has indeed profoundly, and more than any other shock, whether emotional or intellectual, disabused me of the dream of liberty under a socialist state. If these supposedly elevated and detached minds, free of any dread, of any pressure, of any compulsion to choose except between truth and their own mental comfort, can not recognize absolute horror, the absolute degradation of man, the end of science, art, law, human aspiration, and civilized morals, when these arrive in a far country, what will they be worth when the pressure is put upon them at home? They will be worth nothing except to those dark powers which will most certainly undertake to convert state-owned property into an instrument of exploitation beside which the reign of private capital will seem to have been, in truth, a golden age of freedom and equality for all.

To that much emotional shock I plead guilty. But I do not want to leave it there. Many of these delinquent liberals were my friends in past years despite our differences, and I find myself continually puzzling over the problem of their motivation. Why have they betrayed themselves? Why do they promote the interests of a regime under which even they, traitors to democracy though they are, would be shot for half-heartedness, or permitted to die of starvation in a slave camp for having in the past believed, or thought they believed, in freedom?

Up to the Bolshevik Revolution it is not hard to understand what happened to them. The old liberal movement grew out of the struggle against absolutism and feudal oppression. The freedom fought for in that struggle included free trade as a matter of course. But free trade and the industrial revolution soon raised the general wealth so high that idealists began to worry about the living conditions of the poor. Those living conditions were not, in the general average, worse than they had been. The change was in the attitude of civic-minded people toward them. It is not too much to say, as the canny Norwegian, Trygve Hoff, does, that a social conscience was born of this great rise in wealth production. The first sensible step toward bettering the general condition of the poor would obviously have been to increase still more the production of wealth. Then if the pangs of the social conscience had kept pace with this increase all might have been well. What these pangs did was to run way ahead of the increase in wealth. People were attacking the businessman and demanding a better distribution of profits long before such distribution would have made any appreciable difference in the general condition of the poor. As wealth production increased, this state of pained conscience among liberals—themselves businessmen often enough—increased much faster. So fast that their zeal for liberty was gradually replaced by a zeal for a more equal distribution of wealth. Their liberalism became almost indistinguishable from humanitarianism. And this change of mind and mood among liberals was certainly not retarded by Marx's doctrinaire announcement that their interest in freedom had been a fake all along: capitalist profits, not human rights, had been the goal of their struggle against absolutism; their great revolution had been "bourgeois," not democratic.

They still talked the language of liberty—so also did Marx— but their dominant drive was toward a more even-handed distribution of the unheard-of wealth that, under a regime dominated by the idea of liberty, had been piling up. The culmination of this change was, in England, the decline of the Liberal party, the seeping away of its membership into the Labour party with its promise to expropriate the capitalists, and in the United States the transformation of the old liberal press into organs of the New Deal—the government of settlement workers become militant, not in the cause of freedom, but in the battle against "economic royalists." The whole development is summed up in the contrast between Benjamin Franklin's: "Those who would give up essential liberty to purchase a little temporary safety deserve neither liberty nor safety," and Harold Laski's: "Those who know the normal life of the poor . . . will realize well enough that, without economic security, liberty is not worth having."

This much, then, must be said in defense of the delinquent liberals. The edge of their passion for freedom had been growing blunter for decades before the rise of totalitarianism put their loyalties to a test. It is not only freedom that they betray, however, in apologizing for the Soviet tyranny, or pussyfooting about it, or blackening America so savagely that Russia shines in unspoken contrast. They are betraying civilization itself. They are lending a hand in the destruction of its basic values, promoting a return march in every phase of human progress. Reinstitution of slavery, revival of torture, star chamber proceedings, execution without trial, disruption of families, deportation of nations, massacre of communities, corruption of science, art, philosophy, history, tearing down of the standards of truth, justice, mercy, the dignity and the rights of man—even his right to martyrdom—everything that had been won in the long struggle up from savagery and barbarism. How shall I account for this depraved behavior—for that is how it appears to me—on the part of friends and colleagues who were once dedicated to an effort to make society more just and merciful, more truth-perceiving, more "free and equal" than it was?

They shield themselves from facts, I suppose, by a biased selection of the books and newspapers to read. Many violent conflicts of opinion come down to a difference in reading matter. And this is especially so in the case of Soviet communism, for it has been put over with a campaign of All-Russian and International Lying whose extent, skill, efficiency, and consecration is almost harder to believe in than the truth it conceals. Indeed the distinction between truth and the exact fabrications handed down for propagation by the heads of the world party in the Kremlin has disappeared very largely from the minds of its members. Until one has grasped this phenomenon in its full proportions, and learned to distinguish the sincere truth-teller from the sincere lie-teller, it is not easy to be hard-headed about Soviet communism. That too may be advanced in defense of the delinquent liberals—they are the victims of a swindle which nothing in past history had prepared them to detect.

A great many of them, however, are not deceived, but are swallowing the horrors of life under the Soviets with open eyes and a kind of staring gulp that is more like madness than a mistake. In the effort with their soft heads to be hard they have gone out of the world of reasoned discussion altogether. Again I will take the late Harold Laski as an example. No anti-communist has more candidly and crushingly described the blotting out of civilized values and all free ways of life by the Russian Soviet state than he did; and yet no pro-communist has more vigorously defended that state, or brought more intellectual authority to its support. There must be, I suppose, in all the delinquent liberals, a repressed conflict between the impulse to speak those truths that are important to man's civilized survival and the more compelling thirst for a comfortable opinion. In Laski, because of some strange and perhaps bumptious quirk in his nature, this conflict was not repressed, but was naively or insolently blared forth. I met him for the last time in a debate on the "Town Meeting of the Air" September 19, 1946. Knowing about this conflict in his soul, I brought with me, typed out in condensed form, the passage from his *Reflections on the Revolution of Our Time* in which he most eloquently describes the horrors of life under the Soviet communist regime.

In the course of the debate, I made a remark about the crimes of the Russian Communists, and Laski replied: "It's no part of my case that Russia hasn't committed crime and been guilty of grave blunders and committed inconceivable follies; so has the United States, and so has Great Britain."

In answer, I said: "I'm going to read you from Laski's own book some of the crimes that have been committed in the Soviet Union, and you see if any of them have been committed in the United States or England." I then read this passage from Laski's book, or as much of it as I could crowd into the time granted me.

"Despite the pledges of the Constitution of 1936, there is no freedom of speech, except for Stalin's adherents, no freedom of the press or assembly. Everyone knows that the elections are a farce; no candidatures are possible which reject the party line, and even the ballot-papers for them read like a hymn to Stalin. Freedom of movement is gravely restricted. Contact with foreigners is looked upon with suspicion. There is arbitrary arrest; there is long imprisonment and execution without trial. Citizens can not travel abroad without the permission of the government. Most political offences are tried in secret; there is no writ of *habeas corpus,* no right to subpoena witnesses, no right to a professional defence. The death-penalty may be imposed for injury to, or theft of, collective property; and even 'teasing, mocking, or persecuting' a shock-worker may, under Article 58 of the Criminal Code become 'wrecking,' and so punishable with death."

The moderator interrupted me and asked Laski: "Do you care to comment?" And Laski, spreading his hands in a gesture which my friends in the audience described as sickly, answered: "No."

Laski did have, of course, a scheme for convincing himself that in a nation so chained and trampled by power-lustful and unbridled masters of the state, the Revolution of Our Time is bringing to birth a new age of freedom and humane reform. He accomplished it by opposing the words "economic" and "political" as though they designated things happening on different planets. While the above listed horrors filled the sphere called politics, the sphere called economics, he asked us to believe, was brimming with sweetness and light. I quote, also with condensation, from the same book:

"In the narrow economic sphere, there is a more genuine basis for economic freedom for the masses in the Soviet Union than they have elsewhere previously enjoyed. . . . Millions, in every field and factory, help to make the conditions under which they live. There are the effective beginnings of constitutional government in industry. The rules of an enterprise are not made at the discretion of an employer who owns it, but are genuinely the outcome of a real discussion in which men and management participate. . . . Care for the health, sanitation, and safety of the workers in field and factory has been established at a pace which would have been unthinkable in any capitalist society. . . . The administration of justice (political offences apart) . . . is on a level superior to that of most other countries. . . . Bench and bar alike have a more active and sustained interest in the improvement of legal procedure than anyone has displayed in Europe since Jeremy Bentham."

It is obvious that no man thinking about concrete facts could put these two passages into the same book and chapter. How can it be that in a country where "there is no right of *habeas corpus,* no right to subpoena witnesses, no right to a professional defence," nevertheless "the administration of justice (political offences apart) is on a level superior to that of most other countries"? What jocular Deity brings it about that while death may be the penalty for teasing another worker, nevertheless "care for the health, safety and sanitation of the workers" outruns all previous norms? How does it come to pass that where "elections are a farce, freedom of movement is restricted, there is arbitrary arrest, imprisonment and execution without trial," nevertheless "there are the effective beginnings of constitutional government in industry . . . and millions help to make the conditions under which they live"? Would these millions not be

more likely, in a real world, to establish the beginnings of constitutional government by making the rules under which they
can be dragged out and shot?

That this artificial division of society into two halves, political and economic, in which opposite things are taking place,
should have been put before us with obeisances to "Marxism,"
was a prodigy of intellectual acrobatics. Marx might be said to
have spent his life trying to forestall this shallow dichotomy.
But Marx or no Marx, any man of hard sense knows that the
Russian people are not being subjected to those hideous political
repressions for their own good. It is not to bring in the Kingdom
of Heaven that the masters of the state have locked the population in this toothed vise.

I dwell upon this unreal notion of Laski's because I think it
exposes in a raw and yet elaborated form what has happened
in the minds of many of the pro-Soviet liberals. They are not
totally blind to the monstrous things that have happened in
Russia, but they have reasoned their way to a point of tranquil
acquiescence by means of this nonsense about political versus
economic.

This too, then, must be said in behalf of the delinquent liberals: they had a rationalization, a cerebral alibi, so to speak,
for their crime of treason against civilization. They managed
to draw the whole thing up into their heads where it did not
seem so bad.

It is significant that while the pro-communist liberals apol-
ogize for the *political* enslavement of the Russian people on the
ground that they are *economically* free, the pro-socialist liberals
make an opposite use of the same artificial distinction. They tell
us that *economic* enslavement will not deprive us of our real
freedom, which is *political*. Philip Rahv in the *Partisan Review*,
defending the British socialist regime against the assertion of
Dos Passos that "personal liberty has been contracted in Great
Britain," said: "The evidence cited by Dos Passos shows that
the contraction he speaks of has occurred solely in the economic sphere. Socialists, however, do not consider the right to
buy and sell as one pleases to be a significant part of the heri-

tage of freedom."* Stuart Chase took the same line in defending a state-planned society, and to them both Friedrich Hayek made the obvious and conclusive answer: "Economic control is not merely control of a sector of human life which can be separated from the rest; it is the control of the means for all our ends."**

It hardly requires a Marx or a Hayek, however, to reveal the unreality of this dichotomy. It is clear to all who possess "the faculty to imagine that which they know." And I often think that the lack of this faculty or habit, so justly praised by Shelley in his *Defense of Poetry,* is one of the main causes of the delinquency of the liberals. They are predominantly intellectual—and are not intellectuals in general, even when originally moved by sympathy, strangely heartless and conscienceless through the very fact that they make a habit of abstract thinking? A phrase like "workers and peasants," or "kulaks," or "prison camps," or "execution without trial," becomes a bloodless pawn which they move about on the cerebral blueprint of a schemed-out world with as little sense of the human hearts and bodies designated by it as though they were playing a game of chess. This enables them to go on calling themselves "left" and "liberal" after all the original meaning except to their own self-esteem has been drained out of those terms.

Another and cruder motive undoubtedly swung many once refined liberals into the camp of the brutalitarian tyrants. That is an underlying irresistible wish to associate themselves with power. Their early ideals had made spiritual rebels of them in their own country. They were commonly not only against the government and the "vested interests," but in a condition at least of mild demur against the whole established hierarchy of persons and values. To the thinking mind this was valid and exciting, but to mere organic tissue it was a hard attitude to keep up for a lifetime. All human history testifies to the strength and generality of what may be called the hierarchical instinct.

*"Disillusionment and Partial Answers" in *Partisan Review* for May, 1948.
**The Road to Serfdom,* pp. 88 and 92.

Students of comparative psychology have found it to prevail rigidly even in so pre-human a society as is to be found in the henyard. The caste system in a colony of jackdaws, as described by Konrad Lorenz in his book, *King Solomon's Ring*, throws astonishing light on several traits and institutions that we think of as peculiarly human—particularly the disposition to recognize the elite, to fall in line comfortably under those having the prestige of superior power. Its roots seem to be as deep, almost, as the impulse to form a society. Surely this trait can not be ignored in trying to assess the causes of the cultural disaster that I am discussing.

Dwight Macdonald, speaking of a liberal whose delinquency was transitory and need not be advertised here, says: "The spell of communism for people like him seems to have been that at last they could identify themselves with power without feeling guilty. His political language, in America a despised minority dialect, was now spoken throughout a sixth of the globe. A vast international movement backed by a powerful government was going his way—or seemed to be."

Whatever may be the inner truth about the individual in question, the acuteness of this comment on the great wave of enthusiasm for "the proletariat" that struck our liberal intelligentsia in the early thirties, can not be denied. Why did not this wave arise in the early years of the Bolshevik Revolution, when, although violent and brutal deeds were done, they were unsystemized and unusual, and were matched by heroic strides toward ideal reform in almost every phase of life? Hardly a single one of the noted liberals who came so boldly to the defense of Stalin's matured and hardened totalitarian police state had a good word to say for the regime of Lenin and Trotsky. There was a hazard then. Later there was a settled and secure new form of power. It is hard to escape the conclusion that in the depth of them that is what they wanted.

Still I do not think this trait, or all the above traits together fully explain the treachery to civilization of so many distinguished minds in this crisis of man's history. They had not all lost their passion for freedom; they did not all fall for the lie campaign, or swallow the politics-versus-economics moonshine; they are not all excessively cerebral, or swayed by the primitive adoration of power. I think probably the most general explanation lies in a kind of spiritual cowardice. Life is a battle; it is a battle without any final or assured victory, and these aspiring idealists lack the pluck to go down fighting it. Bereaved of other-worldly goals, they have been yearning for some home, some certainty, some Absolute on earth, if it is only the absolute parody of their dreams. And that is about all there is left of the Soviet heaven after they get through listing the qualifications in their adoration of it. The extent of these qualifications makes plain the selfishness of their mental condition. With all their brains, they can not draw the inference that any casual man who cares about other people even a little bit must draw from the continuing horrors suffered by millions of simple-hearted, honest folk under the Kremlin's lash. They can not do it because it would cause a pain in their own safe bosoms. They would have to know, then, that the world is just as bad as it is, and just as fluid too. There is no end-term in the fight to better it. . . .

9 Capitalism and Freedom: A Concluding Note

Milton Friedman

In the 1920's and the 1930's, intellectuals in the United States were overwhelmingly persuaded that capitalism was a defective system inhibiting economic well-being and thereby free-

From Milton Friedman, *Capitalism and Freedom* (Chicago: University of Chicago Press, 1962), Chapter 13, pp. 196–202. Copyright © 1962 by The University of Chicago Press. Reprinted by permission of The University of Chicago Press.

dom, and that the hope for the future lay in a greater measure of deliberate control by political authorities over economic affairs. The conversion of the intellectuals was not achieved by the example of any actual collectivist society, though it undoubtedly was much hastened by the establishment of a communist society in Russia and the glowing hopes placed in it. The conversion of the intellectuals was achieved by a comparison between the existing state of affairs, with all its injustices and defects, and a hypothetical state of affairs as it might be. The actual was compared with the ideal.

At the time, not much else was possible. True, mankind had experienced many epochs of centralized control, of detailed intervention by the state into economic affairs. But there had been a revolution in politics, in science, and in technology. Surely, it was argued, we can do far better with a democratic political structure, modern tools, and modern science than was possible in earlier ages.

The attitudes of that time are still with us. There is still a tendency to regard any existing government intervention as desirable, to attribute all evils to the market, and to evaluate new proposals for government control in their ideal form, as they might work if run by able, disinterested men, free from the pressure of special interest groups. The proponents of limited government and free enterprise are still on the defensive.

Yet, conditions have changed. We now have several decades of experience with governmental intervention. It is no longer necessary to compare the market as it actually operates and government intervention as it ideally might operate. We can compare the actual with the actual.

If we do so, it is clear that the difference between the actual operation of the market and its ideal operation—great though it undoubtedly is—is as nothing compared to the difference between the actual effects of government intervention and their intended effects. Who can now see any great hope for the advancement of men's freedom and dignity in the massive tyranny and despotism that hold sway in Russia? Wrote Marx and Engels in *The Communist Manifesto*: "The proletarians have nothing to lose but their chains. They have a world to win." Who today can regard the chains of the proletarians in the Soviet Union as weaker than the chains of the proletarians in the United States, or Britain or France or Germany or any Western state?

Let us look closer to home. Which if any of the great "reforms" of past decades has achieved its objectives? Have the good intentions of the proponents of these reforms been realized?

Regulation of the railroads to protect the consumer quickly became an instrument whereby the railroads could protect themselves from the competition of newly emerging rivals—at the expense, of course, of the consumer.

An income tax initially enacted at low rates and later seized upon as a means to redistribute income in favor of the lower classes has become a facade, covering loopholes and special provisions that render rates that are highly graduated on paper largely ineffective. A flat rate of 23½ per cent on presently taxable income would yield as much revenue as the present rates graduated from 20 to 91 per cent. An income tax intended to reduce inequality and promote the diffusion of wealth has in practice fostered reinvestment of corporate earnings, thereby favoring the growth of large corporations, inhibiting the operation of the capital market, and discouraging the establishment of new enterprises.

Monetary reforms, intended to promote stability in economic activity and prices, exacerbated inflation during and after World War I and fostered a higher degree of instability thereafter than had ever been experienced before. The monetary authorities they established bear primary responsibility for converting a serious economic contraction into the catastrophe of the Great Depression from 1929–33. A system established largely to prevent bank panics produced the most severe banking panic in American history.

An agricultural program intended to help impecunious farmers and to remove what were alleged to be basic dislocations in the organization of agriculture has become a national scandal that has wasted public funds, distorted the use of resources, riveted increasingly heavy and detailed controls on farmers, interfered seriously with United States foreign policy, and withal has done little to help the impecunious farmer.

A housing program intended to improve the housing conditions of the poor, to reduce juvenile delinquency, and to contribute to the removal of urban slums, has worsened the housing conditions of the poor, contributed to juvenile delinquency, and spread urban blight.

In the 1930's, "labor" was synonymous with "labor union" to the intellectual community; faith in the purity and virtue of labor unions was on a par with faith in home and motherhood. Extensive legislation was enacted to favor labor unions and to foster "fair" labor relations. Labor unions waxed in strength. By the 1950's, "labor union" was almost a dirty word; it was no longer synonymous with "labor," no longer automatically to be taken for granted as on the side of the angels.

Social security measures were enacted to make receipt of assistance a matter of right, to eliminate the need for direct relief and assistance. Millions now receive social security benefits. Yet the relief rolls grow and the sums spent on direct assistance mount.

The list can easily be lengthened: the silver purchase program of the 1930's, public power projects, foreign aid programs of the post-war years, F.C.C., urban redevelopment programs, the stockpiling program—these and many more have had effects very different and generally quite opposite from those intended.

There have been some exceptions. The expressways crisscrossing the country, magnificent dams spanning great rivers, orbiting satellites are all tributes to the capacity of government to command great resources. The school system, with all its defects and problems, with all the possibility of improvement through bringing into more effective play the forces of the market, has widened the opportunities available to American youth and contributed to the extension of freedom. It is a testament to the public-spirited efforts of the many tens of thousands who have served on local school boards and to the willingness of the public to bear heavy taxes for what they regarded as a public purpose. The Sherman antitrust laws, with all their problems of detailed administration, have by their very existence fostered competition. Public health measures have contributed to the reduction of infectious disease. Assistance measures have relieved suffering and distress. Local authorities have often provided facilities essential to the life of communities. Law and order have been maintained, though in many a large city the performance of even this elementary function of government has been far from satisfactory. As a citizen of Chicago, I speak feelingly.

If a balance be struck, there can be little doubt that the record is dismal. The greater part of the new ventures undertaken by government in the past few decades have failed to achieve their objectives. The United States has continued to progress; its citizens have become better fed, better clothed, better housed, and better transported; class and social distinctions have narrowed; minority groups have become less disadvantaged; popular culture has advanced by leaps and bounds. All this has been the product of the initiative and drive of individuals co-operating through the free market. Government measures have hampered not helped this development. We have been able to afford and surmount these measures only because of the extraordinary fecundity of the market. The invisible hand has been more potent for progress than the visible hand for retrogression.

Is it an accident that so many of the governmental reforms of recent decades have gone awry, that the bright hopes have turned to ashes? Is it simply because the programs are faulty in detail?

I believe the answer is clearly in the negative. The central defect of these measures is that they seek through government to force people to act against their own immediate interests in order to promote a supposedly general interest. They seek to resolve what is supposedly a conflict of interest, or a difference in view about interests, not by establishing a framework that will eliminate the conflict, or by persuading people to have different interests, but by forcing people to act against their own interest. They substitute the values of outsiders for the values of participants; either some telling others what is good for them, or the government taking from some to benefit others. These measures are therefore countered by one of the strongest and most creative forces known to man—the attempt by millions of individuals to promote their own interests, to live their lives by their own values. This is the major reason why the measures have so often had the opposite of the effects intended. It is also one of the major strengths of a free society and explains why governmental regulation does not strangle it.

The interests of which I speak are not simply narrow self-regarding interests. On the contrary, they include the whole range of values that men hold dear and for which they are willing to spend their fortunes and sacrifice their lives. The Germans who lost their lives opposing Adolph Hitler were pursuing their interests as they saw them. So also are the men and women who devote great effort and time to charitable, educational, and religious activities. Naturally, such interests are the major ones for few men. It is the virtue of a free society that it nonetheless permits these interests full scope and does not subordinate them to the narrow materialistic interests that dominate the bulk of mankind. That is why capitalist societies are less materialistic than collectivist societies.

Why is it, in light of the record, that the burden of proof still seems to rest on those of us who oppose new government programs and who seek to reduce the already unduly large role of government? Let Dicey answer: "The beneficial effect of State intervention, especially in the form of legislation, is direct, immediate, and, so to speak, visible, whilst its evil effects are gradual and indirect, and lie out of sight. . . . Nor . . . do most people keep in mind that State inspectors may be incompetent, careless, or even occasionally corrupt . . . ; few are those who realize the undeniable truth that State help kills self-help. Hence the majority of mankind must almost of necessity look with undue favor upon governmental intervention. This natural bias can be counteracted only by the existence, in a given society, . . . of a presumption or prejudice in favor of individual liberty, that is, of laissez-faire. The mere decline, therefore, of faith in self-help—and that such a decline has taken place is certain—is of itself sufficient to account for the growth of legislation tending towards socialism."[1]

The preservation and expansion of freedom are today threatened from two directions. The one threat is obvious and clear. It is the external threat coming from the evil men in the Kremlin who promise to bury us. The other threat is far more subtle. It is the internal threat coming from men of good intentions and good will who wish to reform us. Impatient with the slowness of persuasion and example to achieve the great social changes they envision, they are anxious to use the power of the state to achieve their ends and confident of their own ability to do so. Yet if they gained the power, they would fail to achieve their immediate aims and, in addition, would produce a collective state from which they would recoil in horror and of which they would be among the first victims. Concentrated power is not rendered harmless by the good intentions of those who create it.

The two threats unfortunately reinforce one another. Even if we avoid a nuclear holocaust, the threat from the Kremlin requires us to devote a sizable fraction of our resources to our military defense. The importance of government as a buyer of so much of our output, and the sole buyer of the output of many firms and industries, already concentrates a dangerous amount of economic power in the hands of the political authorities, changes the environment in which business operates and the criteria relevant for business success, and in these and other ways endangers a free market. This danger we cannot avoid. But we needlessly intensify it by continuing the present widespread governmental intervention in areas unrelated to the military defense of the nation and by undertaking ever new

[1]A. V. Dicey, *Law and Public Opinion in England* (2d ed.; London: Macmillan, 1914), pp. 257–258.

governmental programs—from medical care for the aged to lunar exploration.

As Adam Smith once said, "There is much ruin in a nation." Our basic structure of values and the interwoven network of free institutions will withstand much. I believe that we shall be able to preserve and extend freedom despite the size of the military programs and despite the economic powers already concentrated in Washington. But we shall be able to do so only if we awake to the threat that we face, only if we persuade our fellow men that free institutions offer a surer, if perhaps at times a slower, route to the ends they seek than the coercive power of the state. The glimmerings of change that are already apparent in the intellectual climate are a hopeful augury.

Part Three

Contemporary Challenges and the Social Order

No list of modern social problems would fail to include the problems of free speech, of democracy, of world communism, of race, of education, of the city, of social justice—and of enlightened criticism. The idea of this section is to tune in on the thinking of highly competent people who have mused on these problems. There is no paradigmatic "conservative" position on any one of them. But rigorous thought, an active imagination, and an anti-ideological disposition are the common denominators. And each of the authors quoted here, in his own way, demonstrates what I would deem to be an aspect of the conservative intelligence examining a particular problem, whether narrow or broad.

Harry V. Jaffa was professor of political science at Ohio University when he wrote his essay "On The Nature of Civil and Religious Liberty." He is, like others of the most able students of political science, a former student of Leo Strauss, from whom he obviously inherited his impatience with the politics that derives from logical positivism. What Jaffa's essay does, and does superbly, is make the case for the nonavailability of the theoretical right to freedom for those who desire to use it in order to destroy—freedom. His is the answer to the assertion of the libertarian totalists that everyone has equally the right to speak, indeed that it is impudent to ask, even, what it is that they wish to say. In a demonstration of transporting lucidity, he undertakes to show that American freedom under the Constitution was by inference promulgated on the understanding that the use of it would not be available as a matter of right to those who seriously threaten (as opposed to merely intend) the abolition of the rights of others; and that therefore the cant phrase about the duty of tolerant men to tolerate intolerance is just that, cant: specious, frivolous. Conservatives who have struggled to formulate a plausible opposition to the extension of freedom to those who desire to use it in order to eliminate freedom, have here an exemplary handling of the apparent dilemma. Mr. Jaffa, by the way, is no mean phrasemaker. He is the author of the most recent version of "Rum, Romanism and Rebellion." It was he who composed, in behalf of Senator Barry Goldwater, the resonant phrase, *"Extremism in the defense of liberty is no vice, moderation in the pursuit of justice is no virtue,"* thus depriving, in the opinion of the embittered, Mr. Goldwater of the freedom to be elected President of the United States.

Willmoore Kendall is already, a very few years after his death, something of a legend. Not only because he made a lasting impression on his students and colleagues, some of whom adored him, some of whom despised him, but because of the workings of his extraordinary mind, which brought a huge theoretical talent to the organization of political problems. He wrote very few books, and his professional reputation rested always on his doctoral dissertation, *John Locke and the Doctrine of Majority Rule.* But he wrote many articles for the academic quarterlies. One of them, "The Two Majorities," is reproduced here.

The essay is read differently by different people. My own feeling is that it is a successful theoretical and sociological attempt to reconcile a set of apparent paradoxes. It is an imaginative attempt to remind us that human beings may appear to be expressing themselves contradictorily at the polls (a liberal President, a conservative Congress), but that the American political mechanism is such as to translate these paradoxes into enduring (and hence conservative) forms. Kendall's prose, by the way, is as controversial as his politics. There are those who dismiss it as plainly impossible. Others differ. For instance Professor Garry Wills, reviewing Kendall's *The Conservative Affirmation* in *Modern Age* in 1963, calls it *"a literary masterpiece, for it is one of the best-kept secrets of our age that one of the best prose stylists of our age is Willmoore Kendall. The long sentence that argues with itself down one page and around the next did not, we find, go out with William Morris wallpaper. Professor Kendall has given the circumspect Victorian periodicity, which disciplines the reader while delighting him, a new lease on life; and this by three means. First, he introduces slang into these staid surroundings. Then, he follows speech rhythms—not the lecturing cadences of a pulpit age, but the lunge of two voices contrapuntally going at each other. Last, he makes fun of his own grammatical arabesques, elaborating them in the most arch fashion. The result is a combination of the colloquial and the baroque that is invariably exciting. His sentences hover somewhere between a ballet and a rumble."*

James Burnham was a professor of philosophy at New York University at age 25 and taught there for twenty years. He went, like others who have contributed to this volume, through socialism and from there to his own brand of conservatism. Although his formal academic qualifications were in philosophy, he became known throughout the academic world as a sociopolitical theorist, and his book *The Managerial Revolution* was treated with the respect given to seminal works. Burnham turned to government service and then back to book-writing *(The Struggle for the World, Congress and the American Tradition, Suicide of the West)* and to journalism. He has been my close associate (and friend) for many years, and in his case (uniquely) I invited him to submit, for this chapter, a selection from his work on the strategic problems posed by the world Communist movement. He replied: "*What I suggest here are three excerpts, the first from* The Struggle for the World *and the last two from, respectively, the introduction and the final chapter of* The War We Are In. *This selection (1) combines writing twenty years old and a recent writing; (2) includes illustrations of the use of historical reference and analogy in relation to historical analysis. I believe this integral incorporation of history to be of the essence of conservatism and almost always absent from ideologism, especially from liberal ideologism; and it is certainly characteristic of my 'method'; (3) includes a summary of the 'nature of communism'; (4) gives a retrospective analysis of global developments and an anticipatory analysis of likely future developments.*"

Ernest van den Haag is a professor of sociology and an active psychologist who teaches at the New School and at New York University. He has written a great deal, including (with Ralph Ross) the ambitious textbook of social science, *The Fabric of Society.*

He is renowned for his incisiveness, which he brings to bear on all subjects including, as in the present essay, the tangled subject of race relations. His approach (which is by no means to be examined as the comprehensive conservative "position" on civil rights and race relations) is unusual in that it weighs not only claims but counterclaims; indeed it externalizes and minutely examines counterclaims which are of enormous emotional and political importance, even if they do not figure in conspicuous discussions of the problem. Van den Haag's technique is relentlessly solomonic. He strives to reconcile, adjust, weigh, grant, withhold; and the intactness of the argument, the impatience with cant, the dogged refusal to be carried along by the Zeitgeist, exhibit something of the moral and intellectual individualism that Oakeshott speaks of.

Mortimer Smith is an evangelist for educational excellence. He has devoted his life to the subject, and he founded the Council for Basic Education which he discovered, to his pleasure, attracted prominent liberals as well as conservatives who shared his indignation against the debasement of learning at the hands of the educationists. It is probably the only fight that has actually been won. At the intellectual level, it is difficult nowadays to find a competent defense of "progressive education." Mr. Smith's first book, *And Madly Teach*, published shortly after the Second World War, caused great scandal because it was in those days unheard of to challenge pedagogical precepts that were presumed to have derived from the (unchallengeable) orthodoxy of John Dewey. His second book, *The Diminished Mind*, provided so much additional evidence of the need for reform that the Council was founded, whose impact has been considerable.

Smith is not in the category of the educational utopianists like Robert Hutchins, although they share the belief that anyone who is not a moron is at least capable of learning how to read, and one sometimes feels that Mortimer Smith, if pressed, would settle for that—for really teaching American students how to read.

I considered, but finally excluded as aristocratic beyond the parameters of this book, excerpting the Page-Barbour lectures of Albert Jay Nock, published in 1932 under the title *The Theory of Education in the United States*. Smith and Nock share, along with a legion of other critics of modern educational attitudes, perhaps most prolific among them Mr. Russell Kirk, the conviction that in education the emphasis should be on excellence, on the primacy of subject matter over technique, and on the thorough mastery of fundamentals.

Jane Jacobs would never classify herself as a conservative,[1] and there is no implicit effort here at conscripting her (or any-

[1]Neither would a few other contributors to this volume. There are those who shrink, usually for good reasons, from what they call "categorization." Then, too, there are those whose special interest does not lodge harmoniously with the general pattern of their concerns. They may attract the co-optive attention of conservatives—or liberals—by something they have written that may be at odds with associated positions they take on other

body else) into the organized or disorganized conservative cause. In fact she argues a thesis concerning the city which is conservative by general understanding, an oversimplification of which is that there are profound human and aesthetic satisfactions to be had in a city that grows as it is disposed to grow, free of the superimpositions and the great allocations of the planners. Mrs. Jacobs makes a powerful case against the current mania for central urban planning, a case made more specifically by Martin Anderson in *The Federal Bulldozer.*

Russell Kirk may well be the best known "professional" conservative in America, by which adjective is meant that he launched his extraordinary career by an act of conscious apostleship to a social and historical and philosophical order which is best described as "conservative." His first spectacular was *The Conservative Mind,* a book on the ideas of prominent English

---

matters. The point is obvious. Although the conservative (and the liberal) syndrome is unquestionably useful (see for instance the chapter, "Who Are the Liberals?" in James Burnham's *Suicide of the West*), still, anomalies are possible, so that you have your *mélanges de genre,* as Babbitt (Irving) called the Darwinian divine; as Buckley (W.) calls the liberal Republican. The label-problem is persistent, but it does not pay to let it overwhelm us. The old categories are still useful for purposes of communication. That they do break down is tribute either to the confusion of thought of an individual writer or to his genuine eclecticism. A complaint from a member of the latter breed was poignantly done a few years ago by Professor Eric Voegelin (see below pp. 438–461), who wrote, *"Once an argument has been classified as 'positional,' it is regarded as having been demolished, since the 'position' attributed to it is always selected with pejorative intent. The choice of the position selected is an expression of the personal antipathies of the individual critic; and the same argument can therefore be attributed to any one of a variety of 'positions,' according to what comes most readily to the critic's hand. The wealth of variation afforded by such tactics is well exemplified by the variety of classifications to which I have myself been subjected. On my religious 'position,' I have been classified as a Protestant, a Catholic, as anti-Semitic and as a typical Jew; politically, as a Liberal, a Fascist, a National Socialist and a Conservative; and on my theoretical position, as a Platonist, a Neo-Augustinian, a Thomist, a disciple of Hegel, an existentialist, a historical relativist and an empirical skeptic; in recent years the suspicion has frequently been voiced that I am a Christian." (Freedom and Serfdom: An Anthology of Western Thought,* ed. Albert Hunold [Dordrecht, Holland: D. Reidel, 1961], p. 280.)

and American conservatives that was arresting in its grasp of intellectual history. It was followed quickly by *A Program for Conservatives* and *Beyond the Dreams of Avarice,* two books of essays the first of which posed the "problems" of conservatism—the problem of "the heart," of "the mind," of whatever. From this book I have taken the chapter on "The Problem of Social Justice," which illuminates the problem of ideological abstractioneering all the more vividly because Mr. Kirk takes on a freemarket professor who has dreamed himself up a neat set of dreams which he would deploy the forces of conservatism to subsidize; warning, again, like Garry Wills, against the dogmatization of social common sense.

Hugh Kenner is the distinguished young critic to whom T. S. Eliot once alluded as perhaps the finest of his generation. He has written numerous books, on Eliot, Wyndham Lewis, Joyce, Beckett, and is completing a magnum opus on the age of Pound. He is a Canadian who took his advanced degree at Yale and went to the University of California at Santa Barbara, where for several years he was head of the English Department.

I selected from his work a not altogether pleasant essay on a young contemporary who has written a widely acclaimed book, *The Reactionaries—Yeats, Lewis, Pound, Eliot, Lawrence: A Study of the Anti-Democratic Intelligentsia.* Not altogether pleasant because Mr. Kenner is very rigorous in his handling of the author whom he accuses of sciolism and great delinquencies of understanding. The essay is relevant here not merely because of its subject matter—Mr. Kenner insists that the geniuses about whom the critic writes are greatly misunderstood by those who fail to see that they are speaking, no less, about the continuing relevance of the Western experience to the future of the world —but because of the form by which Mr. Kenner approaches the problem. He begins by a most meticulous examination of the particular scholarly gaffes of the author; then he takes his criticism to the more generic level, demonstrating the failure of the critic to understand what he was talking about; and then toward a transcendent level, on to his constatation that what in fact they are talking about, learned men must understand: must have some appreciation of, if we are to conserve the heritage. He is impatient with the literary ideologists who sniff about looking for any failure on the subject to pay appropriate obeisance to the reigning symbols of the social order ("All decent people . . ." Mr. William Empson is quoted by Mr. Kenner, the unquoted section almost certainly being, "agree with me"). It is in execution and in substance a defense of excellence and of the maintenance of the highest standard: *"One is inclined to talk of popular taste,"* Kenner quotes Pound as saying in 1934, *"when one should hunt for the chaps working the oracle."* The problem—of the popularization of literary and critical arts—is related to the problems (see above, pp. 96–98) Ortega concerned himself with.

The contributors to this section were selected not only on account of their intellectual and stylistic proficiencies, let us admit; but also because they would appear to illustrate the usefulness of different modes of conservatism. Others, even more markedly in contrast, have already appeared in this volume; others are still to come. But no two of these authors, clearly, came out of the same mould. Jaffa, the historical meticulist; Kendall, the sinuous analytical iconoclast; Burnham, the confident meteorologist of world forces and movements; van den Haag, the tough, honest pawnbroker of the bits and pieces of ideas and passion that are advanced upon him; Smith, the civilized educational fundamentalist; Jacobs, the tenacious challenger of the urban abstractionist; Kirk, the traditionalist skeptic of the passions, substantive or methodological, scourge of the egalitarian; and Kenner, the rigorous unyielding scholarly perfectionist, whose passions, scholarly and philosophical, fuse so terribly when they are simultaneously aroused. A fair sampling. A fine performance. Bravo.

10   On the Nature of
Civil and Religious Liberty

Harry V. Jaffa

There is general agreement among Americans that the central
political issue of our time is the world-wide conflict between
Communist totalitarianism and political freedom, that freedom
whose principles are affirmed in such documents as the Declaration of Independence and the Gettysburg Address. All decent
Americans repudiate Communism and recognize their obligation to do what lies in their power to prevent its ascendancy or
triumph. Yet in the field of civil liberties there is profound
confusion as to what, in crucial cases, decent, freedom-loving
citizens may do. With respect to freedom of speech and the
closely related freedoms of assembly, association, and the right
of petition, the question continually arises: can we deny these
freedoms or rights to Communists, or their agents or coadjutors,
without ourselves ceasing, by that denial and to the extent of
the denial, to constitute a free society? And, conversely, is it not
true that if we do allow Communists the full advantage of these
civil liberties we may allow them so to weaken and confuse our
resistance that Communism may thereby be enabled to succeed?
In short, may it not be true that the indispensable means for
denying success to Communism are at the same time the necessary instruments for the self-immolation of freedom? That we
may be confronted with such a dilemma has certainly puzzled
the will of many conscientious lovers of freedom amongst us.
Perhaps even more serious is the sharp conflict which has de-

From *The Conservative Papers,* edited by Ralph de Toledano and Karl
Hess (New York: Doubleday Anchor, 1964), pp. 250–268. Copyright ©
1964 by Ralph de Toledano and Karl Hess. Reprinted by permission of
Doubleday & Company, Inc.

veloped from time to time between those who have grasped one or another horn of the supposed dilemma.

This difficulty is not a new one in the experience of this republic under its present constitution. We should remember that if Thomas Jefferson opposed the Alien and Sedition Acts, George Washington favored them. The Civil War, however, presented the problem in its most acute form. It would perhaps not be inapt to sum up the experience of the years 1861 to 1865 by saying that no American statesman ever violated the ordinary maxims of civil liberties more than did Abraham Lincoln, and few seem to have been more careful of them than Jefferson Davis. Yet the cause for the sake of which the one slighted these maxims was human freedom, while the other, claiming to defend the forms of constitutional government, found in those forms a ground for defending and preserving human slavery. In his message to Congress on July 4, 1861, President Lincoln propounded the universal problem within the particular crisis in these words:

> And this issue embraces more than the fate of these United States. . . . It forces us to ask: "Is there, in all republics, this inherent and fatal weakness? Must a Government, of necessity, be too *strong* for the liberties of its own people, or too *weak* to maintain its own existence?"

That the liberties Lincoln had in mind were the civil liberties referred to above is shown by his defense, in a major section of that address, of his suspensions of the writ of habeas corpus. All civil liberties depend absolutely upon the privilege of this writ, since no one can exercise his freedom of speech or of association, for example, if he can be detained or imprisoned at the pleasure of any official. It is well then to consider that since the Constitution (Article I, Section 9) provides that the privilege of the writ of habeas corpus may be suspended "when in cases of rebellion or invasion the public safety may require it," the Constitution must contemplate the lawful abridgment under certain circumstances of the freedoms of the First Amendment. It must do so unless the First Amendment is supposed to have cancelled that part of the original Constitution which allows the suspension. No one seriously maintains this, however, because every good thing the people of the United States seek to accomplish in and through their government depends upon the ability of that government to preserve itself. And certainly nothing that led to the adoption of the First Amendment in any way affected the reasons for believing that "in cases of rebellion and invasion" the government might not be able to survive without suspending the writ.

When Lincoln defended his suspensions of the writ of habeas corpus in his Fourth of July message, he was mainly concerned to justify its suspension by the *Executive*. The provision of the Constitution in question is in the article that sets forth the powers (and the limitations upon the powers) of *Congress*. Lincoln's explanation of why the power to suspend cannot be confined to Congress is a masterly example of constitutional construction:

> Now, it is insisted that Congress, and not the Executive, is vested with this power. But the Constitution itself is silent as to which or who is to exercise the power; and as the provision was plainly made for a dangerous emergency, it cannot be believed the framers of the instrument intended that in every case the danger should run its course until Congress could be called together; the very assembling of which might be prevented, as was intended in this case, by the rebellion.

Earlier in the same message, however, Lincoln had taken much broader ground. Provisions of the Constitution, taken literally, can be in conflict, sometimes in direct contradiction, with each other. As we have seen, the command of the First Amendment that "Congress shall make no law . . . abridging the freedom of speech," is in a certain sense incompatible with the proposition that Congress may, in time of rebellion or invasion, suspend the writ of habeas corpus. And so Lincoln, while denying that he had violated the Constitution maintained nonetheless that, if he had done so he would have been justified. For the Constitution also commanded him to "take care that the laws be faithfully executed," and he had sworn an oath so to execute them. All the laws were being resisted, and failing of execution, in nearly one third of the states, and the whole government faced dissolution if its authority could not be restored. But, he asked, if the Constitution denied him the power to suspend the writ of habeas corpus, should he prefer the total destruction of all the laws, and the government, to the very limited violation of this one law? Lincoln summed the matter up in his usual succinct way:

> Are all the laws *but one* to go unexecuted, and the Government itself go to pieces, lest that one be violated?

It is the thesis of this paper that civil liberties are, as their name implies, liberties of men in civil society. As such, they are to be correlated with the duties of men in civil society, and they are therefore subject to that interpretation which is consistent with the duty of men to preserve the polity which incorporates their rights. But the preservation of a civil society does not and cannot mean merely its physical preservation or territorial integrity; nor can it mean merely its freedom from foreign domination or, for that matter, from domestic usurpation. For Lincoln, the preservation of the Union meant all of these things, but it meant above all the preservation of a body whose soul remained *dedicated* to the principles of the Declaration of Independence. The classic example of a dilemma in interpreting the Constitution, and one whose resolution may well serve as a guide for resolving the difficulty with which this paper began, is that afforded by the Fifth Amendment in the decades immediately preceding the Civil War. Among other things, the amendment charges Congress that "No person shall be . . . deprived of life, liberty, or property, without due process of law." The pro-slavery Southerners maintained—and Chief Justice Taney in the Dred Scott decision upheld the assertion— that a congressional prohibition of slavery in any United States territory (as in the Missouri Compromise legislation of 1820) had the effect of freeing slaves that a man had lawfully brought with him into a territory. This, it was held, constituted an arbitrary deprivation of property. The anti-slavery Northerners, on the other hand, pointed to the fact that Negroes were recognized many times by the Constitution as persons (e.g., Article I, Section 2, par. 3; ibid., Section 9, par. 1; and Article IV, Section 2, par. 3). They further insisted that by the terms of the same amendment, no Negro, being a person, might be held in slavery in a territory. The specific and immediate cause of the Civil War was precisely this difference over whether the Fifth Amendment made it the duty of Congress to prohibit or to protect slavery in the territories. Every candid student of this question must come to see, I believe, that the language of the Constitution admits with nearly perfect impartiality of either interpretation. In the so-called fugitive-slave clause of the Constitution—the word slave or slavery never occurs before the Thirteenth Amendment—a sanction undoubtedly is given to state laws which, in turn, treat certain "persons" as if they were not persons, that is, as if they were chattels. In short, the word "person" is treated in the Constitution in such ways that some persons may be either subjects of rights of their own, or mere objects of the rights of others. How to resolve this confusion in the text of the Constitution could not be decided by reference to the Constitution alone. As in many great matters, the meaning of the Constitution had and has to be sought outside the Constitution itself. The great debates that preceded the Civil War, above all the Lincoln-Douglas debates, turned on the question of the authority and meaning of the principles propounded in the Declaration of Independence, as the guide for interpreting the Constitution. For there could be no doubt that if the Declaration was authoritative, and if Negroes were included in the proposition that "all men are created equal," then the free-soil interpretation of the Fifth Amendment had to prevail, Chief Justice Taney to the contrary notwithstanding *(Note: On this whole subject, see my *Crisis of the House Divided: An Interpretation of the Issues in the Lincoln-Douglas Debates.* New York: Doubleday, 1959, esp. Ch. XIV, The Universal Meaning of the Declaration of Independence). It is too little realized that the final word in the greatest of all American controversies is pronounced in the magisterial opening of the Gettysburg Address. Stephen A. Douglas had said, and the pro-slavery Southerners agreed, that we existed as a nation only in virtue of the Constitution, and the Constitution not only tolerated but gave legal guarantees to the institution of human slavery. When Lincoln pronounced "Fourscore and seven years," he forever fixed the year 1776 as the year of the nation's nativity. In so doing he did not downgrade the Constitution, he merely affirmed in the most solemn manner what he held to be the essential cause of the dignity of the Constitution: that it was an instrument for better securing those human rights affirmed in the Declaration, that the Union which was to become "more perfect" took as its standard of perfection, its ends or principles, the "laws of Nature and of Nature's God" invoked in the earlier document.

The Union was created by its dedication to the equality of man. Slavery, Lincoln held, might be tolerated as a necessity, but only so long as it was understood to be a necessary evil. Douglas sought a middle position, a national "don't care" policy which would allow the settlers in the territories to decide as they wished in the matter of slavery. This, Lincoln said with scorn, attempted to treat as a matter of indifference something to which no human being could be indifferent. It was, he said, as vain as the search for a man who should be neither a living man nor a dead one. Lincoln preferred the candid pro-slavery argument, where the issue could be squarely joined, And he argued with unbreakable logic that if the slaveowner's interpretation of the Fifth Amendment were correct, and if the Negroes' humanity were either denied or treated as of no account, then the moral basis of the authority of the whole Constitution had to be called into question, and the American Revolution itself could be regarded as an expression of mere force without right.

Free government rests upon the consent or opinion of the governed. Law is an expression of opinion, and the opinion upon which the law rests is more fundamental than the law itself. "In this and like communities," Lincoln said in the first of his joint debates with Douglas, "public sentiment is everything. With public sentiment, nothing can fail; without it, nothing can succeed. Consequently, he who molds public sentiment, goes deeper than he who enacts statutes or pronounces decisions. He makes statutes and decisions possible or impossible to be executed." The Constitution was the creation of a people committed in the Declaration to the idea of human dignity. Although the people is sovereign, its sovereignty may not be exercised in a manner inconsistent with the moral ground of its own authority.

"All men are created equal," is called a self-evident truth. What does this mean? Not that all men are equal in intelligence, virtue, strength, or beauty. They are equal in certain "rights," and the meaning of these rights can perhaps be most easily expressed today in this negative way: there is no difference between man and man, such as there is between man and animals of other species, which makes any man, that is, any normal adult human being, the natural ruler of any man. Man is by nature the master of dog, horse, cow, or monkey. He is equally the master of the dangerous wild animals he cannot domesticate, because he can kill or capture them as a result of his natural superiority, and not because of mere accident. The rights which men evidently have over other animals, they do not, it is equally evident, have over each other. Men are not angels—who, it may be supposed, would require no government—nor are there angels to govern men. Government, which does not arise directly from *nature,* is then grounded upon *consent.* To repeat, government does not arise *directly* from nature, but it does arise *indirectly,* to the extent that consent, to be the ground of legitimate authority, must itself be based upon a recognition of the essential difference between man and the brutes. If the consent of the governed were given to a regime which treated the rulers as if they were gods or angels, differing essentially in their nature from the ruled, the regime would also be illegitimate. Deception and force are equally incapable of giving rise to legitimate authority. Legitimacy cannot then be claimed for any regime in which the rulers treat the ruled as if they are animals of another species, as if the governed can be used as mere instruments for the advantage of the rulers. Such a regime is illegitimate, we repeat, even if the ruled, for whatever reason, believe that their own highest good consists in gratifying the rulers. The governed, in a civilized regime must, by the principles of our Declaration, be treated as beings with ends of intrinsic worth, which ends the government serves. Cattle may be killed, their flesh eaten, and their skins used to clothe human bodies, because of the indefeasible, objective natural difference between the soul of a man and the soul of a brute.

The Declaration, as we have seen, speaks of the specific nature of man and, inferentially, of its difference from other species, as self-evident. By this it is meant that we cannot demonstrate the essential likeness of men to each other and their difference from other animals. This is because all understanding of the world, all demonstration about the world, proceeds *from* the experience by which we grasp the terms of such propositions as: "This is a man, this is a dog, this is a tree, etc." A self-evident truth is not one which every one necessarily admits to be true; it is one the evidence for which is contained in the terms of the proposition, and which is admitted to be true by everyone *who already grasps the meaning of the terms.* Very young children, lunatics, and savages, are for various reasons deficient in those operations of the mind which issue in the abstractions, man, dog, horse, tree, etc. Hence, until their deficiencies are somehow overcome, they cannot be responsible members of civil society.

The men who founded our system of government were not moral or political relativists, as those terms are understood today. In affirming that all men are created equal, they expressed their conviction that human freedom depends upon the recognition of an order that man himself does not create. Man is not free to disregard the hierarchy of souls in nature. The equality of man flows from and corresponds to the inequality of the human and the subhuman, as it corresponds also to the inequality of the human and the superhuman. For man is part of the order of nature, and his dignity derives from the whole of which he is a part. This whole, being the cause of the dignity of the part which is man, is possessed of a dignity greater than man, for every cause is greater than the effects of which it is the cause. But the whole is not known to us as we and brute creation—the parts—are known. It is a mystery, but a mystery to which man alone in the universe is open. This fact is the ground of freedom of thought, which in turn is the ground of all other freedoms, including civil liberties. Freedom of thought is not freedom to deny that two and two is four. Someone who denies this may be more pitied than censured, but we do not see in his denial a consummation of his freedom. To repeat, all our liberties rest upon the objective fact of the specific difference of the human soul from subhuman souls, and the highest virtue of this difference is the human capacity to confront the mystery of the universe. This is what we mean when we say that the Declaration of Independence affirms the principle of the dignity of man. To call this principle an ideology —which means a mere rationalization of vulgar self-interest— is to demean and debase it. To call it a mere "ideal" is perhaps even worse. An ideal is distinguished from what is real, and the Declaration speaks not of something unreal, but of something real in the highest degree, namely, *truth*. Moreover, there are many ideals, but there is but one truth. To be guided by the laws of Nature and of Nature's God means to be guided not by multiple fantasies but by the unitary ground of actual existence. Present-day skepticism as to the laws of nature mentioned in the Declaration, does not supply us with an alternative ground for justifying civil liberty. Absolute skepticism is a self-devouring monster. Theoretically, it means doubting the ability to doubt. Practically, it teaches that if there is nothing that need be believed as true, neither is there anything that need be disbelieved. Unlimited skepticism quickly transforms itself into unlimited dogmatism. Political freedom exists only upon that wise and tolerant middle ground where men do not treat other men as brutes because they know that they themselves are not gods. But this restraint, this proud humility, is the attribute of those, and only those, who see in the order of nature the ground of the moral and political order.

Let us now turn to the problem with which we began. Does a free society prove false to itself if it denies civil liberties to

Communists, Nazis, or anyone else who would use these liberties, if he could, as a means of destroying the free society? The answer, I believe, is now plain that it does not. In saying this I do not counsel, or even justify, any particular measure for dealing with persons of such description. What is right in any case depends upon the facts of that case, and I am here dealing only with principles, not their application. However, those who think that every denial of civil liberties is equally derogatory of the character of a free society, without reference to the character of the persons being denied, make this fundamental error: they confuse means with ends. Free speech is a priceless and indispensable attribute of a free society because it is a necessary means for deliberating upon public policy. But this deliberation does not extend to everything: above all, it does not extend to the question of whether the community shall exchange its freedom for slavery. Certain ends are fixed, and their fixity is the condition of mutability in other respects. The government may deliberate how to secure the rights to life and to liberty of all; it may never deliberate *whether* they shall be secured. Certain proposals can never be entertained by a civilized community. The essence of all such proposals would be to kill or enslave someone or some group in the community and distribute their property among the rest. Obviously, in any community in which such a proposal were seriously entertained, even for a moment, those who are proposed for proscription might rightfully consider themselves in a state of war with the rest, and feel justified in using every means to preserve themselves. But the right *not to be proscribed* is inherent in every part of the community, severally, and in the whole community, collectively. Hence *no one* ever has the right to introduce or advocate such a thing. Thus speech calling for the proscription of individuals or classes is inherently wrong, and there is an inherent right in every community to treat it as criminal, wholly apart from any consequences which can be foreseen at the moment.

Just as majority rule is a device for deciding matters of common interest where unanimity is impossible, but can never be rightfully used to destroy the minority, so free speech is a device for deliberating upon the common interest, but can never be rightfully employed to propose the destruction of either a majority or minority. Yet this is precisely what both Nazis and Communists do. Both are creeds calling for the proscription of individuals and groups innocent of any crime. The Nazis believe that one so-called race, the Aryan master race, is so superior to all others that it has the right to treat other men as if they were animals of another species. They do not hesitate to exterminate masses of human beings as if they were plague-bearing rats, or to use their skin as parchment, as if they were cattle. And Communists differ morally from Nazis only in proposing a so-called class, the proletariat, instead of a race, as the sole subject of moral right. For Nazis, morality is an intraracial, for Communists an intraclass phenomenon. Neither believe that faith is to be kept or, indeed, that there are any binding moral rules which extend beyond the barriers of race or class. The Nazis would, and have, proscribed every racial strain beyond the pale of their elite; and the Communists do the same with every class which they do not associate with the dictatorship of the proletariat. An American Communist is one who, if he knows the meaning, and accepts the discipline, of the Party, would use power arbitrarily to deprive his fellow citizens of their property and liberty and, if they resisted, their lives.

Communists and Nazis, I maintain, have no right to the use of free speech in a free society. However, whether it is wise or expedient to deny them its use is another matter. I believe that the United States is a sufficiently civilized and a sufficiently stable community to bear the advocacy of almost anything, whether it be National Socialism, Communism, or Cannibalism. I would take my stand with Jefferson, who in his first inaugural address said, "If there be any among us who would wish to dissolve this Union or to change its republican form, let them stand undisturbed as monuments of the safety with which error of opinion may be tolerated where reason is left free to combat it." But Jefferson only tolerated error; he did not in any way concede a right of the enemies of republican government to change it into a contrary form. As the context of this celebrated passage will show, it was only the impotence of the enemies of republican government which, in Jefferson's view, made it expedient, and right only because expedient, to tolerate them. And thus it was not inconsistent, as some critics have charged, for Jefferson to have instituted prosecutions by state officials for sedition, as he did, if experience revealed that the enemies of republican government were not as impotent as he had supposed. I would accordingly contend that, while it is seldom either expedient or wise to suppress the peaceful advocacy even of inhuman doctrines, in a community like ours, it is not for that reason unjust. But in communities very unlike ours—for example, in a new African nation, constantly threatened by relapse into primitive barbarism on the one hand, and by the barbarism of Communism on the other—the advocacy of many inhuman and indecent things would constantly have to be prohibited.

John Stuart Mill is the most famous of those who have or seem to have demanded absolute freedom of thought and expression. Yet, in the first chapter of his essay *On Liberty,* in the very next paragraph after he proposes his great libertarian principle, he adds a qualification which his present-day followers often overlook or disregard. "It is, perhaps hardly necessary to say," says Mill, quite mistaken as to the necessity, "that this doctrine is meant to apply only to human beings in the maturity of their faculties." The principle of liberty does not apply either to children or to those of less than legal age. Mill is very clear that he presupposes moral characters already formed, and not only able to distinguish right from wrong but disposed toward the right by a decent upbringing. Still further, Mill excludes from the application of his principle "those backward states of society in which the race itself may be considered in its nonage." Barbarians, like children, must be guided for their own good. "Despotism," he says, in a classic passage, "is a legitimate mode of government in dealing with barbarians, provided the end be their improvement, and the means justified by actually effecting that end. Liberty, as a principle, has no application to any state of things anterior to the time when mankind have become capable of being improved by free and equal discussion." I would ask those who today consider themselves followers of John Stuart Mill, what principle would exclude from the enjoyment of civil liberties the subjects of Akbar or Charlemagne, but admit the followers of Hitler or Stalin? Mill's great error was not that of believing moral qualifications were not necessary as a basis for the exercise of liberty. His error lay in his failure to discern that barbarism lurked as a potentiality of modern society no less than that of the Dark Ages. He perceived accurately the depth to which the spirit of modern science had penetrated the Western world, and he was right in believing that scientific progress in that world, and even beyond that world, was essentially irreversible. But he was utterly mistaken, in common with nearly all the thinkers of his time, in believing that the effect of the scientific spirit was to make men more temperate and just. The ability to be guided to improvement by conviction and persuasion, he said, had been "long since reached in all nations with whom we need here concern ourselves." He did not think it possible that a highly civilized modern nation could be persuaded to abandon the principle of persuasion. But we, who have seen Weimar Germany, the freest market place of ideas the world has ever known, give itself up to the Nazis, know differently. And we have also seen modern science flourish both in Hitler's Germany and Stalin's Russia. We know today that there is no necessary correlation between modern physics, chemistry, biology, and mathematics, not to mention the many branches of engineering, and a gentle and tolerant temper. Whatever the intention of the founders of modern science, there is nothing in its method which precludes its appropriation by men who are, in every other respect, barbarians.

There is no passage in the literature dealing with civil liberties more celebrated than the dissenting opinion of Mr. Justice Holmes in the Abrams case of 1919. The superlibertarians of our time quote it endlessly, and recite it as a litany, so much so that one wonders if many of them have not utterly forgotten the Declaration of Independence, with which it is, in many respects, in flagrant contradiction. We will present extensive selections.

> Persecution for the expression of opinions seems to me perfectly logical. If you have no doubt of your premises or your power and want a certain result with all your heart you naturally express your wishes in law and sweep away all opposition. To allow opposition by speech seems to indicate that you think the speech is impotent . . . or that you do not care wholeheartedly for the result, or that you doubt either your power or your premises. But when men have realized that time has upset many fighting faiths, they may come to believe even more than they believe the very foundations of their own conduct that the ultimate good desired is better reached by free trade in ideas—that the best test of truth is the power of the thought to get itself accepted in the competition of the market, and that truth is the only ground upon which their wishes safely can be carried out. That, at any rate, is the theory of our Constitution. . . .
>
> . . . I think that we should be eternally vigilant against attempts to check the expression of opinions that we loathe and believe to be fraught with death, unless they so imminently threaten immediate interference with the lawful and pressing purposes of the law that an immediate check is required to save the country.
>
> I wholly disagree with the argument of the Government that the First Amendment left the common law as to seditious libel in force. History seems to me against the notion.

I should like first to notice Holmes' last point. No one today doubts that the First Amendment did leave the common law of seditious libel in force in the states in 1791. Since the publication of Leonard W. Levy's *Legacy of Suppression: Freedom of Speech and Press in Early American History* (Harvard University Press, 1960) all controversy on that subject seems to be at an end. Some doubt remains as to whether the First Amendment, which explicitly laid a prohibition only on *Congress,* allowed the *federal* courts to enforce the common law of seditious libel. But that the *states* remained free to enforce it, and did enforce it, is not in dispute. In his draft of the Kentucky Resolutions of 1798, in the third section, Jefferson cited the language of the Tenth Amendment, and then observed that no power over freedom of religion, freedom of speech, or freedom of the press being delegated to the United States by the Constitution, *nor prohibited by it to the States,* all lawful powers respecting the same did of right remain, and were reserved to the States or the people: that thus was manifested their determination to retain to themselves the right of judging how far licentiousness of speech and of the press may be abridged without lessening their useful freedom . . . [italics added].

Nothing can be clearer than that, according to Jefferson, the First Amendment laid a prohibition *only* on the federal government. So far was Jefferson from any theoretical views that would prevent the people or their governments from abridging freedom of speech and press, that he insisted that the right of judging when and to what degree they ought to be abridged was a right reserved to them by the Tenth Amendment.

In the same section Jefferson went on to speak of religious freedom in a way that distinguished it profoundly from other civil liberties. In the Constitution, he said, the people "guarded against all abridgment by the United States of the freedom of religious opinions and exercises, and retain to themselves *the right of protecting* the same [italics added]. . . ." According to Jefferson the Constitution left to the states and the people the right to judge how far freedom of speech and press might be *abridged,* but left to the same authority the right only of *protecting* freedom of religious opinions. For Jefferson this distinction between religious opinion and other opinions was fundamental. In the *Notes on Virginia,* Query XVII, he says that the legitimate powers of government extend only to those natural rights which we have submitted to government and "The rights of conscience we never submitted, we could not submit." It is in this context that he pronounces the famous dictum, that "Reason and free inquiry are the only effectual agents against error," adding immediately, "Give a loose to them, they will support the true religion by bringing every false one to their tribunal." In the Virginia Statute for Religious Freedom, again referring to religious truth and error, he wrote "that truth is great and will prevail if left to herself . . . errors ceasing to be dangerous when it is permitted freely to contradict them."

Dumas Malone, in the latest volume of his Jefferson biography (*Jefferson and the Ordeal of Liberty*. Boston: Little, Brown and Company, 1962) searches the writings of his hero in vain for even a single statement in which Jefferson defends unconditionally any freedom of opinion other than religious opinion. He finally concludes (p. 393), quoting the "reason and free inquiry" passage, that for Jefferson "freedom of thought was an absolute, and *it may be assumed* that he applied [such maxims] not merely to religious opinion but to all opinion [italics added]." But Malone is wrong. It is no accident that he is forced to make such an assumption. The evidence does not exist because Jefferson did not say what he did not believe.

Freedom of thought was indeed an absolute for Jefferson. "The error seems not sufficiently eradicated, that the operations of the mind, as well as the acts of the body, are subject to the coercion of the laws," he also wrote in Query XVII. "The legitimate powers of government extend to such acts only as are injurious to others. But it does me no injury for my neighbor to say there are twenty gods, or no God. It neither picks my pocket nor breaks my leg." With the purely theoretical question of whether there is no God or twenty, Jefferson says government has no rightful business. But on the practical aspect of the question of whether the mind has a right to entertain such questions, and whether men must be left free by government to entertain them, there was no place in Jefferson's thinking for any neutrality. The error that the mind is not inherently free to speculate, is an error which, Jefferson says, seems not to be "sufficiently eradicated." To deny the power and right of the soul to confront the universe is a denial of human nature. Marxism, for example, by teaching that all opinions on the relation of man to God and to nature are nothing but ideology, that is, devices whereby the mind justifies and thereby co-operates in particular ways of relieving the demands of the body, treats the distinction between body and mind as essentially insignificant. It is no accident that every government professing Marxism therefore attempts to coerce the operations of the mind as well as those of the body. One cannot be equally tolerant then, and certainly Jefferson was not, of opinions destructive, and of opinions not destructive, of the regime of liberty itself. The sphere comprehended by what Jefferson called religious opinions, was essentially the sphere of theory. In his pungent phrase, it was the sphere in which a man's opinion, one way or another, neither picked Jefferson's pocket nor broke his leg. But political opinions, as they bore on the security of the government which preserved men's absolute liberty of theoretical opinion, were not matters of similar indifference. These Jefferson did not entrust to the mere hazard of any "market" of ideas. In his second inaugural address he wrote:

> No inference is here intended, that the laws, provided by the State against false and defamatory publications, should not be enforced; he who has time, renders a service to public morals and public tranquility, in reforming these abuses by the salutary coercions of the law. . . .

Mr. Justice Holmes has written that persecution is perfectly logical if you do not doubt your premises or your power. But there are different kinds of "persecution." Jefferson was sick of the long, melancholy record of human government by superstition and terror. To be blunt, he had no doubt of the premises from which he deduced their illegitimacy, and he recorded his confidence when he proclaimed these premises to be self-evident truths. It was to end persecution that he and his partisans drew the sword of what was indeed a fighting faith. To persecute persecutors, or to be intolerant of intolerance is then not the contradiction that dilettantes of political philosophy sometimes affect.

As the crisis of the Civil War approached, many frenzied efforts were made to placate Southern opinion. In 1860, in the wake of John Brown's raid, Senator Douglas of Illinois proposed a sedition law to punish abolitionist propaganda as an incitement to crime. In the Cooper Union speech, Lincoln argued against any such legislation. But he never even suggested that it would be wrong to pass such a law because it violated freedom of speech or of the press. "If slavery is right," said Lincoln, "all words, acts, laws, and constitutions against it, are themselves wrong, and should be silenced, and swept away. . . . All they ask, we could readily grant, if we thought slavery right; all we ask, they could as readily grant, if they thought it wrong. Their thinking it right, and our thinking it wrong, is the precise fact upon which depends the whole controversy." Freedom of speech was logically subordinate to personal freedom, because a man who was a slave could not demand the right to speak. Lincoln argued over and over, with a logic which no one can now deny, that there was no principle by which the enslavement of Negroes could be justified, which could not also justify the enslavement of white men. The sheet-anchor of our liberties was not the Constitution but the principle of the Declaration of Independence, which alone gave life and meaning to the Constitution. To say that the Constitution protects the right to deny that all men are created equal, is as much as to say that it protects the right to deny any obligations to obey its law.

Lincoln and Jefferson both believed that a free government is the slowest and most reluctant to restrict the liberties even of its most dangerous and fanatical enemies. It is the one which least needs to protect itself by such distasteful means, because it is the one which commands the loyalty of the mass of the citizens by the benefits they feel in their daily lives. Still, it is necessary that our loyalty be enlightened, and to that end we must ever possess ourselves of the true standard by which to measure our blessings. If we fail to see the sanity and nobility of the charter of our own freedom, we will fail to recognize the barbarism of totalitarian doctrines. And it is much better if we repudiate the foul and perverted reasonings that would justify the bestiality of a Hitler or a Stalin, and all their regimes have spawned, by the force of opinion among us. For the more we accomplish by opinion, the less we will have to do by law.

11 Democracy: The Two Majorities

Willmoore Kendall

I

My point of departure is the tension between Executive and Legislature on the federal level of the American political system. My preliminary thesis is that the character and meaning of that tension, as also its role in the formation of American policy, has been too little examined during the period in which the tension has been at its highest; that the explanations of the tension that are, so to speak, "in the air," do not in fact explain it, but rather tend to lead us away from a correct explanation (and, by the same token, away from a correct understanding of our recent political history); that the entire matter, once we have the elements of a correct explanation in hand, opens up a rich field for investigation by our "behaviorists," hitherto unexplored because (in part at least) of the latter's lack of interest in what politics is really about.[1]

First, then, as to the character of the tension:

A. The tension between our "national" Executive and our

From Willmoore Kendall, *The Conservative Affirmation* (Chicago: Henry Regnery, 1963), Chapter 2, pp. 21–49. Reprinted by permission of Henry Regnery Company.

[1]This is almost, but not quite, the same point as that involved in the frequently-repeated charge that the behaviorists spend their time (and a great deal of money) studying the trivial and the obvious, a charge too often put forward by writers who are something less than ready with an answer to the question, "What *is* important?" My point is less that the reader of our behavioral literature finds himself asking "So what?" (though indeed he does), than that he finds himself asking (to quote Arnold Rogow) "What happened to the great issues?" The behaviorists go on and on as if the latter did not exist.

"national" Legislature, though as suggested above it varies in "height" from time to time and at one moment seemed to have disappeared altogether, has in recent decades been a characteristic feature of our politics.

B. The tension typically arises in the context of any attempt or expressed wish on the part of the Executive to "do" something that a majority of one or both houses is inclined to oppose. Typically, that is to say, we have an Executive proposal which—now successfully, now unsuccessfully—a large number of legislators seeks to disallow, either as a whole or in part.[2]

C. The tension is peculiarly associated with certain readily identifiable areas of public policy, and in these areas it is both continuing and predictable.[3] Those that come most readily to mind (we shall ask later what they may have in common) are:

1. The Legislature tends to be "nervous" about internal security. The Executive tends to become active on behalf of internal security only under insistent pressure from Congress; it (the bureaucracy probably more than the President and his official family) here tends to reflect what is regarded as enlightened opinion[4] in the universities and among the nation's intellectuals in general.

2. The Congress adheres unabashedly to the "pork barrel" practices for which it is so often denounced. It tends to equate the national interest, at least where domestic economic policies

[2]A distinction that is indispensable for a clear grasp of the problem. We may call it the distinction between "whether to?" and "how much?" And failure to keep it in mind often results, as I shall argue below, in our seeing Executive "victories" where there are in fact Executive defeats.

[3]We shall have something to say below about what we might call the "latent but always present tension" in certain other areas of public policy, where the Executive would like to do such and such, but because of Professor Friedrich's "law of anticipated reactions" does not dare even to formulate a proposal. Much of what we hear about the so-called "decline" or "eclipse" or "fall" of Congress becomes less convincing when we take into account the matters in which Congress always gets its way because the Executive, much as it would like to do such and such, is not sufficiently romantic even to attempt it.

[4]No implication is intended, at this point at least, as to whether the opinion *is* enlightened, as that question is inappropriate to our immediate purposes.

are concerned, with the totality of the interests of our four-hundred-odd congressional districts.[5] The Executive regards "pork barrel" measures as "selfish" and "particular," and does what it can, through pressure and maneuver, to forestall them. It appeals frequently to a national interest that is allegedly different from and superior to the interests of the constituencies.

3. The Legislature *tends* to be "protectionist" as regards external trade policy. The Executive, again reflecting what is regarded as enlightened opinion among intellectuals, tends to favor ever greater steps in the direction of "free trade," and acceptance by the United States of a general responsibility for the good health of the world economy.

4. The Legislature (again a similar but not identical point) tends to "drag its feet" on foreign aid programs, unless these promise a demonstrable military "pay-off." The Executive seems to be deeply committed to the idea of foreign aid programs as the appropriate means for gaining American objectives that are not exclusively, or even primarily, military.[6]

5. The Congress (though we must speak here with greater caution than has been necessary above because the relevant tension expresses itself in a different and less readily visible way) does not, by its actions at least, reflect what is regarded as enlightened opinion among intellectuals on the complex of issues related to the integration of the southern schools, withholding all action that might ease the Executive's path in the matter. The Executive stands ready to enforce the ruling in the *Brown* case, and seems unconcerned about the difficulty of pointing to any sort of popular mandate for it.

6. The Legislature insists upon perpetuating the general type of immigration policy we have had in recent decades. The Ex-

[5]Cf., *The Federalist,* ed. Edward Mead Earle ("The Modern Library" [New York: Random House, n.d.]), *No. 64:* ". . . the government must be a weak one indeed if it should forget that the good of the whole can only be promoted by advancing the good of each of the parts or members which compose the whole." All subsequent citations to *The Federalist* are by number of the relevant paper.

[6]It perhaps gives to "military objectives" a wider and looser meaning than the congressmen are willing to accept.

ecutive would apparently like to bring our immigration legislation under, so to speak, the all-men-are-created-equal clause of the Declaration of Independence.

7. The Legislature is, in general, jealous concerning the level of the national debt, and thus about government spending; it clings, in principle at least, to traditional notions about sound government finance. The Executive, at least the vast majority of the permanent civil servants (who are, as is well known, in position to bring notable pressures to bear even upon a President who would like, on this or that, to side with Congress), appears to have moved to what we may call a Keynesian position about the national debt and year-to-year spending.

8. The Legislature tends to be "bullish" about the size of the United States Air Force and, in general, about military expenditure as opposed to expenditures for "welfare." The Executive, though no simple statement is in order about its policies, continuously resists congressional pressure on both points.

9. The Legislature tends to be "nationalistic," that is, to be oriented to the "conscience" of its constituents rather than the "conscience of mankind." The Executive tends to be "internationally minded," that is, to subordinate its policies in many areas to certain "principles" concerning the maintenance of a certain kind of international order.

10. The Legislature appears to have little quarrel with Right-wing dictatorships; it tends to favor policies with respect to them based rather upon expediency than upon ideological commitment to democratic forms of government. The Executive, despite the tendencious charges we often hear to the contrary, is disposed to hold governments not based upon free elections at arm's length.

11. The Executive[7] tends to favor each and every component of the current program (the product of what is generally regarded as enlightened opinion among political scientists at our universities) for transforming the American political system into a *plebiscitary* political system, capable of producing and carry-

---

[7]For the sake of simplicity of exposition, I here reverse the previous order, and speak first of the Executive.

ing through *popular mandates*. These components, so well known as to require only the briefest mention, are: Remake our major political parties in such fashion that their programs, when laid before the American people in presidential elections, will present them with "genuine" "choices" concerning policy, and that candidates for office within each party will stand committed to their party's program. (The major public spokesmen for such a reform are the chairmen of the national committees, one of whom is of course the appointee of the President.) Get rid of the Senate filibuster, as also of the seniority principle in congressional committees (which do indeed make it possible for little bands of willful men to "frustrate" alleged majority mandates). Iron out inequalities of representation in Congress, since these, theoretically at least, are capable of substituting the will of a minority for that of the majority. (Although it is perhaps difficult to attribute any policy on the latter two components to the White House itself, anyone who has himself been a permanent civil servant knows that in the executive departments the animosity against the filibuster, the seniority principle, and the alleged "over-representation" of rural folk and white southerners is both intense and deeply-rooted.) Further, assure equal representation and thus genuine majority mandates, by enacting ever stronger "civil rights" legislation calculated to prevent the white southerners from disfranchising or intimidating potential Negro voters, and by putting the Department of Justice permanently into the business of enforcing the "strengthened" civil rights. (The extreme "proposals" here do normally originate with senators and congressmen, but it will hardly be disputed that the White House is consistently on the side of the proponents, and consistently disappointed by Congress' final reply from session to session, to the question, "How much?") "Streamline" the executive branch of government, so as to transform it into a ready and homogeneous instrument that the President, backed up by his "disciplined" majority in Congress, can use effectively in carrying out his mandate, and so as to "concentrate" power and make it more "responsible" (by getting rid of the independent agencies, and eliminating the duplication and competition between agencies that perform the same or very similar tasks). Finally, glorify and enhance the office of President, and try to make of presidential elections the central ritual of American politics—so that, even if the desired reform of the party system cannot be achieved at once, a newly-elected President with a popular majority will be able to plead, against a recalcitrant Congress, that *his* mandate must prevail.

Congress seldom shows itself available to any such line of argument, and off-year congresses like to remind presidents, in the most forceful manner possible, that the system has rituals other than that of the presidential election. For the rest, it resists the entire program with cool determination. With respect to the party system, it is clearly wedded to our traditional system of decentralized parties of a non-"ideological" and non-programmatic character. With respect to mandates, it clearly continues to regard the American system as that which, as I contend below, its Framers intended it to be—that is, one in which the final decisions upon at least the important determinations of policy are hammered out, in accordance with "the republican principle," in a deliberative assembly made up of *uninstructed* representatives, chosen by their neighbors because they are the "virtuous" men. That is, a system which has no place for mandates. As for the filibuster and the committee chairmen, Congress clearly regards as their peculiar virtue that which the Executive and its aggrandizers within the bureaucracy and out among the nation's intellectuals regard as their peculiar vice, namely, that they *are* capable of frustrating an alleged majority mandate. With respect to "streamlining" the executive branch of government, Congress appears to yield to proposals in this sense only when it has convinced itself that further resistance is an invasion of presidential prerogatives rooted in the same constitution from which it derives its own. It clearly clings to the traditional view, again that of the Framers themselves, that power should *not* be concentrated, but rather (since a most efficient Executive might well turn out to be most efficient against the liberties of the people) shared out in such fashion that ambition may counter ambition. With respect to civil liberties, Congress clearly cherishes the notion that the Tenth Amendment has not been repealed, and that, accordingly, there is room in the American system for differences in civil liberties from state to state and even, within a state, for differences in civil liberties from differently situated person to differently situated person. With respect to the aggrandizement of the office of president and the glorification of presidential elections, it again takes its stand with the tradition and the Framers: there is no room in the American system for a presidential office so aggrandized as to be able itself to determine how much farther the aggrandizement shall go. The ultimate decisions on that point, Congress holds, must be made not by the President but by itself, in the course of the continuing dialectic between its members and their constituents: plebiscitary presidential elections cannot become the central ritual of our system without destroying the system.

II

What general statements—of a sort that might throw light on their meaning in the American political system—may we venture to make about these areas of tension?[8]

At least, I believe, these:

A. They all involve matters of policy which, by comparison

[8]I do not forget that the areas of tension are also areas of tension *within* both houses of Congress, where the Executive always, when the big issues are "up," has considerable support, and sometimes "wins" (or at least seems to). It would be interesting, though not relevant to the purposes of the present chapter, to study the incidence of the tensions within Congress (as revealed, e.g., in voting, about which we have a rich and growing literature), particularly with a view to discovering whether there is a discernible "trend" in this regard. As also whether there is any relation, of the kind my analysis below would lead us to expect, between the character of an M.C.'s constituency and the "side" he takes in these mattters. One imagines that the tensions are also repeated within the bosom of the Executive. But we must not get in the habit of permitting our sophistication about such matters to obscure for us the fact that "Congress" acts finally as an institution, whose "behavior" as an institution can and for some purposes must be observed without regard to its internal divisions.

with those involved in areas where tension is not evident and predictable, bear very nearly indeed upon the central destiny of the United States—on the kind of society it is going to become ("open" or relatively "closed," egalitarian and redistributive or shot through and through with great differences in reward and privilege, a "welfare state" society or a "capitalist" society); on the form of government the United States is to have (much the same as that intended by the Framers, or one tailored to the specifications of egalitarian ideology); or on our relatedness to the outside world on points that, we are often told, nearly affect the central destiny of mankind itself. They are all areas, therefore, in which we should expect disagreement and thus tension in a heterogeneous society like ours (though by no means necessarily, I hasten to add, tension between its Legislature and its Executive—not, at least, for any reason that leaps readily to the eye).

B. They are areas in which the Executive (as I have already intimated) is able, with good show of reason, to put itself forward on any particular issue as the spokesman for either "lofty and enlightened principle" or still undiffused professional *expertise,* or both. The Executive tends, that is to say, to have the nation's ministers and publicists with it on "peace," the nation's professors and moralizers with it on desegregation, the nation's economists with it on fiscal policy and redistribution, the nation's political scientists with it on political reform and civil rights, etc. To put it otherwise, Congress at least *appears,* in all the areas in question, to be holding out for either the repudiation or evasion of the moral imperatives that the nation's "proper teachers" urge upon us, or the assertion of an invincibly ignorant "layman's" opinion on topics that are demonstrably "professional" or "expert" in character, or both. The Executive is for world government, for the outlawing of war, for unselfishness in our relations with the outside world, for the brotherhood of man, for majority-rule, for progress, for generosity toward the weak and lowly, for freedom of thought and speech, for equality, for the spreading of the benefits of modern civilization to "underdeveloped" lands, for science and the "scientific outlook," for civil rights. And apparently it is its being for these things that some-how runs it afoul of Congress in the areas in question, so that it is difficult to avoid the impression that Congress is somehow against the things mentioned, and against them because wedded to bigotry, to selfishness both at home and abroad, to oppression, to the use of force, to minority rule, to outmoded notions in science. Because the Executive so clearly represents "high principle and knowledge," the conclusion is well nigh irresistible that Congress represents low principle (or, worse still, no principle at all), reaction, and unintelligence, and does so in full knowledge that the President (both he and his opponent having, in the latest election, asserted the same high principles and the same generally enlightened outlook) has not merely a majority mandate but a virtually unanimous mandate to go ahead and act upon high principle.

C. They are areas that, for the most part, do not lend themselves to what is fashionably called "polyarchal bargaining." For example, the internal security policies that Congress has in recent years imposed upon the Executive have been in no sense the result of protracted negotiations among "groups," conducted with an eye to leaving no group too unhappy; so too, with the policy that it imposes (by inaction) with regard to the desegregation of the southern schools, and that which it imposes (by action) concerning immigration and the armed forces. To put it otherwise, the policy problems involved are by their very nature problems about which everybody can't have a little bit of his way, because we move in either this direction (which some of us want to do) or in that direction (which others of us want to do). The line Congress takes with respect to them seems to be determined much as before, the now fashionable "group interpretation" of our politics took shape, we supposed all policy lines to be determined—that is, by the judgment of individuals obliged to choose between more or less clearly understood alternatives, and obliged ultimately to choose in terms of such notions as they may have of justice and the public weal.

D. They are areas—though we come now to a more delicate

kind of point—in which, little as we may like to think so and however infrequently we may admit it to ourselves, Congress pretty consistently gets its way. Indeed the widespread impression to the contrary seems to me the strangest optical illusion of our politics, and worth dwelling upon for a moment. The question actually at issue becomes, quite simply, whether in recent decades (since, say, 1933) the liberals—for, as intimated repeatedly above, the tension between Executive and Legislature is normally a liberal-conservative tension—have or have not been "winning." I contend that the reason both liberals and conservatives tend (as they do) to answer that question in the affirmative is that we are all in the habit of leaving out of account two dimensions of the problem that are indispensable to clear thinking about it.

First, we cannot answer the question without somehow "ranking" political issues in order of "importance"—without, for example, distinguishing at least between those issues that are most important, those that are important but not most important, those that are relatively unimportant, and those that are not important at all—meaning here by "important" and "unimportant" merely that which the liberals and conservatives themselves deem important or unimportant. In the context of such a ranking we readily see that "winning" in our politics is a matter of getting your way on the matters that are most important to you, not getting defeated too often on those that are merely important to you, and taking your big defeats on those that are relatively unimportant to you or not important at all. Take for instance that liberal "victory" of the period in question that comes most readily to mind: the creation and maintenance of the Tennessee Valley Authority. Everyone familiar with the politics of the period knows that the TVA enthusiasts intended TVA to be the first of a *series* of "authorities," which would have the effect of shifting the entire American economy away from "capitalism" and "free private enterprise." That was what the liberals wanted, and that was what the conservatives, if they meant business, had to prevent. That was what was "most important," against the background of which the creation and maintenance of a single TVA (one, moreover, that men could support out of no animus whatever against private enterprise) was at most "unimportant." And, once we put the question "Who won?" in those terms, and remind ourselves where the White House and the bureaucracy stood, we are obliged to give an answer quite different from that which we are in the habit of giving. The Executive got its TVA in particular, but Congress put a stop to TVA's in general (nor—a point worth making again and again—is there any issue so dead in America today as that of "Socialism").

Secondly, there is the dimension we have mentioned briefly above, that of the things that the Executive would like to propose but has the good sense not to because of its certain foreknowledge of the impossibility of getting the proposals through Congress—it being here that Congress most consistently gets its way, and without anyone's noticing it.[9] James Burnham is quite right in arguing that the capacity to say "No" to the Executive is the essence of congressional power;[10] but he exaggerates the infrequency with which Congress does say "No," partly by ignoring the "No's" that Congress does not have to say for the reason just given, and partly by failing to distinguish between the "No's" that are "most important" to the Congress itself and those that are not.

To summarize: The areas of tension are typically "most important" areas in which this or that application of high principle desired by the Executive gets short shrift from enough congressmen and senators to prevent it or at least to prevent it on anything like the *scale* desired by the Executive. And in these

[9] Let anyone who doubts the point (a) poll his liberal acquaintances on the question, Is it proper for non-believers in America to be taxed for the support of churches and synagogues (which they certainly are so long as churches and synagogues are exempted from taxation)? and, (b) ask himself what would happen in Congress if the Treasury Department were to propose removal of the exemption. There is no greater symbol of Executive-Legislative tension than the fact that the sessions of both houses open with prayer, whereas we cannot imagine a prayer at the beginning of a meeting of, say, an interdepartmental committee of bureaucrats.

[10] Cf., James Burnham, *Congress and the American Tradition* (Chicago: Henry Regnery, 1959), p. 278.

areas the Congress normally "wins," "high principle" seemingly going by the board. Nor would it be easy to show—and this brings us to the nub of the matter—that the tensions are less acute, or produce a notably different result, during the two-year periods that precede presidential elections than during the two-year periods that follow them. The latter, if it were true, might enable us to argue that the tensions arise because of shifts of opinion in the electorate, or that they relate particularly to the two-thirds of the senators who, after any biennial election, are "holdovers." And, that being the case, we are obliged, as I have already intimated, to confront an unexplained mystery of our politics: the fact that *one and the same electorate maintains in Washington, year after year, a President devoted to high principle and enlightenment, and a Congress that gives short shrift to both;* that, even at one and the same election, they elect to the White House a man devoted to the application of high principle to most important problems of national policy, and to the Hill men who consistently frustrate him. More concretely: the voters give an apparent majority mandate to the President to apply principles "x, y, and z," and a simultaneous (demonstrable) majority-mandate[11] to the Congress to keep him from applying them. And the question arises, Why, at the end of a newly-elected President's first two years, do the voters not "punish" the congressmen? Are the voters simply "irrational"? Our political science has, it seems to me, no adequate or convincing answer to these (and many kindred) questions.

III

What is "in the air" in American political science (to return now to the hint thrown out above) because of which my statement of the problem of executive-legislative tension sounds unfamiliar—not to say "against the grain"? Not, I think, any doctrines that clash head-on with such a statement on the

[11]Unless we want to argue that Congress does not have a majority mandate. See below my reasons for thinking such a position untenable, pp. 259–262.

ground that it appears to move in a direction that might be "pro-Congress"; that would be true only if contemporary American political science were "anti-Congress," which I, for one, do not believe to be the case[12] (besides which the statement is not, up to this point, "pro-Congress"). Not either, I think, any specific doctrine or doctrines concerning executive-legislative tensions as such; for though contemporary American political science is certainly not unaware of the tensions (it might, at most, be accused of sweeping them now and then under the rug, contrary to the rules of tidy housekeeping), it seems safe to say that there is no prevailing "theory" of the problem. The answer to our question lies rather, I believe, in this: there are overtones in the statement, perhaps even implications, that simply do not "fit in" with what we are accustomed these days to say or assume—not about executive-legislative tensions, but about some very different matters; namely, elections, majority rule, and the comparative "representativeness," from the standpoint of "democratic theory," of the Executive and the Legislature. And perhaps the best way to bring the relevant issues out into the open is to fix attention on what we *are* accustomed to hear said and assumed about these matters.

I propose to use for this purpose Robert A. Dahl's celebrated Walgreen lectures,[13] which precisely because they are not "anti-Congress" (are, rather, the handiwork of one of our major and most dispassionate experts on Congress) have the more to teach us about the problem in hand. The lectures seem to me to show that we are accustomed now to assume (if not to say) that when we speak of "democratic theory," of majority rule in the United States, we can for the most part simply ignore Congress and congressional elections. This is nowhere asserted in the *Preface*, but I submit to anyone familiar with it *both* that such a tacit premise is present throughout its argument—which goes on and on as if our presidential elections were not merely

[12]There is, of course, an "anti-Congress" literature, but there is also an enormous literature that is friendly to Congress.

[13]Robert A. Dahl, *Preface to Democratic Theory* (Chicago: University of Chicago Press, 1956).

the central ritual of our politics but also the sole ritual—and that Dahl's tacit premise seems, in the present atmosphere, perfectly natural.

But let us think for a moment about that premise, and the resultant tacit exclusion of executive-legislative tension as a problem for democratic theory (Dahl, I think I am safe in saying, nowhere in the *Preface* refers to it).[14] To put the premise a little differently, the majority-rule problem in America is the problem of the presidential elections; either the majority rules through the presidential elections (which Dahl thinks it does not), or it does not rule at all. A book about majority rule in America does not, in consequence, any longer need to concern itself at any point with the possibility that fascinated the authors of *The Federalist*, namely, that of the "republican principle" as working precisely through the election of members to the two houses of Congress. And the effect of that premise, whether intended or not, is to deny legitimacy, from the standpoint of "democratic theory," alike to Congress as a formulator of policy, and to the elections that produce Congress as expressions of majority "preferences." That is, to deny the relevance of those elections to the problem to which the authors of *The Federalist* regarded them as most relevant, i.e., the problem of majority rule in America.[15] Nor is the reason for the premise difficult to discover: for Dahl, and for the atmosphere of which his book may fairly be regarded as an accurate distillation, Congress, especially the lower house, is a stronghold of entrenched minorities[16]—and in

[14]The function of his Congress, in the *Preface* anyhow, is that of "legitimizing basic decisions by some process of *assent*" (italics added), and of registering pressures in the process he likes to call "polyarchal bargaining." See respectively pp. 136, 145.

[15]Cf., *The Federalist, No. 54:* "Under the proposed Constitution, the federal acts . . . will depend merely on the majority of votes in the federal legislature. . . ." Cf., *No. 21:* "The natural cure of an ill-administration, in a popular or representative constitution, is a change of men"—through, of course, elections. Cf. also *No. 44:* If Congress were to ". . . misconstrue or enlarge any . . . power vested in them . . . in the last resort a remedy must be obtained from the people, who can, by the election [in elections where the candidate who gets the largest number of votes wins?] of more faithful representatives, annul the acts of the usurpers."

[16]Dahl, *op. cit.*, p. 142.

any case is, and was always intended to be, a barrier to majority rule, not an instrument of majority rule.[17] It is bicameral; its members are chosen in elections deliberately staggered to prevent waves of popular enthusiasm from transmitting themselves directly to its floors. It "overrepresents" rural and agricultural areas and interests; many of its members are elected in constituencies where civil liberties, including even the liberty to vote, are poorly protected, so that the fortunate candidate can often speak only for a minority of his constituents. And as the decades have passed it has developed internal procedures—especially the filibuster and the seniority principle in the choice of committee chairmen—that frequently operate to defeat the will of the majority even of its own members.[18] It reflects, in a word, the anti-democratic, anti-majority-rule bias of the Framers, who notoriously distrusted human nature (because of their commitment to certain "psychological axioms").[19]

Now the doctrine just summarized is so deeply imbedded in our literature that it may seem an act of perversity to try, at this late moment, to call it into question (as the overtones and implications of my discussion in I and II certainly do). The present writer is convinced, however, that a whole series of misunderstandings[20]—partly about the Framers and partly about majority rule—have crept into our thinking about the matter, and that these have disposed us to beg a number of questions that it is high time we reopened. The Framers, we are being told, distrusted the "people," cherished a profound animus against majority rule, and were careful to write "barriers" to majority rule into their constitution. But here, as it seems to me, the following peculiar thing has happened. Taught as we are by decades of political theory whose creators have been

[17]*Ibid.*, p. 14.

[18]*Ibid.*, p. 15. I am sure Professor Dahl will not object to my mentioning that the point about civil liberties, although not present in his book, he has pressed upon me in private conversation.

[19]*Ibid.*, p. 8.

[20]To which I must plead myself guilty of having contributed, particularly in my *John Locke and the Doctrine of Majority-Rule* (Urbana: University of Illinois Press, 1941).

increasingly committed to the idea of majority mandates arising out of plebiscitary elections, we tend to forget that that alternative, not having been invented yet, was not in the mind of the Framers at all. Which is to say, we end up accusing the Framers of trying to prevent something they had never even heard of,[21] and so cut ourselves off from the possibility of understanding their intention. Above all we forget that what the Framers (let us follow the fashion and accept *The Federalist* as a good enough place to go to find out what they thought) were primarily concerned to prevent was the states' going their separate ways—their becoming an "infinity of little, jealous, clashing, tumultuous commonwealths"[22]—so that there would *be* no union in which the question of majority rule could arise. The "majority rule" they feared was the unlimited majority rule *within the several states* that would, they thought, result from disintegration of the union; and we are misreading most of the relevant passages if we read them in any other sense. We take an even greater liberty, moreover, when we sire off on the Framers the (largely uncriticized) premise that the proper remedy for the evils of some form of majority rule is as a matter of course non-majoritarian. No one knew better than they that the claim of the majority to have its way in a "republican" (or "free") government cannot be successfully denied;[23] indeed what most amazes one upon rereading *The Federalist*, in the context of the

[21]This is not to deny that the "barriers" do, as it turns out, operate to prevent a plebiscitary system. My point is they were not, and could not, have been intended to, but also that a plebiscitary system is not the only possible majority-rule system.

[22]*The Federalist, No. 9.*

[23]Cf., *ibid., No. 58:* ". . . the fundamental principle of free government would be reversed. It would no longer be the majority that would rule. . . ." Cf., *No. 22*, with its reference to the fundamental maxim of republican government as being: that the "sense of the majority shall prevail." Cf., *ibid.:* ". . . two thirds of the people of America could not long be persuaded . . . to submit their interests to the management and disposal of one third." Compare Dahl, *op. cit.*, pp. 34, 35, where after citing various strong pro-majority-rule statements from political philosophers, he concludes that they are all "clearly at odds with the Madisonian view." Note that one of the statements, curiously, is from Jefferson, whom Dahl immediately describes as a "Madisonian."

literature with which we have been deluged since J. Allen Smith, is precisely the degree of their commitment to the majority principle,[24] and their respect and affection for the "people" whose political problem they were attempting to "solve."[25] Their concern, throughout, is that of achieving popular control over government, not that of preventing it.[26] That they thought to do by leaving the "people" of the new nation organized in a particular way,[27] in constituencies which would return senators and congressmen, and by inculcating in that people a constitutional morality that would make of the relevant elections a quest for the "virtuous" men[28]—the latter to come to the capital, normally, without "instructions" (in the sense of that term—not the only possible sense—that we are most familiar with). These virtuous men were to *deliberate* about such problems as seemed

[24]See preceding note. The point has been obscured by our habit of reading the numerous passages that insist on ultimate control by the "people" on the assumption, impossible in my opinion to document, that the authors of *The Federalist* thought they had discovered some way to have matters decided by the people in elections, *without* having them decided by a majority of the people. See following note.

[25]Cf., *ibid.*, *No. 14:* "I submit to you, my fellow-citizens, these considerations, in full confidence that the good sense which has so often marked your decisions will allow them due weight and effect. . . . Hearken not to the unnatural voice which tells you that the people of America . . . can no longer continue the mutual guardians of their mutual happiness. . . . Is it not the glory of the people of America [that they have heeded] . . . the suggestions of their own good sense, the knowledge of their own situation, and the lessons of their own experience?" Such passages abound in *The Federalist*.

[26]Cf., *ibid.*, *No. 40:* ". . . the Constitution . . . ought . . . to be embraced, if it be calculated to accomplish the views and happiness of the people of America." Cf., *No. 46:* ". . . the ultimate authority . . . resides in the people alone. . . ."

[27]Cf., *ibid.*, *No. 39:* "Were the people regarded . . . as forming one nation, the will of the *majority of the whole people* . . . would bind the minority . . . and the will of the majority must be determined either by a comparison of the individual votes, or by considering the will of the majority of the States. . . . Neither of these rules has been adopted" (italics added).

[28]Cf., *ibid.*, *No. 57:* The chosen are to be those "whose merit may recommend [them] to . . . esteem and confidence. . . ." Cf., *No. 64*, with its reference to assemblies made up of "the most enlightened and respectable citizens" who will elect people "distinguished by their abilities and virtue. . . ."

to them to require attention and, off at the end, make decisions by majority vote; and, as *The Federalist* necessarily conceived it, the majority votes so arrived at would, because each of the virtuous men would have behind him a majority vote back in his constituency, represent a popular majority. (My guess, based on long meditation about the relevant passages, is that they hoped the deliberation would be of such character that the votes would seldom be "close," so that the popular majority represented would be overwhelming.) That, with one exception, is the only federal popular majority of which Madison and Hamilton were thinking—the exception being the popular majority bent on taking steps adverse to natural rights,[29] that is, to justice. What they seem to have been thinking of here, however, and took measures (though not drastic ones)[30] to prevent, was precisely *not* an electoral majority acting through a plebiscitarily-chosen president, but rather a demagogically-led movement that might sweep through the constituencies and bring pressure to bear upon the congressmen. Nor must we permit our own emancipation, because of which we know that the difference between unjust steps and just ones is merely a matter of opinion, to blind us to the implied distinction between a popular majority as such and a popular majority determined to commit an injustice. Madison and Hamilton not only thought they knew what they meant, but did know what they meant when they used such language;[31] and we err greatly when we confuse their animus against the popular majority bent on injustice with an animus against the popular majority, the majority of the people, as such.

Ah, someone will object, but you have conceded that the

[29]*I.e.,* a majority "faction." See *ibid., No. 10, passim.*

[30]Indeed, Madison clearly believed (*ibid.*) that nothing could be done *constitutionally* to block a majority "faction."

[31]That is, when they distinguished between just and unjust, and measures adverse to the rights of others and measures not adverse to them. Cf., *ibid.*: ". . . measures are too often decided, not according to the rules of justice and the rights of the minor party, but by the force of an interested and overbearing majority." Cf., Dahl, *op. cit.,* p. 29, where he illustrates the gulf between himself and the Madisonians by writing "good" and "bad," the implication being, I take it, that the distinction is operationally meaningless.

measures they took operate equally against both; the Framers, that is to say, made it just as difficult for a popular majority as such, even a popular majority bent upon *just* measures, to capture the Congress and use it for its purposes, as for an "unjust" majority. But here again we must hold things in their proper perspective—by keeping ourselves reminded that Madison did not think the measures we have in mind (staggered elections and bicameralism in particular) would constitute much of a barrier to either. As Dahl himself points out, Madison placed his sole reliance against the popular movement that snowballs through the constituencies in the hope that the constituencies would, because of the growth and development of the nation, become so numerous, so widely flung, and so diverse as to make it impossible to bring people together into the kind of popular movement he feared. But there are several other dimensions to the thought implicit in *The Federalist* on this matter. There is, first, the constitutional morality suggested in the doctrine concerning the virtuous men; these being, by definition, men bent upon justice, constituency elections turning upon the identification of virtuous men would on the face of them constitute a major barrier to a popular movement bent upon injustice,[32] *but not to a widespread popular movement demanding something just.*[33] Second, there is the fact that the Constitution, being a constitution that limits governmental power, might fairly be expected to bear more heavily upon the prospects of an unjust movement, which as Madison must have known is of the two the more likely to run afoul of the relevant limitations, than on a just one. And there is, thirdly, the fact that so long as the system works as Madison intended it to, bicameralism and staggered elections themselves might be expected to bear more heavily upon an unjust movement than upon a just one. They constitute a "barrier," as far as Congress

---

[32]Cf., *ibid., No. 51:* ". . . a coalition of a majority . . . could seldom take place [except on] principles . . . of justice and the general good."

[33]Cf., *ibid., No. 57,* where it is argued that a political constitution should aim at obtaining for "rulers men who possess most wisdom to discern, and most virtue to pursue, the common good of the society"—and taking the "most effectual precautions for keeping them virtuous. . . ."

is concerned, only to the extent that the hold-over senators and the congressmen from constituencies not yet captured by the spreading popular movement *resist* the relevant popular pressures—which they are most likely to do by debate in the course of deliberation, and can do most effectively precisely when they are able to wrap themselves in the mantle of justice (which by definition they cannot do if the popular movement is itself bent upon justice). In fine, once we grant the distinction between a popular majority in the constituencies bent upon injustice and a popular movement bent upon something just, grant it with all the literalness with which it was intended, there remains no reason to attribute to Madison, or to the Constitution he defended, any animus against popular majorities (as such) having their way. He simply wanted, I repeat, the majority to be articulated and counted in a certain way, and had confidence that so long as it was it would produce just results. And we must, if we are to bring the whole problem into proper focus, recognize that the Madisonian majority, articulated through and counted within the constituencies, is still present in the American political system. Which is to say that we must learn to think in terms of what we may call *two* popular majorities, the congressional and the presidential. And we must accept, as an unavoidable problem for American political theory, the problem of the respective merits of the two (and must not, like Professor Dahl, talk as if one of them did not exist). What is at stake when there is tension between Congress and President is not the majority principle (the "Rule," Dahl calls it), but rather the question of where and how we are to apply it.

IV

What we are always dealing with in the American system is, on the present showing, Two Majorities, two *numerical* majorities,[34] each of which can, by pointing to the Rule, claim what Dahl calls the "last say," and each of which merits the attention

[34]But cf., Burnham, *op. cit.,* p. 316 (and the preceding discussion) for a different view of the two majorities. Burnham, of course, follows Calhoun.

of that part of "democratic theory" that deals with the problem of majority rule. The moment this is conceded, moreover, the problem of executive-legislative tensions begins to appear in the light in which it is presented above.

As for the merits of the respective claims of the two majorities, I content myself here with the following observations:

A. One of the two majorities, the presidential, has (as I have intimated) been *engrafted* onto our political system: it was not intended by the Framers, not even present to their minds as something to be "frustrated" and have "barriers" put in its way. It is, in other words (insofar as we can satisfy ourselves that it exists *qua* majority and eventuates in "mandates"), something new in our politics; something therefore whose appropriateness to the spirit and machinery of our system may fairly be regarded as still open to question. (I hope I shall not be understood to mean that its newness necessarily establishes a presumption against it.)

B. Professor Dahl, for all his fascination with presidential elections, is himself the author of the most brilliant demonstration we have (or could ask for) that nothing properly describable as a majority mandate, sanctioned by the Rule, emerges from a presidential election.[35] Indeed, one way of stating the question concerning the merits of the respective claims of the two majorities is: Is the congressional majority open to the same objections, from the standpoint of the Rule, that Dahl brings so tellingly against the presidential? If not, we should be obliged to view with suspicion Dahl's contention that, there *being* no majority in America, the majority cannot rule (so that we can stop worrying about majority tyranny).[36]

C. It is interesting to notice that some of the claims that Madison (were we, like Professor Dahl, to go, so to speak, to his assistance) might be imagined as making for *his* majority "mandate,"

[35]Dahl, *op. cit.*, pp. 124–131.

[36]*Ibid.*, p. 25, and Chap. V, *passim*. It might be pointed out that Dahl has difficulty deciding just how to phrase the point; "rarely, if ever," does not say the same thing as "rarely," and "ruling on matters of specific policy" does not say the same thing as "ruling."

cannot, as Dahl demonstrates, be made for the side that gets the most votes in a presidential election:

1. Madison's majority mandate does not stand or fall with the possibility of proving that the voters who are its ultimate sanction voted for the same man because they endorse the same policies; the other kind of majority mandate, as Dahl admirably shows, does.[37] Madison's is *heterogeneous* by definition—is supposed to be and was intended to be heterogeneous. Indeed, without its being heterogeneous, it cannot accomplish its intended purpose, which is the ultimate arriving at policy decisions through a process of deliberation among virtuous men representing potentially conflicting and in any case different "values" and interests.

2. It is at least potentially *continuous* in its relation to the voters, whereas, as Dahl shows, the presidential sanction is *discontinuous*[38] (his majority speaks, insofar as it speaks at all, then promptly disappears), and because continuous not sporadic, potentially simultaneous with policy decisions even when they do not coincide with an election. Indeed, the major difference between Madison and Dahl as theorists of majority rule is precisely that Dahl clearly cannot, or at least does not, imagine a popular majority-rule system as working through any process other than that of elections, which, as he himself sees, are in the nature of the case discontinuous and prior to actual policy decisions. Madison, on the other hand, is not in the first place all that preoccupied with elections, and ends up describing a majority-rule process rich in possibilities (as we all know) for what we may, with Burnham, call a continuing dialectical relationship between the virtuous men and their constituents. However, this relationship by no means necessarily takes the form of the member of Congress "keeping his ear to the ground" and seeking to carry out automatically the "will" of a majority of his constituents; he is himself a part of his constituency, potentially "representative" in the special sense of reacting to policy problems just as his constituents *would* were they present, and he also is in-

[37]*Ibid.*, pp. 127–129.
[38]*Ibid.*, p. 130.

formed (which, of course, they often are not). The dialectic, moreover, as Madison could hardly have failed to realize, may take the form of the representative's actually *thinking with* his constituents, whether by communication back and forth or in the course of visits back home.[39] Finally, as again Madison certainly knew, the member of Congress will, if normally ambitious, wish to be reelected, and will not willingly become a party to policy decisions that, when they come to the attention of his constituents, will seem to them foolish or outrageous; which means that he must ask himself continuously how at least his general course of behavior is ultimately going to go down at home.

3. In two senses, Madison's majority mandate does not need to be, and Madison did not expect it to be, "positive" in the way that a writer like Dahl assumes a mandate must be if it is to be really a mandate.[40] First, it is as likely to express itself in prohibitions and "vetoes" as in imperatives. And second, the popular command involved is basically, as Madison conceived it, a command to help produce *just* policy decisions in a certain manner, and normally does not presuppose a positive mandatory relation with respect to particular matters.

4. Madison's is a mandate that emerges from a process that was always intended to emphasize specifically moral considerations, e.g., the kind of considerations involved in deciding who are the virtuous men. To put the point otherwise: it is a process that was originally conceived in terms of a moral theory of politics, while the theorists of the presidential mandate tend, to say the least, to a certain relativism about morals (which is why they can end up insisting that this and this must be done because the majority demands it *tout court*). Its emphasis, therefore, is on the ability of the people (i.e., at least a majority of the people)

---

[39]The essence of *Federalist* thought here is that of a "deliberate sense of the community" (meaning by community, surely, not less than a majority?) formed as problems arise and get themselves discussed in the Congress and out over the nation, and by no means necessarily expressing itself always through elections.

[40]*Ibid.*, pp. 129, 131.

to make sound judgments regarding the virtue of their neighbors, not on their ability to deliberate on matters of policy. (Dahl leaves us in no doubt about their inability to do the latter.)

V

The above considerations seem to me not only to throw light on the respective claims of the Two Majorities, but also to show why (assuming that the older of the two continues to function much as Madison intended it to, which I do believe to be the case) we have no cause to be astonished at the fact of executive-legislative tension in our system. There is no reason *a priori* to expect the virtuous men to be attracted as a matter of course to the proposals put forward by the Executive (with whatever claim to a "majority mandate" for them); at least, that is to say, we see how such tension might occur. But there are some further considerations that seem to me to show why it *must* occur, and at the same time to throw light on how each of us should go about making up his mind as to which of the two to support. These are:

A. The essentially aristocratic character of the electoral process that produces the older of the majorities as over against the essentially democratic character of the electoral process that produces the newer (despite the fact that the electors are in the two cases the same men and women). A moment's reflection will reveal at least one reason for that aristocratic character: although the constituencies and states differ greatly in this regard, they all nevertheless approximate, in a way in which the national constituency cannot do, to structured communities, involving numberless, highly complex face-to-face hierarchical relations among individuals—of superordination and subordination, of capacity to influence or subject to pressure and susceptibility to being influenced or subjected to pressure, of authority and obedience, of economic power and economic dependence, of prestige enjoyed and respect tendered, etc., all of which are patently relevant to the choice of a congressman or senator in a way that they are not relevant to the choice of a president. In the election of the member of Congress, a community faithful to the constitutional morality of *The Federalist* makes a decision about whom to send forward as its most virtuous man, a decision which is the more important, and which it accordingly takes the more seriously, because the community knows that it can have little effect on a presidential election (i.e., its most direct means of defending its own interests and "values" is by sending the right senator or representative to Washington, and sending the right one becomes therefore a matter of sending a man who will represent the hierarchical relations in which those interests and values are articulated). In the congressional election, therefore, the "heat" can and will go on if there is a powerful community "value" or interest at stake in the choice among available candidates; so that although the voters vote as nominal "equals" (one man, one vote) they do so under pressures that are quite unlikely to be brought to bear on their "equal" voting for President (especially as the powerful and influential in the community are normally unable to estimate accurately, for reasons we shall notice below, the probable impact of the presidential candidates upon their interests and "values," whereas they can do so with the candidates for the legislature). This state of affairs is reflected in the notorious fact that congressmen and senators, when they phone home to consult, are more likely, other things being equal, to phone bank presidents than plumbers, bishops than deacons, editors than rank-and-file newspaper readers, school superintendents than schoolmarms—and would be very foolish if they were not more likely to. And the unavoidable result is that the men chosen are likely to be far more conservative, far more dedicated to the "status quo," than the candidate whom the same community on the same day helps elect President (or, to anticipate, than the candidate whom the same community on the same day helps defeat for President). And the chances of their disagreeing with that candidate a few months later on "most important" and "important" questions are, on the face of it, excellent—so that we have at least one built-in reason for expecting executive-legislative tension.

B. The difference in the discussion process as we see it go forward in the constituencies, and the discussion process as we see it go forward in the national forum. This is partly a matter of the point just made (that the constituency is to a far greater extent a structured community), and partly a matter (not quite the same thing) of the sheer difference in size between the local constituency and the nation—or, as I should prefer to put it, of the kind of considerations that led that remarkable "empirical" political theorist, J. J. Rousseau, to declare, at a crucial point in *Du contrat social*, that there is more wisdom in small bands of Swiss peasants gathered around oak trees to conduct their affairs than, so to speak, in all the governments of Europe. One of the questions that that sentence necessarily poses, when we examine it carefully (and that which leads on to what I believe to be a correct interpretation of it), is whether it intends a tribute (which the attribution of wisdom certainly was for Rousseau), (1) to the Swiss, or (2) to peasants, or (3) to peasants who are also Swiss, or (4) to small groups of persons caught up in a certain kind of discussion situation. The context, I suggest, leaves no doubt that the correct answer here is (4): Rousseau certainly thought highly of the Swiss, but not so highly as to claim any sort of monopoly of wisdom for them. He also thought highly of peasants, because of their simplicity of life (if you like—which I don't—because of their closer approximation to the "noble savage"), but precisely *not* because of their native wisdom in the sense intended here, which evidently has to do with wise decisions concerning public affairs. By the same token, as we know from the *Julie*, he thought highly of Swiss peasants in particular, but not so highly as to permit himself the claim that the small bands, merely because made up of Swiss peasants, are the repositories of wisdom. The emphasis, in other words, is upon the "small bands," the fact that each embraces only a small number of individuals, and on the fact of that small number being gathered to dispatch the public business of a small community—the Swiss peasants and the oak tree being simply the symbol, the example, that comes most readily to Rousseau's mind. So we are led on to ask, what difference or differences does Rousseau think he sees between their "deliberation" and other kinds of deliberation? We can, I think, answer with some confidence. First, there is a presumption that each small band is talking about something, not nothing. Second, there is a presumption, because of each band's relatedness to the community whose affairs it is dispatching, that its members are reasonably well-informed about the something they are talking about—the implication being (it is caught up and developed in the *Government of Poland*) that, as a discussion group increases in number and a constituency in size, there is greater and greater danger that the persons concerned will find themselves talking about nothing, not something, and will also find themselves talking about situations and problems that are too large, too complicated, for them to understand. Wise deliberation—the point recurs again and again in Rousseau's political writings—occurs only where people are discussing problems that they can, so to speak, "get outside of," and where the participants in the discussion are not so numerous as to give scope to the gifts of the orator and the rhetorician.

Now: evidently a congressional or senatorial constituency is not a small band gathered around an oak tree; but also nothing can be more certain than that the *national* constituency in America long ago became so large and complex that, even were there candidates who themselves understood it (which is doubtful), the audiences to which they must address themselves do not understand it, cannot even visualize it. Yet we have engrafted upon our constitution an additional electoral process that forces discussion of "national" problems in the national constituency; that obliges candidates to "go to the people" and court votes; and that, for the reason just mentioned, makes it necessary for them to avoid talking about something and leaves them no alternative but to talk about nothing—that is (for this is always the most convenient way of talking about nothing), to talk about high (or at least high-sounding) principle, without application to any concrete situation or problem. Add to this the fact that the candidates, hard put to it to produce in a few weeks enough speeches to see them through the campaign, must enlist the assistance of speech-writers, who come as a matter of course from the intellectual community we have frequently mentioned above, and things—*inter alia,* the sheer impossibility of saying, after a presidential election, what "issues" it has decided—begin to fall into place. There are no issues, because both candidates for the most part merely repeat, as they swing from whistle-stop to whistle-stop and television studio to television studio, the policy platitudes that constitute the table-talk in our faculty clubs. No one, not even the most skilled textual analyst, can tease out of the speeches any dependable clue as to what difference it will actually make which of the two is elected. It seems probable, indeed, that the candidates themselves, unless one of them be a White House incumbent, do not know what use they would make of the vast powers of the presidency. And the inevitable result, as intimated above, is that what you get out of the presidential election is what amounts to a *unanimous* mandate for the principles *both* candidates have been enunciating, which is to say: the presidential election not only permits the electorate, but virtually obliges it, to overestimate its dedication to the pleasant-sounding maxims that have been poured into its ears. Even did the electorate not deceive itself on this point, moreover, it has no way to arrest the process: it must vote for one of the two candidates, and tacitly commit itself, whether it likes it or not, to what they have both been saying.

We now stand in the presence, I believe, of the decisive explanation of executive-legislative tension in the American political system, and the decisive clue to its meaning. Elections for congressmen, and up to now at least most elections for senator, do not and cannot follow the pattern just outlined. With rare exceptions, for one thing, the relevant campaigns are not running debates between the candidates, and thus do not offer them the temptation to raise each other's ante in the matter of principle. For another thing, principle is for the most part *not* what gets talked about, but rather realities, problems, the potential benefits and potential costs (and for whom) of doing this rather than that—all in a context where the principles that are applied are those (very different we may be sure from those of the presidential candidates) upon which the constituents are actually accustomed to act. The talk generated by the campaign, much of it at least, is in small groups made up of persons involved in the actual face-to-face situations we spoke of earlier, and is, therefore, not wholly dissimilar to that of those peasants under the oak tree. So that, insofar as the presidential election encourages the electorate to overestimate its dedication to moral principle, the congressional election encourages them, nay, obliges them, to take a more realistic view of themselves, and to send forth a candidate who will represent, and act in terms of, that more realistic view. By remaining pretty much what the Framers intended them to be, in other words, the congressional elections, in the context of the engrafted presidential election, provide a highly necessary corrective against the bias toward quixotism inherent in our presidential elections. They add the indispensable ingredient of Sancho Panzism, of not liking to be tossed up in a blanket even for high principle, and of liking to see a meal or two ahead even if the crusade for justice has to bide a little. And it is well they do; the alternative would be national policies based upon a wholly false picture of the sacrifices the electorate are prepared to make for the lofty objectives held up to them by presidential aspirants. And executive-legislative tension is the means by which the corrective works itself out.

If the foregoing analysis is correct, the tension between Executive and Legislative has a deeper meaning—one which, however, begins to emerge only when we challenge the notion that the "high principle" represented by the President and the bureaucracy is indeed high principle, and that the long run task is to somehow "educate" the congressmen, and out beyond the congressmen the electorate, to acceptance of it. That meaning has to do with the dangerous gap that yawns between high principle as it is understood in the intellectual community (which makes its influence felt through the President and the bureaucracy) and high principle as it is understood by the remainder of the population (which makes its influence felt through the Congress). To put it differently, the deeper meaning emerges when we abandon the fiction (which I have employed above for purposes of exposition) that we have on the one hand an Executive devoted to high principle and a Legislature whose majority simply refuse to live up to it, and confront the possibility that what we have is in fact two *conceptions* of high principle about which reasonable men may legitimately differ. Whilst we maintain the fiction, the task we must perform is indeed that of "educating" the congressmen, and, off beyond them, the electorate, "up" to acceptance of high principle. Once we abandon it, the task *might* become that of helping the congressmen to "educate" the intellectual community "up" to acceptance of the principles that underlie congressional resistance to executive proposals. In the one case (whilst we maintain the fiction), discussion is unnecessary; in the other case (where we recognize that what we stand over against is two sharply differing conceptions of the destiny and perfection of America and of mankind, each of which conceivably has something to be said for it), discussion is indispensable. And in order to decide, as individuals, whom to support when executive-legislative tension arises, we must reopen (that is, cease to treat as closed), reopen in a context of mutual good faith and respect, the deepest issues between American conservatism and American liberalism. Reopen them, and, I repeat, discuss them; which we are much out of the habit of doing.

12 Communism: The Struggle for the World

James Burnham

The great captains of military history, varied as they have been in every other respect, have all been noted for their grasp of what military writers call "the key to the situation." At each level of military struggle, from a brief skirmish to the grand strategy of a war or series of wars, they have understood that there is one crucial element which is this key to the situation. The key may be almost anything: a ford across a river, or a hill like Cemetery Ridge at Gettysburg; a swift blow at the enemy reserve, or the smashing of the enemy fleet as at Trafalgar or Salamis; stiff discipline on the flanks as at Cannæ, or a slow strangling blockade for an entire war; a long defensive delay to train an army or win an ally, or a surprise attack on a capital; control of the seas, the destruction of supplies, or the capture of a hero.

The great captain concentrates on the key to the situation. He simplifies, even over-simplifies, knowing that, though the key alone is not enough, without it he will never open the door. He may, if that is his temperament, concern himself also with a thousand details. He never allows details to distract his attention, to divert him from the key. Often he turns the details,

From James Burnham, *The Struggle for the World* (New York: John Day, 1947), Chapter 10, pp. 130–135; and James Burnham, *The War We Are In* (New Rochelle, N.Y.: Arlington House, 1967), Chapter 1, pp. 9–23, and Chapter 10, pp. 330–343. *The Struggle for the World.* Copyright © 1947 by James Burnham. Reprinted by permission of the John Day Company, Inc., and James Burnham. *The War We Are In.* Copyright © 1967 by James Burnham. Reprinted by permission of Arlington House, Publishers.

which in quantitative bulk total much larger than the key, over to his subordinates. That is why the genius of the great captain is often not apparent to others. He may seem a mere figurehead, indolent, lethargic, letting the real work be done by those around him. They fail to comprehend that the secret of his genius is to know the key, to have it always in mind, and to reserve his supreme exertion for the key, for what decides the issue.

The principles of political struggle are identical with those of military struggle. Success in both political knowledge and political practice depends finally, as in military affairs, upon the grasp of the key to the situation. The exact moment for the insurrection, the one issue upon which the election will in reality revolve, the most vulnerable figure in the opposition's leadership, the deeply felt complaint that will rouse the masses, the particular concession that will clinch a coalition, the guarded silence that will permit an exposure to be forgotten, the exact bribe that will open up a new Middle Eastern sphere of influence, the precise hour for a great speech: at each stage and level of the political process there is just one element, or at most a very small number of elements, which determines, which decides.

The great political leader (who is often also a great captain)— Pericles or the elder Cato or Mohammed or Cæsar or Henry of Navarre or Bismarck or Hamilton or Lenin or Innocent III or the younger Pitt—focuses on the key. He feels whether it is a time for expansion or recovery, whether the opposition will be dismayed or stimulated by a vigorous attack, whether internal problems or external affairs are taking political precedence. He knows, in each political phase, what is the central challenge.

During the late 12th and for most of the 13th centuries, the Papacy struggled with the Hohenstaufen Empire, and concluded by destroying the Hohenstaufen. For all of Italy that struggle was in those times the key to the general political situation, no matter how it appeared to those whose political sense was distracted by temporary and episodic details. For the first generation of the 5th century B.C., the political key in the Aegean was the attempt of Persia to conquer the Hellenic world. All of the contests among the Greek states, and all their internal city squabbles, were in reality subordinate to the relation with Persia. For a generation in America, until it was decided by the Civil War, the key was the struggle for a united nation. Everything else in politics, foreign or domestic, was secondary. For Western Civilization as a whole at the turn of the 19th century, the key was the contest between England and France. England won, perhaps, because her governing class concentrated on the key, whereas Napoleon, only vaguely glimpsing the key with its shaft of sea power, dissipated his energies.

For a given nation, the political key is located sometimes among internal, sometimes among foreign affairs. For the United States, the key during most of its independent history has been internal: union or slavery or the opening of the West or industrialization or monopoly. For England, quite naturally, it has been more ordinarily, though by no means always, an external relation. It may be the church or the army or the peasant problem, or, for a brief period, a spectacular scandal like the Dreyfus affair or the South Sea Bubble or Teapot Dome.

We have entered a period of history in which world politics take precedence over national and internal politics, and in which world politics literally involve the entire world. During this period, now and until this period ends with the settlement, one way or another, of the problems which determine the nature of the period, all of world politics, and all of what is most important in the internal politics of each nation, are oriented around the struggle for world power between Soviet-based communism and the United States. This is now the key to the political situation. Everything else is secondary, subordinate.

The key is, much of the time, hidden. The determining struggle is not apparent in the form of individual political issues, as they arise week by week. The deceptive surface is the cause of the political disorientation and futility of so many of the observers and actors, which so particularly infect the citizens and leaders of the United States. They base their ideas and actions on the temporary form of political events, not on the controlling reality.

Yugoslavia disputes with Italy over Trieste. Chiang Kai-shek fights with Chou En-lai over North China. Armenians begin to clamor for an independent Armenia. The new Philippine government confronts a revolt of the Hukbalahaps. Poland argues with Mexico in the Security Council. The French Cabinet calls for an immediate break with Franco. Harry Lundberg and the communists fight for control of the United States waterfront. The American Labor Party and the Liberal Party jockey for position in New York State. The British Communists apply for admission to the Labour Party. The World Federation of Trade Unions demands an official voice in the United Nations. The International Harvester Company objects to sending tractors to the Balkans. Japanese printers' unions refuse to set up editorials they don't like. Sweden signs a commercial agreement with Moscow. The United States asks for bases in Iceland or the Azores. Bulgaria, Yugoslavia and Albania arm and succor Macedonian partisans. Joseph Clark Baldwin, ousted by the New York Republicans, is endorsed by Vito Marcantonio. Australia objects to the veto power.

The eyes of the public become entangled in the many-colored surface. The exact ethnic complexion of Venezia Giulia is debated with ponderous statistics. Owen Lattimore proves at length that Chiang is not quite democratic and that many peasants support Yenan. Arthur Upham Pope explains that there are reactionary landlords in Iran. Henry Wallace describes the geography of Siberia. *The Nation* catalogues the villainies of Franco. *PM* sturdily denounces the crimes of Greek Royalists. *The New Republic* gives the history of agricultural oppression in the Philippines. The innocent bystanders send in their dollars, join committees, and sign open letters.

The statistics and records and swarms of historical facts are admirable enough to have at hand. But by themselves they are shadows, ashes. If we do not look through them to the living body, the focal fire, we know nothing. If we do not grasp that

Trieste and Thrace, and Armenia and Iran and North China and Sweden and Greece are the border marches between the communist power and the American power, and that all the statistics and records are filigree work on the historical structure, then we know nothing. We know less than nothing, and we fall into the trap which those who do know deliberately bait with all the statistics and records. It is their purpose to deceive us with the shadows and to prevent us from seeing the body. If we do not know that the American Labor Party has nothing to do with America or with Labor or with any of the issues stated in its program and speeches, but is simply a disguised colony of the communist power planted within the enemy territory, then, politically, we know nothing. If we do not understand that the World Federation of Trade Unions is merely a device manipulated by the N.K.V.D. to further the communist objective of infiltrating and demoralizing the opponents in the Third World War, then we have not begun to realize what is at issue in the world. The central point is not whether Chiang is a democrat—though that too is an important point—but that he is, in his own fashion, a shield of the United States against the thrust of communist power out of the Heartland. The debates in the Security Council are not really over the absurd procedural ritual that appears on the surface of the minutes. The ritual is like a stylized formal dance reflecting in art the battle of the Titans.

Walter Lippmann, after a tour of Europe in the Spring of 1946, told us in a widely publicized series of articles that the main issue of world politics was the contest between England and the Soviet Union, which was coming to a head in the struggle over Germany. The United States he found to be in the comfortable position of an impartial umpire who could generously intervene to mediate and settle the dispute. Mr. Lippmann was right in insisting on the crucial present role of the fight for Germany. But one look at the political map of Europe, with a side-glance at the state of India and the British colonies, should be enough to demonstrate that England could not possibly stand up as principal in a challenge to the communist power. England in Germany, whatever her intentions, functions as a detachment of the greater power which is the only existing rival in the championship class. If it were really England, and if the pressure of the United States were withdrawn from the European arena, the decision over Germany would long since have been announced.

The determining facts are merely these: Western Civilization has reached the stage in its development that calls for the creation of its Universal Empire. The technological and institutional character of Western Civilization is such that a Universal Empire of Western Civilization would necessarily at the same time be a World Empire. In the world there are only two power centers adequate to make a serious attempt to meet this challenge. The simultaneous existence of these two centers, and only these two, introduces into world political relationships an intolerable disequilibrium. The whole problem is made incomparably sharper and more immediate by the discovery of atomic weapons, and by the race between the two power centers for atomic supremacy, which, independently of all other historical considerations, could likewise be secured only through World Empire.

One of the two power centers is itself a child, a border area, of Western Civilization. For this reason, the United States, crude, awkward, semi-barbarian, nevertheless enters this irreconcilable conflict as the representative of Western culture. The other center, though it has already subdued great areas and populations of the West, and though it has adapted for its own use many technological and organizational devices of the West, is alien to the West in origin and fundamental nature. Its victory would, therefore, signify the reduction of all Western society to the status of a subject colony. Once again, the settled peoples of the Plains would bow to the yoke of the erupting Nomads of the Steppes. This time the Nomads have taken care to equip themselves from the arsenal of the intended slaves. The horses and dogs have been transformed into tanks and bombs. And this time the Plains are the entire earth.

Between the two great antagonists there is this other difference, that may decide. The communist power moves toward the climax self-consciously, deliberately. Its leaders understand what is at stake. They have made their choice. All their energies, their resources, their determination, are fixed on the goal. But the Western power gropes and lurches. Few of its leaders even want to understand. Like an adolescent plunged into his first great moral problem, it wishes, above all, to avoid the responsibility for choice. Genuine moral problems are, however, inescapable, and the refusal to make a choice is also a moral decision. If a child is drowning at our feet, to turn away is to decide, as fully as to save him or to push him under. It is not our individual minds or desires, but the condition of world society, that today poses for the Soviet Union, as representative of communism, and for the United States, as representative of Western Civilization, the issue of world leadership. No wish or thought of ours can charm this issue away.

This issue will be decided, and in our day. In the course of the decision, both of the present antagonists may, it is true, be destroyed. But one of them must be. . . .

The War We Are In

The first sentence of my book, *The Struggle for the World*, which was published early in 1947, reads: "The Third World War began in April 1944." . . .

In a more basic sense, however, what began in the spring of 1944 was not so much a "new" Third World War as a new phase in a continuing war that started in November 1917,[*] with the Bolshevik conquest of power in Russia, that might indeed be dated most significantly from Lenin's organization of the Bolshevik faction of the Russian Social Democratic Labor Party in 1903: the protracted war of the communist enterprise for a monopoly of world power. On the coordinates of this longer-term scale, the protracted war is seen as the dominant theme of

---

[*]This is the explicit premise of a detailed study by André Fontaine, Foreign Editor of the leading French newspaper, *Le Monde*, the first volume of which was published in France in 1966 with the title: *Histoire de la guerre froide: De la Révolution d'Octobre à la guerre de Corée.*

twentieth-century history, with its major phases fairly well marked, though overlapping: 1) formation and training of the cadres of the revolutionary army (1903–1917); 2) seizure of the initial base, or beachhead (1917); 3) failure of the first direct attack on the advanced Western powers (1917–1923); 4) consolidation and defense of the base (1917–1944); 5) enlargement of the base (1944–1949 explosively, and irregularly in the years following); 6) indirect attack on the Western powers through support of decolonization and of anti-Western nationalism in the underdeveloped regions of Asia, Africa and Latin America (1944–   ); 7) recognition of the United States as the main enemy, and consequent direction of the main effort to the weakening, isolation and ultimate defeat of the United States (1944–   ). On this same scale the first two "world wars" as well as the post-1956 "Sino-Soviet split" appear as subthemes: disputes *within* one or the other of the two major camps.

The term "Cold War" refers, more or less, to the same set of facts that I have been designating "Third World War." Most people are inclined to interpret either term as an exaggerated metaphor. They feel one doesn't literally mean "war"; that the *real* "Third World War" is something that might happen in the future, when the nuclear bombs start bursting, something that we are trying desperately to avoid while at the same time we prepare for the possibility that it might break out in spite of our best efforts. The communists do not share this conventional view, though they play up to it through the slogan of "peaceful coexistence." Its practical consequences, therefore, are almost necessarily damaging to the non-communist side. By conceiving "the war" as a possible event in the future, which we must prepare to deal with if and when it comes, or preferably find ways to avoid altogether, we are led to minimize the importance of the struggle that we are actually engaged in. That clearly demarcated future "war" may never take place, but meanwhile we can be defeated in stages during the course of the actual struggle.

The Cold War (if we prefer that inexact and inadequate name for the war we are in) has its own special features that, taken in their entirety, distinguish it from other wars, though none of them is unique. It is not formally "declared"—a legalism often dispensed with from tribal days to Hitler's. It is a "limited" war, in the sense that the rivals have not been employing their full weaponry and resources. But this restraint is not unusual in other wars. The "phoney war" period of the Second World War is a notable parallel in recent memory. Such periods of muted operations have been common in the protracted conflicts of the past: the Peloponnesian wars; the Punic wars; the prolonged medieval struggle between the Guelph and the Ghibelline factions; the Thirty Years War; the sixteenth-nineteenth centuries' contest among Britain, France, Spain and Holland for mastery of the seas; prolonged struggles in several epochs of Indian and Chinese history, etc.

If limited in the employment of resources (though the resources that have been brought to bear are in fact greater than in any previous war), the Cold War is not limited in its aim, its geographic scope or the scale of its encounters. The communist side has from the very beginning been unambiguous about its aim: a "World Federation of Soviet Socialist Republics," as it has been expressed in many official programs and manifestoes; a state of affairs in which "the international party shall be the human race," in the words of the hymn of the Revolution; "to bury you," as Khrushchev put it in his peasant-rhetoric; a communist monopoly of world power, as we might summarize it in neutral language, without over-specifying the institutions and internal relationships in which this monopoly might be embodied. If no positive aim has been adopted or stated by the non-communist side, the most basic war aim of all—namely, survival—is implicit both in the actions taken and in the negative programs, such as "containment" or "competitive coexistence," that are from time to time formulated. In any case, it takes only one side to make a war and to define its stakes.

As for geography, the Cold War is the first in history to involve the entire world; the first two World Wars did not live up to their title. And perhaps the easiest way to grasp the scope and significance of the campaigns of the Cold War—the Third

World War, that is—is to consider what has been won and lost as a result of some of them: the communist conquest, in the immediate post-1944 round, of all the nations of eastern Europe, with 100 million inhabitants; communist conquest of mainland China, northern Korea and northern Vietnam, Tibet and, in 1960, a first outpost in the Americas; successful defense by the non-communists (there have been no positive non-communist victories) of Greece, Malaya, the Philippines, Burma, South Korea, Guatemala and Indonesia. In very few wars in history, perhaps in none, have there been victories and defeats affecting such vast areas and populations.

One thing that the Cold War has *not* been is "cold." From the very beginning of this present phase, that is, from 1944, there have been fighting and bloodshed. The fighting has extended to every continent—from Greece to China, Cuba to Zanzibar, Tibet to Venezuela, Indonesia to Hungary, Burundi to Quemoy, Korea and Vietnam to the Congo—and has gone on continuously.

It is hardly surprising that in the conduct of a war there should be shooting and killing. What is perhaps most distinctive about this war we are in is its multi-dimensional, indeed omni-dimensional nature. It is conducted, though with shifting emphases, along every social dimension: economic, political, cultural, racial, psychological, religious as well as military; and the military dimension comprises every sort of guerrilla, terrorist, paramilitary, partisan and irregular combat as well as fighting by conventional forces. The omni-dimensional nature of the war follows from the totalitarian and utterly radical nature of communism. The communist enterprise is simultaneously a secular religion, a conspiracy and a new kind of army. According to communist doctrine, the communist objective is not merely to take power, but to re-create both man and society, to make a new kind of man in a new kind of society. All that has happened to mankind up until now is "prehistory"; true "history" begins only with the advent of communism. Existing non-communist civilization expresses essentially the exploitation and corruption of a class society; it cannot be reformed, but must be over-thrown and destroyed, so that the new communist man can build in its place the new classless communist society. The communist enterprise, therefore, in carrying out both its negative and its positive tasks (*i.e.*, destroying class society and building communism), must concern itself with every social sector and activity, with trade unions as well as armies, churches along with banks, schools and factories as well as governments.

This war we are in is particularly characterized as being omni-dimensional, but it perhaps is even more sharply distinctive for the fact that within the omni-dimensional deployment psycho-political operations have been raised to the level of a primary weapons system. It is very difficult for non-communist military professionals to grasp this fact. According to non-communist military doctrine and practice, psycho-political operations ("propaganda") do have a role in modern warfare, but a minor, non-essential role, merely supplementary to the direct fighting by regular forces. But in communist doctrine, things are often the other way around; the fighting by the regular forces is merely the completing chapter of a struggle that has been conducted for the most part by psycho-political methods plus, perhaps, paramilitary and other irregular military methods.

To the traditionally trained military mind it seems absurd to say that a psycho-political weapon can be stronger than a nuclear weapon. Nevertheless, if we think carefully we will realize that in one sense at least this must always be the case: since the nuclear weapon, and any physical weapon, is nothing at all apart from the human will that decides whether or not to trigger it. The fact of the matter is that the psycho-political operations of the communist enterprise did successfully neutralize American nuclear arms, both when this country possessed an absolute nuclear monopoly—and thereby a more overwhelming relative military supremacy than any nation has held—and during the much longer period when this country had a decisive nuclear superiority. Indeed, communist psycho-political operations continue to block American use of components of its nuclear arsenal that would be dictated by objective strategic considerations.

Stalin conquered Czechoslovakia, as Hitler had done before

him, by exclusively psycho-political means. A long-term global psycho-political campaign that deceived Western opinion and diverted the Western nations from deterrent intervention was an indispensable element in the communist conquest of China. Castro's conquest of Cuba was accomplished through an integral blend of psycho-political and paramilitary measures. The communists in Moscow, Peking and New York as well as in Hanoi have openly admitted that they could not hope to defeat the anti-communist forces in South Vietnam by direct military means, and that their only chance to win would be through the success of psycho-political operations on the American domestic front. All these are dramatic, big-scale examples, but psycho-political operations enter as a primary if not the dominant system into every communist undertaking.

. . . A significant period of the irregular history of the Third World War came to an end and a new period opened in the latter part of 1956. This turning point was marked by two dramatic episodes that took place, in part simultaneously, in the autumn of 1956: the aborted revolt in eastern Europe that swelled up in East Germany and Poland and reached its climax in Hungary; and the aborted Anglo-French invasion of the Suez isthmus (to which the Israeli invasion of the Sinai desert was an incidental appendage). By their outcome these two episodes summarized the net geopolitical results of the preceding period and foreshadowed certain of the trends that were to prevail in the period to follow.

The East European affair proved: 1) The communist regimes had failed to win the allegiance, or even the voluntary adherence, of the peoples of the East European nations. 2) The communist enterprise was prepared to crush opposition by military force wherever and whenever the opposition was serious and the use of military force feasible. 3) The Western powers in general and the United States specifically were not prepared to aid an opposition inside the communist zone by direct or indirect military means, or to furnish any significant quantity of personnel, weapons, supplies or diplomatic assistance to an opposition struggle. This demonstrated—most importantly, to the communist leaders—that there was no substance left in the "policy of liberation" which had figured in the Eisenhower-Dulles rhetoric during the 1952 campaign and had lingered on in some official pronouncements during President Eisenhower's first term. Actually, a policy of liberation had been ruled out in principle, in favor of the policy of containment, as early as the spring of 1950, when President Truman approved National Security Council document NSC-68. But it was the Hungarian revolt that clarified and defined what abandonment (or, at any rate, indefinite postponement) of a perspective of liberation meant in practice.

Moscow, Peking and the global communist enterprise knew, by virtue of the Hungarian affair, that they were guaranteed against outside interference within their household. Within the communist zone they could handle domestic matters in their own fashion, without risking anything worse from outsiders than a routine moralistic scolding. "The imperialists"—so Hungary proved—had swallowed a doctrine cooked up for them by the dialecticians: the doctrine of "the two zones." "The zone of peace" corresponds to the acreage already brought under communist rule, and is off-limits to disturbers; opposition seeking to change or overthrow the government is counter-revolutionary treason, to be crushed by all necessary means. "The zone of war" is the acreage still free from communist rule. Within the zone of war, opposition—from the Left—that seeks to change or overthrow the government is "progressive"; its actions constitute a "struggle for national liberation," deserving support by "all freedom-loving peoples." This doctrine of the two zones, it may be added, is the essence of "the policy of peaceful coexistence."

The two-zone doctrine applies to the Chinese as to the Soviet sectors of the communist domain. When the Tibetans revolted against the Chinese Communist protectorate over their country, the United States and its Western allies kept hands strictly off, exactly as in the earlier case of the Hungarians; the reaction was confined as usual to moral indignation. Although the containment principle seems to call for resistance to an attempted extension of the zone of peace, the two-zone doctrine tends to be applied retroactively if the extension is successfully accomplished, with a resultant communist regime in control of the new area. Even when the extension in the Cuban case, reached inside the strategic threshold of the United States' continental base, the influence of the doctrine prevented a serious effort to reclaim the lost island, and led to the floundering, half-hearted catastrophe of the Bay of Pigs. In the confrontation of the autumn of 1962, upon which his strategic reputation rests, President Kennedy limited himself to getting rid of the missiles that posed a direct and intolerable military threat to United States home territory; in return, he accepted Cuban territory under its communist regime as an integral part of the zone of peace, and therefore off limits for counter-action.

The continuing role of the two-zone doctrine has been evident in the political management of the Vietnam war. Although military necessity has demanded attacks on North Vietnam, these have been kept, for each stage, at the lowest possible intensity—much below what military judgment would ideally call for; and they have been accompanied by repeated formal declarations that the United States does not aim at overthrowing or changing the communist government of North Vietnam. The communist regime in North Vietnam lies within the zone of peace, and is therefore inviolable.

The Suez episode was simultaneous with the Hungarian revolt, as if History were emphasizing that it was merely the other face in the toss of a single coin. If we look at a globe or global map we see at once that the Isthmus of Suez is the land bridge between Asia and Africa, and that the water passage through the isthmus—the Suez Canal—is the link between Europe's sea and the Indian Ocean—which might be more descriptively called "the Afro-Asian Ocean." The isthmus is thus one of the earth's key strategic posts; control of the isthmus is one of the primary strategic prizes.

This is of course why Britain and France, realizing that the isthmus was being taken over by an anti-Western Arab revolutionary closely linked to the Soviet power, attempted to regain control for the West by the joint military expedition. The expedition failed, just as the Hungarian revolt failed. It failed, essentially, because President Eisenhower not merely declined to support or even condone it, but actively vetoed it, and compelled Britain and France to withdraw.

The Suez abortion signified:

1) Africa was henceforth open to Asia; the guard had left the bridge. In 1956—to note one sufficiently significant set of symbols—there did not exist a single independent Communist Party south of the Sahara, except for a small Party in South Africa. There were some communists—mostly whites—but they were attached to one or another of the West European parties. Moreover, there was in 1956 no special bureau in the Soviet Foreign Ministry to handle African affairs; but soon after the Suez episode—in 1958—an African Department was set up, initially under A. V. Budakov. At about the same time, local communist organizations began to be formed in various of the nations-to-be. Some of these were tied to Soviet or East European principals, others to the Chinese, who exploited the Afro-Asian legitimacy they had acquired by their prominence at the 1955 Bandung conference.

2) European colonialism, largely ousted from Asia and the South Pacific in the period from the end of the Second World War to 1956, was on its way out in Africa. The Suez episode was the opening of the floodgate. The tide of "liberation" swept over the continent with a speed much greater than anyone in any camp had imagined possible, much greater than that of any comparable phenomenon in prior history. Suez also gave the signal for clearing up several of the Asian remnants of European colonialism (western New Guinea, Goa).

3) The abject failure of Britain and France in the Suez episode, together with the collapse of their African colonial domains which it foretold, confirmed the fact that, whether acting separately or jointly, they were no longer major world powers. And if Britain and France were not, no other European power

acting separately or in a limited combination, was. Theoretically it remained possible that a western Europe unified or integrated in some fashion might be able to regain the top global level, but the required degree of integration did not exist and was not in prospect.

4) Both the Soviet Union and the United States acted to abort the Suez invasion, but the initiative was taken by the United States. Throughout, it was the United States that played the major role; the Soviet Union merely tagged along. In this respect the Suez affair was not exceptional. In the liquidation of European colonialism—both in the African phase that lay immediately ahead and in the Asian phase of the preceding period—the United States has invariably played an active, and frequently the leading, role. It may be that historically the epoch of European colonialism had ended in any event, but there is no doubt that the active policy of the United States—most conspicuously in relation to Indonesia, India and sub-Saharan Africa—speeded the fall of the curtain.

5) Liquidation of European colonialism left a political vacuum in much of Africa, which the native leadership was neither sufficiently large nor adequately trained to fill. Liberation therefore tended to open the road, in varying measure, to chaos, communism and neo-colonialism.

Throughout this period (and for some years to come) chaos becomes the ally of communism. It is through political and social chaos that the lingering influences, attitudes and institutions tying the decolonialized nations to Europe and more generally to Western civilization can be rooted out. With minor and precarious exceptions (Zanzibar, Congo-Brazzaville) the communists have not yet been in a position to undertake full-scale revolutions in Africa that would result in consolidated communist regimes. The earlier phase of revolutionary development can take the form of the much easier task of promoting chaos, with the accompanying destruction of Western institutional links and pro-Western individuals.

In many of the new African nations, the economic, political and military power of the United States has been drawn in to supplement or replace the declining European power in shoring up against chaos and combating the communist incursions, as well as to advance American economic interest according to the neo-colonial mode: *cf.* Congo-Léopoldville, Kenya, Nigeria, Ghana, Ethiopia, as well as Morocco, Tunisia and Algeria in the African north.

Nikita Khrushchev used the phrase "peaceful coexistence" to describe the state of global affairs that was expressed and symbolized in the dual Hungary-Suez episode. The meaning of "peaceful coexistence" must be understood within the system of revolutionary dialectic. So translated, it is seen to be equivalent to "the Cold War," or what I have called "the Third World War." "Peaceful coexistence" *means* the revolutionary struggle of the communist enterprise against the non-communist world, conducted as this struggle has *in fact* been conducted since 1944: that is, by all the methods of multi-dimensional warfare except for general and thus (in our age) nuclear combat. The concept of "peaceful coexistence" includes the two-zone doctrine that I have discussed: it is a violation of peaceful coexistence if the West attempts to stir up opposition within the communist sphere (the zone of peace); it is a defense of peaceful coexistence when the communists attempt to stir up opposition right to the point of revolutionary struggle ("war of liberation") within the non-communist sphere (the zone of war). Such struggle is "for peace" because it is against "the imperialist warmongers and their puppets" and in defense of "the peace-loving masses," and also because it advances the development of the world socialist society in which war will be impossible. The "defense of peace" is identical to the struggle against the non-communist forces, above all to the struggle against the United States.

The period of "peaceful coexistence" will presumably culminate in "the final struggle": that is, in a general war, when the time is ripe, that will involve nuclear arms. The general war would most probably be initiated by a communist nuclear strike against the decisive non-communist targets. This too would be not a contradiction but a fulfillment of peaceful coexistence: the zone of peace would finally be in a position to liquidate the zone of war, and thereby extend the zone of peace to the entire earth; "the international party will be the human race." Meanwhile, however, the warmongers must be prevented from starting all-out war, most particularly a nuclear war, from their side, or from taking any other action—"aggressive" by definition—that would threaten the frontiers or security of the zone of peace.

In short, peaceful coexistence presupposes a "nuclear stalemate"; and there has in fact been a nuclear stalemate, or what has more lately come to be called a "balance of terror," throughout these years. In the Third World War no one has set off a nuclear weapon for combat purposes; that is the fact of the matter. It is clear, moreover, that the main course of events has presupposed the nuclear stalemate: the stabilization of the East European frontier; the draw in Korea; the post-Suez free-for-all in Africa; the acceptance of communist takeover in China, Tibet and Cuba; the military conduct of the Vietnam war, etc. Whatever might have happened if some or many nuclear weapons of one kind or another had been used, no one will doubt that they would have greatly altered the way things have gone without them. The nuclear stalemate has been a basic parameter of our epoch.

Most persons think of "nuclear stalemate" as a condition in which the non-communist nuclear arsenal is counterbalanced by the communist nuclear arsenal; more specifically, in which United States and Soviet nuclear weapons counterbalance each other—not necessarily because they are equal in quantity, but because each side's nuclear arsenal is capable of visiting "unacceptable" damage on the other side. Such a relationship might induce a nuclear stalemate, but is neither a sufficient nor even a necessary condition. Indeed, "nuclear stalemate" is not fundamentally a quantitative or physical, but a psychological relationship. A nuclear stalemate exists, no matter what the actual weapons situation, when the possessor or possessors of nuclear weapons are not willing to accept the consequences of using them.

In this fundamental sense there seems to have been a nuclear stalemate throughout the Third World War, except perhaps at the time of the Middle Eastern and Quemoy-Matsu crises in 1958, quite independently of the existence, quality or size of the communist nuclear arsenal. For most of the period since the Second World War, it has not been communist nuclear weapons that have counterbalanced United States weapons and thereby created the stalemate. In the early years the communists did not possess any nuclear weapons; and for many years more the comparatively few they had were not part of a useable weapons system. They have never had a first-rate long-range manned aircraft force for weapons delivery, and their intercontinental missiles did not become operational—and then only slowly—until late 1962 or early 1963. At the time of the super-publicized Cuban confrontation (October 1962) no Soviet ICBMs were yet fully operational.

During these years there have been numerous occasions when the actual use of nuclear weapons or a serious and credible threat to use them was militarily relevant, and would have been highly advantageous to the United States and the West from a military or political standpoint: Soviet takeover of Czechoslovakia, Korea, Hungary, Tibet, Cuba, Vietnam, etc. Nevertheless, the United States has never used nuclear weapons, no matter what the "objective" weapons relationship, nor, except perhaps in 1958, has the United States threatened their use seriously and credibly. The record proves that the stalemate is "subjective." What "deters" United States use of the weapons is not necessarily or fundamentally counterbalancing physical weapons on the other side—which may or may not exist—but a subjective unwillingness to accept the consequences of using its own weapons from whatever motive, rational or irrational; in large part, the record indicates, from feelings of guilt in the American scientists and governmental leaders together with fear about the effect on "world opinion." This guilt and this fear are partly spontaneous in origin, but they have been manipulated, exploited and heightened through a continuous psywar campaign conducted by the communists, their fellow travelers and dupes.

What has counterbalanced the United States nuclear armament thus has not been in reality, for most of these years, and is still not in any decisive sense, a physically opposed communist nuclear armament. It has been, and still is principally, an actively employed psywar weapons system. The communist powers do not have to wait for a technological breakthrough to acquire a functioning anti-ballistic missile system. They have all along possessed a demonstratively effective weapons system that was able to take the advent of missiles in its stride.

True enough, the communists also have not used nuclear weapons, though they have possessed them for some years. But the motives deterring the communists and inducing them to accept the stalemate are "dialectically" of a different kind.

There is no sign that the communists share any of the feeling of guilt about the production, possession and possible use of nuclear weapons; quite the contrary, by all one can gather they are very pleased; and they have shown only a minimum of fear of world opinion. However, the communist leaders have been well aware that the United States' nuclear arsenal has been, first infinitely, and then overwhelmingly, superior to their own. What has presumably deterred them has been, not irrational sentiment, but a perfectly rational calculation of the odds: a realization that they have too much to lose, have in fact everything to lose, by initiating use of nuclear arms. Though in their case too the physical facts do not of themselves determine the strategic response (acceptance of the stalemate), the response made by the communist leaders is directly correlated with the physical facts, whereas the response of the United States, as we have seen, is altogether independent of the facts.

This dialectical difference in the communist response suggests a conclusion of some importance. If the physical facts change, if the communist nuclear arsenal becomes significantly superior to the American arsenal, then we may expect the communists to alter their response in accordance with these altered physical facts: that is, to use their arsenal instead of sitting on it.

The nuclear stalemate and the two-zone doctrine (together equivalent to "peaceful coexistence") were the premises for a development that has become more and more conspicuous from 1962 on: the loosening of the blocs. In the first phase of the Third World War, two well-defined and cohesive politico-strategic blocs, expressing in their structures the essential nature of the war, formed up on a global scale: the communists, or Sino-Soviet bloc, dominated by the Soviet Union; and the Western bloc, dominated by the United States. Somewhat later the attempt was made to constitute a third bloc independent of the first two: known variously as "the Afro-Asian bloc," the "non-aligned nations," or "the Third World." In the last few years the internal cement holding each of the blocs together has been noticeably strained and weakened.

In the case of the communist bloc there has occurred what is usually referred to as "the Sino-Soviet split," together with the growth of "polycentrism." The loosening of the Western bloc has been most plainly signaled by the unilateral moves taken by Charles de Gaulle, especially by the partial breakdown of the North Atlantic Treaty Organization which has been one consequence of de Gaulle's policy. . . .

In the years from the Cuban missile crisis of 1962 to 1965, Western opinion very nearly convinced itself that "the Cold War was over." The Soviet Union had obviously settled down, and China, if still talking like a revolutionary adolescent, could be handled by "being made part of the community of nations" through diplomatic recognition, UN membership and expanding trade. If by chance there were big trouble, it would be between the Soviet Union and China, not between either one, or both, and the West. Then came the Chinese nuclear tests and the heated up Vietnam war.

It is only from the past and the present that we can get evidence about the future. Logically it is possible that we are about to begin a decade of global sweetness and light, but nothing that has happened in the past sixty-three years or that is happening today permits us to believe that in actuality things will be so. On the evidence, the probability is overwhelming that the war we are in—Cold War, Third World War, whatever we may prefer to call it—will continue, and that its main theme, though with novel variants, will continue to be the protracted struggle of the communist enterprise to gain global power. It is more likely, on the evidence, that during the next decade the war we are in will increase rather than decrease in scope and ferocity. Is it not true that today, after all the coexisting and people-to-peopling, the biggest fight since 1945 is taking place? And that after all the polycentralizing, the forces against which we are battling have the united support of all communists of every nation, party and faction? Can any rational person suppose that the new Chinese nuclear bombs are a "weapon for peace"? Does Africa look as if it had finished its uhuru pangs and was ready for order and tranquility? Is everybody about to love everybody in the Middle East?

The forms taken by the protracted conflict in the next decade will not be identical to those taken in the last, no doubt. Polycentrism—on both sides—is in some degree a fact; undoubtedly the blocs have loosened. From 1947 until a few years ago the lineup was always simple and obvious: the communist-plus bloc and the Western-plus bloc, with a shifting, rather amorphous grouping in between. Distinctions and divisions within the two primary blocs have now become more apparent and more significant. On limited issues the lineup can now more frequently breach the normal bloc boundaries (though it should be recalled that this happened more than once in the past, beginning with the Suez affair). Thus, on the Vietnam issue, we find France not only opposed to United States policy—which sort of difference in viewpoint occurs normally within all alliances and blocs—but coming close to practical collaboration with the actively fighting enemies of the United States. From the opposite perspective we find the Soviet Union and China snarling at each other in a fairly substantial political warfare sort of conflict—though in their case, they continue practical collaboration with each other against the United States and its fighting allies.

The internal disputes within the communist and Western camps as well as in the Third World have been getting increasingly severe, and it is not excluded that these should escalate into armed struggle of one sort or another. There has of course been a good deal of fighting among the nations of the Third World (U.A.R.-Saudi Arabia, India-Pakistan, Algeria-Morocco, Indonesia-Malaysia, Somalia-Kenya, Sudan-Chad, etc.), but as a rule this is quickly absorbed into the overriding global conflict. There seems to have been occasional border skirmishing between the Soviet Union and China, and it is at least possible that larger-scale fighting between the two will take place during the course of the next decade. This would not, however, alter the fundamental character of the war we are in. Historically, the controlling issue would still be the struggle of the communist enterprise for an effective monopoly of world power.

It is not without precedent that within a dynamic and expanding enterprise there should be internal splits, divisions and conflicts while at the same time the enterprise as a whole maintains its integrity and continues its growth as against the rival enterprises within its field of operation. Indeed, such processes are so usual as to be part of the law of social formation and growth. This happens within every business organization, social club, church, political party and fraternal society. Sometimes the internal dispute develops into a struggle for control of the enterprise; sometimes it becomes so irreconcilable that the dissident faction goes over to a rival or opts out altogether.

Let us add that the Sino-Soviet split and the Castrovian eccentricities are not the first disputes within the communist enterprise. Communists have been disputing among themselves in the most extreme terms since the enterprise started. Several million persons got killed, and thirty million or so sent to concentration camps (where many of them ended up dead also), during the disputes of the late 1920's and the 1930's—a lot more casualties than can be charged against the Sino-Soviet split and polycentrism. But in spite of those millions of casualties, the enterprise as a going concern, an identifiable historical entity, not only maintained its integrity but proved ready to begin a period of astounding growth.

Internal disputes, thus, are not necessarily signs of weakness or decay. They often are, when the enterprise has *already* passed its historical peak, on the way to history's rubbish heap. They can *become* a source of weakness when a rival enterprise is astute enough to exploit the vulnerability that they open up. But frequently they are symptoms of health and vigor—truly "growing pains"—that indicate there is something worth fighting for. Often the internal disputes become sharp and open when the enterprise is in a situation that calls for a strategic turn. In such cases the disputes are correlated with different views about what direction to take.

Stalinist monolithism, after it was successfully consolidated, had elements of great strength, particularly in its ability to concentrate social energies on carefully targeted goals. But a monolithic system is over-rigid; it suppresses much creative energy and—unless it really should transform human nature—it inevitably arouses antagonisms that a looser system might disperse harmlessly. Polycentrism—which is considerably more developed in the writings of the experts than in the actualities of the communist system—can act as a corrective to the excessive global rigidity of the communist enterprise in the past, adapting it better to, for example, newly posed tasks in Africa, Latin America and the Middle East; in fact it has already, in some degree, done so.

It was not long after Mohammed's death that Islam was embroiled in fierce and bloody internal disputes. These did not stop the extraordinary explosion of Islam out of the Arabian desert east to Java and westward through North Africa into Spain and France. Within the frame of reference of Islam itself, the disputes, whether judged as struggles for power or for doctrinal purity, were significant enough. But within the frames of reference of Christendom, Hinduism and paganism, it really didn't matter very much which Islamic wing conquered—which, that is to say, did the burying.

There are—there could not fail to be—differences as well as disputes among Soviet communism, Chinese communism, Castrovian communism, Titoist communism, Polish and Zanzibarian communism. The time and circumstances in which communism took over; the history and culture of the local population; the state of the economy: naturally each of these factors affects the net outcome. But wherever communism takes over and a communist regime is consolidated, no matter what the conditions precedent, certain fundamental traits are invariably found. The important means of production and distribution—factories, mines, banks, businesses—are nationalized; a state monopoly of foreign trade is established; agriculture is brought under some sort of collective scheme; foreign travel is severely restricted, and domestic travel is also limited by job controls, police surveillance, etc.; the private sector of education is eliminated; no organized political opposition is permitted; the press, radio-TV and all other means of communication are made a state or Party monopoly; the state, becoming officially atheist, takes active economic, propagandist and coercive measures to combat and if possible to eliminate religious belief as well as religious organizations; within the judicial system there is no independent legal corps—prosecution and defense, as well as tribunal, are merely agents of the state; there are no civil liberties or civil rights guaranteed against administrative action; the state intervenes pervasively in all or virtually all phases of social and individual life—is, that is to say, totalitarian; the theoretical order, like the practical order, is based on collective ("class") concepts, not on the individual human being.

If our choice were in truth between the Russian form of communism and the Chinese form, presented as sole alternatives, it might seem prudent to settle for (let us say) the Russian form. I rather suspect that back of the refusal to face the challenge of the communist enterprise—a refusal expressed most bluntly in the familiar "Better Red than Dead" slogan—there often does lie the unexpressed conviction that our historical choice is thus restricted, that the only real issue is *which* form of communism, not whether society will become communist. But if we adhere in any meaningful sense to Western civilization, we must reject this restriction, since in their substance all forms of communism are incompatible with the essential ideas, values, traditions and institutions of Western civilization. As Westerners we must, logically, affirm that we decline to choose or accept the Russian or Chinese or Cuban or any other form or variety of communism; that we choose an alternative that is not communism even if the sole actual alternative is death. So long as we are willing to include death among possible alternatives, we shall always be free to choose.

Looked at in this perspective—that is, the perspective of Western metaphysics and civilization—the Sino-Soviet split and communist polycentrism are brought into clearer focus. They are seen to be conflicts *within* the communist enterprise —even if they should sharpen to a point that brought war among communist countries. Skillfully exploited by the non-communist powers, these conflicts might serve to weaken, perhaps even smash, the communist enterprise; but without deliberate intervention from outside, they need not have a permanently weakening effect. In any event, they leave the line between the communist world and the non-communist world far more significant—indeed, of another order of significance—than any line drawn between differing parts of the communist world.

Disputes between this and that variant of communism are not the only type of conflict taking place within the geographical area controlled by communist regimes. There are also disputes which, in tendency at least, go beyond the limits of communism, and which thus pose, wherever they develop, the essential issue of communism *vs.* non-communism. As conspicuous recent examples, there may be cited the Sinyavsky-Daniel episode in the Soviet Union and the Mihajlov episode in Yugoslavia. The activities, writings and proposals of the Soviet writers, Andrei Sinyavsky and Yuri Daniel and of Mihajlo Mihajlov, have remained nominally within the general framework of Marxism, but they advocate rights of intellectual dissent, free publication, even political opposition, affirm the primacy of the individual, and are by implication if not explicitly expressing a fundamental criticism of the communist order. Recognizing this, the communist regimes, at whatever cost to their liberalized images, are sooner or later compelled to silence and jail them.

There is ample evidence that Sinyavsky, Daniel and Mihajlov are only conspicuous representatives of deepening movements of dissent among the intellectuals in all the communist nations, and to some degree among professionals, industrial managers and technicians. We know, moreover, from the 1956 events in Poland, East Germany and Hungary, that this sort of restlessness of the intellectuals is frequently the sign of a rising, quite general social discontent, the sources of which in the mass of the population may lie in economic problems, nationalist sentiment or religious faith that have only an indirect relation to the "demands" articulated by the intellectuals.

It seems likely that in the decade to come these internal tendencies of opposition to the communist order will expand and intensify. It is quite probable that they will result, during the next few years, in public conflicts; on a small scale they have already done so in 1965 and 1966. In the long run these conflicts which breach the communist structure are more important to the non-communist world than the bicentrist or polycentrist struggles of one kind of communism against another. If our experts and policy-makers devoted one-tenth the attention and energy to them that they lavish on polycentrism and Sino-Soviet dialectics, they might discover levers which, properly handled, could bring down the communist enterprise.

Since the war we are in—the Third World War—has not ended, and is not going to end in the decade to come, it is possible to answer a number of subsidiary questions about what will and will not happen. Will there be (for example) serious disarmament? There will continue to be elaborate, expensive and well-publicized talk and negotiations about disarmament, as there have been for the past eighteen years. The United States Government will continue to spend tens of millions of dollars on its Disarmament Agency; many officials in this and other countries will make good livings as disarmament specialists. Dozens of private associations will talk, meet, confer, organize and demonstrate for disarmament. But there will not be much disarmament, just as there has not been during the decade past.

How could there be? It is not arms that make conflicts, but conflicts that prompt men to make arms. Since many and profound conflicts remain, so will arms remain, and abundantly. The sufficient comment on the years of disarmament negotiation is the Vietnam war.

The proclaimed disarmament achievements of the past decade were the nuclear test-ban treaty and the agreement against weapons in space vehicles. No doubt the elimination of atmospheric nuclear fallout would be a good thing, though autos, factories and incinerators produce much more and more lethal atmospheric fallout than anything we have got from nuclear bombs. But the test-ban treaty has not even eliminated atmospheric fallout: France and China have been testing in the atmosphere. And of course the treaty has done nothing at all to reduce nuclear armament. Two additional nations have joined the nuclear club since the treaty was signed; a number more (India, Israel, United Arab Republic, Japan, Brazil, West Germany are among obvious candidates) will probably do so during the next few years. There are more nuclear weapons than ever in existence, and many new sophisticated types have been developed in the post-treaty period.

As for the agreement against weapons in space, it has no enforcement mechanism and is not even a formal treaty. It therefore has only the validity the several powers choose to give it; it will become null whenever any power wishes to nullify it. Meanwhile it exercises little if any inhibiting effect on the development of spatial armament, since this stage of the development would in any case concentrate on the attainment of vehicles (and launching systems) able to mount the arms, toward which goal both major powers are moving as rapidly as they can manage.

The probable net result of disarmament efforts over the next decade is the same as it has been over the last: more arms. The one possibility of an important measure of disarmament would be through acceptance by the United States Government not merely of the words of the disarmament-ideologues—which by and large has already occurred—but of their practical recommendations. Actual disarmament in this case would, it goes without saying, be confined for the most part to the United States and those nations which depend for their arms on the United States.

Will the United Nations, in the next decade, become a genuine "parliament of the nations" and an effective force for global peace, order, liberty and progress? Again, we can judge the future only by what we can learn from the past. Since the United Nations has not been an effective force in the past, since it has not even tried to act in the important episodes (more exactly, since the major powers have not permitted it to act in the important episodes), why should we expect it to be any different in the near future? Self-evidently, a United Nations organization run mostly, in political matters, by the huge General Assembly, as now, rather than by the Security Council, as in the early years, is less rather than more likely to operate effectively. Self-evidently, a General Assembly made up of 120 miscellaneous nations, half of which are not coherent social entities of any sort, is less likely to operate effectively than an Assembly made up, as when the Charter was signed, of fifty or sixty established nations.

The United Nations will continue, as in the past, to perform certain technical tasks that are globally useful in an age of global technology and business. In political affairs it may occasionally, as in the past, aid the settlement or compromise of minor difficulties and furnish facilities for communication among governments, but when things get serious it will either do nothing or, as not infrequently in the past, provoke and exacerbate troubles. Especially in the case of Africa, the United Nations has already proved its trouble-making potential; and in relation to Africa this is likely to be demonstrated often again in the decade ahead.

Will de Gaulle have succeeded in creating a "Europe of the fatherlands," divorced from the Anglo-Saxons and stretching "from the Atlantic to the Urals," which will become the leader of a Third World holding itself independent from the superstates? The answers are No in general and in detail. De Gaulle's "little Europe," without Russia, does not have resources and power enough to construct a new, fully autonomous bloc—especially while Gaullist insistence on total sovereign independence prevents military and economic integration. If little Europe did stretch out to the Urals, then, in the resultant combination, it could never be France that would be the dominant power. By the nature of the relationship of forces, Russia in that case would be dominant; Europe from the Atlantic to the Urals —excluding the Anglo-Saxon nations, and maintaining restrictions on Germany—would inevitably be a Europe brought within the Soviet communist bloc. De Gaulle's professed aims are adapted to lofty rhetoric, but in cold matter-of-fact they are not serious, and will fade away when he fades away, as before long he must.

It is equally illusory to suppose that the Third World will pull itself together and go striding forward into order, progress and power. Some nations of the Third World may do so, and probably will, but the Third World in general will almost surely be in worse rather than better shape as the next decade unrolls. The reasons are not obscure. The population of the underdeveloped and in many cases inherently impoverished nations is rising at historically unprecedented rates, considerably faster than the food supply. Political disorders, resulting from many sorts of internal instability and rivalry, and spurred, often, by both the advanced powers and the United Nations, are increasing rather than quieting down. The interventions and intrigues of the communist enterprise in the Third World are primarily designed at this stage to bring about confusion, civil dissension, breakdown and chaos, as part of the strategy of isolating and encircling the "global cities" (western Europe and North America) by the "liberated" (revolutionized) "global countryside" (Asia, Africa, Latin America); the positive task of building a new communist order in what is now the Third World can be postponed until a later stage.

Indeed, the primary hope for much of the Third World lies in a policy of prudent but vigorous neo-colonialism on the part of the Western nations: a policy that would accept the formal independence and autonomy of the Third World nations, but, for the sake of Western military security and mutually beneficial economic development, would furnish military protection, administrative and technical assistance and productive investment. Thus the Third World will continue to be the arena for the struggle of the great antagonists: the revolutionary attack of the communist enterprise, usually masked in its early phases as "struggle for liberation," will confront the "neo-colonialism" —the term is not without justification—of the West.

. . . The Suez-Hungary episodes of 1956 foreshadowed the major trends of the period that was to follow. In a similar way, the Vietnam war will foreshadow at least some of the major trends in the coming period. I say "will foreshadow" rather than "foreshadows" in order to emphasize that the pattern defined by the episode is not presented statically or in advance. The Suez and Hungarian episodes did not get their particular precognitive significance just because something happened "out there" in history, or because somebody else did something— the Hungarian students and workers rebelling, the French and British armies invading. Their meaning depended also on what we—what the United States, dominant power of the non-communist world—did about what was happening: on the fact that we stood aside from Hungary and that we actively intervened against Britain and France in Suez.

Just so, it is not merely the fact that something is taking place in Vietnam or that somebody else is doing something there—organized communist units fighting—that gives the Vietnam episode a symbolic meaning. What we are doing and will do is an essential part of the pattern that will become significant for the future. When that pattern is sufficiently defined, the Vietnam action will be seen, like Suez-Hungary, as a premonitory crisis or turning point. This is plainly figured by the breadth and intensity of both the domestic and the global disputes over United States intervention in Vietnam. These disputes are, in truth, sharper than any others that have taken place over any previous episode of the Cold War. The fact that they are so demonstrates an almost instinctive general awareness of the crucial importance of what is happening in Vietnam.

So far, since shortly after his election as chief of government in his own name and right, Lyndon Johnson, like Harry Truman in relation to the Greek civil war and unlike Dwight Eisenhower in relation to Suez-Hungary, has acted (however equivocal his talk) firmly and forcefully in relation to Vietnam, and a good deal more firmly than the usually prevailing opinion-makers have approved. The basic alternatives ahead in Vietnam can be very simply put. Either the communists will be beaten badly enough to guarantee that for the next period (there can be no permanent guarantees) there is no chance for a communist or communist-dominated government in South Vietnam, or the communists will get control of South Vietnam. From an anti-communist standpoint, the ideal outcome would include much more than a de facto guarantee against communist domination: overthrow of the communist regime in North Vietnam and perhaps some direct injury to communist China, such as the destruction of her nuclear installations. But these two are the bare, basic alternatives. It is in terms of these that the world will render its judgment and draw its conclusions. If the first comes about, then the judgment will be: victory for the United States, for the anti-communist Vietnamese and for anti-communism generally. If the second, the judgment will be: victory for Ho Chi Minh, for the Vietcong and for the communist enterprise as a whole. It is difficult to see how there can be any compromise, any outcome half-way between these two. No matter which side wins, a diplomatic facade can be, and doubtless will be, erected to make the outcome look like a compromise; this is not "the final conflict," and faces must be saved. The fighting may go on a long while inconclusively. But in the last analysis, the communists either take over South Vietnam or they don't.

If our side wins, our troubles certainly won't be over. But we will have demonstrated that the anti-communist camp, under American leadership and principally through American men and weapons, can stop the present massive drive of the communist enterprise to take over Southeast Asia and break through into the Indian subcontinent and the South Seas. We will have demonstrated that the anti-communist camp, under American leadership and principally through American men and weapons, can handle revolutionary encirclement of the global cities through the global countryside. We will have, not silenced (which is impossible), but refuted the doubters and Softs and cowards and subversives within the anti-communist camp who have argued that a favorable outcome in Vietnam is beyond American capability. We will have enheartened, and rallied around us, many non-communist nations who, because of their own comparative weakness, cannot help guiding their own policies by the way the wind is blowing. Already, in fact, by the unexpected firmness we have shown in Vietnam, this effect is evident in the South Pacific region. A number of the small nations there have sent in their own soldiers to fight alongside ours, and have been feeling their way toward some sort of anti-communist united front. It is certain that the pro-Peking Sukarno regime in Indonesia would not have been over-thrown and the Indonesian Communist Party crushed if we had declined the Vietnam challenge. And who could have guessed beforehand that the Burmese leader, General Ne Win, after a years-long record of anti-Western neutralism, would be a friendly visitor to Washington in the late summer of 1966?

If the communists win in Vietnam, then the sequence of events will be reversed, as nearly everyone really knows. The analysts who spoke of the domino effect were surely right. If the communist advance cannot be stopped in Vietnam, when American power has been committed to that mission, where then is it to be stopped? "Those who do not like the war in Vietnam," commented the authoritative English weekly, *The Economist* (August 20, 1966), "have a duty to ask themselves where else they think the wave can be stopped. Thailand? But the non-communist Thais are not going to call for help from a defeated American army, and in any case it is logistically much harder to get help into Thailand than into Vietnam. Burma? Not in the cards. India, then? But the mind swerves away from the difficulty of doing anything to help that fragile country if the guerrillas once get to work in West Bengal or Kerala or wherever. . . . The deal the Americans cannot reasonably be asked to strike is one that threatens to sell the pass to the whole of southern Asia. This is Mr. Johnson's enormous problem. It is also the problem of those who criticize his decision to take America into the war."

The domino effect would not be confined to southern Asia; it would be world-wide. Everywhere, and rightly, confidence in the will and power of the United States would be shaken; everywhere communists would be emboldened, anti-communists dismayed. If in spite of the United States the Vietcong could succeed—completing the demonstration begun by Fidel Castro—who need respect or fear the American paper tiger? On a world scale, one may predict with certainty, the revolution would take mighty strides forward.

The response of the United States in case of failure is also predictable. The nation would pull back toward the desperate condition of a Fortress America, riven within by fierce conflicts the preliminary lines of which are already being shaped. The two alternatives are so narrowly poised that, just as we can see such anticipations of a possible communist defeat in Vietnam as I have cited, so we can see anticipations of a possible communist victory in the tentative moves already taken toward a Fortress America condition: the widespread call for withdrawal from Vietnam itself, to begin with; the campaign against the President and the Secretaries of State and Defense on the ground that they want the United States to be "world policeman"; the uncritical blanket dissatisfaction with foreign aid and the unanalyzed demand to bring United States troops back from Europe; the switch in strategic defense toward dependence on home-based missiles and submarines. In making his decisions about the Vietnam war, Lyndon Johnson is making also the nation's controlling decisions for the next decade and perhaps the next generation. . . .

13   Race: Claims, Rights, and Prospects

Ernest van den Haag

I. *Legitimate and Illegitimate Claims Distinguished*

Negroes want something—and find something wanting—in American society. Not all their many wants arise from their status as Negroes. Taxes may be too high or wages too low for the poor of any color; but a racial inequity exists only if a hardship is suffered by Negroes because they are Negroes. However, not all disadvantages suffered by Negroes as such can be corrected by public means; only those which can be so corrected justify a demand for public action. Legitimate Negro claims thus must:

1) be directed against an actual hardship;

2) rest on inequity, on rights granted to other Americans and withheld from Negroes because they are Negroes;

3) be satisfiable, or enforceable, by public social means, such as laws, payments, or institutional arrangements which

4) must be effective and rational—likely to help achieve the

From Ernest van den Haag, "Negroes and Whites: Claims, Rights, and Prospects," *Modern Age*, IX, No. 4 (Fall 1965), 354–362. Reprinted by permission of the author and *Modern Age*.

legitimate ends sought without unreasonably impairing rights granted all citizens as such; the effective means which cost (i.e., impair or diminish other rights) least, are the most rational.

Thus, Negro claims are not legitimate as such (whether they be legitimate citizen's claims or not) if the rights claimed are not withheld from Negroes because they are Negroes; or if, although withheld from Negroes as such, the rights claimed cannot be granted by public social means, either because these could not be materially effective, or because the use of these means would unreasonably impair other, no less important, rights or, the rights of others.

At present confusion between illegitimate and legitimate claims prevails among Negroes and whites alike; it is manifest in Congress, in the courts, and among educational authorities and tends to weaken legitimate Negro claims as well as the social fabric as a whole. The tests offered neither exhaust the distinction between legitimate and illegitimate Negro claims, nor clarify it in all instances. They may be useful, however, by drawing attention to such a distinction and indicating the criteria that must be applied.

II. Warranted and Unwarranted Discrimination

All legitimate Negro claims arise from unwarranted discrimination. Discrimination by law, or in public institutions, or by public officials, or even by private persons and means in situations strongly affected with the public interest, is unwarranted if it is irrelevant to the situation or activity at issue, and places a person or group at a material disadvantage. Both elements are necessary: neither a material disadvantage nor an irrelevant distinction alone suffices; the combination does.

Unwarranted discrimination ("discrimination against") can be distinguished from warranted discrimination in the following illustration. If a teacher grades his students according to their scholastic performance, he discriminates among them (and distributes advantages and disadvantages that may ensue) by using a criterion of distinction relevant to the (scholastic) situation or activity. However, if he grades students according to parental wealth, physical attractiveness, race, size, sex, or religion, the students who get low grades would suffer *unwarranted* disadvantages: the criterion of discrimination is not relevant to their activity and to the teacher's task. However, the casting director of a musical would be warranted in discriminating according to sex, beauty, size, or race where this may influence the visual, aesthetic, amusement, or erotic appeal of his show. The criterion irrelevant to one situation is relevant to another. Discrimination according to religion would be relevant in selecting missionaries, but not in casting chorus girls. Discrimination thus gives rise to legitimate claims only (but not always: a claim for public action must also meet tests 3 and 4 noted above) when a person or group is placed at a disadvantage not warranted by his actual task, situation, or activities.

Purely social discriminations by definition cannot be irrelevant, since selectivity in terms of personal preference is the essence of the social, and is displayed in discriminations. To put it paradoxically, the irrelevance (to anything but one's own arbitrary and capricious preference) of social discriminations, being of the essence of the social situation, is that which is relevant to it by definition. Whether social discriminations rest on misjudgments and prejudices, or on correct assessment of one's preferences and of those likely to meet them, the individual has a clear right to discriminate socially in however foolish a manner he wishes—though he might be wiser, and serve his interests better, by not exercising it.[1]

III. Borderline Cases: Employment

There are some borderline cases in which discrimination is warranted in view of one aspect of the situation and unwarranted with regard to another. They can only be sketched here. They occur usually when the situation requires employees to per-

[1]"Social" here means association, or fellowship (social intercourse) for its own sake. Discrimination by social institutions (e.g., clubs) is relevant (and thus justifiable) to the extent to which it expresses the actual social preferences of the individual members.

form services to which race or sex may be irrelevant, and yet also to appeal to and please customers by personality, "rapport," and physical attractiveness. Airline stewardesses, waitresses, and in some cases sales personnel may be in this situation; qualities such as race, sex, or nationality, though irrelevant to the performance of their tangible duties, may have some relevance to the customers' feeling of well being, and thus ultimately to the success of the business.

Such borderline cases require in the first place that the importance of the tangible relative to the intangible tasks of the employee be pondered. Discriminatory practices are potentially justifiable only if the intangible functions have important enough effects to make discrimination in accordance with them economically necessary or rational. To decide their actual legitimacy, the material hardship suffered by those whose job opportunities would be narrowed must be compared with the hardships or losses the employer would suffer if prevented from discrimination among job candidates according to customer appeal, or other intangibles.[2] The same considerations are required if the problem is formulated in terms of the rights of customers to be served by those whom they prefer, versus the right of job candidates to be selected for jobs in terms of their tangible merits.

The case is quite similar if the employer has a business (or, within it, an activity) which relies not only on tangible performance but also on a confidential and friendly rapport, or a social relationship among employees, and between them and their employer. This is the case mostly in small businesses, but may occur in bigger ones if they are organized in small units. In such cases the employer's right to follow personal, i.e., social, preferences irrelevant to the job, or to follow those of the people already employed, must be weighed against the hardship to those discriminated against even though they would be capable of performing the relevant tangible duties.

Employer discrimination unwarranted in terms of tangible

---

[2]"Intangible" does not mean indemonstrable.

tasks and abilities may be allowed without much hesitation if equivalent opportunities are open elsewhere to those discriminated against. For in this case no major hardship is suffered by them. However, if the prospective employee belongs to a group universally discriminated against so that equivalent opportunities are scarce for him, a major hardship is suffered by him; employers should not be allowed to discriminate against him unless they cannot reasonably and profitably operate their business otherwise. It follows that discrimination against Jews, Catholics, or women should be dealt with more leniently than discrimination against Negroes or the aged. For the latter seldom have equivalent employment opportunities.

This kind of borderline case must be distinguished from others in which the ability to perform tangible duties is disputed. Employers may discriminate according to age, sex, race, etc., under the impression that ability to perform the material tasks of the job is correlated with these classifications. Such a belief can be tested by trial performances, or tests which demonstrate the presence or absence of the relevant abilities. Certainly putative class disqualifications must be verified before discrimination among individuals according to class membership becomes warranted.

I should favor applying this rule to educational classifications too. Requiring "college graduates" for jobs for which a college education is of doubtful relevance discriminates unnecessarily against those who have not graduated from college but are quite able to do the job. Irrelevant educational requirements threaten to become quite frequent and should be replaced by *relevant* tests.

IV. Prejudice

The legal prevention or correction of unwarranted discriminatory acts is often presumed to have an educational effect by reducing or eliminating the prejudice which motivates such acts. Such educational effects are never sufficient to justify coercive legal measures. There is nothing in the Constitution to per-

mit the government to coerce adults not actually convicted of
a law violation to change their beliefs (prejudices) or to undergo experiences solely for that purpose; and there is nothing
to authorize coercive laws aimed at the beliefs (prejudices) of
citizens. Thus the government is not entitled to coerce adults
for the sake of their education unless it coerces primarily to
outlaw acts wrong enough to be outlawed; however in this
case, the educational effect is not necessary to justify the law.
(Non-coercive educational activities are beyond my present
scope.)

It seems doubtful anyhow that prejudice can be effectively
influenced by direct educational measures (although it may be
relocated—displaced—and transformed), or by the educational
effects of legal ones. Prejudice is the effect of negative or positive preferences which it rationalizes. Much more rarely, and
secondarily, prejudice is a cause of such a preference. A preference is a liking (or, conversely, disliking) for, say, mountains
over the sea, blondes over brunettes, scotch over bourbon. We
need not and cannot avoid such preferences. They often are defended by attributing to their objects negative or positive
qualities that these do not uniformly possess: the intellect does
not ordinarily fathom the origin of the preference but usually
has a tendency to justify it by a rational argument. Thus we
may asseverate that mountains make for more vigor than the
sea, that blondes have more rhythm or understanding than brunettes, or that the latter steal, or that bourbon is less poisonous
than scotch. Since the prejudice tends to be a secondary elaboration of the preference, it is unlikely to yield to information
(though information may relocate it); nor is information likely
to change the preference itself which is but spuriously linked
to anything cognitive or rational.

Whereas cognition sometimes, and coerced cognition rarely
changes beliefs (of which prejudices are a species), coercion
itself never does. Pico della Mirandola correctly referred to the
attempt to change beliefs by coercion as "*actus tyrannicus vol-
untatis*"—an attempt to produce an (irrelevant and) tyrannical
intrusion of the will into a field in which it must remain powerless (*Apologia* VIII). (Pico, indeed, managed to get the Papal

Curia to revoke an attempted coercion.) Changes in preference depend on the origin and function of the preference in the person that holds it. They are likely to occur in response to emotional changes.

Certainly then, citizens are entitled, in the first place, to whatever prejudices they cherish, and the government is not entitled to correct them coercively, nor to impose its own, or those of the majority. Secondly, such coercion is not effective in changing beliefs. (In spite of coercion, the Christians never managed to shake what they regarded as the Jewish prejudice in favor of Jewish beliefs.) Only when prejudices give rise to practices against which Negroes, or others, have legitimate claims, their *effect* must be corrected, by law if necessary. Such correction is required, regardless of the origin of the practice, or of the effect of its correction on prejudice. Education and propaganda in favor of lawful behavior, and of the moral outlook from which the law springs, facilitate enforcement; but such education can never be the direct or sufficient purpose of criminal law.

V. Corrective Measures, Legitimate and Illegitimate

No doubt Negroes suffer grievously by discriminatory exclusion from desirable dwellings, eating places, and educational institutions, solely because they are Negroes. Such material deprivation, which leaves but inferior dwelling, eating, or educational opportunities for Negroes, can be corrected. Either those who wish to exclude Negroes must be obligated to offer them equally good facilities, or such facilities must be made available through other governmental actions, e.g., subsidies. To these facilities, whites may, but need not, be admitted. Should Negroes wish to exclude whites, each of the two mutually exclusive groups would be obligated to help provide facilities for those members who wish to associate with members of the other.

Thus, unwarranted discrimination can be avoided, without requiring that facilities be used by the two groups together, as long as one wishes to dissociate from the other. This is not easily possible with respect to employment, which, therefore, has been dealt with differently (Section III). But it is possible with regard to the activities at issue. In employment, the tangible effects on those discriminated against cannot be separated from the discriminatory selection, which itself may rest on intangible social preferences. Hence, the effects (hardships) can be avoided only by avoiding the discriminatory (irrelevantly selective) act. Not so with regard to eating, housing, or schooling. The tangible effects—inferior facilities—of discrimination can be avoided, or corrected, without compelling congregation, i.e., without impairing the freedom of social selection (association and dissociation).[3] I cannot see why it should be within the purview of governmental authority to coerce citizens into unwarranted associations (or dissociations) except to avoid or correct material disadvantages to any one group or person discriminated against.

To be sure, legislators and courts have lately held that mere dissociation, in facilities affected with the public interest, places Negroes at a disadvantage not avoided by "equal but separate" facilities. Racial togetherness[4] is becoming obligatory in many aspects of our life, and deliberate separation is regarded as immoral in all and illegal in most cases. There is no evidence, however, that separation *per se* is injurious to Negroes, or that any damage is suffered therefrom.[5] Hence, Negroes have ob-

[3]Certainly housing, schooling, and eating have social aspects.

[4]I am using the social rather than any biological classification of races, which would be irrelevant. Negroes (or whites) are those who are socially so identified.

[5]The courts have held, on the basis of "modern authority," that segregation is "inherently unequal" and injurious to Negroes. And the Civil Rights Act of 1964 holds as much, too. But whatever the courts decree it is, the scientific evidence cited by the courts and the Congress, and indeed whatever evidence is available, does not prove, by accepted scientific standards, that equal things become unequal when used separately or that separation of groups produces a psychological injury. (See my "Social Science Testimony in the Desegregation Cases," and the further references cited therein, *Villanova Law Review*, VI, 1; and my "Negroes, Intelligence and Prejudice," *National Review*, Dec. 1, 1964. (Reprints available from P.O. Box 3495, Grand Central Station, New York, N.Y. 10017.)

tained in the courts (though not in practice) satisfaction for claims that must be regarded as illegitimate. They have persuaded the courts and the Congress to compel unwilling whites to associate with Negroes by insisting that equal but separate facilities would somehow be psychologically unequal, and injurious to Negroes.

VI. Freedom of Association Defined

To insist on compulsory congregation is to unnecessarily reduce the range of voluntary individual and group choices of association. Voluntary association implies free selection by both parties, the right of either party to dissociate from the other regardless of the other's wishes, and the right of both to associate by mutual consent. Voluntary association rests on *mutual* consent; voluntary dissociation requires only the dissent to association by one party. The dissociation remains "voluntary" even if the other party prefers association. Marital choice (association) is free when both parties must agree on marriage, not when one party can impose marriage on the other; rejection by one (dissociation) suffices to prevent marriage. Freedom of association means mutual choice of associates, not unilateral imposition. Legally, association is free when conditions for free mutual choice exist—when the law neither prevents nor imposes choice, and protects the freedom thereof.

It is sometimes argued that, because they are public institutions, schools cannot grant free choice of associations. This argument is without merit. There is nothing in the nature of public, and even of coercive public institutions that requires them to diminish freedom of association beyond what is necessary to their function, or imposed as a penalty (as in jail). And schools can function with all kinds of more or less rational separations, e.g., by sex, age, income, religion—indeed, any sort of desired criterion shared by enough parents. Nor need the desired criterion of association (or separation) be justified rationally, i.e., by more than preference. Although public and presumed to function for instructional purposes, schools are largely social institutions. It follows that the tangible instructional aspects of schooling cannot alone be regarded as decisive. Social preferences have a legitimate role. Else, indeed, the presumption of the Supreme Court that segregation is damaging even when facilities are equal would make even less sense than it does. It rests on recognition that the instructional is not the only function of the schools, and does not exist in isolation from the social.[6] But inasmuch as schools are social institutions, discriminations in terms of social preferences cannot be irrelevant; and, therefore, not illegitimate. The Supreme Court linked its recognition of the social role of schools to its faith in the allegation of "modern authority" that the instructional functions of the school suffer, and that Negroes in particular are injured beyond the purely social, by segregation from white students. If this were true, one would have to ponder (as the Court did not) the injury to Negroes from dissociation versus that to whites from association. But there is no evidence for the contention itself. (See references in Fn. 5.) Thus only the issue of the parental right to follow social preferences remains.

It seems clear that the actions allegedly needed to correct unwarranted discrimination are actually directed against segregation, by simply describing it as discrimination and prescribing compulsory congregation as the legal remedy.[7]

Segregation has become unlawful when deliberate in public facilities, and it may become so even when not deliberate or occurring merely as an effect of incidental factors. The courts which decided that deliberate segregation is injurious to Ne-

---

[6] I take it for granted that private schools can use any criteria of selection they wish. But I see no reason, either, why public schools should narrow the freedom of association more than is needed or indeed rational. (See Fn. 4 *supra*.) The privatization of the school system as proposed by Milton Friedman (see Robert Solo [ed.], *Economics and the Public Interest*, New Brunswick, 1955) would solve this as well as other problems by subsidizing students rather than schools.

[7] *Compulsory* segregation (i.e., segregation, decreed by law) might be illegal, not because inherently discriminatory—it is not—but because it interferes with free association. But where segregation is freely chosen by one of the groups, and where congregated facilities are permitted, freedom of association exists.

groes will have to decide soon whether it is the deliberateness or the segregation that causes the alleged injury. If it is the deliberateness only which is injurious—a difficult doctrine—then non-deliberate *de facto* segregation (imbalance) would be lawful. If it is the segregation that is *per se* unconstitutional—an even more difficult doctrine—then a variety of measures will be required to make sure that students in public schools, tenants in housing developments, etc., be so selected as to avoid any segregation (imbalance) that might occur if not deliberately prevented. Whether this will be the mandate of the courts, and how far it will extend, is at present unknown.[8]

VII. Reverse Discrimination

An informal practice which is illegitimate, and ultimately unlikely to help satisfy legitimate Negro claims, though instituted to do so, is the insistence on proportional representation of Negroes in desirable positions. It is not unreasonable to regard the absence of such representation as suspect enough, *prima facie*, to investigate the possibility of unwarranted discrimination. But under-representation is not itself evidence for unwarranted discrimination, and proportional representation regardless of merit, i.e., of relevant criteria of selection, is not a legitimate demand.

Oddly enough, demands for racial representation are often treated as though legitimate by institutions, such as universities, that ought to know better. Such institutions often diligently look for Negro students and teachers. Sometimes their main qualification is that they are Negroes—there is a tendency to reverse discrimination: unwarranted discrimination in favor of Negroes, who are admitted, hired, or advanced because they are Negroes in preference to equally or even to better qualified non-Negroes.

[8]I should regard student selection by race with "balance" in view certainly as no less irrational than selection by race with the opposite goal in view. Either goal can be defended only as a social preference, and neither, therefore, should be imposed by law; both should be permitted.

Although meant to help, this practice—apart from its obvious inequity—cannot but weaken the Negro cause by perpetuating the common stereotype of Negroes as *ipso facto* less qualified than whites: Negroes actually less qualified than whites are placed into positions where their insufficient or lower qualifications will be displayed. (Note that discrimination against Jews, which demanded higher qualifications from them than from others to occupy any given office, reinforced a stereotype of Jews as particularly intelligent and qualified. In the end that discrimination may have been helpful to them.)

The effects of reverse discrimination on those who are, or might be, directly favored must be psychologically ruinous. A Negro who becomes a professor at City College, say, or perhaps a Ph.D., will never be sure whether he got the title or position because of his merits measured as are those of everybody else in his calling, or whether he got where he is because he is a Negro. There is no question that his self-esteem is likely to suffer from this. On the other hand, the tendency of Negroes who do not get positions for which they are not qualified according to objective criteria, or less qualified than white candidates, to believe that they are unwarrantedly discriminated against, or that they have a right to get the position simply because they are Negroes, is not weakened by indulgence.

The practice of reverse discrimination arises from guilt feelings widespread in the white community as much as from Negro pressure. A practice so clearly irrational in helping either Negroes or whites is indeed best explained as an act of penitence which aims at self-punishment more than at the effective satisfaction of legitimate claims. The underlying guilt feelings are rationalized; we are told that discrimination against Negroes in the past, and the present inferior status of many of them, must be offset by reverse discrimination. Yet discrimination in favor of one person today does not repair the injury done to another 100 years ago. Two inequities do not offset each other, or produce equity. Individual injustices can be offset only by compensating the individuals who suffered them and not some other members of their group. Possibly the expense of compensation should be borne by those who inflicted the injustices; else by the community as a whole, but never by individuals who had nothing to do with the matter. Injustices committed against the group as a whole can be offset only by compensating the group as a whole—i.e., by compensating its communal institutions or otherwise assisting the group as such. The group may be regarded as continuous and identical to itself over time—wherefore it can presently be compensated for past hardships, whereas aid to one individual now cannot offset hardship suffered by another in the past.

VIII. Public Claims and Private Cravings

The most important and personal, and therefore the most stinging problem of Negroes is seldom faced by their spokesmen; it is its unacknowledged presence that explains, or helps explain, the irrationality of many apparent Negro goals—for instance, the insistence on having white people, who do not wish to do so, compelled to eat with Negroes, to go to school with them, or to live in their neighborhood. Such dubious and irrational spokesmen as James Baldwin and Malcolm X also appear to be the product of the psychological defense of Negroes against their unfaced problem—the problem of individual acceptance.

The problem is not faced—and sometimes not consciously felt as such—because it obviously cannot be solved by public social means such as laws or subsidies. Although it affects individuals as group members—as Negroes—there is nothing the group can do to solve this problem, beyond bringing about conditions that may (or may not) make a solution possible. It is here that the problem of individual acceptance differs from that of "discrimination against." Indeed, the main result of the disappearance of unwarranted discrimination is to confront Negroes with the problem of individual acceptance. To avoid facing this problem, Negro leaders have resorted to curious expedients. Among these is the demand for coerced congregation. Unlike claims for equal treatment, demands for compulsory togetherness (however much sanctioned by the courts) are neither legitimate nor fruitful. If gratified, they are more than likely to aggravate the discomfort and strain from which Negroes suffer in American society. Alexis de Tocqueville may have suggested one reason for the demand and the illusoriness of the satisfaction sought, when he wrote:

> Among democratic nations men easily attain a certain equality of conditions: they can never attain the equality they desire. It perpetually retires from before them, yet without hiding itself from their sight, and in retiring draws them on.[9]

What Negroes want—and nothing could be more understandable—is to be accepted by whites as individuals. This is the true and full meaning of equality, equal rights, etc.—the human and concrete meaning that makes "rights" real, and allows a Negro to feel not as somebody who has human or civil rights but somebody who *is* human—a person in his own right. Negroes want to be loved and hated, respected and disdained as individuals. They don't want to be invisible as persons, blacked out by their all too visible color—black shadows or one-dimensional silhouettes. But what they attain by the means now used, is to be formally treated as though equal, and yet, as intruders, not to be truly accepted individually. In public matters the government can compel equal treatment, and even prevent dissociation. But this compulsion does not foster personal acceptance. On the contrary, it throws into relief, more strikingly than ever before, the inability of most whites (including many of those who feel themselves free of "prejudice") to accept Negroes as individuals. As de Tocqueville points out, it is when equality has been attained that resentment will be greatest:

> When inequality of conditions is the common law of society, the most marked inequalities do not strike the eye: when everything is nearly on the same level, the slightest are marked enough to hurt it. Hence the desire of equality always becomes more insatiable in proportion as equality is more complete.[10]

[9]*Democracy in America,* Oxford Univ. Press, p. 347.
[10]*Ibid.*

The external opportunity for acceptance has been created; the presence of Negroes cannot be rejected any longer nor their rights denied. They are equal. Yet the barriers against the group also served the individual members as defenses against individual rejection. Bereft of these barriers, individual Negroes will feel and resent more than ever the remaining purely internal and psychological rejection against which courts and governments are powerless. It will be the more wounding because it will be more continuously experienced under conditions of external equality and frequent and obligatory association.

The question: whence comes the preference for one's own ethnic and national group and the rejection of others? is beyond the scope of this essay. However, this preference is so deeply rooted—in culturally elaborated biological differences —that mere mixing of groups is most unlikely to extinguish it. Measures may be taken, and under favorable circumstances may be successful, to moderate such preferences so as to avoid inequities and aggressive hostilities, perhaps even to permit and foster friendly relations. But coerced mixing is unlikely to have this effect.

Negro intellectuals often and mainly attack white liberals, their allies, the very people who have helped them. Perhaps the Negro intellectuals sense that the white liberals, despite their efforts on behalf of Negroes, feel guilty, feel that, somehow, they owe more to Negroes. They feel guilty about opposing discrimination, segregation, etc., yet being unable to do the one thing they too know Negroes want: accept them as persons and individuals. Official public acceptance is a poor substitute. Indeed, it will cause Negroes to feel their final rejection—by their allies—most stingingly. It is the white liberal who publicly accepts Negroes; private rejection by him is the more resented for this very reason. He would not be necessarily hypocritical were he to insist that Negroes, regardless of one's private feelings, must be granted certain rights. Usually he goes further, however, professing feelings he feels he ought to have but does not feel, and can not fully live up to. In this sense, he is a hypocrite.

Sensing the white liberal's guilt feeling, Negro intellectuals feel free to lambast him for actual or imaginary sins. His guilt feelings will prevent him from fighting back; he will turn his aggressiveness against not-so-liberal whites who do not feel guilty about not loving Negroes. He will attack them and press for new and, recently, quite often unreasonable acts of atonement in favor of Negroes.

14   Planned Mediocrity in the Public Schools

Mortimer Smith

Many of the troubles which beset public education are directly traceable to an etymological phenomenon which has engaged the attention of a host of critics in recent years but does not yet seem to be comprehended by the general lay public: the transfiguration of the word education into Education, an event that first became visible to the naked eye about fifty years ago, was then no bigger than a man's hand, and has now mushroomed into a cloud which envelops our whole educational system. My 1934 edition of Webster's Collegiate Dictionary defines education as "the act or process of education; the impartation or acquisition of knowledge, skill, or development of character, as by study or discipline"; it also refers to education as "pedagogics." The 1951 edition of the same dictionary, while retaining the first part of this definition, has elevated the peda-

From Mortimer Smith, *The Diminished Mind: A Study of Planned Mediocrity in Our Public Schools* (Chicago: Henry Regnery, 1954), Chapter 5, pp. 76–99. Reprinted by permission of Henry Regnery Company.

gogics part to "a science dealing with the principles and practice of teaching and learning." In the process of becoming a science, of acquiring a capital E, education has enhanced its position as a field of study; as the act or process of imparting knowledge it has steadily lost ground. And as the art of pedagogics has developed into the science of education, it has also become a vested interest, supported by a gigantic interlocking bureaucracy which controls public education and is beginning to threaten private education.

Some historians trace the germination of this monstrous growth to some innocent remarks made by President James B. Angell of the University of Michigan to his Board of Regents in 1874. As many graduates of that university went into public school work, he thought that "some familiar lectures" on "the art of teaching and governing a school" might be of "essential service" to the senior class.[1] Four years later Michigan established a chair of "the Science and the Art of Teaching"(apparently the first such chair in this country) but the idea was slow to catch on: twenty years later, in 1900, only about a dozen colleges and universities had established chairs of pedagogy or departments of education. But by 1954 practically every self-respecting university in the country (Princeton is a notable exception) had a booming department of education, with the aim no longer being as simple a one as providing "some familiar lectures on the art of teaching and governing a school." President Angell's modest suggestion was prompted by the realization of a need that is as real now as it was in his day, the teacher's need not only for knowledge of subject matter but for craftsmanship in presenting it and for knowledge of the nature of the recipient of subject matter, the child. I imagine there are very few die-hards who would maintain that all true teachers are born, not made, that thorough knowledge of one's subject automatically equips one to teach it brilliantly or who would deny that some aspects of the art of teaching can be transmitted. But today the art has become more important than

[1]Edgar W. Knight, *Fifty Years of American Education* (New York: Ronald Press, 1952), p. 231.

the matter, the method has taken precedence over the material it was called into being to serve.

Had it not been for one circumstance pedagogics might have remained a relatively minor part of the preparation of teachers and would have continued to be taught by subject matter authorities, with history specialists giving sideline lectures on how to teach history, mathematics professors doing the same for their subject, and so on through the whole field of the liberal arts. But along about the turn of the century education began to be affected by the influence of the new philosophy of pragmatism which was marked, as Santayana observed, by "the dominance of the foreground," by excessive concern with method, with *how* rather than *why*. Of the triumvirate who fathered pragmatism—Charles Peirce, William James, and John Dewey—it was the latter who related it to education; his pioneering book, *The School and Society,* and subsequent books of his, were challenging, indeed revolutionary, for they called into question many of the presumptions on which the older, traditional education was based, especially the education of the very young. Dewey attracted followers and disciples (many of them, as has often been pointed out, far more extreme than the master) and between them they formulated certain philosophical and pedagogical principles which formed the basis of what came to be known as progressive education and is now more commonly referred to as modern education. I do not think anyone will challenge the statement that pragmatism has become the official philosophy of public school education; there may be an occasional maverick scattered here and there but the great majority of the professors of education are committed to this philosophy and they transmit it to the future teachers and administrators whom they train to run the American public school system.[2]

The intricacies of pragmatism do not unravel themselves

---

[2]There were, and still are, well-known figures in professional education opposed to much that goes by the names of pragmatism and progressivism. Several names come to mind: William C. Bagley, Frederick S. Breed, Ross L. Finney, I. L. Kandel, Edgar W. Knight, Robert Ulich. These men, however, are the lonely exceptions.

easily to the amateur in philosophy, especially as set down in the somewhat involuted prose of Professor Dewey, but looming out of the misty and obscure lowlands are discernible certain mountain peaks of meaning for educational philosophy and practice. In some respects the educational conservative and the educational pragmatist can meet on common ground: both believe in the concept of humaneness, that is, that children should be treated with kindness, that cuffing them around and smacking them over the knuckles with rulers is not a sure-fire method of imparting knowledge; the traditionalist can agree that the child needs to live a happy and creative life in the present as well as in some remote future; and he would agree that education in the past often failed to recognize the value of action, the attempt to relate thinking and doing, the mental and the physical, the idea summed up by a nonpragmatist, Jacques Maritain, in the remark that man's intelligence is not only in his head but in his fingers. But beyond these agreements there is a wide gulf separating traditionalist and pragmatist, especially the contemporary pragmatist who in practice often goes beyond anything dreamed of by the founding fathers of the movement.

The pragmatist, following the lead of Dewey, is reluctant to postulate any ultimate values toward which the educational process ought to be aiming, to set up any ends for education; to him the educational process has no end beyond itself. Education is "the reconstruction of experience," it is continued growth. While the concept of growth is central to the pragmatist's position, he is careful to avoid any statement about what direction it should take, except that he sometimes speaks vaguely of "desirable" and "satisfactory" growth; to go beyond this would be to commit oneself to some ultimate values, to absolutes, and this is something the pragmatist refuses to do even though here he runs into a logical absurdity: if you declare something to be desirable and satisfactory you are implying an *ought to be,* you are declaring that there are some desirable ends.

What are the implications of this viewpoint for what goes on in classrooms? If, as the pragmatist maintains, the important thing is the "on-going process" rather than any results obtained, curriculum makers will not acknowledge any hierarchy of values among subjects; no subject will be of any more intrinsic value than any other; courses in pastry-making and basket-weaving will be on a par with courses in history and literature. In the pragmatist's world the important criterion in education is usefulness; the schools should be providing the student with experiences which will contribute in concrete fashion to "successful living" now and in the future. The curriculum will be determined not by any preconceived notion of what is important for all students but by what appeals to the interests, and is compatible with the abilities, of individual students. Effective learning is not something gleaned from books or from contemplation of the dead past but is learning by doing, by re-creating "real-life experiences" in the classroom. The task of schools and teachers must not be the narrowly intellectual one of inculcating knowledge, of transmitting the cultural heritage; it must be nothing less than the attempt to meet the needs of the whole child, not only the intellectual needs, but the emotional, recreational, social, and all other needs. Although the pragmatist often speaks of the ethical and spiritual needs of youth and how they can be met in school, his rejection of transcendental values causes him to think of them solely in secular and social terms; in his lexicon, the ethical and spiritual way becomes an exercise in cooperative living, in how-to-get-along-with-each-other.

I have indirectly touched [elsewhere] on the inadequacies of the pragmatic position as a guide to sound educational practice. For emphasis, I will elaborate briefly on some of those objections. The primary objection is to pragmatism's lack of a value-system, its lack of a sense of direction. That is "true value," the pragmatist asserts, which "works out" beneficently in social fruits, but if we deny that there is an ultimate truth which sometimes transcends time and fact, if we have no absolute standard of what is good and what bad, how are we to judge what is "beneficent"? Won't our answer be determined by our social and cultural conditioning, so that if we are Russians we will decide that communism is beneficent and democracy evil? There are many pragmatists, of course, who do operate as if there were for them ultimate values and who do make moral discriminations but one feels they do this despite their philosophy. It is hard to escape the conclusion of the philosopher Eliseo Vivas: "No Deweyan can give one good, radically theoretical reason, one that goes beyond expedience, why he prefers democracy to totalitarianism or why he regards other men as his moral equals."[3]

Nor is the pragmatist's definition of education as continued growth—Dewey's "experiential continuum"—satisfactory until we set up some goals for growth; one can grow and develop in evil, one can graduate from efficiency at petty thievery to efficiency in murder. Another unsatisfactory criterion is usefulness: who can say what is useful and what isn't? How are we to tell that what seems useless at the moment may not bear unpredictable future fruit, as the young Churchill's painful exposure to grammar and rhetoric bore fruit in his later literary and political career? And if the student gets pleasure from pursuing some obscure aspect of a subject, is that to be dismissed as useless?

I think the pragmatist-schoolman's preoccupation with "real-life experiences" can also be misleading, especially when it fails to take into sufficient consideration the fact that children are not only attracted by the comfortably familiar but by the unfamiliar and the strange, in short, that they are still, despite all the educators have done to undermine them, creatures of imagination and fantasy. When the schoolman agrees with the remark of the American sociologist who intimates that city children can't understand the sentiment in "I remember, I remember the house where I was born" or "over the river and through the wood to grandfather's house we'll go" because they were born in hospitals and spend their holidays in movie palaces,[4] isn't he agreeing that children only appreciate what they know and have no sense of imagination or capacity for vicarious enjoyment? And isn't it comforting to know that this

[3] *The Moral Life and the Ethical Life* (Chicago: University of Chicago Press, 1950), p. 128.

[4] Margaret Mead, *The School in American Culture* (Cambridge: Harvard University Press, 1951), pp. 25–26.

is not so, even in the sociologist's and the schoolman's fast changing world?

I am willing to accept the pragmatist's statement that the curriculum must be based on the child's interests and abilities as a partially valid doctrine; it is uncontestably true that all students do not have the same interests or abilities and that learning will be most effective when these differences are recognized. I am unwilling to accept the current version of this doctrine which is used as justification for the notion that those who (seemingly) lack interest or ability need not be educated but merely adjusted. Nor do I find it easy to accept the companion doctrine that the school must educate the whole child; to do so it would have to assume the functions of the home and community, to the neglect of its own functions.

The traditionalist-humanist asserts that men must be bound together by ties of moral stability and he considers that true education for all men will consist of studies that illumine and strengthen those ties. The educational pragmatist, on the other hand, lacking belief in man's need for such a central moral stability, sees no necessity for a common education which will connect man with man and man with nature. But without this belief in a common bond between man and man education tends to become animal training, with the educator occupying himself more and more in a search for refined *method;* the *content* of education—those studies appropriate to all men—tends to get submerged by the empirical and the "practical," by fragments of information and skills.

It is said that philosophy has no appeal for the average, practical mind, especially the average, practical American mind. When Albert Lynd made the reasonable prediction that the majority of parents would vote against Deweyan pragmatism "if they understood the philosophical ballot" one educationist replied that parents aren't interested in philosophy but are satisfied if the new education "works."[5] Another education-

[5]See "Who Wants Progressive Education?" by Albert Lynd, *Atlantic Monthly,* April, 1953, and the reply thereto in the May, 1953, issue of the same magazine, "How Dangerous is John Dewey?" by Frederic Ernst.

ist refers to "superficial critics" of the schools "with their remote philosophical arguments," and says that "the whole conflict over relative and absolute values is a tempest in a teapot as it applies to the process of education."[6] This cavalier dismissal of philosophical conflict reminds one of John Maynard Keynes' remark that practical men, who believe themselves to be exempt from any intellectual influences, are usually the slaves of some academic scribbler of a few years back. No matter how much educators scoff at philosophy for the masses, or fail to see the philosophical basis of their own actions, the fact remains that conditions in our public schools today stem from a philosophy, from a way of looking at man and the universe; and if we would understand why conditions are what they are we will need to understand the philosophy.

As I have pointed out, the progress of education as Education was slow until about 1900 when the theories of Dewey and his disciples began to be felt. The pragmatists took over public education by following their own precepts; as Dean Marten Ten Hoor has pointed out, they emphasized *pragma,* the *deed,* the *thing done.* These early pragmatists in the colleges were men of action, not content to idle in academic backwaters as were the scholars on the liberal arts faculties. Convinced of the great importance of the *how* of things, of methodology, they proceeded rapidly in the nurture of Professional Education, that infant which has now grown into such an over-sized adult. The progress of this nurture is well described by Dean Ten Hoor:

> The leaders convinced university administrators. They "sold" the school of education to the students and to the public. They organized teacher employment offices on university campuses and refused to recommend students who had not had the requisite number and kind of courses in education and they were thus able to fill the field with their own graduates. They joined forces

[6]Ernest O. Melby, "And the Future of School Administration?" *The School Executive,* January, 1954.

with teachers colleges and normal schools and built up a great, state-wide organization of teachers, principals and superintendents, each of whom was a partisan in his own community. They convinced the public and the state legislatures of the rightness of their cause. They gained virtual control of the laws and the administration of teacher certification. They became a powerful, sometimes a dominating, influence in accrediting associations in the field of higher education. They established their own type of high school curricula and compelled many colleges and universities to alter their admission requirements and even their requirements for graduation. In short . . . the schoolmen acquired control of publicly supported primary and secondary education in the United States, and, as a consequence, considerable influence over the course of private education on these levels.[7]

As the schools of education and the teachers colleges have now become the dominant force in public education by controlling teacher-preparation, it might be well to look a little more closely at their influence. Many parents and laymen, I find, do not seem to realize how a teacher qualifies for a position in our public schools today. Once upon a time bright young girls and boys who did good work in college could go immediately into public school teaching; if they wanted to teach in high school they probably took advanced or postgraduate work in the subject they wanted to teach. Such a preparation no longer qualifies one to teach in public schools; many of these bright young people now go into private school teaching where the salaries are no greater and the hours on duty no shorter but where there is usually some respect for learning and scholarship. A sound education and a knowledge of one's subject is no longer the prime qualification for getting into public school teaching; the modern emphasis on *how* rather than *what* dictates that the prospective teacher must spend about one-fourth of the period of his higher education taking courses in Education; moreover, if he attends a teachers college his work in the traditional subjects will probably be directed not by experts in these subjects but experts in how to teach them.

Preoccupation with methodology and pedagogical gadgetry

[7]"The Stake of the Liberal Arts College in Teacher Certification," *Association of American Colleges Bulletin*, March, 1953.

is certainly not entirely useless. Probably Stephen Leacock was close to the truth of the matter when he described Education as consisting of "10 per cent solid value and 90 per cent mixed humbug and wind." A knowledge of the history of education, of the psychology of learning and growth, and some hours in practice teaching are important in the training of all teachers, but those responsible for teacher training are not content with anything so modest in the way of professional preparation.

Under an ideal system, prospective teachers in their student days would come under the tutelage of the best scholars and authorities in various subject fields. But these scholars, who *do* influence the training of those who are going to teach in private schools or in liberal arts colleges, have practically no effect on the training of public school teachers. By the educators they are often looked upon as old fuddy-duddies, poking around in the trash basket of the stuffy past. The great dichotomy in American education today is between the world of scholarship and learning on the one hand, and on the other, the world of educational *Realpolitik* dominated by the schools of education in our universities, the teachers colleges, the National Education Association and its subsidiaries, the U.S. Office of Education, and the state departments of education, all working together with great unanimity of purpose as the gigantic pressure group which controls public education.

The chief method the Education lobby has used to gain control has been through the certification of teachers; they have so effectively lobbied their point of view in the state legislatures that today only a miracle can get a well-qualified person in the scholastic sense into the schools without exposure to "professional" education. Superintendents, who almost invariably are themselves products of the teacher-training schools, sell their boards the idea that only those teachers should be advanced in the system who go back to the schools of education for periodic doses of indoctrination. (Encouraged by their easy successes of recent years, educators are now lobbying to make "professional" requirements mandatory for teaching in private schools and colleges.)

There is increasing evidence to show that the teacher-training institutions—which have, in the words of the Harvard Report, "taught everything except the indispensable thing, the love of knowledge"—are providing us with teachers who are our most poorly educated citizens. In 1927 Nicholas Murray Butler said that teachers in the United States were "in large part quite uneducated in any large and justifiable sense of that word"; in 1937 William C. Bagley of Teachers College said that of all comparable countries, "the United States may have the least well-selected and least well-educated teachers"; in 1938 Learned and Wood, in a study of conditions in Pennsylvania, said that the teachers in training, compared with the nonteachers, exhibited inferiority in "nearly every department of study."[8] That conditions have not improved since these pessimistic statements were made, is shown by the depressing evidence to be found in the results of the draft deferment examinations given to over 300,000 students in 1951 in which those students majoring in education made by far the poorest showing. According to findings published by the Educational Testing Service, of 97,800 college freshmen tested those who scored highest were students of engineering, with 68 per cent passing; then came the physical sciences, 64 per cent; biological sciences, 59 per cent; social sciences, 57 per cent; the humanities, 52 per cent; general arts, 48 per cent; business, 42 per cent; agriculture, 37 per cent; and then at the end of the procession, education with only 27 per cent. According to the report, seniors in education who took the test did about the same as the freshmen. And from these men we are to draw the future leaders and administrators of our public school system![9]

Many teachers, of course, are not themselves happy about present conditions in the field of teacher training or about the adulteration of real education. Any publicist, lay or schoolman, who touches on these subjects in print is apt to hear immediately from a host of teachers who are only too happy to find a

[8]Knight, *op. cit.*, pp. 279–281.

[9]Henry Chauncy, "The Use of the Selective Service College Qualification Test in the Deferment of College Students," *Science*, July 25, 1952.

sympathetic ear in which to pour their woes. (Many of them request that their names not be used, for fear of reprisals from their educator bosses.) The gist of their complaints is that their training, and supervision after they become teachers, is of a kind to discourage any realistic and fundamental approach to the problem of educating, rather than merely chaperoning, the children under their charge.

It is a healthy sign that many persons both in the field of the liberal arts and of professional education, who cannot by the wildest flight of the imagination be dubbed enemies of the schools, have of late been looking critically at this question of teacher preparation. Harold L. Clapp, of the division of language and literature at Grinnell College, in a trenchant article titled "The Stranglehold on Education," says:

> No dyed-in-the-wool Educationist really seems to believe that knowledge of a subject has much to do with teaching that subject. Subject-matter requirements for teachers are pitifully inadequate, and cannot well be otherwise. There is much too little time to study the *subject* one is to teach when so much time is taken up by courses in *how* to teach. . . .
>
> The appalling fact is that *our most poorly educated college graduates are our teachers.* [Author's italics.] A college which would raise its academic standards is invariably hindered by the plight of the prospective teacher, who because of "professional" requirements cannot carry more than a minimum of academic work. There are reputable colleges in the United States which have established the requirements for their A.B. degree at a high level, but which make a specific exception of the teacher-in-training. While they phrase it less baldly, their catalogues state in effect: "If you are going to be *educated* while in college, you must do this, and this, and this. If you are going to *teach instead*, less is expected of you."[10]

This is what historian Arthur E. Bestor of the University of Illinois has to say:

> American intellectual life is threatened because the first twelve years of formal schooling in the United States are falling more and more completely under the policy-making control of a new

[10]*Bulletin* of the American Association of University Professors, Summer, 1949.

breed of educator who has no real place in—who does not respect and who is not respected by—the world of scientists, scholars, and professional men.[11]

Dean Roger P. McCutcheon of the Graduate School of Tulane University, regretting the tendency to increase Education requirements, says:

> If we really want those who teach our children to have stopped their subject-matter education at the sophomore level, well and good, but we should realize it. We are now face to face with a plan that will require prospective teachers to abandon the Bachelor of Arts degree for an undergraduate degree in education. Furthermore, there is as yet no convincing proof that these education requirements make better teachers.[12]

Criticisms such as the foregoing may, in view of the fact that the critics represent the humanities, be interpreted as the cries of those who see a threat to their own vested interests. Lately, however, some pained voices have been raised from within the temple itself. Frank E. Spaulding, who is a professor of education emeritus (Yale), wrote an article a few years ago in which he deplored the widespread obeisance of superintendents of schools to the dictums of the super-professionals (his term). He feels that superintendents have permitted the super-professionals to determine what is sound preparation for teaching and for advancing in a school system; invariably such preparation means more and more exposure to courses in schools of education. Under the present system, he points out, the poorest teacher in more than 94 per cent of all city school systems in this country, can climb steadily from the foot to the top of the salary scale while the best teacher will remain at the foot if she chooses not to take the courses. The whole present-day setup of salary schedules, says Dr. Spaulding, "is a perfect example of the advantages of cooperation—for those

---

[11]Arthur E. Bestor, *Educational Wastelands* (Chicago: University of Illinois, 1953), p. 121.

[12]"The Master's Degree and the Teacher Requirements," *School and Society*, September 22, 1951.

who cooperate. The prosperity and to a large extent even the livelihood of the super-professionals is dependent on the maintenance of these schedules. Teachers serving under them would be foolish not to take advantage of the large salary increments which result from the hours and years devoted to 'preparation,' and to repeated doses of 'preparation,' which the super-professionals are eager to provide."

Dr. Spaulding, indeed, seems to be a thoroughly disillusioned educationist. In his opinion educators use novel and difficult language and dress up trite thought in new linguistic garments; and he complains that most of them are isolated from the schools, pointing out that of the half-dozen most widely recognized contemporary leaders among the super-professionals, three have never had any direct service in schools and the service of the others was very brief and in each case was completed over forty years ago.[13]

Edgar W. Knight, who until his death in 1953 was Kenan Professor of Educational History at the University of North Carolina, was another educator who felt that all is far from right in the world of teacher training. Complaining of the increased number of courses in education thought up by the teacher-training institutions in cahoots with the certifying bureaus and state departments of education, he said:

> In this fact friendly critics see tendencies toward what would promptly be stamped as crass and vulgar racketeering in less humane activities. It is this condition that causes students to say —generally after they have become bachelor, master, or doctor of education—that the courses they were forced to take were so overlapping and repetitious as to be almost immoral. Out of these and other unhealthy conditions that have grown up and nowadays surround practices in teacher-education, the critics see the rapid tendency for teacher-education institutions to become mere trade-schools and their products often mere mechanics.[14]

[13]"Coping With Modern Educational Ideas," *Teacher Education Quarterly* (Connecticut), Spring, 1950.
[14]"The Obligation of Professional Education to the Schools," *School and Society*, October 6, 1951.

In a later article, Dr. Knight returned to the subject of pro-liferation and inflation of the curriculum in schools of education, stating that these conditions "enable and even encourage indifferent and sometimes quite weak students to become teachers and managers of the schools with comparatively little intellectual effort, if they but learn to give the passwords and pronounce the pedagogical shibboleths."[15]

The educationists, who are the authors of the system, refuse to believe that the poor quality of current teaching has anything to do with the kind of institutions they are running. Their argument is that we are getting poor candidates for teacher training because of the low financial returns. (There is not nearly as great a shortage of teachers in private schools as there is in public ones, even though the financial returns are no greater and often less.) While it is true, and has always been true, that one of the reasons many persons of ability will not enter the profession is that it is a notoriously underpaid one, I believe there are now more compelling deterrents. Any intelligent young person who feels strongly about education wants for himself, and if he becomes a teacher wants to transmit, the best possible sort of education, but he suspects that he is not going to get this kind of education under present teacher-training auspices. The fact seems to be that the greatest deterrent to entering the profession of public school teaching is that it has become intellectually disreputable. If the teacher-training institutions have little regard for real education, for scholastic and intellectual attainment, they will attract individuals who share this disregard—precisely the indifferent and weak students to which Dr. Knight referred. One school of education in a large university states the case frankly in its catalogue: "Students will be admitted to the college of education without reference to high school pattern, only high school education being a requirement."

Under the present scheme of things it is almost impossible for an able, scholarly, and conscientious teacher to advance in

[15]"Some Disturbing Educational Contradictions," *School and Society,* November 29, 1952.

the system without pocketing his or her pride and returning to summer school for further doses of "professional preparation." This usually consists of courses in methodology, often dull, sometimes repellent; and the courses in subject matter are apt to be superficial survey courses, like the summer course in one teachers college which deals with World Literature from ancient times to the twentieth century—all in thirty days! The fashionable gimmick at the moment in professional preparation is something called the "workshop" (sometimes, to add scientific tone, called the "laboratory workshop") which is a sort of round table discussion enabling teachers to get academic credit for agreeing with the educational clichés expressed by the professional educator who presides. The *sine qua non* of these workshops is agreement; the teacher who cannot conform is guilty of the great modern sin in the eyes of educators—non-cooperation with the group.

I imagine that any able teacher is going to be discouraged by the results of a recent "study" which shows that the majority of teacher-training institutions believe they must prepare teachers for "correlated, fused, broad-field, core types of curriculum organization in secondary schools." One can well believe the statement in the same report that "traditional majors and minors" will not help the teacher preparing to teach core, for a knowledge of subject matter may be only a handicap to the teacher who is trying to keep subject matter out of her teaching.[16]

The good teacher is apt to become resentful about all this foolishness and either quit teaching or become embittered and soured—while the ambitious and superficial teachers take all the snap courses, attend the workshops, and become the administrators who set the standards for teaching. Incidentally to some aspiring candidate for an educational doctorate, seeking a subject for a thesis, I make a gratuitous suggestion: why not investigate the high incidence of physical education graduates

[16]*Vitalizing Secondary Education,* Bulletin No. 3, Report of the First Commission on Life Adjustment Education for Youth. Reprinted 1954, U.S. Department of Health, Education and Welfare, p. 27.

among public school administrators and their influence on the intellectual tone of the schools. While I offer no supporting statistics, I have been surprised in travelling around the country how many superintendents of schools are drawn from this field. In one of our largest school systems the deputy superintendent in charge of curriculum is an ex-basketball coach. I don't mean to belittle physical educationists but only to point out that their training is not usually of the sort which qualifies them to set the intellectual character or course of studies of a school system.

I realize that my strictures against the teacher-training institutions may seem too sweeping to some persons, but hardly to those who know something of their character. The surprising thing is that sometimes one will find sound scholars in these institutions, men who quietly resist the nonsense served up by the rest of the staff. If anyone wants to maintain that one of the worst things that ever happened to American education was the formation of Teachers College, Columbia University, I am willing to go along with him and add that I deplore its continuing influence; the fact remains that there have been scholars at Teachers College who made great contributions to education. From my observation, the best people on the staffs of the schools of education are apt to be the professors of educational history (who are often genuine historians) and the professors of educational philosophy (who are sometimes genuine philosophers). The worst seem to be the professors of "administration" most of whom seem to qualify for their jobs by failing as superintendents of schools.

The professional educators are now bent on extending their control beyond teacher certification and seem to be attempting to make the schools entirely autonomous, to divorce them from the natural and normal workings of the political process and put them entirely under the tutelage of the experts. Chiefly through the lobbying efforts of the National Education Association, which with its numerous affiliated associations numbers almost a million in membership, efforts have been afoot for some time to erect a system under which public education is subject to less and less public control. The tendencies for state legislatures, under pressures from the education lobby, to set up provisions whereby the public school system has first call on state revenues; the increasing number of cities where school boards are elected separately from other officials; the tendency to remove all state functions of education from the jurisdiction of the governor and local functions from the jurisdiction of mayor or selectman—all of these things may, at first glance, seem like worthy objectives, as removing education from "politics." But public education, like roads and sanitary arrangements, *is* a part of the function of government, of politics; you can separate it and give it special and preferential treatment only to the detriment of the over-all governmental process. So-called independent school boards (those elected at separate elections) often turn out to be independent of other municipal or town functions but under the domination of educationists; nor are they necessarily less susceptible to political graft as witness the scandals of a year or so ago relating to members of the Los Angeles board of education.[17]

This tendency of the educationists to enhance their position and consolidate their power is one of the reasons I feel we should approach with caution the question of federal aid to education which many Americans feel is the only device that can wipe out unequal educational opportunities. In view of the simple truth, which has been stated by the Supreme Court, that the state is bound "to regulate that which it subsidizes," we may well ask ourselves who the regulators will be; the answer, unfortunately, is that they will be the educationists. Federal aid will be the final step which will put the educationists in undisputed control of American public school education. To some it seems like a very high price to pay for equalization of opportunities.

Even if we get equalization of opportunity I do not think we can be assured that it will mean actual improvement in

---

[17]In this paragraph I have drawn on an excellent article which I recommend to my readers, "Educational Administration and Responsible Government," by Ernest A. Engelbert, *School and Society,* January 19, 1952.

quality of education, if the educationists are to set the tone. In the field of Negro education, for example, the southern states have (largely under threat of what has now come to pass, non-segregation) made tremendous strides in recent years in improving facilities but it remains to be seen if these mechanical advances mean a comparable advance in standards when the standards are set by the educationists. A recent article in a professional magazine, characteristically titled "A High School Diploma for All!" may show which way the wind is blowing. In this article, which describes an "experiment" carried on in a Negro high school in Alabama with the approval of the state department of education, the author rehashes the old familiar arguments about the curriculum being based on the "needs" of the students; as the majority of students in this school become farmers, farmers' wives, or domestics, they don't need to master "theoretical" material, such as history, mathematics, and science but need to learn "socially acceptable manners" and "a few facts, skills, and habits and the acceptance of a few ruling principles." The experiment consists in "awarding a high school diploma to any student who has spent three years in high school. . . . Scholastic achievement is no longer the basis for awarding the diploma."[18] In other words, it's the old trick of the educationists of dividing the sheep and the goats; an attempt will be made to educate the minority who plan to go to college—the sheep—but as for the majority—the goats—they will have to be content with being adjusted to the lowly status they apparently are destined to occupy.

Believers in educational standards who feel that equalization of opportunities can only be achieved by federal aid and who are not, as I confess I am, frightened by state regulation *per se,* ought to give more thought than they seem to be giving to the circumstance that those who will do the regulating under federal aid are those who consistently fight to adulterate standards. One might be less concerned if there was any prospect that the regulators would include those who believe in real

18J. D. Thompson, "A High School Diploma for All!" *The School Executive,* February, 1954.

education, the scholars in the humanities and the sciences; this prospect is not even dim, but nonexistent. I presume that the U.S. Office of Education would fall heir to the bureaucratic functions of federal aid, but if we are really concerned with the improvement of quality wouldn't it be shortsighted to enhance the power of an office which sponsors Life Adjustment, a program based on the assumption that the majority of Americans are incapable of absorbing education?

My severe criticism here of professional education will, as it has on other occasions, undoubtedly be deplored as discourteous in tone and lacking in the spirit of cooperation and conciliation; perhaps some readers will excuse it as a necessary part of the hygiene of the traditionalist, as an aid to circulation of his blood, which is the way Logan Pearsall Smith described the denunciation of the young by the old. Be that as it may, I have felt under the necessity of speaking unequivocally about a situation which is adversely affecting the health of the American public school system and is, unfortunately, but dimly comprehended by the great majority of parents and laymen. When laymen will take the trouble to inform themselves I think they will come to understand the monolithic nature of professional education and will agree with Paul Woodring (one of those rare individuals, a professor in a school of education who is skeptical of current fashions) when he says that under the present system the individual who holds to a minority point of view "is treated as a backward child who must be brought to see the light," that "permanent nonagreement is never tolerated," and that "the validity of pragmatic principles" is never questioned. . . .[19]

[19]*Let's Talk Sense About Our Schools* (New York: McGraw-Hill, 1953).

15   The City: Some Myths About Diversity

Jane Jacobs

"Mixed uses 'look ugly. They cause traffic congestion. They invite ruinous uses."

These are some of the bugbears that cause cities to combat diversity. These beliefs help shape city zoning regulations. They have helped rationalize city rebuilding into the sterile, regimented, empty thing it is. They stand in the way of planning that could deliberately encourage spontaneous diversity by providing the conditions necessary to its growth.

Intricate minglings of different uses in cities are not a form of chaos. On the contrary, they represent a complex and highly developed form of order. . . .

Nevertheless, even though intricate mixtures of buildings, uses and scenes are necessary for successful city districts, does diversity carry, too, the disadvantages of ugliness, warring uses and congestion that are conventionally attributed to it by planning lore and literature?

These supposed disadvantages are based on images of unsuccessful districts which have not too much, but too little diversity. They call up visions of dull, down-at-heel residential areas, pocked with a few shabby, shoestring enterprises. They call up visions of low-value land uses, like junk yards or used-car lots. They call up visions of garish, sprawling, unremitting com-

From Jane Jacobs, *The Death and Life of Great American Cities* (New York: Random House, 1961), Chapter 12, pp. 222–238. Copyright © 1961 by Jane Jacobs. Reprinted by permission of Random House, Inc., and Jonathan Cape Ltd.

merce. None of these conditions, however, represents flourishing city diversity. On the contrary, these represent precisely the senility that befalls city neighborhoods in which exuberant diversity has either failed to grow or has died off with time. They represent what happens to semisuburbs which are engulfed by their cities but fail, themselves, to grow up and behave economically like successful city districts.

Flourishing city diversity, of the kind that is catalyzed by the combination of mixed primary uses, frequent streets, mixture of building ages and overheads, and dense concentration of users, does not carry with it the disadvantages of diversity conventionally assumed by planning pseudoscience. I now intend to show why it does not carry them, and why these disadvantages are fantasies which, like all fantasies that are taken too seriously, interfere with handling reality.

Let us consider, first, the belief that diversity looks ugly. Anything looks ugly, to be sure, if it is done badly. But this belief implies something else. It implies that city diversity of uses is inherently messy in appearance; and it also implies that places stamped with homogeneity of uses look better, or at any rate are more amenable to pleasant or orderly esthetic treatment.

But homogeneity or close similarity among uses, in real life, poses very puzzling esthetic problems.

If the sameness of use is shown candidly for what it is—sameness—it looks monotonous. Superficially, this monotony might be thought of as a sort of order, however dull. But esthetically, it unfortunately also carries with it a deep disorder: the disorder of conveying no direction. In places stamped with the monotony and repetition of sameness you move, but in moving you seem to have gotten nowhere. North is the same as south, or east as west. Sometimes north, south, east and west are all alike, as they are when you stand within the grounds of a large project. It takes differences—many differences—cropping up in different directions to keep us oriented. Scenes of thoroughgoing sameness lack these natural announcements of direction and movement, or are scantly furnished with them, and so they are deeply confusing. This is a kind of chaos.

Monotony of this sort is generally considered too oppressive to pursue as an ideal by everybody but some project planners or the most routine-minded real estate developers.

Instead, where uses are in actual fact homogeneous, we often find that deliberate distinctions and differences are contrived among the buildings. But these contrived differences give rise to esthetic difficulties too. Because inherent differences—those that come from genuinely differing uses—are lacking among the buildings and their settings, the contrivances represent the desire merely to *appear* different.

Some of the more blatant manifestations of this phenomenon were well described, back in 1952, by Douglas Haskell, editor of *Architectural Forum,* under the term "googie architecture." Googie architecture could then be seen in its finest flowering among the essentially homogeneous and standardized enterprises of roadside commercial strips: hot-dog stands in the shape of hot dogs, ice-cream stands in the shape of ice-cream cones. These are obvious examples of virtual sameness trying, by dint of exhibitionism, to appear unique and different from their similar commercial neighbors. Mr. Haskell pointed out that the same impulses to look special (in spite of not *being* special) were at work also in more sophisticated construction: weird roofs, weird stairs, weird colors, weird signs, weird anything.

Recently Mr. Haskell has observed that similar signs of exhibitionism have been appearing in supposedly dignified establishments.

Indeed they have: in office buildings, shopping centers, civic centers, airline terminals. Eugene Raskin, professor of architecture at Columbia University, commented on this same phenomenon in an essay, "On the Nature of Variety," in the Summer 1960 issue of the *Columbia University Forum.* Genuine architectural variety, Raskin pointed out, does not consist in using different colors or textures.

Can it be in using contrasting forms? [he asked]. A visit to one of the larger shopping centers (the Cross Country Shopping Center in New York's Westchester County comes to mind, but pick your own) will make the point: though slabs, towers, circles and flying stairs bound and abound all over the lot, the result has the appalling sameness of the tortures of hell. They may poke you with different instruments, but it's all pain. . . .

When we build, say, a business area in which all (or practically all) are engaged in earning their livings, or a residential area in which everyone is deep in the demands of domesticity, or a shopping area dedicated to the exchange of cash and commodities—in short, where the pattern of human activity contains only one element, it is impossible for the architecture to achieve a convincing variety—convincing of the known facts of human variation. The designer may vary color, texture and form until his drawing instruments buckle under the strain, proving once more that art is the one medium in which one cannot lie successfully.

The more homogeneity of use in a street or a neighborhood, the greater is the temptation to be different in the only way left to be different. Wilshire Boulevard in Los Angeles is an example of one grand exercise after another in superficially contrived distinction, for several miles of innately monotonous office buildings.

But Los Angeles is not unique in presenting us with such vistas. San Francisco, for all its scorn of this kind of thing in Los Angeles, looks much the same at its new outskirts of sorted-out shopping centers and housing developments, and for the same basic reasons. Euclid Avenue in Cleveland, which used to be considered by many critics one of the most beautiful of American avenues (it was, in those days, essentially a suburban avenue of large, fine houses with large, fine grounds), has now been excoriated, with justice, by critic Richard A. Miller in *Architectural Forum*, as one of the ugliest and most disorganized of city streets. In converting to outright urban use, Euclid Avenue has converted to homogeneity: office buildings again, and again a chaos of shouted, but superficial, differences.

Homogeneity of uses poses an unavoidable esthetic dilemma: Shall the homogeneity look as homogeneous as it is, and be frankly monotonous? Or shall it try not to look as homogeneous as it is and go in for eye-catching, but meaningless and chaotic differences? This, in city guise, is the old, familiar esthetic zoning problem of homogeneous suburbs: Shall they zone to require conformity in appearance, or shall they zone to prohibit sameness? If to prohibit sameness, where must the line be drawn against what is too nonconforming in design?

Wherever a city area is functionally homogeneous in its uses, this also becomes an esthetic dilemma for the city, and in more intensive form than in the suburbs, because buildings are so much more dominant in the general scene of cities. It is a ridiculous dilemma for cities, and it has no decent answer.

Diversity of uses, on the other hand, while it is too often handled poorly, does offer the decent possibility of displaying genuine differences of content. Therefore these can become interesting and stimulating differences to the eye, without phoniness, exhibitionism or belabored novelty.

Fifth Avenue in New York between Fortieth Street and Fifty-ninth Street is tremendously diverse in its large and small shops, bank buildings, office buildings, churches, institutions. Its architecture expresses these differences in use, and differences accrue from the varying ages of the buildings, differences in technology and historical taste. But Fifth Avenue does not look disorganized, fragmented or exploded.* Fifth Avenue's architectural contrasts and differences arise mainly out of differences in content. They are sensible and natural contrasts and differences. The whole hangs together remarkably well, without being monotonous either.

The new office stretch of New York's Park Avenue is far more standardized in content than Fifth Avenue. Park Avenue has the advantage of containing among its new office buildings

---

*Its only blatant eyesore and element of disorganization is a group of billboards on the northeast corner of Forty-second Street. These are presumably well meant because, as this is written, they are fatuously exhorting the passing throngs to pray in family groups, to save for a rainy day, and to fight delinquency. Their power to reform is questionable. Their power to blight the view up Fifth Avenue from the library is unquestionable.

several which, in themselves, are masterpieces of modern design.* But does homogeneity of use or homogeneity of age help Park Avenue esthetically? On the contrary, the office blocks of Park Avenue are wretchedly disorganized in appearance, and far more given than Fifth Avenue to a total effect of chaotic architectural willfulness, overlaid on boredom.

There are many instances of city diversity that include the use of residences and come off well. The Rittenhouse Square area in Philadelphia, Telegraph Hill in San Francisco, parts of the North End in Boston, afford examples. Small groups of residential buildings can be similar or even identical to each other without imposing a pall of monotony, so long as the grouping takes in no more than a short street block, and is not thereupon immediately repeated. In such a case, we look at the grouping as a unit, and see it as differing, in content and appearance, from whatever the next use or residential type may be.

Sometimes diversity of uses, combined with diversity of age, can even take the curse of monotony off blocks that are far too long—and again without the need for exhibitionism because differences of real substance exist. An example of this kind of diversity is Eleventh Street between Fifth and Sixth Avenues in New York, a street admired as both dignified and interesting to walk on. Along its south side it contains, going west, a fourteen-story apartment house, a church, seven three-story houses, a five-story house, thirteen four-story houses, a nine-story apartment, five four-story houses with a restaurant and bar at the street level, a five-story apartment, a little graveyard, and a six-story apartment house with a restaurant at street level; on the north side, again going west, it contains a church, a four-story house with a nursery school in it, a nine-story apartment house, three five-story houses, a six-story apartment house, an eight-story apartment house, five four-story houses, a six-story residence club, two five-story apartment houses, another five-story apartment house of very different vintage, a nine-story

*Lever House, Seagram, Pepsi-Cola, Union Carbide.

apartment house, a new addition to the New School for Social Research with a library at street level and a public view to the interior courtyard, a four-story house, a five-story apartment house with a restaurant at street level, a mean- and cheap-looking one-story laundry and cleaner, a three-story apartment house with a candy and newspaper store at street level. While these are nearly all residential buildings, they are broken into by instances of ten other uses. Even the purely residential buildings themselves embrace many different periods of technology and taste, many different modes and costs of living. They have an almost fantastic array of matter-of-fact, modestly stated differences: different heights at first-floor levels, differing arrangements for entrances and sidewalk access. These arise directly out of the fact that the buildings actually are different in kind and age. The effect is both serene and unself-conscious.

Still more interesting visual effects, and again without any need for exhibitionism or other phoniness, can and do arise in cities from mixtures in building types far more radical than those of Eleventh Street—more radical because they are based on more radical inherent differences. Most landmarks and focal points in cities—of which we need more, not fewer—come from the contrast of a use radically different from its surroundings, and therefore inherently special-looking, happily located to make some drama and contrast of the inherent difference. This, of course, was what Peets was talking about . . . when he advocated that monumental or noble buildings be set within the matrix of the city, instead of being sorted out and withdrawn into "courts of honor" with other inherently similar neighbors there.

Nor are the innate radical differences of humbler elements in city mixtures to be scorned esthetically. They too can convey the pleasures of contrast, movement and direction, without forced superficialities: the workshops that turn up mingled with residences, the manufacturing buildings, the art gallery next to the fish market that delights me every time I go to buy fish, the hoity-toity gourmet shop in another part of town that peacefully contrasts and coexists with a robust bar of the kind where new Irish immigrants come to hear about jobs.

Genuine differences in the city architectural scene express, as Raskin says so excellently,

> . . . the interweaving of *human* patterns. They are full of people doing different things, with different reasons and different ends in view, and the architecture reflects and expresses this difference—which is one of content rather than form alone. Being human, human beings are what interest us most. In architecture as in literature and the drama, it is the richness of human variation that gives vitality and color to the human setting. . . .
>
> Considering the hazard of monotony . . . the most serious fault in our zoning laws lies in the fact that they *permit* an entire area to be devoted to a single use.

In seeking visual order, cities are able to choose among three broad alternatives, two of which are hopeless and one of which is hopeful. They can aim for areas of homogeneity which look homogeneous, and get results depressing and disorienting. They can aim for areas of homogeneity which try not to look homogeneous, and get results of vulgarity and dishonesty. Or they can aim for areas of great diversity and, because real differences are thereby expressed, can get results which, at worst, are merely interesting, and at best can be delightful.

How to accommodate city diversity well in visual terms, how to respect its freedom while showing visually that it is a form of order, is the central esthetic problem of cities. . . . The point is this: City diversity is not innately ugly. That is a misconception, and a most simple-minded one. But lack of city diversity is innately either depressing on the one hand, or vulgarly chaotic on the other.

Is it true that diversity causes traffic congestion?

Traffic congestion is caused by vehicles, not by people in themselves.

Wherever people are thinly settled, rather than densely concentrated, or wherever diverse uses occur infrequently, any specific attraction does cause traffic congestion. Such places as clinics, shopping centers or movies bring with them a concentration of traffic—and what is more, bring traffic heavily along the routes to and from them. A person who needs or wants to use them can do so only by car. Even a grade school can mean traffic congestion in such a milieu, because children must be carried to school. Lack of wide ranges of concentrated diversity can put people into automobiles for almost all their needs. The spaces required for roads and for parking spread everything out still farther, and lead to still greater uses of vehicles.

This is tolerable where the population is thinly spread. It becomes an intolerable condition, destructive of all other values and all other aspects of convenience, where populations are heavy or continuous.

In dense, diversified city areas, people still walk, an activity that is impractical in suburbs and in most gray areas. The more intensely various and close-grained the diversity in an area, the more walking. Even people who come into a lively, diverse area from outside, whether by car or by public transportation, walk when they get there.

Is is true that city diversity invites ruinous uses? Is permissiveness for all (or almost all) kinds of uses in an area destructive?

To consider this, we need to consider several different kinds of uses—some of which actually are harmful, and some of which are conventionally considered to be harmful but are not.

One destructive category of uses, of which junk yards are an example, contributes nothing to a district's general convenience, attraction, or concentration of people. In return for nothing, these uses make exorbitant demands upon the land—and upon esthetic tolerance. Used-car lots are in this category. So are buildings which have been abandoned or badly underused.

Probably everyone (except possibly the owners of such objects) is agreed that this category of uses is blighting.

But it does not follow that junk yards and their like are therefore threats which accompany city diversity. Successful city districts are never dotted with junk yards, but that is not *why* these districts are successful. It is the other way around. They lack junk yards *because* they are successful.

Deadening and space-taking low economic uses like junk yards and used-car lots grow like pigweed in spots which are *already* uncultivated and unsuccessful. They sprout in places that have low concentrations of foot traffic, too little surrounding magnetism, and no high-value competition for the space. Their natural homes are gray areas and the dwindled-off edges of downtowns, where the fires of diversity and vitality burn low. If all controls were lifted from housing-project malls, and these dead, underused places found their natural economic level, junk yards and used-car lots are exactly what would sprout in many of them.

The trouble represented by junk yards goes deeper than the Blight Fighters can plumb. It achieves nothing to cry "Take them away! They shouldn't be there!" The problem is to cultivate an economic environment in the district which makes more vital uses of the land profitable and logical. If this is not done, the land might as well be used for junk yards, which after all have *some* use. Little else is apt to be successful, and this includes public uses, like parks or school yards, which fail catastrophically precisely where the economic environment is too poor for other uses that depend on magnetism and surrounding vitality. The kind of problem symbolized by junk yards, in short, is not solved by fearing diversity, or by suppression, but rather by catalyzing and cultivating a fertile economic environment for diversity.

A second category of uses is conventionally considered, by planners and zoners, to be harmful, especially if these uses are mingled into residential areas. This category includes bars, theaters, clinics, businesses and manufacturing. It is a category which is not harmful; the arguments that these uses are to be tightly controlled derive from their effects in suburbs and in dull, inherently dangerous gray areas, not from their effects in lively city districts.

Thin smatterings of nonresidential uses do little good in gray areas, and can do harm, because gray areas are unequipped to handle strangers—or to protect them either, for that matter. But again, this is a problem that arises from too feeble a diversity in the prevailing dullness and darkness.

In lively city districts, where abundant diversity has been catalyzed, these uses do not do harm. They are positively necessary, either for their direct contributions to safety, public contact and cross-use, or because they help support other diversity which has these direct effects.

Work uses suggest another bugaboo: reeking smokestacks and flying ash. Of course reeking smokestacks and flying ash are harmful, but it does not follow that intensive city manufacturing (most of which produces no such nasty by-products) or other work uses must be segregated from dwellings. Indeed, the notion that reek or fumes are to be combated by zoning and land-sorting classifications at all is ridiculous. The air doesn't know about zoning boundaries. Regulations specifically aimed at the smoke or the reek itself are to the point.

Among planners and zoners, the great shibboleth in land use was formerly the glue factory. "Would you want a glue factory in your neighborhood?" was the clincher. Why a glue factory I do not know, except possibly that glue then meant dead horses and old fish, and the reference could be counted upon to make nice people shudder and stop thinking. There used to be a glue factory near us. It was in a small, attractive brick building and was one of the cleanest-looking places on its block.

Nowadays, the glue factory has been replaced by a different bogy, the "mortuary," which is trotted out as a crowning example of the horrors that insinuate their way into neighborhoods which lack tight controls on uses. Yet mortuaries, or funeral parlors as we call them in the city, seem to do no harm. Perhaps in vital, diversified city neighborhoods, in the midst of life, the reminder of death is not the pall it may be on waning suburban streets. Curiously, the proponents of rigid use controls, who object so firmly to death in the city, seem to object equally firmly to life breaking out in the city.

One of the blocks of Greenwich Village which happens to be spontaneously upgrading itself in attractiveness, interest and economic value, happens also to have a funeral parlor on it as this is written, and has had for years. Is this objectionable? Obviously it has been no deterrent to the families who have put money into the rehabilitation of town houses on the street, nor to the businessmen who have been investing money in opening or refurbishing quarters there, nor to the builder erecting a new high-rent apartment.*

The strange idea that death should be an unnoticeable or unmentionable part of city life was apparently debated in Boston a century ago, when city improvers advocated the removal of the small old graveyards of Boston's downtown churches. One Bostonian, Thomas Bridgman, whose views prevailed, had this to say, "The burial place of the dead, so far as it has any influence, is on the side of virtue and religion. . . . Its voice is one of perpetual rebuke to folly and sin."

The only clue I can find to the presumed harm wrought by funeral parlors in cities is contained in *The Selection of Retail Locations*, by Richard Nelson. Nelson proves statistically that people visiting funeral parlors do not customarily combine this call with shopping errands. Therefore, it is of no extra retail advantage to locate next to a funeral parlor.

In low-income neighborhoods of big cities, such as New York's East Harlem, funeral parlors can, and often do, operate as positive and constructive forces. This is because a funeral parlor presupposes an undertaker. Undertakers, like druggists, lawyers, dentists and clergymen, are representatives, in these neighborhoods, of such qualities as dignity, ambition and

---

*This particular block, incidentally, is always spoken of locally as a nice residential street, and residence is indeed its predominant use, both in fact and in appearance. But consider what else it has, as this is written, tucked among its residences: the funeral parlor of course, a real estate office, two laundries, an antiques shop, a savings and loan office, three doctors' offices, a church and synagogue (combined), a little theater in the rear behind the church and synagogue, a hairdresser, a vocal studio, five restaurants, and a mysterious building that could be anything from a school to a craft-factory to a rehabilitation center, and isn't telling.

knowledgeability. They are typically well-known public characters, active in local civic life. Quite often, they eventually go into politics too.

Like so much of orthodox planning, the presumed harm done by this use and that use has been somehow accepted without anyone's asking the questions, "Why is it harmful? Just how does it do harm, and what is this harm?" I doubt that there is any legal economic use (and few illegal ones) which can harm a city district as much as lack of abundant diversity harms it. No special form of city blight is nearly so devastating as the Great Blight of Dullness.

Having said this, I shall bring up a final category of uses which, unless their location is controlled, are harmful in abundantly diversified city districts. They can be numbered on one hand: parking lots, large or heavy trucking depots, gas stations, gigantic outdoor advertising* and enterprises which are harmful not because of their nature, exactly, but because *in certain streets* their scale is wrong.

All five of these problem uses are apt to be profitable enough (unlike junk yards) to afford, and to seek, space in vital, diversified areas. But at the same time they usually act as street desolators. Visually, they are disorganizing to streets, and are so dominating that it is hard—sometimes impossible—for any countering sense of order in either street use or street appearance to make much impression.

The visual effects of the first four of these problem uses are easily seen and often thought about. The uses themselves are the problem because of the *kinds* of uses they are.

However, the fifth problem use I have mentioned is different, because in this case the problem is *size* of use rather than *kind* of use. On certain streets, any disproportionately large occupant of street frontage is visually a street disintegrator and desolator, although exactly the same *kinds* of uses, at small scale, do no harm and are indeed an asset.

For example, many city "residential" streets shelter, along

---

*Usually, but not always. What would Times Square be without its huge outdoor advertising?

with their dwellings, all kinds of commercial and working uses, and these can and do fit in well so long as the street frontage which each one occupies is no greater, say, than that taken up by the typical residence. Literally, as well as figuratively, the uses fit in. The street has a visual character which is consistent and basically orderly as well as various.

But on just such a street, a use that abruptly takes street frontage on a large scale can appear to explode the street— make it fly apart in fragments.

This problem has nothing to do with use, in the usual zoning sense of use. A restaurant or snack place, a grocery, a cabinet-maker, a printer's shop, for instance, can fit well into such a street. But exactly the same *kind* of use—say, a big cafeteria, a supermarket, a large woodworking factory or a printing plant— can wreak visual havoc (and sometimes auditory havoc) be-cause it is on a different *scale*.

Such streets need controls to defend them from the ruin that completely permissive diversity might indeed bring them. But the controls needed are not controls on kinds of uses. The con-trols needed are controls on the scale of street frontage per-mitted to a use.

This is so obvious and so ubiquitous a city problem that one would think its solution must be among the concerns of zoning theory. Yet the very existence of the problem is not even recog-nized in zoning theory. As this is written, the New York City Planning Commission has been holding hearings on a new, progressive, up-to-the-minute comprehensive zoning resolu-tion. Interested organizations and individuals in the city have been invited to study, among other things, the proposed zoning categories into which streets fall and to make recommendations for shifts from one category to another if that seems desirable. There are several dozen use categories, each differentiated most carefully and thoughtfully—and all of them are irrelevant to the real-life problems of use in diverse city districts.

What can you recommend, when the very theory behind such a zoning resolution—not merely its detail—needs drastic over-haul and rethinking? This sad circumstance has given rise to many a ludicrous strategy session, for instance, in the civic organizations of Greenwich Village. Many well-loved and popular residential side streets contain mixtures and sprinklings of small establishments. These are generally present by exemption from existing residential zoning, or are in violation of the zoning. Everybody likes their presence, and no arguments arise over their desirability. The arguments, rather, revolve around the question of what kind of categories in the new zoning will be least at odds with the needs of real life. The drawbacks of each offered category are formidable. The argument against a commercial category for such streets is that, although it will permit the small-scale uses that are an asset, it will also permit uses purely as uses, without regard to scale; for instance, large supermarkets will be permitted and these are greatly feared by residents as explosive to such streets and destructive to residential street character—as they are. Ask for residential categories, this argument continues, and then small establishments can infiltrate in violation of the zoning as they have in the past. The argument against a residential category is that somebody might actually take it seriously and the zoning against "nonconforming" small-scale uses might be enforced! Upright citizens, with the civic interests of their neighborhoods genuinely at heart, sit soberly plotting as to what regulation will offer the most constructive circumvention of itself.

The dilemma posed is urgent and real. One Greenwich Village street, for example, recently came up against a version of precisely this problem because of a case in the Board of Standards and Appeals. A bakery on this street, at one time mainly retail and small, has grown vigorously into a substantial wholesaler, and was applying for a zoning exemption to expand considerably farther (taking over the quarters of a former wholesale laundry next door). The street, which has long been zoned "residential," has been upgrading itself recently, and many of its property owners and renting residents, in their growing pride and concern with their street, decided to fight the exemption request. They lost. It is no wonder they lost, for their case was blurry. Some of the leaders of the fight, who owned property or lived in property with small-scale nonresidential uses on the ground floors, were themselves in conflict, actual or sympathetic, with the "residential" zoning—just as surely as the relatively big bakery was. However, precisely the many small-scale nonresidential uses on the street, which have been increasing, are responsible for much of the increased attractiveness and value of the street for residence. They are acquisitions, and the people on the street know it, for they make the street interesting and safe. They include a real estate office, a small publishing company, a bookshop, a restaurant, a picture framer, a cabinetmaker, a shop that sells old posters and prints, a candy store, a coffee house, a laundry, two groceries, and a small experimental theater.

I asked a leader of the fight against the bakery exemption, a man who is also the principal owner of rehabilitated residential property on the street, which alternative in his opinion would do greater harm to his residential property values: the gradual elimination of all "nonresidential" uses on the street, or the expansion of the bakery. The first alternative would be more destructive, he answered, but added, "Isn't an implied choice of that kind absurd!"

It is absurd. A street like this is a puzzle and an anomaly under conventional use-zoning theory. It is a puzzle even as a commercial zoning problem. As city commercial zoning has become more "progressive" (i.e., imitative of suburban conditions) it has begun to emphasize distinctions between "local convenience shops," "district shopping," and the like. The up-to-the-minute New York resolution has all this too. But how do you classify such a street as this one with the bakery? It combines the most purely localized conveniences (like the laundry and the candy store) with district-wide attractions (like the cabinetmaker, the picture framer, the coffee house) and with city-wide attractions (like the theater, the art galleries, the poster shop). Its mixture is unique, but the pattern of unclassifiable diversity which it represents is not in the least unique. All lively, diversified city areas, full of vitality and surprises, exist in another world from that of suburban commerce.

By no means all city streets need zoning for scale of street frontage. Many streets, particularly where large or wide buildings predominate, whether for residential or for other uses or both, can contain enterprises of large street frontages, and mix them with small ones too, without appearing to explode and disintegrate, and without being functionally overwhelmed by one use. Fifth Avenue has such mixtures of large and small scale. But those city streets that do need scale zoning need it badly, not just for their own sake but because the presence of streets with consistent character adds diversity to the city scene itself.

Raskin, in his essay on variety, suggested that the greatest flaw in city zoning is that it *permits* monotony. I think this is correct. Perhaps the next greatest flaw is that it ignores *scale* of use, where this is an important consideration, or confuses it with *kind* of use, and this leads, on the one hand, to visual (and sometimes functional) disintegration of streets, or on the other hand to indiscriminate attempts to sort out and segregate kinds of uses no matter what their size or empiric effect. Diversity itself is thus unnecessarily suppressed, rather than one limited manifestation of it, unfortunate in certain places.

To be sure, city areas with flourishing diversity sprout strange and unpredictable uses and peculiar scenes. But this is not a drawback of diversity. This is the point, or part of it. That this should happen is in keeping with one of the missions of cities.

Paul J. Tillich, professor of theology at Harvard, observes:

> By its nature, the metropolis provides what otherwise could be given only by traveling; namely, the strange. Since the strange leads to questions and undermines familiar tradition, it serves to elevate reason to ultimate significance. . . . There is no better proof of this fact than the attempts of all totalitarian authorities to keep the strange from their subjects. . . . The big city is sliced into pieces, each of which is observed, purged and equalized. The mystery of the strange and the critical rationality of men are both removed from the city.

This is an idea familiar to those who appreciate and enjoy cities, although it is usually expressed more lightly. Kate Simon, author of *New York Places and Pleasures*, is saying much the same thing when she suggests, "Take the children to Grant's [restaurant] . . . they may bump into people whose like they may never see elsewhere and may possibly never forget."

The very existence of popular city guidebooks, with their emphases on the discovery, the curious, the different, are an illustration of Professor Tillich's point. Cities have the capability of providing something for everybody, only because, and only when, they are created by everybody.

16   The Problem of the New Order

Russell Kirk

A friend of mine has the misfortune of owning a number of stone cottages. I say "misfortune" because the cottages are in Scotland, and their rents are fixed at the level of 1914. The cottages were built long before 1914—some of them are eighteenth-century work, with their pantiled roofs and thick rubble walls and irregular little windows; but they are good to look upon still, with their white door-sills and their little gardens along the path to the road. The law compels my friend to keep them in tolerable repair, if they are tenanted, and to pay most

From Russell Kirk, *A Program for Conservatives* (Chicago: Henry Regnery, 1954), Chapter 7, pp. 164–192. Reprinted by permission of Henry Regnery Company.

of what rent he receives either to local authorities or to the Exchequer, in the form of rates and income-taxes. But the rent of each cottage amounts to a mere five shillings a week—seventy cents, at the present rate of exchange. This is not particularly depressing to my friend, for the rents of his farms are fixed at levels no higher than they were during the Napoleonic wars, let alone the First World War. The cottages are a cause of expense to him, of course, rather than a source of income; but persons of his station are now resigned to being ruined, and for some of his cottages he asks no rent at all, letting them to old people who can afford to pay next to nothing. Some of his tenants, however, are better off, according to their lights, than my friend himself: they have risen in the economic scale while he has descended. His income is still much greater than theirs, but his expenses are much greater, and his responsibilities. These tenants now have better wages and shorter hours than ever they did before; they can afford their little luxuries, extending sometimes to television-sets. Some of them have come to look upon rent as a luxury—for, after all, many of their neighbors are the recipients of my friend's charity, paying nothing for their cottages. Accordingly, my friend's agent occasionally has his difficulties when he goes from door to door, on Mondays, collecting five shillings here and five shillings there. One morning the agent knocked at the door of a tenant who was in good health and employed at good wages. The tenant came to the door and announced that he had decided to pay no more rent; he could not afford it; prices were high, and he could use that five shillings himself.

"Will you be honest with me?" the agent asked.

The tenant said he would.

"Well, then," said the agent, "how much do you spend a month on cigarettes?"

"Thirty shillin's," replied the tenant, in righteous defiance, "and not a penny more."

When a man feels that he is entitled to withhold his rent, though he spends on tobacco fifty per cent more per month than he does for his cottage, his notion of Justice seems to be confused. This is not so serious a confusion, however, as the revolution of belief in nearly the whole of eastern Europe, where the possessor of property has come to be looked upon as an enemy of society, and is lucky if he escapes being driven out into the woods to die of pneumonia, or herded off to a labor-camp. My friend is in no immediate danger of such a fate, though, as things are going, the old farms that have been in his family for two hundred years will have to be sold at auction when he dies, and perhaps the roof will be taken off the big handsome house that his fathers knew before him. In Scotland, fortunately for my friend, the destruction of old institutions is gradual, not violent. But at bottom the same force which has effaced traditional life in eastern Europe is ruining my Scottish friend: a confusion about first principles. Among these principles which have sustained our civilization and our very existence ever since man rose above the brutes, the principle of Justice has been the great support of an orderly and law-abiding society.

From the time when first men began to reflect upon such matters, the nobler and more serious minds have been convinced that Justice has some source and sanction more than human and more than natural. Either Justice is ordained by some Power above us, or it is mere expediency, the power of the strong over the weak—

> . . . . the simple plan,
> That they shall take, who have the power,
> And they shall keep who can.

A great part of mankind, nowadays, has succumbed to this latter concept of Justice; and the consequence of that belief is plain to be seen in the violence and ruin that have overtaken most nations in this century.

Now our traditional idea of Justice comes to us from two sources: the Judaic and Christian faith in a just God whom we fear and love, and whose commandments are expressed in unmistakable language; and the teachings of classical philosophy, in particular the principles expressed in Plato's *Republic* and

incorporated into Roman jurisprudence by Cicero and his successors. The concept of Justice upon earth which both these
traditions inculcate is, in substance, this: the idea of Justice is
implanted in our minds by a Power that is more than human;
and our mundane Justice is our attempt to copy a perfect Justice that abides in a realm beyond time and space; and the general rule by which we endeavor to determine just conduct and
just reward may be expressed as "To each man, the things that
are his own."

Plato perceived that there are two aspects of this Justice:
justice in private character, and justice in society. Personal or
private justice is attained by that balance and harmony in
character which shines out from those persons we call "just
men"—men who cannot be swayed from the path of rectitude
by private interest, and who are masters of their own passions,
and who deal impartially and honestly with everyone they
meet. The other aspect of justice, *social* justice, is similarly
marked by harmony and balance; it is the communal equivalent of that right proportion and government of reason, will,
and appetite which the just man displays in his private character. Socrates says to Glaucon, "And is not the creation of justice
the institution of a natural order and government of one faculty
by another in the parts of the soul? And is not the creation of
injustice the production of a state of things at variance with the
natural order?" The happy man, Socrates maintains, is the just
man; and the happy society is the just society. It is the society
in which every man minds his own business, and receives always the rewards which are his due. The division of labor is a
part of this social justice; for true justice requires "the car-
penter and the shoemaker and the rest of the citizens to do each
his own business, and not another's." Injustice in society comes
when men try to undertake roles for which they are not fitted,
and claim rewards to which they are not entitled, and deny
other men what really belongs to them. Quite as an unjust man
is a being whose reason, will, and appetite are at war with one
another, so an unjust society is a state characterized by "med-
dlesomeness, and interference, and the rising up of a part of the

soul against the whole, an assertion of unlawful authority, which is made by a rebellious subject against a true prince, of whom he is the natural vassal—what is all this confusion and delusion but injustice, and intemperance and cowardice and ignorance, and every form of vice?"

It is perfectly true, then, both in the eyes of the religious man and the eyes of the philosopher, that there is a real meaning to the term "social justice." The Christian concepts of charity and obedience are bound up with the Christian idea of a just society; while for the Platonic and Ciceronian philosopher, no government is righteous unless it conforms to the same standards of conduct as those which the just man respects. We all have real obligations toward our fellow-men, for it was ordained by Omniscience that men should live together in charity and brotherhood. A just society, guided by these lights, will endeavor to provide that every man be free to do the work for which he is best suited, and that he receive the rewards which that work deserves, and that no one meddle with him. Thus cooperation, not strife, will be the governing influence in the state; class will not turn against class, but all men will realize, instead, that a variety of occupations, duties, and rewards is necessary to civilization and the rule of law.

As classical philosophy merged with Christian faith to form modern civilization, scholars came to distinguish between two types or applications of justice—not divine and human justice, not private and social justice, precisely, but what we call "commutative" justice and "distributive" justice. "Commutative" justice, in the words of old Jeremy Taylor, three centuries ago, is "that justice which supposes exchange of things profitable for things profitable." It is that righteous relationship by which one man gives his goods or services to another man and receives an equivalent benefit, to the betterment of both. Now "distributive," justice, again in Jeremy Taylor's words, "is commanded in this rule, 'Render to all their dues.'" Distributive justice, in short, is that arrangement in society by which each man obtains what his nature and his labor entitle him to, without oppression or evasion. Commutative justice is righteous dealing between particular individuals; distributive justice is the general system of rewarding each man according to his deserts. Both concepts of justice have been badly misunderstood in our time, but distributive justice has fared the worse.

Edmund Burke, a hundred and sixty-five years ago, perceived that radical reformers suffered from a disastrous misconception of the idea of justice. The followers of Rousseau, asserting that society is simply a compact for mutual benefit among the men and women who make up a nation, declared that therefore no man has any greater rights than his fellows, and that property is the source of all evil. Burke turned all the power of his rhetoric against this delusion. Men do indeed have natural rights, he answered; but those rights are not what Rousseau's disciples think they are. The foremost of our *true* natural rights is the right to justice and order, which the radical fancies of the French revolutionaries would abolish:

> Men have a right to the fruits of their industry, and to the means of making their industry fruitful. They have a right to the acquisitions of their parents; to the nourishment and improvement of their offspring; to instruction in life, and to consolation in death. Whatever each man can separately do, without trespassing upon others, he has a right to do for himself; and he has a right to all which society, with all its combinations of skill and force, can do in his favour. In this partnership all men have equal rights; but not to equal things. He that has but five shillings in the partnership, has as good a right to it, as he that has five hundred pounds has to his larger proportion. But he has not a right to an equal dividend in the product of the joint stock; and as to the share of power, authority, and direction which each individual ought to have in the management of the state, that I deny to be amongst the direct original rights of man in civil society; for I have in my contemplation the civil social man, and no other. It is a thing to be settled by convention.

This is the Christian and classical idea of distributive justice. Men have a right to the product of their labors, and to the benefits of good government and of the progress of civilization. But they have no right to the property and the labor of others. The sincere Christian will do everything in his power to relieve the distresses of men and women who suffer privation or injury; but the virtue of charity is a world away from the abstract *right* of equality which the French radicals claimed. The merit of charity is that it is voluntary, a gift from the man who has to the man who has not; while the radicals' claim of a *right* to appropriate the goods of their more prosperous neighbors is a vice—the vice of covetousness. True justice secures every man in the possession of what is his own, and provides that he will receive the reward of his talents; but true justice also ensures that no man shall seize the property and the rights that belong to other classes and persons, on the pretext of an abstract equality. The just man knows that men differ in strength, in intelligence, in energy, in beauty, in dexterity, in discipline, in inheritance, in particular talents; and he sets his face, therefore, against any scheme of pretended "social justice" which would treat all men alike. There could be no greater injustice to society than to give the good, the industrious, and the frugal the same rewards as the vicious, the indolent, and the spendthrift. Besides, different types of character deserve different types of reward. The best reward of the scholar is contemplative leisure; the best reward of the soldier is public honor; the best reward of the quiet man is the secure routine of domestic existence; the best reward of the statesman is just power; the best reward of the skilled craftsman is the opportunity to make fine things; the best reward of the farmer is a decent rural competence; the best reward of the industrialist is the sight of what his own industry has built; the best reward of the good wife is the goodness of her children. To reduce all these varieties of talent and aspiration, with many more, to the dull nexus of cash payment, is the act of a dull and envious mind; and then to make that cash payment the same for every individual is an act calculated to make society one everlasting frustration for the best men and women.

How was it that this traditional concept of social justice, which took into account the diversity of human needs and wishes, came to be supplanted, in the minds of many people, by the delusion that social justice consists in treating every man as if he were an identical cog in a social machine, with precisely the same qualities and hopes as his neighbor? One can trace the fallacy that justice is identical with equality of condition far back into antiquity, for human folly is as old as human wisdom. But the modern form of this notion arose late in the eighteenth century, and Burke and John Adams and other conservative thinkers foresaw that it was destined to do immense mischief in our world. Condorcet, for example, eminent among the philosophers who ushered in the French Revolution, proclaimed that "Not only equality of right, but equality of fact, is the goal of the socialist art"; he declared that the whole aim of all social institutions should be to benefit physically, intellectually, and morally the poorest classes. Now the Christian concept of charity enjoins constant endeavor to improve the lot of the poor; but the Christian faith, which Burke and Adams held in their different ways, does not command the sacrifice of the welfare of one class to that of another class; instead, Christian teaching looks upon the rich and powerful as the elder brothers of the poor and weak, given their privileges that they may help to improve the character and the condition of all humanity. Instead of abolishing class and private rights in the name of an abstract equality, Christian thinkers hope to employ commutative and distributive justice for the realization of the peculiar talents and hopes of each individual, not the confounding of all personality in one collective monotony.

Karl Marx, casting off the whole moral legacy of Christian and classical thought, carried the notion of "social justice" as pure equality further yet. Adapting Ricardo's labor theory of value to his own purposes, Marx insisted that since all value comes from "labor," all value must return to labor; and therefore all men must receive the same rewards, and live the same life. Justice, according to this view, is uniformity of existence. "In order to create equality," Marx wrote, "we must first create inequality." By this he meant that because men are *not* equal in strength, energy, intelligence, or any other natural endowment, we must take away from the superior and give to the inferior; we must depress the better to help the worse; and thus we will deliberately treat the strong, the energetic, and the intelligent unfairly, that we may make their natural inferiors their equals in condition. Now this doctrine is the callous repudiation of the classical and Christian idea of justice. "To each his own": such was the definition of justice in which Plato and Cicero and the fathers of the Church and the Schoolmen agreed. Each man should have the right to the fruit of his own labors, and the right to freedom from being meddled with; and each man should do that work for which his nature and his inheritance best qualified him. But Marx was resolved to turn the world inside out, and a necessary preparation for this was the inversion of the idea of Justice. Marx refused to recognize that there are various kinds and degrees of labor, each deserving its peculiar reward; and he ignored the fact that there is such a thing as the postponed reward of labor, in the form of bequest and inheritance. It is not simply the manual laborer who works: the statesman works, and so does the soldier, and so does the scholar, and so does the priest, and so does the banker, and so does the landed proprietor, and so does the inventor, and so does the manufacturer, and so does the clerk. The highest and most productive forms of labor, most beneficial to humanity both in spirit and in matter, commonly are those kinds of work least menial. Only in this sense is it true that all value comes from labor.

In the history of political and economic fanaticism, there are few fallacies more nearly transparent than the central principle of Marxism. But the publication of Marx's *Capital* coincided with the decay of established opinions in the modern world, and with all the confusion which the culmination of the Industrial Revolution and the expansion of European influence had brought in their train. Thus men who had repudiated both the old liberal educational disciplines and the bulk of Christian teaching embraced Marx's theories without reflection; for men long to believe in *something*, and the declaration that everyone is entitled by the laws of social justice to the possessions of his more prosperous neighbor was calculated to excite all the power of envy. The doctrinaire socialists and communists began to preach this new theory of justice—the dogma that everything belongs of right to everyone. That idea has been one of the chief causes of our modern upheaval and despair, throughout most of the world. In its milder aspect, it has led to the difficulties of my Scottish friend in collecting his rents; in its fiercer aspect, to the dehumanization of whole peoples and the wreck of ancient civilizations.

True distributive justice, which prescribes the rights and duties that connect the state, or community, and the citizen or private person, does not mean "distribution" in the sense of employing the power of the state to redistribute property among men. Pope Pius XI, in 1931, made it clear that this was not the Christian significance of the phrase. "Of its very nature the true aim of all social activity," the Pope wrote, "should be to help individual members of the social body, but never to destroy or absorb them. The aim of social legislation must therefore be the re-establishment of vocational groups." This encyclical, in general, urges the restoration of *order*, through the encouragement or resurrection of all those voluntary associations which once interposed a barrier between the Leviathan state and the puny individual. The state ought to be an arbiter, intent upon justice, and not the servant of a particular class or interest. The late William A. Orton, in his last book, *The Economic Role of the State*, discussing commutative and distributive justice in the light of Papal encyclicals, reminds us of how sorely the concept of distributive justice has been corrupted:

> Distributive justice does not primarily refer, as does the economic theory of distribution, to the sharing-out of a given supply of goods and services, because the state has no such supply. Yet that is the conception which tends to develop in the late stages of all highly centralized societies, including our own: the notion that the masses can and ought to receive from the state goods and services beyond what they could otherwise earn for themselves. The popularity of this notion has obvious causes, ranging from genuine altruism through political expediency to undisguised class interest. It is noteworthy that, as organized labor becomes a major political force, it is no longer content—as Gompers might have been—to rely on the economic power of the trade-unions but goes on, while resisting all limits on that,

to make demands for state action in the interests of wage-earners as a class. And the point is not whether those demands are justifiable as desiderata; quite possibly they are, since, like the king in wonder-working days of old, we would all like everybody to have everything. The point is that this whole notion of the providential state invokes and rests upon the coercive power, regarded solely from the standpoint of the beneficiaries. Furthermore, there are practical limits to this sort of procedure; and it is less painful to recognize them in advance than to run into them head on.

And Orton proceeds to examine the necessity of re-asserting moral principles in the complex economic negotiations of our time. It is impossible to determine a "fair wage," or the proper relationship between employer and union, or the aims of social security, or the boundary between a just claim and extortion, or the proper regulation of prices, or the degree of freedom of competition, without reference to certain definitions that depend upon moral sanctions. Of those definitions, "justice" is the cardinal term. The Benthamite delusion that politics and economics could be managed on considerations purely material has exposed us to a desolate individualism in which every man and every class looks upon all other men and classes as dangerous competitors, when in reality no man and no class can continue long in safety and prosperity without the bond of sympathy and the reign of justice. It is necessary to any high civilization that there be a great variety of human types and a variety of classes and functions.

A true understanding of what "social justice" means would do more than anything else to guard against that bitter resentment of superiority or differentiation which menaces the foundations of culture. We hear a good deal of talk, some of it sensible, some of it silly, about the "anti-intellectualism" of our time. But it is undeniably true that there exists among us a vague but ominous detestation of the life of the mind—apparently on the assumption that what one man has, all men must have; and if they are denied it, then they will deny it to the privileged man. The late C. E. M. Joad, a writer scarcely given to reactionary or anti-democratic opinions, noted with alarm this resentment of the masses against anything that they cannot share; and they now have it in their power, he suggested, to topple anything of which they disapprove. It is not even necessary for the masses to employ direct political action; the contagion of manners works for them: formerly a class of thinkers and artists could flourish in the midst of general ignorance, but now the mass-mind, juke-box culture, penetrates to every corner of the Western world, and the man of superior natural talents is ashamed of being different.

One could elaborate upon Joad's suggestion almost interminably. The gradual reduction of public libraries, intended for the elevation of the popular mind, to mere instruments for idle amusement at public expense; the cacophony of noise which fills almost all public places, converting even the unwilling into a part of the captive audience, so that only by spending a good deal of money and travelling some distance can one eat and drink without being oppressed by blatant vulgarity; the conversion of nominal institutions of learning to the popular ends of sociability and utilitarian training—all these things, and many others, are so many indications of the advance of the masses into the realm of culture. The nineteenth-century optimists believed that the masses would indeed make culture their own, by assimilating themselves to it; it scarcely occurred to the enthusiasts for popular schooling that the masses might assimilate culture to themselves. The magazine-rack of any drug-store in America would suffice to drive Robert Lowe or Horace Mann to distraction. Now we cannot undo the consequences of mass-schooling, even if we would; but what we can contend against is the spirit of vulgar intolerance which proclaims that if the masses cannot share in a taste, that taste shall not be suffered to exist. And this is closely bound up with the idea of social justice. If justice means uniformity, then the higher life of the mind which is confined to a few has no right to survival; but if justice means that each man has a right to his own, we ought to try to convince modern society that there is no injustice or deprivation in the fact that one man is skilled with his hands, and another with his head, or that one man enjoys baseball and another chamber music. We must go beyond the differences of taste, indeed, and remind modern society that differences of function are as necessary and beneficial as differences of opinion. That some men are richer than others, and that some have more leisure than others, and that some travel more than others, and that some inherit more than others, and that some are educated more than others, is no more unjust, in the great scheme of things, than that some undeniably are handsomer or stronger or quicker or healthier than others. This complex variety is the breath of life to society, not the triumph of injustice. Poverty, even absolute poverty, is not an evil; it is not evil to be a beggar; it is not evil to be ignorant; it is not evil to be stupid. All these things are either indifferent, or else are occasions for positive virtue, if accepted with a contrite heart. What really matters is that we should accept the station to which "a divine tactic" has appointed us with humility and a sense of consecration. Without inequality, there is no opportunity for charity, or for gratitude; without differences of mind and talent, the world would be one changeless expanse of uniformity; and precisely that is the most conspicuous feature of Hell.

I am inclined to believe, then, that the need of our time is not for greater progress toward equality of condition and distribution of wealth, but rather for the clear understanding of what commutative and distributive justice truly mean: "to each his own." It is very easy to run with the pack and howl for the attainment of absolute equality. But that equality would be the death of human liveliness, and probably the death of our economy. I know, of course, that we have all about us examples of wealth misspent and opportunities abused. In our fallen state, we cannot hope that all the members of any class will behave with perfect rectitude. But it would be no wiser to abolish classes, for that reason, than to abolish humanity. We do indeed have the duty of exhorting those who have been placed by a divine tactic in positions of responsibility to do their part with charity and humility; and, before that, we have the more pressing duty of so exhorting ourselves. There are signs, in most of the countries of the Western world, that what remains of the old leading classes are learning to conduct themselves with courage and fortitude. If they are effaced utterly, we shall not be emancipated totally from leadership, but shall find ourselves, instead, at the mercy of the commissar. The delusion that justice consists in absolute equality ends in an absolute equality beneath the weight of a man or a party to whom justice is no more than a word.

At the back of the mind of the man who declined to pay his rent, I think, was the notion that under a just domination, all things would be supplied to him out of a common fund, without the necessity of any endeavor on his part. It is easy enough to describe the genesis of such concepts; it is much more difficult to remedy them. The real victim of injustice, in this particular case, was my friend the landed proprietor—though he never thought of complaining. No one subsidizes him; his garden lies choked with weeds; he has sold his Raeburns and Constables and his ancestors' furniture to keep up his farms and pay for his children's education; he continues to serve in local office at his own expense; he labors far longer hours than his own tenants; he can indulge, nowadays, very few of his tastes for books and music, though the cottagers can gratify theirs, in comparable matters, beyond anything they dreamed of in former days. My friend endures these things—and the prospect that when he is gone, everything which his family loved will pass away with him—because of the ascendancy of the idea that justice consists in levelling, that inherited wealth and superior station are reprehensible, and that society and culture can subsist and flourish without being rooted in the past. He himself, to some extent, is influenced by this body of opinion. Thus the unbought grace of life may be extinguished by the power of positive law within a single generation.

Probably the traditional leading classes of Europe were at their worst in the Russia of the czars. But what humane and rational man can maintain that the leading classes of Soviet Russia constitute an improvement upon their predecessors? And who dares maintain that all the graces and beauties of life have been nurtured there by the doctrinaire principle of equalitarian "justice"? Man was created not for equality, but for the struggle upward from brute nature toward the world that is not terrestrial. The principle of justice, in consequence, is not enslavement to a uniform condition, but liberation from arbitrary restraints upon his right to be himself.

There is no injustice in inequality, as such; the only unjust inequality is that in which a man is denied the things for which his nature is suited in favor of a man whose claims to those things is inferior. And precisely this latter sort of inequality is what the radicals would establish, depriving a great many men of the occupations and rewards to which their nature entitles them, for the sake of a ridiculous division of all things among all men. Socialism would deprive those persons who have a legitimate expectation of inheritance of the rights of heirs, one of the most ancient rights in all systems of justice. More, socialism would deprive those persons of superior talents of the rewards which their energies and endowments deserve. On this latter topic, one cannot do better than to read the books of W. H. Mallock, particularly *A Critical Examination of Socialism* (1908) and *The Limits of Pure Democracy* (1919).

Ability is the factor which enables men to lift themselves from savagery to civilization, and which helps to distinguish the endeavors of men from the routine existence of insects. Ability is of various sorts: there are philosophical ability, mechanical ability, commercial ability, directive ability, and persuasive ability. But all these are various aspects of the special talent, produced by intelligence, which is independent of routine or of brute strength. In any age, some men possess unusual abilities, which they may employ, if they choose—or if they are persuaded—for the benefit of everyone. But these men commonly are few in number; and though it is impossible to create such Ability by state action, it is altogether too possible that state action may succeed in extirpating the Ability of a whole generation—or, indeed, of a whole people. The thing has been done before.

There is only one way to find and encourage Ability, and that is to reward it. It does no good to punish men of abilities for not doing their very best; for then they either conceal their peculiar talents, or sink into apathy. This, too, is a very old story, and a perfectly true one. And I think that invariably a principal error of the masters of the total state is their failure to provide for the reward of Ability. When that reward no longer is forthcoming, a society stagnates.

The rewards of Ability are several. There is the reward of a good conscience, brought about by duty done. There is the reward of public praise, and that of power, and that of security, and that of advantage to one's family and one's posterity; and there is the reward of material gain. This last may sound mean, but we are hypocritical if we refuse to admit that it always has been the reward most likely to attract the great mass of men— even men of talent. Edmund Burke observes that ordinary service must be secured by the rewards to ordinary integrity. If we refuse to pay for service, then we are going to be afflicted with the service of men deficient in integrity, which is worse than no service at all.

Yet the total state, and in particular the sprawling socialist state of modern times, commonly refuses to pay for economic services in proportion to the abilities required to furnish those services; therefore the modern total state soon finds itself drained of men of integrity; and the state is served, instead, by the contact-man, the charlatan, the incompetent, the brutal, and the ruthless—by anyone but the man of ordinary integrity. In any state except the most thoroughly immoral, there always remain a few persons who will serve simply out of conscience, and a few more who will serve for praise or power. But these are not enough to sustain the intricate concerns of society, if those incentives which attract common integrity are lacking. Having failed to reward Ability, the state, fatigued, descends toward the routine of insect-life. In the long run, man (not being made physically or morally or psychologically for insect-life) fails to adjust satisfactorily to this attempt at supporting the state by mere routine, and then society disintegrates.

Why do the masters of the total state, and the men who would like to convert their free society into a total state, fail to recognize the necessity for rewarding Ability? It is in part the consequence, I think, of their notion that men are interchangeable units in a social machine, and that if one unit fails to function, another unit may be thrust into the vacated place. They think in terms of the "mobile labor-force" when they ought to be thinking in terms of particular persons with particular talents. Society is not a machine; it is, rather, a delicate growth or essence; and men of ability are not cogs in a machine, but the blood or life-spirit of society.

And in part their error is consequent from their false conception of Justice. Under the influence of Marx, the doctrinaire radical has maintained that the source of all wealth and power is Labor—the physical labor of the unskilled workman, if they are pressed to a closer definition; and therefore Justice dictates that all wealth and power should return to Labor. Yet this concept is ludicrously wrong. For it is not Labor which lifts man above ant-level; it is not Labor which is responsible for the world's work; it is not Labor which elevates a society from savagery to civilization. The real factor which accomplishes these things is Ability.

It is Ability—the ability of the statesman, the scholar, the economist, the inventor, the scientist, the industrialist—which has brought to civilized peoples justice, tranquility, and prosperity. The savage has Labor, but his way of life prevents the development of Ability, without which Labor is mere clumsy and inefficient brute force. Men prosper in proportion as they participate in the rewards of Ability.

The advances made by men of remarkable talent are shared, in some considerable degree, by everyone in society, even by those who contribute only manual labor. As the workingman himself acquires Ability by increasing his skills and technical knowledge, he too receives the rewards of Ability. Thus the incomes of workingmen, in the past century, have increased proportionately far faster than those of any other class; and this is because the workingman, for the most part, has ceased to be a mere manual laborer, and has become a skilled participant in Ability.

An omnipotent state always can command Labor, for Labor

can be exacted through force. The exercise of Ability, however, can be secured only through a system of adequate rewards. The experience of this century, particularly in Russia, has demonstrated how rapidly socialistic governments turn to force to compel labor. In England, the vaticinations of certain collectivistic writers, among them Mr. G. D. H. Cole, and Mr. P. C. Gordon Walker, and Mr. E. H. Carr, suggest that, given the opportunity, they would be anything but reluctant to apply compulsion to labor there. When the ordinary rewards for integrity are lacking, even the commonest forms of labor can be obtained only through compulsion. But can Ability, under such conditions, be obtained at all? There is good reason to doubt that the Soviets are obtaining the Ability necessary to give their experiment vigor, even the mere vigor of material production. And any careful observer of Britain today must be alarmed for the future. The serious journals in England have awakened to the danger of suppressing or ignoring Ability, but the process already is far advanced. Taxation that even Fabian economists call "savage," death-duties that wipe out agricultural estates and family businesses, regulations and subsidies that are driving the population out of private homes and into state-built housing, a general fear that nothing a man does will endure and nothing that he saves will be worth anything to him—these influences, though moderated under the present Conservative government, continue to discourage the exertion of private abilities.

Now the rewards of Ability, as I suggested earlier, are various. The society which desires its own survival will do everything in its power to increase these rewards, not to diminish them; for Ability, given its head, pulls the whole of society upward, intellectually and materially. But Ability discouraged will decrease its efforts proportionately, to the detriment of every class and occupation. We need to respect that reward of Ability which comes from a sense of duty done, and we need to recognize that reward which consists of public honor, and we need to appreciate fairly that reward which consists of just power. But beyond these rewards, which are desired by a comparative few, we need to insure that the ordinary rewards of ordinary integrity, material rewards for material accomplishments, are not neglected; it is for such rewards, after all, that most of the material business of life is carried on. This does not mean simply a sedulous attention to profits and salaries and wages, though of course direct monetary income matters. There exist concrete rewards, however, which are not expressed simply in terms of money. One of these rewards is the ownership of private property, in its many forms; another is membership in a reputable undertaking, as distinguished from impersonal employment by the all-embracing state; another is the sense of security and permanence of possession; another is the assurance that thrift and diligence will bring some degree of decent independence, as distinguished from the uneasy condition of pensioners of the state. All these things are among the material rewards of genuine Ability, and they have been recognized as the due of able men and women for many centuries. It has remained for the arrogance of the doctrinaire socialist and the state planner, in our time, to deal contemptuously with the traditional incentives to ordinary integrity. But they will be paid back in their own coin, once Ability has been reduced to mere Labor—labor with the mind as well as the hands, dull and routine. The total state can carry on, after a fashion, so long as a reservoir of Ability is supplied by the surviving private enterprises; but in proportion as state industry increases, private industry shrinks, and with it those abilities which make possible all the material achievements of our modern life, and most of our intellectual achievements. In the total state, everything may be dedicated to Labor; but with the crushing of Ability, that dedication will result in the rapid impoverishment of Labor, too, and probably in consequences yet more grave.

To whom, precisely, would this New Order be just? In the name of Justice, as in that of Liberty, every conceivable crime has been committed. The doctrinaire radical would risk the whole fabric of society for the sake of an abstract Justice which never existed and never can, and which would be hateful to the radical if ever it did arrive. But it is not only the doctrinaire radical who entertains curiously unreal notions of the meaning of Justice. The professor brought up in the doctrines of Manchester, but warmed by the climate of opinion into humanitarianism, may try to make the best of both worlds by redefining Justice. For an instance of this, we may take an odd little article by Professor Bruce Knight, published in *Faith and Freedom* (May, 1954)—not because of any merits of cogency, but because it suggests what a Babel our world is become. Professor Knight, in many respects a thoroughgoing disciple of the classical economics, is disturbed because "there are *unjust* inequalities in the personal distribution of the *means* of choosing," and therefore recommends that we regularly take away from the prospering and give to the indigent, in hard money. This, he thinks, is distributive justice.

Now Professor Knight is falling into the trap of what President Gordon Chalmers of Kenyon College calls "disintegrated liberalism." Mr. Knight carries down the doctrines of Bentham and James Mill, rigidly, to the present day—embellishing them, however, with a sentimental humanitarianism which inverts the original purpose of those doctrines. I am not reproaching Mr. Knight for being liberal, or for being humane. What alarms me is the degeneration of liberal economic doctrines into the praise of a "freedom" which makes men the wards of the state, and the corruption of the idea of charity by the invasion of compulsion and impersonality into a realm which ought to be governed by love. Mr. Knight's confusion is the consequence, I think, of his ignoring the classical definition of justice and the Christian definition of charity. What Mr. Knight is preaching, behind his dialectic, is the redistribution of wealth, by direct grants of money from the public purse, to gladden the hearts of the poorer people (we are not told who the "poor" are, or how far this redistribution is to go), upon the principle of an alleged distributive justice. Mr. Knight believes that those who are more favored with the goods of fortune have a moral obligation (the adjective "moral" is mine, not his) to assist those who have fallen behind in the race for prosperity.

But Mr. Knight detests price-fixing, price-supports, state

housing, state medical treatment, and even state education, since these tend to interfere with the freedom of the market, and sometimes do not succeed in aiding the poor at all. We shall subsidize the poor directly, then, thus preserving their "freedom of choice"—which is a dogma with the rigid Benthamite—the assumption being that nearly every man is fit by nature to choose for himself in all things.

This is specious reasoning: if one accepts Dr. Knight's premises, these conclusions follow without much forcing; but I am afraid that his premises, however agreeable they may seem at first glance to religious and generous people, are perversions of true justice and generous people. I think that Mr. Knight, with the best will in the world, is invoking the dogmas of doctrinaire individualism to bring about practical collectivism. I do not want to live in either society; I do not relish the concept of society which looks upon us as so many equipollent economic units governed by sheer self-interest, nor yet the concept of society as an equalitarian tapioca-pudding.

I doubt if Mr. Knight foresees the practical consequences which would follow upon the adoption of his system. The doctrines he advocates, practically applied, would lead toward an actual collectivism which Mr. Knight himself could not possibly endure; and since collectivism destroys all the old motives to integrity, presently we would find ourselves saddled with force and a master, the utter negation of that ideal of "freedom of choice" of which Dr. Knight dreams.

Professor Knight's initial blunder is his loose usage of the grand old word Justice. He does acknowledge that inequality and injustice are not identical; but he thinks that it is a chief function of the state to "equalize opportunities"; and this will be accomplished by taking away from the prosperous and giving to the poor until all opportunities are equal—whatever that may mean. I do not know, for my part, how we are to draw a line of demarcation between "opportunity" and "attainment," or how a mere grant of money can bring men and women equality of opportunity. The real causes of inequality, in nine cases out of ten, are differences of intelligence, strength, swiftness, dexterity, beauty, perseverance, and other physical and moral qualities. How can money provide equal "opportunities" in this competition? Are we to give an extra-large grant to a stupid man, or an ugly woman?

But Mr. Knight does not descend to particulars, and I shall endeavor to emulate him. I think, in fine, that he has no very clear idea of what constitutes justice. He employs the Schoolmen's "distributive justice" to advocate a levelling process which would have been infinitely repugnant to the Christian philosophers who made that concept part of our moral and juridical heritage. *True* distributive justice, as I have said already, does not mean "distribution" in the sense of employing the power of the state to redistribute property among men. I feel sure that Dr. Knight's motive is altruism, not political expediency or class interest; yet, his proposals adopted, he would find himself swept aside brutally by men with very different motives, who would employ his altruistic notions of grants to the poor to establish, not equality of opportunity, but rather equality of condition; and, since enforced equality is an unnatural condition, ruinous politically and economically, this interim state of equality would soon be succeeded by a regime of central direction and compulsion.

I am not much afraid that Communists are going to conquer the United States from without, or that the American Communists are going to overthrow our liberties by boring from within. What I fear, rather, is the muddy thinking of gentlemen like Mr. Knight, who, with the best intentions in the world, would so confuse and injure the moral and political and economic system within which we exist, as to open the way for the doctrinaire radical and the ruthless adventurer. Mr. Knight's notions are dangerous in this, that they tend to stir up a complex of envy and senseless resentment which no amount of money could satisfy. In Burke's words, these schemes are "a monstrous fiction, which, by inspiring false ideas and vain expectations into men destined to travel in the obscure walk of laborious life, serves only to aggravate and embitter that real inequality, which it never can remove; and which the order of civil life establishes as much for the benefit of those whom it must leave in a humble state, as those whom it is able to exalt to a condition more splendid, but not more happy."

Besides, I cannot imagine how "equality of opportunity," in Mr. Knight's sense, can possibly stop short of that absolute equality of condition which Mr. Knight himself confesses to be unjust. A man who drives a new Cadillac has rather a better chance for material success than a man who drives a decayed Chevrolet; a man who lives in a house with five bedrooms impresses his fellows more than a man who has but one bedroom. Are we, then, to give everyone the money to purchase these instruments of opportunity? And who is to supply the cash? I confess myself aghast, indeed, that in 1954, with the ruin of Europe before our eyes, a well-known professor of economics still can indulge in these airy speculations. Surely we learn from history that we learn nothing from history.

And there is another aspect of the idea of justice which we ought not to neglect, even though Mr. Knight ignores it. That is the juridical principle that no man ought to be judge in his own cause. Yet in any democratic state, the comparatively poor outnumber the comparatively rich; one man is one vote; and the very people who have the most to gain from Dr. Knight's projected redistribution of "opportunity" would have it in their power to carry his leveling operation so far as they might please. Dr. Knight's confidence in human rationality is nothing short of astounding, exceeding even Bentham's and Mill's, if he really believes that men who have been told that they have a right to a redistribution of money will restrain themselves out of an abstract regard for posterity, or for the theoretical working of the economy. A nation infatuated with such economic concepts will devour its own seed-corn.

Let us not deceive ourselves. Precisely the reason why we do not allow a man to be judge in his own cause is the reason why we dare not allow the recipients of charity to be the administrators of charity. It may be asked, of course, why the mass of men do not adopt some such scheme of redistribution immediately, the political power already being in their hands. And the answer to this question is that most men still believe that schemes like Mr. Knight's are grossly unjust. Most men still are governed by prescription and habit, and they retain to our own day a prejudice against coveting their neighbor's goods. If, however, professors like Mr. Knight keep assuring men that they have an absolute right to grants of money from the state, then presently men will proceed to act upon Mr. Knight's precepts; and that will be the end of the "freedom of action" and the "market economy" which he extols.

My second profound disagreement with Professor Knight is this: he invokes the idea of charity to defend his notion of distributive justice, but he seems to have no clear apprehension of what religious charity really is. "Free men," he says, "stand responsible for the consequences of their choices, not only to themselves and their families but to their fellow men in general. Otherwise social freedom is social nonsense. A free man is his brother's keeper. The strong are responsible for protecting the weak, and the lucky are obligated to help the unfortunate."

Now this is very true, according to the dictates of Christianity and most other religions. The question is one of degree and method. But we need to remember that Christianity looks upon poverty as no evil, and inequality as no evil, and obscurity as no evil, and even physical suffering as no evil. These things, in truth, may be positive advantages if we employ them for the improvement of the soul and the inculcation of obedience to God. Thus it is that, to the understanding Christian, charity works for good unto the *giver;* it is an opportunity for the sacrifice of self in obedience to the ordinances of God. The high merit of true charity is that it is voluntary, a deliberate act of will. If someone snatches our money and gives it to a beggar, we are not being charitable and neither is the thief: it is no virtue to be liberal with someone else's money.

If our money is taken from us by taxes, that is no credit to our hearts, unless we personally approved those taxes; indeed, such compulsion may harden hearts to the very idea of personal and private charity. And the man who receives a state distribution of money as a *right,* from an abstract central authority, will not feel gratitude. Why should he? And how could he? We cannot really love abstractions; we can love only particular persons.

I think, then, that Mr. Knight—still with the best intentions in the world—would do us incalculable harm by distorting the Christian idea of charity out of all meaning. We have a way of forgetting, nowadays, what the road to hell is paved with. Mr. Knight would destroy, in the name of charity, the ideal of charity. I am aware that we already employ the agency of the state, as Mr. Knight suggests, to relieve the necessities of the poor in certain respects—in schooling, in medical attention, even in food and clothing. We do so because it is convenient to have a regular and efficient means of supplementing private endeavor and private charity. We think that such supplementary activities, kept within proper limits, are for our common benefit. But here in America we have kept a jealous eye on the extension of these functions, and wisely. We have endeavored to relieve only cases of actual distress, not to afford everyone a largess to secure an indefinable "equality of opportunity."

In some respects, Dr. Knight seems to have a Hegelian concept of the state, though in other matters he is a Utilitarian (and a curiously old-fashioned one, at that). He talks much and vehemently of "free choice"; but in the realm of moral action, where free choice matters most of all, he would reduce us to servility. His general yearning after freedom of choice is an abstraction so divorced from reality that I really am puzzled to find anyone entertaining it today. It is as idealized and as false a concept of human nature as that held by William Godwin a century and a half ago. It is disintegrated liberalism.

Christian thinkers always have known that man is a creature of mingled good and evil, frequently weak of will, easily misled, and in need of the guidance of good persons. Man does not exist by pure rationality; he is governed, much more commonly, by immediate appetite, and he cannot possibly be expected to perceive even his own remote self-interest. Most of the leading lights of contemporary liberalism are anxious to disavow their old confidence in the automatic wisdom and virtue of the average man when he is divorced from tradition and leadership. I wonder, then, if Mr. Knight really finds it possible to believe what he writes when he insists that "We can hardly argue that taxpayers have a 'right' to control the form of aid if the aid itself is deserved." For the only alternative to having some such control over charitable grants is to let the recipients spend the cash as their immediate impulse dictates. But whatever is eleemosynary tends to be held cheap. The British government, for some years, has made a free distribution of milk to families of school children during the summer vacation. I have seen row upon row of bottles of soured milk standing untouched on doorsteps. If the parents were given a cash grant, would they spend it on something better than milk? Well, that depends on whose betterment one has in mind. A great deal of it, I know, would go to purchase liquids of a different description.

We ought to concern ourselves with flesh-and-blood men and women and their needs, not with idealized abstractions. If the alleged "ill-fed, ill-clothed, ill-housed" third of the American people were made the beneficiaries of a substantial cash grant, how would the money be spent? Upon the education and self-advancement schemes Mr. Knight seems to have in mind? I doubt whether we could expect so much. I am not aware that most rich people employ a cash windfall very prudently, and so I do not expect most poor people to exhibit superior wisdom or control. I have no objection whatever to a man spending his money, within the law, as he chooses—so long as it is *his* money.

Mr. Knight reduces to absurdity the concept of human nature popularized by the Utilitarians. This, after all, is not hard to do; the experience of the past several generations has given the Benthamites the lie. But I object to Mr. Knight's endeavor to combine the silliest delusions of the Bleak Age with the most consummate follies of sentimental socialism. However generous of impulse, persons like Professor Knight contribute to the confusion of modern social thought, and to the degradation of the true meaning of words, by confounding charity with political compulsion, and justice with an undefined ideal of redistribution.

And what is the conservative program where the problem of social justice is concerned? Why, to endeavor to insure that there shall be some rational relationship between endeavor and reward. Material values, not to mention moral values, are somewhat confused in a society which tolerates a barbers' association fixing the price of haircuts at two dollars, but lets its liberal-arts colleges starve to death and its judges receive the emoluments of janitors. The first step toward recovery of values is to make it clear we are not Marxists, and have no intention of making one hideous equalitarian table-land of modern life. To each man, a just society preserves the things that are his own.

17   The New Scholarship: The Relevance of "The Reactionaries"

Hugh Kenner

"Sort of ignorance," said the old priest to Yeats in a railway train, "is spreading every day from the schools!"
                                                                    —Ezra Pound, *Canto 101*

Look here upon this picture and on this: here on the right hand, many dozen books, the work of five difficult, prolific writers, the effort of five lifetimes, four of them long; and here, on the left, the synthesis achieved by an Englishman* whose

Adapted from Hugh Kenner, "The Sleep Machine," *Triumph*, II, No. 8 (August 1967), 32–34. Copyright © 1967 by Hugh Kenner. Reprinted by permission of the author.
    *John R. Harrison's *The Reactionaries—Yeats, Lewis, Pound, Eliot, Lawrence: A Study of the Anti-Democratic Intelligentsia* (New York: Schocken, 1967).

report of his immersion in all those books, all those intricate mental landscapes, an experience achieved in his late twenties, has won him the grateful applause of Walter Allen in the *New York Times Book Review* ("especially interesting . . . a cool look"), Graham Martin in *The Listener* ("steady good sense, and total eschewal of liberal rhetoric"), Anthony Burgess in the *Spectator* ("really very good and very fair"); moreover, an introductory chortle by William Empson (who finds the evidence presented "coolly, with justice and understanding"), the imprint of Schocken, and a discreet effusion of ticker tape sponsored by the *New York Review of Books* Chowder and Marching Society.

An impressive feat, that; no previous book on Yeats, Lewis, Eliot, Pound, Lawrence, whether singly or in any of the twenty-six remaining combinations, has drawn such a harmony of approbation from that array of oracles. Mr. Harrison has managed it, what is more, without really knowing his subjects very well. When they find, for instance, in his chapter on Wyndham Lewis, the statement, "Lewis is fond of quoting Henry Ford's advice to young writers—get a dictionary and study the meaning of words" (p. 94), the innocent may need telling that the quoter wasn't Lewis, it was Pound; and the Ford (Detroit will be sorry to hear) not Henry but Ford Madox.

We have at least, in this bungle, the echo of something Mr. Harrison has heard of. Other stretches of wording are attributable to what he hasn't heard of. Though it has been a commonplace of Eliot scholarship for twenty years that the sequence of antique phrases in *East Coker* is taken from *The Boke Named the Governour* by the poet's collateral ancestor Sir Thomas Elyot, incorporated into a poem whose motif is personal ends and beginnings, Mr. Harrison can only brush "the archaic spelling" aside without patience ("no doubt this marks a quotation but tracing it does not seem likely to be much help," p. 154).

Again, glossing Pound's *Usury Canto,* he writes (p. 132), "The great leaders of society had nothing to do with this kind of financial exploitation:

> Pietro Lombardo
> came not by usura
> Duccio came not by usura."

One may see Pietro's stonework in Venice and Duccio's in Rimini, but for all one can tell Mr. Harrison supposes they were both politicians. (This canto is by way of becoming a *pons asinorum*; I once read for an American publisher a manuscript whose author supposed that Duccio was Il Duce.)

Here and there, if you can stand it, his fatuity is like a window into the monkey-house. Thus the resonant lines in *Gerontion*—

> To be eaten, to be divided, to be drunk
> Among whispers; by Mr. Silvero
> With caressing hands, at Limoges
> Who walked all night in the next room;
> By Hakagawa, bowing among the Titians;
> By Madame de Tornquist, in the dark room
> Shifting the candles; . . .

prompt within his thin skull no sacred dread, but only chatter about acculturation: "Certainly it is often hard to combine different cultures, but the idea that the Japanese ought not to see European paintings is silly. If the different levels and types of culture are to interact and foster one another, and Eliot says they should, then somebody has to become familiar with them" (p. 151).

Doing his stint at becoming familiar with culture, Mr. Harrison not only explains the line about Hakagawa ("he presumably means that it is useless for a Japanese to study Titian"), but also specifies what we are to infer from the name "Rachel née Rabinovitch" in another poem, "that a Jewess ought not to marry a Gentile." These exegeses derive no doubt from some remembered schoolroom injunction to isolate the Lesson the Poet is Teaching. We are also given help with the hard words ("By usury, Pound means the charging of interest on loans by banks"; p. 131), and set straight on history, lest for instance we suppose that the taste of the unprivileged was in any way connected with the success of the Northcliffe press: "R. C. Churchill has shown that working class reading, though not widespread, was of a high standard in the nineteenth century. It is wrong to assume that Northcliffe's productions had widespread popularity because they were of a low standard; they were the first to be deliberately aimed at the new reading public" (p. 91). Let no one ask where that new public came from or how the low standard and the deliberate aim were related if they were not synonymous. Mr. Harrison, scenting an aristocratic devil somewhere, is reciting formulae of exorcism, and if they've gotten a little jumbled through much repetition the devil at least will understand them.

With formulaic jumble goes rhetorical deadness, an interesting disability in a writer whose claim is to skill in penetrating the rhetoric of others. Reread that sentence—"working class reading, though not widespread, was of a high standard," query the applicability of "widespread" (spread wide?), then note this word's recurrence, like a tick on the record, two lines later; what you sense in our author is a pewter ear for idiom, which helps explain the trouble reading gives him. Thus his dealings with the Poundian hyperbole are always unhappy. "And as for Venice," wrote Pound in 1912, celebrating with beneficent irony American expansiveness: "as for Venice; when Mr. Marinetti and his friends shall have succeeded in destroying that ancient city, we will rebuild Venice on the Jersey mud flats and use the same for a tea-shop." Mr. Harrison, after clearing his throat with remarks about braggadocio and parochialism, reports this as follows: "He believed then that the Americans were the dominant people, and said that they would rebuild Venice on the Jersey mud flats and use it as a tea shop" (p. 122). A critic who can miss the magisterial fun with which "the same" (not "it") inflects Pound's semantics is simply not to be trusted. Yet William Empson and Anthony Burgess of all people, enviable in their own command of idiomatic nuance, here they are, gladly trusting him. They seem not to care, so potent is ideological sympathy, that he's very vague indeed about what his authors mean.

He is vaguest about Wyndham Lewis, to master whose complex career is indeed rather a chore, entailing as it does the vigors of some fifty books and a good many paintings. There is no sign that Mr. Harrison has looked at any of the pictures, though their iconic severity takes one by the shortest route into the cosmos of that great Manichaean. Nor does his bibliography list even half the books (the *Letters* are an especially conspicuous omission). Nor should his treatment of the Lewis books he does venture to summarize inspire with confidence any but the most innocent (Mr. Empson, say, or Mr. Allen or Mr. Burgess). *The Revenge for Love* is said (p. 97) to satirize "the pseudo-bohemian society of rich idlers who profess to be painters or writers, who rent studios, and make it impossible for real painters to find anywhere to live and work"; but the critic's notes have gotten shuffled: the novel that sentence describes is *The Apes of God*. Of *The Revenge for Love*, furthermore, we are told that "one of the parlor communists kicks Hardcaster's stump where he has had his leg amputated," though in fact Jack Cruze, the kicker, is no communist, merely a hearty lecherous tax-consultant defending his investment of time in an adulterous girl friend.

The reader will have gathered that Mr. Harrison is rather scantily equipped for a public performance and may wonder how he mustered the nerve. But his nerve is as the nerve of ten, because his heart is pure, and the ideas that come at need to the pure in heart fill in so readily all those little chasms in his mere information that he is on the whole not really aware of deficient insight. Pound, for instance, is perpetually fascinated by strong undercurrents of pagan survival in Italy, where early in the twentieth century the black shawls of Venetian women still betokened a survival of the cult of Demeter, and Mr. Harrison, who does not know this, also seems not to know that he does not know it, so transparent to his eye is the Demeter allusion. For *black* plus *Italy* equals *Fascist*, does it not? Remember those shirts! And so we have, to explain the line "Black shawls still worn for Demeter in Venice," this gloss: "Demeter is here used as a symbol of the fascist ideal. She was the Greek goddess of agriculture, and the National Socialists placed great emphasis on the soil in their political tracts" (p. 128).

Once we understand that their writings are full of code words like "black" (not conspiratorial code words, however, but words blurred by an ideological penumbra, words used as Mr. Harrison uses words), we can read ahead rapidly through all those books, over hill, over dale, as a beam penetrates mist or a knife, cheese. Take the word "society," for example. What does it mean, what can it conceivably mean, but what socialists mean by it? The question need not even be asked, does not even arise; and when Wyndham Lewis writes of "Society" (his capital letter, his quotation marks) that it is "an organized pettiness . . . a defensive organization against the incalculable . . . so constituted as to exclude and to banish anything, or any person, likely to disturb its repose," why, clearly we are to introduce the quotation with "He attacks democratic society in this way"; and we may even concede him a certain measure of truth, protesting, however, that "It is wrong to limit such criticism to democratic society. It is a charge which could be leveled at any society, even a revolutionary one, which tends to banish everything that is not revolutionary." (Connoisseurs may note the handsome concessiveness of that "even." Mr. Harrison, as the *Listener* reviewer said, eschews liberal rhetoric.) And a free-form litany may be appended: "Democracy at least attempts to treat each member of society as an individual with certain rights and responsibilities. Modern democracies have more consideration for the individuals which make up the mass than practically any other society in history. The aim of a democracy is to end the state of affairs where the mass is a dead thing and not to be considered. To treat it so has been a principle of the ruling class in many past societies, and would become an important principle in the kind of society Lewis advocates" (p. 79).

Transported by the blaze of the monstrance that enshrines that transubstantiated word "democracy," the catechumens at the close of this prim ritual give themselves over to silent responsive affirmation, in the hush of which no one is going to go thumbing after chapter and verse; so no one, any more than does Mr. Harrison, is going to know what Lewis was actually talking about, on pages 260–261 of *The Apes of God*. Mr. Harrison, it turns out, has quoted from the top of p. 261 (where the word "Society" caught his eye) without having looked back to the bottom of p. 260. For there we learn that, far from attacking "democratic society," Lewis was anatomizing "Society" as Cholly Knickerbocker understands it: the cozy cenacle of a Mayfair or a Bloomsbury, where "in place of the life of the world-at-large—of so-called public events, and of the executive values of men's traditional ambitions—you get the values of the women's world of social life, and the Public Opinion of the salon." And "the atmosphere of the salon has been adapted always to providing a place where the little can revenge themselves upon the great." It was an elite that he was disparaging, a self-appointed elite: that was the "organized pettiness" that was at that moment under his microscope. Mr. Harrison will have it that Lewis believed in nothing but elites, probably nasty and jackbooted ones. To make that case one would have to pick one's quotations more carefully, if one were writing for people at all scrupulous about the context of quotations. Mr. Harrison, however, is writing for the likes of Mr. Allen, Mr. Martin, Mr. Burgess and Mr. Empson (for whom the evidence is presented "coolly, with justice and understanding"), folks who will never notice, any more than he does himself, if a quotation is made to mean just the opposite of what its author had in mind.

When words like "society" and "democracy" bemuse one, meanings are apt to swerve 180 degrees. Paraphrasing Pound's social diagnosis, Mr. Harrison glosses, "The only solution is to examine the society in which these evils occur, and discover their cause in the society itself, not in the individuals who comprise that society:

> like an arrow
> Missing the bull's eye seeks the cause in himself,
> only the total sincerity, the precise definition,

will solve these problems" (p. 115). But the quotation from *Canto 77* and the surrounding paraphrase contradict one another completely ("seeks the cause in himself": Pound is quoting his elected master Mencius), and one can only suppose that his utter certainty about what Pound must have meant (for was he not a fascist? and does fascism not shape societies while crushing individuals?) has made Mr. Harrison, in some manner inaccessible to analysis, misread the quotation completely.

Indeed knowledge of what misguided genius *must* have meant has a way of controlling Harrisonian reading, to an extent that ought to have given even Mr. Empson pause. When Eliot, in the passage from *East Coker* we have already alluded to, offers a midnight vision of an antique ritual—

> In that open field
> If you do not come too close, if you do not come too close,
> On a summer midnight, you can hear the music
> Of the weak pipe and the little drum
> And see them dancing around the bonfire

—he would seem to a normal mind to be recommending the normal caution with which one approaches apparitions, so as not to scare them; but Mr. Harrison helps us understand how the land really lies: "Such ancient, pagan rites are part of lower cultural levels,

> Lifting heavy feet in clumsy shoes
> Earth feet, loam feet, lifted in country mirth,

and so a certain detachment from them (the repeated 'do not come too close') is necessary" (p. 153). For Eliot was, a priori, a Snob. How indispensable is a grasp of general ideas, when you have difficult poetry to interpret!

There are times when only the guidance of his general ideas enables us to interpret Mr. Harrison. "Lewis objected to the uniformity and standardization that moulds separate individuals into indistinct masses. This hatred of the mass of people . . ." (p. 78). We rub our eyes: Is his attention span so short that he misreads even the phrase he has himself just set down? But no, on pondering the context (on pondering, for that matter, any stretch of Harrisonism we may choose to sample) we realize that nice discriminations between process and product are out of place here; Mr. Harrison does not really ask to be read more rigorously than he reads anyone else. It is not Harrison creeping on fly's feet over someone else's text, but Harrison executing acrobatics some inches above the panorama of intellectual history that gives us the following: "Later romantics embraced the liberal cause. Shelley enshrined the old Jacobin doctrines in *Prometheus Unbound,* and Byron preached a gospel of boundless liberty and hatred of all existing governments" (p. 23). Let no one scrutinize the entrails of *that* in search of the semantics of liberalism. We are to nod in a comfortable approving doze as the woolly words tumble by, like long ago's teddy bears and teething rings restored in a dream: *liberal, enshrined, Jacobin, gospel, liberty.* And *hatred* makes with *government,* in this pinkpainted nursery lexicon, a Siamese twin, does it not?

Would anyone accept such summations from an undergraduate in a good university as better than C-plus work, the plus for freedom from syntactic errors? But keepers of the Establishment tablets have accepted it, and accepted in consequence this summary of the book's premises: "What Yeats, Pound, Lewis and Eliot wanted in literature was bareness, a hard intellectual approach ruled by the authority of strict literary principles. They rejected the humanist tradition in literature, and in society, the democratic humanitarian tradition. The same principles governed their social criticism as their literary criticism, and led them to support the fascist cause, either directly, as Pound and Lewis did, or indirectly, as Yeats and Eliot did" (p. 33).

Here quite a few terms have undergone mutation. What is that "humanist tradition in literature" which they rejected? What possible set of strict principles, moreover, can encompass the approbations of Yeats (the Romantics, especially Shelley and Blake, plus the Symbolists plus Donne) *and* Eliot (the English seventeenth century, especially its drama, Dante, the latter half of the French nineteenth, but not the Romantics) *and* Pound (Homer, Dante, troubadours, Chaucer, Shakespeare's historical plays, the Shelley of the fifth act of *The Cenci,* Gautier and Laforgue but not Baudelaire) *and* Lewis (Shakespeare and Chapman, and Russian novelists, which latter Eliot read with approval but Pound with a conviction of their inferiority to Flaubert)? And the authors of *Ash Wednesday* and *The Apes of God* sought bareness, of all qualities? And Yeats and Eliot supported the fascist cause? Ah, but it was "indirectly"? Ah, so. How useful a word is "indirectly."

This fatuity, this ignorance, this silliness, this stark insensibility, none of it would be worth five minutes' attention but for the highly symptomatic fact that reviewers paid it no heed at all in their headlong endorsement of Mr. Harrison's attitudes. *The Reactionaries* is not only a tract of writing thought publishable in 1967, it's something influential pundits in that year were willing to endorse. That is its interest. In itself it's negligible. Were it a doctoral thesis its contribution to knowledge would be this, that we should know how unqualified was its director. The author is imperfectly acquainted with his material, grossly unacquainted with the existing scholarship surrounding it, and not always free from the suspicion of having leafed through big books looking for telling things to quote. And yet, that gratitude, those plaudits, those reviews! Can we conclude anything from those, beyond the fact that reviewers read rather fast?

We can, as it happens, conclude a few things. First of all, approbation of *The Reactionaries* springs from a certain relief at seeing the topic—the political orientations of major writers—even ventured on. The subject deserves a book, though not this book. It deserves a book that considers not what general propositions about reaction their words can be made to serve, but rather what in particular they are talking about: the fact that Yeats, for example, had his mind so wholly on Ireland that one extrapolates his remarks on noble families only at great peril, or the fact that Lewis, who thought that people do not *want* responsibility (I know of no evidence for the statement in Mr. Martin's review that Lewis "thought that being treated cruelly was what the masses really liked") was thinking almost exclusively of just those Englishmen whose united clamor for more pay, more services, and less or little work has caused successive postwar Labor governments such embarrassment.

The subject deserves, moreover, a temperate book, free from snarls and glares: and it is no doubt in particular his unfeigned air of temperance and patience that has given such relief to Mr. Harrison's grateful claque. He seems a mild-tempered man, so convinced of the self-evident righteousness of his redbrick attitudes that he feels no need to mobilize the "liberal rhetoric" his eschewal of which pleased *The Listener*. (Who nowadays expends passion against Draco? Everyone knows better than Draco.) He supposes, really, that his authors have nothing to tell us, so that their attitudes constitute nothing more than a problem for history.

And that is the real secret of *The Reactionaries*. It comes to tranquil undisturbing conclusions. It finds its subjects, all of them, reprehensible in their lack of "sympathy for one's fellow human beings, whether individually or in the mass" (p. 208)— ignoring especially, here, Pound's long record of benefactions, unless we are to understand that his beneficiaries weren't human beings—and at the same time finds this attitude more or less understandable; *and* frees us thereby from any obligation to attend to their words in their contexts and make the effort of extrapolation to other contexts; *and* offers no particular objection to anyone's enjoying, if he chooses, what is left of their work.

And what *is* left of their work? What is left of any writer's work, for any reader, is the difference it has made to that reader's mind. To a Harrisonian mind nothing makes much difference; a blob of ideological convention, it receives, like Silly Putty, transient impressions, but subsides again into symmetry when it can. We can watch this happen in a single sentence: first the show of arousal—"Precisely because the value of 'the knowledge derived from experience' is limited (such is the answer to Eliot)"; then the limp subsidence—"we must try to go forward by means of practical social reform" (p. 155). It is immune, so far as we can tell, to cadences, this mind, impermeable to noble rhetoric, and so little arrested by diction that confronting Yeatsian audacity of phrase—

> . . . And haughtier-headed Burke that proved the State a tree . . .

it can commit, and then pass without question in typescript, galley proofs, page proofs, the ludicrous mistranscription "Laughter-headed" (p. 60).

That minds like that are being produced, or anyway validated, at universities like Sheffield, and occupying Lectureships —in English!—at such universities as Bradford, and moreover uttering books the oracles take seriously, is the kind of fact a historian will one day have to explain. Such a historian will understand, as Mr. Harrison (p. 61) does not, Yeats's lack of enthusiasm for the sort of education the century was dispensing:

> The children learn to cipher and to sing,
> To study reading-books and histories,
> To cut and sew, be neat in everything
> In the best modern way. . . .

He will understand, too, how the aetiology of such minds was documented by Lewis and Pound and Eliot and Yeats and Lawrence, whose complex urgencies included prophetic insight. "Few people realize," Eliot wrote in 1920, "that the Greek language and the Latin language, and, *therefore*, we say, the English language, are within our lifetime passing through a critical period. . . . We need someone . . . to explain how vital a matter it is, if Aristotle may be said to have been a moral pilot of Europe, whether we shall or shall not drop that pilot." He spoke in synecdoche: the assumption he confronted was simply that the entire Western past had grown irrelevant for progressive people: had become a "subject" for the optional attention of specialists. Sure enough, a lifetime later we find a Lecturer in English grimacing with the effort to be fair-minded each time he copies down the word "tradition," and informing us that "the social reformers of the twentieth century in the main derive their faiths from Marx and Darwin," for whom "the past . . . is not important in itself, but only in so far as it has produced the present state of affairs, and may give some indication of what might be ahead in the future" (p. 154). Thus "certain evils which exist in our society ought to be destroyed. Society would then be better, inasmuch as those evils would no longer exist." Has he heard of the Hydra? Or of Cadmus? Perhaps not. Or perhaps he has: "A succession of such changes will probably cause new evils to appear, but this ought not to deter us from doing the best we can" (p. 155). This, for a man educated, indeed academically consecrated, at mid-century, is how we are to regard the present and the past it contains: this, plus some sniffing about "minority culture," and about elites. On the other hand, he says, "Eliot prefers to go back. . . ." He has been quoting from *The Dry Salvages*; he does not quote,

> Not fare well,
> But fare forward, voyagers.

With so much understanding in the process of being lost, one can understand the concern of Yeats and Pound and Eliot with the viability of the past, the fury of Lewis taxonomizing present ideologies, the quest of Lawrence, whom silly specialists irked, for a myth of continuities felt in the blood. Each of them had seen the future, and it was (more or less) John Harrison. More or less: it was also the Messrs. Empson, Martin, Burgess and Allen, not to mention The *New York Review of Books*, where one defers only to sociologists.

For it does no good to fulminate against elites. That claque *is* an elite; it instructs the public, to be sure not very reliably. Against two pages of Harrisonizing (118–119) on the folly of Pound's early concern with the taste of the tastemakers (rather than "with trying to raise the level of taste of the public" so as "to be intelligible to a majority of voters"), we may set the obvious fact that five decades later the tastemakers are the focus of infection: men so numb and bland that a Harrison's patent lack of sensibility, or of simple information, doesn't inhibit them in the slightest from seconding his literary judgments. ("One is inclined to talk of popular taste," wrote Pound in 1934, "when one should hunt for the chaps working the oracle.") Not even Norman Podhoretz' constatation (*Making It*) of what one set of oracle-workers really values—cozy prestige within a cozy cenacle—inspired, so far as I know, even one complaint that the public water supply, not some remote lake, was the sewer for those golden streams. *Making It* got widely reviewed, but only as gossip.

What was being done, in 1912 and later, to the public mind; what might, by the 1960's, be done to it every weekend as a matter of course, by an elite so fatuous, so—in the etymological sense—so brutalized, that key words are meaningless, values to hold in the mind irrelevant, demogogic mantrams the sole radiant forms ("All decent people . . ." Mr. Empson has said in public): that was what exercised the writers whose concern with where the word comes from and how it is handed down is now called rejection of "the democratic humanitarian tradition." It was not on behalf of dictators, but on behalf of a public he thought was being betrayed, that Pound adopted the frantic expedient of broadcasting to America from enemy soil. (What he chiefly had to say then he had formulated long before the war: that people were being driven frantic by a needless clog in the distribution of purchasing power. Decades later we find Milton Friedman working out the mechanics of a Negative Income Tax.)

Platitudes about fascism contribute to no one's understanding of that complex event. Nor need platitudes about democracy conceal forever the pertinence of what Lewis had to say about the actualities of power. The revolutionary movements amid which we live nervously today—Black Power, Student Power, the Theater of Happenings—were described by Lewis so long before anyone else could discern them that he was thought merely paranoid, and so accurately that dozens of his pages might have been written yesterday afternoon. Trim out of *Paleface, The Doom of Youth,* or *The Dithyrambic Spectator* the mere topicalities of 1929–32, and you have in schematic form a world then forty years in the future, the world of Eldridge Cleaver and Mark Rudd. Lewis affirmed—not in approval, in glacial detachment—that it was by such means as theirs, and not by democratic processes, that actual power to effect events was actually brought to bear, and today Mr. Cleaver—not in detachment, in paranoid advocacy—would agree. But Lewis spoke at the wrong time and is stigmatized in death as in life as insufficiently sympathetic toward his fellow human beings.

Whoever can read (is that a stern qualification?) and moreover can rid his mind of tastemakers' cant, will find a pertinence in the books Mr. Harrison deplores that is wholly lacking in the likes of Mr. Harrison. It is the current elite that is old-fashioned. It is the thought of the Pound Era that is pertinent today: more pertinent, curiously, than it was to its own time. With Hitler, Mussolini and General O'Duffy at last out of the way, with the magnetic fields their names commanded now for all time collapsed, one can see what were the real subjects of concern. That such totems are now discredited does not discredit men who once found some of their doings paradigmatic. Milton's concern for liberty, in the same way, survives his commitment to Cromwell's way of implementing it.

Milton is perhaps the most accessible parallel. To survey his harsh tracts is to understand anew how a writer's way of expressing his sympathy for fellow human beings may be to write what will often be found disturbing, what will prevent his fellows from accepting with too great an ease the words, perpetually repeated around them, to persuade them, so long as they are fed, that all is well. Mr. Harrison opens his chapter on Lawrence by calling for concern with "what a writer is saying, rather than the way in which he says it." But the quality of his own concern with what five writers were saying has principally this effect, that it seals off the most variegated chapter in the twentieth-century life of the mind, and restores it, along with those who pretend concern with it, to what Lewis called "the sleep of the machine."

Part Four

The Relevance
of Social
Science

A disabling feature of modern social science is its exaggerated devotion to the quantitative methods of the physical sciences. No doubt this happened on account of the high prestige of the physical sciences during the nineteenth century, which prestige remains high at the present time. Yet this imitativeness, in one sense, has not been thoroughgoing enough. Even in the physical sciences, empiricism does not stand alone; it is employed to test theory. But the hypothesis comes first, then the experiment validates or denies it. Without the prior hypothesis the testing process would have no direction.

The incompletely digested empiricism of much social science has had pernicious effects of varying degrees of seriousness. There is the persistent triviality of much of it. Lacking criteria of relevance, the social scientist bemuses himself with marginal or microscopic subjects. The empirical method itself can establish priorities leading to extensive work on, say, voting behavior—where empirical measurement is easy—while directing attention away from other more important areas. Often the empiricist has an unacknowledged theory that directs his operations in a clandestine way and issues in self-confirming pseudoscientific conclusions about, say, the authoritarian personality; or, as Leo Strauss points out, the method can have pernicious political implications precisely because of what it ignores. A laborious comparative study of coercion and freedom in the United States and Soviet Russia would issue in the conclusion that there is more coercion and less freedom in the USSR. But the implication would be that the difference between the two societies was merely quantitative; the entire question of goals, of the informing vision of society, would be ignored.

The empirical method has dominated academic social science, most particularly American social science, perhaps because American culture generally has (its famous pragmatism) favored fact at the expense of theory. Yet this domination has not gone unchallenged—by writers who have pointed out that the trouble with pragmatism is that it does not work, and that it cannot establish the truth of empiricism empirically, and that neither approach by itself raises the questions that matter. The stupendous essay by Leo Strauss here reproduced is the epilogue of a book called *Essays on the Scientific Study of Politics* edited by H. J. Storing. The contributors are all, or most of them, former students of Professor Strauss, always assuming that there is such a thing as a former student of Strauss. Leo Strauss was born in Germany but came to America in the late thirties and settled down at the University of Chicago where he taught political theory. He is unquestionably one of the most influential teachers of his age.

In Christopher Dawson's early essay, "Sociology and the Theory of Progress" (1921), you can count all the elements that even the latest challenges include. Dawson is the renowned British historian (he is one of only two—the other is Oakeshott —completely foreign contributors to this book, having been born in England and lived there all his life; though to be sure he taught a year or two at Harvard, in the Divinity School). Among his major works are *The Age of the Gods, Beyond Politics,* and *Religion and Culture.* Dawson sees the bankruptcy of the doctrine of progress—and, importantly, recognizes it as a doctrine. He thus anticipates Eric Voegelin's work in *The New Science of Politics*, which establishes the religious roots of the doctrine in the ancient heresy of Gnosticism. This was a pattern of religious speculation that conceived of the creation of an earthly paradise through human endeavor. It flourished in antiquity, was revived in the later Middle Ages, and played an informing role in modern political ideology. It is a perennial heresy of the West.

Dawson also points out that the implicit or explicit metaphysic of nineteenth-century social thought prevents it from understanding human society in its historical actuality, that a materialist bias prevents it from acknowledging that *"behind every civilization there is a vision"* which provides its form. Dawson called for a *"scientific investigation"* of that vision, with the aim of understanding human civilization. He called upon science, in other words, to stop excluding a part of reality. That is, he called for true, rather than pseudo, social science.

Such an investigation has been, in different ways, the life work of both Eric Voegelin and Leo Strauss.

In his masterwork, *Order and History*, which is nearing completion in a fourth volume, Voegelin has set himself the task of studying man's different conceptions of cosmic order and of how they changed from epoch to epoch. He has found that lines of meaning can be discovered in time. A development in time, in the direction of a *telos*, becomes evident and forms not only a legitimate subject for investigation, but a necessary one. Certain moments stand out as irruptions of the transcendent into man's existence, and these moments can be linked with one another. By taking human experience seriously—by taking man seriously—Voegelin avoids that hypostatization of history so common to modern ideologies, from Condorcet to Hegel, Marx, and Toynbee. Voegelin is, as he himself sees, in *"the Platonic position"*—engaged in a restoration similar to Plato's, yet confronted by the hostility of those still bound by materialist assumptions and ideology. Voegelin was born in Germany and, like Strauss, became a naturalized citizen in the forties. His tetralogy is *Israel and Revelation, The World of the Polis, Plato and Aristotle,* and *In Search of Order.*

Leo Strauss also sees the limits of empiricism and the bankruptcy of the modern ideology. He recognizes that we must move in the direction of a careful reconsideration and reconstruction of theory, but in contrast to Voegelin, who takes all of the world's cultures as his subject of study, Strauss has proceeded by means of a close analysis of the central tradition of Western political theory, ancient and modern. His approach has had two results. He has shown the relevance, indeed recovered the meaning, of many classic texts. In addition, his unequaled ability as an analyst of the text has given rise to an entire school of political scientists who have brought his methods to bear on their disciplines. He has thus presided over a renaissance of political theory even within the walls of the American academy.

Should such a renaissance of theory become general, however, it should not cause us to ignore the valid role of empiricism, an a posteriori role. Empirical investigations test, and may expand and deepen, theoretical insights. Jeffrey Hart, professor of English at Dartmouth College, in an essay on Burke, places him at the beginning of one distinctively modern tradition of social speculation, a tradition formed in response to the theory and events of the French Revolution. Burke knew that the French Revolution was not only a political, but a spiritual, cultural, and psychological event, and this essay depicts him as initiating a great conversation about the nature of man and society. A conversation deeply engaging, now, those who, like Dawson and Voegelin and Strauss, have a glimpse of the whole meaning of social science. And given the parameters of this discussion, empirical work has played, Hart insists, a significant role. Perhaps to their chagrin (one does not know), the empirical studies of modern academicians like Almond, Verba, Merton, and Broom, quoted by Hart, tend to confirm Edmund Burke.

18   The New
Political Science

Leo Strauss

... [The] new approach to political things emerged shortly before World War I; it became preponderant and at the same
time reached its mature or final form before, during, and after
World War II. It need not be a product or a symptom of the
crisis of the modern Western World—of a world which could
boast of being distinguished by ever broadening freedom and
humanitarianism; it is surely contemporary with that crisis. ...

... To state that issue means to bring out the fundamental
difference between the new political science and the old. To
avoid ambiguities, irrelevancies, and beatings around the bush,
it is best to contrast the new political science directly with the
"original" of the old, that is, with Aristotelian political science.

For Aristotle, political science is identical with political philosophy because science is identical with philosophy. Science
or philosophy consists of two kinds, theoretical and practical or
political; theoretical science is subdivided into mathematics,
physics (natural science), and metaphysics; practical science is
subdivided into ethics, economics (management of the household), and political science in the narrower sense; logic does
not belong to philosophy or science proper but is, as it were,
the prelude to philosophy or science. The distinction between
philosophy and science or the separation of science from philosophy was a consequence of the revolution which occurred in
the seventeenth century. This revolution was primarily not the

From *Essays on the Scientific Study of Politics*, edited by H. J. Storing
(New York: Holt, Rinehart and Winston, 1962), Epilogue, pp. 307–327.
Copyright © 1962 by Holt, Rinehart and Winston, Inc. Reprinted by per-
mission of Holt, Rinehart and Winston, Inc.

victory of Science over Metaphysics but what one may call the victory of the new philosophy or science over Aristotelian philosophy or science. Yet the new philosophy or science was not equally successful in all its parts. Its most successful part was physics (and mathematics). Prior to the victory of the new physics, there was not the science of physics simply: there was Aristotelian physics, Platonic physics, Epicurean physics, Stoic physics; to speak colloquially, there was no metaphysically neutral physics. The victory of the new physics led to the emergence of a physics which seemed to be as metaphysically neutral as, say, mathematics, medicine, or the art of shoemaking. The emergence of a metaphysically neutral physics made it possible for "science" to become independent of "philosophy," and in fact an authority for the latter. It paved the way for an economic science that is independent of ethics, for sociology as the study of non-political associations as not inferior in dignity to the political association, and, last but not least, for the separation of political science from political philosophy as well as the separation of economics and sociology from political science. Secondly, the Aristotelian distinction between theoretical and practical sciences implies that human action has principles of its own which are known independently of theoretical science (physics and metaphysics) and therefore that the practical sciences do not depend on the theoretical sciences or are not derivative from them. The principles of action are the natural ends of man toward which man is by nature inclined and of which he has by nature some awareness. This awareness is the necessary condition for his seeking and finding appropriate means for his ends, or for his becoming practically wise or prudent. Practical science, in contradistinction to practical wisdom itself, sets forth coherently the principles of action and the general rules of prudence ("proverbial wisdom"). Practical science raises questions that within practical or political experience, or at any rate on the basis of such experience, reveal themselves to be the most important questions and that are not stated, let alone answered, with sufficient clarity by practical wisdom itself. The sphere governed by prudence is then in principle self-sufficient or closed. Yet prudence is always endangered by false doctrines about the whole of which man is a part, by false theoretical opinions; prudence is therefore always in need of defense against such opinions, and that defense is necessarily theoretical. The theory defending prudence is misunderstood, however, if it is taken to be the basis of prudence. This complication—the fact that the sphere of prudence is, as it were, only *de jure* but not *de facto* wholly independent of theoretical science—makes understandable, although it does not by itself justify, the view underlying the new political science according to which no awareness inherent in practice, and in general no natural awareness, is genuine knowledge, or in other words only "scientific" knowledge is genuine knowledge. This view implies that there cannot be practical sciences proper, or that the distinction between practical and theoretical sciences must be replaced by the distinction between theoretical and applied sciences—applied sciences being sciences based on theoretical sciences that precede the applied sciences in time and in order. It implies above all that the sciences dealing with human affairs are essentially dependent on the theoretical sciences—especially on psychology, which in the Aristotelian scheme is the highest theme of physics, not to say that it constitutes the transition from physics to metaphysics—or become themselves theoretical sciences to be supplemented by such applied sciences as the policy sciences or the sciences of social engineering. The new political science is then no longer based on political experience but on what is called scientific psychology. Thirdly, according to the Aristotelian view, the awareness of the principles of action shows itself primarily to a higher degree in public or authoritative speech, particularly in law and legislation, rather than in merely private speech. Hence Aristotelian political science views political things in the perspective of the citizen. Since there is of necessity a variety of citizen perspectives, the political scientist or political philosopher must become the umpire, the impartial judge; his perspective encompasses the partisan perspectives because he possesses a more comprehensive and a clearer grasp of man's natural ends and their natural order than do the partisans. The new political science, on the other hand, looks at political things from without, in the perspective of the neutral observer, in the same perspective in which one would look at triangles or fish, although or because it may wish to become "manipulative"; it views human beings as an engineer would view materials for building bridges. It follows that the language of Aristotelian political science is identical with the language of political man; it hardly uses a term that did not originate in the market place and is not in common use there; but the new political science cannot begin to speak without having elaborated an extensive technical vocabulary. Fourthly, Aristotelian political science necessarily evaluates political things; the knowledge in which it culminates has the character of categorical advice and of exhortation. The new political science, on the other hand, conceives of the principles of action as "values" which are merely "subjective"; the knowledge it conveys has the character of prediction and only secondarily that of hypothetical advice. Fifthly, according to the Aristotelian view, man is a being *sui generis,* with a dignity of its own: man is the rational and political animal. Man is the only being that can be concerned with self-respect; man can respect himself because he can despise himself; he is "the beast with red cheeks," the only being possessing a sense of shame. His dignity is then based on his awareness of what he ought to be or how he should live. Since there is a necessary connection between morality (how a man should live) and law, there is a necessary connection between the dignity of man and the dignity of the public order: the political is *sui generis* and cannot be understood as derivative from the sub-political. The presupposition of all this is that man is radically distinguished from non-man, from brutes as well as from gods, and this presupposition is ratified by common sense, by the citizen's understanding of things; when the citizen demands or rejects, say, "freedom from want for all," he does not mean freedom from want for tigers, rats, or lice. This presupposition points to a more fundamental presupposition according to which the whole consists of essentially different parts. The new political science, on the other hand, is based on the fundamental premise that there are no essential or irreducible differences: there are only differences of degree; in particular there is only a difference of degree between men and brutes or between men and robots. In other words, according to the new political science, or the universal science of which the new political science is a part, to understand a thing means to understand it in terms of its gene- sis or its conditions and hence, humanly speaking, to under- stand the higher in terms of the lower: the human in terms of the sub-human, the rational in terms of the sub-rational, the political in terms of the sub-political. In particular the new political science cannot admit that the common good is some- thing that is.

Prior to the emergence of the new political science, political science had already moved very far from Aristotelian political science in the general direction of the new political science. Nevertheless it was accused of paying too much attention to the law or to the Ought, and of paying too little attention to the Is or to the actual behavior of men. For instance it seemed to be exclusively concerned with the legal arrangements regard- ing universal suffrage and its justification and not to consider at all how the universal right to vote is exercised; yet democracy as it is is characterized by the manner in which that right is exercised. We may grant that not so long ago there was a po- litical science which was narrowly legalistic—which, for exam- ple, took the written constitution of the USSR very seriously —but we must add immediately that that error had been cor- rected, as it were in advance, by an older political science, the political science of Montesquieu, of Machiavelli, or of Aristotle himself. Besides, the new political science, in its justified pro- test against a merely legalistic political science, is in danger of disregarding the important things known to those legalists: "voting behavior" as it is now studied would be impossible if there were not in the first place the universal right to vote, and this right, even if not exercised by a large minority for very long periods, must be taken into consideration in any long-range prediction since it may be exercised by all in future elections taking place in unprecedented and therefore particularly interesting circumstances. That right is an essential ingredient of democratic "behavior," for it partly explains "behavior" in democracies (for example, the prevention by force or fraud of certain people from voting). The new political science does not simply deny these things but it literally relegates them to the background, to "the habit background"; in so doing it puts the cart before the horse. Similar considerations apply, for instance, to the alleged discovery by the new political science of the importance of "propaganda"; that discovery is in fact only a partial rediscovery of the need for vulgar rhetoric, a need that had become somewhat obscured from a few generations which were comforted by faith in universal enlightenment as the inevitable by-product of the diffusion of science, which in its turn was thought to be the inevitable by-product of science. Generally speaking, one may wonder whether the new political science has brought to light anything of political importance which intelligent political practitioners with a deep knowledge of history, nay, intelligent and educated journalists, to say nothing of the old political science at its best, did not know at least as well beforehand. The main substantive reason, however, for the revolt against the old political science would seem to be the consideration that our political situation is entirely unprecedented and that it is unreasonable to expect earlier political thought to be of any help in coping with our situation; the unprecedented political situation calls for an unprecedented political science, perhaps for a judicious mating of dialectical materialism and psychoanalysis to be consummated on a bed supplied by logical positivism. Just as classical physics had to be superseded by nuclear physics so that the atomic age could come in via the atomic bomb, the old political science has to be superseded by a sort of nuclear political science so that we may be enabled to cope with the extreme dangers threatening atomic man; the equivalent in political science of the nuclei are probably the most minute events in the smallest groups of human beings, if not in the life of infants; the small groups in question are certainly not of the kind exemplified by the small group that Lenin gathered around himself in Switzerland during World War I. In making this comparison we are not oblivious of the fact that the nuclear physicists show a greater respect for classical physics than the nuclear political scientists show for classical politics. Nor do we forget that, while the nuclei proper are simply prior to macrophysical phenomena, the "political" nuclei, which are meant to supply explanations for the political things proper, are already molded, nay constituted by the political order or the regime within which they occur: an American small group is not a Russian small group. We may grant that our political situation has nothing in common with any earlier political situation except that it is a political situation. The human race is still divided into a number of the kind of societies that we have come to call states and that are separated from one another by unmistakable and sometimes formidable frontiers. Those states still differ from one another not only in all conceivable other respects but above all in their regimes and hence in the things to which the preponderant part of each society is dedicated or in the spirit which more or less effectively pervades each society. These societies have very different images of the future so that for all of them to live together, in contradistinction to uneasily coexisting, is altogether impossible. Each of them receiving its character from its regime is still in need of specific measures for preserving itself and its regime and hence is uncertain of its future. Acting willy-nilly through their governments (which may be governments in exile), these societies still move as if on an uncharted sea and surely without the benefit of tracks toward a future that is veiled from everyone and which is pregnant with surprises. Their governments still try to determine the future of their societies with the help partly of knowledge, partly of guesses, the recourse to guesses still being partly necessitated by the secrecy in which their most important opponents shroud their most important plans or projects. The new political science which is so eager to predict is, as it admits, as unable to predict the outcome of the unprecedented conflict peculiar to our age as the crudest soothsayer of the most benighted tribe. In former times people thought that the outcome of serious conflicts is unpredictable because one cannot know how long this or that outstanding leader in war or counsel will live, or how the opposed armies will act in the test of battle or similar things. We have been brought to believe that chance can be controlled or does not seriously affect the fate of societies. Yet the science that is said to have rendered possible the control of chance has itself become the refuge of chance: man's fate depends now more than ever on science or technology, hence on discoveries or inventions, hence on events whose precise occurrence is by their very nature not predictable. A simply unprecedented political situation would be a situation of no political interest, that is, not a political situation. Now if the essential character of all political situations was grasped by the old political science, there seems to be no reason why it must be superseded by a new political science. In case the new political science should tend to understand political things in non-political terms, the old political science, wise to many ages, would even be superior to the new political science in helping us to find our bearings in our unprecedented situation in spite or rather because of the fact that only the new political science can boast of being the child of the atomic age.

But one will never understand the new political science if one does not start from that reason advanced on its behalf which has nothing whatever to do with any true or alleged blindness of the old political science to any political things as such. That reason is a general notion of science. According to that notion, only scientific knowledge is genuine knowledge. From this it follows immediately that all awareness of political things that is not scientific is cognitively worthless. Serious criticism of the old political science is a waste of time; for we know in advance that it could only have been a pseudo science, although perhaps including a few remarkably shrewd hunches. This is not to deny that the adherents of the new political science sometimes engage in apparent criticism of the old, but that criticism is characterized by a constitutional inability to understand the criticized doctrines on their own terms. What science is, is supposed to be known from the practice of the other sciences, of sciences that are admittedly in existence and not mere desiderata, and the clearest examples of such sciences are the natural sciences. What science is, is supposed to be known, above all, from the science of science, that is, logic. The basis of the new political science then is logic, that is, a particular kind of logic; the logic in question is not, for instance, Aristotelian or Kantian or Hegelian logic. This means, however, that the new political science rests on what for the political scientist as such is a mere assumption that he is not competent to judge on its own terms, namely, as a logical theory, for that theory is controversial among the people who must be supposed to be competent in such matters, the professors of philosophy. The political scientist is competent, however, to judge it by its fruits; he is competent to judge whether his understanding of political things as political things is helped or hindered by the new political science that derives from the logic in question. He is perfectly justified in regarding as an imposition the demand that he comply with "logical positivism" or else plead guilty to being a "metaphysician." He is perfectly justified in regarding this epithet as not "objective," because it is terrifying and unintelligible like the war cries of savages.

What strikes a sympathetic chord in every political scientist is less the demand that he proceed "scientifically"—for mathematics also proceeds scientifically and political science surely is not a mathematical discipline—than the demand that he proceed "empirically." This is a demand of common sense. No one in his senses ever dreamt that he could know anything, say, of American government as such or of the present political situation as such except by looking at American government or at the present political situation. The incarnation of the empirical spirit is the man from Missouri, who has to be shown. For he knows that he, as well as everyone else who is of sound mind and whose sight is not defective, can see things and people as they are with his eyes, and that he is capable of knowing how his neighbors feel; he takes it for granted that he lives with other human beings of all descriptions in the same world and that because they are all human beings, they all understand one another somehow; he knows that if this were not so, political life would be altogether impossible. If someone offered him speculations based on extrasensory perception, he would turn his back more or less politely. The old political science would not quarrel in these respects with the man from Missouri. It did not claim to know better or differently than he such things as that the Democratic and Republican parties are now, and have been for some time, the preponderant parties in this country, and that there are presidential elections every fourth year. By admitting that facts of this kind are known independently of political science, it admitted that empirical knowledge is not necessarily scientific knowledge or that a statement can be true and known to be true without being scientific, and, above all, that political science stands or falls by the truth of the pre-scientific awareness of political things. Yet one may raise the question of how one can be certain of the truth of empirical statements that are pre-scientific. If we call an elaborate answer to this question an epistemology, we may say that an empiricist, in contradistinction to an empirical, statement is based on the explicit assumption of a specific epistemology. Yet every epistemology presupposes the truth of empirical statements. Our perceiving things and people is more manifest and more reliable than any "theory of knowledge"—any explanation of how our perceiving things and people is possible—can be; the truth of any "theory of knowledge" depends on its ability to give an adequate account of this fundamental reliance. If a logical positivist tries to give an account of a "thing" or a formula for a "thing" in terms of mere sense data and their composition, he is looking, and bids us to look, at the previously grasped "thing"; the previously grasped "thing" is the standard by which we judge his formula. If an epistemology, for example solipsism, manifestly fails to give an account of how empirical statements as meant can be true, it fails to carry conviction. To be aware of the necessity of the fundamental reliance that underlies or pervades all empirical statements means to recognize the fundamental riddle, not to have solved it. But no man needs to be ashamed to admit that he does not possess a solution to the fundamental riddle. Surely no man ought to let himself be bullied into the acceptance of an alleged solution—for the denial of the existence of a riddle is a kind of solution of the riddle—by the threat that if he fails to do so he is a "metaphysician." To sustain our weaker brethren against that threat, one might tell them that the belief accepted by the empiricists, according to which science is in principle susceptible of infinite progress, is itself tantamount to the belief that being is irretrievably mysterious.

Let us try to restate the issue by returning first to our man from Missouri. A simple observation seems to be sufficient to show that the man from Missouri is "naïve": he does not see things with his eyes; what he sees with his eyes are only colors, shapes, and the like; he would perceive "things," in contradistinction to "sense data," only if he possessed "extrasensory perception"; his claim—the claim of common sense—implies that there is "extrasensory perception." What is true of "things," is true of "patterns," at any rate of those patterns which students of politics from time to time claim to "perceive." We must leave the man from Missouri scratching his head; by being silent, he remains in his way a philosopher. But others do not leave it at scratching their heads. Transforming themselves from devotees of *emperia* into empiricists, they contend that what is perceived or "given" is only sense data; the "thing" emerges by virtue of unconscious or conscious "construction"; the "things" which to common sense present themselves as "given" are in truth constructs. Common sense understanding is understanding by means of unconscious construction; scientific understanding is understanding by means of conscious construction. Somewhat more precisely, common sense understanding is understanding in terms of "things possessing qualities"; scientific understanding is understanding in terms of "functional relations between different series of events." Unconscious constructs are ill-made, for their making is affected by all sorts of purely "subjective" influences; only conscious constructs can be well-made, perfectly lucid, in every respect the same for everyone, or "objective." Still, one says with greater right that we perceive things than that we perceive human beings as human beings, for at least some of the properties which we ascribe to things are sensually perceived, whereas the soul's actions, passions, or states can never become sense data. Now, that understanding of things and human beings which is rejected by empiricism is the understanding by which political life, political understanding, political experience stand or fall. Hence, the new political science, based as it is on empiricism, must reject the results of political understanding and political experience as such, and since the political things are given to us in political understanding and political experience, the new political science cannot be helpful for the deeper understanding of political things: it must reduce the political things to non-political data. The new political science comes into being through an attempted break with common sense. But that break cannot be consistently carried out, as can be seen in a general way from the following consideration. Empiricism cannot be established empiricistically: it is not known through sense data that the only possible objects of perception are sense data. If one tries therefore to establish empiricism empirically, one must make use of that understanding of things which empiricism renders doubtful: the relation of eyes to colors or shapes is established through the same kind of perception through which we perceive things as things rather than sense data or constructs. In other words, sense data as sense data become known only through an act of abstraction or disregard which presupposes the legitimacy of our primary awareness of things as things and of people as people. Hence, the only way of overcoming the naïveté of the man from Missouri is in the first place to admit that that naïveté cannot be avoided in any way or that there is no possible human thought which is not in the last analysis dependent on the legitimacy of that naïveté and the awareness or the knowledge going with it.

We must not disregard the most massive or the crudest reason to which empiricism owes much of its attractiveness. Some adherents of the new political science would argue as follows:

One cannot indeed reasonably deny that pre-scientific thought about political things contains genuine knowledge; but the trouble is that within pre-scientific political thought, genuine knowledge of political things is inseparable from prejudices or superstitions; hence one cannot get rid of the spurious elements in pre-scientific political thought except by breaking altogether with pre-scientific thought or by acting on the assumption that pre-scientific thought does not have the character of knowledge at all. Common sense contains genuine knowledge of broomsticks; but the trouble is that this knowledge has in common sense the same status as the alleged knowledge concerning witches; by trusting common sense one is in danger of bringing back the whole kingdom of darkness with Thomas Aquinas at its head. The old political science was not unaware of the imperfections of political opinion, but it did not believe that the remedy lies in the total rejection of common sense understanding as such. It was critical in the original sense, that is, discerning, regarding political opinion. It was aware that the errors regarding witches were found out without the benefit of empiricism. It was aware that judgments or maxims which were justified by the uncontested experience of decades, and even of centuries, or millennia, may have to be revised because of unforeseen changes; it knew, in the words of Burke, "that the generality of people are fifty years, at least, behind hand in their politics." Accordingly, the old political science was concerned with political improvement by political means as distinguished from social engineering; it knew that those political means include revolutions and also wars, since there may be foreign regimes (Hitler Germany is the orthodox example) that are dangerous to the free survival of this country, regimes that would be expected to transform themselves gradually into good neighbors only by the criminally foolish.

Acceptance of the distinctive premises of the new political science leads to the consequences which have been sufficiently illustrated. . . . In the first place, the new political science is constantly compelled to borrow from common sense knowledge, thus unwittingly testifying to the truth that there is genuine pre-scientific knowledge of political things which is the basis of all scientific knowledge of them. Secondly, the logic on which the new political science is based may provide sufficient criteria of exactness; it does not provide objective criteria of relevance. Criteria of relevance are inherent in the pre-scientific understanding of political things; intelligent and informed citizens distinguish soundly between important and unimportant political matters. Political men are concerned with what is to be done politically here and now in accordance with principles of preference of which they are aware, although not necessarily in an adequate manner; it is those principles of preference which supply the criteria of relevance in regard to political things. Ordinarily a political man must at least pretend to "look up" to something that at least the preponderant part of his society looks up to. That which at least everyone who counts politically is supposed to look up to, that which is politically the highest, gives a society its character; it constitutes and justifies the regime of the society in question. The "highest" is that through which a society is "a whole," a distinct whole with a character of its own, just as for common sense "the world" is a whole by being overarched by heaven of which one cannot be aware except by "looking up." There is obviously, and for cause, a variety of regimes and hence of what is regarded as the politically highest, that is, of the purposes to which the various regimes are dedicated. The qualitatively different regimes, or kinds of regimes, and the qualitatively different purposes constituting and legitimating them, then, by revealing themselves as the most important political things, supply the key to the understanding of all political things and the basis for the reasoned distinction between important and unimportant political things. The regimes and their principles pervade the societies throughout, in the sense that there are no recesses of privacy which are simply impervious to that pervasion as is indicated by such expressions, coined by the new political science, as "the democratic personality." Nevertheless, there are political things that are not affected by the difference of regimes. In a society which cannot survive without an irrigation system, every regime will have to preserve that system intact. Every regime must try to preserve itself against subversion by means of force. There are both technical things and politically neutral things (things that are common to all regimes) that are necessarily the concern of political deliberation without ever being as such politically controversial. The preceding remarks are a very rough sketch of the view of political things that was characteristic of the old political science. According to that view, what is most important for political science is identical with what is most important politically. To illustrate this by a present-day example, for the old-fashioned political scientists today, the most important concern is the Cold War or the qualitative difference, which amounts to a conflict, between liberal democracy and communism.

The break with the common sense understanding of political things compels the new political science to abandon the criteria of relevance that are inherent in political understanding. Hence, the new political science lacks orientation regarding political things; it has no protection whatever, except by surreptitious recourse to common sense, against losing itself in the study of irrelevancies. It is confronted by a chaotic mass of data into which it must bring an order alien to those data, an order originating in the demands of political science as a science anxious to comply with the demands of logical positivism. The universals in the light of which the old political science viewed the political phenomena (the various regimes and their purposes) must be replaced by a different kind of universals. The first step toward the finding of the new kind of universals may be said to take this form: what is equally present in all regimes (the politically neutral) must be the key to the different regimes (the political proper, the essentially controversial); what is equally present in all regimes is, say, coercion and freedom; the scientific analysis of a given regime will then indicate exactly—in terms of percentages—the amount of coercion and the amount of freedom peculiar to it. That is to say, as political scientists we must express the political phenomena par excellence, the essential differences or the heterogeneity of regimes, in terms of the homogeneous elements which pervade all regimes. What is important for us as political scientists is not the politically important. Yet we cannot forever remain blind to the fact that what claims to be a purely scientific or theoretical enterprise has grave political consequences—consequences which are so little accidental that they appeal for their own sake to the new political scientists: everyone knows what follows from the demonstration, which presupposes the begging of all important questions, that there is only a difference of degree between liberal democracy and communism in regard to coercion and freedom. The Is necessarily leads to an Ought, all sincere protestations to the contrary notwithstanding. The second step toward the finding of the new kind of universals consists in the following reasoning: all political societies, whatever their regimes, surely are groups of some kind; hence, the key to the understanding of political things must be a theory of groups in general. Groups must have some cohesion and groups change; we are then in need of a universal theory which tells us why or how groups cohere and why or how they change. Seeking for those why's or how's we shall discover n factors and m modes of their interaction. The result of this reduction of the political to the sociological—a reduction that, it is claimed, will make our understanding of political things more "realistic"—is in fact a formalism unrivaled in any scholasticism of the past. All peculiarities of political societies, and still more of the political societies with which we are concerned as citizens, become unrecognizable if restated in terms of the vague generalities which hold of every conceivable group; at the end of the dreary and boring process we understand what we are interested in not more but less than we understood it at the beginning. What in political language are called the rulers and the ruled (to say nothing of oppressors and oppressed) become through this process nothing but different parts of a social system, of a mechanism, each part acting on the other and being acted upon by it; there may be a stronger part but there cannot be a ruling part; the relation of parts of a mechanism supersedes the political relation. We need not dwell on the next, but not necessarily last, step of the reasoning which we are trying to sketch, namely, the requirement that the researches regarding groups must be underpinned, nay, guided by "a general theory of personality" or the like: we know nothing of the political wisdom or the folly of a statesman's actions until we know everything about the degree of affection which he received from each of his parents, if any. The last step might be thought to be the use by the new political science of observations regarding rats: can we not observe human beings as we observe rats, are decisions which rats make not much simpler than the decisions which humans frequently make, and is not the simpler always the key to the more complex? We do not doubt that we can observe, if we try hard enough, the overt behavior of humans as we observe the overt behavior of rats. But we ought not to forget that in the case of rats we are limited to observing overt behavior because they do not talk, and they do not talk because they have nothing to say or because they have no inwardness. Yet to return from these depths to the surface, an important example of the formalism in question is supplied by the well-known theory regarding the principles of legitimacy which substitutes formal characteristics (traditional, rational, charismatic) for the substantive principles which are precisely the purposes to which the various regimes are dedicated and by which they are legitimated. The universals for which the new political science seeks are "laws of human behavior"; those laws are to be discovered by means of "empirical" research. There is an amazing disproportion between the apparent breadth of the goal (say, a general theory of social change) and the true pettiness of the researches undertaken to achieve that goal (say, a change in a hospital when one head nurse is replaced by another). This is no accident. Since we lack objective criteria of relevance, we have no reason to be more interested in a world-shaking revolution that affects directly or indirectly all men than in the most trifling "social changes." Moreover, if the laws sought are to be "laws of human behavior" they cannot be restricted to human behavior as it is affected by this or that regime. But human behavior as studied by "empirical" research always occurs within a peculiar regime. More precisely, the most cherished techniques of "empirical" research in the social sciences can be applied only to human beings living now in countries in which the governments tolerate research of this kind. The new political science is therefore constantly tempted (and as a rule it does not resist that temptation) to absolutize the relative or peculiar, that is, to be parochial. We have read statements about "the revolutionary" or "the conservative" which did not even claim to have any basis other than observations made in the United States at the present moment; if those statements had any relation to facts at all, they might have some degree of truth regarding revolutionaries or conservatives in certain parts of the United States today, but they reveal themselves immediately as patently wrong if taken as they were meant—as descriptions of the revolutionary or the conservative as such; the error in question was due to the parochialism inevitably fostered by the new political science.

At the risk of some repetition, we must say a few words about the language of the new political science. The break with the political understanding of political things necessitates the making of a language different from the language used by political men. The new political science rejects the latter language as ambiguous and imprecise and claims that its own language is unambiguous and precise. Yet this claim is not warranted. The language of the new political science is not less vague but more vague than the language used in political life. Political life would be altogether impossible if its language were unqualifiedly vague; that language is capable of the utmost unambiguity and precision, as in a declaration of war or in an order given to a firing squad. If available distinctions like that between war, peace, and armistice prove to be insufficient, political life finds, without the benefit of political science, the right new expression (Cold War as distinguished from Hot or Shooting War) that designates the new phenomenon with unfailing precision. The alleged vagueness of political language is primarily due to the fact that it corresponds to the complexity of political life, or that it is nourished by long experience with political things in a great variety of circumstances. By simply condemning pre-scientific language, instead of deviating from usage in particular cases because of the proven inadequacy of usage in the cases in question, one simply condemns oneself to unredeemable vagueness. No thoughtful citizen would dream of equating politics with something as vague and empty as "power" or "power relations." The thinking men who are regarded as the classic interpreters of power, Thucydides and Machiavelli, did not need these expressions; these expressions as now used originate, not in political life, but in the academic reaction to the understanding of political life in terms of law alone: these expressions signify nothing but that academic reaction. Political language does not claim to be perfectly clear and distinct; it does not claim to be based on a full understanding of the things which it designates unambiguously enough; it is suggestive: it leaves those things in the penumbra in which they come to sight. The purge effected by "scientific" definitions of those things has the character of sterilization. The language of the new political science claims to be perfectly clear and distinct and, at the same time, entirely provisional; its terms are meant to imply hypotheses about political life. But this claim to undogmatic openness is a mere ceremonial gesture. When one speaks of "conscience" one does not claim to have fathomed the phenomenon indicated by that term. But when the new political scientist speaks of the "Superego," he is certain that anything meant by "conscience" which is not covered by the "Superego" is a superstition. As a consequence he cannot distinguish between a bad conscience which may induce a man to devote the rest of his life to compensating another man to the best of his powers for an irreparable damage and "guilt feelings" which one ought to get rid of as fast and as cheaply as possible. Similarly he is certain to have understood the trust which induces people to vote for a candidate to high office by speaking of the "father image"; he does not have to inquire whether and to what extent the candidate in question deserves that trust—a trust different from the trust which children have in their father. The allegedly provisional or hypothetical terms are never questioned in the process of research, for their implications channel the research in such directions that the "data" which might reveal the inadequacy of the hypotheses never turn up. We conclude that to the extent to which the new political science is not formalistic, it is vulgarian. This vulgarianism shows itself particularly in the "value-free" manner in which it uses and thus debases terms that originally were meant only for indicating things of a noble character—terms like "culture," "personality," "values," "charismatic" and "civilization."

The most important example of the dogmatism to which we have alluded is supplied by the treatment of religion in the new political or social science. The new science uses sociological or psychological theories regarding religion which exclude, without considering, the possibility that religion rests ultimately on God's revealing Himself to man; hence those theories are mere hypotheses which can never be confirmed. Those theories are in fact the hidden basis of the new science. The new science rests on a dogmatic atheism which presents itself as merely methodological or hypothetical. For a few years, logical positivism tried with much noise and little thought to dispose of religion by asserting that religious assertions are "meaningless statements." This trick seems to have been abandoned without noise. Some adherents of the new political science might rejoin with some liveliness that their posture toward religion is imposed on them by intellectual honesty: not being able to believe, they cannot accept belief as the basis of their science. We gladly grant that, other things being equal, a frank atheist is a better man than an alleged theist who conceives of God as a symbol. But we must add that intellectual honesty is not enough. Intellectual honesty is not love of truth. Intellectual honesty, a kind of self-denial, has taken the place of love of truth because truth has come to be believed to be repulsive and one cannot love the repulsive. Yet just as our opponents refuse respect to unreasoned belief, we on our part, with at least equal right, must refuse respect to unreasoned unbelief; honesty with oneself regarding one's unbelief is in itself not more than unreasoned unbelief probably accompanied by a vague confidence that the issue of unbelief versus belief has long since been settled once and for all. It is hardly necessary to add that the dogmatic exclusion of religious awareness proper renders questionable all long-range predictions concerning the future of societies.

The reduction of the political to the sub-political is the reduction of primarily given wholes to elements which are relatively simple, that is, sufficiently simple for the research purpose at hand yet necessarily susceptible of being analyzed into still simpler elements *in infinitum*. It implies that there cannot be genuine wholes. Hence it implies that there cannot be a common good. According to the old political science, there is necessarily a common good, and the common good in its fullness is the good society and what is required for the good society. The consistent denial of the common good is as impossible as every other consistent manifestation of the break with common sense. The empiricists who reject the notion of wholes are compelled to speak sooner or later of such things as "the open society," which is their definition of the good society. The alternative (if it is an alternative) is to deny the possibility of a substantive public interest but to admit the possibility of substantive group interests; yet it is not difficult to see that what is granted to the goose, "the group," cannot be consistently denied to the gander, "the country." In accordance with this, the new political science surreptitiously reintroduces the common good in the form of "the rules of the game" with which all conflicting groups are supposed to comply because those rules, reasonably fair to every group, can reasonably be admitted by every group. The "group politics" approach is a relic of Marxism, which more reasonably denied that there can be a common good in a society consisting of classes that are locked in a life and death struggle overt or hidden, and therefore found the common good in a classless and hence stateless society comprising the whole human race. The consistent denial of the common good requires a radical "individualism." In fact, the new political science appears to teach that there cannot be a substantive public interest because there is not, and cannot be, a single objective approved by all members of society: murderers show by their action that not even the prohibition against murder is, strictly speaking, to the public interest. We are not so sure whether the murderer wishes that murder cease to be a punishable action or rather that he himself get away with murder. Be this as it may, this denial of the common good is based on the premise that even if an objective is to the interest of the overwhelming majority, it is not to the interest of all: no minority however small, no individual however perverse must be left out. More precisely, even if an objective is to the interest of all but not believed by all to be to the interest of all, it is not to the public interest: everyone is by nature the sole judge of what is to his interest; his judgment regarding his interest is not subject to anybody else's examination on the issue whether his judgment is sound. This premise is not the discovery or invention of the new political science; it was stated with the greatest vigor by Hobbes, who opposed it to the opposite premise which had been the basis of the old political science proper. But Hobbes still saw that his premise entails the war of everybody against everybody and hence drew the conclusion that everyone must cease to be the sole judge of what is to his interest if there is to be human life; the individual's reason must give way to the public reason. The new political science denies in a way that there is a public reason: government may be a broker, if a broker possessing "the monopoly of violence," but it surely is not the public reason. The true public reason is the new political science, which judges in a universally valid, or objective, manner what is to the interest of each, for it shows to everyone what means he must choose to attain his attainable ends, whatever those ends may be. It has been shown earlier in this volume what becomes of the new political science, or of the only kind of rationality which the new political science still admits, if its Hobbian premise is not conveniently forgotten: the new form of public reason goes the way of the old.

The denial of the common good presents itself today as a direct consequence of the distinction between facts and values according to which only factual judgments, not value judgments, can be true or objective. The new political science leaves the justification of values or of preferences to "political philosophy" or, more precisely, to ideology on the ground that any justification of preferences would have to derive values from facts and such derivation is not legitimately possible. Preferences are not strictly speaking opinions and hence cannot be true or false, whereas ideologies are opinions and, for the reason given, false opinions. Whereas acting man has necessarily chosen values, the new political scientist as pure spectator is not committed to any value; in particular, he is neutral in the conflict between liberal democracy and its enemies. The traditional value systems antedate the awareness of the difference between facts and values; they claimed to be derived from facts—from Divine Revelation or from similar sources, in general from superior or perfect beings which as such unite in themselves fact and value; the discovery of the difference between facts and values amounts therefore to a refutation of the traditional value systems as originally meant. It is at least doubtful whether those value systems can be divorced from what present themselves as their factual bases. At any rate, it follows from the difference between facts and values that men can live without ideology: they can adopt, posit, or proclaim values without making the illegitimate attempt to derive their values from facts or without relying on false or at least unevident assertions regarding what is. One thus arrives at the notion of the rational society or of the non-ideological regime: a society that is based on the understanding of the character of values. Since this understanding implies that before the tribunal of reason all values are equal, the rational society will be egalitarian or democratic and permissive or liberal: the rational doctrine regarding the difference between facts and values rationally justifies the preference for liberal democracy—contrary to what is intended by that distinction itself. In other words, whereas the new political science ought to deny the proposition that there can be no society without an ideology, it asserts that proposition.

One is thus led to wonder whether the distinction between facts and values, or the assertion that no Ought can be derived from an Is, is well founded. Let us assume that a man's "values" (that is, what he values) are fully determined by his heredity and environment, that is, by his Is, or that there is a one-to-one relation between value *a* and Is A. In this case the Ought would be determined by the Is or derivative from it. But the very issue as commonly understood presupposes that this assumption is wrong: man possesses a certain latitude; he can choose not only from among various ways of overt behavior (like jumping or not jumping into a river to escape death at the hands of a stronger enemy who may or may not be able to swim) but from among various values; this latitude, this possibility has the character of a fact. A man lacking this latitude—for example, a man for whom every stimulus is a value or who cannot help giving in to every desire—is a defective man, a man with whom something is wrong. The fact that someone desires something does not yet make that something his value; he may successfully fight his desire or if his desire overpowers him he may blame himself for this as for a failure on his part; only choice, in contradistinction to mere desire, makes something a man's value. The distinction between desire and choice is a distinction among facts. Choice does not mean here the choice of means to pre-given ends; choice here means the choice of ends, the positing of ends or, rather, of values. Man is then understood as a being which differs from all other known beings because it posits values; this positing is taken to be a fact. In accordance with this, the new political science denies that man has natural ends—ends toward which he is by nature inclined; it denies more specifically the premise of modern natural right, according to which self-preservation is the most important natural end: man can choose death in preference to life, not only in a given situation, out of despair, but simply: he can posit death as his value. The view that the pertinent Is is our positing of values, in contradistinction to the yielding to mere desires, necessarily leads to Oughts of a radically different character from the so-called Oughts corresponding to mere desires. We conclude that the "relativism" accepted by the new political science according to which values are nothing but objects of desire is based on an insufficient analysis of the Is, that is, of the pertinent Is; and, furthermore, that one's opinion regarding the character of the Is settles one's opinion regarding the character of the Ought. We must leave it open here whether a more adequate analysis of the pertinent Is, that is, of the nature of man, does not lead to a more adequate determination of the Ought or beyond a merely formal characterization of the Ought. At any rate, if a man is of the opinion that as a matter of fact all desires are of equal dignity since we know of no factual consideration which would entitle us to assign different dignities to different desires, he cannot but be of the opinion—unless he is prepared to become guilty of gross arbitrariness—that all desires ought to be treated as equal within the limits of the possible, and this opinion is what is meant by permissive egalitarianism.

There is then more than a mysterious pre-established harmony between the new political science and a particular version of liberal democracy. The alleged value-free analysis of political phenomena is controlled by an unavowed commitment built into the new political science to that version of liberal democracy. That version of liberal democracy is not discussed openly and impartially, with full consideration of all relevant pros and cons. We call this characteristic of the new political science its democratism. The new political science looks for laws of human behavior to be discovered by means of data supplied through certain techniques of research which are believed to guarantee the maximum of objectivity; it therefore puts a premium on the study of things which occur frequently now in democratic societies: neither those in their graves nor those behind the Curtains can respond to questionnaires or to interviews. Democracy is then the tacit presupposition of the data; it does not have to become a theme; it can easily be forgotten: the wood is forgotten for the trees; the laws of human behavior are in fact laws of the behavior of human beings more or less molded by democracy; man is tacitly identified with democratic man. The new political science puts a premium on observations which can be made with the utmost frequency, and therefore by people of the meanest capacities. Thus it frequently culminates in observations made by people who are not intelligent about people who are not intelligent. While the new political science becomes ever less able to see democracy or to hold a mirror to democracy, it ever more reflects the most dangerous proclivities of democracy. It even strengthens those proclivities. By teaching in effect the equality of literally all desires, it teaches in effect that there is nothing that a man ought to be ashamed of; by destroying the possibility of self-contempt, it destroys, with the best of intentions, the possibility of self-respect. By teaching the equality of all values, by denying that there are things which are intrinsically high and others which are intrinsically low as well as by denying that there is an essential difference between men and brutes, it unwittingly contributes to the victory of the gutter. Yet this same new political science came into being through the revolt against what one may call the democratic orthodoxy of the immediate past. It had learned certain lessons which were hard for that orthodoxy to swallow regarding the irrationality of the masses and the necessity of elites; if it had been wise it would have learned those lessons from the galaxy of anti-democratic thinkers of the remote past. It believed that it had learned in other words that, contrary to the belief of the orthodox democrats, no compelling case can be made for liberalism (for example, for the unqualified freedom of such speech as does not constitute a clear and present danger) nor for democracy (free elections based on universal suffrage). But it succeeded in reconciling those doubts with the unfaltering commitment to liberal democracy by the simple device of declaring that no value judgments, including those supporting liberal democracy, are rational, and hence that an iron-clad argument in favor of liberal democracy ought in reason not even to be expected. The very complex pros and cons regarding liberal democracy have thus become entirely obliterated by the poorest formalism. The crisis of liberal democracy has become concealed by a ritual which calls itself methodology or logic. This almost willful blindness to the crisis of liberal democracy is part of that crisis. No wonder then that the new political science has nothing to say against those who unhesitatingly prefer surrender, that is, the abandonment of liberal democracy, to war

Only a great fool would call the new political science diabolic: it has no attributes peculiar to fallen angels. It is not even Machiavellian, for Machiavelli's teaching was graceful, subtle, and colorful. Nor is it Neronian. Nevertheless one may say of it that it fiddles while Rome burns. It is excused by two facts: it does not know that it fiddles, and it does not know that Rome burns.

19 Sociology and the Theory of Progress

Christopher Dawson

As the modern world gradually lost touch with the organized Christianity which had been the governing spirit of European civilization in the past, it began to find new inspiration for itself in the ideal of Progress. From the second quarter of the eighteenth century onwards through the nineteenth, faith in human progress became more and more the effective working "religion" of our civilization; a religion fundamentally the same under the more or less philosophic or scientific disguise of the

From Christopher Dawson, *The Dynamics of World History,* edited by John J. Mulloy (New York: Sheed & Ward, 1956), Chapter 3, pp. 43–52. Copyright © 1956 by Sheed & Ward, Inc. Reprinted by permission of Sheed & Ward, Inc., The Society of Authors, and Christopher Dawson.

Encyclopaedists or of Herbert Spencer as in the Messianic rhapsodies of the *Légende des Siècles.*

It is true that, alongside of this religious current and inter-mingling confusedly with it, there has been a genuine attempt to study the laws of social change and the positive development of civilizations, but this scientific theory of progress has nat-urally been slower in developing and less fertile in results than its more emotional companion. The latter, which we may call the Gospel of Progress to distinguish it from the scientific theory of social development, had the advantage of finding for its apostles a series of great men of letters. From the time of the Abbé St. Pierre and Voltaire down to that of Victor Hugo, it was the dominant inspiration of the great literary movements of the age, most of all in France, but to a considerable degree in Germany and England also. Nor is this surprising: for it was the culmination of a literary tradition; its roots lie deep in the Renaissance culture, and if the Gospel of Progress itself was not explicitly held by the men of the sixteenth century, that was because the Renaissance as a whole only came to complete fulfillment in the eighteenth-century Enlightenment.

The dominant characteristic of the culture of the eighteenth century, and one that it had received as a direct heritage from the earlier Renaissance, was a conception of Civilization as something absolute and unique—a complete whole standing out in symmetrical perfection, like a temple by Poussin or Claude, against a background of Gothic confusion and Oriental barbarism.

It was the old dualism of Hellenism and barbarism rendered abstract by generations of Renaissance culture; but whereas the sixteenth-century scholar still looked back to the classical past as to a golden age, the eighteenth-century philosopher had ceased to despise the present. He looked forward to the imme-diate advent of a civilization which should be no less "polite" (urbane) than that of Greece or Rome, while it would be far richer in knowledge and in material resources. This ideal was well suited to the temper of the age, but it tended to diverge from and even stand in antagonism to the dispositions of a

scientific sociology. It introduced a cleavage between the facts
of social development and the ideals of the cultured world. The
same spirit that Molière expressed regarding mediaeval art

> *Le fade goût des monuments gothiques*
> *Ces monstres odieux des siècles ignorants*

was shown towards all the social institutions of the immediate
past, and the offspring of the historic life of Europe was merci-
lessly hacked about on the Procrustean bed of eighteenth-
century reason and "good sense." When Condorcet sets himself
to write a complete history of the progress of humanity, he condemns almost every institution which the societies of the past
had evolved, and attaches supreme importance to the progress
of intellectual enlightenment in the mind of the individual. As
pure taste could create the perfect work of art, so pure reason
would construct a perfect society. The history of the past was
little more than a dismal catalogue of absurdities and crimes
against humanity, all of which would have been avoided if man
had been content to follow his innate good sense. When once
he had learned that simple lesson, an Apocalypse of Reason
would usher in the true Millennium.

This absolutism of method was as characteristic of the na-
ture-worship of Rousseau, as it was of the rationalism of the
champions of progress, and both these currents united in the
French Revolution in an attempt to make a clean sweep of the
past and to construct a perfect society on the foundations of
pure doctrine.

In spite of the failure of these hopes and the powerful reaction that the experiment aroused, in spite of the work of Burke
and de Maistre and the German thinkers of the period of
national awakening, the temper of the eighteenth-century Enlightenment did nevertheless survive into the nineteenth century, and provided the main doctrinal foundation for the creed
of Liberalism. The scientific temper of the new age could not,
however, rest very contented with the purely abstract conception of progress which had satisfied the eighteenth century.
The need was felt for a scientific law of progress which should

be deducible from the observation of material phenomena, and numerous attempts were made to discuss the external forces which were responsible for social change. Hence the character-istic nineteenth-century Theories of Progress elaborated by Buckle in 1856, by Karl Marx in 1867, and by Herbert Spencer between 1851 and 1876. It was the latter who brought the idea of social progress systematically into relation with a general theory of evolution (that of Lamarck rather than Darwin), and treated it as the culminating branch of a universal develop-ment, physical, organic, social. But all these theories, we now see, were biassed by a certain "materialism," that is to say a more or less one-sided externalism in their attitude to history; hence their failure to attain a truly vital conception of society. It is true that Spencer insists at length on the idea of society as an organism, yet his prevailing externalism and individualism is seen in that he had no difficulty in reconciling the idea with his mechanical, utilitarian and individualistic views of the State.

To Buckle and Spencer civilization was primarily a state of material well-being such as they saw around them in the suc-cessful members of the community; and the greater spiritual currents that historically have moulded the higher civilizations were either neglected by them, or else were treated as forces which more or less retarded and distorted the normal develop-ment of society. Thus they regarded the civilization of their own age and country not as the result of the psychical develop-ment of a single, highly peculiar period, but as an absolute thing which was susceptible of improvement, but yet was in the main lines final and immutable. More than half a century before Spencer wrote, Herder (doubtless not a little influenced by Montesquieu) had given a far deeper and richer analysis of the movement of social development. He had shown "that the happiness of man is in all places an Individual good; that it is everywhere climatic and organic, the offspring of tradition and custom,"[1] but his thought was unsystematic and confused. Like

[1]Herder's *Ideas Towards the Philosophy of the History of Mankind*, Bk. viii, ch. 5.

Vico, he founded no school, and he stands by himself as the inspired precursor rather than the creator of a true theory of social evolution.

It was in fact during the second and third quarters of the nineteenth century in France that the foundations of a genuinely sociological science were laid for the first time. The post-Revolution period was a time of intense intellectual activity. Social thought had been stimulated not only by the catastrophes of the Revolution itself but also by the new movement which had rediscussed the Middle Ages and shaken the complacency of the eighteenth-century attitude towards the past. Moreover, new foreign influences—Lessing and Herder, Fichte and Hegel, and even the long unrecognized Vico—were being felt for the first time.

Thus it was that men like St. Simon and Comte while retaining all the eighteenth-century enthusiasm for Humanity and Progress, were able at the same time to combine with it a sense of the past at once realistic and appreciative and a recognition of the relativity of contemporary civilization, as one phase in the secular evolution of humanity.

The whole philosophy of Comte hinges on a Theory of Progress, but it was no longer Progress conceived in the external eighteenth-century fashion. He had made the discovery that all social development is the expression of a spiritual *consensus* and it is this which creates the vital unity of society. Consequently the emphasis of Progress is neither on an improvement in material well-being as the Abbé St. Pierre believed nor an increase in the freedom and enlightenment of the individual such as Condorcet had traced in his *Tableau Historique*; the accent now is on the formation and growth of a living community which embraces every aspect of human life and thought, and in which every age has a living and internal connection with the past and the future. In other words, in order to construct a genuine sociology, the study of social institutions must go hand in hand with the study of the intellectual and spiritual forces which give unity to the particular age and society in question.

Unfortunately, in his own attempt to give scientific form to a general theory of Progress, Comte failed to free himself altogether from the vices of the older method. His survey of the whole field of social phenomena was made in the light of a brilliant generalization based on the history of Europe, and indeed of Western Europe alone, which is after all but one term of the social development of the human race. But though his actual interpretation of history was, as it were, pre-sociological, he had at least defined the true nature of social science, and had shown what were the tasks that it had to accomplish in the coming age. An adequate analysis of social life was only possible when the way had been prepared by the progress of the new sciences of anthropology, social geography and social economics, in the second half of the nineteenth century.

Frederic Le Play, the man who, more than any other, first brought social science into touch with the concrete bases of human life, was a striking contrast to the earlier sociologists, or rather social philosophers. He was not concerned with theories of progress, and he had no general philosophy to serve. He was at once a man of faith, and a man of facts, a traditionalist, who loved his Europe, and desired to bring it back to the ancient foundations of its prosperity. In his patriarchalism, he came closer to Confucius and the classical teachers of China than to any modern Western thinker.

His method is well expressed in that saying of Fontenelle's which he chose as the motto of his great work: "He enquired with care into the value of soils, and their yield, into the aptitude of the peasants, their common fare and their daily earnings—details which, though they appear contemptible and abject, nevertheless belong to the great art of government."

It was by these enquiries, by the observation of the simplest forms of life in their natural economic relations, that Le Play and his school arrived at a clear conception of the natural region, as the mother and nurse of every primary social type. And this discovery was of capital importance for the future development of sociology since it supplied that concrete basis, the lack of which had vitiated all earlier social thinking. Without a true grasp of regional life and regional individuality, history becomes a literary exercise and sociology a theorizing in the void. For we have to study not Man in the abstract, nor "the Aryan race," nor even the national type, but men in their fundamental local relations to the earth and the life of Nature.

This does not, of course, mean that social science must envisage man as the passive product of geographical and economic factors. Le Play himself would have been the first to deny it. Social progress and the very existence of society itself are the results of the creative force of human personality. The vital principle of society is spiritual, and the causes of progress must be sought, as Comte sought them, in man's physical development rather than in the play of external circumstance. True social science must synthesize not only social geography and economics but also social psychology and ethics.

Nor can we limit ourselves to studying the psychology and ethics of the regional society alone. That is only adequate in the case of the Nature Peoples: as soon as the beginnings of culture are reached it is necessary to consider not only the relation of the regional society to its environment, but also the actions and reactions that take place between the regional society and the individualities of the wider social units—the nation and the civilization.

It is, of course, highly necessary to give a regional interpretation to the history of even the most advanced peoples, if it is to be properly understood. For example the change which transformed the Spain of the twelfth and thirteenth centuries into the Spain of the sixteenth century is much more than a political change from separatism to absolutism, it is above all the transformation of a culture which was based on the regional life of the Guadalquivir valley and the Valencian coast, into one based on the Castilian plateau and the Galician and Biscayan coasts. In each age both these elements were present, but the one dominated, and gave its character to the Spain of the early Middle Ages, the other to the Spain of the sixteenth century.

Nevertheless this interpretation of Spanish civilization is not exhaustive. If we take two typical artistic products of the two regions, such as the Great Mosque at Cordova and the Cathedral of Burgos, we find that while each of them could only have been produced in that particular region, yet neither of them is explicable from the life of the region itself. They are both of them local variants of world types. Behind one stands the world movement of mediaeval Christendom, behind the other the faith and culture of Islam.

Or take the case of the local men of genius. In Averroes of Cordova we see the final flowering of an intellectual movement which goes back to Avicenna of Bokhara and to the Syriac scholars of Mesopotamia, while his Castilian contemporary, St. Dominic, worked side by side with Italians and Frenchmen and Germans in a common task of spiritual reconstruction which affected all Western and Central Europe. Here again then we have spiritual world forces expressing themselves in local forms, and what is true of the works of art and the men of genius is equally true of the societies which gave them birth.

This brings us near to the famous generalization of Ibn Khaldun, the historian of the Berbers, according to which the Tribe which is the product of the region, and the Religion, which is a world force, are the two main factors in history. Under the breath of a common religious inspiration the tribes are bound together into a civilization, and when the inspiration passes the tribes fall back into their natural separatism. They live on, but the civilization dies.

Civilization is essentially the co-operation of regional societies under a common spiritual influence. This influence need not be religious in the ordinary sense of the word, for the Hellenic world and the civilization of modern Western Europe, as well as Islam and mediaeval Christendom, form genuine spiritual unities.

But on the other hand a true civilization is much more than a mere piecing together of the different cultural elements, supplied by different regions. It has an individuality of its own, which is capable of moulding, as well as being moulded by, the life of its component parts.

In the case of primitive civilizations, like that of Egypt, the expression of this individuality takes a symbolic religious form which it is difficult for the modern mind to comprehend; but as soon as these closed local civilizations had been brought into close contact with one another, and had begun to be united into more composite cultural wholes, we find behind every such unity a common view of life and a common conception of human destiny which give psychological unity to the whole social complex.

Behind every civilization there is a vision—a vision which may be the result of the joint labour of many minds, but which sometimes springs from the sudden flash of inspiration of a great prophet or philosopher. The faith in Progress and in human perfectibility which inspired the thinkers of the eighteenth and nineteenth centuries in Europe, was essentially of this order, just as much as was that great vision of the vanity of human achievement which Mohammed saw in the cave of Mount Hira and which made civilization and all temporal concerns as meaningless as "the beat of a gnat's wing," in comparison with the splendour of Eternal Power, burning alone like the sun over the desert. Nor can we doubt that the material progress of modern Europe as opposed to the material stagnation of Islam is, at least to some extent, the result of the different psychological effects produced by these two different visions.

Of course it may be argued with considerable truth that the inspiration of Mohammed was itself the product of his environment—of the desert caravan routes and the close juxtaposition of civilization and emptiness which is characteristic of the life of the oasis, but we must also remember that, only a century or two after its appearance, this vision had become the dominant spiritual power in Syria, Babylonia and Egypt, the three richest and most populous regions of the Middle East. For a vision to be so universal in its effects there must be also something universal in its causes, and we cannot suppose it to be a merely fortuitous product of local circumstance. It is a world phenomenon that, in spite of its individuality, is in some sense governed by general laws which are susceptible of scientific investigation.

This is one of the main tasks in front of the social sciences, for while, thanks to the school of Le Play and to the anthropologists, great progress has already been made in the study of the evolution of regional life, little has been done to study, in the method of Science, the problem of the formation of the higher social unities. Hitherto historical science has concerned itself not with the spiritual unities, *i.e.*, the Civilizations, but with the political unities, the State and the Empire, and these moreover it has sought to interpret in terms either of race or of politics instead of in terms of world culture or of regional life. If once we begin to consider Race apart from Region and Civilization, it becomes a pernicious abstraction which falsifies the whole view of history. Witness the false generalizations of the mid-nineteenth-century historians of England and Germany, and still more the curious race-mysticism of such writers as Houston Stewart Chamberlain. And even commoner and more dangerous than this is the political or imperialist misreading of history, which justifies whatever is successful and measures social values in terms of material power. This is the error that lies at the root of most of our current misconceptions of progress, by substituting a false idea of social unification for the true one. Unlike civilization which is a spiritual co-operation of regional societies, Imperialism is an external forced unification, which may injure or destroy the delicate organisms of local life. It can only be of real value to culture, if it acts as the servant of a cultural unity or a spiritual force which is already existent, as the Roman Empire was the servant of Hellenism, the Byzantine of Christianity and the Chinese of Confucianism. During the last fifty years Imperialism, whether military or economic, has tended to predominate over the spiritual element in the European world-society. The economic organization of the world has far outstripped its spiritual unity, and the natural development of regional life has been repressed or forced away by a less vital, but mechanically stronger world-power. Thus it is that the great modern city, instead of fulfilling the true vocation of the city, which is to be the meeting and the marriage of region and civilization, is neither regional nor cultural, but is merely the misshapen product of world industry and economic imperialism.

These forces are in fact part of a movement of degeneration as well as of growth, yet they have been hailed all over the world as the bringers of civilization and progress. True progress, however, does not consist in a quantitative advance in wealth and numbers, nor even in a qualitative advance in technology and the control of matter, though all these play their subsidiary parts in the movement. The essential fact of Progress is a process of integration, an increasingly close union between the spirit of the whole civilization and the personality of the local society. This evolution of a richer and fuller group-consciousness we can trace through the history of all the ages that are known to us. Partial lines of progress, continuous improvement in the arts for instance, are obscure and often impossible to trace, but this great movement of integration which has proceeded almost without a break from the dawn of civilization in the river valleys down to the present day is real and incontestable. Nor can we set aside as merely Utopian the idea that this process is likely to continue until humanity as a whole finds social expression—not necessarily in one State—but in a common civilization and a common consciousness—a synthesis in which every region can bring its contribution to the whole, without losing its own soul under the pressure of the dead hand of world imperialism.

This progressive realization of the unity of mankind was indeed Comte's interpretation of the historical process, and in this at least he was not simply misled by an abstract theory. Where he failed was in his attempt to determine the exact form of this final unification, in his ambition to draw up a constitution for the human race, and to create the spirit that was to animate it. But the laws by which a further synthesis may be reached are not to be determined by abstract theory, they are discoverable only by the study of the formation and disintegration of similar syntheses in the past—unities such as Hellenism and Islam, or China and India, which were but partial syntheses, it is true, but were universal in their aim.

In the militant world-state of Islam, and in the pacific social culture of China, in the free communion of the Hellenic cities, and in the life of mediaeval Christendom with its common spiritual unity and its infinite diversity of local and civic forms, we may find not only more instruction, but more inspiration for the future of our civilization than in all the Utopias that philosophers and poets have ever dreamed.

—1921.

20   Gnosticism— The Nature of Modernity

Eric Voegelin

The clash between the various types of truth in the Roman Empire ended with the victory of Christianity. The fateful result of this victory was the de-divinization of the temporal sphere of power. To anticipate, the advent of modernity would bring about a re-divinization of man and society. It is important at this point to define our terms, especially since both the concept of modernity and the periodization of history depend upon the meaning of re-divinization. Therefore, by de-divinization we mean the process by which the culture of polytheism died from experiential atrophy, and human existence in society became reordered, through the grace of the world-transcendent God, by the experience of man's destination as eternal life in

From Eric Voegelin, *The New Science of Politics* (Chicago: University of Chicago Press, 1952), Chapter 4, pp. 107–132. Copyright © 1952 by The University of Chicago. Reprinted by permission of The University of Chicago Press.

beatific vision. By re-divinization, however, we do not mean a revival of polytheistic culture in the Greco-Roman sense. The characterization of modern political mass movements as neo-pagan, which has a certain vogue, is misleading because it sacrifices the historically unique nature of modern movements to a superficial resemblance. Modern re-divinization has its origins rather in Christianity itself, deriving from components that were suppressed as heretical by the universal church.

Within Christianity itself, then, there has existed a tension between the central tradition which viewed man's destiny as transcendent and eternal and a suppressed tradition which looked forward in time to the establishment of a Kingdom of God in the world. Historically, the tension derives from the origin of Christianity as a Jewish messianic movement. The experience of the early Christian communities oscillated between the eschatological expectation of the Parousia that would bring the Kingdom of God and the understanding of the church as the apocalypse of Christ in history. Since the Parousia did not occur, the church actually evolved from the eschatology of the Kingdom of God in history toward the eschatology of transhistorical, supernatural perfection. In this evolution the specific essence of Christianity separated from its historical origin.[1] This separation began within the life of Jesus itself,[2] and it was on principle completed with the Pentecostal descent of the Spirit. Nevertheless, the expectation of an imminent coming of the Kingdom was stirred to white heat again and again by the suffering of the persecutions; and the most grandiose expression of eschatological pathos, the Revelation of St. John, was included in the canon in spite of misgivings about its compatibility with the idea of the church. The inclusion had fateful consequences, for with the Revelation was accepted the revolutionary annunciation of the millennium in which Christ would

[1] On the transition from eschatological to apocalyptic Christianity see Alois Dempf, *Sacrum Imperium* (Munich and Berlin, 1929), pp. 71 ff.
[2] Albert Schweitzer, *Geschichte der Leben Jesu Forschung* (Tübingen, 1920), pp. 406 ff.; and Maurice Goguel, *Jésus* (2d ed.; Paris, 1950), the chapter on "La Crise galiléenne."

reign with his saints on this earth.[3] Not only did the inclusion
sanction the permanent influence within Christianity of the
broad mass of Jewish apocalyptic literature but it also raised
the immediate question how chiliasm could be reconciled with
idea and existence of the church. If Christianity consisted in
the burning desire for deliverance from the world, if Christians
lived in expectation of the end of unredeemed history, if their
destiny could be fulfilled only by the Realm in the sense of
chapter 20 of Revelation, the church was reduced to an ephemeral community of men waiting for the great event and hop-
ing that it would occur in their lifetime. On the theoretical
level the problem could be solved only by the tour de force of
interpretation which St. Augustine performed in the *Civitas
Dei.* There he roundly dismissed the literal belief in the millennium as "ridiculous fables" and then boldly declared the Realm
of the thousand years to be the reign of Christ in His church in
the present saeculum that would continue until the Last Judgment and the advent of the eternal Realm in the beyond.[4]

The Augustinian conception of the church, without substantial change, remained historically effective to the end of the
Middle Ages. The revolutionary expectation of a Second Coming that would transfigure the structure of history on earth was
ruled out as "ridiculous." The Logos had become flesh in Christ;
the grace of redemption had been bestowed on man; there
would be no divinization of society beyond the pneumatic
presence of Christ in His church. Jewish chiliasm was excluded
along with polytheism, just as Jewish monotheism had been
excluded along with pagan, metaphysical monotheism. This left
the church as the universal spiritual organization of saints and
sinners who professed faith in Christ, as the representative of
the *civitas Dei* in history, as the flash of eternity into time.
And correspondingly it rendered the power organization of
society merely temporal—a manifestation of that part of

[3]On the tension in early Christianity, the reception of Revelation, and
its subsequent role in Western revolutionary eschatology see Jakob Taubes,
Abendländische Eschatologie (Bern, 1947), esp. pp. 69 ff.
[4]Augustinus *Civitas Dei* xx. 7, 8, and 9.

human nature that will pass away with the transfiguration of time into eternity. The one Christian society was articulated into its spiritual and temporal orders. In its temporal articulation it accepted the *conditio humana* without chiliastic fancies, while it heightened natural existence by the representation of spiritual destiny through the church. . . .

2

Western Christian society thus was articulated into the spiritual and temporal orders, with pope and emperor as the supreme representatives in both the existential and the transcendental sense. From this society with its established system of symbols emerge the specifically modern problems of representation, with the resurgence of the eschatology of the realm. Such resurgence had a long social and intellectual prehistory, but the desire for a re-divinization of society produced a definite symbolism of its own only toward the end of the twelfth century. Our analysis here will start from the first clear and comprehensive expression of the idea in the work of Joachim of Flora.

Joachim broke with the Augustinian conception of a Christian society when he applied the symbol of the Trinity to the course of history. In his speculation the history of mankind had three periods corresponding to the three persons of the Trinity. The first period of the world was the age of the Father; with the appearance of Christ began the age of the Son. But the age of the Son will not be the last one; it will be followed by a third age of the Spirit. The three ages were characterized by intelligible increases in spiritual fulfilment. The first age unfolded the life of the layman; the second age brought the active and contemplative life of the priest; the third age would bring the perfect spiritual life of the monk. Moreover, the ages had comparable internal structures and a calculable length. From the comparison of structures it appeared that each age opened with a trinity of leading figures, that is, with two precursors, followed by the leader of the age himself; and from the calculation of length it followed that the age of the Son would reach its end in 1260. The leader of the first age was Abraham; the leader of the second age was Christ; and Joachim predicted that by 1260 there would appear the *Dux e Bablyone*, the leader of the third age.[5]

In his trinitarian eschatology Joachim created the aggregate of symbols which govern the self-interpretation of modern political society to this day.

The first of these symbols is the conception of history as a sequence of three ages, of which the third age is intelligibly the final Third Realm. As variations of this symbol are recognizable the humanistic and encyclopedist periodization of history into ancient, medieval, and modern history; Turgot's and Comte's theory of a sequence of theological, metaphysical, and scientific phases; Hegel's dialectic of the three stages of freedom and self-reflective spiritual fulfilment; the Marxian dialectic of the three stages of primitive communism, class society, and final communism; and, finally, the National Socialist symbol of the Third Realm—though this is a special case requiring further attention.

The second symbol is that of the leader.[6] It had its immediate effectiveness in the movement of the Franciscan spirituals who saw in St. Francis the fulfilment of Joachim's prophecy; and its effectiveness was reinforced by Dante's speculation on the *Dux* of the new spiritual age. It then can be traced in the paracletic figures, the *homines spirituales* and *homines novi*, of the late Middle Ages, the Renaissance, and Reformation; it can be discerned as a component in Machiavelli's *principe;* and in the period of secularization it appears in the supermen of Condorcet, Comte, and Marx, until it dominates the contem-

---

[5]On Joachim of Flora see Herbert Grundmann, *Studien über Joachim von Floris* (Leipzig, 1927); Dempf, *op. cit.,* pp. 269 ff.; Ernesto Buonaiuti, *Gioacchino da Fiore* (Rome, 1931); the same author's "Introduction" to Joachim's *Tractatus super quatuor evangelia* (Rome, 1930); and the chapters on Joachim in Jakob Taubes' *Abendländische Eschatologie* and Karl Löwith's *Meaning in History* (Chicago, 1949).

[6]For further transformations of Joachitism see Appendix I, "Modern Transfigurations of Joachism," in Löwith, *op. cit.*

porary scene through the paracletic leaders of the new realms.

The third symbol, sometimes blending into the second, is that of the prophet of the new age. In order to lend validity and conviction to the idea of a final Third Realm, the course of history as an intelligible, meaningful whole must be assumed accessible to human knowledge, either through a direct revelation or through speculative gnosis. Hence, the Gnostic prophet—or, in the later stages of secularization, the Gnostic intellectual—becomes an appurtenance of civilization. Joachim himself was the first instance of the species.

The fourth symbol is that of the brotherhood of autonomous persons. The third age of Joachim, by virtue of its new descent of the spirit, will transform men into members of the new realm without sacramental mediation of grace. In the third age the church will cease to exist because the charismatic gifts that are necessary for the perfect life will reach men without the administration of sacraments. While Joachim himself conceived the new age concretely as an order of monks, the idea of a community of the spiritually perfect who can live together without institutional authority was formulated on principle. The idea was capable of infinite variations. It can be traced in various degrees of purity in medieval and Renaissance sects, as well as in the Puritan churches of the saints; in its secularized form it has become a formidable component in the contemporary democratic creed; and it is the dynamic core in the Marxian mysticism of the realm of freedom and the withering-away of the state.

The National Socialist Third Realm is a special case. To be sure, Hitler's millennial prophecy authentically derives from Joachitic speculation, mediated in Germany through the Anabaptist wing of the Reformation and through the Johannine Christianity of Fichte, Hegel, and Schelling. Nevertheless, the concrete application of the trinitarian schema to the first German Reich that ended in 1806, the Bismarck Reich that ended in 1918, and the *Dritte Reich* of the National Socialist movement sounds flat and provincial if compared with the world-historical speculation of the German idealists, of

Comte, or of Marx. This nationalist, accidental touch is due to the fact that the symbol of the *Dritte Reich* did not stem from the speculative effort of a philosopher of rank but rather from dubious literary transfers. The National Socialist propagandists picked it up from Moeller van den Bruck's tract of that name.[7] And Moeller, who had no National Socialist intentions, had found it as a convenient symbol in the course of his work on the German edition of Dostoevski. The Russian idea of the Third Rome is characterized by the same blend of an eschatology of the spiritual realm with its realization by a political society. This other branch of political re-divinization must now be considered.

Only in the West was the Augustinian conception of the church historically effective to the point where it resulted in the clear double representation of society in the spiritual and the temporal powers. The fact that the temporal ruler was situated at a considerable geographical distance from Rome certainly facilitated this evolution. In the East developed the Byzantine form of Caesaropapism, in direct continuity with the position of the emperor in pagan Rome. Constantinople was the Second Rome, as we see from the declaration of Justinian concerning the *consuetudo Romae:* "By Rome, however, must be understood not only the old one but also our royal city."[8] After the fall of Constantinople to the Turks, the idea

[7]Moeller van den Bruck, *Das Dritte Reich* (Hamburg, 1923). See also the chapter on "Das Dritte Reich und die Jungen Völker" in Moeller van den Bruck, *Die politischen Kräfte* (Breslau, 1933). The symbol gained acceptance slowly. The second edition of the *Dritte Reich* appeared only in 1930, five years after the author's death through suicide; see the "Introduction" by Mary Agnes Hamilton to the English edition, *Germany's Third Empire* (London, 1934).

[8]*Codex Justinianus* i. xvii. 1. 10. We are quoting the legal formalization of the idea. On the nuances of meaning with regard to the foundation and organization of Constantinople, in 330, see Andrew Alföldi, *The Conversion of Constantine and Pagan Rome,* trans. Harold Mattingly (Oxford, 1948), chap. ix: "The Old Rome and the New." The tension between the two Romes may be gathered from Canon 3 of the Council of Constantinople in 381: "The Bishop of Constantinople to have the primacy of honor next after the Bishop of Rome, because that Constantinople is New Rome" (Henry Bettenson, *Documents of the Christian Church* [New York, 1947], p. 115).

of Moscow as the successor to the Orthodox empire gained ground in Russian clerical circles. Let me quote the famous passages from a letter of Filofei of Pskov to Ivan the Great:

> The church of the first Rome fell because of the godless heresy of Apollinaris. The gates of the second Rome at Constantinople were smashed by the Ishmaelites. Today the holy apostolic church of the third Rome in thy Empire shines in the glory of Christian faith throughout the world. Know you, O pious Tsar, that all empires of the orthodox Christians have converged into thine own. You are the sole autocrat of the universe, the only tsar of all Christians. . . . According to the prophetic books all Christian empires have an end and will converge into one empire, that of our gossudar, that is, into the Empire of Russia. Two Romes have fallen, but the third will last, and there will not be a fourth one.[9]

It took about a century to institutionalize the idea. Ivan IV was the first Rurikide to have himself crowned, in 1547, as czar of the Orthodox;[10] and in 1589 the patriarch of Constantinople was compelled to institute the first autocephalous patriarch of Moscow, now with the official recognition of Moscow as the Third Rome.[11]

The dates of the rise and institutionalization of this idea are important. The reign of Ivan the Great coincides with the consolidation of the Western national states (England, France, and Spain), and the reigns of Ivan IV and of Theodore I coincide with the Western Reformation. Precisely at the time when the Western imperial articulation ultimately disintegrated, when Western society rearticulated itself into the nations and the plurality of churches, Russia entered on her career as the heir of Rome. From her very beginnings Russia

---

[9]On the Third Rome see Hildegard Schaeder, *Moskau—Das Dritte Rom: Studien zur Geschichte der politischen Theorien in der slavischen Welt* (Hamburg, 1929); Joseph Olšr, *Gli ultimi Rurikidi e le base ideologiche della sovranità dello stato Russo* ("Orientalia Christiana," Vol. XII [Rome, 1946]); Hugo Rahner, *Vom Ersten bis zum Dritten Rom* (Innsbruck, 1950); Paul Miliukov, *Outlines of Russian Culture,* Part I; *Religion and the Church* (Philadelphia, 1945), pp. 15 ff.

[10]George Vernadsky, *Political and Diplomatic History of Russia* (Boston, 1936), p. 158.

[11]*Ibid.,* p. 180.

was not a nation in the Western sense but a civilizational area, dominated ethnically by the Great Russians and formed into a political society by the symbolism of Roman continuation.

That Russian society was in a class by itself was gradually recognized by the West. In 1488 Maximilian I still tried to integrate Russia into the Western political system by offering a royal crown to Ivan the Great. The Grand Duke of Moscow refused the honor on the grounds that his authority stemmed from his ancestors, that it had the blessing of God, and, hence, that there was no need of confirmation from the Western emperor.[12] A century later, in 1576, at the time of the Western wars with the Turks, Maximilian II went a step further by offering Ivan IV recognition as the emperor of the Greek East in return for assistance.[13] Again the Russian ruler was not interested even in an imperial crown, for, at that time, Ivan was already engaged in building the Russian Empire through the liquidation of the feudal nobility and its replacement by the *oprichnina,* the new service nobility.[14] Through this bloody operation Ivan the Terrible stamped on Russia the indelible social articulation which has determined her inner political history to this day. Transcendentally Russia was distinguished from all Western nations as the imperial representative of Christian truth; and through her social rearticulation, from which the czar emerged as the existential representative, she was radically cut off from the development of representative institutions like those of the Western national states. Napoleon, finally, recognized the Russian problem when, in 1802, he said that there were only two nations in the world: Russia and the Occident.[15]

Russia developed a type of representation which was *sui generis* in both the transcendental and the existential respects. The Westernization since Peter the Great did not change the

[12]*Ibid.,* p. 149.
[13]Rahner, *op. cit.,* p. 15.
[14]Vernadsky, *op. cit.,* pp. 169 ff.
[15]Napoleon, *Vues politiques* (Rio de Janeiro, *s.a.*), p. 340.

type fundamentally because it had practically no effect with regard to social articulation. One can speak, indeed, of a personal Westernization in the ranks of the high nobility, in the wake of the Napoleonic Wars, in the generation of Chaadaev, Gagarin, and Pecherin; but the individual servants of the czar did not transform themselves into an estate of the nobility, into an articulate *baronagium*. Perhaps the necessity of co-operative class action as the condition of a political Westernization of Russia was not even seen; and certainly, if the possibility for an evolution in this direction ever existed, it was finished with the Dekabrist revolt of 1825. Immediately afterward, with Khomyakov, began the Slavophilic, anti-Western philosophy of history which the apocalypse of the Third Rome, reconceived with broad effectiveness in the intelligentsia of the middle nobility, as the messianic, eschatological mission of Russia for mankind. In Dostoevski this superimposition of messianism crystallized in the curiously ambivalent vision of an autocratic, orthodox Russia that somehow would conquer the world and in this conquest blossom out into the free society of all Christians in the true faith.[16] It is this ambivalent vision which, in its secularized form, inspires a Russian dictatorship of the proletariat that in its conquest of the world will blossom out into the Marxian realm of freedom. The tentative Western articulation of Russian society under the liberal czars became an episode of the past with the revolution of 1917. The people as a whole have become again the servants of the czar in the old Muscovite sense, with the cadres of the Communist party as its service nobility; the *oprichnina* which Ivan the Terrible had established on the basis of an agricultural economy was re-established with a vengeance on the basis of an industrial economy.[17]

[16]For this view of Dostoevski see Dmitri Merezhkovski, *Die religiöse Revolution* (printed as Introduction to Dostoevski's *Politische Schriften* [Munich, 1920]), and Bernhard Schultze, *Russische Denker* (Wien, 1950), pp. 125 ff.

[17]Alexander von Schelting, *Russland und Europa* (Bern, 1948), pp. 123 ff. and 261 ff.

3

From the exposition of Joachitic symbols, from the cursory survey of their later variants, and from their blending with the political apocalypse of the Third Rome, it will have become clear that the new eschatology decisively affects the structure of modern politics. It has produced a well-circumscribed symbolism by means of which Western political societies interpret the meaning of their existence; and the adherents of one or the other of the variants determine the articulation of society domestically as well as on the world scene. Up to this point, however, the symbolism has been accepted on the level of self-interpretation and described as a historical phenomenon. It must now be submitted to critical analysis of its principal aspects, and the foundation for this analysis must be laid through a formulation of the theoretically relevant issue.

The Joachitic eschatology is, by its subject matter, a speculation on the meaning of history. In order to define its special character, it must be set off against the Christian philosophy of history that was traditional at the time, that is, against Augustinian speculation. Into the traditional speculation had entered the Jewish-Christian idea of an end of history in the sense of an intelligible state of perfection. History no longer moved in cycles, as it did with Plato and Aristotle, but acquired direction and destination. Beyond Jewish messianism in the strict sense the specifically Christian conception of history had advanced toward the understanding of the end as a transcendental fulfilment. In his elaboration of this theoretical insight St. Augustine distinguished between a profane sphere of history in which empires rise and fall and a sacred history which culminates in the appearance of Christ and the establishment of the church. He, furthermore, imbedded sacred history in a transcendental history of the *civitas Dei* which includes the events in the angelic sphere as well as the transcendental eternal sabbath. Only transcendental history, including the earthly pilgrimage of the church, has direction toward its eschatological fulfilment. Profane history, on the other hand, has no such direction; it is a waiting for the end; its present mode of being is that of a *saeculum senescens,* of an age that grows old.[18]

By the time of Joachim, Western civilization was growing strongly; and an age that began to feel its muscles would not easily bear the Augustinian defeatism with regard to the mundane sphere of existence. The Joachitic speculation was an attempt to endow the immanent course of history with a meaning that was not provided in the Augustinian conception. And for this purpose Joachim used what he had at hand, that is, the meaning of transcendental history. In this first Western attempt at an immanentization of meaning the connection with Christianity was not lost. The new age of Joachim would bring an increase of fulfilment within history, but the increase would not be due to an immanent eruption; it would come through a new transcendental irruption of the spirit. The idea of a radically immanent fulfilment grew rather slowly, in a long process that roughly may be called "from humanism to enlightenment"; only in the eighteenth century, with the idea of progress, had the increase of meaning in history become a completely intramundane phenomenon, without transcendental irruptions. This second phase of immanentization shall be called "secularization."

From the Joachitic immanentization a theoretical problem arises which occurs neither in classic antiquity nor in orthodox Christianity, that is, the problem of an eidos of history.[19] In Hellenic speculation, to be sure, we also have a problem of essence in politics; the polis has an eidos both for Plato and for Aristotle. But the actualization of this essence is governed by the rhythm of growth and decay, and the rhythmical em-

[18]For an account of the Augustinian conception of history see Löwith, *op. cit.*

[19]On the eidos of history see Hans Urs von Balthasar, *Theologie der Geschichte* (Einsiedeln, 1950), and Löwith, *op. cit., passim.*

bodiment and disembodiment of essence in political reality is the mystery of existence; it is not an additional eidos. The soteriological truth of Christianity, then, breaks with the rhythm of existence; beyond temporal successes and reverses lies the supernatural destiny of man, the perfection through grace in the beyond. Man and mankind now have fulfilment, but it lies beyond nature. Again there is no eidos of history, because the eschatological supernature is not a nature in the philosophical, immanent sense. The problem of an eidos in history, therefore, arises only when Christian transcendental fulfilment becomes immanentized. Such an immanentist hypostasis of the eschaton, however, is a theoretical fallacy. Things are not things, nor do they have essences, by arbitrary declaration. The course of history as a whole is no object of experience; history has no eidos, because the course of history extends into the unknown future. The meaning of history, thus, is an illusion; and this illusionary eidos is created by treating a symbol of faith as if it were a proposition concerning an object of immanent experience.

The fallacious character of an eidos of history has been shown on principle—but the analysis can and must be carried one step further into certain details. The Christian symbolism of supernatural destination has in itself a theoretical structure, and this structure is continued into the variants of immanentization. The pilgrim's progress, the sanctification of life, is a movement toward a telos, a goal; and this goal, the beatific vision, is a state of perfection. Hence, in the Christian symbolism one can distinguish the movement as its teleological component, from a state of highest value as the axiological component.[20] The two components reappear in the variants of immanentization; and they can accordingly be classified as variants which either accentuate the teleological or the axiological component or combine them both in their symbolism. In the first case, when the accent lies strongly on movement, without clarity about final perfection, the result will be the pro-

[20] For the distinction of the two components (which was introduced by Troeltsch) and the ensuing theological debate see Hans Urs von Balthasar, *Prometheus* (Heidelberg, 1947), pp. 12 ff.

gressivist interpretation of history. The aim need not be clarified because progressivist thinkers, men like Diderot or D'Alembert, assume a selection of desirable factors as the standard and interpret progress as qualitative and quantitative increase of the present good—the "bigger and better" of our simplifying slogan. This is a conservative attitude, and it may become reactionary unless the original standard be adjusted to the changing historical situation. In the second case, when the accent lies strongly on the state of perfection, without clarity about the means that are required for its realization, the result will be utopianism. It may assume the form of an axiological dream world, as in the utopia of More, when the thinker is still aware that the dream is unrealizable and knows why it is; or, with increasing theoretical illiteracy, it may assume the form of various social idealisms, such as the abolition of war, of unequal distribution of property, of fear and want. And, finally, immanentization may extend to the complete Christian symbol. The result will then be the active mysticism which envisions a state of perfection to be achieved through a revolutionary transfiguration of the nature of man, as, for instance, in Marxism.

4

Our analysis can now be resumed on the level of principle. The attempt at constructing an eidos of history will lead into the fallacious immanentization of the Christian eschaton. The understanding of the attempt as fallacious, however, raises baffling questions with regard to the type of man who will indulge in it. The fallacy looks rather elemental. Can it be assumed that the thinkers who indulged in it were not intelligent enough to penetrate it? Or that they penetrated it but propagated it nevertheless for some obscure evil reason? . . . Obviously one cannot explain seven centuries of intellectual history by stupidity and dishonesty. A drive must rather be assumed in the souls of these men which blinded them to the fallacy.

The nature of this drive cannot be discovered by submitting

the structure of the fallacy to an even closer analysis. The attention must rather concentrate on what the thinkers achieved by their fallacious construction. On this point there is no doubt. They achieved a certainty about the meaning of history, and about their own place in it, which otherwise they would not have had. Certainties, we know, are demanded for the purpose of overcoming the anxiety of uncertainty; and the next question then would be: What specific uncertainty was so disturbing that it had to be overcome by the dubious means of fallacious immanentization? One does not have to look far afield for an answer. Uncertainty is the very essence of Christianty. The feeling of security in a "world full of gods" is lost with the gods themselves; when the world is de-divinized, communication with the world-transcendent God is reduced to the tenuous bond of faith, in the sense of Heb. 11:1, as the substance of things hoped for and the proof of things unseen. Ontologically, the substance of things hoped for is nowhere to be found but in faith itself; and, epistemologically, there is no proof for things unseen but again this very faith.[21] The bond is tenuous, indeed, and it may snap easily. The life of the soul in openness toward God, the waiting, the periods of aridity and dulness, guilt and despondency, contrition and repentance, forsakenness and hope against hope, the silent stirrings of love and grace, trembling on the verge of a certainty which if gained is lost—this entire mode may prove too heavy a burden. . . . The danger of a breakdown of faith to a socially relevant degree will increase as Christianity becomes a worldly success: that is, it will grow when Christianity penetrates a civilizational area thoroughly, supported by institutional pressure, and when, at the same time, it undergoes an internal process of spiritualization, of a more complete realization of its essence. The more people are drawn or pressured into the Christian orbit, the greater will be the number among them who do not have the

---

[21]Our reflections on the uncertainty of faith must be understood as a psychology of experience. For the theology of the definition of faith in Heb. 11:1, which is presupposed in our analysis, see Thomas Aquinas *Summa theologica* ii–ii. Q. 4, Art. 1.

spiritual stamina for the heroic adventure of the soul that is Christianity. In addition, the likeliness of a fall from faith will increase when education, literacy, and intellectual debate bring the full seriousness of Christianity to the understanding of ever more individuals. Both of these processes characterized the high Middle Ages. Historical detail is not our present concern here; it will be sufficient to refer summarily to the growing town societies with their intense spiritual culture as the primary centers from which the danger radiated into Western society at large.

If the predicament of a fall from faith in the Christian sense occurs as a mass phenomenon, the consequences will depend on the content of the prevailing culture. A man cannot fall back on himself in an absolute sense, because, if he tried, he would find very soon that he has fallen into the abyss of his despair and nothingness; he will have to fall back on a less differentiated culture of spiritual experience. Under the civilizational conditions of the twelfth century it was impossible to fall back into Greco-Roman polytheism, because it had disappeared as the living culture of a society; and the stunted remnants could hardly be revived as a substitute for Christianity, because they had lost their spell precisely for those men who had tasted of Christianity. The fall could be interrupted only by experiential alternatives, sufficiently close to the experience of faith that only a discerning eye would see the difference, but receding far enough from it to remedy the uncertainty of faith in the strict sense. Such alternative experiences were at hand in the gnosis which had accompanied Christianity from its very beginnings.[22]

The economy of this essay does not allow a description of the gnosis of antiquity or of the history of its transmission

---

[22]The exploration of gnosis is so rapidly advancing that only a study of the principal works of the last generation will mediate an understanding of its dimensions. Of special value are Eugène de Faye, *Gnostiques et gnosticisme* (2d ed.; Paris, 1925); Hans Jonas, *Gnosis und spätantiker Geist* (Göttingen, 1934); Simone Pétrement, *Le Dualisme chez Platon, les Gnostiques et les Manichéens* (Paris, 1947); and Hans Söderberg, *La Religion des Cathares* (Uppsala, 1949).

into the Western Middle Ages; it is enough to say that at the time gnosis was a living religious culture on which men could fall back. The attempt at immanentizing the meaning of existence is fundamentally an attempt at bringing our knowledge of transcendence into a firmer grip than the *cognitio fidei*, the cognition of faith, will afford; and Gnostic experiences offer this firmer grip in so far as they are an expansion of the soul to the point where God is drawn into the existence of man. This expansion will engage the various human faculties; and, hence, it is possible to distinguish a range of Gnostic varieties according to the faculty which predominates in the operation of getting this grip on God. Gnosis may be primarily intellectual and assume the form of speculative penetration of the mystery of creation and existence, as, for instance, in the contemplative gnosis of Hegel or Schelling. Or it may be primarily emotional and assume the form of an indwelling of divine substance in the human soul, as, for instance, in paracletic sectarian leaders. Or it may be primarily volitional and assume the form of activist redemption of man and society, as in the instance of revolutionary activists like Comte, Marx, or Hitler. These Gnostic experiences, in the amplitude of their variety, are the core of the re-divinization of society, for the men who fall into these experiences divinize themselves by substituting more massive modes of participation in divinity for faith in the Christian sense.[23]

A clear understanding of these experiences as the active core of immanentist eschatology is necessary, because otherwise the inner logic of the Western political development from medieval immanentism through humanism, enlightenment, progressivism, liberalism, positivism, into Marxism will be obscured. The intellectual symbols developed by the various types of immanentists will frequently be in conflict with one another, and the various types of Gnostics will oppose one another. One can easily imagine how indignant a humanistic liberal will be when he is told that his particular type of im-

---

[23]For a general suggestion concerning the range of Gnostic phenomena in the modern world see Balthasar, *Prometheus*, p. 6.

manentism is one step on the road to Marxism. It will not be superfluous, therefore, to recall the principle that the substance of history is to be found on the level of experiences, not on the level of ideas. Secularism could be defined as a radicalization of the earlier forms of paracletic immanentism, because the experiential divinization of man is more radical in the secularist case. Feuerbach and Marx, for instance, interpreted the transcendent God as the projection of what is best in man into a hypostatic beyond; for them the great turning point of history, therefore, would come when man draws his projection back into himself, when he becomes conscious that he himself is God, when as a consequence man is transfigured into superman.[24] This Marxian transfiguration does, indeed, carry to its extreme a less radical medieval experience which draws the spirit of God into man, while leaving God himself in his transcendence. The superman marks the end of a road on which we find such figures as the "godded man" of English Reformation mystics.[25] These considerations, moreover, will explain and justify the earlier warning against characterizing modern political movements as neopagan. Gnostic experiences determine a structure of political reality that is *sui generis*. A line of gradual transformation connects medieval with contemporary gnosticism. And the transformation is so gradual, indeed, that it would be difficult to decide whether contemporary phenomena should be classified as Christian because they are intelligibly an outgrowth of Christian heresies of the Middle Ages or whether medieval phenomena should be classified as anti-Christian because they are intelligibly the origin of modern anti-Christianism. The best course will be to drop such questions and to recognize the essence of modernity as the growth of gnosticism.

[24]On the superman of Feuerbach and Marx see Henri de Lubac, *Le Drame de l'humanisme athée* (3d ed.; Paris, 1945), pp. 15 ff.; Löwith, *op. cit.*, especially the quotation on p. 36 concerning the "new men"; and Eric Voegelin, "The Formation of the Marxian Revolutionary Idea," *Review of Politics*, Vol. XII (1950).

[25]The "godded man" is a term of Henry Nicholas (see Rufus M. Jones, *Studies in Mystical Religion* [London, 1936], p. 434).

Gnosis was an accompaniment of Christianity from its very beginnings; its traces are to be found in St. Paul and St. John.[26] Gnostic heresy was the great opponent of Christianity in the early centuries; and Irenaeus surveyed and criticized its manifold variants in his *Adversus Haereses (ca.* 180)—a standard treatise on the subject that still will be consulted with profit by the student who wants to understand modern political ideas and movements. Moreover, besides the Christian gnosis there also existed a Jewish, a pagan, and an Islamic gnosis; and quite possibly the common origin of all these branches of gnosis will have to be sought in the basic experiential type that prevailed in pre-Christian Syriac civilization. Nowhere, however, has gnosis assumed the form of speculation on the meaning of immanent history as it did in the high Middle Ages. Gnosis does not by inner necessity lead to the fallacious construction of history which characterizes modernity since Joachim. Hence, in the drive for certainty there must be contained a further component which bends gnosis specifically toward historical speculation. This further component is the civilizational expansiveness of Western society in the high Middle Ages. It is a coming-of-age in search of its meaning, a conscious growth that will not put up with the traditional view that civilization was declining, senescent. And, in fact, the self-endowment of Western civilization with meaning closely followed the actual expansion and differentiation. The spiritual growth of the West through the orders since Cluny expressed itself, in Joachim's speculation in the idea of a Third Realm of the monks; the early philosophical and literary humanism expressed itself in Dante's and Petrarch's idea of an Apollinian Imperium, a Third Realm of intellectual life that succeeds the imperial spiritual and temporal orders;[27] and in the Age of Reason Condorcet conceived the idea of a unified civilization

[26]On gnosis in early Christianity see Rudolf Bultmann, *Das Urchristentum im Rahmen der antiken Religionen* (Zurich, 1949).

[27]On the Apollinian Imperium as a Third Realm see Karl Burdach, *Reformation, Renaissance, Humanismus* (2d ed.; Berlin and Leipzig, 1926), pp. 133 ff.; and the same author's *Rienzo und die geistige Wandlung seiner Zeit* (Berlin, 1913–28), Vol. II/I; *Vom Mittelalter zur Reformation,* p. 542.

of mankind in which everybody would be a French intellectual.[28] The social carriers of the movements, in their turn, changed with the differentiation and articulation of Western society. In the early phases of modernity they were the townspeople and peasants in opposition to feudal society; in the later phases they were the progressive bourgeoisie, the socialist workers, and the Fascist lower middle class. And, finally, with the prodigious advancement of science since the seventeenth century, the new instrument of cognition would become, one is inclined to say inevitably, the symbolic vehicle of Gnostic truth. In the Gnostic speculation of scientism this particular variant reached its extreme when the positivist perfector of science replaced the era of Christ by the era of Comte. Scientism has remained to this day one of the strongest Gnostic movements in Western society; and the immanentist pride in science is so strong that even the special sciences have each left a distinguishable sediment in the variants of salvation through physics, economics, sociology, biology, and psychology.

5

This analysis of the components in modern Gnostic speculation does not claim to be exhaustive, but it has been carried far enough to enable us to recognize the experiences which determine the political articulation of Western society under the symbolism of the Third Realm. . . . Following the Aristotelian procedure, the analysis started from the self-interpretation of society by means of the Joachitic symbols of the twelfth century. Now that their meaning has been clarified through theoretical understanding, a date can be assigned to the beginning of this civilizational course. A suitable date for its formal beginning would be the activation of ancient gnosticism through Scotus Eriugena in the ninth century, because his works, as well as those of Dionysius Areopagita which he

[28]Condorcet, *Esquisse* (1795), pp. 310–18.

translated, were a continuous influence in the underground Gnostic sects before they came to the surface in the twelfth and thirteenth centuries.

This is a long course of a thousand years, long enough to have aroused reflections on its decline and end. These reflections on Western society as a civilizational course that comes into view as a whole because it is moving intelligibly toward an end have raised one of the thorniest questions to plague the student of Western politics. On the one hand, as you know, there begins in the eighteenth century a continuous stream of literature on the decline of Western civilization; and, whatever misgivings one may entertain on this or that special argument, one cannot deny that the theorists of decline on the whole have a case. On the other hand, the same period is also characterized by an exuberantly expansive vitality in the sciences, in technology, in the material control of environment, in the increase of population, of the standard of living, of health and comfort, of mass education, of social consciousness and responsibility; and again, whatever misgivings one may entertain with regard to this or that item on the list, one cannot deny that the progressivists have a case, too. This conflict of interpretations leaves in its wake the adumbrated thorny question, that is, the question how a civilization can advance and decline at the same time. A consideration of this question suggests itself, because it seems possible that the analysis of modern gnosticism will furnish at least a partial solution of the problem.

Gnostic speculation overcame the uncertainty of faith by receding from transcendence and endowing man and his intramundane range of action with the meaning of eschatological fulfilment. As this immanentization progressed experientially, civilizational activity became a mystical work of self-salvation. The spiritual strength of the soul which in Christianity was devoted to the sanctification of life could now be diverted into the more appealing, more tangible, and, above all, so much easier creation of the terrestrial paradise. Civilizational action became a *divertissement,* in the sense of Pascal, but a *divertisse-*

ment which demonically absorbed into itself the eternal destiny of man and functioned as a substitute for the life of the spirit. Nietzsche most tersely expressed the nature of this demonic diversion when he raised the question why anyone should live in the embarrassing condition of a being in need of the love and grace of God. "Love yourself through grace—was his solution —then you are no longer in need of your God, and you can act the whole drama of Fall and Redemption to its end in yourself."[29] And how can this miracle be achieved, this miracle of self-salvation, and how this redemption by extending grace to yourself? The great historical answer was given by the successive types of Gnostic action that have made modern civilization what it is. The miracle was worked successively through the literary and artistic achievement which secured the immortality of fame for the humanistic intellectual, through the discipline and economic success which certified salvation to the Puritan saint, through the civilizational contributions of the liberals and progressives, and, finally, through the revolutionary action that will establish the Communist or some other Gnostic millennium. Gnosticism, thus, most effectively released human forces for the building of a civilization because on their fervent application to intramundane activity was put the premium of salvation. The historical result was stupendous. The resources of man that came to light under such pressure were in themselves a revelation, and their application to civilizational work produced the truly magnificent spectacle of Western progressive society. However fatuous the surface arguments may be, the widespread belief that modern civilization is Civilization in a pre-eminent sense is experientially justified; the endowment with the meaning of salvation has made the rise of the West, indeed, an apocalypse of civilization.

On this apocalyptic spectacle, however, falls a shadow; for the brilliant expansion is accompanied by a danger that grows apace with progress. The nature of this danger became apparent in the form which the idea of immanent salvation assumed

---

[29]Nietzsche, *Morgenröthe*, § 79.

in the gnosticism of Comte. The founder of positivism institutionalized the premium on civilizational contributions in so far as he guaranteed immortality through preservation of the contributor and his deeds in the memory of mankind. There were provided honorific degrees of such immortality, and the highest honor would be the reception of the meritorious contributor into the calendar of positivistic saints. But what should in this order of things become of men who would rather follow God than the new Augustus Comte? Such miscreants who were not inclined to make their social contributions according to Comtean standards would simply be committed to the hell of social oblivion. The idea deserves attention. Here is a Gnostic paraclete setting himself up as the world-immanent Last Judgment of mankind, deciding on immortality or annihilation for every human being. The material civilization of the West, to be sure, is still advancing; but on this rising plane of civilization the progressive symbolism of contributions, commemoration, and oblivion draws the contours of those "holes of oblivion" into which the divine redeemers of the Gnostic empires drop their victims with a bullet in the neck. This end of progress was not contemplated in the halcyon days of Gnostic exuberance. Milton released Adam and Eve with "a paradise within them, happier far" than the Paradise lost; when they went forth, "the world was all before them"; and they were cheered "with meditation on the happy end" of salvation through Christ. But when historically man goes forth, with the Gnostic "Paradise within him," and when he penetrates into the world before him, there is little cheer in meditation on the not so happy end.

The death of the spirit is the price of progress. Nietzsche revealed this mystery of the Western apocalypse when he announced that God was dead and that He had been murdered.[30]

---

[30]On the "murder of God" passages in Nietzsche, prehistory of the idea, and literary debate see Lubac, *op. cit.*, pp. 40 ff. For the most comprehensive exposition of the idea in Nietzsche's work see Karl Jaspers, *Nietzsche: Einführung in das Verständnis seines Philosophierens* (Berlin and Leipzig, 1936), under the references in the register.

This Gnostic murder is constantly committed by the men who sacrifice God to civilization. The more fervently all human energies are thrown into the great enterprise of salvation through world-immanent action, the farther the human beings who engage in this enterprise move away from the life of the spirit. And since the life of the spirit is the source of order in man and society, the very success of a Gnostic civilization is the cause of its decline.

A civilization can, indeed, advance and decline at the same time—but not forever. There is a limit toward which this ambiguous process moves; the limit is reached when an activist sect which represents the Gnostic truth organizes the civilization into an empire under its rule. Totalitarianism, defined as the existential rule of Gnostic activists, is the end form of progressive civilization.

21   Burke and Radical Freedom

Jeffrey Hart

I

As everyone knows, an enormous revival of interest in Edmund Burke has taken place during the past twenty years or so, the period, roughly, since the end of the Second World War.

Jeffrey Hart, "Burke and Radical Freedom," *The Review of Politics,* XXIX, No. 2 (April 1967), 221–238. Reprinted by permission of *The Review of Politics.*

Scholars, to be sure, have always been interested in him, and he was widely admired for his style, and by some for his "practical wisdom," during the nineteenth century. But the point is that in our time he has come to be read not merely as one among a large number of other important figures in the history of political thought, but as a thinker of intense, of special, contemporary relevance. Burke is our contemporary, he is an *issue,* in a way that Locke is not, and Leibniz is not, and even Mill is not. Burke has not receded into what Lovejoy called the pathos of time, by which he meant that benign and even tender feeling we have for thought that is now completely, forever, a part of the past—and so neither defines us nor menaces us.

In part, of course, Burke is a beneficiary of the revival of critical and scholarly esteem for eighteenth-century writing generally, and especially of eighteenth-century writing on the conservative side. Like Dryden and Pope and Swift and Johnson, he speaks, we see, for civilization, for a high and elegant and traditional civilization, and this is a welcome to us in our age of cultural democratization, and corruption of manners. In part, too, Burke is a beneficiary—as is conservative thought generally—of the fact that in the world arena today America is irreversibly a conservative nation, with everything to gain from the maintenance of order and nothing from its dissolution. Yet neither of these reasons quite accounts for the atmosphere of passion and polemic that surrounds the subject of Burke. Attitudes toward him among otherwise sober-seeming scholars tend to suggest total commitment—for him, or against him. Individuals whom one would never suspect of much capacity for feeling transform themselves when the question of Burke is up. And this, I will maintain, is because Burke was the first to recognize the deep moral division of the West, which was just then opening up, and which today, across the board, is decisive for our moral, political, and metaphysical opinions: and because Burke, having recognized the division and defined its doctrinal grounds, took sides.

II

Burke's break with Charles James Fox in 1791 may be taken as a kind of symbol of the division then opening in the West itself, and I think that Burke himself so understood it. Burke, of course, had always been known as an advocate of reform. He had urged a moderate and conciliatory policy toward the American colonies. A recently uncovered note among his papers at Sheffield in England demonstrates that Burke actually had a good deal of sympathy with the American Revolution. "The Americans," he noted,

> as I have and do repute them the first of men, to whom I owe eternal thanks for making me think better of my nature—tho they have been obliged to fall down at present before the professional armies of Germany, have yet afforded a dawning hope by the stand they have made, that in some corner of the globe, at some time, or in some circumstance or other, the Citizen may not be the slave of the Soldier.

In his parliamentary career Burke had fought for the independence of Parliament against what he thought to be the unconstitutional influence of the Crown. In economic matters, Burke was reformist as against the older mercantilist economic theory; he inclined to the theories of Adam Smith, who said, indeed, that Burke was the only man in England who really understood him. Burke's reformist politics even involved him in some friendly friction with his associates in Dr. Johnson's circle, who were very largely Tories. (Dr. Johnson, you will recall, remarked only half-playfully that the first Whig was the Devil, and that Patriotism—by which he meant the so-called Patriot political group, that is, the critics of George III, and not what we mean today by patriotism—was "the last refuge of a scoundrel.") Burke was the friend of Dr. Johnson, but he was the friend and political ally of the reformers—of Sir Philip Francis (the probable author of the Junius letters), of Sheridan, of Charles James Fox. Jeremy Bentham had read with approval and copiously annotated his reformist speeches;

and Burke was admired from afar by Tom Paine. If we could transport the pre-French Revolutionary Burke to our own times we would consider him a moderate and a reformer, humanitarian in his sympathies; he was, as against politics, half in love with philosophy and literature; but the French Revolution did occur: and it changed all this. Burke's principles did not change, but the deep transformation of the world cast him into an entirely different role.

Dramatically, Burke found himself separated from his former allies, who sympathized with the Revolution—and separated from them not only politically but personally, so far-reaching and decisive did the issues seem to him. In the spring of 1791, during a parliamentary debate on matters unrelated to France, Charles James Fox, well known to be an admirer of the Revolution, interpolated into a speech some comments favorable to it. Burke decided to reply to Fox at the earliest opportunity, and on May 6, during a debate on the Canada Bill, Burke rose to speak on the Revolution. As he spoke, Fox's followers repeatedly interrupted him and created an atmosphere of general disorder in the House. Irritated by this, Burke commented angrily on Fox's eulogies of the Revolution, and finally spoke these irrevocable words: "It is indiscreet," he said, "at any period, but especially at my time of life, to provoke enemies or give friends occasion to desert me. Yet firm and steady adherence to the British Constitution places me in such a dilemma; I am ready to risk it, and with my last words to exclaim, 'Fly from the French Constitution.' " Charles James Fox eagerly called to him that there need not be any loss of friends. "Yes, yes," replied Burke, "there is a loss of friends. I have done my duty at the price of my friend. Our friendship is at an end." Aghast at these proceedings, the members watched Burke stalk from the Chamber. This was an unexpected and dramatic but by no means fortuitous event: only a few months before, after a sharp argument over the *Reflections on the Revolution in France*, Burke's long friendship with Sir Philip Francis came permanently to an end.

No doubt Fox and Francis, worthy enough men, but certainly

not thinkers of the first order, were perplexed by Burke's behavior. They were men of generous spirit, they wished well to the people of France. Fox in particular was a sympathetic and colorful character. He was fat, he gambled for enormous sums in the front window of Brooks', he stabled a string of racehorses, he kept a mistress, and after relentlessly attacking Lord North for years he reversed himself, in the genial manner of the time, and formed a coalition with him. But men of this sort, good men though they were, possessed we might say of all the Dickensian virtues—the very creatures, indeed, of the old order—were not equipped either imaginatively or intellectually to understand the implications of the revolutionary threat to the European order, or of the doctrine that informed the threat.

Burke was. The focus of the *Reflections* is on final political things. We do not go to it for a definitive account of the economic conditions of France in 1789, or for a character sketch of Marie Antoinette, or for an apt account of the members of the Assembly. We do go to it for Burke's insight into the intellectual and spiritual issues. For the French Revolution seemed momentous to Burke not because of its violence, or because it threatened the peace of Europe: these things were derivative. Burke was, as he says, "alarmed into reflection" by what he considered a "revolution of doctrine and theoretic dogma," by emotions which, it seemed to him, would render impossible any stable and settled condition of society, and which would issue, indeed, in *permanent* revolution. As he says, near the beginning of the *Reflections,* in a sentence which reverberates in the mind like the opening bars of a great and dark symphony, this was "a great crisis, not of the affairs of France alone, but of all Europe, perhaps of more than Europe."

III

I think the best way of stating Burke's fundamental objection to the Revolution would be to say that it turned on a definition of "freedom"—that for Burke, freedom was a concrete and historical thing, the actual freedoms enjoyed by actual Englishmen: they enjoyed the historic rights of *Englishmen*. What revolutionary theory proposed, he thought, was a freedom that was abstract and unhistorical: not the rights of Englishmen but the Rights of Man. For Burke, there was no such thing as an abstract man, and to evoke one, as Rousseau had done in the famous first sentence of *The Social Contract*, was to construct a battering ram against all normal social relationships: "Man is born free," said Rousseau, "but everywhere he is in chains."

I do not mean to suggest, idiotically, in the remarks that are to follow, that Rousseau caused the French Revolution. That is not the role of ideas in relation to historical events. In addition, I know very well that there is a good deal of discussion among Rousseau scholars today on the precise intention behind that sentence. Nevertheless I think it remains true that in the *Rhetoric* of that sentence we may find articulated the longings that were at the heart of the Revolutionary ethos, and continue, today, to inform the modern revolutionary spirit.

In what sense was man "born free"? we might well ask with Burke. The infant does not look free; he seems completely dependent. And the violence of the statement is suspicious: *everywhere* in chains? *Everywhere?* And it is significant that the chains—man's social circumstances "everywhere"—are concretely imagined in Rousseau's metaphor, but that the "freedom"—man is "born free"—remains hypothetical, abstract, a mere proposition, whatever its rhetorical authority as the opening statement of the sentence. Just what is this freedom? It evidently is not the concrete, historical *freedoms* which Burke has in mind, but rather the hypothetical, indeed mythical, freedom of a presocial self. It is the freedom of man as an essence, not as an existence. Traditional thought—and this is the real reason why religion is necessary to any viable conservative politics—envisioned man as achieving essential being (that is, being as an essence) only outside of time: in eternity. Obviously this is logically consistent and intellectually respectable. But what Revolutionary theory sought, and this was the source—is the source—of its deep appeal in the West, was the experience of *essential freedom,* the freedom of man as an essence, *within* time. And that is why it proved, and has proved, to be so powerful a weapon. Any concrete circumstance standing in the way of *that* freedom—and any concrete circumstance would have to stand in the way of that freedom—would at best be regarded as a bothersome and interim thing, and at worst as contemptible and intolerable, something to be spat upon and smashed.

The theoreticians of the Revolution proposed, as Taine put it, to strip from man his artificial garments, all those fictitious qualities that made him "ecclesiastic or layman, noble or plebeian, sovereign or subject, proprietor or proletarian." Only when these supposed fictions had been stripped away could "natural man," man *qua* man, make his appearance in history— man liberated from false appearance, and so spontaneous, innocent, and free. The actual results of the French Revolution did not diminish the vitality of this hope; nor have the results of subsequent revolutions done so. There is, indeed, a sense in which the revolutionary hope cannot *be* defeated historically, since it is fundamentally unhistorical. By the time Shelley wrote *Prometheus Unbound* the French Revolution was part of history, and it had not transformed human nature. Yet the revolutionary vision retained all of its original vitality, and Shelley longed for another revolution, a final and successful one, which would liberate man at last from the "masks" of actual social existence:

> The loathesome mask has fallen, the man remains
> Scepterless, free, uncircumscribed, but man
> Equal, unclassed, tribeless, and nationless,
> Exempt from awe, worship, degree, the king
> Over himself; just, gentle, wise; but man
> Passionless? no, yet free from guilt or pain.

But if Shelley is a poet of the revolutionary vision, Burke is a poet of man conceived of as a social being, man as we have actually known him *in* history. He identified the revolutionary vision with great precision, and in the *Reflections* launched a powerful attack upon it. In a passage reminiscent of *Lear,* and employing the traditional metaphor of *clothes* to signify—as in Shakespeare or Swift—man's social aspect, Burke describes the informing impulse of the Revolution:

> All the decent drapery of life is to be rudely torn off. All the superadded ideas, furnished from the wardrobe of a moral imagination, which the heart owns and the understanding ratifies as necessary to cover the defects of our naked, shivering nature, and to raise it to dignity in our estimation, are to be exploded. . . .

In Burke's metaphor, clothes—what he calls "the decent drapery of life"—correspond to Shelley's "loathesome mask" and to Rousseau's "chains"; that is, they are our actual social roles. When they are stripped away, there remains "our naked shivering nature"—or in Shelley's terms, "man . . . scepterless, free"; or in Rousseau's terms, man "free" as he supposedly was when he was born.

At the center of the *Reflections*, then, is this issue: if indeed that "self" does exist, can it really be divested of its "artificial" attributes, and if it can be, will its nakedness be productive of joy? Burke was one of the first to understand that the spirit of the Revolution—and, as I wish to insist, the spirit of revolutionary modernity (which is not here a merely chronological concept)—was at its roots characterized by a hatred of the very idea of *society.* He knew that the defense of what the *philosophes* called "appearances" or "masks" is the defense of society itself, that the reality of society consists of appearances, of "roles." The natural man of revolutionary theory is only a myth, though a powerful one, and a destructive one—for the critique of roles, of forms, the assault upon Rousseau's "chains" (an element of his sentence which I will explicate shortly) has issued, precisely because natural man is a fiction, not in a more intense experience of selfhood but in the experience of emptiness, disgust, and alienation, in a deep hatred of the actual circumstances of social life, in a deep hatred, indeed, for historical existence itself; that is to say, in the special anger of the revolutionary spirit, which we daily feel all around us.

This spirit, as Christopher Dawson has remarked, is characterized by a disgust with the concreteness of man's being. Jean

Paul Sartre, a very great man in my view, conceives of himself, quite correctly, as a continuator of the Revolutionary tradition, as the heir of the *philosophes,* and he has made immense contributions by way of deepening and expanding that tradition intellectually. He is certainly a much more formidable figure than Camus, whose sensibility, much more traditional in character, surely strikes many as more attractive. Now it is characteristic of the Sartrean hero as we meet him in, say, Roquentin of *Nausea,* that he feels a deep revulsion in the presence of what he regards as "absurd" limitations on his freedom. "I see," says Roquentin in a moment of illumination, "I recall better what I felt the other day at the seashore when I held the pebble. It was a sort of sweetish sickness. How unpleasant it was! It came from the stone. I'm sure of it. It passed from the stone to my hand. Yes, that's it, that's just it—a sort of nausea in the hands!" Mere things seem to Roquentin simply to be there, without reason or purpose, devoid of consciousness. "The world of *Nausea,*" as Francis Jeanson has said, "is the world as it threatens to appear to us when we look at it passively, when we refuse to project a future for it. It becomes a petrified consciousness." The man of Sartrean sensibility, as he moves away from consciousness toward the unconscious, experiences increasing "viscosity"—we hear of "the stickiness," "the rising triumph of the solid over the liquid," "thoughts made sticky by their own objects," as well as, even more frequently, of "bloatedness," "insipid flesh," "pink flesh," "clammy flesh," and so on. Consciousness for Sartre is freedom, experienced as complete lucidity, while unconsciousness is a prison of "facticity." And the emotion includes his own body: "a dull and inescapable nausea perpetually reveals my body to myself."

This polarity between freedom and imprisonment is the reality of human experience for Sartre, but against it men of bad faith, whom Sartre calls "salauds"—stinkers—and who are principally to be identified with the middle class, erect the barriers of habit, conventional assumption, social role. All these constitute refusals of consciousness and freedom. Thus, in a characteristic gesture the Sartrean hero (Roquentin, Mathieu, Goetz) asserts his freedom from facticity by actually stabbing himself:

"My saliva is sweetish, my body lukewarm; I feel insipid. My penknife is on the table. I open it. Why not? In any case it would change things a bit. I place my left hand on the writing pad and dispatch a good knifethrust into the palm." It is by asserting himself against all forms of facticity and unconsciousness that the Sartrean hero becomes a free and spontaneous individual. "Sartre's essential philosophical trend," observes Wilfrid Desan, "is one of *negation,* a negation of all limitations to freedom, all hampering of man's free movement." Surely Desan is correct in this, for the attitude in question pervades Sartre's philosophical writings, his drama and his fiction, and even his criticism, which is savagely moral rather than aesthetic: Genet is a "saint" because of his negation of conventional morality; Giacometti is a great sculptor, for his wiry, fragile figures show man stripped of all "artificial" attributes.

This radical dualism between consciousness and object, lucidity and density, or, in Sartre's terminology, the *Pour-soi* and the *En-soi,* tends, by implication, toward a rejection of the social possibility, as Merleau-Ponty pointed out in his famous critique of Sartre, *Les Adventures de la Dialectique.* In accepting only *man* and *things* Sartre overlooks the *entremonde,* the both-and, that in-between-world of symbolism, value, and history—all that "man" finds and has found to be true. It is as if the individual consciousness alone counts, and both history and the social order are something extraneous. And of course, this sensibility takes the individual consciousness as something that, "naturally," does not incorporate into itself history (its memory) or the social order (its roles). That is to say, any memory, and any social role, is unnatural. Sartre defines integrity as *permanently* revolutionary, revolutionary against any of its conceivable concrete circumstances. That is why he is the greatest and deepest of the *philosophes,* and probably the last.

This hatred of the physical and limiting, of the concrete and irreducible, represents at its deepest reaches—to shift into another idiom—a rejection of the doctrine of the Incarnation, which in one of its meanings expresses the possibility that the concrete and the limiting—the flesh—may enter into union with spirit. To enter into the world at all, the spirit must become flesh—concrete and embodied. We know no naked essences. This union constitutes, in Donne's phrase, "that subtle knot" which makes us man. The Incarnation is the epitome of the very both-and which Sartre has it in mind to split apart. But it is Sartre's power, even perhaps his greatness, that he can move us with his dream of radical freedom, and make us, for a moment, desire to untie that knot.

No one can doubt in reflecting upon Burke's penetration of these matters that he illuminated the heart of portentous issues, that he played, indeed, a prophetic role. If his revolutionary opponents conceived of the self as an entity separate from, and hidden behind, false appearances, their modern intellectual descendants have professed what, to coin a phrase, we might call a conspiracy theory of reality. Not the appearances of society, they have maintained, but the secret and hypothetical economic or sexual basis is the "reality." Our naive experience of the world, we hear, is deceptive: the truth is behind the appearances, waiting to emerge under the proper auspices, and when the proper key is turned. Marx, for example, conceives of society as it has heretofore existed as a constricting thing, inimical to spontaneity and freedom—the derivation of these terms in Marxist thought should now be familiar—and he argues that all historical societies at best have helped to move toward, at worst have culpably blocked, the emergence of the ultimate "freedom." This we are to enjoy in the future. Marx's "natural man" is the worker—not, of course, actual workers as these are known to us: *they* often have to be dealt with very severely—but a kind of ideal worker. The artificial thing he is to be liberated from is called "capitalism." And its overthrow will bring about a classless and stateless condition (no "roles") in which we will all be "free"—that is to say, liberated from the false appearances which now imprison us. In Marx and Sartre, however, much as in Rousseau, the negation is considerably more vivid than the affirmation. The "chains" are concrete, but the "freedom" abstract and vague. These writers are much more successful in telling us what we must not be than what we ought to be. The "free" man who is to emerge from all entangling alienations remains unknown.

Freudian theory too belongs to this tradition, though it has special characteristics of its own, and though it is deeply suspect from the point of view of the Marxist or the Sartrean. (Sartre's position, of course, is philosophically irreconcilable with Marxism, but that is not the point here. More significant from the point of view of this essay are his heroic attempts to reconcile them in the *Critique de la Raison Dialectique.* Clearly, he recognizes their common tendency.) But Freud's system also conceives of society as repressive. Here "natural man" is the infant, and "civilization" painfully confines him; the pain, however, is to be alleviated not by revolution but by psychoanalysis. In matters of detail, some striking analogies appear—as between the Labor Theory of Value and the psychoanalytical theory which holds culture to be a product of sublimation: both theories describe the valuable as proceeding from a source customarily rated as "low" (the libido and the worker). Freud, to be sure, defected from the revolutionary tradition in not holding out—in explicitly rejecting—the possibility of revolutionary freedom or radical liberation. He said, in *Civilization and Its Discontents,* that we must *endure* our historical pain. (There is an amusing passage somewhere in his correspondence, in which he remarks to a friend that he is "half" a Marxist. Asked for an explanation he replied that Marx had said that history would be marked by wars, revolutions, and vast suffering, but that the process at last would issue in the bliss of the classless society. Freud said he believed only the first part.) From their different points of view, therefore, both Sartre and the Marxists regard Freud's work as a piece of theoretical backsliding and bourgeois bad faith, particularly his positing of an unconscious that cannot be finally transformed, and that, even worse, is *inherited.* The unconscious, in Freud, is recalcitrant, it is connected with the past, it is a *donnée,* a given; it is, in fact, a reactionary idea; and it has, as we will see, some interesting connections with the idea of habit in Burke. Sartre's psychoanalytic theory in contrast, issues in a theoretical denial of the existence of the unconscious.

IV

Earlier in this essay I quoted Rousseau's famous sentence, "Man is born free, but everywhere he is in chains," and the foregoing remarks have constituted a kind of meditation (perhaps, out of filial piety, we should say a reflection), under the auspices of Burke, on the first four words of that sentence: "Man is born free." I would like to turn now to the second part, "but everywhere he is in chains." Because it is precisely those chains, quite differently judged, that Burke's political philosophy in its positive aspect is concerned to protect. There is a much older figure, familiar to everyone, which occurs prominently in Shakespeare, Hooker, Milton, and Pope, among many others, and, like Rousseau's sentence it too, oddly enough, employs the "chain" metaphor. I speak of course of the "chain of being." The older thought conceived of life as arranged in a great hierarchy, with God at the top, the angels below him, man in a "middle state," and the lower forms of life below him. Ontologically, man was thus one "link" in the chain. This older thought also conceived of society as a hierarchy, in which social roles were links, this time in the "chain" of society. In each order, ontological and social, man's identity depended upon his limitations: he was a man, ontologically, and not an angel or an ape; and socially his identity was constituted by his roles. He was not "free"; he was a king or a soldier, or a merchant or a farmer; he belonged to a neighborhood and perhaps to a guild, and so on. The metaphor recognizes that man is not an abstract essence, and, beyond that, connects his "being" with the "chain" —with, in other words, his concrete relations. The metaphor thus *confirms his historical existence:* he is this and not that, he has one identity and not another. Though he certainly enjoys freedoms, constitutional or customary ones, he is not in the radical sense free.

To continue to employ the chain metaphor, we may say that Burke views man as naturally involved with links, and he considers that as those links dissolve, man's identity does too.

One such link in Burke's thought is the link in time. "People will not look forward to posterity," he says in the *Reflections*, "who never look back to their ancestors," and he thinks that men isolated from their past are little better than "flies of a summer." A man's sense of his place in a succession of generations gives him an awareness of being located in a coherent chronology which is not just a sequence of mechanical clock-minutes or calendar days. The past is not anonymous, and so neither will the future be. "Respecting your forefathers," he said to the revolutionaries, "you would have been taught to respect yourselves." Clearly, his position here is correct. We know from the work of modern sociologists and psychologists the role the father plays in the formation of identity, and Freud has a great deal to say about the father's role with regard to ego and superego formation; that is, with the establishing of identity and of principles. The father's own identity, in turn, is the result of his own ancestry. Groups in which the family structure is weak, or the father's sense of identity uncertain, or in which the father is actually likely to desert the family—as in the case of the American Negro at the present time—tend to be characterized by identity "crises" and deep uncertainty about goals and values. As Burke argues repeatedly in the *Reflections*, imaginative awareness of the links between himself and his past prevents the individual from feeling that his existence is arbitrary, or, in the fashionable term, absurd.

Another link, in Burke's thought, is the link to one's contemporaries: to the family, first of all, but extending beyond that to the neighborhood and the region, and thence to the nation and the civilization. Burke characteristically moves outward, from the immediate to the more remote, insisting upon the importance of the group closest to the individual: "To be attached to the subdivision, to love the little platoon we belong to in society, is the first principle (the germ, as it were) of public affections. It is the first *link* [my italics] in the series by which we proceed towards a love to our country, and to mankind." Concerned to protect the various groups to which the individual is most immediately linked, and which help to constitute his identity, Burke characteristically refuses to begin in the abstract, unhistorical way with Mankind or the Brotherhood of Man. Here again Burke anticipated some of the best in modern social thought, and in particular that which may be said to derive from Georg Simmel's *The Web of Group Affiliation*. Simmel argues that a person's identity is formed by the "pattern" of his group affiliation, and that individuality is maintained by variety among the patterns. The more distinctive groups there are—clubs, professional associations, church congregations, and so on—and the more independent they are, the more various will be the patterns of affiliation, and the wider, therefore, will be the possibilities of individuality. Other social scientists—I particularly have in mind the work of Almond and Verba— have pointed out that independent groups, by fostering commitments on levels below the political and the ideological help to defanaticize the political order. They produce a kind of tolerance through complexity of commitment.

Still another link, for Burke, was the link to place. A man's identity is very much involved with his attachment to place, his sense of himself as associated with a geographic locality. The length of time he has lived there has much to do with the strength of such local feeling, as do the distinctive characteristics of the place itself: Burke was attached to the "irregularities" of things, and instinctively rejected a uniformitarian idea of "reason." But the link to place also has much to do with ownership: the man who owns his house is likely to have a deeper imaginative involvement with the neighborhood than one who does not. And here we may observe that Burke, drawing upon Locke, perhaps, but also on his own common sense, put a very high valuation on the protection of property. He did not make that grotesque but familiar distinction between property rights and human rights, but viewed property as a human right. It is not, after all, a vegetable or a mineral right.

In proportion as such links as these were dissolved, Burke

thought, man's identity would be dissolved as well. The links prevented him from floating away psychologically as a kind of angry abstraction, or, to put it another way, from resembling, psychically, those odd modern sculptures, composed of coat hangers, tin cans, and stove bolts. And we may indeed suppose that much of the distinctive pain of modern existence does proceed from the assault that has been carried forward against such links. They sometimes have been weakened or broken, of course, by historical developments of a nonideological character—by industrialization, by urbanization, by the widening possibilities of geographical and social mobility. But the point to be made here is that the bad effects of these developments have been intensified, rather than moderated, by the ideology Burke fought. A moral assault as well has been conducted on these natural links, a moral assault that would seem to have as its intention the isolation of the individual, the reduction of him to a "free" self. Think of the deeply antidomestic implications of progressive pressure for sexual freedom and for relaxed divorce laws and for more abortions. Or the implications of the advocacy, by R. H. Tawney, on moral grounds, of a 100 percent death tax.

V

I would like to turn now to the matter which plays a very important role in Burke's political thought; it is, like the links I have been talking about, a psychological point primarily, but also, like them, it issues in a political principle. For Burke's politics, like any genuinely conservative politics, places a high valuation on *habit*. "Prejudice," he says in the *Reflections*, "renders a man's virtues his habit, and not a series of unconnected acts. Through just prejudice, his duty becomes a part of his nature." This high valuation of habit proceeds from an awareness of the complexity of social life, and from the elementary observation—though Burke was the first to make it; in a sense *he* was the discoverer of the unconscious—that habit performs complex tasks with greater ease and efficiency than does the conscious reason. The daily tasks that we perform most easily (we say, usually, that we perform them "naturally"), from tying our shoes to handling the day's social encounters, we perform habitually. If we were forced to think them through analytically, our activities would come rapidly to a halt. There is a sense, indeed, in which it is really habit, paradoxically enough, that renders one free, since freedom actually is experienced only as a quality of an activity. One is free to do this or that; one is not "free" in an abstract way apart from activity. Castiglione spoke of the courtier's quality of *sprezzatura,* by which he meant his ability to perform his role with ease; through long practice, that is, he could perform it *with ease*— "naturally." And in a similar way Lord Chesterfield advised his son to practice entering a drawing room properly, so that he could do it with ease. A skillful musician is "freer" to play his instrument than a novice. And these examples may be taken as synecdochic of our other activities.

It will be seen, therefore, that considerable advantage will reside in circumstances that permit social roles themselves to be rooted in habit, though no conceivable circumstance of course could render them entirely habitual. And the sort of society advocated throughout Burke's works operates to strengthen the element of habit in social role. Wealth, property, and power are not to pass with great rapidity from one hand to another. He opposed mobility rapid enough to endanger social habit. "I do not hesitate to say," he wrote in the *Reflections,* "that the road to eminence and power from obscure condition ought not to be made too easy, nor a thing too much of course. If rare merit be the rarest of all things, it ought to pass through some sort of probation." In the society thus adumbrated, a man might be a soldier, a merchant, a landholder, or a nobleman, and would expect to remain one. His sense of himself would be that his identity was to a considerable degree "given" rather than willed. But in a more fluid condition of society this is much less the case. Individuals become to a much greater degree free to create themselves, become, in Don Quixote's marvellous phrase, the children of their deeds rather than the children of their actual parents. But to the extent that careers are open to talents, to the extent, that is, that one's social role is the result of one's own talent and will, one's identity must be experienced as *arbitrary*. One might just as well have willed something else. And when identity thus partakes of the quality of the willed and the arbitrary, it is experienced as a kind of mask, or even as a lie. One's roles seem absurd, perhaps even hateful. The self comes to stand in an ironic or antagonistic relationship to all its social manifestations. Perhaps this is one reason why the literature of the Enlightenment, responding at once to actual conditions of increasing social mobility, but also to the ideological assumption that mobility is simply *good,* has as one of its central themes the critique of roles and appearances. Even such ostensibly conservative writers as Swift and Goldsmith shock conventional views by examining society through the wrong end of a telescope or from the perspective of a Chinaman.

Nevertheless, as Burke saw, there is an intimate connection between habit and ease, and this applies as much to society at large as to the individual. The vast majority of its activities, from delivering the mail to running a legislature, go forward smoothly so long as they follow habitual procedures. It is the habits of society—its customs, institutions, and prejudices—that embody the results of its historical experience and enable it to function and preserve its coherence in the present. It was one of Burke's great accomplishments as a political philosopher to show that Hobbes and Locke erred in assigning to reason rather than to habit the function of maintaining the stability of a society. Habit, to be sure, is not an appropriate instrument for dealing with *novel* experience; but on that very account, as Burke saw, a society is better off if it can absorb novelty in small and manageable amounts.

At the beginning of this essay, I spoke of the moral division of the West. We may observe here that that division is less exacerbated even though present, in England and America than in France, say, or Italy. A study entitled *The Civic Culture* which was published recently by Gabriel Almond and Sidney Verba, makes a Burkean point about this. Ideological division is less comprehensive in those two countries precisely because they have not had revolutions, and have attempted, so to speak, to solve their problems *one at a time.* In consequence, such solutions have had less tendency to become features of a comprehensive program. Novelty was absorbed gradually. Almond and Verba, moreover, agree with Burke in viewing revolutionary ideology as the mortal enemy of stable representative government, which depends, they argue, on a number of quite subtle "informal" factors—upon a general atmosphere of trust among the citizens, upon a tradition of political legitimacy, and upon a tacit agreement to "play by the rules." Paradoxically, they argue, representative institutions thrive only in an atmosphere of *limited* political commitment on the part of most people. A political commitment cannot become so powerful that it refuses to subordinate itself to the assumptions about trust, legitimacy, and playing by the rules. Most persuasively, Almond and Verba define the attitude appropriate to the citizen in what they call a "civic culture": he simultaneously does *not* participate in politics and assumes that *he could if he wanted to.* The civic culture thus balances activity and passivity by a norm Almond and Verba call "the potentially active citizen." We may notice, moreover, the contrast between this attitude and the one recommended by civics texts and democratic ideologists, who urge participation and activism.

It is only recently, it seems to me, that scholars and social scientists have recovered anything like Burke's imagination of the delicacy and complexity of our social arrangements. I have in mind the works of Talcott Parsons, Leonard Broom, Robert Merton, and Almond and Verba, among others, as well as the resurgence of interest in those aspects of such older writers as Bagehot and Simmel which bear on the question of the sources of social stability.[1] In society, as Burke put it, "there are often

[1]Merton and Broom, for example, have provided the theoretical framework for a sociology of anger which would be highly relevant to American society at the present time and which in a variety of ways confirms Burke's insights. Our common sense assumption is that non-neurotic anger proceeds from a "grievance" and would disappear if the grievance were "corrected." In his classic study *Suicide,* however, Emil Durkheim showed that feelings

some obscure and almost latent causes, things which appear at first of little moment, on which a very great part of its prosperity or adversity may most essentially depend." And further, that "it is with infinite caution that any man ought to venture upon pulling down an edifice which has answered in any tolerable degree for ages the common purposes of society."

VI

The emphasis in Burke's writing upon man in his historical existence and his denigration of "abstract" speculation have led many to suppose that his thought is pragmatic in character, and informed by no permanent principles. John Morley, for example, who wrote a good short book on Burke during the nineteenth century, was of this opinion. But this view is quite mistaken and ignores the special way in which Burke made use of history.

---

of grievance and deprivation are relative to goals—that, paradoxically, such feelings intensify as possibility is enhanced. Robert Merton moved a step further in the relativization of grievance in his development of "reference group theory." The individual feels deprived, he shows, relative to those with whom he is accustomed to compare himself. The feeling of deprivation flows from the comparison, for it is the comparison which gives the meaning to the objective circumstance (see Merton's great essay "Notes Toward a Theory of Reference Group Behavior" in *Social Theory and Social Structure*). Leonard Broom has added a further dimension to our understanding of social anger by, in effect, internalizing Merton's conception of relative deprivation. Broom applies the theory of relative deprivation to the question of social status. Pointing out that an individual's status is not a monolithic thing, but is made up of manifold components— wealth, education, ethnicity, occupation, neighborhood, and so forth— Broom shows that comparisons can be made between one component and another. An individual might be "high" in one—say education—and "low" in another: perhaps ethnicity. Comparing one with the other, he would feel *relatively* deprived as regards his low component. Consistency among the components of an individual's status produces a better social "fit"; conversely, status inconsistency is generative of social anger. It is worth noticing that rapid mobility—as on the campus today—almost inevitably generates status inconsistency (see Broom's "Social Differentiation and Stratification" in *Sociology Today*, eds. Merton, Broom, and Cottrell).

Burke considered that an "eternal law" is discoverable in history. Men, he says, "attain to the moral reason in their collective experience, they realize and embody it in their stable social relations and organization." For Burke, that is to say, the moral law is eternal and universal, though men cannot, because of their limited reason, apprehend it directly. The moral law does, however, acquire concrete existence and so may be apprehended, historically—in man's stable (and the word is crucial) social arrangements. The stability of those arrangements demonstrates that the moral law is being obeyed. Thus there exists for Burke two sources of our knowledge of the "eternal law"— Christian revelation and our historical experience. From this perspective, novel theories of government and human nature, though they may be the product of brilliant thinkers, can scarcely compare in validity either with revelation or with institutions that have been the creation of many generations. Such novel theories are presumptuous in attempting to set up as rivals of "eternal law," and their inadequacy is proved by the catastrophes that result when they are used as principles of government.

When the statesman acts in conformity with the eternal law, Burke thinks, *tranquility* is fostered in society. Running through his work is a vocabulary indicative of a set of fundamental polarities. On the one hand are the qualities to be desired in society: stability, public tranquility, peace, quiet, order, harmony, regularity, unity, decorum. Opposed to these are the symptoms of social disease: discord, contradiction, confusion, violence, excess, the need for coercion. The task of the statesman is to promote "tranquility."

The attitudes and doctrines that informed the French Revolution, Burke thinks, make tranquility impossible. Asserting against an actual society rights derived from a mythical state of nature, and celebrating a freedom equally mythical—"man is born free"—the theorists wielded a weapon to which any society would be vulnerable. Against such demands, he said, "no agreement is binding; these admit no temperament and no compromise; anything withheld is so much fraud and injustice." On the other hand, the rights Burke was defending were rights he had known as historical facts. It was those rights that he put in the path of a permanent shattering of tranquility, a permanent revolution.

Of course, the belief that tranquility is man's social goal has by no means been a matter of universal agreement. There are those, and Burke knew them well, who delight in agitation; there are literary and intellectual *voyeurs* of revolution; there are temperaments for which, as Burke said, it "is a war or a revolution or it is nothing." There are those who, finally, agree with Goethe that the achievement of tranquility represents the defeat of the human spirit. Faust, that symbol of much, at least, in the modern temper, is never to say to the moment, "*Verweile doch, du bist so schön*" ("Stay, thou art so fair."). Only a perpetual dissatisfaction, for the Faustian spirit, is truly human. Faust represents the deep antiontologicality which is, as we have seen, one feature of the modern mind—its hatred of what *is*, of the given: its impatience with what it regards as "irrational" differences of nationality, social class, race, or sex (modernity is coeducational, as, indeed, was Faust). And of course it is differences that define particular existence—this, and not that. Yet in opposition to this temper, there is another and older sense of things, an alternative to the restless spirit of transformation, and which most certainly is willing to say to the moment, to the world, "Stay, thou art so fair." Do not change: *Be*. In his splendid brief study of Piero della Francesca, Bernard Berenson speaks of a quality to be found in many of the greatest portraits that date from before the nineteenth century. A kind of silence surrounds those figures, he says; they do not gesture or grimace at us from the canvas. A portrait by Piero or Botticelli, Velasquez or Murillo, Reynolds or Gainsborough, seems to say that the existence of its subject in no way appeals to *our* presence before the canvas. Those dukes and cardinals and princesses and statesmen take their existence as a matter of course. They are *there*, self-contained; their being is concrete, actual, accepted. And it may be that sense of being which really is in harmony with the deepest intuitions of the West about the proper mode of the human, for it is that sense which comes to us from the oldest and most continuous of our moral traditions—from Plato and Aristotle, Cicero, Aquinas, Hooker, Elyot, Samuel Johnson, Burke; and so, in politics, it is to Burke that we logically turn as we seek to reconstitute that tradition in the teeth of another revolution.

Part Five

The Spiritual Crisis

I have quoted Voegelin as saying that somewhere along the line it has even been whispered by his critics that he is a Christian. The Christianity of T. S. Eliot was an acknowledged thing quite a while ago, after he had attained an irrevocable reputation, but his critics tended to put it down as one of those larger mannerisms that went with his whole way of life as an Anglophile, and anyway, hasn't Christianity become, as Canon Bernard Iddings Bell once remarked, *"merely a pastime, preferred by some to golf or canasta"*?

But when his *Notes Toward the Definition of Culture* appeared, it became clear to his critics that he had something very concrete in mind in stating his preference for Christianity, that, far from thinking of it as of purely subjective importance, he held religion to be essential to the flowering of any culture. He held, indeed, that where religion is excluded, so is true culture; that such cultures as attempt to endure without religion are undefinable; and that they are most emphatically undesirable. T. S. Eliot was a poet, not an exegete. And it helps in understanding him to think of religion as meaning to him, among other things, the incarnation of the Word—even as, to the historian, spirit is the incarnation in history. Eliot's expressive sense of the horrors of metaphysical desolation, with which, through a single poem, he scarred an entire generation early in his life, suggests also the hunger he felt for the spiritual consolation that finally he took from Christianity.

The essay I have selected from Whittaker Chambers is not altogether typical, because the major part of it is written in the didactic mode with which Chambers was uncomfortable (he did not like schoolmasterish idiom). But in this essay, published posthumously as a part of the collection *Cold Friday*, he felt the need to relate, with A-B-C directness, the phenomenon of Communism to the spiritual desolation of the West; and he did so simply, without ornament, not so much pleading with the reader to understand, for it was a part of his understanding that the reader would not do so, as advising the reader that it was part of the author's witness to say it as he understood it, and that this is the way it was.

Then, suddenly—and completely—the legendary Chambers surfaces, and the magic begins to flow. The keenest human understanding, reflected in the numinous prose, baptized in tragedy . . . He had received a letter from an old friend, an intelligent and devout Christian, who wrote him: *"The Epiphany has fizzled."*

"I found this a lapidary line: 'The Epiphany has fizzled.' Yet, when the amusing novelty has worn off, it is seen to express chiefly a disconsolate exasperation. It is a kind of continental sadness, like the wail of a locomotive whistle, rushing off (where?) in the night—haunting, yet not true music, a very American sound, just as the locomotive whistle is (or was) perhaps the most American of sounds. . . .

" 'The one essential condition of human existence,' " Chambers quotes Stefan Trofimovitch, a character in Dostoevsky's *The Possessed, " 'is that man should always be able to bow down before something infinitely great. If men are deprived of the infinitely great, they will not go on living and will die of despair.' It is for this that we crave reality. . . . 'I want to know why,' [Sherwood Anderson] asked. I want to know why. It is*

*for this we seek a little height, and because of this we do not
feel it too high a price to pay if we cannot reach it crawling
through a lifetime on our hands and knees, as a wounded man
sometimes crawls from a battlefield, if only so as not to die as
one more corpse among so many corpses.*

*". . . And if the old paths no longer lead to a reality that en-
ables men to act with meaning, if the paths no longer seem to
lead anywhere—have become a footworn, trackless maze, or,
like Russian roads, end after a few miles of ambitious pavement leading nowhere but into bottomless mud and swallowing distance—men will break new paths, though they must
break their hearts to do it. They will burst out somewhere, even
if such bursting-out takes the form of aberration. For to act in
aberration is at least more like living than to die of futility, or
even to live in that complacency which is futility's idiot twin.
We all know those grand aberrations of our time. We have
plenty of names for them. . . . But all the aberrations have one
common cause, and point, in the end, in one direction."*

Albert Jay Nock's essay, "Isaiah's Job," is surely the best expression of a pessimist's serenity in modern times. The thesis—
that it is only The Remnant who understand, but that they
most surely do understand, and hear every uncorrupted word
that you utter—makes Remnant-serving a most honorable and
useful vocation. A close friend of Nock's, the aforementioned
Bernard Iddings Bell, once told me that Nock had written this
essay whole from a sermon he had heard Bell preach; but
never mind, said Bell, the plagiarism doesn't matter, it does
matter that the idea was so superbly set down.

Frederick Wilhelmsen, professor of philosophy and author of
The Metaphysics of Love, closes this volume with an essay, one
part history, one part poetry, one part an act of devotion, which
I reproduce here believing that no volume on conservatism in
America should omit an example of felt Christianity, an example of how it feels to believe those ancient religious axioms
which are, for so many, the intellectual and spiritual basis of

conservatism. Wilhelmsen is not satisfied to praise religion. He sees it as Chesterton did, and he is the only American writing today who combines Chesterton's powers of historical discrimination and religious animation—the mystic enthusiasm of the religion of joy, despising the accretions of puritanical dourness, straining to adore: and succeeding.

And as an epilogue, a personal letter, the final letter, from Whittaker Chambers, dispatched a few weeks before his death.

22 The Direct Glance

Whittaker Chambers

I speak with a certain urgency both because I believe that history is closing in on this people with a speed which, in general they do not realize or prefer not to realize, and because I have a sense that time is closing in on me so that, at this point, I do not know whether or not I shall be given time to complete what I seek to say. I feel, too, a sense of my own inadequacy in many ways. I cannot claim to speak with the authority of many whose learning is greater, whose competency is certified by years of devout effort in special acreages of the mind. I may not claim for the larger meanings of what I shall say: This is truth. I say only: This is my vision of truth; to be checked and rechecked (as I myself continually check and recheck it) against the data of experience. Every book, like every life, is issued ultimately, not to those among whom it appears and lives, but to the judgment of time, which is the sternest umpire. What serious man could wish for his life or his book a judgment less final?

I write as a man who made his way back from a special experience of our time—the experience of Communism. I believe the experience to be the central one, for whichever side prevails the outcome will be shaped decisively by what Communism is and meant to be, and by the conditions that made it possible and made possible the great conflict. *Man's Fate* (or *La Condition Humaine*, to use its French title, which fixes its

From Whittaker Chambers, *Cold Friday* (New York: Random House, 1964), pp. 67–88. Copyright © 1964 by Esther Chambers. Reprinted by permission of Random House, Inc., and Brandt & Brandt.

meaning more clearly) seems to me one of the few books*
which have placed a surgical finger upon the problem of man
in this century—the problem of the terms on which man can
wrest some semblance of his human dignity (some would say:
save his soul) in a mechanizing world, which is, by force of the
same necessity, a revolutionary world. After he had read *Witness*, André Malraux, the author of *Man's Fate*, wrote me: "You
are one of those who did not return from Hell with empty
hands." I did not answer him. How is one man to say to another: "Great healing spirit"? For it is not sympathy that the
mind craves, but understanding of its purposes. I do not know,
it is not even for me to say, what value may be set on those
scraps and tatters of experience that I brought back with me.
They, too, are issued for time to judge. I do not know how they
may serve, or whether they have any power to prevail against
the many voices in the West today that say, "These are scraps
and tatters," and deny them any further meaning.

In *Witness* I sought to make two points which seemed to me
more important than the narrative of unhappy events which,
time has compelled me to conclude, chiefly interested most
readers. The first point had to do with the nature of Communism and the struggle against it. The crux of this matter is the
question whether God exists. If God exists, a man cannot be a
Communist, which begins with the rejection of God. But if
God does not exist, it follows that Communism, or some suitable variant of it, is right.

More follows. A man is obligated, if he seeks to give any
effect to his brief life, to tear away all mystery that darkens or
distorts, to snap all ties that bind him in the name of an untruth, to push back all limiting frontiers to the end that man's
intelligence may be free to realize to the fullest of its untrammeled powers a better life in a better world. I did not spell this

*Some others: Arthur Koestler's *Darkness at Noon* and *The Invisible
Writing*; Czeslaw Milosz's *The Captive Mind*; the Abbé Henri de Lubac's
Drama of Atheist Humanism; Manes Sperber's *The Burned Bramble*,
whose French title, *Et le Buisson Devient Cendre* (*And the Burning Bush
Sank to Ash*), again seems to me more meaningful than the English
rendering.

out in *Witness*. "Be sure that nothing can be told to any who divined it not before." It is pointless and, indeed, impossible to press anything upon those who are unprepared for it. I set up the proposition and left it to those who could to draw the inference. Precisely, the enlightened community of the West, as could be expected, drew them first. That proposition was, in my opinion, the chief cause of the lightnings that darted at *Witness* and still play about it. They darted not only from the political Left. In time, elements of the Right began to sense that a question had been posed to them. That proposition questioned the whole materialism of the West, and the West is heavily materialist. It is, in fact, this materialism that Communism constantly appeals to and manipulates, not in terms of any easily defined political lines of Left or Right but in terms of a common investment in a materialist view of life, which an important section of the West shares with Communism, and which Communism has simply carried to its utmost logical conclusion in thought and action. This common interest in a common materialism—which nevertheless differs in the West and in Communism in form, degree, qualifications, and reservations—is the grain of truth and sincerity in the West's resentment against Communist "witch hunts." For it feels an affinity and a respect for a materialism which it finds liberating to the mind, while it feels itself unfairly threatened or hurt because reprisals against Communism inevitably touch it as a sympathetic form, though it does not share Communism's political aims. This is a distinction which the non-Communist materialism of the West does not trust the anti-Communists to grasp or respect—the more so since, in action, the line is frequently blurred, so that even when the materialism of the West is assertively anti-Communist it often serves Communist ends.

From this proposition—that the heart problem of Communism is the problem of atheism—followed the second proposition which I set up in *Witness*, also without developing its conclusions. This proposition implied that the struggle of the West with Communism included its own solution. That is to say, in the course of its struggle with Communism, the West would develop or recover those resources (in the main, spiritual and moral) which it held to constitute its superiority to Communism, or in the struggle it would go under. Going under might, I suppose, take one of two forms. The West might simply lose the war in political or physical terms. But I also allowed for the fact that the West might win the war in such terms and still lose it, if the taxing necessities of the conflict brought the West to resemble what it was struggling against, *i.e.*, Communism. A turn in this direction has been perfectly visible in the West for several decades.

The margin of success in the struggle, it seemed to me, lay less in an equality of technology and weapons (so long as weapons paced themselves approximately) than in certain factors within Communism which are little appreciated in the West. These factors were also spiritual and moral even though they expressed indirectly contrary terms, even though Communism expressly denied man's spirit and morality as the West uses the words. These resources I believed to be peculiarly inherent in the Russian Communist Party.

For scale, complexity, and depth, the struggle between Communism and the West is a conflict without any precedent of human record. Other conflicts have unsettled continents. The rise and sweep of the Mongol hordes comes at once to mind and is often cited as a parallel. This was a great surface fire, fed by the dry rot of all the lands it swept, having no plan and purpose beyond plunder and the raw play of ferocious energies, dying out as those purposeless energies died out, and leaving upon history little more than the literal ashes of its passage and a haunting memory of heaps of human bones. It is most like a catastrophe in nature, hurricane or flood; and has, in fact, no parallel at all. Communism first of all asserts a purpose and a plan. Both feed a will to victory that operates on as many multitudinous levels as life is capable of. There is no human creature living in any region so remote that he is not, in some way, affected by that force which each one, sooner or later, faces in what Sir Thomas Browne called "the areopagy and dark tribunal of our hearts." For the distinctive feature of Communism is not that it threatens all continents as no other force has ever done or even that it seeks a radical readjustment of all societies. Its distinctive feature is that it seeks a molecular rearrangement of the human mind. It promotes not only a new world. It promotes a new kind of man. The physical revolutions which it once incited and now imposes, and which largely distract our attention, are secondary to this internal revolution which challenges each man in his mind and spirit. Thus, the phenomenon of Communism is closest in the experience of the West to the rise of Christianity and its gradual transformation of the mind of the ancient world. Hence our puzzlement before the discrepancy between the ends of Communism and its visible personnel, which more or less reflects the bafflement of Pliny in his well-known letter to Trajan about the early Christians. Hence our large-handed contempt for Communists wherever they do not yet hold political power, which almost echoes Lucian's remarks about the Christians in the second century A.D.: "They waste their days, running from Romanism to ism, and imagine that they are achieving great things in treating their friends to children's fairy tales. In the squares, where they all shout the same thing in the same way, they are eaten up with envy. From their dirt, their lousiness, their mendacity, they argue with conviction that they are called to redeem the world."

For the war of Communism with the rest of mankind is first of all a war of ideas. In that war, Communism rejects few means of any kind, or none (its system of ideas justifies this practice). But its first assault is always upon the minds of men; and it is from the conversion of minds that it advances to the conquest of mass bodies and their living space. Each advance enables Communism to expedite conversion by political control since, for those whom it controls, Communism has become the one reality. The West (whatever value the captive may give that word) becomes at most a hope, but a hope that has been defeated (that is why the captives are captive); and it is a hope continuously deferred. Hope deferred not only maketh the

heart sick; it stirreth profound suspicions that there is something radically wrong with it. In this case, it stirs a suspicion
that exactly to the degree that Communism is felt to be evil and
monstrous in its effects, there must be something organically
wrong with the West that is unequal to prevailing against a
power so conspicuously condign.

This failure to grasp that the basic struggle with Communism
is a struggle of ideas has led, in the West, to the failure to
grasp the signal fact of the conflict. That fact is that Communism, which in all material ways has been for decades weak to
a degree almost unimaginable to the average American, has
rallied strength and made its staggering advances precisely at
the expense of that West which is in all material ways overwhelmingly superior. With this goes the boundless complacency of the West in supposing that the struggle will be decided
in its favor by material means. I cannot remember a time when
there was not a lively conviction in the West that the Communist state was about to fall by reason of its own malevolence
and inadequacy. This stems from the easily observable fact that
Communism is a philosophy of thoroughgoing materialism,
brutal in its practical manifestations, because it denies the sanc-
tity of the individual in terms of the self-interest of the community, which, in practice, is the arbitrary will of the shifting
consortia that run the state. Communism is a philosophy of
brute materialism. But if we ask: "What is the philosophy of
the West?" is there not a certain embarrassment? What *is* the
philosophy of the West? In a war for men's minds, what is it
that we are offering whose inherent force is so compulsive that
it instantly seizes on the imagination of men and incites them
to choose it in preference to Communism? In the name of what
do we expect them to rise and overthrow Communism which
can be done only by an effort of incalculable suffering—and not
the suffering of faceless millions (as we so easily think of such
things), but the suffering of this father or that mother who love
their children whose lives, rather than their own, are the first
sacrifice in so one-sided a conflict? Is it Christianity? There are
millions of Christians in the Communist Empire whose Western

populations are overwhelmingly Christian. Some 40 million must be practicing Catholics. I remember no appeals to the Christians in the name of their common faith with the West. Individual freedom is often mentioned. It is well, perhaps, to remember that freedom, in our understanding of the term, has been restricted largely to the United States and the fringe of Western Europe. In the rest of the world it has no accepted currency, and over large areas of Europe the Second World War and the revolutions that preceded it utterly destroyed the conditions of freedom and raised strong questions in many minds whether or not freedom is practicable in the conditions of our times. *"Der Fahneneid,"* said General Groner to the Kaiser in 1918, suggesting that his swift abdication would be well-viewed, *"ist jetzt nur eine Idee"* (The oath on the colors is now only an idea).

Moreover, these people are not children. They have the acute realism of those who live daily under impending tank treads. The satellite populations can look westward and see that individual freedom is constantly being whittled down in the West in the interest of centralizing government, and they are perfectly competent to infer that this is the result of the play of the same basic forces and factors that have destroyed their own freedom.

We tend to forget—life has been, in general, so good to us, we are so appalled by life under Communism—that thousands of acute intelligences in the East are also peering back at us. We tend to forget what spectacle we present to those eyes which weigh us with the close harshness of men facing awful alternatives. It is not necessary to particularize that spectacle here. But if we think about it a moment, think about it as those others may see it, adding in their sense that our failure fixed their fate on them, is it strange if they do not find the spectacle that the West presents overly reassuring?

When, in History, there appear in swarms such commanding and ferocious types as the Communist, and his bastard brother, the Fascist, our habit of viewing them first of all with aversion, a habit of mind very widespread, especially in the United States, is no longer helpful. The moral judgment may be justified. But is largely pointless. It condemns us to see them continually in terms of effect instead of cause. We limit ourselves to seeing the effects that the Communist, for example, creates. We keep pretty carefully away from the causes that create the Communist. This resolute flight from causes, and resolute dwelling only in effects leads us into the plight of a man in a maze or a squirrel in a revolving cage. We go round and round; we never come out anywhere. It leads, in thought, to a defeating confusion. In practice, it leads to some pretty extravagant hypocrisy. The spectacle of the West encouraging cultural exchanges with a Communism, which in the next breath it condemns as a barbaric and criminal force, is, to say the least of it, puzzling. It is sometimes argued that with respect to Communism, the West is merely stupid. But stupidity isn't good enough.

Surely it is not too sweeping to say that there is nothing secret about Communism. For decades, its motives, purposes, and specific strategies have been explicitly stated by Communists themselves, and freely disseminated in the West. Even its guiltiest secrets are known in wearisome detail. Seldom in history can the actions of any cause have been subjected to so minute a picking-over in the very course of their occurrence. It makes not the slightest practical difference. On one hand, the disclosures lead to a hue of moral outrage. On the other hand, the West continues to deal with the Communist center as if this were not true. Thus, the West itself engages with respect to Communism in a kind of double-think which it supposes to be one of Communism's distinctive faculties. This singular behavior is paced by another even more singular. This is the cherishing of a notion, constantly blighted, ever ready to flower anew, that Communism and Communists are about to undergo a change of mind (or "heart") so that henceforth they will no longer act like Communists; they will be like us.

Yet we have seen this manifestation occur on a mass scale more than once. When it does, we enter the realm of illusion.

There is a clinical name for it, but it is not stupidity. Stupidity cannot explain; such stupidity has to be explained itself. This persistent flight into fantasy and resistance to reality, accompanied by an emotional play like the boiling of an overheated engine, suggest much more the energy, now dogged, now frantic, with which certain patients sometimes resist knowing the facts of their condition and its causes because they find the facts too painful to bear. A suspicion stirs that we resist knowing about Communism because we do not wish to know about ourselves; that, in fact, we need scarcely fear Communism if we did not secretly fear ourselves.

This suspicion is fortified by an arresting fact, one which requires no special knowledge to see (it is inescapable), and one, incidentally, that is not often referred to. That fact is that the Communist Empire, born in chaos, backward and weak beyond the imagination of the average man of the West in all the resources that make a modern industrial state powerful—this desperately weak state has, nevertheless, in the course of four decades, rallied its strength, organized a modern industry almost from scratch, and possessed itself of a third of the earth's land surface and hundreds of millions of new population precisely at the expense of the West which, in all material ways, is enormously superior to it and whose survival it now challenges. Moreover, the fall-out of its influence affects millions beyond its official frontiers.

There is a further fact. Communism has achieved this fear at the expense of a West which is not only vastly superior in material, but a West which believes itself to be vastly superior in moral and spiritual resources. It is popular to dismiss Communism as a grubby materialist philosophy imposed by force on slaves whom we expect, sometimes indifferently, sometimes hopefully (we are in one of our hopeful phases) to revolt and overthrow it. But what is the philosophy of the West? In the name of what are we inviting the slaves of the East to revolt? We speak of freedom. Every day that the Communist Empire endures, the word becomes more meaningless for millions.

It is the business of the Communist theoretician, with his eye on the whole sweep of history, to try to assess the relationship of forces in the world at every given moment, to calculate their rate of drift and general direction as a guide to action—in order to take advantage of the constantly changing relationships of force to promote a revolution which the Communist holds to be beneficent and, in some degree, fated.

This process in history, and this view of it, Communists call dialectical materialism (or, in that Communist shorthand that we commonly call jargon, Diamat). It is dialectic because it deals with quantities of force in motion, sometimes violent, sometimes gradual. It is called materialism because the Communist mind, like the scientific mind, rejects any supernatural factor in his observation of experience. In short, God is rigorously excluded from the equations of changing force in which the Communist mind tirelessly seeks to grasp, to express, and to act on history at any and every moment.

To try to explain Communism and the Communist while ignoring dialectical materialism is like trying to explain a man's actions while leaving out the chief clue to his mind and his motives and general viewpoint. Dialectical materialism is the central fact of Communism. Every Communist is a dialectical materialist. Ultimately, he cannot be understood in any other terms. This does not mean that all Communists are consistent or successful dialecticians. There are millions of Communists in the world and they show the same gradations of intelligence and character as millions of anybody else. There are millions of Christians, too, of whom only a comparative handful are theologians (Communists say: theoreticians). The mass of Christians is held together by a faith in what suffices to explain to them the meaning of their lives and history, although even highly intelligent communicants may be quite vague about the doctrines of their faith, or even specific articles of it. This is made possible because the center of efficacy of their faith is the Cross, using that symbol in its most inclusive sense. The Cross makes them one in faith even though at thinner fringes of Christendom the efficacy of the Cross is questioned or tends to fade. In much the same way, dialectical materialism is the effective force of Communism, and even when understanding is weak or lacking, it operates as a faith which explains satisfactorily to millions of Communists the meaning of life and history—reality, as Communists say. By this they always mean reality in a state of flux, usually violent. Dialectical materialism is the crux of Communism, and not to understand this means never truly to understand the Communist. It is one reason why the West still does not understand the Communist despite the heaps of other highly accurate data about him. Such data remain extraneous, almost irrelevant, because they miss, or by-pass, the central fact which makes the Communist a Communist.

This is the fact which absolutely sunders the mind of the Communist from the traditional mind of the West—which makes him in the mass a new breed in history. For our breeds, in this sense, are defined by the view we hold, unconsciously or not, of the world and its meaning, and the meaning of our lives in it. Obviously, a breed of men who hold that everything is in violent flux and change, moving by laws and in a pattern inherent in matter, and having nothing to do with God—obviously, that breed of men is different in kind from the rest of mankind. It is closest, in our time, to the viewpoint of the scientist for whom a simple, solid chair represents a form of energy whose particles, seemingly solid and commonplace, are in fact in violent motion. This, incidentally, rather than the "progressive" elements in Communism which are usually brought forward in such cases, is the instant point of appeal which Communism so often has for the scientists of the West. They feel in Communism the force of a faith based on a material reality which more or less matches their own vision of reality. It is an abstruse view, and the scientists who hold it are lonely men, since the masses of the West cannot possibly understand or sympathize with what the scientists are talking about. The intelligent Communist knows exactly what they are talking about though he may know little or nothing about abstruse physics. Similarly, the scientist may know little or nothing about the niceties of dialectical materialism. Yet each senses that the other's basic view of reality is much the same. The affinity is strong.

In the years when Communism was advancing successfully against the West there were those who believed that its disruptive power was its power to manipulate a Fifth Column composed of non-Soviet Communists, sympathizers, fellow travellers, dupes, opportunist politicians, hitchhiking with Communism as they would in any other vehicle that seemed to be going part of their way—in short, the kind of debris and dust that almost anything with sufficient gravitational pull attracts and keeps whirling around it. I held that such elements, while dangerous, were not Communism's chief power in the West. I held that power to be something else—the power of Communism to manipulate responsive sections of the West to check, counteract, paralyze, or confuse the rest. Those responsive sections of the West were not Communist, and never had been. Most of the minds that composed them thought of themselves as sincerely anti-Communist. Communism manipulated them, not in terms of Communism, but in terms of the shared historical crisis—peace and social justice being two of the most workable terms. They were free to denounce Communism and Communists (and also anti-Communists) after whatever flourishes their intellectual innocence or arrogance might choose. Communism asked no more. It cared nothing, at this point, about motives. It cared about results.

Unlike Communism, the West held no unified solution for the crisis. In face of the crisis, part of the West reacted with inertia—inertia, in the simple terms of the physics primer, that is, the tendency of a body to remain at rest or in a straight line of motion. But the responsive section offered a solution for the crisis. This solution, whatever differences it assumed from place to place and time to time, whatever disguises political expediency or preference draped or phrased it in, was always the same solution. It was the socialist solution. Derived, as doctrine, from the same source—the historical insights of Karl Marx—the socialist solution differed from the Communist solution chiefly in political methods. One difference consisted in the slower rate of speed at which socialism proposed to apply its solution. Another difference concerned the kind and degree of coercion that socialism would apply to impose its solution. In practice, no socialist government had yet pushed its solution to the point where full coercion must come into play. Therefore, this difference had not yet stood the test of reality. Otherwise, between the end solution that socialism and Communism both hold in view for mankind—the matured planned economy of the future—the difference was so slight that it would be difficult to slip a razor blade between them.

It was no innate charm of socialism that made millions in the West espouse it, just as it was no innate charm of Communism that recruited its millions. It was the force of the historical crisis that made masses of men entertain the socialist solution, which, in fact, sundered the West. It divided the West as a whole against itself. And it divided against itself every nation that might still qualify, in a diminished world, to the rank of great power. In fact, it split almost every great nation into almost equal halves, as major sections more and more tended to show. Hence the intensity of feeling, the swollen pain as around any unhealing fracture.

The divisions in the West passed beyond matters of opinion. The arguments had all been made; the returns were in. The division of the West was organic; it turned upon different breeds of men. The sundering point was a choice between political liberty and economic security. One breed of man held freedom to be the greatest good to the point where regimentation seemed to him the touch of spiritual death, so that he would prefer to die rather than live under the socialist state. The other breed of man held social security, and hence regimentation, to be a simple necessity if he were to live at all in a modern world. The difference had nothing to do with logic of argument. The difference had to do with breeds of men. One or the other principle would determine the future of the West. One would be paramount—one or the other; both could not be. It was increasingly clear that those who held the latter

view were in the majority. But when masses of men are so
evenly and fiercely divided, the readjustment of reality can
scarcely occur without an earthquake, even if the revolution
takes a form no more violent than mass balloting. . . .

I received a letter from a close friend of many years standing
who is, as I once wrote of him to Rebecca West, "a Conservative by cell-structure." Though he talks about the matter only
among intimates, he is an intensely religious man. This religion,
too, forms a family climate. He and his family lived actively
within their church, decades before church-going became a
renewed fashion among us. My friend, though highly literate,
is simply devout. In my experience, this combination of high
intelligence and devotion is—though the fact may be somewhat dismaying to face—rather unusual.

It was this man who wrote me as follows. "The rector of our
church took a reading of the so-called rebirth of religion in the
U.S., which he thought had started about 1950 . . . 'The Epiphany has fizzled,' was the way he phrased it. This is sad, but
the 'rebirth' was a phoney to begin with." My friend then men-
tions, as a peculiar token of the failure, the name of a celebrated divine, the author of immensely popular books of a kind
of fatuous Couéism, which he turns out in such quantity that
he may almost be said to farrow rather than to write them.

I found this a lapidary line: "The Epiphany has fizzled." Yet,
when the amusing novelty has worn off, it is seen to express
chiefly a disconsolate exasperation. It is a kind of continental
sadness, like the wail of a locomotive whistle, rushing off
(where?) in the night—haunting, yet not true music, a very
American sound, just as the locomotive whistle is (or was) perhaps the most American of sounds. But for any depth of meaning, "The Epiphany has fizzled" isn't good enough.

A decade or so ago the eminent French Catholic theologian,
Father Henri de Lubac, published a book called *The Drama of
Atheist Humanism,* a study of rare understanding of certain of
the great questioners or lay-sages of our age—Kierkegaard,
Feuerbach, Marx, Nietzsche, Dostoevsky.

Father de Lubac quotes a letter of Jacques Rivière to the poet Paul Claudel, written in 1907 (when incidentally my generation was about seven years old; and such dates are meaningful for those of us who have survived so long into this frightful age). "I see," Rivière wrote, "that Christianity is dying. . . . We do not know why, above our towns, there still rise those spires which are no longer the prayer of any one of us. We do not know the meaning of those great buildings (*i.e.,* religious institutions—Tr.) which today are surrounded by railroad stations and hospitals, and from which the people themselves have chased the monks. And on the graves, we do not know what is made manifest by those stucco crosses, frosted over with an execrable art."

"And, no doubt," says Father de Lubac, "Claudel's reply to that cry of anguish was a good one: 'Truth is not concerned with how many it persuades.' "

Then Father de Lubac goes on to cite "an almost daily experience" which shows that "certain of the harshest reproaches made against us come both from our worst adversaries and from men of good will. The tone, the intention, the inspiration are profoundly different. But the judgments come to much the same thing. An astonishing and significant convergence." There is more. Father de Lubac goes on to another experience, one that bears directly on the so-called rebirth of religion among us and thrusts close to the heart of an instant problem. It is the plight of those seekers who, in deepest sincerity, approach the churches in a need and craving, often desperate, for truth and a haven. They approach, but then they hesitate and stand still. In the end they go no farther.

There follows an eloquent passage. "Among those who thus disappoint us," says Father de Lubac, "some of the clearest-sighted and most spiritual find themselves torn by conflicting feelings. We see them ravished [*seduits*] by the Gospel whose teachings seem to them still full of force and novelty; drawn to the Church in which they sense a more than human reality and the sole institution capable of bringing, together with a remedy for our ills, the solution to the problem of our destiny.

But, on the threshold, see what stops them: the spectacle that we make, we, the Christians of today, the Church that we are, that spectacle repels them. . . . It is not that they condemn us violently. It is, rather, that they cannot take us seriously."

This needs no commenting on by me. But I submit that it needs long and careful reflecting on, and that this is inescapable wherever the question of the rebirth of religion, which is raised in general statistically, must be weighed qualitatively. For here is raised a question which lies at the heart of our conflict with Communism. The question is: What is the West's answer to Communism? It is pretty clear, I think, that the more or less anonymous thousands who yearly flee Communism (about whom and whose later fate we rather prefer not to think unless we are compelled to) are fleeing a misery, rather than embracing an alternative idea. Though it works out of necessity in rather different ways, much the same is true of many former Communists whose defections or later testimony makes a week's news. It is the wretchedness of life for them under Communism which impels them; it is Communism's failure in their terms that drives them to the West. This is clearly not the same thing as an answer to Communism. The lack of such an answer defeats our propaganda at the core—and the word "propaganda" used in this sense, is itself suggestive. By an answer I mean a rallying idea, capable of being grasped by, and so overmastering, millions of men of the most diverse kinds because its single force persuades that it brings "together with a remedy for their ills, the solution to the problem of their destiny." In the West, taken as a whole, this idea does not exist. We know this whenever the problem arises, as it does daily, to the people of Asia and Africa, for example—a sense-making notion of what the West stands for, so that they quickly grasp it, and it stirs them to a willingness to die for it, rather than live for any other. Does such an idea exist? Let us not deceive ourselves, but answer truthfully: "It does not exist." "But what about Freedom?" you say. You are saying it to millions who never have been free in your sense, and grasp chiefly that they are free to starve. They will reach quicker for an idea that promises them an end to hunger, even if they suspect that the promise is over-blown (for even the most primitive starvelings are, in general, not fools; they are merely not sophisticated in your terms; but they catch on quickly).

So long as such a central rallying idea does not exist, we in the West are likely to go on defending frontiers, even if we are no longer losing provinces. And that regardless of how elaborately the frontiers are manned and weaponed. Maginot Lines are butts to ideas.

On the eve of our time, Stefan Trofimovitch saw our problem clearly enough, even though, as sometimes happens, it took him a pointless lifetime to reach the insight and his last strength to frame it: "The one essential condition of human existence is that man should always be able to bow down before something infinitely great. If men are deprived of the infinitely great, they will not go on living and will die of despair." It is for that we crave reality, for the infinitely great may not be on any less terms. It remains otherwise lies and illusion. It is for that we crave a little height, to reach some notion of the meaning of our reality, and so as not to die of despair. So that we can rise above the paralyzing mood of our time, which we feel as a sense that none of us can really do anything; that things are merely going to happen to us.

If the voice says: "But that is what men have always craved," we will answer: "Yes, always craved." But the problem presents itself in different terms to different generations. Yet the root problem remains always the same. It is: On what terms consistent with their reality men can have God, or whether they must seem for a time even not to have Him. When, also on the eve of our time, another voice cried: "God is dead," the unthinkingly shallow heard in that cry the wildest blasphemy, and the unthinkingly intelligent heard it as a stupid promise of emancipation. But Nietzsche was only reading aloud the transcript of his time. That time comes whenever men remake God so much in their own image that He no longer corresponds to reality. For, of course, God never dies. The generations simply seek how they can have Him in terms of their reality. You cannot offer to the half-starved millions of Asia God as a sole solution to their plight, with the best of them turning away with pity for your stupidity if not with contempt for your dishonesty. But something else is also true: You cannot replace God with Point Four. If you fed the starving millions four square meals a day and studded their primitive lands with automated factories, men would still die of despair.

"I want to know why," one of the most native of our voices [Sherwood Anderson] asked in a line that rises out of all else he did and said because it sums up all the rest. I want to know why. It is for this we seek a little height, and because of this we do not feel it too high a price to pay if we cannot reach it crawling through a lifetime on our hands and knees, as a wounded man sometimes crawls from a battlefield, if only so as not to die as one more corpse among so many corpses. Happy is he who finds any height, however lowly.

That craving for the infinitely great starts with the simplest necessity. It is the necessity to know reality in order, by acting on it directly, to find the measure of men's meaning and stature in that single chance of some seven decades that is allotted them to find it out in. Since, by reason of the irrevocable briefness of that span, life is inherently tragic, the effort to wrest meaning from reality is tragic, too, and means always the necessity to rise above reality at any cost. But it is not the commonplace of tragedy, it is anything that blocks their freedom to enact it meaningfully that kills men with despair. And if the old paths no longer lead to a reality that enables men to act with meaning, if the paths no longer seem to lead anywhere—have become a footworn, trackless maze, or, like Russian roads, end after a few miles of ambitious pavement, leading nowhere but into bottomless mud and swallowing distance—men will break new paths, though they must break their hearts to do it. They will burst out somewhere, even if such bursting-out takes the form of aberration. For to act in aberration is at least more like living than to die of futility, or even to live in that complacency which is futility's idiot twin. We all know those grand aberrations of our time. We have plenty of names for them, political and invective. Communism is one of them. But all the aberrations have one common cause, and point, in the end, in one direction.

Suffering is at the heart of every living faith. That is why man can scarcely call himself a Christian for whom the Crucifixion is not a daily suffering. For it is by the hope that surmounts suffering that true tragedy surmounts pain and has always had the power to sweep men out of the common ugliness of ordeal to that exaltation in which the spirit rises superior to the agony which alone matures it by the act of transcending it. This is what we loosely call greatness. And it is the genius of Christianity to recognize that this capacity for greatness inheres in every man in the nature of his immortal soul, though not every man is called upon to demonstrate it. For it is by the soul that, at the price of suffering, we can break, if we choose, the shackles that an impersonal and rigid Fate otherwise locks upon us. It was the genius of Christianity to whisper to the lowliest man that by the action of his own soul he could burst the iron bonds of Fate with which merely being alive seemed to encase him. Only, it could never be done except at a price, which was suffering. It was because Christianity gave meaning to a suffering endured in all ages, and otherwise senseless, that it swept the minds of men. It still holds them, though the meaning has been blurred as Christianity, in common with the voices of a new age, seeks new escapes from the problem of suffering. But the problem remains and the new escapes circle back to the old one. For in suffering, man motivated by hope and faith affirms that dignity which is lit by charity and truth. This is the meaning of the eternal phrases: lest one grain perish, and unless a man die, he shall not live—phrases as hackneyed as history and as fresh as the moment in which they rose upon the astonishments of the saints.

Nothing is more characteristic of this age than its obsession with an avoidance of suffering. Nothing dooms it more certainly to that condition which is not childlike but an infantilism which is an incapacity for growth that implies an end. The mind which has rejected the soul, and marched alone, has brought the age to the brink of disaster. Let us say it flatly: What the age needs is less minds than martyrs—less knowledge (knowledge was never so cheap) but that wisdom which begins with the necessity to die, if necessary, for one's faith and thereby liberates that hope which is the virtue of the spirit.

But let us not suppose, like children, that suffering must not take its toll. Suffering implies growth and all growth is an hourly and daily dying. Age is its price as maturity is its crown. Both enjoin their blessings, among which is, supremely, a liberation from the interminable compromise in which all life is lived. Thus, at the end, or with the end in sight, truth alone becomes the compelling need and the quest for truth the only worthwhile occupation, while those engaged in it achieve that good humor of the spirit which most of those achieve who are engaged in any engrossing labor. For they know that constancy rather than energy is the cost of accomplishment in an art so difficult and so long to learn, while tolerance becomes a function of that infinity that opens up to them so near at hand. Truth too is a suffering and may not be had for less. The quest for it is a labor, life's only permanently valid one, and like any labor humbling because only the laborer knows how many mistakes have to be undone or unlearned to make anything, or supposes that he can ever really learn the mystery of his craft.

But I have reached an age, in one sense or another, and a condition where I have no other real interest. The first men who thought at all knew that the sadness of life is inseparable from its beauty—so that wisdom always implies the reaching of a point where a man can smile at both, while minimizing neither. But leave-taking is also the great liberator. The grown man who looks around for the last time has no room in his mind, and no time, for more than reality. And he wants it plain. He has no longer any reason to share it as men do to make it endurable in life, and no reason to care how others share it. This is the ultimate freedom; and what man can count that suffering a cost which has led him to the direct glance that measures what it leaves without fear and without regret?

23 Isaiah's Job

Albert Jay Nock

One evening last autumn I sat long hours with a European acquaintance while he expounded a politico-economic doctrine which seemed sound as a nut, and in which I could find no defect. At the end he said with great earnestness, "I have a mission to the masses. I feel that I am called to get the ear of the people. I shall devote the rest of my life to spreading my doctrine far and wide among the populace. What do you think?"

An embarrassing question in any case, and doubly so under the circumstances, because my acquaintance is a very learned man, one of the three or four really first-class minds that Europe produced in his generation, and naturally I, as one of the unlearned, was inclined to regard his lightest word with reverence amounting to awe. Still, I reflected, even the greatest mind cannot possibly know everything, and I was pretty sure he had not had my opportunities for observing the masses of mankind, and that therefore I probably knew them better than he did. So I mustered courage to say that he had no such mission and

From Albert Jay Nock, *Free Speech and Plain Language* (New York: William Morrow, 1937), pp. 248–265. Copyright © 1937 by Albert Jay Nock; renewed 1965 by S. A. Nock. Reprinted by permission of William Morrow and Company, Inc.

would do well to get the idea out of his head at once; he would find that the masses would not care two pins for his doctrine, and still less for himself, since in such circumstances the popular favourite is generally some Barabbas. I even went so far as to say (he is a Jew) that his idea seemed to show that he was not very well up on his own native literature. He smiled at my jest, and asked what I meant by it; and I referred him to the story of the prophet Isaiah.

It occurred to me then that this story is much worth recalling just now when so many wise men and soothsayers appear to be burdened with a message to the masses. Dr. Townsend has a message, Father Coughlin has one, Mr. Upton Sinclair, Mr. Lippmann, Mr. Chase and the planned-economy brethren, Mr. Tugwell and the New Dealers, Mr. Smith and the Liberty Leaguers—the list is endless. I cannot remember a time when so many energumens were so variously proclaiming the Word to the multitude and telling them what they must do to be saved. This being so, it occurred to me, as I say, that the story of Isaiah might have something in it to steady and compose the human spirit until this tyranny of windiness be overpast. I shall paraphrase the story in our common speech, since it has to be pieced out from various sources; and inasmuch as respectable scholars have thought fit to put out a whole new version of the Bible in the American vernacular, I shall take shelter behind them, if need be, against the charge of dealing irreverently with the Sacred Scriptures.

The prophet's career began at the end of King Uzziah's reign, say about 740 B.C. This reign was uncommonly long, almost half a century, and apparently prosperous. It was one of those prosperous reigns, however, like the reign of Marcus Aurelius at Rome, or the administration of Eubulus at Athens, or of Mr. Coolidge at Washington, where at the end the prosperity suddenly peters out, and things go by the board with a resounding crash. In the year of Uzziah's death, the Lord commissioned the prophet to go out and warn the people of the wrath to come. "Tell them what a worthless lot they are," He said. "Tell them what is wrong, and why, and what is going to happen unless they have a change of heart and straighten up. Don't mince matters. Make it clear that they are positively down to their last chance. Give it to them good and strong, and keep on giving it to them. I suppose perhaps I ought to tell you," He added, "that it won't do any good. The official class and their intelligentsia will turn up their noses at you, and the masses will not even listen. They will all keep on in their own ways until they carry everything down to destruction, and you will probably be lucky if you get out with your life."

Isaiah had been very willing to take on the job; in fact, he had asked for it; but this prospect put a new face on the situation. It raised the obvious question why, if all that were so, if the enterprise were to be a failure from the start, was there any sense in starting it? "Ah," the Lord said, "you do not get the point. There is a Remnant there that you know nothing about. They are obscure, unorganized, inarticulate, each one rubbing along as best he can. They need to be encouraged and braced up, because when everything has gone completely to the dogs, they are the ones who will come back and build up a new society, and meanwhile your preaching will reassure them and keep them hanging on. Your job is to take care of the Remnant, so be off now and set about it."

II

Apparently, then, if the Lord's word is good for anything—I do not offer any opinion about that—the only element in Judaean society that was particularly worth bothering about was the Remnant. Isaiah seems finally to have got it through his head that this was the case; that nothing was to be expected from the masses, but that if anything substantial were ever to be done in Judaea, the Remnant would have to do it. This is a very striking and suggestive idea; but before going on to explore it, we need to be quite clear about our terms. What do we mean by the masses, and what by the Remnant?

As the word *masses* is commonly used, it suggests agglomerations of poor and unprivileged people, labouring people, proletarians, and it means nothing like that; it means simply the majority. The mass-man is one who has neither the force of intellect to apprehend the principles issuing in what we know as the humane life, nor the force of character to adhere to those principles steadily and strictly as laws of conduct; and because such people make up the great, the overwhelming majority of mankind, they are called collectively *the masses*. The line of differentiation between the masses and the Remnant is set invariably by quality, not by circumstance. The Remnant are those who by force of intellect are able to apprehend these principles, and by force of character are able, at least measurably, to cleave to them; the masses are those who are unable to do either.

The picture which Isaiah presents of the Judaean masses is most unfavourable. In his view the mass-man, be he high or be he lowly, rich or poor, prince or pauper, gets off very badly. He appears as not only weak-minded and weak-willed, but as by consequence knavish, arrogant, grasping, dissipated, unprincipled, unscrupulous. The mass-woman also gets off badly, as sharing all the mass-man's untoward qualities, and contributing a few of her own in the way of vanity and laziness, extravagance and foible. The list of luxury-products[1] that she patronized is interesting; it calls to mind the women's page of a Sunday newspaper in 1928, or the display set forth in one of our professedly "smart" periodicals. In another place[2] Isaiah even recalls the affectations that we used to know by the name of the "flapper gait" and the "debutante slouch." It may be fair to discount Isaiah's vivacity a little for prophetic fervour; after all, since his real job was not to convert the masses but to brace and reassure the Remnant, he probably felt that he might lay it on indiscriminately and as thick as he liked—in fact, that he was expected to do so. But even so, the Judaean mass-man must have been a most objectionable individual, and the mass-woman utterly odious.

If the modern spirit, whatever that may be, is disinclined

[1]Isaiah iii. 18–23.
[2]Chap. iii. 16.

towards taking the Lord's word at its face value (as I hear is the case), we may observe that Isaiah's testimony to the character of the masses has strong collateral support from respectable Gentile authority. Plato lived into the administration of Eubulus, when Athens was at the peak of its great jazz-and-paper era, and he speaks of the Athenian masses with all Isaiah's fervency, even comparing them to a herd of ravenous wild beasts. Curiously, too, he applies Isaiah's own word *remnant* to the worthier portion of Athenian society; "there is but a very small *remnant*," he says, of those who possess a saving force of intellect and force of character—too small, precisely as in Judaea, to be of any avail against the ignorant and vicious preponderance of the masses.

But Isaiah was a preacher and Plato a philosopher; and we tend to regard preachers and philosophers rather as passive observers of the drama of life than as active participants. Hence in a matter of this kind their judgment might be suspected of being a little uncompromising, a little acrid, or as the French say, *saugrenu*. We may therefore bring forward another witness who was preeminently a man of affairs, and whose judgment cannot lie under this suspicion. Marcus Aurelius was ruler of the greatest of empires, and in that capacity he not only had the Roman mass-man under observation, but he had him on his hands twenty-four hours a day for eighteen years. What he did not know about him was not worth knowing, and what he thought of him is abundantly attested on almost every page of the little book of jottings which he scribbled offhand from day to day, and which he meant for no eye but his own ever to see.

This view of the masses is the one that we find prevailing at large among the ancient authorities whose writings have come down to us. In the eighteenth century, however, certain European philosophers spread the notion that the mass-man, in his natural state, is not at all the kind of person that earlier authorities made him out to be, but on the contrary, that he is a worthy object of interest. His untowardness is the effect of environment, an effect for which "society" is somehow responsible. If only his environment permitted him to live according to his best lights, he would undoubtedly show himself to be quite a fellow; and the best way to secure a more favourable environment for him would be to let him arrange it for himself. The French Revolution acted powerfully as a springboard for this idea, projecting its influence in all directions throughout Europe.

On this side of the ocean a whole new continent stood ready for a large-scale experiment with this theory. It afforded every conceivable resource whereby the masses might develop a civilization made in their own likeness and after their own image. There was no force of tradition to disturb them in their preponderance, or to check them in a thoroughgoing disparagement of the Remnant. Immense natural wealth, unquestioned predominance, virtual isolation, freedom from external interference and the fear of it, and, finally, a century and a half of time—such are the advantages which the mass-man has had in bringing forth a civilization which should set the earlier preachers and philosophers at naught in their belief that nothing substantial can be expected from the masses, but only from the Remnant.

His success is unimpressive. On the evidence so far presented one must say, I think, that the mass-man's conception of what life has to offer, and his choice of what to ask from life, seem now to be pretty well what they were in the times of Isaiah and Plato; and so too seem the catastrophic social conflicts and convulsions in which his views of life and his demands on life involve him. I do not wish to dwell on this, however, but merely to observe that the monstrously inflated importance of the masses has apparently put all thought of a possible mission to the Remnant out of the modern prophet's head. This is obviously quite as it should be, provided that the earlier preachers and philosophers were actually wrong, and that all final hope of the human race is actually centred in the masses. If, on the other hand, it should turn out that the Lord and Isaiah and Plato and Marcus Aurelius were right in their estimate of the relative social value of the masses and the Remnant, the case is somewhat different. Moreover, since with everything in their favour the masses have so far given such an extremely discouraging account of themselves, it would seem that the question at issue between these two bodies of opinion might most profitably be reopened.

III

But without following up this suggestion, I wish only, as I said, to remark the fact that as things now stand Isaiah's job seems rather to go begging. Everyone with a message nowadays is like my venerable European friend, eager to take it to the masses. His first, last and only thought is of mass-acceptance and mass-approval. His great care is to put his doctrine in such shape as will capture the masses' attention and interest. This attitude towards the masses is so exclusive, so devout, that one is reminded of the troglodytic monster described by Plato, and the assiduous crowd at the entrance to its cave, trying obsequiously to placate it and win its favour, trying to interpret its inarticulate noises, trying to find out what it wants, and eagerly offering it all sorts of things that they think might strike its fancy.

The main trouble with all this is its reaction upon the mission itself. It necessitates an opportunist sophistication of one's doctrine which profoundly alters its character and reduces it to a mere placebo. If, say, you are a preacher, you wish to attract as large a congregation as you can, which means an appeal to the masses, and this in turn means adapting the terms of your message to the order of intellect and character that the masses exhibit. If you are an educator, say with a college on your hands, you wish to get as many students as possible, and you whittle down your requirements accordingly. If a writer, you aim at getting many readers; if a publisher, many purchasers; if a philosopher, many disciples; if a reformer, many converts; if a musician, many auditors; and so on. But as we see on all sides, in the realization of these several desires the prophetic message is so heavily adulterated with trivialities in every instance that its effect on the masses is merely to harden them in

their sins; and meanwhile the Remnant, aware of this adulteration and of the desires that prompt it, turn their backs on the
prophet and will have nothing to do with him or his message.

Isaiah, on the other hand, worked under no such disabilities.
He preached to the masses only in the sense that he preached
publicly. Anyone who liked might listen; anyone who liked
might pass by. He knew that the Remnant would listen; and
knowing also that nothing was to be expected of the masses
under any circumstances, he made no specific appeal to them,
did not accommodate his message to their measure in any way,
and did not care two straws whether they heeded it or not. As a
modern publisher might put it, he was not worrying about circulation or about advertising. Hence, with all such obsessions
quite out of the way, he was in a position to do his level best,
without fear or favour, and answerable only to his august Boss.

If a prophet were not too particular about making money out
of his mission or getting a dubious sort of notoriety out of it,
the foregoing considerations would lead one to say that serving
the Remnant looks like a good job. An assignment that you can
really put your back into, and do your best without thinking
about results, is a real job; whereas serving the masses is at
best only half a job, considering the inexorable conditions that
the masses impose upon their servants. They ask you to give
them what they want, they insist upon it, and will take nothing
else; and following their whims, their irrational changes of
fancy, their hot and cold fits, is a tedious business, to say
nothing of the fact that what they want at any time makes very
little call on one's resources of prophecy. The Remnant, on the
other hand, want only the best you have, whatever that may
be. Give them that, and they are satisfied and you have nothing
more to worry about. The prophet of the American masses must
aim consciously at the lowest common denominator of intellect,
taste and character among 120,000,000 people; and this is a
distressing task. The prophet of the Remnant, on the contrary,
is in the enviable position of Papa Haydn in the household of
Prince Esterhazy. All Haydn had to do was to keep forking out
the very best music he knew how to produce, knowing it would

be understood and appreciated by those for whom he produced it, and caring not a button what anyone else thought of it; and that makes a good job.

In a sense, nevertheless, as I have said, it is not a rewarding job. If you can touch the fancy of the masses, and have the sagacity to keep always one jump ahead of their vagaries and vacillations, you can get good returns in money from serving the masses, and good returns also in a mouth-to-ear type of notoriety:

Digito monstrari et dicier, Hic est!

We all know innumerable politicians, journalists, dramatists, novelists and the like, who have done extremely well by themselves in these ways. Taking care of the Remnant, on the contrary, holds little promise of any such rewards. A prophet of the Remnant will not grow purse-proud on the financial returns from his work, nor is it likely that he will get any great renown out of it. Isaiah's case was exceptional to this second rule, and there are others, but not many.

It may be thought, then, that while taking care of the Remnant is no doubt a good job, it is not an especially interesting job, because it is as a rule so poorly paid. I have my doubts about this. There are other compensations to be got out of a job besides money and notoriety, and some of them seem substantial enough to be attractive. Many jobs which do not pay well are yet profoundly interesting, as, for instance, the job of the research-student in the sciences is said to be; and the job of looking after the Remnant seems to me, as I have surveyed it for many years from my seat in the grandstand, to be as interesting as any that can be found in the world.

IV

What chiefly makes it so, I think, is that in any given society the Remnant are always so largely an unknown quantity. You do not know, and will never know, more than two things about them. You can be sure of those—dead sure, as our phrase is—

but you will never be able to make even a respectable guess at anything else. You do not know and will never know who the Remnant are, or where they are, or how many of them there are, or what they are doing or will do. Two things you know, and no more: first, that they exist; second, that they will find you. Except for these two certainties, working for the Remnant means working in impenetrable darkness; and this, I should say, is just the condition calculated most effectively to pique the interest of any prophet who is properly gifted with the imagination, insight and intellectual curiosity necessary to a successful pursuit of his trade.

The fascination and the despair of the historian, as he looks back upon Isaiah's Jewry, upon Plato's Athens, or upon Rome of the Antonines, is the hope of discovering and laying bare the "substratum of right thinking and well-doing" which he knows must have existed somewhere in those societies because no kind of collective life can possibly go on without it. He finds tantalizing intimations of it here and there in many places, as in the Greek Anthology, in the scrapbook of Aulus Gellius, in the poems of Ausonius, and in the brief and touching tribute *Bene merenti* bestowed upon the unknown occupants of Roman tombs. But these are vague and fragmentary; they lead him nowhere in his search for some kind of measure of this substratum, but merely testify to what he already knew a priori, that the substratum did somewhere exist. Where it was, how substantial it was, what its power of self-assertion and resistance was—of all this they tell him nothing.

Similarly, when the historian of two thousand years hence, or two hundred years, looks over the available testimony to the quality of our civilization and tries to get any kind of clear, competent evidence concerning the substratum of right thinking and well-doing which he knows must have been here, he will have a devil of a time finding it. When he has assembled all he can get and has made even a minimum allowance for speciousness, vagueness, and confusion of motive, he will sadly acknowledge that his net result is simply nothing. A Remnant were here, building a substratum, like coral insects—so much he knows—but he will find nothing to put him on the track of who and where and how many they were, and what their work was like.

Concerning all this, too, the prophet of the present knows precisely as much and as little as the historian of the future; and that, I repeat, is what makes his job seem to me so profoundly interesting. One of the most suggestive episodes recounted in the Bible is that of a prophet's attempt—the only attempt of the kind on record, I believe—to count up the Remnant. Elijah had fled from persecution into the desert, where the Lord presently overhauled him and asked what he was doing so far away from his job. He said that he was running away, not because he was a coward, but because all the Remnant had been killed off except himself. He had got away only by the skin of his teeth, and, he being now all the Remnant there was, if he were killed the True Faith would go flat. The Lord replied that he need not worry about that, for even without him the True Faith could probably manage to squeeze along somehow, if it had to; "and as for your figures on the Remnant," He said, "I don't mind telling you that there are seven thousand of them back there in Israel whom it seems you have not heard of, but you may take My word for it that there they are."

At that time probably the population of Israel could not have run to much more than a million or so; and a Remnant of seven thousand out of a million is a highly encouraging percentage for any prophet. With seven thousand of the boys on his side, there was no great reason for Elijah to feel lonesome; and incidentally that would be something for the modern prophet of the Remnant to think of when he has a touch of the blues. But the main point is that if Elijah the Prophet could not make a closer guess on the number of the Remnant than he made when he missed it by seven thousand, anyone else who tackled the problem would only waste his time.

The other certainty which the prophet of the Remnant may always have is that the Remnant will find him. He may rely on that with absolute assurance. They will find him without his doing anything about it; in fact, if he tries to do anything about

it, he is pretty sure to put them off. He does not need to adver-
tise for them, or resort to any schemes of publicity to get their
attention. If he is a preacher or a public speaker, for example,
he may be quite indifferent to going on show at receptions, getting his picture printed in the newspapers, or furnishing autobiographical material for publication on the side of "human
interest." If a writer, he need not make a point of attending any
pink teas, autographing books at wholesale, or entering into
any specious freemasonry with reviewers. All this and much
more of the same order lies in the regular and necessary routine laid down for the prophet of the masses; it is, and must be,
part of the great general technique of getting the mass-man's
ear—or as our vigorous and excellent publicist, Mr. H. L.
Mencken, puts it, the technique of boob-bumping. The prophet
of the Remnant is not bound to this technique. He may be quite
sure that the Remnant will make their own way to him without
any adventitious aids; and not only so, but if they find him
employing such aids, as I said, it is ten to one that they will
smell a rat in them and will sheer off.

The certainty that the Remnant will find him, however,
leaves the prophet as much in the dark as ever, as helpless as
ever in the matter of putting any estimate of any kind upon the
Remnant, for, as appears in the case of Elijah, he remains ignorant of who they are that have found him, or where they are, or
how many. They do not write in and tell him about it, after the
manner of those who admire the vedettes of Hollywood nor yet
do they seek him out and attach themselves to his person. They
are not that kind. They take his message much as drivers take
the directions on a roadside signboard; that is, with very little
thought about the signboard, beyond being gratefully glad that
it happened to be there, but with very serious thought about
the directions.

This impersonal attitude of the Remnant wonderfully en-
hances the interest of the imaginative prophet's job. Once in a
while, just about often enough to keep his intellectual curiosity
in good working order, he will quite accidentally come upon
some distinct reflection of his own message in an unsuspected

quarter; and this enables him to entertain himself in his leisure moments with agreeable speculations about the course his message may have taken in reaching that particular quarter, and about what came of it after it got there. Most interesting of all are those instances, if one could only run them down (but one may always speculate about them), where the recipient himself no longer knows where or when or from whom he got the message; or even where, as sometimes happens, he has forgotten that he got it anywhere, and imagines that it is all a self-sprung idea of his own.

Such instances as these are probably not infrequent, for, without presuming to enroll ourselves among the Remnant, we can all no doubt remember having found ourselves suddenly under the influence of an idea, the source of which we cannot possibly identify. "It came to us afterward," as we say; that is, we are aware of it only after it has shot up full-grown in our minds, leaving us quite ignorant of how and when and by what agency it was planted there and left to germinate. It seems highly probable that the prophet's message often takes some such course with the Remnant.

If, for example, you are a writer or a speaker or a preacher, you put forth an idea which lodges in the *Unbewusstsein* of a casual member of the Remnant, and sticks fast there. For some time it is inert; then it begins to fret and fester until presently it invades the man's conscious mind and, as one might say, corrupts it. Meanwhile he has quite forgotten how he came by the idea in the first instance, and even perhaps thinks he has invented it; and in those circumstances the most interesting thing of all is that you never know what the pressure of that idea will make him do.

V

For these reasons it appears to me that Isaiah's job is not only good but also extremely interesting; and especially so at the present time when nobody is doing it. If I were young and had the notion of embarking in the prophetical line, I would certainly take up this branch of the business; and therefore I have no hesitation about recommending it as a career for anyone in that position. It offers an open field, no competition; our civilization so completely neglects and disallows the Remnant that anyone going in with an eye single to their service might pretty well count on getting all the trade there is.

Even assuming that there is some social salvage to be screened out of the masses, even assuming that the testimony of history to their social value is a little too sweeping, that it depresses hopelessness a little too far, one must yet perceive, I think, that the masses have prophets enough and to spare. Even admitting in the teeth of history that hope of the human race may not be quite exclusively centred in the Remnant, one must perceive that they have social value enough to entitle them to some measure of prophetic encouragement and consolation, and that our civilization allows them none whatever. Every prophetic voice is addressed to the masses, and to them alone; the voice of the pulpit, the voice of education, the voice of politics, of literature, drama, journalism—all these are directed towards the masses exclusively, and they marshal the masses in the way that they are going.

One might suggest, therefore, that aspiring prophetical talent may well turn to another field. *Sat patriae Priamoque datum*— whatever obligation of the kind may be due the masses is already monstrously overpaid. So long as the masses are taking up the tabernacle of Moloch and Chium, their images, and following the star of their god Buncombe, they will have no lack of prophets to point the way that leadeth to the More Abundant Life; and hence a few of those who feel the prophetic afflatus might do better to apply themselves to serving the Remnant. It is a good job, an interesting job, much more interesting than serving the masses; and moreover it is the only job in our whole civilization, as far as I know, that offers a virgin field.

24 Christmas in Christendom

Frederick D. Wilhelmsen

Let us now go even unto Bethlehem, and see this thing which is come to pass, which the Lord hath made known unto us. And they came with haste, and found Mary, and Joseph, and the babe lying in a manger.

A note of haste sounds clearly in the staggering text of St. Luke: the shepherds run to the new-born God as would an army of men, upon the breaking out of peace after a long war, run to their hearths and to their own.

The early Church was in a hurry to celebrate Christmas. Pagan antiquity had become bankrupt spiritually and intellectually by the time that God deigned to become Man. Philosophy had failed. The handful of sages who had made Greek *episteme* their own and who actualized the lofty moral precepts of Stoicism lived out their lives in a quiet desperation, convinced that human existence is little more than the lot of a condemned prisoner who waits in his cell upon the call of the executioner. A cold wind full of despair whistles through Marcus Aurelius' contention that "it is possible to be a good man, even in a palace." The final irony of classical antiquity consisted in its having wrought civilization out of barbarism as it chiseled palaces out of stone quarries: it had to suffer stoically, as does a man a burden or a secret tragedy, the very glory that it created.

Frederick D. Wilhelmsen, "Christmas in Christendom," *Triumph*, II, No. 12 (December 1967), 10–12. Reprinted by permission of the author and *Triumph*.

So it was a very tired and sad world that hurried to the Good News of Bethlehem: "For unto you is born this day in the city of David a Saviour, which is Christ the Lord."

Observers from another world would presume that the doctrines of the Incarnation and the Resurrection, and their promise of a final victory over the tomb, would have fixed the eyes of the men of this time upon a distant but guaranteed salvation—and blinded them, consequently, to the world. And this did happen, of course: the flight of the monks to the Egyptian desert, the severe and often savage asceticism of the early Fathers, the joy of the martyrs as they elbowed aside their fellow Christians in the colosseum and then embraced the lions in the service of a final crown—all bespoke a contempt for this world by men whose faith was so palpable that things visible were but a pale screen between them and an Eternity they already experienced in the flesh.

But Christianity—formed as is its Cross of a cluster of tensions that are never resolved—while permitting and even encouraging this flight from the world, simultaneously exalted Creation as the work of God, and therefore judged it to be very good indeed, as did the Father when He rested on the seventh day. Although the *"world"* might be very evil (the terminology is Pauline), *"Creation"* was sacred. And it was Christmas that made possible—better yet, that concentrated within itself— this distinction. For if the Son of God, the Eternal Glory and the Wisdom of the Father, He in Whom all things are made, was born of a Virgin, and thus entered time as a Perfect Man, then there was a double reason for saluting existence. Not only are all things made in His Image, but He entered time and as a man became one with these things of the world as He mixed Divinity with the clay of the earth. In those first moments of His Birth as a Child thrashing about in swaddling clothes, He sanctified not only the straw upon which He lay and the clothes of His Mother as he groped for her milk, but He hallowed all reality unto the most distant solar system.

Christmas, in the early centuries of the Church, thus focusing attention on Christ's humanity, lifted the sadness that had settled over the world due to the failure of classical paganism. Before the Child at Bethlehem no real Christian could doubt that the Nicene formula, "true God and true Man," knits together our most daring theological convictions . . . with that moment of blinding innocence and joy which is the Christmas of a child in Christendom.

The Church was in a hurry about Christmas in those early centuries; but many churchmen were not. There was a quite natural hesitation about assigning a specific date to the birth of Christ for fear that it would be confused with the innumerable "birthdays of the gods." The first evidence of the feasting of Christmas comes from Egypt around the year 200, where the sacred date was thought to have been May 20 in the twenty-eighth year of the reign of the Emperor Augustus. But the sermons of St. John Chrysostom in Antioch show that by the fourth century, the December date was firmly fixed. The famed Golden Tongue publicly urged the Faithful to unite with their brothers in the West in the celebration of Our Lord's birthday on December 25. There had been a reaction by the Christians in that city back to certain Jewish rites and feasts; but from Thrace to Cadiz, argued Chrysostom, the churches have united around December 25 as the birthday of Christ. This very spontaneity, he went on, was a sign of the genuineness of the day. His vigor won over the doubting brothers of Antioch. And December 25 it was to be: Christ was born on that day liturgically and the subject was then closed forever. But the Church came to this decision, rather boldly, less for reasons of historical accuracy than out of a desire to replace popular pagan feasts.

There is strong evidence that the solar feast of *Natalia Invicti*, in honor of the Unconquered Sun and observed on December 25 throughout the Mediterranean world, is responsible for our Christian date. A solar cult of the Mithraic religion competed with Christianity for dominance within the Empire. Set up to climax the older Saturnalia which lasted from December 17 to December 24, the feast of the Sun climaxed a period of merrymaking when all classes of society mingled together in a carnival spirit of gift exchanging, the carrying of torches, and the wearing of colorful and outlandish costumes. In grafting the spirit of that pagan celebration onto Christmas, the early Fathers transmuted heathen revelry into Christian joy.

Far from the warm Mediterranean, beyond the frontiers of the Empire, the Germanic tribes in the vast forests that covered half of Europe would break the monotony of a bitter winter by observing the solstice. This festival centered around the old barbaric worship of "the mother tree," which grew in the center of every settlement and was thought to be the source of all life, its roots reaching down to the springs of being itself. When baptized by missionaries, the Teutons retained their feast, but transmuted its nature into the custom that survives today in the Germanic Yule log and tree. This tradition, linked with the Latin fig tree (descendant of the tree under which Romulus and Remus had been suckled by the she-wolf), came in time to be associated with the burning bush of Exodus, where God told Moses His Name; and all of them together mingled with the Tree of Life in the Garden of Eden; and the combined symbolism looked forward to the Tree of the Cross. Thus the entire weight of the tradition of the Christmas Tree, *Weinachtsbaumum*, reminds us that with the birth of Our Lord all Creation was born again.

By the twelfth century Christmas was celebrated in every nation in Europe, reflecting warmth and humanity and the good will of man to man. But the thirteenth century deepened profoundly these emotions in a new celebration of Creation that not only emphasized the humanity of Christ and the cult of the Virgin, but that gloried in His helplessness as a baby, and His poverty, born as He was in a cave. It was at this time that Christmas became the feast of the poor and the outcasts, of defiance against the cold blasts of winter. Thus did the pain of God's poor—humbled and in misery—defy the mystery and cruelty of the powers of this world. But this defiance was never bitter. Rather it was filled with good cheer, comforted by the knowledge of the conditions surrounding the birth of Christ.

The English Christmas of Dickens, of Tiny Tim, rescued in the end by a Scrooge converted by the Spirit of Christmas Future, extends backwards in a straight line to the High Middle Ages.

We owe to those centuries our first Christmas carols, and also Saint Nicholas, whose feast falls on December 6. This bishop whose bones lie in peace in the Antalya Museum in Turkey was renowned in his time for his charity toward the poor and for his love of children; but he came into his own only many centuries later. St. Nicholas—Father Christmas in England, *Papa Noël* in France, *Pelznickel* in Germany, *Sinter Klaus* in Holland, our Santa Claus—was most loved by children, for whom he occupied the position held in the earlier tradition by the Christ Child: bearer of gifts, "Christ bundles" full of good things to eat and wear. As Daniel Foley says in his splendid little book, *The Christmas Tree,* "the gifts were given on the basis of good behaviour. Thus, children at an early age were introduced to the basic tenets of theology."

Gift-giving was the prerogative of Saint Nicholas and of the Child Jesus in the north of Europe; but the children of Spain have always had to wait for the Three Kings to come at Epiphany. Heralded by fireworks and by the illumination of the walls of the town, Gaspar, Melchior, and Baltasar have ridden out of the centuries into the plazas of every city and village of the Hispanic world. Surrounded by servants groaning under enormous casks and trunks filled with presents, the Kings of the Orient still scatter largesse in the streets, often to the booming of cannons from the town walls, climaxing the Twelve Days— Christmas to Epiphany—formally sanctified by the Second Council of Tours in 566.

The three Masses said on the day of *Christ's Mass* date from 1110. St. Thomas Aquinas defended the liturgical custom of saying such a plethora of Masses on Christmas—at midnight, at dawn, and *in die*—by alluding to the triple "birth" of Christ: in Eternity, in Time and in the Souls of the Faithful. It was at the third Christmas Mass, in the year 800 of our Lord, that Leo III crowned Charlemagne Holy Roman Emperor and thus knit altogether into one the history of the West.

Christmas thus became the central festival within Christendom. Easter advanced what were possibly better abstract and liturgical grounds for preeminence within the Christian Year, but the popular conscience seized upon Christmas as its own proper day, knowing intuitively that the sense of the Incarnation circles around and is one with Christmas. And the Church, always wise, judged the dissertations of the theologians in the light of the truth of our popular Christmas. That defiance of the poor against the bleakness of a life grim and harsh, a defiance bent upon a happiness that would not be gainsaid, found in the Mother and Child a reality deeper than all symbols, because it united into one things never mixed otherwise—fecundity embraced innocence and thus banished the price that each must pay for being at all. This was the popular Catholicism that stormed heaven with the spires of the Gothic, the same faith that sought the wisdom of children before the manger. "Little children will enter the gates of heaven, and unless you become as one. . . ."

The Puritan heresies smashed this Christmas of ours. Although Lutheranism had done little to alter the old feast, the French, Dutch and English Puritans, burnt from within by the bitterness of their hatred for Creation, confused by what they viewed as the Roman myth of the Virgin, forbade the celebration of Christ's Mass and of His Day. An Act of Parliament in 1644 declared Christmas a *fast* day, of all things. Shops were forced to remain open, plum puddings and mince pies were condemned as heathen and popish (which, of course, they are). Even before Oliver Cromwell legislated Christmas out of England, the deed was done in the American Colonies. Cotton Mather denounced Christmas in sermon after sermon, and the General Court of Massachusetts levied its stamp of disapproval of the popish holiday by enacting, democratically, a statute "for preventing disorders" (i.e., fun) on that Day. The peculiar fanaticism of these our ancestors makes interesting reading:

> For preventing disorders arising in several places within the jurisdiction by reason of some still observing such festivities as were

superstitiously kept in other communities, to the great dishonor of God and offense to others; therefore that whosoever shall be found observing any such day as Christmas or the like, either by forbearing of labor, feasting or any other way upon any such account aforesaid, every such person so offending shall pay for every offense five shillings as a fine to the county.

Five shillings from the poor of the colonies! This was the gigantic fraud out of which grew our modern world, a world dour and grim, devoid of an older code of honor that it repudiated along with Rome. In this concerted attack upon the hallowed traditions of Christmas past, launched in the name of Bible Worship and Money, Puritan capitalism fingered the central issue with all the nervous brilliance of the mind of its founder, Calvin: if Creation is evil (and John Calvin and John Knox and Cotton Mather would have it so); if God is an awful Transcendence, a Totally Other, removed as is innocence from the taint of sin, the world; if this popish plot, the world, is concentrated in a unique fashion within the body of Woman (Did not sin come into the world through a woman? They looked into their Book and found the answer.); if this evil spills out in the bodies of small children, full of evil and marked with the sign of predestination; if the vast bulk of humanity, unwashed and filthy with sin, is condemned from all eternity by our God who told us all this out of His Book; and if but a handful are elected to be lifted out of the caldron and signed with salvation (a visible effect of which is cleanliness and earthly wealth, for does not the Book write of filling the barns of the just?)—then it follows: first, that the Incarnation—God's coming into the world—was totally superfluous and in fact an utter waste of time; second, that children are nothing other than potential adults, fields for education by the Elect with their Book, in themselves depraved little devils rotted by original sin and without any claim to special wisdom into the true meaning of the real; third, that the Romish cult of the Virgin simply perpetuates and deepens through the feast of Christmas a silly love affair with Creation which covers over the sin of the Woman, all women, and the depravity of the Child, all children. If all of this be true (and John Calvin and the Holy Writ would have it so) then carols as well as the Masses, the tree along with the manger, the Mother along with the Child must go. If the world is utterly hideous, then man must build another one. When the technocratic secularists today, in the name of the "modern world," strike at Christmas and attempt to prohibit its public celebration, they can take comfort in being in a tradition that goes back to the fining of poor men five shillings because they danced on Christmas Eve. Secularism and all the mythology about the "absolute separation of church and state" is simply a Puritanism debased, its original corruption compounded.

But in this ghastly simulacrum of civilization that we call the twentieth century, where all honor is forgotten, there are still children in the high plains of Castille who are romping now through cobbled streets covered in snow, the night bitter and cold under a sky swept clean of clouds. And they are singing, these children: *"Ande, ande, ande, la Maria morena; ande, ande, ande, qu'es la Nochebuena."* Dark Mary, Our Lovely, please hurry and give birth to Your Son, because tonight is the Good Night. Like the first shepherds, in haste, they flee from a tired and sick world in order that they might find Emmanuel, our Great God. Stumbling and falling along the roadside, fleeing the banalities of a world without Him, they bear Her along and buoy Her up. Tonight they will fling themselves before His Manger and sate themselves, gluttons for God, in adoration. Come, Dark Mary, deliver us tonight Christ, Our God, Our Lord, Our King.

25 Epilogue

Whittaker Chambers

Il Faut le Supposer Heureux

(*The following is from the last letter I received
from Whittaker Chambers.*—W.F.B.)

Pipe Creek Farm
Westminster, Md.
April 9, 1961

Dear Bill,

Weariness, Bill—you cannot yet know literally what it means.
I wish no time would come when you do know, but the balance of experience is against it. One day, long hence, you will
know true weariness and will say: "That was it." My own life
of late has been full of such realizations: "So that was why he
did that"; "So that was why she didn't do that"; about the past
acts of people with whom my own age (and hence understanding) has only just caught up. There's a kind of pathos about it—
a rather empty kind, I'm afraid; the understanding comes too
late to do even the tardy understander much good.

Our kind of weariness. History hit us with a freight train.
History has long been doing this to people, monotonously and
usually lethally. But we (my general breed) tried, as Strachey
noted, to put ourselves together again. Since this meant out-

Whittaker Chambers, "Il Faut le Supposer Heureux," *National Review,* XI,
No. 4 (July 29, 1961), 47. Reprinted by permission of *National Review.*

witting dismemberment, as well as resynthesizing a new life-view (grandfather, what big words you use), the sequel might seem rather remarkable, rather more remarkable than what went before. But at a price—weariness. People tend to leave Oedipus, shrieking with the blood running down his cheeks—everybody nicely purged by pity and terror, and so home and to bed. But I was about 23 when I discovered, rather by chance, that Oedipus went on to Colonnus. But each of us, according to his lights, was arrested in time by the same line—the one in which Oedipus, looking out from precarious sanctuary after long flight, sums up: "Because of my great age, and the nobility of my mind, I feel that all will be well." That is the Oedipus largely overlooked. Of course, I can say nothing of the nobility of my mind, or even Koestler's or Camus'; and I realize, too, that Oedipus spoke at a grateful moment of rescue. One cannot pretend to live at that height. And yet, to reach it even at times is something. One must have got rid of great loads of encumbering nonsense and irrelevance to get there; must have learned to travel quite light—one razor, one change, etc. And I suppose the "well" of the quotation is almost wholly a subjective value. And there remains the price—the weariness I mentioned which none of us complains about, but should take good care not to inflict on other people's lives. I did and I'm sorry about it. We're grateful too.

Something quite different which struck me—what seems to have been your desolation by *Man's Fate* [by André Malraux]. But Hemmelrich goes back (supreme tenderness) to close the door left too hastily open on the bodies of his murdered wife and son. Tchen, about to throw himself and bomb under the automobile, believes that Pei (spared to life because Tchen acts alone) will be able to write more meaningfully by reason of Tchen's act. Kyo takes the cyanide with the sense that the concept of man's dignity enjoins control over his own death. Katow, surrendering even that ultimate, divides his cyanide with those less able to bear man's fate; and walks toward the locomotive through a hall of bodies from which comes something like on unutterable sob—the strangled cry. It may also be phrased: "And the Morning Stars sang together for joy." It may also be phrased: *"Il faut supposer Katow heureux,"* as Camus wrote: *"Il faut supposer Sisyphe heureux."* For each age finds its own language for an eternal meaning.

As always,
Whittaker

✒ INDEX

534